50 GREAT
AMERICANS

Great Americans

THEIR INSPIRING LIVES
AND ACHIEVEMENTS

By

HENRY THOMAS

and

DANA LEE THOMAS

Garden City, N. Y.
DOUBLEDAY & COMPANY, INC.

Contents

Introduction	vii	Andrew Carnegie	230
Benjamin Franklin	1	John Wanamaker	242
George Washington	12	John Davison Rockefeller	250
Paul Revere	23	Oliver Wendell Holmes	258
Daniel Boone	32	William James	268
Thomas Paine	41	Joseph Pulitzer	275
Thomas Jefferson	50	Alexander Graham Bell	283
John Paul Jones	58	Thomas Alva Edison	294
John Marshall	67	Eugene Victor Debs	303
Alexander Hamilton	76	Woodrow Wilson	312
John Jacob Astor	88	Theodore Roosevelt	321
Robert Fulton	97	Jane Addams	330
Andrew Jackson	105	Henry Ford	339
Daniel Webster	116	George Washington Carver	348
Sam Houston	127	Charles Proteus Steinmetz	358
Brigham Young	136	The Wright Brothers	368
Ralph Waldo Emerson	145	Bernard Mannes Baruch	376
Robert Edward Lee	156	Alfred Emanuel Smith	386
Edgar Allan Poe	164	George Michael Cohan	395
Abraham Lincoln	173	Will Rogers	406
Walt Whitman	183	Helen Keller	414
Susan B. Anthony	194	George Catlett Marshall	421
Stephen Collins Foster	203	Franklin Delano Roosevelt	431
James Abbott McNeill		Knute Rockne	440
Whistler	209	Dwight David Eisenhower	449
Mark Twain	219	George Gershwin	460

Introduction

S WE look upon America, the most impressive thing about it
is the vastness and the variety of its scene. The American
landscape is a picture not only of material grandeur, but of
mental adventure, artistic achievement, and spiritual growth.
It is almost a world in itself—a panorama of diversified crops
and climates, rivers and harbors and highways, fruitlands and grasslands,
farms and factories, mines and machines and cities and statues and poems
and churches and schools, plantations and prairies, forests and deserts
and canyons and mountains and tempests and floods—soul-testing labors,
undaunted souls. A miniature of man's struggle on earth. America's summons to human ingenuity. All sorts of material, to challenge all manner
of men.

It would seem as if Destiny had kept this continent hidden away until
1492 in order to prepare it as a laboratory for the rest of the world. An
experiment in the fusion of many diverse elements into a unit of progressive democracy. The United States is perhaps the first international
nation of history. It offers a practical demonstration of the truth that all
the warring races can be welded together into a single unwarlike family.
Here in this country, it seems, we may be able to find the answer to the
philosopher's eternal quest for a united mankind. The love of freedom
that is England, the beauty that is France, the science that is Germany,
the mysticism that is Russia, the music that is Italy, the poetry that is
Ireland, the passion that is Africa, the courage that is Norway and
Sweden, the peacefulness that is Holland, and the thirst for the divine
that is the Orient—all these ingredients have been poured into the cruci-
ble of America and are being transmuted into the gold of a new civilization.

And the emergence of a new type of man—*Homo Americanus*. This
book is an effort to present a composite picture of this American type.
The material builder, the esthetic dreamer, the spiritual fighter, the
inspired teacher, and the heroic defender of the American way. This

American way has a horizon wide enough to embrace such varied personalities as Henry Ford, the inventor, and Walt Whitman, the poet; Tom Paine, the breaker of the old images, and Thomas Jefferson, the builder of the new; George Gershwin, the maker of music, and Andrew Carnegie, the maker of steel; Dwight Eisenhower, the military leader, and Eugene Debs, the dreamer of peace; Al Smith, the Catholic, Benjamin Franklin, the Protestant, Bernard Baruch, the Jew, and George Washington Carver and Jane Addams, the seekers of new paths toward a clearer vision of Justice and Humanity. These, and thirty-seven other exponents of American democracy at work. Considered one by one, these fifty examples of distinguished Americans might have appeared to pull each in a different—and often antagonistic—direction. Yet all of them, taken together, compose a united group representative of a united nation. A new kind of nation, with a new kind of dream—to replace the Old World idea of Might with the New World idea of Right. Of every one of the personalities included in this book it may be said—"Here at last is something in the doings of man that corresponds with the broadcast doings of the sun and the stars."

For the vastness of the American scene—as we shall observe—has tended to produce a corresponding vastness in the American soul.

50 GREAT
AMERICANS

Benjamin Franklin

[1706-1790]

THE Yankee "Thunder-Master" was on one of his official visits to England. Everywhere the people looked with openmouthed astonishment at this magician who, with his electrical wand, had snatched the lightning from the heavens. He was rated among the famous enchanters of history—Moses, Merlin, Paracelsus, Cagliostro, King Solomon, the Devil himself. And just now he had offered to perform a trick which even the Devil would have found beyond his power. "I shall repeat one of the miracles of the Bible," he said with a quiet smile. "With this walking stick I shall calm the raging waters."

They were standing on the edge of the lake at Bowood, the palatial estate of Lord Shelbourne. Among the guests on that occasion were famous scientists, clergymen, poets, statesmen, scholars, and a handful of cynics who "believed in the gospel of disbelief." One of these cynics turned to Dr. Franklin. "You're just trying to diddle us, sir, are you not?"

"On the contrary, I'm quite serious," rejoined Franklin, raising his cane above his head. "Look."

Thrice he whirled the cane over the water whose surface was being plowed up by a spanking breeze. As he did so, he muttered a "magic formula." The cynics laughed as they looked on at this childish farce. But suddenly their laughter was changed to a cry of amazement. "By Jove, he has done it!" With the waving of his cane, Benjamin Franklin had smoothed the ruffled waters although the breeze was blowing as lustily as ever.

"How did you manage it?" asked the Abbé Morellet a few minutes later, when they were alone.

"By filling my hollow cane with oil," remarked Franklin simply. "I just scattered the oil over the water, and the water became calm." And then, with a twinkle in his eye, he added: "Almost every problem can be solved if you know how to go about it."

This was the secret of Franklin's success. Throughout his life he made it his business to know how.

II

FRANKLIN was born with a good physical and mental endowment. On his father's side he came of a race of blacksmiths, and from them he inherited his iron constitution. His grandfather on his mother's side was a poet, and from him he derived his fine feeling for words. As for his humor, he must have extracted it from his native soil. For it was flavored with the pungency of the pine grove and it crackled like a fire over a bundle of evergreens.

He rode into the world on the wings of a northeaster in the winter of 1706. It required a tough constitution to survive in that primitive little city of Boston, "squeezed between the Atlantic and the marshes." But the new Franklin baby was equal to the job. He "learned to walk on frozen toes" and liked it. And he liked the wrangling and the tangling companionship of his brothers and his sisters—there were sixteen of them. From infancy he was well trained in the art of getting along with people.

His father, the candlemaker Josiah, preferred Benjamin to all his other children. He was such a precocious little tyke. At five he could read the Bible, and at seven he could already interpret it in his own way. "Father," he said once at the dinner table, "why waste all this time giving your daily blessing? Why not give one general blessing once and for all? I think this would save your time and the Lord's time." He would make a good clergyman, thought Josiah.

And so he sent him to the Boston Latin School for a classical education. But after a while Josiah realized that it was beyond his purse to indulge his son in a "gentleman's" career. He transferred him from the Latin School to George Brownell's School, an institution which specialized in the practical rather than in the liberal arts. But even this sort of education proved to be too expensive for Benjamin. No use trying to cultivate a Franklin mind when there were so many Franklin mouths to feed. Two years of schooling were enough. Let Benjamin be a toiler instead of a tattler. Josiah took his son out of school and into his candle shop.

But Benjamin disliked the smell of the tallow. He looked around for an apprenticeship at a more congenial trade and found it in his brother James's printing shop.

At this early age (twelve) Ben Franklin was already somewhat of a personality. He wrote poetry and printed it and sold it in the streets of Boston. He played with the boys and generally beat them at their games. And he discussed books with his elders and generally beat them at their discussions. He was an excellent swimmer, a handy mechanic, a voluminous reader, and a skeptic. He argued about everything and he took nothing for granted. He stopped going to church on Sundays, because he wanted to spend the day in reading. A good book, he said, is more educational than a bad sermon. Yet he was not irreligious. Throughout his life he showed a deep reverence for God—the Creative Power of the World and the Father of Mankind.

His apprenticeship in his brother's shop kept Franklin busy and out of mischief. For, in accordance with the contract which he had signed with his brother, he had indentured himself body and soul to his job—not only *during* but also *after* his working hours. "Taverns, inns, or alehouses"—thus ran the contract—"he shall not haunt. At cards, dice, tables, or any other unlawful games he shall not play. And"—continued the curious document—"matrimony he shall not contract."

In return for these prohibitions his brother had promised to keep him until his twenty-second year, to "teach him the art of printing," and to supply him with "meat, drink, washing, lodging, and all other necessaries during the said term." As for salary, there was to be none.

But Franklin wanted ready cash. And before long his ingenious mind hit upon a plan which would not only provide him with the necessary cash but would also supply his brother with extra funds. It was his brother's custom to take his meals, together with his workmen, at a neighbor's boardinghouse. "Suppose you let me eat by myself," said Benjamin, "and pay me only half of what my meals cost you."

His brother, like a regular Franklin, jumped at the idea. And thus both James and Benjamin saved money—James through his complacency, and Benjamin through his frugality. For, by changing his former diet of roast beef and cider to a strict regimen of vegetarian broth, the young apprentice was able to lay aside many a pretty penny for future use.

He enjoyed his vegetarian food—for ideal as well as for practical reasons. It soothed his conscience at the same time that it filled his pocket. "To eat meat," he had read in a book by a certain Mr. Tryon, "is a crime. For animals have souls. When you kill the body of a living creature, you do an injury to its soul." Throughout his life the son of the Yankee chandler maintained a double objective for his conduct: he tried to achieve moral purity and financial security. His motto was—a life full of good deeds and of good dollars. He was a perfect child of New England.

Yet he was unhappy in his New England surroundings. He couldn't get along with his brother. "This place isn't big enough for the two of us." And so on a September night in 1723, while the Bostonians were busy entertaining a delegation of Indians, the seventeen-year-old apprentice slipped quietly out of the city and boarded a sloop bound for new scenes and new services.

He disembarked at New York; but after surveying the "little village" of seven thousand inhabitants and finding it not at all to his liking, he fared on and finally landed in Philadelphia.

He was hungry and dirty and ragged, and he had used up all his capital with the exception of a single Dutch dollar. But he had a more important possession—the capital of a tenacious perseverance and a penny-counting thrift. Money, he said, is the most prolific thing in the world. A dollar married to a dollar results in healthy offspring. And it didn't take him long to prove the validity of this motto in his own case. He worked for some years as a printer in the Quaker City, saved his pennies, went to

London for more capital and experience, and finally returned to Philadelphia to open a printing shop of his own. Some of his friends tried to
discourage him. "We are in the midst of a Great Depression," they said.
"The country has stopped growing. Everything is going to the dogs." But
while these people sat idly *bewailing* conditions, Franklin worked steadily
to *improve* them. He familiarized himself with every phase of his business
—typesetting, presswork, engraving, binding. He even learned to make
the type. And, above all, he learned to make friends. Friendship, he said,
is the most precious thing in the world. Both spiritually and financially,
it pays.

His friendships really did pay. He organized a club—the Junto—whose
members exchanged ideas and brought business to one another. Franklin
was now sufficiently prosperous to think of marriage. He became engaged
to a charming young lady—and broke the engagement because she
couldn't bring him a dowry. And then he married a rather uncharming
but homelike and motherly young woman, and gave her one of his illegitimate children as a wedding present. He continued to increase his family
both by legitimate and by natural means, and to attend to his printing,
and to multiply his friendships, until he was ready at forty-one to retire
from business with an assured and comfortable income for life.

And then he really began to live.

III

FRANKLIN's business activity was the least important aspect of his many-
sided personality. The character of Franklin is a veritable kaleidoscope of
dazzling colors. The eighteenth century produced only one other man of
that universal type—Voltaire. But Franklin, though perhaps the less talented of the two, was the more versatile. He interested himself in almost
every phase of human activity. And in everything he undertook he became
a master. It seemed as if Nature, having experimented on every possible
type of American, decided at last to combine them all into one and created Benjamin Franklin. He was a journalist, statesman, philanthropist,
philosopher, scientist, inventor, humorist, and ambassador. And for a time
he even thought seriously of becoming the founder of a new religion.

His career in journalism had begun at sixteen. At that time he was engaged as a printer's apprentice on his brother's paper, the *New England
Courant*. One morning, when brother James opened his office, he found
an article that somebody had slipped under the door. The article was
signed—Mrs. Silence Dogood. "Sir," began Mrs. Dogood, who described
herself as the modest widow of a country parson, "it may not be improper
. . . to inform Your Readers that I intend once a Fortnight to present
them, by the help of this Paper, with a short Epistle, which I presume will
add somewhat to their Entertainment . . ."

This was the beginning of a series of letters, written in an unassuming
style that sheathed many a subtle sting at the follies of the day. Each of
these letters arrived at the office of the *Courant* via the selfsame crack

under the door. In vain the editor published a request that Mrs. Dogood bring the articles in person, so that "he might have the pleasure of her acquaintance." It was not until all the articles had been published that the "moralistic old lady" revealed herself to be none other than young Ben Franklin.

These cynical letters of Mrs. Dogood were the beginning of a cataract of political and social satires that tumbled from his laughter-loving pen throughout his life.

He wielded his pen in the service of his politics. Benjamin Franklin was one of the shrewdest of American politicians. And one of the noblest of her statesmen. He entered upon his public career at thirty, when he was elected clerk of the Pennsylvania Assembly. A few years later he became a member of that body. His constituents liked his forthright honesty in the declaration of his principles. Years before the Revolution he was the incarnation of the American spirit of independence. As early as 1737 he wrote in his *Poor Richard's Almanack:* "An innocent plowman is more worthy than a vicious prince"—a sentiment which the plowmen and the pioneers of America found after their own hearts. He advocated (1753) the confederation of the American colonies into a political union. He wrote an article—which was published in nearly all the newspapers of the colonies—representing the disunited colonies by the picture of a serpent cut into wriggling but helpless segments. Under this symbol he inscribed the words—"Join or Die." He tried to interest not only the American colonies but the English Government in this Confederated Dominion of the New World. But at that period both the American and the English politicians were too shortsighted to accept his plan.

Having failed in his national plan, the philosopher-statesman proceeded to look after the local interests of his people. The proprietary colony of Pennsylvania was going through a stormy crisis. The question of taxation was threatening to scuttle the Holy Experiment of the Quakers. The king demanded his taxes from Pennsylvania as well as from the other colonies. The people of Pennsylvania were willing to pay these taxes provided the proprietors of Pennsylvania—the two sons of William Penn who had inherited their father's colony but not his character—would contribute their proportional share. This the proprietors refused to do. Whereupon Franklin shouldered the responsibility of teaching the proprietors their lesson. He went to England, presented to the king the case of the people versus the proprietors, and won his point. From that time on the sons of Penn as well as the sons of penury were obliged to pay their share of the taxes.

As a member of the Assembly and later as Postmaster General, Franklin devoted himself as usual to a double service—to extend his own glory and to further the interests of the people. He had learned early in life the important fact that kindness is a profitable investment. "It is good business to do good." And thus he accumulated his dollars and his honors through the simple device of accumulating his friends.

Yet his motives were not altogether selfish. There was a strange admixture of idealism in the character of this practical Yankee. He was the first of the modern Americans—that delightful combination of sentimentalism and common sense. He promoted the happiness of his fellows because in this way he promoted a happy feeling in himself. He used his politics as a soil for the growth of his philanthropy. As a result of his influential position he was able to institute a police force, to inaugurate a fire department, to organize a street-cleaning division, to open an academy which later developed into the University of Pennsylvania, to improve the postal system, to build a lecture hall for free political and religious discussion, to establish one of the earliest colonial hospitals, and to create the first public library in America. Franklin was justly proud of these practical achievements—especially of the part he played in the education of the people through the library system. "These libraries," he tells us in his *Autobiography,* "have made the common tradesmen and farmers as intelligent as most gentlemen from other countries, and perhaps have contributed in some degree to the stand so generally made throughout the colonies in defense of their privileges." Through all his public career Franklin made it his business, insofar as he was able, to eliminate the physical and the mental imperfections of mankind. He regarded himself as an apprentice—God's apprentice. God had created the world, and Franklin tried to add the improvements and to keep the machinery in running order.

His interests were speculative as well as practical. He was one of the foremost philosophers and scientists of his day. Unschooled though he was in formal knowledge, he received honorary degrees from Harvard and Yale as well as from several of the leading universities of Europe. His Junto Club—a "modest gathering of artisans for mutual self-improvement"—developed later into the American Philosophical Society. Franklin's own achievement as a philosopher was second only to that of Voltaire. He was a Yankee Socrates. His philosophical papers, like the dialogues of Socrates, were marked by a forthright honesty and homespun simplicity. Like the Athenian sage who had made it his purpose to bring wisdom down from heaven as an everyday tool for his fellow men, the Yankee philosopher made it his business to interest himself in the human rather than in the divine problems of the world. He liked to speculate on the needs of men rather than on the nature of God.

Franklin's philosophy, in other words, is utilitarian. It takes a practical turn. His primary concern was to make the world a better place to live in —materially as well as morally. Accordingly he interested himself in all sorts of scientific experiments with a view to improving and to prolonging human life. He lived in an age when everybody was excited over that "new mysterious substance—electricity." People wrote texts of polysyllabic pretentiousness in which they discussed the theoretical question as to whether there is any analogy between electricity and lightning. Franklin read none of these texts—he probably wouldn't have understood their Greek and Latin terminology if he *had* read them. Instead he resorted to the only simple and direct treatise which dealt with the question—the lightning itself. In the midst of a thunderstorm he went out with a kite in his hand to seek the answer to the problem. And the answer came flashing down from the heavens by way of the metal key attached to the end of the kite: *Lightning and electricity are one.*

Always he tried to reduce the mysteries of nature to their simplest equations. And in revealing these mysteries to his fellows he employed no subtle formulas but presented plain facts. And he made these facts *interesting.* While the pedants huddled in their dusty rooms, Franklin invited his friends to an "electrical picnic" on the banks of the Schuylkill. At this picnic he announced, "Spirits are to be fired by a spark sent from side to side through the river, without any other conductor than the water . . . A turkey is to be killed for our dinner by the electrical shock and roasted by the electrical jack, before a fire kindled by the electrical bottle . . . And the healths of all the famous electricians in England, Holland, France, and Germany are to be drank in electrified bumpers, under the discharge of guns from the electrical battery."

But Franklin didn't confine his experiments to electricity. His investigations extended into the fields of pathology and anatomy; he studied the nature and the velocity of the winds and the current and the temperature of the Gulf Stream. Blessed with skillful hands as well as with a versatile mind, he developed several of his experiments into practical inventions. Even as a boy he had devised a pair of hand paddles which enabled him to outswim his playfellows. When he was an assemblyman in Pennsylvania he invented a street lamp which turned the narrow lanes of Philadelphia into "great white ways" as compared with the dimly lighted thoroughfares of metropolitan London. Aiming always, as he did, at the comfort of his fellows, he invented an iron stove which consumed less fuel and gave greater heat. And—here is an interesting phase of his personality—this "greatest inventor of the colonial period" refused to take out a patent on any of his inventions. The human race, he said, is one brotherhood; no one should receive pay for the presents he gives to his brothers.

Franklin was not only the leading scientist of the colonial period, but he was its greatest humorist as well. In his humor he was the forerunner of Mark Twain. Like Mark Twain, he told some of his best stories orally, for men's ears only. But even in his written work we can frequently observe the hearty flavor and the unrestrained laughter of the outdoors. It is the humor of a pioneer country. Practically all his writings are sprinkled with the spice of his pointed aphorisms. He is at his best in his *Poor Richard's Almanack.* To be sure, many of the adages contained in this *Almanack,* like many of the stories in Shakespeare's plays, are not original. They are, as Franklin himself confesses, "the gleanings . . . of the sense of all ages and nations." But Franklin took this universal wisdom and whittled it into something distinctly American. He expresses the deepest truths in the fewest words. As a rule, Franklin's aphorisms deal with the homely virtues—such as duty, thrift, industry, honesty, and common sense. Every American school child is familiar with Poor Richard's truisms that *honesty is the best policy,* that *God helps them that help themselves,* that *there are no gains without pains,* and that in order to succeed, *you must keep your nose to the grindstone.* These, and many others like them, are mixed like tasty raisins into the pudding of our everyday American thought. But not all his maxims are of the type that inculcate the simple constructive virtues. Many of them are as cynical as the darts of Voltaire's or of Swift's destructive satire. Again and again Franklin expresses his contempt for courtiers and kings "and other such useless trash." *He who would rise at court,* he tells us, *must begin by creeping.* He is amused at the endless royal squabbles over petty causes. *Children and princes,* he observes, *will quarrel over trifles.* He is disgusted with the extravagance of the kings at the expense of their subjects. *The king's cheese,* he writes, *is half wasted in parings.* But, adds Franklin sarcastically, this is of no concern to the king. For his cheese *is made of the people's milk.* With a hearty American disdain, he laughs at purple blood, or blue blood, or "ancient ancestral" blood. *All blood,* he points out, *is alike ancient.* Ancestry, aristocracy, and royalty have no place in the democratic philosophy of his American humor.

Franklin's disdain for royalty was equaled by his dislike for war. To the colonial American, war was a distasteful business—sometimes necessary, perhaps, but always disgusting. The American settlers had more important jobs to attend to. They were interested not in destroying but in building. Yet the American frontier had to be protected—and Franklin was above all a realist. Accordingly he was active in the organization of an American militia. When General Braddock came with his British soldiers to defend the colonies against the French and the Indians (1755), Franklin not only raised a large sum of money for his army but helped to supply him with guns and wagons. Civilian though he was, he had the military foresight to advise Braddock that his European manner of fighting in close ranks would only be playing into the hands of the Indians, accustomed as they were to shooting from behind the shelter of trees and rocks. Unfortunately Braddock disregarded this advice—with disastrous results.

Franklin's military experience was not confined to giving advice. For several months during the French and Indian War he commanded a division of troops in defense of the northwestern frontier. He engaged in no actual battles but he won the respect and the discipline of his men. He restrained them with a witty tongue rather than with an iron fist. On one occasion the chaplain of the division complained that the soldiers refused to come to the prayer meetings. "I have a good remedy for that," said Colonel Franklin. "Offer them rum after their prayers." The remedy worked. From that time the prayer meetings enjoyed a perfect attendance.

Franklin, however, felt more at home in the diplomatic arena than in the military camp. In 1765 he was at the British court as the unofficial ambassador of the American colonies. The Stamp Act had just been passed against America. This act provided that all bills, legal documents, marriage certificates, and the like were to be written only on stamped and taxed paper. The colonists were indignant, and Franklin undertook to point out to Parliament the injustice and the folly of such an act. It would prove to be an excessive burden, he argued, to the people of the American frontier, who had become impoverished as a result of the French and

Indian War. The English Government, he insisted, had no right to impose taxation without representation.

"Do you think," he was asked, "that the people of America would submit to pay the stamp duty if it was moderated?"

"No, never," replied Franklin. "The people of America would never submit unless compelled by force of arms."

The British Parliament heeded Franklin's words. The Stamp Act was repealed, and for the time being the Revolutionary War was averted.

At first Franklin was not favorable to the American Revolution. He was afraid it might fall into the hands of the unthinking mob. "A mob," he had written in *Poor Richard's Almanack*, "is a monster—heads enough but no brains." What he aimed at for his country was a confederation that would be a peaceful, free, and integral part of the British Empire. Franklin hated war. But when, against his advice, the war was declared, he threw himself heart and soul into the American cause. For he realized at last that America was compelled to choose between foreign rule and freedom. Franklin's love for freedom proved to be greater than his regard for England. Once more he urged upon his people a confederation—this time, however, not as an integral part of the British Empire but as an independent unit. "If you do not all hang together, you will be hung separately."

During the course of the Revolution he was inspired to some of his most pungent satire. In his attitude toward the conduct of the (German) Hessian leaders in the British Army—King George III himself, it must be remembered, was a German—Benjamin Franklin outswifted even Swift himself. He directed a satirical pamphlet against the brutality of the German princes who sold their Hessian soldiers to the British Army. The pamphlet is written in the form of a letter directed by a petty German prince to his Hessian general in America, urging him not to spare the lives of his men, since England gave him thirty guineas apiece for each soldier killed, and he needed this money for his coming opera season:

"I am about to send you some new recruits," writes the prince. "Don't economize them. Remember glory before all things. Glory is true wealth. There is nothing that degrades the soldier like the love of money. He must care only for honor and reputation, but this reputation must be acquired in the midst of dangers. A battle gained without costing the conqueror any blood is an inglorious success, while the conquered cover themselves with glory by perishing with their arms in their hands. Do you remember that of the three hundred Lacedaemonians who defended the defile of Thermopylae, not one returned? How happy should I be could I say the same of my brave Hessians!"

At the time when he wrote this denunciation of the military-minded brutality of the Prussians, Franklin was serving as the American ambassador in Paris. When Congress had elected him to this post he had said, "I am old and good for nothing; but, as the storekeepers say of their remnants of cloth, I am but a fag end, and you may have me for what you please." Yet this "fag end" of a precious personality succeeded in performing a double service in Paris: he enlisted the aid of the French in the American Revolution, and he helped to sow the seeds of the French Revolution. Thanks to Benjamin Franklin, the New World was the teacher of the Old World in the experimental science of self-government.

Throughout his stay in Paris, Franklin was the sensation of the day. Everybody flocked to see the strange son of an American tallow chandler who looked like a peasant and talked like a god. The populace cheered him, the ladies lionized him, and even the king addressed him with respect. And Franklin, as of old, took his cheers and his honors with his tolerant smile and his whimsical humor. One day a gushing old lady congratulated him on the beautiful spectacle the "fighting Americans" were giving to the world. "Yes," replied Franklin dryly. "It's a beautiful show, but the spectators haven't paid the price of admission."

His person, like his style, was simple and unadorned. On only one occasion—when invited to a royal function—did he condescend to go shopping for a wig, since a wig was the absolute rule at court. But he was not able anywhere to be fitted. "It isn't that the wigs are too small, sir," remarked a clerk at one of the stores, "but your head is too big."

One day the "biggest head in America" met the "biggest head in France." This encounter between Franklin and Voltaire was, in the words of a contemporary journalist, "the event of the eighteenth century." The two old philosophers—Franklin was seventy-one and Voltaire eighty-four —shook hands and then impulsively embraced, while the spectators "burst into tears." Franklin had his grandson with him at the time. Voltaire placed his hands upon the child's head and in a voice trembling with emotion said: "My boy, dedicate yourself to God and Liberty."

IV

WHEN Franklin returned to America (1785), he was nearly eighty years old. But his work was not yet over. At eighty-two he attended the Constitutional Convention. He was too weak now to stand long on his feet, so his speeches were read out by a friend while he sat and nodded his wise white head in approval.

When the convention was over he felt that he had outstayed his welcome in a world that had proved so hospitable to him. "I seem to have intruded myself into the company of posterity," he said, "when I ought to have been abed and asleep."

But there was one more thing to do before he went to bed. He must inaugurate one more crusade before he could lay down his trembling pen. A crusade against human bondage. He gathered enough strength to finish his *Plea for the Abolition of Slavery*—and then the summons came.

His last hours—he was suffering from pleurisy—were painful. When one of his attendants tried to turn him on his side so he could breathe more easily, he observed, "A dying man can do nothing easy."

Yet he was cheerful to the end. "These pains will soon be over." And after that? "I cannot suspect the annihilation of souls . . . I believe I shall in some shape or other always exist."

IMPORTANT DATES IN THE LIFE OF BENJAMIN FRANKLIN

1706—Born, Boston.

1723—Broke away from his printer's apprenticeship in Boston and set up for himself in Philadelphia.

1730—Married Deborah Reid.

1730-44—Established the *Pennsylvania Gazette,* the Philadelphia Library, the American Philosophical Society.

1732-57—Published *Poor Richard's Almanack.*

1746-52—Investigated nature of lightning.

1753—Appointed Postmaster General of the colonies.

1754—Introduced a project for uniting the thirteen colonies under a central government.

1766—Aided in bringing about the repeal of the Stamp Act.

1775—Appointed to the Continental Congress.

1776—Served on committee to draw up the Declaration of Independence.

1776-85—Minister to France.

1782—Negotiated, together with Adams and Jay, the treaty of peace with England.

1785-88—President of the Supreme Council of the State of Pennsylvania.

1787—Delegate to the Constitutional Convention.

1790—Signed, as President of the Abolition Society, a petition to Congress to suppress the slave trade and to abolish slavery.

1790—Died, Philadelphia.

George Washington

[1732-1799]

WE BEGIN our story of George Washington with three scenes:

First scene, shortly after Brandywine:

Washington has been riding furiously all day. A lashing rainstorm has arisen. Washington has taken shelter in a farmhouse. He is about to change into dry clothes when the farmer knocks at the door. "Pardon me, sir, but would you mind stepping into the parlor when you are ready? My little daughter is anxious for a peep at our great visitor."

"Glad to oblige," laughs Washington. And without waiting to take off his rain-drenched clothes he proceeds to present himself to the little girl.

"Well, my dear," he says, "you see a very tired old man in a very dirty shirt."

*   *   *

Second scene, just before Trenton:

The American cause is on the brink of disaster. A member of the Philadelphia Congress is waiting upon Washington. "The general appeared much distressed," writes this congressman, "and he lamented the ragged and dissolving state of his army in affecting terms. I gave him assurances of the disposition of Congress to support him . . . While I was talking to him I observed him to play with his pen and ink upon several small pieces of paper. One of them by accident fell upon the floor near my feet. I was struck with the inscription upon it. This inscription was—'victory or death.'"

*   *   *

Third scene, at Valley Forge:

For weeks now his half-naked men have eaten no meat. The Congress at Philadelphia has taken no steps to supply the army with food or clothing or shelter. The rank and file are ready to desert. Even Washington has come to the reluctant conclusion that the case is hopeless. He has just written his resignation as commander in chief. He sits toying with his white-handled penknife as he discusses his resignation with General Knox. "This penknife," observes Knox, "is the best argument against your resignation."

Washington looks at Knox with a puzzled expression in his eyes. And then he remembers. The penknife is an old present from his mother. Years ago, at the age of fifteen, he wanted to enlist in the navy. His kit had already been taken aboard and he himself was on the point of following when his mother, in a final plea, induced him to remain. As a reward his mother ordered a "good penknife" from England; and when it arrived, she presented it to him with the words, "Always obey your superiors."

Washington's friends have often heard this story from his lips. And now, when he is about to resign from the army, General Knox reminds him of his knife as the symbol of his duty. Always obey your superiors. "Congress has commanded you to lead the army. Nobody has commanded you to lay down this leadership."

"You are quite right," agrees Washington. "It is not for me to make the decision." And picking up the resignation from the table, he tears it into pieces.

* * *

These episodes represent three of the outstanding facets of Washington's many-sided character. When we try to pierce through the legendary mists that surround his figure, we see him stand forth as a man of simplicity, determination, duty.

But this is only a small part of the living picture that is George Washington.

II

OF ALL the great men of the past, George Washington is perhaps the most difficult to visualize in the living flesh and blood. He stalks like a shadow through the pages of history. The fault, we believe, lies with two of his earliest biographers: Parson Weems and Professor Sparks. The parson depicted him as a bundle of Sunday-school maxims, and the professor displayed him as a glorified wax dummy. Both of them made the unwise attempt to deify him and succeeded only in dehumanizing him. Most of his later biographers, taking their cue from their earlier models, have pumped the hot red blood out of his veins and refilled them with a cold preservative fluid. They have even mutilated his own words and transformed them from living tones into dead echoes.

For example:

One day, when aroused over the conduct of Edmund Randolph, he declared: "A damneder scoundrel God Almighty never permitted to disgrace humanity." His editors changed this to, "A greater scoundrel never disgraced humanity."

On another occasion, when he discussed a proposed appropriation by Congress, he observed: "One hundred thousand dollars will be but a flea-bite." His editors expurgated this into, "One hundred thousand dollars will be totally inadequate."

And thus his early biographers edited not only Washington, by their invention of words that Washington never said, but they also edited God, by their creation of an image that God never made. If we are to understand Washington as a living personality, we must at the very outset recognize the fact that he was human and not divine. He had human faults as well as human greatness. He was not a paragon of virtue. On occasion he lied, he swore, he flirted, he gambled, he lost his temper, and he whipped his unruly slaves. And he did not look, as he is almost universally pictured, like a flawless ancient statue dressed in a Continental uniform. As a matter of fact, his jaw was somewhat out of shape as the result of a poorly fitting set of false teeth. And—a point which most of his painters and his sculptors have tried to conceal—his face from early youth was disfigured with pockmarks.

He was a poor looker and a poor speller. He rarely got his *es* and his *is* correct in such words as *believe, receive, ceiling.* The color *blue* he always spelled as *blew.* The word *lie* generally appeared in his papers as *lye.* He referred to London as the great *matropolis.* And once, when he was disappointed in love, he wrote that he would *eliviate* his sorrow by staying away from the ladies.

Yet all these blemishes, far from belittling the Father of Our Country, only tend to make him more approachable, more lovable, more human. Knowing Washington as he really was, we shall stop adoring a manikin and begin to admire a man.

III

As a boy he was shy, reserved, and unprecocious. His early acquaintances remembered him as a gangling youngster with a gawky nose. "His nose," remarked his mother, "seems to grow faster than all the rest of his body." As a result of this defect he always felt inferior in company. And determined. "Someday, somehow, I'll make them like me in spite of my nose."

At eleven he lost his father. And then he was more determined than ever. In accordance with the inheritance laws of the day, his brother Lawrence, the eldest of the Washington children, had received the bulk of his father's estate. Young George would have to carve out his own fortune. And he meant to do it! "For all my handicaps, I must get people to respect me."

But in the meantime he must get through with his education. A practical education, fit for a youngster who meant to live a practical life. Reading, writing, arithmetic—especially arithmetic. Two acres plus two acres equals four acres. Four plus four equals eight. When he grew up he would add acre to acre, house to house, plantation to plantation. He would be a rich man. *That* was the way he would get the respect of his neighbors. He would take after his brother Lawrence. This young man, George's senior by fourteen years, was already one of the most respected citizens of Virginia. A landowner, an aristocrat, a soldier. A shining hero for a shy but energetic, proud, and ambitious young fellow.

At his brother's invitation he went to live with him. Here, at the spacious estate of Mount Vernon, he met all the fine gentry of Virginia. They treated him as one of them. He rode with them after the foxhounds, rode at breakneck speed, and they applauded him for his horsemanship. He was glad now he had given up his momentary impulse to go to sea. He was too fond of the land, of galloping through the pathless forests, of dancing over the polished floors of the drawing room.

Yet it wasn't often he got an opportunity to dance. He was too awkward—over six lanky feet of bones and sinews and knuckles, with size thirteen shoes and "the biggest hands in the colony of Virginia." And he was too bashful. Instead of speaking boldly to the girls he wrote verses to them, hinting—in a manner that would delight the modern psychoanalysts—at conquests and flirtations that he dared not bring to fulfillment.

In deluding sleepings let my eyelids close
That in an enraptured dream I may
In a rapt lulling sleep and gentle repose
Possess those joys denied by day.

He soon gave up his poetry, however, and returned to the field in which he was much more adept—mathematics. He took up surveying. As a preliminary to *owning* land he would learn to *measure* land.

At this point a stroke of good fortune came to him in the guise of Lord Thomas Fairfax. This nobleman owned an estate amounting to the almost incredible figure of five million acres. He hired young Washington to survey this land. The job, with interruptions, lasted about two years—a period, to a penniless youngster, of "lavish" earnings. "A Dubleloon," wrote Washington, "is my constant gain every day that the weather will permit my going out and sometimes Six Pistoles." A doubloon was worth about seven dollars, and six pistoles amounted to about twenty-one dollars.

When finally he returned from his surveying he felt "comfortable in purse and rich in experience." It was his first protracted contact with the hardships of the wilderness. On the first night out, he tells us, he was put up at a farmhouse where he was surprised to find his blanket "with double its weight of vermin, such as Lice, fleas, and so forth." On several occasions, "after Walking a good deal all the Day, I lay down before the fire upon a Little Hay, Straw, Fodder, or Bearskin . . . with Man, Wife, and Children like a Parcel of Dogs and Catts, and happy is he that gets the Birth nearest the fire." After experiences such as these he "made a promise . . . to sleep in ye open air."

IV

In 1751, George Washington accompanied his brother Lawrence to the island of Barbados, in the West Indies. His brother had contracted tuberculosis and had decided upon this trip to the "flowery garden of the tropics" in an effort to rid himself of the disease.

The trip did neither of them any good. Lawrence came home a dying man, and George a marked man. He had caught the smallpox at Barbados, and his face remained disfigured for life.

When Lawrence died he left his Mount Vernon estate to his little daughter, with George as her manager. In the event of his daughter's death, Lawrence had provided, George was to inherit the property. Within a short time the child died, and George became the owner of a sizable plantation and a flock of slaves.

But he was not satisfied. In order to gain the respect of his fellows it was necessary not only to *own* things but to *do* things. His brother Lawrence had been a soldier. George, too, wanted to be a soldier. He possessed a stronger body than Lawrence's—indeed, one of the strongest in the colony. "I have a constitution," he wrote to Governor Dinwiddie, "hardy enough to undergo the most severe trials." And he enjoyed the dangers of an exposed life. Once as a surveyor in the wilderness he had met a company of Indians returning from battle. And instead of terror he had experienced, to quote his own words, "an agreeable surprise." He had mingled with them and asked them "to give us a War Daunce." George Washington was insensitive to fear.

His reputation as a fearless explorer of the wilderness had reached the ears of Governor Dinwiddie, who appointed him as a messenger to warn the French away from the British territory in America. His mission was unsuccessful, but it gave him an invaluable lesson in the taming of an ice-filled river. "There was no way for getting over but on a Raft," he writes. "We set about building it with but one poor hatchet . . . Before we were halfway over we were jammed in the Ice . . . The Rapidity of the Stream . . . jerked me out into ten feet of water . . ."

A prophetic rehearsal for the crossing of the Delaware, many years later.

Shortly after his return from his mission to the French he was appointed aide-de-camp to General Braddock. He considered it a rare privilege "to attain some knowledge in the military profession . . . under a gentleman of General Braddock's abilities and experience."

He was disappointed, however, in his commander's abilities and experience when he witnessed Braddock's European methods in fighting an American war. In vain he pointed out to the general that in attacking the Indians you must adopt the backwoods style of fighting—that is, you must scatter your ranks and take advantage of the sheltering rocks and trees. But Braddock, a man "devoid of both fear and common sense," disdained the "skulking cowardice" of his American soldiers. He would meet the enemy in regular battle order, platoon formation, mass attack, and full face!

Such was his order at Turtle Creek (1755). His army was almost annihilated. How Washington escaped alive from this massacre is one of the
miracles of history. Three horses had been shot from under him. His
uniform had been punctured with several bullet holes. But his body had
received not a scratch.

And, in spite of his chagrin at the disaster, he had thoroughly enjoyed
the fight! "I have heard the bullets whistle," he wrote to his brother Jack,
"and believe me, there is something charming in the sound."

He reveled in the whistling of the bullets, but he shrank from the sound
of applause. For he had not yet overcome his bashfulness. In 1759, as a
reward for his "coolness under fire," he was elected to the Virginia House
of Burgesses. Mr. Robinson, the Speaker of the House, greeted the new
member in words of glowing praise. In answer to the cheers that followed,
Washington rose, cleared his throat, blushed, and sat down in embarrassed silence. "Mr. Washington," said the Speaker gently, "we quite understand. Your modesty is equal to your valor. And both are beyond the
power of words."

V

WASHINGTON was jilted by several young women because of his pockmarks
and the length of his nose. Finally, however, he succeeded in winning the
affections of Martha Custis, a personable young widow who possessed an
enormous estate and two little children. Their marriage was one of the
social events in colonial history.

George Washington's time was now divided between the management
of his Mount Vernon plantation and the care of his wife's estate (which
was called the White House). He took his place among the Virginia
gentry, he raised fine horses, he followed the foxhounds, he bought his
slaves—but he didn't sell them, for fear that they might fall into his
hands of an unkind master—and on the whole he seemed to be a safe and
sane exponent of British Toryism in America.

But somewhere within him there flickered the spark of rebellion. Just
when and where this spark had entered his heart we don't know. Perhaps
it was during his adolescent days of surveying among the pioneers that he
had learned to understand and to pity the lot of the underprivileged. Perhaps it was in the French and Indian War that he had come to despise the
superciliousness and the cruelty of the British officers in America. He was
a man of few words and he rarely made a display of his emotions. Yet
once or twice, in his campaigns with the British against the French, he
had expressed his resentment at the arrogance of the British officers
toward their American soldiers. "Captain Mackay," he wrote to Governor
Dinwiddie, "refuses to oblige his (British) men to work upon the road
. . . whilst our (American) soldiers are laboriously employed." On another occasion he wrote that it irked him, a colonel in the American
Army, to swallow the insults of the majors and the captains in the British
Army—men inferior to him "both in rank and in courtesy." The British,

he felt, looked upon themselves as a master race, and upon the Americans as their slaves.

And so he went about his business and observed much and thought much, but said little. He read about the British atrocities in Massachusetts and kept silent. He ready the fiery speeches of Patrick Henry and went back in silence to his plantation. And when, on June 15, 1775, he was appointed commander in chief of the American Army, he went silently to place himself at the head of the rebels. He had little confidence in himself as a military leader. "I do not think myself equal to the command I am honored with," he wrote at the time of his appointment. But he had the greatest confidence in the cause he was fighting for and the most implicit faith in the ability of his soldiers to win the war. At the Battle of Turtle Creek he had learned that the British soldiers knew how to run. And now he learned that the American soldiers knew how to stand. While he was on his way to Boston to take command of the army, he heard of the Battle of Bunker Hill. "Did the militia fight?" he asked.

"Yes," was the reply.

"In that case," said Washington, "the liberties of the country are safe."

VI

ONE of the chief characteristics of Washington as a military leader was his ability to outsmart his opponents. It was not without reason that they called him the Old Fox. The enemy was never able to guess at his plans, or to calculate the time or the place of his next attack, or to ascertain the size of his army. And, in order to keep the British in a continual state of befuddlement, he didn't *withhold* information but fed them with *wrong* information. He prepared false reports about his army and deliberately allowed the enemy to capture the messengers who carried these reports. And thus the British were always acting upon "certainties" that turned out to be illusions.

Yet let us not be unfair to the British. Their army was compelled to struggle under three disadvantages: a set of officers who didn't believe in their cause; a mob of Hessians who had been shipped to fight in America against their will; and a military campaign whose general outlines were planned not by the experienced commanders in the field but by the clerks of the War Department in London.

The officers of the British Army did not care to fight against the Americans. They wanted to conciliate them rather than to kill them. Had their hearts been in the war, they might have won it on several occasions by a decisive blow. For, in spite of Washington's brilliant maneuvers, they had the American Army trapped over and over again. But they never could find the energy to spring the trap. There was too much unnecessary danger on the battlefield, and too much fun in the cities where they were so comfortably stationed. They believed they could *starve* the Americans, instead of *shooting* them, into submission. In the meantime let the American rebels suffer while they themselves were living literally "on the fat of the land"—good food, jolly parties, pretty women, fine music, and excellent wine. To the Americans the Revolutionary War was a tragedy. But to the British officers it was a comic opera. It was a splendid show while it lasted; and, for all they cared, let it last forever.

Added to the heedlessness of the British officers was the listlessness of their Hessian troops. These Hessians had been sold by their German princes, like so many slaves, to fight for a nation whose language they didn't understand and for a cause in which they hadn't the slightest interest. Their princes got about fifty dollars apiece for selling them, but all that the Hessians got for their fighting was danger and sickness and death. Accordingly they developed their strength in their legs rather than in their arms. The Hessians in the British Army were among the best runners in military history.

But the greatest obstacle against which the British Army had to contend was the stupidity of the War Department which insisted upon mapping out in England the campaigns that were to be fought in America. It was a case of absentee generalship. The Englishmen in London knew nothing about the geography of the American wilderness, with its swamps and hills and gullies, its pathless forests and its impassable rivers. Accordingly they planned out a preposterous campaign (in the summer of 1777) whereby General Burgoyne, General Howe, and Colonel St. Leger, each one starting from a different point, were to meet at a certain date at Albany. The Tories were exultant. At last there would be a consolidation of the British forces, and the American Army would be crushed.

But things didn't work out as planned. The British commanders lost their way in the American bogs—a contingency unforeseen by the British War Department—and General Burgoyne, as he tried to find his way out again, was attacked and decisively defeated at Saratoga. Obliged to surrender, he agreed to ship his entire force back to England.

One of the English armies was now gone. But the other two still remained in America, and to Washington the situation looked as desperate as ever. For he, too, was beset with seemingly insurmountable difficulties and handicaps. The Congress, whenever he requested help, kept "nibbling and quibbling" and ended by refusing his requests. Neither in the Congress nor in the country was there a united consecration to the cause. The national crisis, like all other national crises the world over, had daily become the more critical through the obstructionism of the ill-disposed traitors and the well-disposed fools.

The Revolution, in other words, far from being the divine vision of "rosy pillars and patriotism," was in reality a very human mixture of grandeur and graft. Within the army, as in the Congress, there was backbiting, incompetence, dissension, and fraud. And the low ebb in this morale, both within and outside of the ranks, was reached at the Valley Forge period. Again and again during this period Washington complained of the desertions of the soldiers and of the "speculation and the peculation" of the profiteers. "Shall a few designing men . . . to gratify their own avarice, overset the goodly fabric we have been rearing at the expense of so much time, blood, and treasure?" On another occasion:

"General Fry . . . has drawn three hundred and seventy-five dollars, never done one day's duty, scarce been three times out of his home." And still again: "Different regiments were upon the point of cutting each other's throats . . . Many of the soldiers are deserting . . . Such a dearth of public spirit I never saw . . . and pray God I may never be witness to again."

But—and here we have Washington in his most admirable mood—"we must bear up . . . and make the best of mankind as they are, since we cannot have them as we wish."

And so he took his soldiers as they were and transformed them into a conquering army. They called him the "Necessary Man." As time went on he became to them more precious than their very lives. Again and again they begged him not to expose himself to the bullets of the enemy. But he laughed off their fears. *Their* danger, he said, was *his* danger; and *their* suffering, *his* suffering. He insisted upon sharing their risks, just as he insisted upon their sharing his triumphs. And even his very food. "One day," writes the Chevalier de Pontgibaud, "we were at dinner at headquarters. An Indian entered the room, walked round the table, and seized a large joint of hot roast beef. We were all much surprised, but General Washington gave orders that he was not to be interfered with. 'Gentlemen,' he said, 'let him be. He, too, it seems, is a hungry man.'"

The comfort of his soldiers was always a thought nearest to Washington's heart. An aide-de-camp who had come down with a heavy cold lay coughing in his cot, unable to fall asleep. Suddenly he became aware of a towering, night-clad figure approaching his cot. It was General Washington, who had got out of his bed to prepare a hot bowl of tea for his suffering "comrade."

VII

AT LAST George Washington, the "Old Fox" to the enemy, the "Gentle Father" to his own people, defeated Cornwallis (Yorktown, 1781) and won the freedom of America. And then, like the ancient Cincinnatus, he took off his military uniform and became once more a private citizen. His zest for battle was over. He wanted to be left alone, to end his days in the peaceful retreat of his Mount Vernon plantation, to raise his crops, to look after his slaves, to entertain his guests—"a glass of wine and a bit of mutton are always ready." He was old now, and his sight was impaired. "I have not only grown gray but blind in your service," he had said to the soldiers upon his retirement from the army. But he asked for no reward, and he refused to speak of his conquests. A guest remarked about his "thoughtful silence, with lips moving, as if wrapped in an inward isolation." It was in this mood of thoughtful silence that he met his friends and rejoiced in their joys and helped them in their sorrows. He dispensed his favors and distributed his charities with the request—as Bishop White informs us—"that this be done without ostentation or mention of my name." The noblest kind of charity, said the great Jewish philosopher Maimonides, is to give without revealing the identity of the giver.

And thus George Washington lived in peace, enjoying his declining years under his "vine and fig tree," as he expressed it, when unexpectedly his country drafted him once more into the turmoil of public life. His old "modest diffidence" was still upon him when he was elected to the presidency. "I wish," he declared in a public address, "that there may not be reason for regretting the choice." And in a private conversation with General Knox he remarked: "My movement to the chair of Government will be accompanied by feelings not unlike those of a culprit who is going to the place of his execution."

But he accepted his duty and like a good soldier fulfilled it to the best of his ability. He was not, as he himself readily admitted, among the greatest of statesmen, just as he was not among the greatest of generals. But he had one of the most solid characters in history, both as a statesman and as a soldier. He was that rarest type of individual who could win the admiration of his enemies as well as of his friends. He was *wholesome,* a *whole* man—just the sort of leader necessary in an infant republic. His personality was like a healthy mortar which cemented all the separate states, with their conflicting local differences and interests, into a national unit. His attitude toward national and international questions was conservative and, for that day, sound. The reactionaries thought him too liberal; and the liberals, too reactionary. But he wisely selected a middle course and persisted in that course to the very end of his administration. For his cabinet he appointed conservatives like Hamilton and radicals like Jefferson; and between the two extremes he was able to watch the pulse of the normal thought and temper of the people. He signed a treaty with England and he was charged with being an Anglophile. He refused to endorse the Reign of Terror in France and he was accused of being a counter-revolutionist. But in everything he did he had a single definite aim—to keep his nation independent and respected and *at peace.*

Throughout his two terms in the presidency there was a hysterical fear in many parts of the country that he wanted to become king. Washington made repeated attempts to dispel this "insane" fear. "I would rather be back on my farm," he said, "than to be seated on the throne of the *entire world.*"

And he meant it. At the end of the second term he flatly refused to be re-elected. "Although I have abundant cause to be thankful for the good health with which I am blessed, yet I am not insensible to my declination in other respects. It would be criminal, therefore, in me . . . to accept an office . . . which another would discharge with more ability."

And so John Adams took the presidential oath and George Washington, "his gray hair streaming in the wind," stepped down from the public gaze. As he passed through the cheering crowd, "his eyes were bathed in tears"—this picture comes from the lips of one of the bystanders, as quoted by Washington Irving—"his emotions were too great for utterance, and only by gestures could he indicate his thanks and convey his farewell blessing."

He had finished his job. "With God's help I have lived to see the

United States as one great whole . . . *a nation which may bid defiance in a just cause to any power on earth."*

IMPORTANT DATES IN THE LIFE OF
GEORGE WASHINGTON

1732—Born, Westmoreland County, Virginia.

1748—Became surveyor in the employment of Lord Fairfax.

1752—Received from Lieutenant Governor Dinwiddie commission as major in colonial forces.

1754—Defended Fort Necessity against an attack by the French.

1755—Fought under Braddock in disastrous battle at Turtle Creek.

1759—Married Martha Custis.

1774—Delegate to the First Continental Congress.

1775—Chosen commander in chief of the Continental Army.

1776-83—Led Continental Army to victory.

1783—Bade farewell to army and returned to private life in Virginia.

1787—Chosen president of the Constitutional Convention.

1789—Inaugurated as the first President of the United States.

1792—Re-elected for a second term.

1797—Retired from the presidency.

1799—Died, Mount Vernon, Virginia.

Paul Revere

[1735-1818]

EIGHT o'clock of a fine clear morning, and all's well!" Along Boston's water front trudged the town crier, bell ringing. Tar, fish, and rum mingled their spices with the tang of the clean salt air. Sailors from many ports jostled one another as Fish Street woke to life. "Sweep o' sweep," sang a black boy, brandishing his chimney broom. From the shop of Paul Revere, silversmith, came the clang of metal. The town's artisans were up betimes and at their tasks since dawn.

By the side of his father, young Paul worked. A swarthy boy, with strength in his stocky frame. A bewigged and powdered gentleman gazed at him in approval. "A likely lad," he observed. "Aye, likely. And industrious withal," agreed the father.

Paul's white teeth flashed in a ready smile. He was a sociable lad, and he liked the shop where usually there was plenty of company. His clever face wore a contented look, for he loved his work. The ring of metal and the faintly acrid odor—as bellows pumped to a rosy glow the embers in the forge—were well to his liking.

At sixteen Paul had finished what schooling was available. He was gregarious, and popular with his fellow apprentices. It was a good mixture that flowed in his veins. The father (christened Apollos Rivoire), refugee from the Huguenot persecutions in France, and the mother, a woman of Yankee stock, had produced fine sturdy offspring. And the finest of them was Paul—honest, fearless, and firm.

They were God-fearing, these Reveres, but not bigoted. They attended the church called the Cockerel, after the weather vane atop its spire. But the new Christ Church had eight bells in its tower. Enthralled by their soft mellow music, Paul organized five of his friends into a society of bell ringers. A secret society, with badges and salutes. The elders' tales of persecution had left their mark on the new generation.

When Paul was nineteen his father's death left him head of the family.

But adventure called. Turning the business over to his younger brother, he followed fife and drum into the wilderness. The hated French Jesuits in Canada were making trouble, razing border towns and stirring up the Indians. In blue jacket and red breeches, hatchet at his belt, Paul joined the volunteers to battle for the colonists' hard-won privilege to worship as they pleased.

A year of soldiering, and Paul was back at his trade—happy amid the familiar sounds and smells of his shop. He had taken to himself a bride, Sary Orne. Sary was a frail woman, but she knew what was expected of a wife. Skipping the odd numbers, she presented him with a child on each of the even years. Paul loved them all and awaited every new arrival with impatience. He also loved a ringing song and a "chearful glass." Every evening saw him at the Green Dragon or at some other favorite dram-shop. After general greetings Paul could be seen slipping unobtrusively into a back room. There he found his Masonic Brethren and members of other secret orders. Several of these societies were banded together into a league which they had named the Sons of Liberty.

II

PAUL WAS INVITED to join the Long Room, advisory council of the many secret orders. A tribute to his ability. This group was composed of Harvard graduates, professionals, and men of means. Paul was the only artisan in their midst. Times were bad, unjust taxes were being levied, the Stamp Act was causing indignation. Everywhere people were muttering.

At the head of the council was Sam Adams. Practical and farseeing, Adams argued for preparedness. "This state of public submissiveness cannot long endure," he declared. "The colonists must be organized to defend themselves in the eventuality of war." Many people shied away from the "Wild Radical," but Paul Revere stood resolutely by his side. Every new act of oppression swung him more firmly in the direction of revolt.

The Stamp Act was repealed, and there was great rejoicing. The lukewarm among the Sons of Liberty began to drift away. But Adams and Revere knew that this was merely the lull before the storm. Everywhere there were undercurrents of unrest, street fights, tarring and feathering, threats of death. In the midst of this turmoil Sary completed the pattern of her days. Having presented Paul with a daughter in one of her even years, she died the next. A time of vigorous demands. With a large family to rear, a man could not long grieve for his wife. Within a few months Paul married Rachel Walker—an intelligent, vigorous woman, with a mind of her own and a tongue that dared to speak. He was delighted with this woman who could "stand up to him."

They were prosperous, the Reveres. For though there was a decline in the silversmithing trade, Paul's Yankee ingenuity had enabled him to add two side lines to his business. Copperplate engraving, and dentistry. New England was pitifully tooth-shaken, and there was much work for Paul Revere. A simple profession, dentistry, as practiced then. It consisted mostly in extracting the corrupted tooth, and in substituting a tooth from a sheep or part of a walrus tusk. The operation lent an odd appearance to the patient, but enabled him to partake of solid food. Little skill was required for this work, and Paul had but little interest in the performance.

More to his taste was the engraving. Though he never attained real artistry in this handicraft, he did acquire a certain skill. Since practically all the work done was political propaganda, he gave himself with zest to its execution.

Paul had prospered steadily. He now possessed a mare, and had "bult a barne." His political sympathies, however, veered ever more strongly toward the left as the storm gathered for the inevitable crash against England. Paul loved his family, but his love for freedom was even greater. Rachel stood by his side—fit helpmeet for this stalwart son of a stalwart age.

III

PAUL had many calls upon his time. The tea act had again brought together the Sons of Liberty. Ships had lately arrived from England, their decks scarlet with soldiers. These "lobsterbacks" had come, not to protect, but to police. The townsfolk resented their insolent parade, and streets and taverns were loud with brawling. Even the weaker spirits among the colonists seethed under the insult of the "British invasion." Now it was that the Sons of Liberty had real need of their organization. The tea ships were arriving. The time had come when America must knuckle under or assert her rights. The colonists demanded that the ships depart from their shores. But there was in effect a law that ships could not sail unloaded. A deadlock? No. The Sons of Liberty had an answer ready for His English Majesty.

Like clockwork the secret society functioned. The grapevine buzzed with instructions. At dusk a crowd of Indians in war paint gathered at the docks. Strange that the populace did not challenge them. Strange, too, that many a white hand and face were visible underneath the Indian trappings. Surely that leader of the Mohawks had the figure and stride of Paul Revere. Onto the ships swarmed the "white" Indians. As the town watched in silent approval, the last leaf of tea went into the water. It was more than a bitter cup for His Majesty that had been brewed at that tea party. It was a message to the world that men can organize to combat oppression.

The people of Boston, washing paint from their faces and removing feathers from their hair, prepared for bed. But for Paul Revere there was to be no sleep that night. As Rachel placed cold meat and a flagon of wine in his saddlebag, he tightened his belt and fastened on his spurs. Embracing his "dear girl" and receiving her Godspeed, he swung into the saddle and was off on the first of his many rides. The Courier of Liberty.

To New York and Philadelphia he rode, and back, in twelve days, bringing heartening news. These port towns did not need his warnings that the tea ships might attempt to unload their cargoes there. For already the English ships were anchored at the wharves. But the two cities had sworn to resist this "greatest of all plagues." They voiced approval of the Bostonians' act and pledged their allegiance in the dark days ahead.

IV

PAUL FOUND that the New Yorkers "talk quick, and of an altogether." And that the Quakers "are inclined to be cautious." He was almost constantly in the saddle now, riding between the three cities. On each return to Boston he beheld ominous signs that the crisis was at hand. Many English ships rode at anchor in Boston harbor. There was "not a topsail to be seen—naught save ships of war."

General Gage had replaced Governor Hutchinson and, landing thousands of troops, had declared a state of martial law. Frantically the citizens were laying in supplies. Boston was closed to traffic, and Paul must make his journeys surreptitiously. Sometimes he slipped past the British sentries disguised as a farmer; at other times by means of a boat which he kept hidden at the riverbank.

There were other riders who kept the rebels informed of the British activities. With one of these riders Paul watched the fortifications that were being built by the "lobsterbacks." He was unimpressed. "They are mere beaver dams," he scoffed.

"We will kick them over with our stout boots," boasted his companion.

Concord and Lexington were gathering large stores of guns and ammunition. Undoubtedly, therefore, these towns would be the targets at which the British would aim. Signals were arranged. Paul and his fellow riders inside the city were to watch the troops. When they prepared to move, lanterns were to be hung in the belfry of Christ (now Old North) Church. Two lanterns if they left by water; one if they moved by land.

Tense days now, with troops drilling constantly on the common. And in the country British supplies mysteriously disappeared. Food wagons were overturned, flour and bacon hurled into swamps. Paul worked little at his trade, but he kept unrelaxing vigil.

And now a day dawns when the air is electric with suspense. There is movement everywhere. A tense quiet strains nerves as, all day long, redcoats mass on the common—hundreds, thousands of them. It is the long-awaited hour. Unseen eyes watch, to note what route the redcoats will follow. By water! Now the Sons of Liberty slip silently along side streets, each to his appointed task. At a back door Paul Revere stands waiting in the shadows. He is joined by Robert Newman. Together they hurry to Christ Church. Paul waits below until Newman hangs the two lanterns in the belfry. Then up another side street he glides and two more conspirators join him. They are to row him across the Charles River, to where his horse is being held in readiness.

But what is this? Our calm Paul so excited he has forgotten the cloth with which to muffle the oars! " 'Tis no matter," a companion whispers. "Wait!" Underneath a window he gives a low whistle, and a woman's head appears. A few whispered words, a few minutes of suspense, and a ruffled petticoat descends upon their heads.

"It is still warm from the wearer," Paul laughs.

"An ardent-hearted wench," chuckles his companion.

Now they are off again, and rowing under the very guns of the *Somerset*, British man-o'-war. From upstream float the sounds of the redcoats crossing. The three laugh silently, for the slightest sound would sign their death warrant. Across now, and Paul is mounting his horse. Their farewells are heartfelt, for they may be the last; this night's work may cost every one of them their heads.

Off into the path of the pale moonlight and straight into the pages of history gallops Paul Revere.

V

PAUL'S RIDE was not without mishap. Challenged by two British officers, he easily gave them the slip—his light mare taking to the swamps, where the heavy English animals could not follow. Man and beast blended as one, they sped onward to "alarum every house as far as Lexington."

And now the war had broken out in earnest, and Paul was a marked man. No longer could he go in and out of Boston, but must stay and get whatever news of his family the other blockade-runners were able to bring. That same family must be fed. In addition to Sary's children and his sister's, Rachel had generously contributed to the number. Paul rode post and was commissioned to print money for the new Congress. Gunpowder was needed, and Paul learned the secret of its manufacture. It was a war to the hilt now. The rebels must win their fight or lose their lives.

Through the Battle of Bunker Hill—cannon fire dinning in his ears— Paul worked steadily.

Events marched on. A new name was upon all lips. Young General George Washington was leading his ragged forces to victory after victory. The bright day dawned when Boston fell. The British had departed. From all sides, in carts and afoot, amid laughter and tears, the exiles streamed back into their city. Families were reunited, and once more the numerous Reveres occupied the house in North Square.

But not yet was Paul to settle down. General Washington ordered him to take command of Castle Island. Across this narrow strip of water separating the island from the town, Lieutenant Colonel Revere gazed wistfully at the mainland. He longed for his family and for the feel of satin-smooth silver in his hands. Paul could learn a new craft "as quick as you could turn about," and he made an excellent soldier. He had learned to cast cannon, of which the new Republic was in great need. But his heart was in Boston. Now and then he slipped over at night, to fire his forge and to fashion a pepper pot or a porringer—rejoicing that his hands had retained their skill.

The Fourth of July. Anniversary of the signing of the Declaration of Independence. Boston was gay in triumphant celebration. Cannon and fireworks saluted the dawn of a new life. From Castle Island, Paul fired cannon and musket, hailing the first birthday of the robust infant, Liberty.

And then—the fortunes of war took an unexpected turn for Paul Revere. After an unsuccessful foray against the British at Penobscot, Paul's commission was withdrawn. He was ordered to "repair to his dwelling," charged with having deserted his men in battle. For two years he petitioned for a court-martial, that he might clear his name. Yet the charges against him did not weigh too heavily on his mind, for they were unfounded. Primarily an artisan, he was happy in his work.

Foreseeing a demand for luxuries with the coming of peace, he placed in England large orders for goods that had long been absent from the Boston shops. "The old order changeth," and Paul keeps pace with the new. With the signing of peace his goods arrived, and he set up shop as a side line, never forsaking his forge for his new pursuits.

George Washington died, and the nation mourned as he was given a hero's burial. The Masons requested from his widow a lock of Washington's hair, that they might preserve it in memory of their beloved leader. Paul fashioned an urn of gold, within which—beneath a glass cover—they placed the cherished relic.

A new social life was arising in Boston. The China trade was in full flourish, bringing prosperity and foreign culture. Old fortunes were disappearing, new faces dominated the scene. These *nouveaux riches* had a tendency to bury their homespun past under a veneer of genteel elegance. Old comrades waxed bitter at this outcome of their heroic struggle. But Paul's bright eye surveyed the scene and found it all to the good. He perceived many new fields awaiting the exploration of his practical mind.

VI

STILL there was unrest, and Paul had much to do. The states were quarreling among themselves. The Federal Constitution had not yet been ratified by Massachusetts. Sam Adams found it inadequate and withheld his signature. He saw therein the seeds of future strife and advised changes and additions. Once more the Green Dragon received its secret guests. After a lengthy council the leaders emerged, Paul among them, and paraded to Adams's house. They demanded immediate ratification. Bowing to the will of the people, Adams signed.

Paul was engrossed in a new project. In his shop he sold hardware and envisioned the time when this would all be made at home, not imported. Day and night he was busy in a shed he had rented. One bright morning he emerged to face an indignant housewife, her arms akimbo. "Pray, what is the meaning of this, Mr. Revere?" she demanded. "Filthy soot all over my clean linen every time the wind is about."

Paul pointed jubilantly to the belching smokestack. "We've got our furnace agoing!" he shouted.

Frowning, the woman surveyed the soot-smeared wash. She covered her ears against the clanging sounds and her nose against the smells that issued from the shed. But to Paul these sounds and smells were perfumed music. He moved his home, to be closer to them. Modern industry had come to Boston.

In the midst of all this activity Paul was granted his court-martial and was exonerated of the charge of desertion.

Faster now. Everyone was in a rush. The Industrial Age was ushering in new modes and greater needs. Paul cast his first bell. It was "panny, harsh, and shrill." But Boston and Revere were inordinately proud of it. It made an excellent fire alarm. Enchanted by his new work, Paul was determined to perfect his art until his bells would outmatch the sweetness of the English bells.

The Reveres were right prosperous now. Paul had established a copper foundry in Canton. There they spent their summers, returning to Boston for the winter. Rachel had time for "lolling" a bit, and attired herself in the latest Paris mode. Paul had been elected Grand Master of the Masons, and attended banquets and parades. On the nights when he was at home there were backgammon and whist to while away the hours. Rachel's tongue was as quick as ever, her tart observations still bringing a twinkle to Paul's eye. Only five children and three grandchildren remained with the old folks. The others had scattered inland, where industrialization was opening up the country.

Paul clung to the knee breeches and the cocked hat of his youth, even though the fashion in men's clothing had changed. In all things else he was in the vanguard. The ban on card playing, dancing, and the theater had been lifted, thanks to a committee of which he was the heart and the head. Valiantly he campaigned for prison reform, for the better treatment of the insane, for every cause that seemed to him liberal and just. Nor were personal problems too much for him. Deborah Gannett, the only woman to fight in the Revolution, had fallen into a pitiable state of poverty. Paul petitioned Congress and won a pension for her. The apprentice system was still in effect. Paul told his fellow artisans that higher wages and shorter hours would make better workmen—and he set the example in his own factories. "A strange creature, Paul Revere. He really practices what he preaches."

VII

PAUL had more time now for cultural pursuits. His many ventures were well organized. Paul Revere III carried on the tradition in the silversmith shop. Joseph Warren Revere supervised the copper foundry. This gave their father leisure to write poetry. Though mediocre, Paul's verses were full of good will, reflecting deep contentment with his lot.

His correspondence had become voluminous. Interested in genealogy, he exchanged letters with his relatives in Europe. To one relative, John Rivoire, he lamented that there would be no more young Reveres. A mere sixteen children, when a man could well have done with a good even twenty.

Civic affairs still claimed him. With other workers, he organized a League of Artisans. Their first object was to institute reforms beneficial both to apprentices and to employers. And thus the merit system was inaugurated.

Life was shaping itself at last into a pattern of quiet and contented usefulness. But, after a short illness, Rachel died—and Paul was left to "trudge on alone."

He had almost reached his eightieth birthday now. But with his round, ruddy face topped by a mane of thick white hair, he looked scarcely more than sixty. The hale man was a familiar sight to Bostonians. He was to be seen everywhere, his knee breeches and ruffles conspicuous amid the fashionable long trousers. "As regularly as comes Sabbath" he attended church.

Ever ready with a jest, eye twinkling in merriment, this patriarch playboy was a great favorite with the neighborhood children. Especially on those days when a new bell was being tested before the purchasing committee. When some fascinated youth drew too close, Paul would prod him gently with his cane. "Stand back, lad," he would warn. "If that hammer hits your head, you will make more noise than the bell."

Gone were all his old comrades—those valiant men whose sacrifices had built a nation. And perhaps it was for the best. Many would have lamented the turn of events. For the great leveling process had begun. Beacon Hill, that gallant landmark, was disappearing bit by bit. All day long the carts trundled up and down, dumping their loads of earth into the Charles River. With hands folded behind his back, legs astraddle, Paul watched—interested only in the engineering feat.

At night he sat in the spacious parlor, glancing now and then at Rachel's empty "lolling chair." At times his gaze rested on the small gold urn containing the lock of George Washington's hair. And a sigh or two would escape him.

VIII

"Eight o'clock of a fine clear morning, and all's well!" Bostonians in their Sunday best are churchward bound. From every quarter of the city, bells summon the worshipers—Revere bells, most of them. But hold now!—a new voice joins the chorus—the Passing Bell. It is Paul's masterpiece and hangs in King's Chapel. Many civic-minded citizens have added their family silver to the casting, to give it that fine mellow tone.

Churchgoers pause to listen, counting the strokes. A male! Eighty-three years! Paul Revere has made another silent crossing—this time over the Dark River—and is departed on his last great ride.

IMPORTANT DATES IN THE LIFE OF
PAUL REVERE

1735—Born, Boston.

1756—Served at capture of Crown Point.

1774—Patrolled Boston streets to watch British troops. Urged seizure of British military stores at Portsmouth, New Hampshire.

1775—April 18—Entered upon famous Midnight Ride.
Set up powder mill at Canton, Massachusetts.

1776—Commissioned major in Massachusetts Militia.

1779—Took part in Penobscot expedition.

1795—Laid cornerstone of new State House in Boston.

1818—Died, Boston.

Daniel Boone

[1735-1820]

DEEP silence, and the snow-blanketed forest brooding in mystery. A young man finished carving letters on the bark of a huge oak. Sheathing the long hunting knife, he stepped back to view the handiwork.

D. Boone kilt a bar hear 1754

A sound reached the youth's ears. He slipped noiselessly behind the tree. Frontiersmen, with senses trained to detect the faintest signs of danger, hid first and investigated afterward. It was no childish game they played, but a grim battle for existence where a few seconds' negligence might cost a life.

Within a few feet of his hiding place an Indian passed, townward bent and, therefore, probably friendly. So quietly did the Indian make his way through the snow that his footsteps would have been inaudible to ears untrained in forestcraft. All too often had some townsman been caught unaware, never to be heard from again. Nor could the settlers be too sure even of the friendly Indians who might, upon slight provocation, turn to relentless enemies. In Daniel's mind all this knowledge was instinctive. A sixth sense guided his actions. Taking a course parallel to that of the savage, and careful always to keep a good distance, he walked toward the village. Inured since infancy to hardship, he was unmindful of the wet clothing that, stiff with freezing, grazed his hard young body. From his belt hung knife and powder horn. The small bear hung head downward, its feet pegged across the long gun which Daniel carried over his two shoulders, yoke fashion.

Here in the Yadkin Valley was true wilderness. After the settled towns of Pennsylvania, Daniel's heart thrilled to the vast unexplored tracts of woodland—the abode of wild beasts and savages. The old restlessness had seized him again. Of late more settlers had arrived in his neighborhood. With cabins springing up as fast as mushrooms, some scarcely a mile apart, he felt cramped. "A good gun, a good horse, and a good wife" were all that were necessary to a man's happiness, he had said. And now the homesteaders were thronging in, bringing with them the customs and appurtenances of civilization. Time to move on and find elbowroom.

A roving tribe, the Boones. Solid Quaker stock, migrated from lovely Devon, in England, to Pennsylvania. Thence to North Carolina. And always with an eye to the surveying of more land. Here was young Daniel, in whom all the wanderlust of his forebears seemed concentrated and whose foot ever tingled with the urge to be off.

That urge had been stilled for a while when, as a wagoner, he followed Gage's men into the campaign against the Indians. A fateful trip. The ghastly slaughter of Gage's men had filled him with horror. The trip had been fateful in more ways than one. For then he had met and talked with Finley, first white man to travel beyond the mountains and deep into the wilderness. By the flickering campfire and on the hot dusty trail he had listened to Finley's tales of Kaintuck—that lush virgin land where the wild cane grew far above a man's head, where forest and river teemed with game. A man must be careful lest he kill more than he had need for.

Emerging from the forest, Daniel could see in the distance the smoke curling from his own chimney. Rebecca would be waiting with a sigh for his safe return. What would she say to this news, that the wilderness was beckoning him with a lure he no longer had the strength to resist? A grand wife, Rebecca! Smiling, he slackened his pace and allowed his mind to travel back over the days of their meeting. Surely there never had been such another courtship!

II

WITH DANIEL it had been love at first sight, and all evidence pointed to reciprocation on the part of the bright-eyed Rebecca. But while the Boones were courageous, they were also cautious—looking well before they leaped. He laughed aloud now, remembering the little drama he had staged to test her patience. Playing with his hunting knife, he had cut her most treasured article of clothing—a fine white cambric apron, irreplaceable finery here on the frontier. Rebecca, with never a rebuke, had smiled sweetly. "Don't you worry, Daniel. The tear is nothing at all." And so she had the gentle nature he sought, and he could proceed to carry out the gesture required of a young man seriously courting.

Bringing to the cabin of his betrothed a deer which he'd slain, he skinned and quartered the beast before the assembled friends. Proof that he could provide for a family. Much comment accompanied the operation. The girls teased Daniel about the amount of blood and grease he had smeared on his shirt. Daniel smiled good-naturedly, biding his time. When all were set about the festive board, he stared soberly into his jug of milk. "You, too, like my shirt, have missed many a washing." A gasp, and then laughter. He was a one who could jest as well as be serious.

So then they had been married. In symbolic gesture, Rebecca was transferred from the back of her father's horse to that of her new husband.

After this ceremony the feasting began. Liquor flowed freely and tongues wagged gaily. The young couple were escorted to their loft quarters, recipients of much sound advice and many a coarse jest. On the frontier there was no room for delicacy. Men needed sons to help in the fields, to join the hunt. That was why men married, and none ever thought to pretend otherwise.

Daniel was nearing his cabin now, his thoughts back to the present. Crossing the threshold, he was aware of an atmosphere of festivity. In the semidarkness he saw by the fireplace a peddler, his pack open on the floor. The family stood about, yearning over the merchandise. And the peddler himself—surely he was fate in disguise, to have appeared on this day of all days. For when his eyes had accustomed themselves to the twilight, Daniel recognized in the peddler that very man Finley upon whom his thoughts had dwelt all day—that adventurer whose tales of Kaintuck were the source of his restlessness to be off and away. A restlessness, however, about which he was afraid to speak to Rebecca.

Daniel need never have felt hesitancy where his wife was concerned. When the supper things were cleared and Rebecca had seated herself at her spinning wheel, they talked. Finley's words painted a picture of a friendly fertile land, waiting for the mere claiming of it. As the logs crackled in the fireplace, sending dancing shadows about the cabin, husband and wife listened. Rebecca's foot became still upon the treadle, her hand holding the thread, as she looked at Daniel. Almost fearfully he met her gaze. She smiled and nodded. Daniel knew that she saw the thoughts in his mind, that she gave her consent. Knew, too, that always there would be this understanding between them. His heart filled with love and pride.

III

OTHER EYES than Daniel's were turned toward the new land. And there were other ears willing to listen to the tales of plenty. Taxes in North Carolina were high, and money was scarce. Then, too, the coming of so many settlers had driven the game away. Daniel's love for land did not include the tilling of it. Hunting was not only a necessity, it was also the very lifeblood of Daniel. As soon as his son James was able to walk, Daniel had taken him on long trips, imparting to him his own knowledge of woodlore. In the bitter cold he had carried the boy beneath his leather coat for warmth. And now James had attained to manhood and would make a fine companion for adventuring into the wilderness.

There were many who had listened to Daniel's stories and were ready to follow him. Among them were a few rich adventurers who saw that civilization would be spreading beyond its present boundaries and that there would be purchasers later for lands claimed now. If ever there was a man who could lead them to the Kaintuck and appraise the most valuable tracts, that man was young Boone.

And so a band of men set forth across the mountains, along the Warrior's Trace, under the leadership of Daniel and Finley. They had the utmost confidence in Daniel Boone as their shepherd. For he had mastered the art of gunsmithing and had learned to make his own powder. The forest was a book to him, each snapped twig or crushed leaf a page to be read and its message acted upon. None more familiar than Daniel with the tricks that the Indians might employ, and with the safest means for outwitting them.

For the savages he had a deep liking, calling them brothers. In return they admired the Great White Hunter, tales of whose prowess had gone before him. They considered it a happy day when they could outmaneuver him. It would be fine sport to capture him. You could admire a man and scare him at the same time. Besides, what business had he in their territory?

But the white men under Daniel Boone had grown careless. They camped at Dreaming Creek—symbolic name. Hunting in small parties and maintaining several camps, they piled high stacks of pelts that would bring them wealth. Around their campfires at night they permitted themselves to relax. For as yet they had been unmolested by Indians. . . .

When the blow came it was sudden. A band of Shawnees attacked Daniel Boone and one of his companions, John Stuart, who had gone ahead of the rest of the party. Goaded by the upraised tomahawks and the pricking of menacing arrows, Daniel and Stuart were compelled to disclose the several camps to their captors. Helplessly they looked on as the Indians plundered their camps. They had little doubt as to the fate that awaited them in the village to which they were being led. Every frontiersman was familiar with the tales of torture suffered by the white captives at the hands of the Indians. Few expected quarter when taken.

But the Shawnees meant no real harm to the Great White Hunter. They would just frighten him away from their land, that's all. Within a few days they released him, with a warning to return whence he had come and to trespass no more on Shawnee soil.

IV

DISHEARTENED by their losses, many of the men turned homeward. A few, still confident, pushed on. But as weeks lengthened into months the constant attacks of the Indians wore down their courage. In small companies they turned their footsteps back, until only Daniel and his brother Squire remained.

And now a new danger confronted them. Their ammunition was almost exhausted. Without the tools to hunt, a man must starve. Squire, it was decided, would return for supplies, while Daniel would travel as far as possible alone. Left by himself in the wilderness, with a volume of *Gulliver's Travels* for his only company, he hunted and explored by day. By night he hid in caves or in secluded camps. There were surprise attacks, but Daniel's sixth sense was functioning. Many a time he saved himself by rolling into the underbrush just as the enemy entered his camp.

His brother at last returned with supplies—which were promptly stolen by Indians who had pretended friendship. Back again to the settlement went Squire for new supplies, and Daniel forged on alone. He explored the whole of the lush Kaintuck. Returning to North Carolina, he brought glittering reports of that rich terrain. There were many who listened eagerly, and they were ready to follow into the "Promised Land."

Again he set forth, this time with a group of forty adventurers, to build the wilderness road. Several groups of surveyors had preceded this party. The Indians, infuriated by the ever-increasing numbers of white men who poured into their hunting grounds, had grown hostile. Daniel was now for the first time to meet with personal tragedy. His son James, while en route for supplies, was captured and tortured to death by a band of Shawnees. . . . Yet Daniel still called the Indians his brothers, nor could he feel any great enmity toward them. "Forgive them, Father, they know not what they do."

At long last the party reached the Great Salt Licks—the river where buffalo, in countless numbers, came to lick at the salt deposits. Boonesborough they named the spot, and set about building a fort and staking out claims. They organized a government and a militia. Daniel was appointed lieutenant, and then captain. Disputes arose and Daniel was appointed judge. Beneath a huge elm tree he meted out justice. Of the law he had but slight knowledge; his system of jurisprudence was as individual as his spelling. But the settlers were satisfied in their choice, and no one ever disputed his decisions.

Under the elm the small community held its first religious service, on an April day in 1776. The eighteenth it was—a fateful day here as well as in faraway Boston.

V

IN THE KAINTUCK, as in Massachusetts, the settlers were suffering at the hands of the British. But with a difference. Here in Kaintuck the English were stirring up the Indians against the white men, providing them with arms and liquor and—indispensable fighting material to the savage—war paint by the hundreds of gallons. Renegade Englishmen organized and directed the Indians in raids against Daniel and his men.

The Indians harassed the settlers constantly—for the most part in small marauding bands that stole livestock and destroyed crops. No open warfare had, as yet, taken place. Once, on a summer Sunday morning, Daniel's fourteen-year-old daughter Jemima, together with two companions, went out for a paddle in a canoe. So quiet was the countryside that they drifted farther then they had intended. Laughing and chatting in the sunlight, they were unaware of the sharp eyes that watched them from the tall cane along the bank. A too swift current, a short struggle with the unmanageable canoe, and the trippers were caught in shallow water. Swiftly and silently brown bodies rushed into the shallows, clapped hands over the girls' mouths and carried them into the cane. It was evening before the girls were missed and the alarm was spread. Daniel rushed from his cabin without stopping to don his moccasins.

For days they trailed the kidnaping party. At times it was possible to follow the trail by bits of torn clothing that the girls had managed to leave dangling from the bushes. But soon these signs stopped. The Indians, growing suspicious, had begun to watch them more closely. They were delighted with their prize and did not intend to lose so valuable a captive as the daughter of "Wide Mouth." But Daniel plodded on, his woodcraft and his knowledge of Indian tricks guiding him instinctively in the right direction.

At last, a definite clue. A snake, freshly killed and still wriggling, showed Daniel that they were practically within earshot of the redskins. Cautioning his companions to silence, he whispered plans for a surprise attack. They crept silently forward to a clearing where the captors were preparing their midday meal of buffalo meat. The savages, thinking that they had thrown their pursuers off the trail, had grown incautious. The girls had already given themselves up to despair, when a shot rang out in the noonday stillness. "That's my father!" Jemima cried exultantly. At Daniel's warning—"On the ground, quick!"—they threw themselves face downward. It was but a matter of minutes before all the Indians were dead or scattered and the girls safe in the midst of their rescuers.

Again Daniel had outguessed his wily red brothers in the game that meant death or enslavement in some smoke-grimed wigwam.

VI

TIDINGS were slow to reach this outpost of civilization. The settlers knew nothing of the events that had taken place in the north until a much-worn, much-traveled copy of the *Virginia Gazette* arrived at Boonesborough, its pages weighty with the Declaration of Independence. Solemnly to the assembled company the great document was read aloud. That, and the news that America was now a nation, and Kentucky a part of it. Triumphantly the tricolor flag graced the rude stockade, the settlers of Boonesborough rejoicing in their new status as citizens of a free America.

But the Indian troubles were starting anew and in earnest. Everywhere signs and messages gave warning that the Shawnees and the Cherokees were preparing for attack. Food at Boonesborough was becoming scarce. Now and then a brave hunter was able to slip past the lurking enemies and bring back some game. But these expeditions were becoming more and more infrequent; mostly the settlers went meatless. And saltless. When the last salt had been used it became necessary for some of the settlers to go in groups far down the river to replenish the supply. A slow, tedious process. The river water was scooped into great iron kettles, boiled, and allowed to evaporate, leaving an almost infinitesimal deposit of the precious crystals. Always a hazardous undertaking, the danger was now multiplied by watchful enemy eyes. Daniel led the first relay to the salting grounds. A month at this arduous task, and the group was ready, with filled sacks, to return to the fort.

Several scouts, Daniel among them, had set out in different directions to secure game for the homeward journey and to make certain that the way was clear. At evening Daniel turned his horse toward the camp, pushing through a blinding snowstorm. The horse seemed nervous. Daniel looked back, to find four Shawnee braves upon him. There was no time to reach for his rifle. Rejoicing over their capture of "Wide Mouth," the braves gave promise not to attack the fort if Daniel would lead them to the "salt makers" and persuade them to surrender without a fight. This Daniel did, and the white men were led off to the Shawnee village. Fortunately all of them were strong and used to hardship; for the trip was harrowing, and it was an Indian custom to tomahawk any prisoner who lagged by the wayside.

Daniel was adopted by Chief Blackfish. At an impressive ceremony his name was changed to Sheltowee (Big Turtle); and, as a full-fledged Shawnee, he received the admiration and respect of his red brothers. In all good faith the Shawnees accepted Daniel's promise that if they waited until spring he would persuade the white men at the fort, just as he had persuaded the party of salt makers, to surrender. Blackfish and his squaw sincerely loved their foster son and were pleased with his seeming contentment in their home. Daniel's knowledge of firearms proved invaluable. He was entrusted with the repair of their guns. Amazing his captors with his tricks and delighting them with his promises of easy victory, he blinded them to the fact that he was secretly appropriating arms and ammunition—and biding his time.

As winter melted into spring it became apparent that the Indians, too, were making secret preparations. Everywhere Daniel saw unmistakable signs that the savages were preparing a mass attack on the fort. He must make good his escape quickly, he decided. The opportunity arose when a hunting party surprised a flock of wild turkeys. The braves rushed after the frightened birds and Daniel was left alone with the squaws. His foster mother looked up to see him mounting a horse. "Where are you going, Sheltowee?" she demanded. "Blackfish will be angry."

"I must see my squaw and children," he answered calmly. "In a moon and a half I will bring her back to live with you." Then Daniel was off, riding furiously home to save his people.

VII

DANIEL had spent four months as a prisoner and four days of unspeakable hardship returning to the fort. His overworked horse had collapsed under him, and most of the journey had to be made afoot. But all this was as nothing to the anguish he felt as he gazed about an empty cabin. Rebecca, having given up hope of his return, had left for North Carolina, taking with her all the children, with the exception of Jemima, now a staid matron of fifteen. As desolation spread through him, something soft rubbed against his leather stocking. The cat, left behind. He stroked the purring creature, grateful for one living thing in the house.

Daniel roused himself. No time for sorrow in the face of coming danger.

Gathering his people about him, he urged them to rush completion of the fort. And none too soon. Blackfish, with a large army of braves, arrived to demand that Sheltowee make good his promise of peaceful surrender. The atmosphere at the fort on Daniel's return had been strained. A few escaped prisoners had told of his friendliness with the Indians, and there were those who were inclined to believe him a traitor. Now, as Daniel palavered with the enemy—creating a delay until promised reinforcements came—there were glances that mistrusted him. But Daniel was their natural leader, and this was no time to split ranks.

After days of parleying, Blackfish became suspicious that Sheltowee did not mean to surrender. Quickly events shaped into open warfare, and a ghastly siege began—a seven-day torment for the white men who listened to the sound of the digging as the Indians tunneled their way beneath the stockade. The eighth day seemed likely to mark the end, for the redskins were now under the fort. Flaming arrows had found their mark, and the sun-dried cabins were a roaring furnace. The last drop of water had been squeezed from its vessel. Determined not to surrender, the white men awaited their death, each in his own fashion. Some were praying, others still fighting, when a merciful rain came to their aid. Underneath the drenching downpour, the tunnel collapsed and the flames were extinguished. Admitting their defeat, the Indians departed. And now all the white men prayed—a prayer of thanksgiving.

But Daniel's troubles were just beginning. The seeds of suspicion, once sown, had found fertile soil. Daniel had been too friendly with his red brothers; this was something the white men could not understand. Daniel's cause received a further setback when a number of redskins, caught in the act of thievery, boasted that Sheltowee would take care of them. Daniel's spirits had reached a low ebb.

At last Rebecca returned; and Daniel, together with a handful who were still loyal to him, moved farther into the wilderness. And into further trouble. Called into court to bear witness in land disputes, he earned the enmity of those against whom he testified. Moreover, through his negligence in recording claims, he lost one by one the tracts to which he claimed ownership. And thus the passionate lover of the land was left in his old age landless and alone.

With the ever-faithful Rebecca he took to the woods, living in a camp so primitive as to seem remarkable even to pioneer eyes. There in the forest, away from men's bewildering laws—laws in which there appeared to be no justice—Daniel's spirits returned. Laughter came to his lips again, and a spring to his walk. And to his soul, a new longing for adventure. The Spanish governor of the Missouri wilderness had invited him to make his home there. The coming of such a man as Boone would bring other settlers in his wake. Land grants and official honors awaited him. Toward Missouri, then, Daniel and Rebecca set their steps—leaving once more behind them the civilization which they could not understand and the laws which had robbed them of all they possessed.

VIII

IT WAS HEART-WARMING for Daniel to find that there were people who still loved and trusted him. A hundred white families followed him into Spanish territory. True to their word, the Spaniards bestowed on him huge land grants and titles. One son had preceded him, and the rest followed. As the young Boones married and the grandchildren multiplied, Daniel became the center of an adoring circle. His tales were a never-ending source of delight to the worshipful youngsters.

Late into his eighties Daniel hunted. So crippled was he with rheumatism that Rebecca went along to carry the rifle. After she died, a Negro attendant accompanied him. Even at this late date a new adventure set Daniel dreaming. Tales of the Great Salt Lake had fired his imagination, and Daniel planned a trip to see the salt mountains and the salt springs. But his body, strong as it was, must eventually yield to the years. Partially paralyzed, he was confined to a chair.

A young artist, commissioned to paint his portrait, found him so palsied that a grandchild must stand behind the chair to hold his trembling head. Now and then he steadied, the old fire gleamed in his eyes, and his stories of the wilderness held listeners spellbound. His long white hair was still thick; a granddaughter combed it for him.

"Weren't you ever lost, Colonel?" inquired the young painter.

"Cain't say as I was." Daniel's eyes twinkled. "But I was bewildered once, for nigh on four days."

Daniel's last outing was a gay one. Attending a party at his daughter's house, the old man overindulged. Adoring grandchildren saw to that. He insisted on riding home, though he had to be helped onto his horse and propped there. For three days he lay ill, and then died peacefully—surrounded by a loving family.

"A good gun, a good horse, a good wife." Daniel had had them all, and great adventure as well.

IMPORTANT DATES IN THE LIFE OF DANIEL BOONE

1735—Born, Pennsylvania.

1753—Moved, with father, to North Carolina.

1754—Married Rebecca Bryan.

1765—Explored the Tennessee wilderness.

1769–71—Explored Kentucky.

1773—Started with family for Kentucky.
    Son slain by Indians.

1775—Founded the stockade of Boonesborough.

1776—His daughter captured by Indians.

1777—Fought Indians.

1778, January 1—Captured by Indians.
    June 16—Escaped.

1780—Brother killed by Indians.

1795—Moved farther West.

1820—Died, Missouri.

Thomas Paine

[1737-1809]

CAGE Lane, Thetford, England, is a short street at the end of which stands a meetinghouse. On a Sunday in 1774 the sedate Quakers, in decent gray, gathered quietly at its portals. In a small garden, halfway down the lane, a tall, lean man watched the procession. His shrewd, long-nosed face was sad, but his lips were softened in a tolerant smile. It was a long time since Tom Paine had bidden farewell to the faith of his fathers. Through the years his mind had ventured into the realms of thought, seeking a religious truth greater than sects. And now he was bidding farewell to the *homeland* of his fathers.

He patted his pocket, making certain that his letter was safe. A letter of introduction from Benjamin Franklin, who was living in England at the time. Tom Paine thought of their many talks and of Franklin's encouragement. America was a new land, where men's minds were open to new ideas—where resolute spirits were needed and would find response. Truly the place for an inspired adventurer whose life was dedicated to his fellow men.

He strolled slowly to the back of the house, to stand before the grave of a crow. He smiled in reminiscence. At eight he had already questioned the religious formulas taught him, had doubted the vengefulness attributed to the Almighty—and in that mood of doubting irony had carved an epitaph upon the tombstone of the bird.

> *Here lies the body of John Crow,*
> *Who once was high, but now is low;*
> *Ye brother crows, take warning all,*
> *For as you rise, so must you fall.*

And now, in review, the events of his life passed before his mind's eye. As corset maker, like his father before him, he had worked here and there about England. As assizeman he had felt the injustice of the long hours and the small pay of the government clerks. But his petitions to Parliament had proved of no avail.

About the garden he wandered, saying good-by to all his childhood haunts. His mind then traveled on to his courtships and his marriages. An orphaned servant girl had been his first wife. She had died within a year. His second marriage, to Elizabeth Ollive, had lasted three years and then, quietly and with mutual consent, had been dissolved.

It is hard to leave the familiar crucibles in which our daily lives have been molded. A small sadness smote him as he closed the gate for the last time and strolled down the street. But exultation sped him on. He had heard the call of America, where men's destinies were being decided. A growing country which, like unshaped clay, awaited the creative influence of minds like Thomas Paine's.

II

A GREAT GIFT was Thomas Paine's—the ability to analyze a situation and to translate the salient fact into living words. In pithy, epigrammatic sentences he reached the people with a language comprehensible to the least of men. No small voice in the wilderness his, but the voice of destiny pointing out the straight path through the maze of bewildering events and conflicting causes.

From Cage Lane to Philadelphia was a logical and not too drastic transition. From the street of Friendly Devotion to the city of Brotherly Love. In Philadelphia, Tom Paine found himself comfortably surrounded by the familiar Quaker gray. Having sworn allegiance to the "state of Pennsylvania" (he would not swear allegiance to the Crown, although Pennsylvania was still a colony), and having assured himself of a livelihood through tutoring, he wielded his pen in the cause of justice. His terse, pungent phrases fell on fertile soil. In his fight for the truth, he spared neither riches nor rank. For a pen name he adopted the picturesque caption Common Sense, and he bombarded the colonists with a barrage of thought-provoking pamphlets. How, he challenged America, could she justify her fight for freedom, when she herself was indulging in the traffic of Negro slaves?

As tension grew, and the inevitable day of reckoning approached, his pen flew ever faster. His impassioned words penetrated even to the shores of England, kindling into fire the sympathies of those who championed America's right to independence. "The American cause is the cause of God and humanity," he wrote, "and God will separate America from Britain."

And now the thunderclouds had burst and America was riding the whirlwind of open revolt. As cannon and musket fire reverberated over the once quiet countryside, a new emotion stirred within the heart of Tom Paine. The man of peace, who but lately had exhorted his Quaker brethren not to kill, now laid down his pen to take up a gun. With George

Washington and his ragged troops he experienced all the horrors of war: the near starvation—the bitter cold that froze men's bodies—the bitter defeats that froze their souls.

One day, shortly before the fateful Christmas that turned the tide of war, the Continental Army was bivouacked near the Delaware River, across from the English-held city of Trenton. With sinking heart George Washington had observed the ill-fed and poorly equipped soldiers deserting in ever-increasing numbers. Tom Paine realized that his country still needed the service of his pen. Laying down his sword, he clasped the mightier weapon. There in the snow, by a flickering campfire which threw ghostly shadows on the bleeding feet of the half-starved men— a drumhead for his desk—he penned the immortal words whose meaning grows clearer with the advancing years:

"These are the times that try men's souls. The summer soldier and the sunshine patriot will, in this crisis, shrink from the service of their country; but he that stands it now deserves the love and thanks of man and woman. Tyranny, like hell, is not easily conquered; yet we have this consolation with us, that the harder the conflict, the more glorious the triumph."

III

TOM PAINE'S sincerity and quiet humor attracted the attention of the congressional leaders. "A man to tame the savage heart." And so they took him out of the ranks and sent him to negotiate with the Indians. Seated before their council fires, courteously observing their customs and addressing them as brothers, he was able to secure the respectful cooperation of these proud people.

And of *all* people. Wherever he went he was met with appreciation. A prophet who found honor in all countries—a citizen of the world, Thomas Paine.

He was secretary of the Committee on Foreign Affairs—a post created at his own suggestion. His flying pen was never still. His ceaseless volley of pamphlets blasted the complacency of the manufacturers in England. Could they not see, he asked them, that it was to their interest to foster American independence? A *peaceful* America would be a *prosperous* America that would provide a vast market for their export trade.

Upon Lord Howe especially he trained his guns and fired away. Were they not both born Englishmen and writers? Could not the general see that he was battling in a lost cause? How much better, then, to lay down arms and to settle differences by the weapons of common sense!

Another target of his rapid-fire reasoning was Silas Dean. A profiteer, this Dean, wresting a private fortune from the commercial transactions between the Americans and the French. The verbal marksmanship against Silas Dean proved somewhat disturbing to a new and uncertain Assembly. Anticipating a reprimand, Tom Paine resigned his secretaryship.

A discharged soldier without a job. But there was no need for worry. Temperate living and Quaker frugality had stood him in good stead.

There was enough money saved to keep him alive while he planned a history of the American Revolution.

But first there was another important pamphlet to be written. The people of America were staggering underneath the taxes imposed by the burden of the war. These taxes, he wrote, could be lightened by levying a duty on liquor and by selling crown lands in Virginia.

This pamphlet done, he paid a visit to the University of Pennsylvania, where he was honored with the degree of Master of Arts. And now he was ready for the history.

But his versatile mind could never resign itself to but a single task at a time. He spent his leisure hours in discussing, with William Henry, the marvels of that astounding new giant—steam—whose powers were as yet but dimly glimpsed. Time now to experiment. Together they envisioned the day when this unchained power would speed friendly ships across the seven seas. For Tom Paine's prophetic eye saw a new world—a world bound into a closer unit not only in spirit but in fact.

IV

THE DESTINIES of Thomas Paine and Benjamin Franklin were inextricably intertwined. From the very first day when the threadbare youngster had stood before America's representative in England, the two lovers of liberty had labored in a common cause. They sought the same end, but with a difference. The portly Franklin, with tongue in cheek, dispensed his puritanic maxims for the masses whilst he himself dallied with the decadent aristocracy. Paine, on the other hand, wrote with a sincerity so deep it lent to his eye an almost fanatical gleam.

"Where liberty is, there is my country," Franklin said.

"Where liberty is *not*, there is my country," Paine replied.

Together they had drafted a new constitution for the state of Virginia. Now they had come to France to negotiate a loan for the newborn Republic, each working in his own way. Franklin paced out a minuet in gilded and tapestried salons, kissing titled hands and regaling royalty with his salty humor. Paine spent his time among the people, writing and speaking at every possible opportunity, unsparing of himself in the pursuance of his goal. He lived and worked in meager lodgings.

At last Benjamin Franklin and Tom Paine accomplished their purpose. At Brest a ship lay at anchor, laden with silver. On the morrow she would set sail for the States. Paine's eyes turned wistfully toward the white cliffs of Dover. He longed to take his ideas to England, to stir in the hearts of his former countrymen the will to freedom. Reluctantly, however, he allowed himself to be persuaded that England was not ready and that America still had great need of his services.

There was much to be done. A liberal Society of Political Study had to be organized. The Bank of North America had to be curtailed in its activities so that it would not threaten the very structure of the Republic.

And the young Republic offered tangible proof of its appreciation for his services. The state of New York presented him with a mansion in New Rochelle. Its two hundred and seventy-seven acres spread graciously about the fine stone manor. Pennsylvania made him a gift of twenty-five hundred dollars. Another grateful constituency gave him a splendid horse—a luxury for which he had always yearned.

And now a new idea had gripped this amazing adventurer of the spirit. He declared that iron could be built into bridges that would safely span the widest of rivers. Taking a model made by his friend John Hall, Paine set sail for Europe to find backers for his bridge. The voice that had fomented political revolution was now enlisted in a cause that would one day, he hoped, revolutionize industry.

V

THE WORLD was ripe for progress. The imagination of the people, especially in France, had become inflamed with Tom Paine's exhibition of the new bridge—a structure that in a single arc could link shore to shore. The ninety-foot model of this projected bridge drew enormous throngs. So popular had this "eighth wonder of the world" become that the admission fees alone paid for the entire construction.

England, too, was quick to perceive the possibilities of this hitherto-unexploited metal. Contemplating the hundred-and-twenty-foot model on view in that country, manufacturers and merchants realized that a new field of endeavor had been opened up to the inventive genius of man.

While in England, Paine paid a short visit to Thetford, attending the funeral of his stepmother. Again he reflected upon the narrowness of some of the religious sects. "If the taste of a Quaker could have been consulted at the Creation, what a silent and drab-colored creation it would have been! Not a flower would have blossomed, nor a bird been permitted to sing."

He returned to the exhibition. But in the midst of the popular approval of his bridge, he yearned for the fresh green fields of America. Longed for an early-morning canter with his horse, Button. His new project had been successfully launched. Time now to go home and rest and play.

A sudden eruption—and all thought of play was erased from Tom Paine's mind. The smoldering volcano of French discontent had finally burst into revolt. The Bastille had fallen!

No one was more sensitive than Tom Paine to the implications of this startling event. It meant another forward step in humanity's heroic battle for freedom. Wherever liberty's flag was unfurled, there Tom Paine was ready to serve. He decided to remain in France.

To George Washington he wrote that he hoped soon to see the day on which the French people would march in triumph through the streets of Paris. On that day he, Tom Paine, would be in the vanguard "holding aloft the American flag, shouting aloud a cry to arms" to which all the world must hearken and respond.

Surely, he felt, England must now see that liberty for all men was the coming order. Setting aside his bridgebuilding for the present, he took up his pen and poured out a new flood of pamphlets not only into France but into England as well. Now at long last he could do for Britain what he had done for America. His barbed words whizzed about the head of George III. "Why pay impoverishing taxes to keep upon the throne a foreign brute that, like a paralysis, sits astride your bright land?"

The king trembled; and with him, all the lords and masters of privilege throughout the world. Tom Paine had become a marked man.

VI

HE WAS EVERYWHERE, this gaunt pamphleteer. Side-curled and powdered, he was the center of the intellectual life of London. He was most often to be found at the bookshop of Thomas Richman—the center of an admiring group. His nimble mind played over the contemporary scene, carrying his listeners into a future full of inspiration and hope. He held these small gatherings spellbound with his anecdotes and his brilliant epigrams. But for platform speaking he had no talent. His was the still, small voice of reason and not the thundering bluster of the orator's command.

And so he went on, in his quiet way, to reason the world into a new era of justice. He penned and published a New Testament for thinkers—*The Rights of Man*—and rocked two continents to the very foundations. He dedicated the work to that gallant friend of freedom, Lafayette—"in gratitude for your services to my beloved America."

There was no mincing of words in this revolutionary book; its import was all too clear. He spoke of the "ridiculous insignificance into which all literature would sink were their authors made hereditary; and I carry the same idea into governments." Bewigged heads bent over these passages, beringed hands wrote the word *seditious* across the pages.

Paine had stirred England as mightily as ever he wished, but in the process he had achieved a martyrdom for himself. Great applause from the liberals who hailed him as a Messiah, and violent execration from the royalists who denounced him as a dangerous radical. They burned him in effigy and then pelted him with stones. Before his lodgings they staged many a riot. Heaving missiles, they failed to shatter his spirit.

And then came the climax. Through the mob an officer of the king pressed his way. A loud knock upon the door, and in an ominous hush Paine received the summons to trial, charged with sedition.

VII

TO THE CHARGE Paine pleaded not guilty. Fearing, however, that this firebrand might slip through their fingers, king and court hastened the trial.

In the meantime a world-shaking upheaval had taken place across the channel. France had been declared a republic. Paine was elected a member of the Assembly. What now did the trial of one man matter? Republicanism was on trial, and Paine must go to plead its cause. Aided by his many friends, he eluded the police and set sail for France.

As the boat plowed through the choppy water Paine grasped the railing and steadied himself against the pitching of the deck. Unmindful of the present, he projected his vision to travel ahead. Of what concern to him were riots and demonstrations? Behind him lay Britain with her social conscience now fully awake; ahead of him loomed France, where revolution had raised the common man into a position of power. And beyond stirred a small but powerful country that might someday join her larger sister republics. Surely it was not too much to dream of—a United France, England, Holland, and America. And from that dream was it not possible for the imagination to leap to a still greater vision—all mankind united into a federated Republic of the World?

After that the next step was logical and inevitable. Away with sects and narrow creeds, in whose name neighbor shuns neighbor and nation wars against nation. The entire human family must remold itself into the image of one God whose word is Love. . . .

But what were those guns on the shores of France? What were those mobs that gathered at the dock? The name they shouted from hoarse throats was "Paine, Paine!" More rioting? No, not that. They were the citizens of France, proud in their new estate, come to welcome the newest member of the Assembly—to voice their appreciation of the friend whose courageous pen had helped them through the hours of their greatest tribulation.

In triumph they escorted him to the waiting coach, showering gifts and praises upon him. For a moment those glittering eyes were dimmed by a happy tear and that athletic frame was bowed beneath a storm of emotion.

VIII

In paris he was overwhelmed with honors and banquets and parades. To his lodgings came the cream of intellectual France. In the Assembly his words were greeted with joyful shouts. On the surface all was serenity and peace; but underneath, the practiced eye could see the preliminary stirrings of a new tidal wave.

And the wave was to break sooner than he had expected. In the Assembly he pleaded for the life of Louis XVI. The deposed king was now powerless, he argued. Of what benefit would his death be to the Republican cause? "Send him to America. Give not the Tyrant of England the triumph of seeing the man perish on the scaffold who has aided my much-loved America to break her chains!" Coldly Danton replied that revolutions are not won with rose water.

Danton and Robespierre had gained in power, firing the people with a thirst for blood. With bowed head and a sense of defeat, Paine contemplated the execution of the French king. The Reign of Terror had begun. As the fury mounted, the guillotine was scarcely ever still. The people danced madly through the streets, drunk with blood. Little by little Paine withdrew from public life and secluded himself within his apartment. In his small garden he received those who had retained their sanity in the midst of this dance of death. There they indulged in quiet games and discussed a future when the world once more would come into the possession of its senses. Some solace he found in the flowering fruit trees and the blossoming vines of the garden. But the echoes of the tempest beyond the walls penetrated even to this peaceful retreat.

Added to this was a tempest now blowing in from London. In his absence Tom Paine was tried and found guilty. A price was set on his head. Condemned by the reactionaries in England, unheeded by the radicals in France, Tom Paine found himself a commander without an army —a lone soldier enlisted in a battle for common sense.

A courageous fight, in which Tom Paine was determined never to yield an inch. He secluded himself from his friends and sat down to write the *Age of Reason*. Into that pamphlet he poured all his spiritual passion for a sane and sober world.

Arrest cut short this labor. Giving the manuscript into the keeping of his friend Barlow, Paine was incarcerated in the Luxembourg Prison—a victim of the French terrorists who preached the doctrine of salvation through blood.

IX

TERROR reigned supreme, and Paine was subjected to one of its cruellest manifestations. In the dead of night the guards removed a number of prisoners, herding them like cattle to their execution. At bedtime every prisoner retired with the thought that tonight it might be his turn. Anxious ears strained for the sound of footsteps that would mean death. Under this tension, tortured nerves made sleep impossible and sensitive minds broke down.

Paine wrote to his old friend and comrade in arms, George Washington, to intercede in his behalf. But Washington was now courting England, and Paine's letters went unnoticed. Under these harrowing conditions— the uncertainty of his fate, the dampness of the prison, and the ingratitude of man—the powerful intellect of Tom Paine could no longer urge the body onward. He succumbed to a raging fever, out of which the devoted attentions of the prison doctor drew him back to partial health.

In direst distress now, Tom Paine petitioned James Monroe, the American ambassador to France, to get him sugar, soap, and a few candles. Monroe secured more than these homely articles for the petitioner—he secured his release. For eighteen months Paine remained a guest in the home of his benefactor. With boundless hospitality, Monroe made possible his recovery and the completion of his work on the *Age of Reason*.

But his generation had drifted into an age of *un*-reason. People everywhere, even in America, were tired of revolution. Other times, other interests, but the same old snobbery of class distinction. A new aristocracy had arisen, founded upon wealth. Tom Paine's call to clear thinking and plain living was drowned out in the blatant shouting of the money marts. What people wanted was not a new approach to God but a new scramble for gold. Tom Paine's book fell upon heedless ears. Another prophet forgotten in his own day.

X

TOM PAINE was now preparing for his final journey—saddened by the outcome of the struggles to which he had given so unreservedly of himself. "While I beheld with pleasure the dawn of liberty rising in Europe, I saw with regret the luster of it fading in America."

Stones and jeers awaited him in the country to which he had consecrated his life. His plea for a higher interpretation of religion was misinterpreted as a descent into the "gutter of atheism." People pulled their skirts about them as he passed by.

But he went doggedly ahead. He founded a movement in America— "to place *essential* religion in radiance and reverence." He named this organization the Theophilanthropist Society—a body dedicated to the love of humanity and God. The society was suppressed.

He retired to the seclusion of New Rochelle—to dream of a day when men would have saner heads and more understanding hearts.

The spirit had grown too tired to carry on; disillusionment had taken too heavy a toll. He fell into an apoplectic paralysis from which he never recovered. Nursed by a blind old woman, he lingered for a while. But, unable to take nourishment, he sank gradually.

The release came on June 8, 1809. He left to the world a handful of rags and a heritage of reason.

IMPORTANT DATES IN THE LIFE OF THOMAS PAINE

1737—Born, Thetford, England.
1774—Came to America.
1774-76—Edited *Pennsylvania Magazine*.
1776—Wrote *Common Sense*. Joined staff of General Green.
1777—Wrote *Crisis*.
1779—Became secretary to Committee of Foreign Affairs.
1787—Went to Europe, with model of iron bridge.

1792—Published *Rights of Man*. Went to France; became member of National Convention.
1793—Expelled from Convention. Imprisoned in the Luxembourg.
1794—Released from prison.
1794-1807—Wrote *Age of Reason*.
1802—Returned to America.
1809—Died, New Rochelle, New York.

Thomas Jefferson

[1743-1826]

WHEN Jefferson ran for the presidency (1800), the following "intimate portrait of his character came from the lips of an opposition stump orator:

"Tom Jefferson . . . is nothing but a mean-spirited, low-lived fellow, the son of a half-breed Indian squaw, sired by a Virginia mulatto father, as is well known in the neighbourhood where he has been raised wholly on hoe-cake . . . bacon and hominy, with an occasional change of fricasseed bullfrog, for which abominable reptiles he has acquired a taste during his residence among the French at Paris, to whom there can be no question he will sell his country at the first offer made to him cash down, should he be elected to fill the Presidency . . ."

Jefferson, continued his opponents, was not only a half-breed but a scoundrel. "He has defrauded the widows and the fatherless children!" And—they added—he was not only a scoundrel but an atheist. "If Jefferson is elected, the ties of marriage will be dissolved, our wives and daughters will be thrown into the stews, our children will be cast into the world and forgotten. Can the imagination paint anything more dreadful this side of hell?" The women of America were warned, in the event of his election, to bury their Bibles in their gardens, or he would confiscate and burn them "in a general holocaust of infidelity."

And what was Jefferson doing all this time? Quietly sitting at home and compiling the *Morals of Jesus*. He made no effort to reply to the avalanche of accusations that had been let loose against him. "While I should be answering one, twenty new ones would be invented." It is a common human failing, he observed, "to transfer to the person the hatred they bear to his political opinions."

And they hated his political opinions for but a single reason. He believed in the protection of the weak against the strong.

II

ON HIS MOTHER'S SIDE he was descended from the aristocracy; on his father's, from farmer and pioneer stock. His heritage therefore was two-fold. He possessed a genteel love for beauty and a rugged respect for work. His father, a giant of a man morally as well as physically, had expressed three wishes for his son. He wanted Tom to have a strong body, a classical education, and a gentle heart. Although he died when Tom was only fourteen, his three wishes were granted. For he had taken care to give the boy a proper start in life. He had taught him to ride hard, to study diligently, and to put himself whenever possible "in the other fellow's place."

At seventeen he entered William and Mary College at Williamsburg —Jefferson referred to it as "Devilsburg." Here, at the "headquarters of the aristocracy," he lived a studious, observant, and somewhat aloof life. He took frequent rides into the countryside, in order to escape from the "drinking and the gambling and the fox-hunting gentry" into the homes of the farmers and the trappers dressed in their coonskin caps, moccasins, and buckskin breeches. Much of his time he whiled away playing on his fiddle. He was very fond of his music. In one of his early letters he complained that while he slept at a friend's house during the Christmas holidays, "the cursed rats" had eaten up his pocketbook, his "jemmy-worked silk garters and half-a-dozen new minuets I had just got." But then he added good-naturedly, "Oh well, rats will be rats."

Good-natured, tall, rangy, soft-spoken, shy, freckled and blue-eyed and redheaded, young Tom Jefferson made a favorable impression on Dr. William Small, professor of mathematics at William and Mary. And Dr. Small, in turn, made a favorable impression on Tom Jefferson. "From his conversation," wrote Jefferson many years later, "I got my first views . . . of the system of things in which we are placed." Thanks to Dr. Small, Jefferson became acquainted with a "young lawyer named George Wythe" (who was later to be one of the signers of the Declaration of Independence). This man of inflexible integrity, wrote Jefferson, inspired within him a feeling of "warm patriotism" and a respect for "the natural and equal rights of man."

Such were some of the influences that went into the growth of the character that was Thomas Jefferson. Yet when he left college his character was still in the formative stage. He couldn't make up his mind as to his future career—whether to become "a lawyer, a farmer, or a lover." He settled his perplexity by becoming all three—he passed the bar, he enlarged his inherited farm, and he began to pay court to Rebecca Burwell. In the first two ventures he was fairly successful, but in the third he failed. Rebecca married his rival, and for a time he plunged into the "dissipation of dancing and flirting" with the pretty girls at "Devilsburg." Jefferson, however, was not cast in the character of a devil's disciple. He enjoyed neither smoking nor drinking nor gambling. Before long he found himself out of step with the light-footed denizens of the primrose path. He returned to his studies and his hard work. "His working day," we are told, "averaged fifteen hours." Although he had a great many servants, as became a landed aristocrat at that period, he always rose early to build his own fire in his bedroom. "For what purpose have our hands been given us if not for labor?"

Man is made for labor—and for love. At thirty Jefferson once more began to pay court to a young woman. And this time he was successful. On New Year's Day, 1772, he married the twenty-three-year-old Martha Skelton, and carried his "personable little bride" over the threshold of his newly built home on the hilltop of Monticello.

It was a journey of a hundred frosty miles from her home in Charles City to Monticello. They had started in a phaeton, but they had been obliged to abandon it and to go forward on horseback. The last stage of the journey was over a footpath two feet deep in snow. When they arrived at Monticello late at night, there were no servants, no fire, no food to greet them. But the bride and the bridegroom were happy in the warmth of a mutual affection.

This wedding journey to Monticello was symbolical of their wedding journey through life—sad and bleak and affectionate. And tragically short. Within ten years they lost three of their children. And then the mother followed them. Jefferson never married again.

III

SHORTLY after his marriage Jefferson gave up his law and went into politics. "The lawyer tries to take advantage of *bad* laws. The politician—or rather the statesman—tries to bring about the adoption of *good* laws." He regarded his politics as an adjunct to his farming. It is the business of the farmer to produce the proper food for the nation. It is the business of the politician to see that the nation is properly fed. The immortal Declaration of Independence, which Jefferson wrote, was but a step in this direction. This Gospel of Justice, based upon the philosophy of Plato, Locke, Montesquieu, Rousseau, and Voltaire, "will enable the citizenry . . . to understand their rights, to maintain them, and to exercise with intelligence their parts in self-government." And in self-sustenance. His objective was not only political and social independence, but economic independence as well. He was anxious to "prevent the accumulation and perpetuation of wealth in select families."

It was this spirit that animated his entire political life. He endeavored to transform America from an *aristocracy* to a *democracy*—from the arbitrary rule of *private wealth* to the equitable rule of the *commonwealth*.

Jefferson entered upon his political career with no personal hope of gain. Statesmanship in those days was not an attractive profession. It meant hard work, inadequate pay, and neglect of one's private affairs at a time when such neglect might prove very costly. Many a well-to-do statesman found himself, at the end of his official career, financially ruined. This was to prove true in the case of Jefferson, and he probably knew it from the very start. It was with reluctance, therefore, that he accepted his political jobs. He would have preferred the uninterrupted enjoyment of "my family, my friends, my farm, and my books." Nature, he observed in one of his letters, had intended him "for the tranquil pursuits of science." But the nation demanded his services, and Jefferson accepted his job as a public duty.

He first served his nation as the governor of Virginia (1779). Plunged into his gubernatorial duties in the middle of the Revolution, he had little opportunity to display his constructive statesmanship. But even at this early period of his career he distinctly showed the democratic trend of his philosophy. He stood for free education, free libraries, religious tolerance, the emancipation of the Negroes, and the abolition of primogeniture—that is, the custom of handing down the entire inheritance of an estate to the first-born. Through the abolition of primogeniture he hoped to keep the land of the nation divided into small parcels among a large number of people, instead of allowing it to pass into the hands of a few owners of enormous estates. "Ill fares the land, to hastening ills a prey, where wealth accumulates and men decay." Like the English poet, Jefferson wanted to see a land of distributed blessings rather than one of concentrated glory. And that was why the Tories—the men who held the reins of concentration in their hands—so heartily detested Jefferson. "He was the first American," as Claude G. Bowers points out in his *Jefferson and Hamilton,* "to invite the hate of a class."

It was as an enemy of the exploiting class that he was hailed in Paris when he arrived there as ambassador in 1784. He came there both as a student and as a teacher of revolution. He traveled over the countryside, observed the life of the peasants, sat with them at table to see what they ate, rested on their beds to note whether they were comfortable, and inquired into their ideas and their hopes and their fears. As a result of his study he came to the conclusion that "every man here is either the hammer or the anvil." And he threw himself heartily into the cause of the "ever-beaten, ever-resisting" anvils. The government of France, the governments of all the other European countries, he observed, are "mere devices for taking money out of one man's pocket and putting it into another's." They are "governments of wolves over sheep." He returned from France more firmly convinced than ever that "the republican is the only form of government which is not eternally at open or secret war with the rights of mankind."

IV

On his return to America he was invited to enter George Washington's Cabinet as Secretary of State. He arrived in New York, the temporary capital, in the winter of 1790. And immediately he found himself with a first-class fight on his hands. America had won the war, but it had not attained its independence. The country was now threatened by a new tyranny—the absolute power of wealth. The people who had shed their blood in the Revolution now discovered, to their dismay, that they had exchanged an English *autocracy* for an American *aurocracy*—a government of gold. There was an open struggle between the *producers* of wealth on the one hand and the *exploiters* of wealth on the other. Jefferson aligned himself on the side of the producers—the manufacturers, the farmers, and the laborers—all those who used either their money or their hands to make goods. The other side had found their leader in Alexander Hamilton, who represented the interests of the exploiters—the monopolists, the bankers, and the speculators—all those who used either their capital or their ingenuity to make money. Jefferson was an idealist, a dreamer ahead of his day. Hamilton was a realist, a perfect product of his day.

And, strangely enough, the idealist was triumphant over the realist. When the smoke of the battle had lifted, America was seen heading diffidently but definitely in the direction of democracy. And out of the fight emerged two opponents worthy of one another's respect. For both of them were sincere, and each of them respected the sincerity of the other. "Alexander Hamilton," wrote Jefferson of him some years later, "was disinterested, honest, and honorable in all private transactions." As for his public acts, "Mr. Hamilton formed his conclusions after the most mature consideration . . . His principles were conscientiously adopted." And Hamilton, though given to invective in the heat of battle, retired after his defeat with the acknowledgment that America might have been put into less trustworthy hands than Jefferson's. "After all, Jefferson has . . . character."

V

JEFFERSON had character. This was clearly shown in his relations toward his servants. And in the relations of his servants toward their master. He is on his way to Monticello, returning home for a spell after a term of public service. The slaves, "all adorned in their Sunday splendor," are waiting for him at the foot of the hill. The carriage appears around a bend in the road. The slaves, singing, laughing, shouting, weeping for joy, rush forward to greet "Marse Jeff'son." Unhitching the horses, they pull and push the carriage up the hill. "Glory be you'se back home safe!" They kiss his hands, his feet, the hem of his cloak. And now they have arrived at the summit. Lifting their beloved master on their shoulders, they carry him in to a banquet fit for a king. "Only you'se no king, praise de Lawd, you'se a republican."

And it was as a republican—a believer in the public administration of the public affairs—that Jefferson was elected to the presidency. Almost the entire press had fought against him. "With Jefferson holding the reins our civilization will be wrecked . . . It is dreadful to contemplate the results of his election."

But there was nothing dreadful either in the ideas or in the acts of President Jefferson. His first inaugural may be not inaccurately described as a political Sermon on the Mount. In this inaugural he outlines his policy as the servant of a free and democratic country. "I approach my task," he begins, "with those anxious and awful presentiments which the greatness of the charge and the weakness of my powers so justly inspire." For he realizes that his country, young and inexperienced and none too vigorous, is entering upon a career among nations "who feel power and forget right." Yet this country, he goes on, "is the world's best hope." The republican government is "the strongest government on earth."

And what is this republican government that he envisions in this inaugural? It is a government in which the will of the majority shall rule, the rights of the minority shall be protected, religious intolerance shall be abolished, labor shall not be exploited, justice shall be dispensed equally to all men, peace and honest friendship shall be maintained with all nations, and entangling alliances shall be made with none. And then he ends his inaugural with a simple and sincere prayer to the Infinite Power "to lead our councils to what is best, and to give them a favorable issue for our peace and prosperity."

In Washington—which had now become the seat of the government —Jefferson lived as peacefully and as simply as he had lived at Monticello. The British minister to the United States, a sullen individual by the name of Merry, was scandalized one day when, calling on business at the White House, he was received by Mr. Jefferson in slippers and a dressing gown.

"I want to be known as plain Mr. Jefferson . . . I hope that the terms of Excellency, Worship, and Esquire have disappeared from among us forever." He disliked official kowtowing and ceremonial formality. "We have suppressed," he wrote to Kosciusko, "those public forms and ceremonies which tended to familiarize the public eye to the . . . less democratic forms of government."

He was a plain man administering justice from a plain city. "Washington," wrote Gouverneur Morris sarcastically, "is the best city in the world to live in—in the future." One could travel through the city for miles, remarked Abigail Adams, without seeing a human being. Washington was indeed a capital of "magnificent distances." The streets were "unlighted swamps and forests." A party of Federalist leaders, returning home from a friend who lived only two miles away, lost their bearings in the "impenetrable blackness" and wandered all night over the wastelands. The inhabitants of the city were few and widely scattered. "From the steps of the Capitol one could count seven or eight boardinghouses, one tailor's shop, one shoemaker's, one printing establishment, the home of a washerwoman, a grocery shop, a stationery store, a drygoods house, and an oyster market." A symbol of American democracy at that period. And of Jefferson's character. Wide horizons, and an all-inclusive sympathy from printer to President.

Jefferson's two terms in Washington were on the whole uneventful. His great liberalizing work had been completed before his election to the presidency. One of the events of his administration, however, was of the greatest importance. This was the Louisiana Purchase (1803) from Napoleon, who had previously acquired it from the Spanish king. The territory which then became a part of the United States is not to be confused with the present state of Louisiana. The land which Jefferson's envoys purchased from Napoleon, and which at that period went under the name of Louisiana, comprised an enormous territory reaching all the way from the Mississippi to the Rockies and from Canada to the Gulf of Mexico. It more than doubled the size of the United States, and it opened up the West to the flood of pioneers who poured in from the East. And all this territory Jefferson was able to get for only fifteen million dollars. It was "the most stupendous bargain in history."

VI

JEFFERSON retired from political life "with hands as clean as they are empty." He had always as a public servant refused presents, however small. For he was anxious, as he wrote to Samuel Hawkins, "to retain that consciousness of a disinterested administration of the public trusts which is essential to perfect tranquillity of mind."

And so it was with perfect tranquillity of mind that he departed from his public duties. "Nothing is more incumbent on the old," he observed, "than to know when they should get out of the way, and relinquish to younger successors . . . the duties they can no longer perform."

He returned to Monticello—and to financial ruin. Far from enriching himself at the expense of the government, he had paid out of his own pocket for the many social functions necessitated by his official duties. And his plantation, under the inefficient management of his overseers during his absence, had sunk into a deep morass of red ink. He now found himself burdened with a debt from which he was unable to emerge to the end of his days. In order to pay off a part of this debt, he was obliged to sell his entire library—a collection of books he had accumulated during a lifetime of diversified interests.

Yet in spite of his poverty he retained the catholic scope of his interests. Echoing the ancient Latin poet, he said, "I am a man, and therefore everything human is within my horizon." He devoted his declining years to farming, philosophy, science, art, music, literature, religion—and, above all, education. For "education, the ploughing and the planting of human thought, produces the universal food of human progress."

With this object in mind, he not only conceived the idea, but drew up the architectural plans, for the University of Virginia. His chief interests, he said, were intellectual and ethical rather than political. He requested that his tombstone should proclaim nothing of his career as governor and ambassador and President. He wanted the inscription to mention only three things by which he hoped to be remembered: his writing of the Declaration of Independence, his fighting for Religious Freedom, and his founding of the University of Virginia.

And now, in his eighty-fourth year, he found himself face to face with the prospect of being turned out-of-doors. He was obliged to sell his estate in a lottery in order to save his "home in Monticello to lay my head in, and a plot of land for my burial."

Assured at last of his home and his grave, he was ready for the end—
"that great adventure, untried by the living, unreported by the dead."
He was tired, he said, of "pulling off my shoes and stockings at night, and
putting them on again in the morning." He prayed for only one thing—
that "the Benevolent Being who presides over the world" might spare his
life until the next Independence Day.

And God heard his prayer. Thomas Jefferson died on the Fourth of
July, 1826.

IMPORTANT DATES IN THE LIFE OF
THOMAS JEFFERSON

1743—Born, Albemarle County, Virginia.

1760-62—Student at William and Mary College, Williamsburg, Virginia.

1762-67—Studied law.

1769-75—Member of the Virginia House of Burgesses.

1775-76—Delegate to the Second Continental Congress at Philadelphia.

1776—Wrote the Declaration of Independence.

1779-81—Governor of Virginia.

1785—Succeeded Benjamin Franklin as Minister to France.

1790—Appointed Secretary of State in the first administration of President Washington.

1793—Resigned from Cabinet in protest against Hamilton's financial policy.
Founded party of "Democratic-Republicans."

1796—Elected Vice-President in administration of John Adams.

1800—Elected third President of the United States.

1801-02—Successful war against Barbary pirates.

1803—Purchased Louisiana Territory from France.

1807—Declared embargo against French and British to retaliate against their impressment of American sailors.

1809—Retired to private life after two terms in the White House.

1819—Established the University of Virginia.

1826—Died, Monticello, on the Fourth of July, same day as John Adams.

John Paul Jones

[1747-1792]

I T WAS a strange destiny that pursued the life of John Paul Jones.
In war he never suffered a defeat, and in peace he rarely won a victory. A peculiar paradox of a man—dainty as a woman, ferocious as a
tiger, naïve as a child—a man of great sadness and not a little madness.
His role as a romantic adventurer was regal and reckless and swift.
"I will not have anything to do with ships which do not sail fast," he
once wrote, "for I intend to go in harm's way." Always he went in harm's
way, and always he came out bloody and unbowed and ready for the next
fight. And all the reward that he ever got for his triumphant fights was
a frosty "thank you" followed by a winter of neglect.

II

FROM HIS INFANCY he was driven by a "great and mighty restlessness." He
inherited this restlessness from his mother, Jeanne MacDuff—"a Hieland
lassie" with a strong Gaelic strain in her blood. His father, John Paul, was
a Scotch landscape gardener, a prosaic but gritty product of the soil. It
was his mother who gave him his love for adventure. His cradle songs
were not lullabies of gentle relaxation, but ballads of impetuous motion.

> *Come hither, Evan Cameron,*
> *Come stand beside my knee;*
> *I hear the river roaring down*
> *Unto the wintry sea.*

His formal schooling was of the scantiest. Almost as soon as he learned
to read a book, he learned to row a boat. The family of John Paul was
none too blessed in worldly goods. There were seven children to support,
and the boys were compelled to help replenish the larder out of the waters

of Solway. At twelve he was an expert boatman. One stormy day in the summer of 1759 a number of villagers were attracted to a fishing yawl that was trying to make the shelter of a creek against a stiff northeaster. Among the spectators were John Paul and a visiting shipowner by the name of James Younger. "I'm afraid they'll never make it," said Mr. Younger as he watched the "crew"—a young boy who was steering and handling the sheets and a grown man who was "trimming" the boat by sitting on the weather rail.

"You're wrong, sir," observed John Paul. "They'll make it all right. That's my boy steering."

As soon as the boat was landed, Mr. Younger offered the "little captain" a berth as master's apprentice on his new brig, the *Friendship,* which was about to sail for Virginia and the West Indies. A tempting offer, not only to young John Paul, but to his parents. For this voyage would give their boy the opportunity to visit his eldest brother, William. A successful young man, this brother Will—the adopted son of a rich plantation owner, William Jones, and the manager of Mr. Jones's huge colonial estate in Virginia.

The parents yielded to Mr. Younger's suggestion; and John Paul, a sturdy though undersized little fellow of twelve, got his first salt taste of the sea.

Arrived in Virginia, he so ingratiated himself with everybody at the plantation that Mr. Jones offered to adopt him also. But John Paul refused the offer. "Thank you, sir, but I am afraid I am too fond of my ship."

So back to the ship he went; and so rapid was his seafaring progress that at seventeen he was appointed second mate, and at eighteen first mate. The following year, when Mr. Younger retired from the shipping business, he presented John Paul with a sixth interest in a ship called *King George's Packet.* "This, my boy, for your faithfulness and intelligence as a seaman."

And so we see John Paul, at nineteen, launched upon a new adventure as part owner—and first mate—of a merchant ship.

And the merchandise? Black slaves from Africa. A none-too-savory, but in those days considered a perfectly legitimate, business. Two profitable voyages to Africa, and John Paul had had enough of slaving. He sold his interest in the ship for a thousand guineas (about five thousand dollars), and paid a visit to his brother in Virginia.

Another offer of adoption, another refusal, and John Paul set out for England in the brig *John o'Gaunt.* A sad voyage; yet it turned out to John Paul's advantage. An outbreak of yellow fever carried off all but five of the sailors, including the captain and the mate. John Paul took charge of the ship, brought it safely to Whitehaven, and received as a reward a ten-per-cent share of the cargo.

Thus far his career had been stormy, but safe. Now, however, there came upon him the first of his many misfortunes. It happened during one of his voyages in the *John o'Gaunt.* An epidemic of fever had reduced the crew to five men. One of these men, a mulatto by the name of Mungo Maxwell, had mutinied; and Captain Paul, in an effort to keep the mutiny from spreading, found it necessary to punish the culprit with a belaying pin. Shortly thereafter Maxwell died. John Paul, upon his arrival in port, surrendered to the authorities, made a full statement, and was ordered to stand trial for willful murder on the high seas.

Prosecuting Attorney: "Captain Paul, are you, in conscience, satisfied that you used no more force than was necessary to preserve discipline in your ship?"

John Paul: "I would say that it became necessary to strike the mutinous sailor, Maxwell. Whenever it becomes necessary for a commanding officer to strike a seaman, it is also necessary to strike with a weapon. I may say that the necessity to strike carries with it the necessity to kill or to completely disable the mutineer . . ."

The court acquitted him of willful murder. John Paul felt vindicated and subdued. He was resolved never in the future to strike any man under his command. And he stuck to this resolution for the rest of his life. From that day on he ruled his men through the persuasiveness of his talk rather than through the power of the whip.

But for a while he felt a bit nauseated with the idea of ruling men on the high seas. For there was a feminine softness at the core of this resolute man of steel.

III

A CHANGE OF OCCUPATION, and a change of name. Old William Jones had died (1760) in Virginia, leaving his entire estate to John Paul's brother, William. He had made John Paul, however, the residuary legatee in the event of his brother's death, provided John Paul would assume, like his brother, the name of Jones. In the spring of 1773 his brother died; and John Paul, who from that day called himself Paul Jones, became the owner of a Virginia plantation consisting of "3000 acres, 20 horses and colts, 80 neat-cattle and calves, sundry sheep and swine, and 30 Negroes."

Paul Jones proved himself, both to his white neighbors and to his Negro slaves, an exacting, generous, aristocratic democrat. Like the fringe of land which he owned between the forest and the sea, he was a perfect blending of the wilderness and the garden. And a perfect "catch" for the young ladies of Virginia. A gay life of boating and dancing and drinking and flirting at the carefree age of twenty-eight in the carefree atmosphere of a colonial plantation. A stormy affair with Betty Parke, a relative of Martha Washington's—and then the call of a greater storm.

Paul Jones was not unprepared for the coming storm of the Revolution. In his leisure hours he had attended the sessions of the Virginia House of Burgesses and listened to the eloquence of Patrick Henry and to the logic of Thomas Jefferson. Fine men, these homespun Americans, so different from the snobbish officers of the British Army and Navy! Paul Jones had had a scuffle with one of these naval officers at a public ball in Norfolk. "This officer, Parker by name"—we are quoting Paul Jones himself—"declared that in case of a revolt or insurrection it would be easily suppressed, if the courage of the Colonial men was on a par with the virtue of the Colonial women! I at once knocked Mr. Parker down . . ."

Paul Jones was certain, in the event of a showdown, as to which side he would take. On April 21, 1775, he was on a visit to New York. And there he heard the astounding news that made the heart leap. The Battle of Lexington. America had decided to be free!

He returned home and offered his services to the Continental Congress. "It is, I think, to be taken for granted that there can be no more temporizing . . . Nothing now is in store for us except either war to the knife or total submission to complete slavery . . .

"I cannot conceive of submission to complete slavery; therefore only war is in sight . . .

"Such being clearly the position of affairs, I beg you to keep my name in your memory . . . and in any provision that may be taken for a naval force, to call upon me in any capacity which your knowledge of my seafaring experience and your opinion of my qualifications may dictate."

He was able to offer to the American cause more than his seafaring experience. In his trips to the various countries he had picked up not only an ability to speak foreign languages but a capacity to handle foreign men. He would be an ideal master of a heterogeneous crew. Moreover, his active mind had absorbed a knowledge of navigation unsurpassed in his own day. He was a student not only of the open sea but of the open book. His was that rare blending of genius—a scholarly head and an impetuous heart.

Vaguely, though not fully, aware of his genius, the Continental Congress invited him to express his views on the organization of an American navy and the selection of its personnel. He outlined his views in a long and carefully studied report. The report was approved. The navy was organized. And then, to add gall to his glory—a bane that was to pursue him to the end of his days—he was appointed to the subordinate post of first lieutenant in the new fleet.

A keen blow to his hopes. But Paul Jones took it in stride. "I am here to serve the cause of human rights, not to promote the fortunes of Paul Jones." On February 17, 1776, Lieutenant Jones set sail on the *Alfred,* one of the four ships of the pioneer American fleet. The captain of the *Alfred* was Dudley Saltonstall, a fine gentleman but mediocre sailor. A brief cruise of seven weeks, an unsuccessful brush with the British sloop of war, the *Glasgow,* and Captain Saltonstall was temporarily retired from active service. This "demotion" of Saltonstall led to a reshuffling of the naval personnel and to the promotion of Paul Jones to a captaincy.

And then began a *real* cruise for Paul Jones. The *Providence*—the ship of which he was now the commander—set sail on June 14, 1776; and before she returned to port she had defeated sixteen British vessels, of which eight were sunk and eight manned out of the meager crew of the *Providence* and sent in as prizes to America.

A triumphant voyage, a sad return. During his absence his plantation had been destroyed by the Tory soldiers under Lord Dunmore. This misfortune, too, he took in stride. "It appears," he wrote to his friend Joseph

Hewes, a member of the Continental Congress, "that I now have no fortune left but my sword, and no prospect except getting alongside the enemy."

"Getting alongside the enemy" was from now on the chief pursuit of his life.

IV

ON NOVEMBER 7, 1776, he set out on an enemy hunt as the commander of his old ship, the *Alfred*. A short cruise of only five weeks, and a "bag" of seven British ships.

And then he was assigned (June 14, 1777) to a still more important ship, the *Ranger*—an assignment which Paul Jones regarded as the greatest distinction of his life. For the circumstances of the assignment, inadvertently perhaps, linked his name forever with the birth of the new Republic. A twofold resolution passed by Congress, not in honor of Paul Jones but in an effort to transact as much business in as short a time as possible:

"*Resolved,* That the Flag of the Thirteen United States of America be Thirteen Stripes, Alternate Red and White, and that the Union be Thirteen Stars in a Blue Field.

"*Resolved,* That Captain John Paul Jones be Appointed to Command the Ship *Ranger.*"

Paul Jones took this as a sacred omen. "That flag and I are twins; born in the same hour from the same womb of destiny. We cannot be parted in life or in death. So long as we can float, we shall float together. If we must sink, we shall go down as one!"

V

PAUL JONES had traveled far from his slave-trading days. Though a fighter by profession, he was by nature a man of friendly generosity. And his friendliness extended not only to his equals but to his so-called "inferiors" as well. In one of his victorious reports to Robert Morris he cited his entire crew for "extraordinary courage" under fire. "Where all behaved so well, I cannot bring myself to single out individuals." And yet he goes on to single out three men "who, belonging to races considered inferior, may be more entitled to credit than their shipmates of the higher race. These are Anthony Jeremiah, a full-blooded Narragansett Indian, and Cato Jones and Scipio Jones, Negro boys, formerly my own slaves, but set free by me on the 10th of this month."

His devotion to his sailors inspired an equal devotion on their part. It was this inspiration that turned them into fighting demons, even against the greatest of odds. On April 24, 1778, his little boat, the *Ranger,* ran down and captured the *Drake,* a twenty-gun British sloop of war. The entire world rubbed its eyes in amazement at the sight of "a poodle leading a tiger by the leash." It was the turning of a new page in history—the capture of a larger by a smaller ship.

But this was only a rehearsal for a far greater achievement—the capture of a ship afloat by a crippled ship that was sinking. It was in the famous battle between the British warship, the *Serapis,* and Paul Jones's ship, the *Bonhomme Richard.* The *Serapis* carried 50 guns, throwing 315 pounds of metal in a single broadside. As against this, the *Bonhomme Richard* carried 42 guns, throwing only 258 pounds of metal in a single broadside. An uneven battle. Yet Jones loved uneven battles. "Where's the fun when my opponent isn't stronger than myself?"

The battle began on Thursday, September 23, 1779. "Sea smooth"—we are quoting from the log of the *Serapis*—"moon full, sky clear, time 7:15 P.M. We hail the enemy, the enemy answers with a broadside." A furious fight, the two ships sailing side by side, answering broadside to broadside. Heavy shots from the *Serapis,* weak barks from the *Richard.* "Many of our guns were smashed, or else so jammed as to be unserviceable," reports Henry Gardner, the quarter gunner of the *Richard.* "Of the 140 officers and men stationed on the main gun-deck, 80 were killed or wounded. The whole deck was slippery with blood and littered with fragments of heads, bodies, and limbs."

At this rate the end is just a matter of minutes. Something drastic must be done. Paul Jones barks out a command. "Let us close with the enemy. We must get hold of him!"

A reckless maneuver, but it's the only chance. Paul Jones sails close to the *Serapis,* spanks out the grappling hooks, and pins the enemy ship alongside of his own. The *Richard* is now a wreck. The wheel has been shot away, the masts are gone, the sides are gaping with holes. The ship is beginning to list.

Captain Pearson, of the *Serapis:* "Are you ready to surrender?"

Paul Jones: "No, I have just begun to fight!"

And now he is not only directing the fight, but showing them how to do it by his own example. Six marines are busy loading their muskets and handing them to the commodore. And Paul Jones, as rapidly as he receives them, fires them from the shoulder and speeds every shot along with an ear-splitting oath. By Jove, not a man but a flame! A spirit of vengeance disguised in human shape for the righting of human wrongs!

And still the battle hangs in the balance. But now a lucky chance turns the tide in our favor. A lucky chance, and the daredevil skill of Midshipman Fanning of the *Bonhomme Richard.* Once more, let Gardner tell the story:

"Fanning lay out on the yardarm of our ship. The hatch of the *Serapis* was not entirely open, the cover only having been slewed around, probably by one of our shots earlier in the action, leaving a triangular opening about two feet at the widest part. As the ships were rocking in the swell, it took a pretty good aim to throw a grenade through so small an opening. Still, Fanning did it at the third trial."

A terrific explosion. The hatch flies open, and the air is filled with the fragments of fifty men.

There is no more stomach for fighting on the *Serapis.* "Come on, boys," shouts Paul Jones to his crew, "let's go in!"

They clamber over the sides of the *Serapis*. A halfhearted attempt at resistance, and then Captain Pearson strikes his flag. He surrenders his sword to Paul Jones . . .

The American commodore was now master of the *Serapis*. From her deck he watched his own ship going down to her glorious grave. "No one," he writes, "was now left aboard the *Richard,* but our dead. To them I gave the good old ship for their coffin, and in her they found a sublime burial. She rolled heavily in the long swell . . . settled slowly by the head, and sank peacefully in about forty fathoms.

"Our torn and tattered flag had been left flying when we abandoned the ship. As she plunged down at the last, her taffrail momentarily rose in the air; so the very last vestige mortal eyes ever saw of the *Bonhomme Richard* was the defiant waving of her unconquered and unstricken flag."

VI

"The greatest achievement in naval history!" This was the universal verdict at the time of the capture of the *Serapis*. Yet Paul Jones remained poor and obscure. When he tried to collect the pay for his sailors he was knocked about from pillar to post. He wrote a volume of letters—to Benjamin Franklin, to Robert Morris, to Arthur Lee, to the leaders of the allied governments of Holland and of France—begging them, arguing with them, accusing them of neglect of their fighting men. But everybody passed the burden along to everybody else. "The whole expense," wrote Franklin in a letter that was characteristic of them all, "will fall upon me, and I am ill provided to bear it, having so many unexpected calls upon me from other quarters." Blank refusals, or else polite promises to pay at some time in the indefinite future. Paul Jones had a twofold obstacle to overcome: the poverty of the exchequer throughout the world, and the thoughtless ingratitude of the human heart.

And in his futile struggle against these two obstacles, his health broke down. "My greatest trouble in those years," he wrote in his journal, "was inability to get sound or refreshing sleep." Continual trips between France and America, America and Holland, Holland and France. And always the same results—acclamation when he appeared before an audience, neglect the moment he got out of sight.

Yet throughout it all he retained an irresistible gaiety and gusto for life. His tact, his effervescence, his graciousness, and his wit made him a favorite among the ladies. And he was not averse, on occasion, to reciprocate their favors. We have a vivid picture of him at this time, as described in the words of an Englishwoman, Miss Edes-Herbert:

"Having been taught to regard Captain Jones as a rough, desperate renegade, if not pirate, I was amazed to meet a most courteous, graceful gentleman of slight build and rather delicate, not to say effeminate, cast of features, faultlessly dressed, exquisitely polite, altogether handsome, and speaking French fluently . . . By way of compliment, I suppose, he said that, while under the circumstances that existed he was compelled to be indifferent to the estimation in which Englishmen held him, he was as sensitive as ever to the sentiments of Englishwomen; also that, while he might be at war with my countrymen as a nation, he could never be anything but at peace with their daughters . . ."

He was popular with the daughters of Englishmen and of all other men. Queen Catherine of Russia, having heard of this "gallant sea-wolf," invited him to an important command in the Russian Navy. He eagerly accepted the invitation, for he had heard many glowing reports of the "Great Queen." Driven by his old impetuosity to meet a situation, he made a wild dash for Russia, disregarding ice, snow, personal danger, even death. "You can't cross the Gulf of Finland," the natives warned him. "It's full of ice. Nobody attempts it this time of the year."

"Well, *I* shall attempt it!" Setting out in a small boat with a number of daredevils like himself, he started the crossing at the dawn of an April day (1788). There was a strong wind blowing from the northwest. In the course of the day the wind became a gale; by nightfall it was a tempest. A blinding fury of snow lashed over the unprotected deck. Huge cakes of ice, swirling together like the jaws of a nutcracker, threatened to crush the boat. "We must turn back," cried the terrified boatmen.

"We will do nothing of the kind!" With pistol in one hand and his other hand on the steering wheel, he held his men to their task until they reached the opposite shore.

A dash through the snow-covered forests of Russia, an enthusiastic reception at the palace—and then, further trouble. Russia was at war with Turkey. The commander in chief of the Russian forces, Prince Potemkin, had promised Paul Jones the full command of the Baltic fleet. But, having heard of Catherine's partiality for the "American adventurer," Potemkin gave way to a fit of jealousy. He now offered Paul Jones a divided command—that is, Jones was to share the command with two other men, Prince Nassau and Brigadier Alexiano.

These two colleagues of Paul Jones turned out to be men of feeble hands but of valiant tongues. They let Jones do all the fighting—and much gallant fighting he did!—and then they took upon themselves all the credit for his victories. They poisoned against him the ear of Potemkin, and Potemkin poisoned against him the ear of Catherine. She sent him an order of dismissal, couched in the disguise of a promise for "a better command in a more important field of action."

At first the unsuspicious American admiral, accustomed as he was to honest thoughts expressed in honest words, was unaware of the double meaning implied in the queen's command. He actually believed he was being promoted to a better post. When the truth dawned upon him, he was heartbroken. Catherine had dismissed him in favor of a couple of cowardly braggarts! Desperately he tried to regain the queen's favor. To no avail. Potemkin had done his job. Potemkin, and the British ambassador at the Russian court. They distorted old stories and manufactured new ones, in order to prejudice the queen against him. They revived the Mungo Maxwell case, they insinuated that Paul Jones was a self-seeking egotist, a bully, and a lecherous beast. They concocted a plot which implicated Paul Jones in a fictitious attempt at rape. In vain the distracted admiral offered irrefutable evidence to disprove every one of the charges brought against him. Queen Catherine believed them and condemned him on all points. Especially on the charge of the alleged rape. Herself the most lecherous woman in Europe, she castigated her own guilty conscience in castigating Paul Jones. "After this nasty incident (of the alleged rape)," she wrote to Baron Grimm, "it would be difficult to find in the Royal Navy a man who would consent to serve under him."

But the men in the Royal Navy thought quite otherwise. To them it was a sad day when he left them. "On this day," one of them lamented, "we have lost our light."

VII

THE REST OF HIS LIFE was the sinking of the sun in a heavy mist. Illness, poverty, frustration, neglect. But no despair. To the very end he hoped to be recognized for the man he was.

It was not until after his death, however, that this recognition came to him. At his burial in the Protestant Cemetery of Paris (July 20, 1792), a French clergyman referred to him as "one of the first champions of American liberty, one of the first harbingers of the liberty of the world."

IMPORTANT DATES IN THE LIFE OF
JOHN PAUL JONES

1747—Born, Scotland.
1759—Went to sea.
1766—Became chief mate of a slave ship.
1768—Became captain of a trader.
1773—Came to America.
1775—Appointed lieutenant in Continental Navy.
Took command of brig ship, the *Providence*.
1776—Commissioned captain in navy.

1778—Commanding the *Ranger*, conquered British sloop of war, the *Drake*.
1779—Took command of the *Bonhomme Richard*.
Captured British warship, the *Serapis*.
1788—Served under Catherine of Russia.
1790—Went to France.
1792—Died, Paris, France.

John Marshall
[1755-1835]

HIS father was a soldier and a pioneer. He could display no emblazoned coat of arms or match his plebian origin with the pedigreed aristocracy of Virginia. But his wife could boast a family tree whose bark was coated with silver and whose leaves were ingots of gold. She was descended from the earls of Scotland—a clan of fighters who had served under some of the greatest military heroes in British history. It was a strange and powerful union—this marriage between the red blood of the New World and the blue blood of the Old.

When John was ten years old his parents moved from their dank log cabin in Virginia to the heart of the Blue Ridge Mountains. It was a terrifying place where "the weeds of disease and the wiles of the Indians" lay in ambush for the white settlers. But Mary Marshall spoke reassuringly to her children, especially to the eldest who would be able to understand. "Don't be afraid, Johnny. The pioneers of the past have shown us the way. And, God helping us, we will show the way to the pioneers of the future."

II

YOUNG JOHNNY loved his mother, but he simply adored his father. Tom Marshall, a flame of defiant courage, had served his community successively as vestryman, sheriff, and member of the Virginia House of Burgesses. His heart had leaped high on that never-to-be-forgotten day when Patrick Henry had stood up to denounce the injustice of the British king against the American colonies.

On his return home, Tom Marshall had gravely considered the issue. He had heard rumors that the Bostonians had sent a shipload of British tea to the bottom of the harbor. And that a handful of farmers in Lexington had chased the British regulars twenty miles. Soon these rumors were confirmed. American blood had been spilled. Massachusetts was at war. There was no doubt as to where Virginia would stand.

One day he spoke to John, who was now twenty years old. "Son, they tell me you're one of the best shots around here."

"Well, I guess I have a *little* bit of skill."

"You'll need it, son." He handed him the rifle which he had taken down from the wall. "There's war with England."

"Thanks, Father, I will march with you."

III

TOGETHER the two militiamen, Lieutenant John Marshall and his father, helped to hold the bridge over the Elizabeth River against the charge of Governor Dunmore and his Virginia regulars. Together they enrolled in the Third Virginia Regiment and threw aside their homespun shirts and bucktail caps for the Continental blue and buff. Together they marched north to help the hard-pressed Washington. And together they starved and froze at Valley Forge.

Many fathers and sons had enlisted as partners in this uncertain adventure for freedom. Fathers of the colonial past, sons of the republican future, comrades in the hard-fighting moments of the present.

When John Marshall resigned from the service, the war was not quite over. But he was the hero of a dozen tales of glory. Among the fashionable Virginians everybody knew that old Tom Marshall's son had proved himself an exemplary soldier. His stoical conduct at Valley Forge had been a model for all his fellow soldiers. His coolness under fire had won the praise of all the officers. The young ladies of Yorktown talked about his exploits with heightened pulses and flushed faces.

Especially the three Ambler girls, the daughters of the treasurer of the colony. They could scarcely sleep when they heard that young Marshall was coming to town—"resplendent in his gold braids and epaulettes, and carrying a dazzling sword."

What was their chagrin when they were introduced to a tall, gangling youth in ill-fitting homespun clothes, a "country bumpkin" who stumbled in his speech and shambled in his walk! And yet there *was* an undeniable charm about him. He came often to see the girls. He read them poetry in a pleasant, "soulful" voice while the two older girls knitted with lowered eyes. But Mary, the youngest of the Ambler sisters—a pert little hoyden of fourteen—looked boldly upon him as he read. "I will marry him," she decided.

She set her cap for him with the clever audacity of a young woman who had made up her mind. And poor John, for all his experience in war, was no match for her attack. The tall young oak tree fell at the stroke of a wisp of a girl. He found himself desperately in love.

But she was too young. They would have to wait for marriage. Moreover, it was high time he looked around for something to do in the way of a career. The soldiers at Valley Forge had told him he was born with a legal mind. They had laid their squabbles before him, and never once had they dissented from his decisions as they sat on their straw mattresses and munched their "firecakes" and listened to those masterpieces of logic that came out of his untutored mouth. "Anybody can tell you were cut out for a lawyer."

Ah, wouldn't his Mary's eye glow with pride when, in the presence of the learned jurors, he pitted his mind against the minds of the most distinguished lawyers in Virginia!

It was love that gave the final spurt to law. He entered the College of William and Mary, a school with a fine tradition and congenial customs. "No liquor shall be furnished or used at table," read one of the regulations, "except beer, cider, toddy, or spirits and water." In hot weather the students attended classes without their coats, shoes, or stockings. For John Marshall it was always hot weather. He came to his classes regularly, and with many notebooks. But hardly a page did he fill with the wise utterances of his professors. On every line appeared the name of Mary Ambler. "Miss M. Ambler," written upside down. "Miss Mary A.—J. Marshall," scrawled on the margins. And sketches of her face from a hundred different angles graced the covers.

Finally he could stand it no longer. He was certain she would give her heart and her future to someone else unless he really got down to making a living. His studies at William and Mary were a waste of time and energy. Bother the *theory* of law. He knew enough already of the *practice* of law to get his license and begin to hunt up clients.

He applied for admittance to the bar and—such were the standards of the time—his application was successful. American jurisprudence directly after the Revolution was a field not for scholars but for pioneers. A tough intellectual fiber, a sympathetic insight into human emotions, and a dauntless energy—these rather than scholastic learning were the requirements for a legal career in 1783. And John Marshall possessed, in addition to these requirements, a fourth asset not infrequently to be found among the pioneering folk who spent many hours around the campfire telling tall stories—the gift of an eloquent tongue.

There were many claims and much business for the struggling young lawyer—but no cash. Cash was a scarce commodity, and men paid for their services in land and in durable goods. For three years Marshall collected his goods. And then he joined hands with his beloved. He was twenty-seven. The bride was seventeen. When he had finished paying the minister, he had one guinea left in his pocket.

IV

JOHN MARSHALL'S RISE to prominence was rapid. By his marriage he had become allied to one of the most powerful families in Virginia. But the deep respect he commanded in his profession was due to his native genius and not to his acquired family connections. Within a short while his reputation for controversy was known throughout the state.

A distinguished visitor from another part of the country had come to Virginia to appeal a lawsuit in her courts. He looked around for a suitable attorney. The landlord of the hotel where he was staying recommended young John Marshall. "There comes young Marshall himself," added the landlord as they were chatting on the piazza. The client looked down the street. The lawyer strode slowly by. He was dressed carelessly in a black blouse and unpressed trousers. His hair was disheveled and his shoes were untied. He carried his hat in one hand and nibbled at a bag of cherries which he held in the other. So this was "the famous" Mr. Marshall! The guest had been introduced to another advocate—a venerable patriarch of the law, dressed in a powdered wig and a fashionable cloak. There was no doubt in his mind as to which man he would choose. But before his case was called he had an opportunity to be present when both the "aristocrat" and the "roughneck" argued before the judge. "Mr. Marshall," he said right after the latter had finished his argument, "I have made a dreadful mistake. I have already given my lawyer half of his fee. I will give you the remainder if you stay away from the courthouse and eat cherries until my case is closed."

But the unfortunate visitor was not alone in his initial estimate of John Marshall. The learned members at the bar, long used to judging all manners of men, confessed that their young colleague defied analysis. "Without a commanding presence in the courtroom, with a dry, hard voice and clumsy gestures, possessing not a single ornament of the orator, John Marshall is one of the most eloquent men in the world." And the reason for this eloquence was not far to seek. John Marshall possessed one original and almost supernatural faculty—the power to encompass a subject by a single glance of his mind. "His genius is not forensic. Nor is it artistic. It is the charm of his intellect that casts forth a potent spell." No matter how complex and confusing a subject, "though ten times more knotty than the 'gnarled oak,' the lightning of heaven is not more rapid or more resistless than his astonishing penetration." Folks responded to the logical development of his pleadings with a fervor that was almost evangelical. The stuff of his genius was no less scientific than that of Euclid's. His brain cut away at a fact with a series of swift, simple, energetic strokes. "The audience is never permitted to pause for a moment . . . Every sentence is progressive; every idea sheds new light on the subject." The dawn advances. One by one the salient features of the argument take shape until the entire body is touched into flame by the sudden sunburst of a magical phrase. And the audience, spellbound, is witness to a new miracle—the lifeless word transformed into living flesh.

John Marshall's genius was bound to make itself felt not merely in the courtroom but in the entire life of the newly awakened nation. The principles for which he had fought against the British were still (in 1788) in abeyance. His countrymen had thrown off the burden of the British Government, but they had not as yet assumed the responsibilities of a national government of their own. The states were zealous of their sovereignty and refused to yield any essential rights to a central power. While they loudly insisted upon their independence from foreign slavery, the American people were allowing themselves "to sink into a galling domestic bondage"—the bondage of anarchy, and impotency, and disunion. George Washington, the patriarch who had given up all considerations of personal freedom in order to lead his countrymen to Canaan, had declared for a strong national government as the only instrument for the realization of a people's true liberty. "For men are truly free only when they have the courage to surrender voluntarily as much of their private rights as is commensurate with the public good."

Yet when Washington and Madison and Jefferson and the other students of political science drew up a Constitution for the "public government" of the United States, the majority of the people at the outset were strongly opposed to accepting it. It required the combined brilliance and persuasiveness of the greatest minds among the supporters to win over the necessary nine states for the ratification of this Constitution.

Foremost among the Virginians in pleading the cause of the Constitution was John Marshall. To the incessant fulminations of the opposition he entered a lucid and classic argument: "What are the objects of the national government? To protect the United States and to promote the general welfare. Protection in time of war is one of its primal objects. Until mankind shall cease to have avarice and ambition, wars shall rise . . . The honorable gentlemen say that we need not be afraid of war. But look at history . . . Look at the great volume of human nature. They will both tell you that a defenceless country cannot be secure."

Finally the Virginia delegates accepted the Constitution by a majority of ten votes—and Marshall returned to the business of making a living at the bar. But he no longer practiced in the comparative privacy of a local reputation. He had become a national figure. With the formation of a republican government and the election of a President and a Congress of the United States, the necessity arose for a new type of American—a man who could rise to the stature of statesmanship. And John Marshall proved to be the man. The Federalist Alexander Hamilton, committed to the philosophy that the men of solid property alone should rule the state, had found in John Marshall a fellow Federalist. For Marshall was a lawyer whose mind tended naturally to honest and solid conservatism—not the ostentatiously elegant conservatism of the Boston, New York, and Philadelphia Federalists, but the "homespun stability" that fitted into a slack attire and uttered words of wisdom in a rustic vernacular.

Marshall was still a man of rustic sensibilities. He loved his common neighbors of the countryside. And he was eager for their happiness. Even now he awoke nights with a moan as he felt the chill of the winter at Valley Forge seep through his veins. And he resolved that he would do his part to build a solid and substantial nation in which this terrible catastrophe of ice and blood must never happen again.

V

JOHN MARSHALL'S SUN was rapidly climbing to its zenith. He had been a strong supporter of President Washington's foreign policy, and he was appointed by President John Adams to a commission whose job it was to keep the hotheaded revolutionary government of France at peace with the United States. When the members of the French foreign office brazenly demanded a bribe of good American coin before they talked business, Marshall replied by demanding his passports back to the United States.

He came home in a halo of martyred glory, served a term in the House of Representatives, and accepted the portfolio of Secretary of State in the final Cabinet of President Adams.

And then fate played her familiar role of irony. The Federalists who had held the reins of power for ten years, ever since the formation of the government in 1789, now saw themselves rapidly slipping into the discard. In the fall of 1800, Thomas Jefferson, the candidate most obnoxious to all men of property, was elected President over John Adams. It was a complete victory for the party of "farmers and day laborers." For they had won not only the presidency and the vice-presidency, but the Congress as well. To the Federalists it was tantamount to a revolution. There was one branch of government they might still retain in the face of the avalanche, however, and that was the judiciary. As Adams's term of office neared its end, he frantically signed permanent appointments for his "old-guard Federalists" to the principal judgeships of the nation. In the arms of the law, at least, the principles of property would be protected.

And then, at the last moment, Adams produced his master stroke. Looking around for someone of his own persuasion to be selected as the final guardian of the American Constitution, he decided there was one man in the country pre-eminently suited for the office—John Marshall.

And so at forty-five, still robust, still fond of his game of quoits, John Marshall found himself Chief Justice of the Supreme Court—an institution new in the history of government and of law. There was no precedent for his office, no guide for his action. What good would all the learning of Blackstone and all the experience of Mansfield do him? Until this appointment he had never even held a judicial office. And now, as he donned the judge's robes, he felt the same nameless fear that had paralyzed him as a child when he moved from the comfortable log cabin in the Tidewater into the Western Wilderness through the paths of the Unknown. Once again he was called upon to take an unknown road, to break new ground. This was the scourge—and the sublimity—of being an American.

After all, what a man needed was merely a deep sense of justice. Here was the Constitution of his government. Interpret its definitions as to the rights and the duties of four million Americans not with subtlety nor with sophistry, but with justice.

In 1789, when the Constitution became the supreme law of the land, many people predicted openly—and some of them with malice—that it would fail within a decade. The shortsighted Americans had never understood the serious purpose of the Constitution-makers—not to present the substance of a dogma, but to preserve the spirit of an ideal, the soul of human independence resurrected out of the scarred body of the American Revolution. And Marshall, as he sat down for the first session of the Supreme Court held under his leadership, was conscious of the great creative task before him. For the Constitution would become potent only through the interpretative genius of the philosopher-judge who could transform its *written words* into *living thoughts*.

One of John Marshall's shrewdest associates on the bench, Judge Story, looked at him inquisitively as the Chief Justice donned his robes. "He will see the law through honest eyes," he decided. "I love his laugh; it is too hearty for an intriguer."

VI

FOR THIRTY-FOUR YEARS John Marshall saw justice and made it into American constitutional law. In his major decisions he gave full affirmation to the ties that solidified the great and efficient family of the United States. Opponents argued loudly that the United States was a government of *enumerated powers*. Marshall answered, "It is a government of great *national purposes*." And such it has remained by the verdict of the Supreme Court.

In the first major case presented to him, Chief Justice Marshall set a precedent for calling his court *Supreme*. For he proclaimed the *final right* of the judiciary to pass on the constitutionality of an act of Congress. In a subsequent decision he extended the powers of the federal government by affirming the right of the Supreme Court to pass on the constitutionality of a measure enacted by a state legislature. In still another historic instance he further broadened the basic power of the central government when he declared that the establishment of a national bank was quite in accord with the spirit of the Constitution. There were those, indeed, who charged that 90 per cent of his decisions were marked by "a Federalist bias," and that he had deliberately turned away "from the democracy of the individual to the autocracy of the state." But this was a fault (if fault it was) of his nature, not of his morals. The particular shape of his personality had stamped him as an *honest Federalist*.

Yet in one instance, it must be confessed, he allowed himself to yield to the flames of prejudice. It was at the trial of Aaron Burr, whom the Jeffersonian administration had labeled as a traitor endeavoring to carve a Mexican empire out of the Western territories of the United States.

Marshall presided at the trial. He was completely impartial in his feelings toward the defendant. But he was a lifelong political enemy of Thomas Jefferson, the President who, as the Federalists alleged, had engineered the trial. Marshall had received his appointment as Chief Justice from John Adams just before the inauguration of President Jefferson—in order, ran the Republican gossip, "to entrench federalism in those regions where the long arm of the people can not reach." Ironically enough, the new President and the Chief Justice were cousins by birth. And during the course of the trial Marshall proceeded to make things "very hot" for Cousin Jefferson. Burr had asserted that some of the evidence necessary to his defense was in the hands of the President. And he had demanded that the President be subpoenaed as a witness in the trial. Marshall sustained the plaintiff and thus bade fair to set a pretty precedent. "Only the King of England is exempt from giving evidence in common law," he asserted. "The American President can claim no exception to the rules." And he ordered a subpoena to be served on Jefferson. The country waited to see what would happen. Would Titan bend the knee to Titan? The issue was not long left in doubt. The President wrote a stormy reply to the subpoena. "The Constitution enjoins the President's agency in the concerns of six millions of people. Is the business paramount to this which summons him as witness in the behalf of a single one?" He threatened among his friends to arrest Marshall and to throw "the whole meddling court" out of the country. He fumed and fulminated. "Yet in spite of all this," one of Marshall's friends remarked to the Chief Justice, "I am sure your subpoena is constitutional."

"Yes," replied Marshall with a wry smile. "But read the Constitution again. I am compelled under its authority to *issue* the order. But there is no authority in the land that can compel the President to *obey* this order."

VII

FOR THE REST OF HIS LIFE the stalwart descendant of the earls of Scotland and of the carpenters of America brought his decisions to every man's fireside. And in this way he sealed a glorious verdict "on his property, his reputation, his life, his all." Every morning, with republican simplicity, the distinguished Federalist walked on foot to market and fetched home a basket of vegetables under his arm. In the rainy season he carried a faded green umbrella; and on sunny days he paused a bit by the wayside, placed his bundles on the ground, and rolled up his sleeves to pitch horseshoes.

And once, in the late afternoon of his public life, he descended from his judicial bench to the assembly floor. His native Virginia had called a convention to revise her local constitution. He was a very old man. But he stood beside the youngest delegates—"tall, in a long surtout of blue, with a face of genius and an eye of fire."

But the fire was burning low. He had been stricken by an ailment in the kidney. His years made the prospect of a successful operation doubtful. At any rate, the doctor told him, it would be a painful procedure.

"I have no anxiety over the result. I have not the slightest desire to live, suffering as I do."

He emerged successfully from the operation. But he could not escape his suffering. The death of his wife, followed by the passing of his oldest son—one of ten children—hastened his final journey.

At the age of seventy-two he was asked to write an autobiographical sketch. He commenced with an apology. "The events of my life are too unimportant, and have too little interest for any person not of my immediate family, to render them worth communicating or preserving."

He finished his last lines and was laid to rest amid imposing ceremonies and weighty tributes.

"What was there about him that impressed you most?" a female relative was asked at the funeral.

"His great humility," she replied.

IMPORTANT DATES IN THE LIFE OF JOHN MARSHALL

1755—Born, Germantown, Virginia.

1776—Lieutenant in the Continental Army.

1778—Captain in the Continental Army.

1781—Admitted to the bar.

1782—Elected to the Virginia Assembly.
Married Mary Ambler.

1788—Member of the Federal Convention appointed to discuss the ratification of the United States Constitution.

1797-98—Special envoy to France, to adjust commercial relations between France and United States.

1798—Elected to the United States House of Representatives.

1800—Appointed Secretary of State under President Adams.

1801—Appointed Chief Justice of the Supreme Court.

1804-07—Wrote five-volume biography of George Washington.

1831—His wife died on Christmas Day.

1835—Died, Philadelphia.

Alexander Hamilton

[1757-1804]

I T WAS a hot, haze-ridden morning when he crossed the Hudson
River in his boat. Mr. Pendleton, his second, was peering anxiously
from the bow at the gleaming outlines of the Palisades on the Jersey
side. Dr. Hosack, the surgeon, was quietly inspecting his bandages.
Alexander Hamilton looked at Dr. Hosack and his first-aid kit. The
good old surgeon would be very busy in just a few minutes, trying to
stanch the blood from a mortal wound. No question that it would be
mortal. Hamilton's lips moved as if to say, "This will not be a duel, it will
be a suicide." But instead he merely murmured, "Isn't the Hudson beautiful today?"

He had first seen the Hudson thirty-two years ago, in 1772, when he
had reached New York after a passage from his native island of Nevis in
the West Indies. How broad and tranquil the river had seemed in contrast
to the surging waves of feeling in his own heart! It was the heart of a lad
of fifteen, pounding like a hurricane at his venture into the New World.
And now at forty-seven he was preparing to pass to another world. His
hair was streaked with gray, and his lips were compressed with the sadness of a man who had lived too long and who refused any further extension of life.

He turned one more glance toward the city he was leaving just as the
boat was beached on the red clay soil of New Jersey. Back toward the
island where he had waged the most exciting battles of his political
career, where his wife and his children were now asleep. That was his
magic city. For fifteen years he had held it in the palm of his hand. Hamiltonopolis! The capital of his Empire. He had shuffled the destiny of its
people like dice. No guardian deity of any ancient Greek citadel had exercised a more absolute power or compelled a more profound reverence
than he. But now he had left his sanctuary. He was traveling in the dawn
to a duel of honor at Weehawken. He had determined that he would die

under Colonel Burr's fire. He would point his gun to the sky. There would be no uncertainty about his death, just as there had been no uncertainty about his life. He had planned out every conscious hour, from the moment he had realized the strength of his will. It was no small satisfaction for him to dictate to the destinies just how and when he, Alexander Hamilton, would end his career. It was no small triumph to flaunt the gift of life right back into the face of the gods who had bestowed it upon him. He disdained their gift. At forty-seven he was ready to die. Let Aaron Burr live on.

The haze lifted as Hamilton, together with his party, reached Weehawken in the Palisades. Colonel Burr and Mr. Van Ness, his second, were already clearing the brush. Burr nodded to his antagonist in a warm friendliness. And Hamilton replied with a stiff bow—as if he had made a gallant little speech and was now awaiting applause. "I feel it is my religious duty to oppose his political career," he had repeatedly told his closest friends.

Mr. Pendleton handed him a pistol. Mr. Van Ness marked off ten paces.

What in the world had the final quarrel been about? Oh, bother! There was a breath of expectancy in the air. It warmed his blood. It was going to be another hot day, another day of life and women and wine. . . .

"No quarrel," he muttered as he allowed himself to be carried gently to the boat. He felt his head growing light and he heard the whisper of Dr. Hosack. "A mortal wound." Overhead the blue of the sky had broken into a rainbow of colors through the prism of his tears.

II

WHEN Alexander stood in the tropical sunset of his last night on the island of Nevis and bade farewell to his aunt, there were no tears in his eyes. Tears do not come readily to a proud, ambitious lad of fifteen fired with the expectation of conquest. He was leaving the store at Christianstadt and going to America for a college education. He had no regrets at parting company with his uncle and his job. He had shed his last tears over his mother when they had buried her four years ago. He might have clasped the hand of a father with something of a lump in his throat. But his father, having suffered financial misfortune, had left his family to the care of wealthy relatives and had sought employment on another island. Alexander knew that while his mother lived his father had occasionally corresponded with her. But after her death he was heard from less frequently, until finally he became somewhat of a legend.

There had been tears in the voice of his mother just before she died. But they had been chilled by a look of cold determination in her eye. "No matter what anyone may say to you, Alexander, your father is a good man." And when she had gone he heard ugly mutterings about himself from his acquaintances. "Illegitimate. Born out of wedlock." And he had come to his aunt, his cheeks on fire, demanding to know.

"Your mother and your father loved each other very deeply, Alexander.

But they were never married in the eyes of the law. In the eyes of God I'm sure they were forgiven!"

And then she went gently on with her story. "You see, Alexander, your mother was a very sad and beautiful lady, compelled by her parents when she was little more than a child to marry a wealthy old landowner whom she detested. And before she was out of her teens she separated from him. But she was unable to get a divorce. The Parliament in England was too busy passing budgets to listen to the pleadings of a woman's heart . . ."

And his eyes glistened with pride as she continued with the story of his origin. "Your father was a Hamilton. James Hamilton, of the Scotch aristocracy. When he came adventuring to the island, he was only a year older than your mother. They made a bonny handsome couple, those two."

A fierce sense of grandeur stirred the fires of his spirit as he heard this story. So he was no common boy! He would wear his irregular origin as a badge of distinction and not as a mark of shame.

He had formed his plans to go off adventuring like his father. When a close friend of his had left the island to get a college education in America, Alexander knew that he too must acquire this most powerful weapon for social mastery—a trained mind. He worked ever more assiduously at the hateful business of piling up money for his uncle and dreamed of the day when he too would be able to leave for America.

At times, when he wrote to his friend in college, his hand trembled with the impatience of his desire to get away. ". . . For to confess my weakness, Ned, my ambition is prevalent, so that I contemn the grovelling condition of a clerk, or the like, to which my fortune condemns me . . . I would willingly risk my life . . . to exalt my station."

His relatives knew only the outside of him. What they knew they liked. Hair a glorious shade of red just like his mother's. Patrician nose. Determined chin. A dandified little gentleman. Quite the finest breed of the rich tropics. Why not send him away to college? He had written a very fine descriptive essay on the hurricane that had lately swept the islands. A newspaper in St. Kitts had published it. Let the winds blow him westward to America. He had been born of a tropical passion. Let him rise to success through a hurricane.

III

IN THE glittering parlors of New York he lost much of his sensitivity. He had arrived with the best of credentials from his uncle and he met the most promising people. "Born of a plantation aristocracy in the West Indies," the Schuyler, Livingston, and Witherspoon families were told. The result of an irregular affair. But an affair of the finest blood. Mother, a Huguenot; father, a Hamilton of the old Scottish clans.

The ladies, Kitty and Judith and Sarah and Susan, made much of a fuss over him. What an interesting eye! Like a violet half frozen in the spring. And what an enviable complexion! "My dear Hamilton," breathed Kitty

Livingston, "have a care. You are far too fortunate. You will rise rapidly to the highest places. And the jealous gods will smite you."

He bore himself correctly. The boys at King's College, where he studied for his degree, envied the unerring grasp of his mind. And Hamilton was quite comfortable, for he envied no one. When his fellow students fancied themselves swept away in a crusading spirit against the British Parliament, it was Hamilton who found the most fitting arguments with which to plead their case from the college steps. He had been in America only three years, and he already had a more comprehensive understanding of the controversy between the colonies and England than "these heathen," as he contemptuously called the native students.

In the moments when he rested from his lawbooks he wrote pamphlets on the problem of taxation without representation, adding the reflections of his eighteen years to the wisdom of the leading patriots and scholars of America.

He had not forgotten his studies in Demosthenes. "As a general marches at the head of his troops, so ought wise politicians, if I dare use the expression, to march at the head of affairs." He would take more and more of an active part, even join the army if open rebellion was decided on. No question, he had concluded, that the inhabitants of America had the right to the disposal of their own lives and property, without being imposed upon by a Parliament sitting three thousand miles away. And moreover—he calculated—those who stood solidly by their guns, though now they were in the minority, would someday become the very saints of the people. There was a mob of harebrained patriots, to be sure, men who were ready to risk their lives for emotional slogans. "A reliance on pure patriotism has been the source of many errors," he reasoned. Well, he would take up arms on a calculation that had nothing of the heart's voice in it. The financial classes in America were bound by every right of the history of financial groups everywhere to free themselves from the domination of foreign capital. There was only one issue in doubt. Could the British force the colonies into subjugation? Hamilton thought not. And so with remarkable shrewdness he joined a company of "rebels," and shortly received a commission as captain of artillery. It was in the skies of a free America that his star would rise.

"Dear Hamilton will never look natural in a military uniform," declared Kitty Livingston. "And his cheeks are too rosy to be stained in the smoke of battle."

"You do not know your soldier," whispered one of her friends. "His lips are severe. He will get along."

The Battle of Long Island. The retreat to Jersey. Grime, sweat, blood, tears, despair. Hamilton marched beside his cannon with his cocked hat pulled down over his brilliant eyes, lost in thought.

The American cause in the deepest shadow. George Washington was strolling along the ranks on the lookout for an aide-de-camp. He saw Hamilton digging at a breastwork. Their eyes met. "I will have you."

The members of Washington's family were fascinated by the new aide-de-camp. He sat at the general's table along with Lafayette. He spoke little, looked silently at his food, blushed on occasion when he was complimented. Washington valued Hamilton's services highly. He got out more letters and attended to more business than any dozen of his other aides. "He is my high priest of energy," Washington often told his friends.

And Hamilton sat writing the general's dispatches and learning much of the inside detail of the American campaign for independence. He had a genius for campaign strategy. Not only on the battlefield but in the terrain of the hearts of those who suited him. Which was the greater battle—the fight of the Continental Army or his own fight? To his friends in the West Indies, with whom he corresponded regularly, he gave an account of the army's military policy. "We are retreating step by step in the face of superior numbers. We are avoiding a general engagement with the enemy. Our hopes are not placed in any particular city or spot of ground, but in the preserving of a good force, furnished with proper necessaries, to take advantage of favorable opportunities, and to waste and defeat the enemy by piecemeal. Every new post they take requires a new division of their forces. In the end we will be successful." But to no one did he reveal the tactics of his own advance.

On official duty he was sent to General Schuyler, the head of one of the wealthy patroon families in New York and one of the leading politicians of the country. Schuyler admired Hamilton's businesslike manner. And Schuyler's second daughter, Betsy, completely lost her heart to him.

"I must have a wife," Hamilton had declared to a fellow aide, "who believes in God and hates a saint." And in his effort to secure his wife, he dispatched to Betsy letters of love in a handwriting of legible beauty. Everything about him was so neat and precise. And calculated. Before the British had surrendered, the Schuylers were united with the Hamiltons.

But the war had not reached its end when Hamilton suffered a minor disagreement with Washington and resigned from his desk to go into the field. He received the command of an infantry company and distinguished himself in battle. He played the role of a conscious hero. "Two nights ago," he wrote to his wife, "my duty and my honor obliged me to take a step in which your happiness was too much risked. I commanded an attack upon one of the enemy's redoubts; we carried it in an instant and with little loss."

At the cessation of hostilities he was regarded as a soldier who had offered himself wholly to his country. There were few who could go back to civil life—and politics—boasting a more distinguished record of patriotic service.

IV

During the months following the treaty of Yorktown, Hamilton became a father and a lawyer. "I have been employed for the last ten months," he wrote, "in rocking the cradle and studying the art of fleecing my neighbors." His efficiency in matters commercial as well as in matters political had won him the eye of the financier of the Revolution, Robert Morris, who asked him to draw up a financial account for the state of New York. And within a short time he had become prominent enough in state politics to be appointed as a delegate to the Convention of the States at Annapolis, held in 1786.

At this convention he became the leading proponent of a federal constitution for the thirteen states. In his advocacy of a firm and centralized machinery of government by a few men, he confessed candidly that "our prevailing passions are ambition and self-interest." And, he continued, "it will ever be the duty of a wise government to avail itself of those passions."

In order to explain and to "sell" the new constitution to the people of New York, he wrote a series of *Federalist Papers* under the pseudonym of Caesar. And he bit his lip in anguish when he realized the blunder he had committed. Caesar! His political opponents had caught up the name and the blunt philosophy it expressed and had hurled it back at him in a thousand different ways.

"Why, this dapper little fellow possesses the very subtlety of a Caesar. His perfumed glove conceals an iron hand. Come to think of it, it was he who first proposed a centralized government—in other words, a tyranny—even before the end of the war." Could this sort of agitation please the people who had just waged a war to rid themselves of *another* tyranny?

And Hamilton stood before the mirror powdering his hair and tying it into a queue. Why should he be ashamed? A man must always advocate the politics that *benefit* a country, not the slogans that *please* it. He carefully placed a flower in his lapel. Was that the reason for the continual whispers about him? "Beware of Alexander Hamilton. He is an exotic flower who will poison the soil into which he has been transplanted." He frowned. How poetic! And how silly! He would far rather be called a tyrant—if he *must* be called names—than a flower. There was nothing static or flowerlike about *his* genius.

The state of New York had finally voted to accept the constitution. But only with reluctance. And only after Alexander Hamilton had spoken briefly but effectively in its favor at the Convention Hall. He had played his game well. With his pen and with the assistance of his able political lieutenants he had won the cityfolk of Manhattan over to his cause. And then he had faced the "die-hard" residents of upper New York. "I therefore announce to you, gentlemen, that if you do not ratify this constitution without further talk, then Manhattan, Westchester, and Kings counties shall withdraw from the State of New York and form a state by themselves, leaving the rest of you without a seaport for your commerce." That was sufficient. New York entered the union.

To be sure, Hamilton was not completely satisfied with the constitution he had saved. He had desired a president and a body of senators modeled after the British monarch and the House of Peers, and elected on the basis of their property holdings to serve for the duration of their lives. Yet, "with all its imperfections," he regarded the adoption of this constitution as a personal triumph. Some of his friends dared to call him "Alexander the Great." The city whose political opinion he had swayed was his very own "Hamiltonopolis." He stood at the window in the sunset and watched the parade of thousands of demonstrators in the street—celebrating the victory of the new national government. Shipbuilders and blacksmiths and stonemasons marched singing through the streets. He felt pleased—and yet annoyed at the same time. What were these commoners celebrating for? He hated mobs and their celebrations. Did these masses of humanity think that *they* were going to rule the new government? He laughed outright at this "amusing" thought. "Poor heathen!"

V

IT WAS NOT in the hands of the people he would place the future security of his country, vowed Alexander Hamilton as he came to his desk. He had just been appointed Secretary of the Treasury in the administration of President Washington. This was no time for shilly-shally sentiment. The monarchies all over Europe were looking with expectant and greedy eyes upon this "foolish" experiment of the United States of America. If it failed to survive, the day of kings had only just begun.

Ill-wishers abroad predicted that this government would die in an excess of simple and childish idealism. But Hamilton thought differently. "No, we shall outwit you as we have outfought you. This is no attempt at a Utopia—to perish in a day. We realize that all men unfortunately are *not* created equal. We shall build a government that will appeal to the one stable element in human society—the self-interest of influential men. Our country will outlast your hopes."

He sat fourteen hours a day preparing a report for Congress on the new financial system of the nation. This nation would survive through the law of the survival of all the strong nations. "This government, like all (solid) governments, shall be an administration of the few. But the few in America are not, as in Europe, an aristocracy of *land* owners; they are an aristocracy of *money* owners. The past has been with you, your kings and your warriors; the future is with us, our merchants and our bankers. I shall attach the money owners so closely to the government that the success of all their *personal* fortunes will be identical with the success of the *national* fortune."

During the Revolution many of the rank and file had invested all their savings in government certificates. But as the fortunes of the government seemed to wane and the investors found themselves in need of ready cash, they sold their bonds to speculators at a fraction of their original value. When Hamilton came into the Cabinet as Secretary of the Treasury, he decided that it was "a matter of principle and honor, in laying the cornerstone of our financial policy, to redeem these bonds at their full original value." This full value, however, was to be paid not to the first purchasers of the bonds, but to their present owners. "It is true that a great proportion of the poor people's money has passed into the hands of adventurers and that we shall therefore by a stroke of the pen create a new class of rich men. But we must compromise with the evil. Government must always depend upon a group of faithful retainers. And the new class of financiers will be our strongest supporters."

Thus reasoned Hamilton. "I will propose also that the Federal Government take over every dollar of the debts contracted by the states during the war and that it share the total obligation directly and equally with all . . . In this way I shall create for each a stake in the national government, a common revenue and a common obligation to see the Union through to the finish. I shall get the necessary votes for this measure in Congress even if I have to transfer the capital from New York to the South . . . I shall recommend the creation of a national bank. This shall be a business man's government, a government of buying and selling and investing. It is a disgrace the way our poor heathen hoard their goods in their cellars and hide their money in their stockings. Out in the open with all the citizens' assets. A citizen with savings invested in a national bank will never be a *rebellious* citizen."

And Hamilton went on with his reasoning. "When I have thus assured the allegiance of the bankers and the speculators, I shall broaden the basis of our wealth. I shall introduce a system of protective tariffs that will create a new class of manufacturers and owners of merchandise. I shall increase the numbers of the ruling classes. For in numbers alone there is security."

Security created by measures of finance. Security sealed by the creation of an army and the rigid enforcement of the law.

He rose in the subdued splendor of his library to his full height.

VI

Side by side with Alexander Hamilton in the Cabinet sat Thomas Jefferson, the Secretary of State. As the plans of the "little Treasurer" unfolded, a volcano of feeling blazed through Jefferson's pale blue eyes. The hand that had written the Declaration of Independence trembled and curled into a fist. "This man would be Monarch of America," he told his lieutenants in Congress, Madison and Monroe. And Alexander Hamilton measured his opponent coolly. "This man shall be the monarch's fool." Methodically he rallied his followers for the life-and-death struggle to come.

Never was his pen more desperately needed. The Jeffersonians had organized a newspaper which sounded the key for a mass campaign to force Hamilton from the Cabinet into private life. And Hamilton hurled pamphlet after pamphlet into the battle for the defense of his financial policy. Finally the Jeffersonians, in their effort to oust him, engineered a congressional resolution compelling him to make a public accounting of his treasury expenses. "Jefferson has raised the devil," he blazed to his friends. "He has become a colossus of hate." Yet he submitted his accounts to the public scrutiny—and cleared himself to the satisfaction of everyone.

In the meantime ill winds were blowing from abroad. The French Revolution! Here was Jefferson's faith in the nobility of the people being put to the test. The streets were slippery with the blood of those who, like Hamilton, disagreed with the philosophy of liberty, equality, fraternity. "What philosopher," argued Hamilton, "ever meant sincerely that the voice of the people is the voice of God?" Hamilton walked triumphantly into the "parlors of the elect" as the news of the French Reign of Terror reached America. "Your people, sir, is a beast." At bottom, he admitted, the masses are no more beastly than the classes. But they are *hungry, exploited, bruised,* and *beaten* beasts, and therefore when they are let loose they are more dangerous than the sleek and the well-fed. "The vices of the rich are far more congenial to good government than the vices of the poor."

But Jefferson stayed away from the "unwholesome brilliance" of society. He sat by his dim candlelight and refused to lose his faith in the people. A stubborn fanatic!

They met again at a Cabinet session when the ambassador from the French Republic arrived in Washington and asked that the American people take definite sides with the French people in their struggle against the counter-revolutionary forces of the world. Hamilton insisted that America, as a neutral nation, must refuse to take part in foreign quarrels. But, Jefferson wanted to know, had not France taken part in the American quarrel by sending Lafayette over to our aid? "The people's fight against dictatorship is not merely a European or an American issue. It is a *world* issue."

Hamilton jumped to his feet. "You have no business, sir, to sit in this Cabinet by day and hire henchmen by night to fill the press with scurrilous attacks against constituted order!"

"Why, sir, do you despise the common folk?" retorted Jefferson. "Why do you endeavor to turn our dream of organized justice into a nightmare of organized wealth?"

When Washington supported the foreign policy of the Secretary of the Treasury, Jefferson resigned from the Cabinet in a white wrath. And all "Hamiltonopolis" applauded. The "little lion" had won a mighty victory. "You have driven this dangerous rabble rouser from the government into the streets where he belongs!"

The Secretary of the Treasury remained in the Cabinet. And he turned with an iron hand to domestic affairs. He recommended a direct tax on liquors. The farmers of western Pennsylvania stormed into rebellion. At a series of mass meetings they determined to resist rather than to pay the tax. President Washington hesitated. "Call out the army," demanded Hamilton, "and permit me to march at its head."

Hamilton marched. The farmers quickly dispersed and paid the tax. And Hamilton smiled once again in the parlors. "To perpetuate the United States of America there must always be a man on horseback."

"But if you are to play the role, my dear Alexander," said Kitty Livingston, "you must remember this: the man on horseback must sooner or later face a hostile army. And more often than not he falls to earth."

"Have no fear about my future. I am resigning from the government. I am going back to my private law practice. For my family." He chuckled mournfully. "I suppose my enemies do not realize how much money I have sacrificed by giving up my practice and taking a thirty-five-hundred-a-year government job. I have made a fortune for my country—and I have impoverished myself."

He retired to private life. But events skidded rapidly on the greased wheels of irony. He was still recognized by the rank and file of his supporters as the creator and the very personification of the Federalist party. And yet there was one man who challenged his supremacy in silence, who refused to take the second place in the party hierarchy. This man was John Adams, delegate to the old Continental Congress, signer of the Declaration of Independence, minister to England under the Confederation. In Washington's first administration he had been elected Vice-President of the United States. And now, upon Hamilton's retirement to private life, he became the President of the United States. In silence he had watched the development of Hamilton's control over the party. He knew that the Secretary of the Treasury had tried to pull every wire to block his election to the presidency. And he suspected—with good reason—that every member of his own Cabinet was sworn to the "little lion" in New York. With a touch of malice he wrote in his private notes: "Hamilton is commander-in-chief of the Senate, of the House of Representatives, of the heads of departments, of General Washington, and least, if you will, of the President of the United States."

Clearly the Federalist party was not big enough for two such men. And a series of political skirmishes led to a final break between them.

This final quarrel grew out of the international position of the American Government. In spite of Washington's declaration of the country's neutrality in foreign affairs, American relations with France had become strained to the breaking point. Preparations were being made to raise a large army against the possibility of a Franco-American war. Hamilton had applied for a commission second to that of General Washington. But Adams, venting his spite, appointed his Secretary of War instead of Hamilton to that commission.

The Franco-American war failed to materialize. But war to the finish had been declared within the ranks of the Federalists. Hamilton replied to Adams's rebuff by writing a pamphlet in which he attacked the character of the President more scurrilously than he had ever attacked Tom Jefferson. It was a fatal blunder, for the attack had been made on the eve of a national election. He had bitten off the nose of the Federalist party to spite the face of his personal enemy. In the picturesque words of Hamilton himself, "For the first time I have taken off the head of a statesman and assumed the ears of an ass."

The Federalists, having already aroused the resentment of the public with their restrictive laws against the freedom of the press, now split themselves wide open with their foolish fratricidal strife. The Jeffersonians were quick to seize their opportunity. Into the split they thrust a wedge and widened the gap still further. At the polls their two candidates —Aaron Burr and Thomas Jefferson—had received the highest number of votes for the presidency. The two were deadlocked with an identical number of electoral votes. According to the law of the land, the election would be decided by a poll of the House of Representatives. But the majority in the House was still in the hands of the Federalists. And therefore Hamilton, as party director, controlled the election.

When the leaders of the House of Representatives called on him for his decision he remarked graciously: "Is there any doubt as to what my vote will be? I have nothing against Aaron Burr except that he is a political demagogue with unlimited personal ambition, completely unfit for high office. I have nothing in favor of Thomas Jefferson except that he is an honest man. I charge you to make him President of the United States."

VII

THE BOAT carrying the man with the mortal wound slowly crossed the Hudson in the morning.

Dr. Hosack looked down. "From the day of Jefferson's election," he remarked to Pendleton, "Alexander Hamilton was marked for death. Two years later he stopped Aaron Burr from becoming governor of New York. And Burr, who wouldn't hesitate to kill on far slighter provocation, just waited for the opportunity to shoot it out. A strange and compelling man, this Hamilton."

They were approaching the New York landing. "For many years he knew Burr's domestic and political life intimately. He was thoroughly convinced that Burr was an unscrupulous demagogue, a Caesar who would destroy the country. Well, Mr. Pendleton, we may agree or disagree with many of Hamilton's ideas. That's an American privilege. But here is an action that speaks much louder than any philosophy. This was an American duty."

Duty. . . . The air was wringing wet. The heat burned slow madness into the veins. Mr. Pendleton drew his snuff. "He was a little hard on the people, sir. He believed they had taxes to pay before they could receive their liberties, duties to perform before they could claim their rights." He looked lengthwise down the peaceful river. "This country will be a going concern as long as we pay our debts *his* way."

IMPORTANT DATES IN THE LIFE OF
ALEXANDER HAMILTON

1757—Born, West Indies.

1769—Entered the countinghouse of his uncle, Nicholas Cruger.

1772—Came to New York.

1774—Entered King's College.

1777—Became Washington's aide-de-camp.

1780—Married Elizabeth Schuyler.

1782-83—Served in the Continental Congress.

1786-87—Delegate to the Constitutional Convention.

1787-88—Interpreted the Constitution in a series of articles, the *Federalist Papers*.

1790—Appointed Secretary of the Treasury.

1795—Resigned to practice law in New York.

1800—Blocked attempt of Aaron Burr to become President of the United States.

1801—His oldest son was killed in a duel at Weehawken, New Jersey.

1804—Killed in duel with Aaron Burr, Weehawken, New Jersey.

John Jacob Astor
[1763-1848]

Y A roadside a boy of sixteen sat and gazed at the village he had just left. Tears blurred his vision; the tiled roofs of Waldorf, and the old Roman road that led down to it, danced in the sunlight. Behind it rose Germany's famed Black Forest, whence Wald-Dorf (Forest Village) had taken its name. Out of sight of friends and family, the boy could let the tears fall unrestrained. But America beckoned, and John Jacob Astor was not the kind to turn back once he had set his mind on some objective. His brother in America had written him time and again about the place where a man could be whatever he liked, if only he worked hard. There was no end to the amount of money a man could make, and Jacob wanted passionately to make money. He was determined not to be a butcher like his father.

Fair-haired and thickset, Jacob had the slow deliberation of the European peasant. His blue eyes were merry with the promise of good humor, but the mouth and the chin bespoke an obstinacy that would carry him to whatever end he had set for himself. First he would go to England. Jacob was thorough—a few years with the firm of his brother in London would give him mastery over the English language. It would also give him the fare to the New World. In his pocket reposed the sum of his worldly wealth—two dollars. Tied in a handkerchief, and carried across his shoulders on a stick, was his wardrobe. In his head he carried visions of success, a stubborn self-confidence, and a capacity for hard work.

A cart lumbered up the road. Jacob hailed the driver. His friendliness and youth earned him a lift, and he was taken one step nearer to the Rhine. From there he would work his way to Britain. And then to America. As he sat quietly beside the driver, wrapped in his dreams, no one could have guessed that he would someday be the richest man in America.

Jacob was the last of four sons to leave the paternal roof. Rebellious against a drunken autocratic father, each of the Astor boys had struck out for himself at the earliest possible moment. And every one of them was successful in his chosen field. In London brother George Peter dealt in musical instruments. With open arms he welcomed young Jacob into his employ. Jacob learned the business quickly. A music lover and flute player in his own right, he was a decided help in the business. For four years he worked for his brother. And then, having saved sufficient funds, he prepared for the next lap of his journey toward wealth. George Peter urged his young brother to stay, offering him a partnership in the firm. But Jacob's dreams were too big for a mere partnership. Dressed in a suit of English make, he invested a third of his savings in seven flutes and set sail—in the steerage—for the land of opportunity.

Aboard the vessel were a number of fur traders. In fascination Jacob listened to their stories of the wild lands teeming with fur-bearing wild life. He listened, and learned. His practical eye pierced beyond the adventure that would have contented most boys. His alert mind stored away facts and figures. He had no vision for the beauty of the rainbow. He saw only the pot of gold that lay beckoning at the further end.

On an early spring morning (1784) Jacob strode up Broadway, New York. Cool underneath the rustling poplar trees, musical with the cries of vendors, colorful with brightly clad Negroes, Broadway was a place of fascination. Jacob felt immediately at home in the bustling, busy town. He clutched the flutes tightly against his side. In his pocket there remained only fifty cents, but in his heart there was a capital of high hope. He smiled as he envisioned the future. Someday all these hurrying strangers would harken to the name of John Jacob Astor.

II

BROTHER HEINRICH was doing very well as a butcher; he offered "Yawcob" a place in his shop. But butchering was not included in Jacob's plans. His first job was as a baker's boy. Carrying baskets of buns and bread through the streets, he vociferously peddled his wares. Though he hated the work, he applied himself to it diligently. But not for long. In two weeks he had found employment with a fur merchant, a Quaker named Brown. At the same time romance had found Jacob. It was at the lodginghouse of the Widow Todd, a lady of good birth but straitened circumstances. She had a daughter, Sarah, who helped her with her chores. Sarah was the type of young lady that Jacob could understand and appreciate. A hard worker, with a sweet disposition and a practical mind. Before long the two young people were strolling arm in arm along the Bowery—an ideal setting for lovers, with the tulip trees nodding overhead and pedestrians nodding a friendly "good day" from the sidewalks. Jacob was getting on in Quaker Brown's fur business. All he had learned on shipboard he now remembered and put to good use. To this knowledge he added the observations of a quick eye. So well did he acquit himself that Quaker Brown sent him on buying trips into the Iroquois country. With German thoroughness, Jacob learned the many dialects of the tribes he dealt with, and thus made

himself a welcome guest in the Indian villages. Unlike the buyers who had
gone before him, he treated the red men as friends and equals. He had
learned, too, that "music hath charms to soothe the savage breast." Many
a time his flute gained him the confidence of some stony-faced chief who
would not traffic with other white men. His efforts brought pleasing results. He returned with loads of fur far more valuable than those which
the average trader was able to obtain. Quaker Brown, delighted with
Jacob's industry, widened the range of his activities and raised his salary.
It seemed that Jacob was once more to receive the offer of a partnership.

In the meantime Jacob and Sarah were married. They took rooms on
the first floor of the Widow Todd's house. But Sarah was not the one to
sit back and let a struggling young husband support her. She kept on
working for her mother. Smiles followed them everywhere, and approval
from the older folks. "Here is a likely couple, bound to succeed." Ambition burned in both their breasts with an equal flame. Jacob was outgrow-
ing Quaker Brown's establishment. He was planning for the day when he
would have his own business. Sarah was all encouragement. Why wait
longer? There were the three hundred dollars of her dowry money, the
two hundred dollars that Jacob had saved, and the rooms on the first
floor of the lodginghouse for a shop. A small enough grubstake, to be
sure, from which to build a fortune. But everything is possible when two
young people are healthy, ambitious, and very much in love.

The seven flutes had long reposed in the window of a store where
Jacob had placed them to be sold on commission. Though there had been
neither sale nor inquiry, he had not lost his faith in them. Now, with
other musical instruments from England, he placed them on sale along
with a handful of furs. The papers began to carry an announcement that
Mr. J. J. Astor had opened his doors to the public. Sarah proved herself
the perfect helpmeet—never idle, always ready with a smile and a mouth-
ful of good sound advice.

As children began to make their appearance at regular intervals, Sarah
took their coming in her stride and somehow found room for them.
There was no time for coddling, as she had to tend the shop—sometimes
for six months at a stretch—when he was away in the fur country. Sarah
had an eye for furs. "It is better than my own," Jacob cheerfully admitted
—and he never concluded a deal without the benefit of her practical
judgment.

The harder the Astors worked, the more genial they became. Jacob's
home-comings were scenes of great rejoicing. Toward his wife and his
children he was full of tender playfulness. His affectionate gestures,
though somewhat heavy, were nonetheless deeply appreciated. A family
of loving bears.

One sorrow had entered their otherwise perfect domestic happiness.
Their first son, whom they had named after John Jacob, had been born
an idiot; he must be confined to an upper room. Upon Astor's arrival, his
first thought was always for the unfortunate child. "How iss de boy?" he
would ask in the guttural accent which he had never lost. "Just the same,
Jacob," Sarah would reply, wiping away a tear with her apron.

Jacob adhered to the principles which he had early formulated for himself. "To be honest, to be industrious, and never to gamble." But things were getting away from him. The business had expanded so rapidly that Jacob asked for a loan from Heinrich to keep up with his obligations. Two hundred dollars was all he wanted; but Heinrich was outraged, delivering a long lecture on gambling and refusing the loan. Jacob listened to the tirade. With head bowed, he saw all that he had worked for slipping away for want of a few dollars. At last Heinrich compromised. "I will not lend you the two hundred," he said, "but I will give you one hundred, on condition that you promise never to borrow again." Jacob took the one hundred, choking down his humiliation, and went to Sarah. Sarah was optimistic. They would find the other hundred somehow, she said. And somehow they did. But the bitterness of the incident had burned itself into Jacob's breast. He never again permitted himself to be placed in a position where he would be forced to borrow.

At the beginning of his career the accent had been on musical instruments. But as the fur business advanced, the music business receded into the background and eventually was discarded altogether. And then came real estate. Jacob's first venture into this field was modest enough—two lots in lower Manhattan, bought for little more than a song. At about the same time George Washington was elected first President of the United States. An auspicious year—the birth of a vast American fortune, the beginning of a great American institution.

III

As HE FRATERNIZED with the trappers, Jacob listened to their tales of richer fur lands beyond those yet penetrated. Fired by their stories of the fabulous fur trade in Canada, he went to Montreal. He established contact directly with the Canadian trappers, setting up his own trading posts in the great Northwest. The Astor empire was spreading, the stacks of furs in New York grew higher, and his competitors dropped one after another by the wayside. No longer was the first floor of his mother-in-law's home large enough to house the project. He rented another warehouse, and then another, and still another.

One large stock of furs lay in the attic of his new home. Jacob hated to see merchandise lying around without earning money. He knew there was a large demand for that particular fur in England. But his thrift had hardened into parsimoniousness, and he refused to hire a London agent to transact the deal. Restlessly he paced the floor, telling Sarah about his problem. She looked at him, thinking. Jacob had been showing signs of discontent. With the first approach of spring he had grown restless, and the restlessness had lasted through the summer. Staid and respected citizen that he was, he had often absented himself from his place of business. Perhaps a European voyage would do him good, she thought; and she suggested that he make the trip by himself. Jacob acted eagerly upon the suggestion. He bought a ticket for England—in the steerage, though he was already one of the richest men in America. Generous to his children, and indeed to all his relatives, he was a miser to his own needs.

In London, Jacob heard mention of the governor of the East India Company—that vast enterprise which dominated the sea trade between Europe and Asia. The name of the governor sounded familiar. It was that of a German immigrant whom Jacob had known in his own poor years. Jacob visited the all-powerful governor. Sure enough, it was the same man. Invited to dine, Jacob refused. He did not own evening clothes and would not spend money on any such frivolous fripperies. The governor, wishing to present Jacob with some memento of their former struggles, gave him a permit to trade in Canton. The document meant nothing to its recipient. He tucked it into a pocket and for a time forgot its existence. On his return to New York he showed it casually to Sarah. At once she recognized its value. "We will trade in Canton," she said.

"But ships," Jacob protests. "Where will we get ships?"

Didn't James Livermore have ships? she asked. And weren't they resting idle at the wharves, because of the trouble with the French?

As usual, Sarah's advice was sound, and Jacob effected one of his typical deals. James Livermore would furnish the ships and the cargo. Jacob would furnish the permit, and both of them would share the profits equally.

At first James Livermore refused the obviously unfair bargain. But anything was better than having his ships idle, and so finally he agreed. A few days after the arrival of the first ship from Canton to New York, a dray deposited on the Astor doorstep a number of small, heavy kegs. "What are these?" Sarah asked, astonished. "The fruits of the East India passage," Jacob answered. "Fifty thousand dollars." Sarah could only gasp.

Jacob's appetite had been whetted; he now proceeded to satisfy it. He chartered ships, he bought ships, he built ships, until at last he dominated the Canton trade. While his competitors wondered, Jacob chuckled over a secret that made his transactions so much more profitable than theirs. For he not only shipped furs to Canton, bringing back the precious cargo of tea, but he docked many of his ships at the Sandwich Islands, loading them with the sandalwood so prized by the Cantonese.

The Astors now were solid citizens, received in the best of society. Jacob's children attended the most exclusive colleges and finishing schools. As Jacob's wealth increased, so did his thirst for respectability and his childish vanity. A director of the Bank of the United States, he didn't like to be reminded of his beginnings. When a sister arrived from Germany and her husband went into the distilling business, Jacob was outraged. This business was not respectable, he stormed. It was an insult to his position. His sister only shrugged her shoulders. "Jacob is not such a much of a much himself," she scoffed. "Didn't he start as a baker's boy, yelling in the streets for a few pennies?" And Jacob could only wince and pocket his pride along with his wealth.

And his wife Sarah, though she didn't share his pride, was always eager to share his wealth. She loved nothing better than to receive presents of large sums; but, being practical and trade-minded, they both enjoyed a little domestic bargaining. "You look ofer dot new lot of skins, yah, Sarah?" Jacob would urge.

"I'm a busy woman, Jacob; my time is worth money."

"Von tousand dollars an hour. Two." Sarah would shake her head solemnly. "Eight, ten, Sarah." Then, smiling, Sarah would inspect the pelts, pocketing the sum with extra relish, because she had earned the money.

As Jacob's empire spread, on land through the Northwest into Canada, and by sea to the Indies and Canton, his life grew more simple. With leisure to do as he liked, he roamed the countryside. Saddling his horse every clear day, he would ride beyond the city, up through Greenwich Village and further, to the very hills of Harlem. Yet even in this simple exercise he had an eye to business. He foresaw the day when the town would spread. While his friends scoffed at the money Jacob was spending on useless tracts out in the country, he was buying land, and yet more land, laying down the firm basis for the fortune that the later generations of Astors were to enjoy. On Wall Street he sold two lots, and with the proceeds he bought hundreds of acres of wasteland. The purchaser of the Wall Street lots enjoyed the bargain; it was a red-letter day when somebody could put something over on Jacob. Jacob chuckled. "Your lots vill not increase much in falue," he said. "But in tventy years mine acres vill be vort a hundert times vat I paid for dem." He was right.

Jacob cherished the idea that he never cheated. Yet he was capable of welching on a small promise. A captain of one of his ships, while trading in Canton, was able to save Jacob much money at the cost of his own time and some expense. Jacob was delighted. There was some fine madeira ripening in his cellar, he said. When it was good, the captain should have some. Many times the captain called on Jacob. "Is the madeira ready?" he would inquire. "No, nod ready yet," Jacob would reply. He could not bring himself to part with so precious a thing as a bottle of wine.

IV

As JACOB's POWER increased, so did his disrespect for law and government. He grew to think of himself as above such restrictions, to believe that they were for the little men without the money or audacity to flout institutions. His first overt act was somewhat in the nature of a joke. To his friends it brought chuckles of appreciation, but it raised a general furore that earned him the hatred of the public. Because of the embargo on shipping, all merchant vessels lay idle in the harbor. Competitors who observed that one of Jacob's Canton ships was being outfitted questioned him. "Yah, she just need a leetle repairs," he explained. A few days later the papers carried a notice that Jacob's vessel had sailed for Canton. Public indignation demanded an accounting. Special government permission had been given, Jacob explained, because his boat was carrying home a Chinese mandarin who had visited the country. Inquiries reached the President himself, and investigation proved that Jacob's mandarin was a Chinese deck hand he had dressed in silks and exhibited as an official in order to make good his ruse. It was too late to do anything; the vessel was on her way, and returned laden with tea which was then selling at a dollar a pound.

Jacob's fur trade, practically a monopoly, was spreading across the whole continent. He envisioned the time when his trading posts would reach from Canada to Oregon, and he set in motion the wheels which would accomplish this end. Dreamer of big dreams, he nevertheless skimped on the little things—and therein lay the seeds of disaster. French Canadian labor was cheaper than American labor, and so Jacob hired Canadians to man his boats and his trading posts. The first contingent of Jacob's hirelings arrived in New York, throwing the town into an uproar. The rowdy "Canucks" marched through the streets, bellowing lascivious songs and molesting women with their amorous advances. New Yorkers protested the invasion. But Jacob clung stubbornly to his policy —even when his ships were endangered by the brawling of the sailors who refused to accept discipline from their Yankee captains. His overland parties fared no better. The tales of their quarrels, their racial dissensions, and their mistreatment of the natives are legend. But Jacob still refused to pay the price for American labor. He was self-righteously indignant when his Canadian lieutenants sold him out to their own Northwest Company, his most powerful competitors.

A hated nabob—a beloved wife. Sarah had not changed much with the years. Wealth sat easily upon her shoulders. The same warm smile and friendly manner, the same simple domestic routine. She felt sorry to see her husband's unpopularity—"Old Skinflint" was the name most often applied to him. She upbraided him for his readiness to foreclose small mortgages held against the property of poor widows. But Jacob went on, driven by a power he could not himself understand. "More money, more houses, more land. Yah, Sarah, more, more, more!"

But more happiness? "Ach, Sarah, I am nod happy." His youngest daughter, Eliza, had fallen victim to his social ambition. Eliza loved a young dentist; but Jacob, feeling that the Astor millions deserved a European title, demanded that she marry a Swiss nobleman. Sarah sided with her daughter, but Jacob was not the one to be thwarted by his women. Eliza married the nobleman. Her health, never too robust, began to fail alarmingly from the moment of her marriage. With some feeling of remorse, Jacob spent a goodly part of his fortune in taking her from one European health resort to another. But not even his money could save her. When Eliza died, it was a sorrowful father that embarked upon his homeward journey. His one consolation was that Sarah would be there to solace him. As though Fate had conspired against the man who had so flagrantly defied the laws of generosity, she now punished him with one blow after another. The ship hit heavy seas, was tossed about for days. Jacob, his blustering vanity forgotten, begged the captain to turn back and set him ashore. "I vill pay you a tousand dollars, five tousand, ten tousand." The other passengers enjoyed themselves hugely at the spectacle of the mortgage miser reduced to unreasoning terror.

While these negotiations were being carried on, the storm subsided and the vessel continued on her homeward passage. But more tragedy awaited Astor upon his arrival. There was no Sarah to greet him. Instead his son William met him at the pier, to break the news of Sarah's death.

An end to happiness. But no end to greed. There were definite indications that the scramble for excessive fortunes was coming to a halt. Industry was about to settle into the era of small business and small profit. The East had been opened to many merchants, and prices had become stabilized. The fur trade, as Jacob had known it, was over. In England he had observed that silk was beginning to take the place of fur in the manufacture of hats. Moreover, the very magnitude of the fur trade had been the cause of its decline. Jacob's trappers had killed off the fur-bearing animals so recklessly that they threatened to become extinct. The man who dreamed of unlimited golden eggs had killed the goose that laid them.

And so he sold his interest in the fur trade and dedicated his voracity to the real-estate business. By his foresight he had acquired vast holdings of land which were growing in value beyond his wildest expectations. The narrow little island of Manhattan, unable to push outward, began to push upward. And Jacob held most of the strategic points. For anyone foolish enough to mortgage a piece of property that he could foreclose, he felt only contempt. *"Dumkopf!"*

Life was drawing to a close. Something must be done to perpetuate his name. He commissioned Washington Irving to write a book about him and to call it *Astoria*. And he ordered a whole block of houses to be torn down on lower Broadway, to be replaced by a building called the *Astor House*.

But there was one thing he could not order. A new lease on life. As his age increased he yearned for the company of young people. After a good dinner he loved to join the youngsters at the piano and sing sentimental songs. The fact that he had just put some widow out of her home would in no way detract from his enjoyment of the maudlin ballads that he sang. He liked nothing better than the deference paid him by the young. Whenever he finished a song he stood shaking with the effort, saliva drooling from his colorless old lips, and beamed like a schoolboy at the compliment of some pretty girl. "I sing gut, *nicht wahr?*" It never occurred to him that his presence was undesirable, especially when partial paralysis made it necessary for a footman to stand beside him and guide the food to his trembling mouth.

Jacob fought death with the same dogged determination with which he had fought poverty. Paralyzed, suffering from insomnia, he clung to the bare threads of existence. Unable to digest any solid food, he was kept alive on breast milk. With almost no blood left in the worn-out frame, but with a fierce glitter in his eye, he was tossed in blankets to stimulate circulation. One day, from the heaving blanket, he berated an agent who complained that he could not collect rent from a poverty-stricken woman.

"You could get it if you vas firm enough," Jacob managed to gasp. "Go back und try again, und don't come here till you get it." In desperation the agent appealed to Jacob's son, William. William counted out the money, handing it to the distracted man. "See," Jacob said gleefully, "you just have to be smart with these lazy dumkopfs."

At last, in his eighty-sixth year, death triumphed over his stubborn resistance. He had come to America with fifty cents. He went to his grave leaving behind him thirty million dollars.

IMPORTANT DATES IN THE LIFE OF JOHN JACOB ASTOR

1763—Born, Waldorf, Germany.
1784—Came to America.
1788—Went with cargo of furs to London.
1794—Started shipping furs all over the world.
1798—Worth quarter of a million.
1802—Worth half a million.

1809—Started American Fur Company.
1811—Founded Astoria at mouth of Columbia River.
Engaged in shipbuilding, fur and tea trade, and real estate.
1848—Worth thirty million dollars. Died, New York.

Robert Fulton

[1765-1815]

ONE night in 1806, Robert Fulton was lecturing to a large audience in New York. He had just returned from Europe, where he had astounded the scientific world with his experiments on steamships, torpedoes, and submarines. The public was especially interested in that "most diabolical" of his inventions—an "underwater contraption of cylinders and explosives" which, regulated by clockwork, could be placed under an enemy ship and blow it up. He was explaining to his audience the mechanism of this invention. "The torpedo which you see before you is charged with a hundred and seventy pounds of powder. Attached to it, as you will note, is a bit of clockwork which regulates the timing of the explosion. Now let me remove the peg which plugs up the powder charge." An apprehensive stir in the auditorium. "Next," he continued, paying no attention to the uneasiness of his audience, "let me set the clock ... There ... And now, ladies and gentlemen, if I let this clock run ten minutes longer, we shall all be blown into kingdom come . . ." He tried to go on with his lecture, but there was no one left to listen to him. At the words "blown into kingdom come," the entire audience, in a panic, had made for the nearest exits. "Robert Fulton and the Devil are in league to destroy the world!"

II

HIS FATHER was Scotch and his mother was Irish—a background which gave Robert the combined advantage of a tenacious will and a vivid imagination. He had need of both these characteristics from the start, for at the age of three he was left fatherless—a tough proposition for a youngster whose widowed mother had five children to feed and no income to fall back upon. Poor food, a frail body, and an everlasting itch to be doing something with his fingers. He didn't care for the three Rs, which his mother taught him, nor for his lessons in school—which he entered at the age of eight. "This child," said his teacher, "will not even have an ordinary education." No, his education was most extraordinary— and through his own choosing. He never knew how to spell correctly; but he knew how to make a lead pencil superior to the one that his teacher gave him. "Why don't you study your books?" his teacher asked him.

"I dunno, sir. Guess there are so many thoughts in my head, I can't crowd no thoughts into it out of my books."

"Can't crowd *any* thoughts into it! And no more of your impertinence, young man!"

"Yes, sir. Can't crowd *any* thoughts into it. And I won't be impertinent no more."

Incorrigible child. Just *wouldn't* learn his grammar. But he learned how to make all sorts of little gadgets in the blacksmith shops and the tinsmith shops of Lancaster (Pennsylvania). And he drew original designs for ornamenting the rifles that were manufactured in the village arsenal. "A pretty good draughtsman and a very good mechanic."

And a youngster with an inventive mind. One Fourth of July he decided to have a new kind of celebration all by himself. Bringing to the general store a number of candles which he had saved up for the occasion, he exchanged them for a bag of gunpowder and several sheets of pasteboard. "Please don't roll up these sheets, Mr. Howard," he said to the storekeeper.

"All right, if you say so," replied the storekeeper. "But tell me what you're going to do with them."

"Wait till tonight, and you'll see."

That night the villagers were startled to see Robert's "newfangled shooting candles" flashing through the air. The thirteen-year-old inventor had become the celebrity of the town.

Always inventing things. Always drawing pictures. And oftentimes getting into trouble because of his too fertile imagination. On one occasion he precipitated a fight between the townspeople and the Hessian soldiers who were quartered in the neighborhood. The town authorities, in order to avoid trouble between the civilians and the soldiers, had stretched a rope at a designated place with instructions that neither the townspeople nor the Hessians were to cross that rope. Whereupon Robert drew a picture of the townspeople invading the Hessian side of the rope and putting the enemy to the sword. This provocative picture, displayed in the public square, served as an instigation to both sides. A serious riot broke out, and it was only with difficulty that the cooler heads among the two factions were able to prevent bloodshed.

Stirring times, and stirring thoughts. Robert couldn't make up his mind as to his future career. Should he devote himself to mechanics or to painting? Or, perhaps, to fighting? General Washington needed plenty of fighting men. But Robert was neither strong enough nor old enough for the rigors of a military life. "You are meant for the peaceful pursuits, my boy," said his mother. She sent him to Philadelphia, where for three years he knocked about as a jeweler's apprentice, an architect's assistant, and an occasional painter of miniature portraits.

One of the men whose portraits he painted was Benjamin Franklin. The elderly statesman encouraged him in his work and secured him commissions from several personages of "manners and means." Robert was on the way to making for himself a tidy sum when his career was cut short for the time being. An inflammation of the lungs, accompanied by the spitting of blood, sent him to the warm springs of Virginia.

Recovery, and a return trip to Philadelphia. He had planned, during his convalescence, to try his fortune in England. He wanted to ask Franklin's advice about this plan. "You are right, young man. England is the place for an artist. America is too young, too eager to achieve. We have no time here for the leisurely appreciation of art."

He gave Fulton a letter of introduction to Benjamin West, the American painter who had made his mark in England. Fulton thanked his benefactor, invested the greater part of his savings in a farm for his mother, and set sail for England with a capital of forty guineas (about two hundred dollars) in his purse. "How foolish of him," said a friend, "to have decided upon the two most unprofitable careers in the world."

"Yes," nodded another. "Painting and inventing—a wild-goose chase with an empty gun in either hand."

III

LONDON, and a devoted intimacy with Benjamin West. Under the elder artist's inspiration, Fulton made rapid progress as a portrait painter. On two occasions his pictures were exhibited at the Royal Academy. His American friends had been wrong in their predictions. His artistic career was bringing him not only profit but prestige. "His portraits," wrote an eminent critic (Charles Henry Hart), "are well drawn, good in design, delicately colored, and well executed technically."

Yet Fulton was not content. If he stuck to his art, he would remain a competent painter all his life. But that was not enough. What he wanted was not competency, but mastery. And so he gave up the promise of his artistic career for the uncertainty of his engineering adventures. "Now at last," said everybody, "young Fulton has gone definitely mad."

Definitely and stubbornly mad to turn his creative ability into constructive good. Fulton possessed that rare combination of genius— Leonardo da Vinci was another man who possessed it—he was at once scientific in his art and artistic in his science. He reduced every object to a specific design and developed every design into a provocative picture. It was therefore an easy transition for him to transform his canvases into blueprints—to advance from the copying of existing shapes to the shaping of new existences. In rapid succession he invented a machine for spinning flax, an appliance for twisting ropes, and a mill for polishing marble.

First the thought, then the plan, and finally the finished product. "He never made a model of an invention until he had completed a drawing which showed every part projected on the proper scale."

All these inventions, however, were but a preparation for his life's work—the lessening of the distance, both mental and material, between man and man. It was his ambition from now on to facilitate travel, to stimulate commerce, and to discourage dissension and war. For his interests were not only artistic and scientific; they were also political. "The establishment of Republicks throughout Europe . . . and the study of the Art of Peace should be the aim of everybody." Certainly it was the aim of his own inventive labors. He tried to develop a system of canals in England and on the European continent, so that the Old World might be more closely united into a confederation of free and friendly states. He spent a number of years on the invention of the submarine and the torpedo—two weapons whose destructiveness, he hoped, would bring about "the end of naval oppression and the establishment of peace through an agreement of nations." And he worked incessantly on his new "eagle of the sea"—a steam-propelled ship whose speed would "narrow the sea into a strait and turn America and Europe into next-door neighbors."

The dreams of a deranged mind, was the almost universal verdict when he spoke of his plans. One day he was invited to dinner at a friend's house. Next to him at the table sat Prince Talleyrand. The two men conversed about Fulton's inventions, especially the steamboat. After the dinner the host asked Talleyrand for his opinion of Robert Fulton. "A charming man and brilliant conversationalist. But"—and Talleyrand shook his head sadly—"I'm afraid the poor fellow's cracked."

This fear that Fulton was cracked compelled many an influential person to fight shy of him. Owing to the high cost of his materials, he was always in need of funds. And almost always he was refused when he requested a loan. "My money," said one of the wags who denied his request, "would only float away on the sea or go up in flames." Once, when he was working on the steamboat, he was in absolute need of a thousand dollars. He went to a wealthy friend and asked him to advance this sum as an investment. "You don't expect me to throw away a thousand dollars," said his friend. "But I'll tell you what I'll do. I'll give you a hundred dollars if you can get me the names of nine other people who will advance a hundred dollars each." With great difficulty Fulton succeeded in raising the nine hundred dollars. But he couldn't get the money from the friend who had offered the original hundred. For he couldn't give him the names of the other nine contributors. Every one of them had refused to subscribe publicly to "so crazy an adventure."

IV

IN THE COURSE of his travels to interest people in his inventions, Fulton had an interesting episode with a French noblewoman—the wife of the Vicomte de Gontaut. It was during the crossing of the English Channel that he met her. We have the story in her own words: "Our family having been proscribed at the time of the [French] Revolution, I was returning to Paris in connection with the management of our property. In order to avoid detection, I had assumed the name of Madame François, 'a dealer in laces going to Paris on business.' One day, as I was sitting on the deck, an Englishman of striking appearance and charming demeanor came and spoke to me in halting French. He was delighted when he learned that I could speak English. 'Madame,' he said to me, 'you could do me a great favor if you would act as my interpreter.' I promised him I would. He then told me that he was an inventor of amazing machines —boats that could sail under the water and blow up ships on the surface, vessels driven by steam power that could outspeed any sail-driven craft, and several other devices that sounded like tales out of the *Arabian Nights*. I listened to his talk with genuine interest, and I agreed to introduce him to various important Parisians who might help him to further his plans."

On her arrival in Paris, however, she was arrested as a noblewoman in disguise. Fulton visited her in the detention room. He had in his possession, he told her, a letter recommending him to Monsieur Barthélemy, one of the Directors of the French Republic. "With this letter, madame, I can set you free—provided you will do me the honor to become my wife."

"But, monsieur, I am still married to my husband."

"What a pity, Madame François, what a pity! I would make you rich. My inventions are going to set the world agog. Just say the word. Divorce Monsieur François and come to me. I will marry you, and that will be the end of your troubles."

But "Madame François" shook her head. "I didn't dare at the time to tell him that I was traveling under a fictitious name, and that in reality I was the wife of a French nobleman."

A few weeks later she managed to secure her release through the influence of one of her friends—Herr Schemelpeninck—the German consul to Paris. She had now, for safety's sake, assumed her maiden name. One day as she was walking in the street with her brother-in-law her "English inventor" rushed up and seized both her hands. "Ah, Madame François, I am so happy to see you!"

"Pardon, monsieur," said her brother-in-law, "but zis is not Madame François. You have ze honor to address Mademoiselle de Montault."

Fulton shrugged his shoulders and walked away. He couldn't make out the mystery. Was it the same woman or a twin sister?

Several months elapsed. Fulton had returned to London. One night at the opera he saw his "mysterious lady" sitting in the box of a friend of his. He made his way to her side. "What an unexpected pleasure to meet you here, Mademoiselle de Montault!"

"Monsieur is mistaken," said her escort. "The lady you are addressing is the Vicomtesse de Gontaut."

"What, triplets?" muttered Fulton under his breath. Aloud, however, he said with a smile: "Madame, allow me to congratulate your husband on being married to the three most beautiful women in France."

V

IT WAS THROUGH Madame de Gontaut that Fulton was able to interest the French ministers in his submarine and steamboat experiments. In December 1797 he made his first attempt—on the Seine—to blow up a ship with a submarine. The attempt was a failure, both Fulton and his assistant escaping narrowly with their lives. Undeterred by the setback, he went ahead and built another submarine. This "undersea battleship" aroused the interest of Napoleon, who was at the time (1801) planning an invasion of England. "The sea which separates you from your enemy," Fulton wrote to Napoleon, "gives him an immense advantage over you. Aided . . . by the winds and the tempests, he defies you from his inaccessible island. I have it in my power to cause this obstacle which protects him to disappear. In spite of all his fleets, and in any weather, I can transport your armies to his territory (and destroy his ships) in a few hours . . . I am prepared to submit my plans."

Napoleon invited him to submit the plans and to demonstrate their effectiveness. In the summer of 1801, Fulton succeeded in "blowing a boat into atoms." The submarine was a proved success. Fulton was elated. "At long last we have an instrument that will do away with the erroneous system of exclusive commerce and distant possesions . . . the obstacles which hinder nations from arriving at a lasting peace."

But Napoleon and his ministers were not so sanguine about the usefulness of the submarine. "It would be impossible," said the Minister of Marine, "to give commissions to men using such an instrument in war, as these men would surely be hanged if captured." Fulton's invention was turned down.

Disappointed with his failure to interest the world in the submarine, Fulton now turned his entire effort to his next idea—the steamship. In this idea—the possibility of steam navigation—he was not alone. Both in America and in Europe there were a number of scientists preoccupied with experiments in this field. One of these scientists, Robert R. Livingston, was in 1801 appointed minister to France. The two Roberts—Fulton and Livingston—were drawn together through their similarity in temperament and taste. Fulton had the ideas, and Livingston had the funds. They formed a partnership which turned out to their mutual advantage and to the benefit of the entire world.

At the outset, however, they had anything but smooth sailing. In the early spring of 1803 they were ready with their model steamboat. It was anchored on the Seine, waiting for its initial experiment. One morning Fulton was roused from his bed. His boat, he was told, had sunk in the night. He rushed to the spot. Sure enough, the boat was split in two. The iron machinery in the center had proved too heavy for the wooden structure.

Plunging into the icy water and working incessantly for twenty-four hours, Fulton succeeded in raising the boat. The machinery was intact, but the framework was a wreck. So too, for a time, was his health. But Fulton went right on rebuilding the boat, and in the summer of that same year was ready for the test.

On August 10, 1803, the following account of the historic event appeared in the *Journal des Débats*:

". . . During the past two or three months there has been seen at the end of the quay Chaillot (on the Seine) a boat of curious appearance, equipped with two large wheels, mounted on an axle like a chariot, while behind these wheels was a kind of large stove with a pipe, as if there was some kind of a small fire engine intended to operate the wheels of the boat . . .

"The day before yesterday, at six in the evening, the inventor . . . put his boat in motion . . . and for an hour and a half he produced the curious spectacle of a boat moved by wheels, like a chariot, these wheels being provided with paddles or flat plates, and being moved by a fire engine . . .

"The boat ascended and descended the stream four times from Les Bons-Hommes as far as the pump of Chaillot; it was maneuvered with facility, turning to the right and left, came to anchor, started again, and passed by the swimming school . . .

"This mechanism, applied to our rivers—the Seine, the Loire, and the Rhone—will have most advantageous consequences upon our internal navigation. The tows and barges which now require four months to come from Nantes to Paris would arrive promptly in ten to fifteen days . . ."

Again Fulton had offered a valuable gift to the French Government, and again the offer was turned down. Napoleon and his ministers gave due consideration to the "experiment on the Seine," and decided that the steamship, like the submarine, was a "useless toy."

Fulton was now thoroughly disgusted with France—not only for personal but also for political reasons. When he had first visited that country the Reign of Terror had given way to the promise of freedom. His democratic spirit had thrilled to the hope of a new day for Europe when despotism would be a thing of the past. It was a great shock to him, therefore, to see the accession of Napoleon to the office of First Consul. "The French Revolution is dead. The French people have merely exchanged one despot for another." Fulton longed to breathe once more the air of a free country. He took passage to America.

And to final glory. Together with Livingston, who had returned from his diplomatic post in the Old World, he built a steamship—the *Clermont* —in the East River, and one day quietly sailed around the tip of New York and over to the New Jersey shore. It was a most successful trip. Fulton and Livingston were now ready for their first public test.

The public, however, had nothing but jeers for "Fulton's Folly"— the nickname given to the boat by one of the New York wit-snappers. "The thing," wrote a journalist who had gone down to examine the boat, "is an ungainly craft looking precisely like a backwoods' sawmill mounted on a scow and set on fire."

Yet on the day of the trial—August 17, 1807—a large number of spectators gathered on the banks of the Hudson River. "While we were putting off from the wharf," wrote Fulton in a letter to a friend, "I heard a number of sarcastic remarks." Excitement, incredulity, ridicule, scorn—and then silence, followed by a shout of spontaneous applause. "Holy Jupiter, the thing does work!" yelled one of the spectators hysterically as the *Clermont* wheeled across the river, made a clean-cut turn upstream, overtook sloop after sloop and "parted with them as if they had been at anchor."

Three weeks after the trial—from the seventh to the eleventh of September—the *Clermont* sailed up the Hudson to Albany and back. The trip was a continuous triumph. Throngs of people on the banks and in boats looked on "with awe almost amounting to terror," as the water chariot rolled over the Hudson, her funnel spouting forth a pillar of cloud by day, a pillar of fire by night. A scene reminiscent of the Old Testament—the finger of God pointing the way to a new Canaan, the Promised Land of speedier communication and better understanding between man and man. "The power of propelling boats by steam," as Fulton wrote to one of his sponsors, "is now fully proved."

VI

THE REST of Fulton's life may be summed up in a few words. A late marriage and an early death. He was forty-two when he married—there were four children resulting from the union—and only forty-nine when he died. As a mark of respect, the only one of its kind ever shown to a private citizen, the New York Legislature passed a resolution that both houses should wear mourning for six weeks.

IMPORTANT DATES IN THE LIFE OF ROBERT FULTON

1765—Born, Pennsylvania.
1778—Invented paddle wheels.
1782–85—Painted miniature portraits.
1786—Went to London.
1793—Interested in canal navigation.
1794—Patented mill for polishing marble.
1796—Interested in bridgebuilding.
1797—Built submarine in Paris.

1801—Experimented with submarines at Brest.
1803—Launched a steamboat on the Seine.
1806—Returned to the United States.
1807—Sailed steamboat *Clermont* on the Hudson.
1809—Took out patent on steam navigation.
1815—Died, New York.

Andrew Jackson

[1767-1845]

HE WAS Scotch and Irish, shrewd and fearless. His ancestors had migrated from Carrickfergus, North Ireland, to Twelve Mile Creek in the Carolinas. Here in the wilderness his father gave away his life clearing land and hauling trees and gathering food. Andrew was born a posthumous child in a neighbor's hut.

From the time he learned to walk he was a "nuisance and a troublemaker"—the one disharmonious note among the children in his uncle's house. They sent him to a woodland shanty known as the Settlement School. They wanted him to be "a learner." But he enjoyed a fight better.

His fellow pupils knew him for a tough one. "I could throw him on the ground three times out of four," said a schoolmate, "but he never would stay throwed. Game, that's what he was." As iron-willed as anyone on the frontier. In his eyes there was a fire which turned the blue to steel at the slightest affront. And when he was angry he looked like "an avenging angel." His hair threw an ash-blond halo around his head. A fighting, two-fisted angel. He would thrash anyone and everybody for a principle. "He was the only bully ever seen who was not also a coward."

His folks decided they would make a Presbyterian minister out of him. They sent him to the "Academy"—a larger shanty than the primary school. Here taught the Reverend Dr. Humphrey, who whitened at the words of his "swearing pupil." By heck, there was not another lad on the frontier who could string together so picturesque a combination of oaths as Sandy Andy!

Before he was fifteen the Revolutionary War had reached the South. And some of the bloodiest skirmishes took place in Andy's neighborhood. His older brother, Hugh, gave his life in battle. Andy collected an arsenal of angry-looking weapons—long-bladed knives, tomahawks, stone clubs—and counted the months until he'd be old enough to join in the fighting.

Especially he liked his scythe, with which he cut down the heads of the tall grasses near his home. He'd mow down the redcoats this way, too, when he was a man!

One day a party of British dragoons had swept into his home town. A squadron rushed into Andy's dwelling, ransacked the furniture, crushed a baby's crib. An officer bawled to Andy an order to clean his boots.

The boy looked up calmly. "Sir, I'm a prisoner of war and claim to be treated as such." He'd black no man's boots.

The officer raised his sword and swung it down over Andy's head. But Andy deflected the blow and the sword slashed his cheek instead of his skull. Together with his brother Robert and with a number of other unfortunates, he was thrown into prison. An epidemic of smallpox broke out among the prisoners. One of the victims who succumbed to it was Robert. Andy, too, had caught the disease. When he recovered he received another shock—the news that his mother, his only friend in the world, had died while attending the sick and the wounded Americans aboard a British prison ship.

II

It is a tough and cruel world. But the lad is even tougher. Now, at fifteen, he is an orphan and destitute. None of his relatives wants to take him in. He is growing too fast and developing too much muscle for a peaceful home life. He is a swaggerer and a fighter who expects no quarter from anyone. And no one may expect any quarter from him.

He got a job in a saddler's shop. But he left it for the "more exciting adventures of the big city"—Charleston. His relatives were only too glad to get him out of the way. They presented him with a horse for the trip. Now they were clear of all responsibility. He gambled and swigged and bet on the horses and the cockfights. And then he decided—of all things —to teach school.

He knew precious little about education. But the men and the boys around him knew even less. He cleared the backwoods and erected a schoolhouse. But after a spell he picked up his belongings and wandered on.

He couldn't stay put. Something was driving him forward. He set his horse toward Salisbury, Rowan County, seeking a teacher with whom to study the law. For out of the welter of his experiences and the turmoil of his feelings he had developed a legalistic mind. A lawyer can become quite a "big gun" in the settlements on the frontier. He can protect a squatter's land rights and he can "spring a fellow free" from a murder charge.

He settled down with several other students in a "cross between a henhouse and a Negro cabin," littered with books, documents, and pamphlets. But he didn't trouble the books much. In a society of roughriders, horse sense alone would do well enough.

He paid his rent by winning large sums of money from his landlord at cards. The mere mention of his name brought a blush to the cheeks

of the "respectable" ladies in Rowan County. At a Christmas ball sponsored by the social elite, Jackson appeared arm in arm with two women
of the streets. "And why not?" he reasoned. "All women are created
equal." The town bouncers showed the tall young "terror" to the door
in an atmosphere of stunned silence.

Two years of this life, and Andy is ready for his license to practice law.
He has left a bill of mounting debts in every tavern of the town and a
record of exciting memories in every "disreputable" haunt.

Now he is ready for his first assignment in justice. He is offered a position as public prosecutor in the wildest section of the Union, five hundred
miles from the nearest outposts of civilization—the Bad Lands of Tennessee.

III

MOST of the "legal" disputes in Tennessee were settled by an arbitration
of the bullet. "The chief ambition of every man is to find a good pretext
for the shooting of his neighbor." No respectable man's life was safe. This
was an ideal country for Jackson. The majority of his clients were people
to whom other people owed land or money. And Jackson rode out after
the debtors and brought them into court at the point of the pistol. In
addition there was the fashionable crime of mayhem—the biting of the
nose and the ears of one's opponent. Jackson was magnificent in his duties
as an officer of the law.

And while he thus earned his living, love came to him. He boarded at
the home of an attractive young woman, Rachel Donelson, whose husband
was insanely jealous of her and accused her of all sorts of intrigues. But
for all that, Rachel was a "sweet and childlike girl who read her Bible
regularly and smoked a long-stemmed clay pipe."

The chivalry of Jackson appealed strongly to Rachel. His sympathy for
her unhappy married life overwhelmed her. Her husband had gone to
Virginia to sue for a divorce. He was "raging mad" at the woman whom
he accused of "communing with" the public prosecutor of Tennessee.
But he preferred to defend his honor through the legal procedure of a
divorce rather than to risk it in a duel.

Word reached Rachel from Virginia that she was a free woman, and
when Jackson asked for her hand she readily consented.

They were married in a simple ceremony at Natchez, Mississippi. Two
years after their marriage they learned that Rachel's divorce from her
former husband had only recently been legalized. Andrew Jackson bristled
up and cleaned the barrels of his pistols. Would anybody make anything
out of it? His friends advised him to get "married genuinely" now, to
still the breath of scandal that was inevitable.

"By the Eternal, I've been married for two years and everyone around
here knows it!" he shouted.

But wiser counsels prevailed. He underwent the ceremony a second
time and then threatened to shoot any "pickle-herring" who dared to
capitalize on the humor of the situation.

In the meantime there were big political events in Tennessee. The population of the Bad Lands had grown materially, and the settlers had begun to clamor for admission into the Union. Representatives from every county had assembled at Knoxville to draw up a constitution that would transform their territory into a state. Jackson was one of the delegates selected for the framing of the document.

Andrew is sitting by the fireplace, puffing at his pipe and poring over a sheaf of papers. Rachel's lips are puckered around the stem of her own clay pipe as she sits knitting a shawl.

"What are you reading, Mr. Jackson?" she asks him.

"Constitution, wife," he answers.

She looks up anxiously. "Ain't you well, Mr. Jackson?" In her cupboard she has several medicines for his constitution.

Tennessee was admitted into the Union, and Jackson was chosen to represent it in the Congress of the United States. He bought himself a suit of broadcloth, plastered down his unruly hair, tied it into a queue with an eelskin ribbon, and set out on horseback for Philadelphia, the "metropolis of urbane manners."

He created quite a sensation in the capital city. The polished Easterners stared with amazement at this "filthy democrat" from Tennessee, with his pugnacious jaw and his arrogant stride. If this was a sample of the new West, they muttered, God help the future of the country!

Andrew Jackson had no greater admiration for the Easterners than the Easterners had for him. He longed to return to his cockfights and his two-fisted legal jousts. But his constituents wouldn't let him be. When his term as representative was over, they elected him senator. Rachel must continue to sit lonesomely by the fireside, waiting for her man to come back.

Finally he returned and was appointed judge of the State Supreme Court in recognition for his services "abroad." But he found the life on the bench too sluggish for his adventurous spirit. When he secured an offer to serve as major general of the state militia he fairly leaped at the chance. To be sure, his spirits were somewhat dampened by the fact that there was peace on Tennessee's borders at the time. But he hoped for the best. Sooner or later war was bound to come. The quarrelsome human family would see to that.

And so he waited for his fighting chance. In the meantime he opened two retail stores—at Clover Bottom and at Gallatin. He sold hardware, gunpowder, whisky, salt, and grindstones and received in exchange not money—for the Tennesseans distrusted the federal currency—but the more satisfactory currency of foods and goods, such as pork and wheat and potatoes, tobacco, cotton, and skins. In addition to these activities, he built boats and he traded in horses and in Negro slaves. No matter what the polite society of Philadelphia might think of him, out here in Tennessee, Andrew Jackson was regarded as a *gentleman*—an outstanding citizen of the frontier. Lord help anyone who questioned this!

And one man *did* question Jackson's claim to being called a gentleman. This skeptic, a handsome young devil of a rake named Charles Dickinson, was a political and business rival of Jackson's. Jealous of his success, he one day in his cups blurted out an innuendo about Jackson's irregular marriage to Rachel.

The idol of Tennessee challenged Dickinson to a duel. It was a rash thing to do, for Dickinson was known to be the best shot in the state. In the taverns the experts were laying heavy odds against Jackson's chances. Dickinson himself wagered five hundred dollars that he would kill his opponent at the first shot.

The day before the duel Andrew kissed his wife and told her he must leave on business. But he kept from her the nature of this business. All day long he rode with a party of friends to the meeting place in Logan County. He knew that Dickinson's aim would be true. "But by the Eternal, I too can aim." And then he added: "I'll get him even if he shoots me in the head!" At least there would be two graves instead of one.

He stops at the inn, eats a hearty supper, and enjoys a long smoke before he goes up to bed. In the dawn he throws a loose black cloak around him. Its folds, he trusts, will conceal the outlines of his long lank body from Dickinson, who will be aiming at his heart.

He meets his adversary. "Ready, aim, fire!" Dickinson's shot has been good. He smiles as he sees his opponent clutching at his breast. But then his face grows ghastly. His stricken adversary hasn't dropped to the ground. Instead he takes deliberate aim and pulls the trigger of his gun.

There is no explosion, and Dickinson breathes more easily. Jackson's pistol has been half cocked.

There is a look of derision in Dickinson's eyes. He is about to say something, but his words remain unspoken. For Jackson has now fired his pistol. A spurt of blood from Dickinson's mouth, and his seconds carry away his dead body from the field.

Andrew Jackson walked to the inn with his friends. One of them noticed that a trickle of blood was dripping from his shoe. Jackson smiled. "Yes, he pinked me a little," he confessed.

They took him to his room and pulled off his clothes. Two of his ribs were shattered. The bullet had lodged near his heart. But not near enough to prove fatal. "He missed me," laughed Jackson, "by a fold of my loose black cloak."

To the end of his life Andrew kept a pistol over the mantelpiece in his parlor. And when any visitor looked at it he took the pipe from his lips long enough to say casually, "That's the gun that stopped an evil tongue."

IV

THE INDIAN TRIBES in the West, goaded by the British in 1812, had broken out in mass hostility against the frontier settlements. Andrew Jackson, without waiting for the orders of the War Department, gathered the Tennessee militia around him and started on an expedition of vengeance. His pistols were his "passports." His arm was in a sling and he was weak from the loss of blood—which he had suffered in another of his interminable brawls. It had cost him physical agony to get out of his bed. The soldiers worshiped him for his courage. "Old Hickory" was their nickname for him from that day on.

These soldiers of Jackson's were reckless and ruthless fighters. They were bent upon exterminating the Creeks who had been massacring the whites in Alabama. The battles of this Creek War were holocausts of murder. In village after village the "Tiger Men" left not a single warrior alive. As Jackson rode through one of these devastated villages he came upon a little papoose clutched tightly in the embrace of its dead mother.

He picks up the papoose and rides with it to his tent. He feeds him milk, wraps him in blankets, and watches over him like a father until the Indian wars are over. Then he takes him home to his wife Rachel and brings him up as a playmate to his son.

But Andrew is not often tender. Not when he faces an army of sullen, snarling men who threaten to mutiny. Tired, disgusted, and half starved on their rations of roasted acorns, they have started against his orders to march back home. Whirling around on his horse and pointing a gun at the rebels, Jackson shrivels them into submission with an outburst of invectives. "The first blackguard who stirs a foot marches straight into hell!"

The rebels cringe before his look. They growl and sulk but dare not turn their steps homeward. For they know that he means what he says. What they do not know, however, is the fact that the gun which he has pointed at them was not loaded.

He marches them to New Orleans, where he hears that the British will try to effect a landing for a drive up the Mississippi. His swashbuckling campaign in the West has gained him a sensational reputation, and when he enters New Orleans he is wined and dined by the fashionable society. "Huzzah for General Jackson!" The tables "groan under the weight" of the dishes prepared by the French cooks in his honor. But the general pushes aside the viands and calls for a bowl of hominy.

The British are now approaching the Queen City of the South. They are bent—so it is rumored—upon booty and beauty. But Old Hickory takes an oath that the redcoats will never reach New Orleans except over his dead body. Up go the fortifications. Bales of cotton are rolled from the warehouses and piled into bastions. One of the owners rushes over to Jackson's quarters loudly complaining that the cotton which has been commandeered is his property. The general thrust a gun into his hands. "Since this is your property, sir, it is your business to defend it. Get into the ranks!"

In the meanwhile the federal government had sent commissioners to meet the British at Ghent. Negotiations to end the war had been under way for some time. And finally they were concluded. Peace had come. But neither the commander of the British nor Andrew Jackson knew anything of this peace as they prepared for the battle. Such was the penalty of slow communication in the days before the Atlantic cable.

The British charged the American fortifications with drawn muskets and left over seven hundred killed and fourteen hundred wounded within a quarter of an hour. For them it was relatively the bloodiest battle of the century. The Americans suffered eight killed and thirteen wounded.

When the announcement of the armistice reached New Orleans, Andrew Jackson was furious. By the Eternal, he would like to hang all those meddling politicians who made peace just when he was getting into his stride!

Crestfallen, he disbanded his army; cheerlessly he received the plaudits of the multitude. There were no more Creeks to kill. The British were departing. He had nothing left to do. If only the government gave the word, he'd march into Florida and take it from the Spaniards. "By the Eternal, that's an idea!"

V

OLD HICKORY had now become the Hero of New Orleans. The entire country gave him a roaring welcome. He sent a letter to Rachel enclosing a piece of chipped bone to remind her of his wounded arm which was now rapidly healing. And then he set out for Washington. In Virginia old Tom Jefferson invited him to a banquet. In the White House, Dolly Madison presided over a celebration in his honor. But for all his prestige, he still hadn't learned to spell or to speak grammatically. He wrote a letter of advice to his nephew, a young man who had just entered West Point. "You are now—amonsht Strangers, where it behoves you to be guarded at all points. Amonsht the vituous females, you ought to cultivate an acquaintance . . . and shun the intercourse of the others as you would the society . . . of a base charector. . . ."

But why worry about his illiteracy? The common man throughout the United States had learned to respect and love him. And he had become a powerful influence in federal politics. Ignoring the War Department and the State Department, he marched his troops into Florida and drove the Spanish garrison out of St. Marks and the Spanish governor out of Pensacola. And then, just for good measure, he hanged two Englishmen whom he accused of being spies. And the government at Washington didn't dare to court-martial him, so great was his popularity with the people. A man on horseback!

In the meantime Spain had resigned herself to the loss of the Florida territory. She consented to sell it in good grace and collected indemnities. And Jackson was appointed governor of this new acquisition. But he was definitely out of his element in civil office. He handed in his resignation.

It was the sixth administrative job from which he had resigned. President Monroe was at a loss as to what to do with this "trouble shooter." He considered giving him the portfolio as minister to Russia and asked Jefferson's opinion.

"My God," exclaimed the aged sage, "if you do this you will have a war on your hands inside of a month!"

But awaiting Old Hickory was another destiny far removed from the ambassadorship to Russia. The shrewd political friends of the homespun soldier had no less an aim for him than the presidency of the United

States. Was not Andrew the incarnation of the common man, the very image of the millions of uncouth and unlettered pioneers who dreamed of fighting their way to glory with their own right arm? The ideal candidate for the People's President!

As for his illiteracy, his managers observed, they would edit his speeches and his statements to the press. They would "polish his eccentricities, keep his mouth shut on every social occasion, restrain his impulses. . . ." There was a great deal of work to be done before they could succeed in hoisting Andrew Jackson from the people's shoulders into the White House.

And in their first attempt (in 1824) they failed. To be sure, Andrew Jackson had received a plurality of the popular vote over John Quincy Adams, Calhoun, Crawford, and Clay. But he failed to get a majority of the electoral votes. The election was thus thrown into the House of Representatives. Henry Clay yielded in favor of Adams, the Eastern Conservative, and Jackson was thus "cheated"—as his friends alleged—out of the presidency.

This "conspiracy against the will of the people" only served to enhance the popularity of Jackson. Over the country like wildfire swept the insinuation—"a corrupt bargain of politicians"—for Adams had appointed Clay as his Secretary of State. The country was divided into "Adams men" and "Jackson men." When Adams was sworn into office, it was amid a tempest of hisses and catcalls. Wherever Adams turned, whenever he laid his head upon a pillow, the jeers of the multitude thundered in his ears. The Forgotten Man had made a vow never to forget. In 1829, John Quincy Adams relinquished his office, a nervous and broken man, and Andrew Jackson rode triumphantly to the White House on the crest of a landslide vote.

But the victory was costly. The press of the East had poured forth a slanderous broadside in an effort to keep the "honest savage" from occupying the President's chair. The editors had revived the old whispering campaign about his peculiar marriage to Rachel. People had smacked their lips and whispered "Adultery!" And Rachel's heart had been fatally wounded. Not long after the election she found a resting place in the family cemetery; and together with Rachel, all the gentleness of Andrew Jackson was laid to rest. He stood with wet eyes at the burial of his wife and of his heart. He was hungry to sit down with her once more in the long shadows by the fireside of heaven, but first he must attend to some unfinished business. . . . Grimly he looked toward Washington.

VI

WHEN President Jackson galloped into the White House, a whole tornado whirled in along with him. His inauguration was the most amazing in American history. The prim and stately minuets of the earlier inaugural balls were swept away in the hurricane of a frontier carnival. Jackson was the man of the people, and the people came to Washington to rejoice. They pushed their way past the doorkeepers into the White House; they stormed the punch bowls and broke the glasses and spilled the contents on the floor; they shuffled over the carpets with their muddy boots; they leaped on the damask chairs to have a look at their President; and they sang and shouted and rejoiced that a new day had dawned for the common folk.

And, indeed, a new day *had* dawned for them. One of Jackson's first official acts was to dismiss a whole cabinet because their wives had stuck up their noses at Peggy Eaton, the wife of the Secretary of War. Peggy was the daughter of a tavern keeper and therefore taboo in Washington society. But Jackson was more interested in humanity than he was in society. He remembered the injustice that had killed his own wife. He therefore took up the cudgels for Peggy Eaton, scandalized the higher social circles, and won for himself the adoration of the scorned and the oppressed throughout the land.

He had struck a vigorous blow against snobbery. But now he found himself with another, and more serious, fight on his hands. A civil rebellion was brewing in America. The people of South Carolina were displeased with the federal tariff laws (1832) and they threatened to secede unless these laws were nullified. But Jackson, the queller of mutinies, would hear of no such thing. "The laws of the United States must be executed," he declared. "For any state to disregard these laws," he went on, "is disunion; and disunion by armed force is treason." And, as a warning that he meant business, he dispatched seven revenue cutters and a ship of war to South Carolina with orders that if the gentlemen of that state persisted in their disobedience of the law, they were to be "hanged by their elegant necks."

This prompt and decisive action on the part of Old Hickory prevented a war of secession in 1833. South Carolina saw the light and returned to the fold.

Once more the strong man had won. But the malcontents continued to grumble against his "highhanded actions." They called him "demagogue" —"dictator"—"czar." Very well, he retorted, the czar would fight against the emperor. Emperor Nicholas Biddle, head of the United States Bank, controller of the United States finances, and manipulator of the invisible strings of the United States Government. Under the influence of "Emperor Biddle," America had become a plutocracy—the very thing that Thomas Jefferson had feared and fought against. And now Jackson took up the fight and carried it to a finish. The old charter for the bank was to expire in 1836, and as early as 1832 the board of directors had applied for a recharter. They paved the way for favorable action by means of extensive loans—Jackson called them bribes—to fifty-nine members of Congress. They also made "good-will loans" to the leading newspapers in order to insure a friendly press. The plan worked. Congress voted in favor of the recharter. But the board of directors had reckoned without Jackson, who promptly and emphatically vetoed the bill. In his veto he made it clear to the "farmers, mechanics, and laborers" of America that he was "unalterably opposed" to any law which would "make the rich richer and the potent more powerful."

The veto created a sensation. An avalanche of editorials, full of fire and brimstone, descended upon his head. But Old Hickory stood firm. In 1832 he came up for re-election; and, in spite of a hostile press, he was swept into office by the overwhelming acclamation of the people.

But Jackson was not yet through with his fight. Immediately after his re-election he withdrew all the government deposits from the United States Bank. It was like withdrawing water from a fish. The bank gasped and floundered and expired.

The fight was over. The financial monopoly was smashed. But so was the strength of Andrew Jackson. He had spent too many months in the saddle sloshing through the malarial swamps at the head of his militia, he had suffered too many festering wounds in his duels and his battles, he had wasted too many sleepless nights in the taverns. And finally he had lost the residue of his vigor in the death of his wife. There was nothing but the backbone of an iron will that kept his head from drooping over his shoulders. During the last years of his office his lungs had been slowly bleeding to death. Tuberculosis.

Yet he remained active. He took trips through the country to contact the people, to learn how they felt about him, to discover whether their lives had been made in a little measure happier for his endeavors.

In due course he completed the "reign" which he had never wanted, which he had accepted only at the solicitations of his friends. He was happy now to retire to the affections of his constituents in the West—the untrained idol of an untrained folk.

VII

AGAIN AND AGAIN Andrew Jackson had promised his wife that he would join the Church. But thus far his life had been too full of fights and exasperations for the fulfillment of such a promise. Now at last, in the quiet of The Hermitage, he took long walks with the parson and discussed the plans for his religious conversion.

"General," remarked the parson on one of these walks, "there is a question which it is my duty to ask you. Can you forgive your enemies?"

Old Hickory bent his head in meditation, and then he looked up with his eyes flashing fire. "By the Eternal, I am not *that* old yet!"

Finally he softened. He was willing to compromise. "Well, I'm ready to forgive the whole crew of them collectively, but not as individuals. No, sir, not as *individuals*."

The good parson smiled but accepted him nonetheless into the Presbyterian Church of his fathers.

And when the general was ready to depart for his final High Office in the West, there was an ardent prayer on his lips: "May I find that there, too, the Good Fight will go on!"

IMPORTANT DATES IN THE LIFE OF
ANDREW JACKSON

1767—Born, Union County, North Carolina.

1780—Volunteered to serve in Revolutionary War.

1786—Admitted to the bar.

1788—Appointed public prosecutor in Tennessee Bad Lands.

1791—Married Rachel Donelson.

1796—Elected first representative from the newly admitted state of Tennessee.

1797—Appointed to the United States Senate.

1798—Elevated to the bench of the Supreme Court of Tennessee.

1801—Appointed major general of the militia.

1814—Named "Old Hickory" as a result of his victory over the Creek Indians.

1815—Defeated the British at New Orleans.

1821—Governor of the territory of Florida.

1824—Received largest popular vote among four candidates for the presidency, but failed to obtain a majority.

1828—Elected the seventh President of the United States.

1832—Frustrated plan of South Carolina to secede from the Union.
Re-elected President.
Vetoed bill to renew charter of the Bank of the United States.

1837—Retired from public office.

1845—Died, The Hermitage, Tennessee.

Daniel Webster

[1782–1852]

"THAT large, dark forehead may not be a sign of greatness in your son, but of rickets." His head grows ever larger and his skin darker. Can it be Negro blood somewhere in Ebenezer's lineage that has come out in his son Dan'l? "Surely there's something of the dark South in this New Hampshire Yankee lad." Doesn't act as though he were baptized in the bracing East Wind. Looks as if the lazy South Wind had cradled him in his infancy.

But laziness doesn't thrive well in the loam of a New Hampshire farm. It just won't grow in the salty air. There are no lotus islands in the dreams of the New England farmer when he puts his muddy shoes by the bed. Come on, Daniel, you weren't meant to dream, but to pitch hay!

"He's so damn lazy, I'll send him off to school," decided old Ebenezer. "Ain't got enough brains to be of much use around here, anyhow."

"The child is so weak in body," supplemented his mother. "He'll be much better off larnin' than pickin' whortleberries with his sisters."

Come to think of it, education isn't such a bad thing after all. Take Ebenezer Webster, for example. See what it might have done for him. An old veteran of the Revolution, he had been selected in a guard of honor to keep post near Washington's tent. But did it get him to Congress when the whole business was over? Not at all! "I sweat and toil tryin' to grow vegetables out of the sand, while Old Abiel Foster from Canterbury gets six dollars a day in Washington." All because Abiel had gone to school.

So Daniel went to school with his father's blessing. And how Eben could bless—and curse! Daniel sat at the foot of the freshman class at Phillips Academy. And it was an expensive seat. It took all his father's savings to keep him there. Cheaper by far to sit on a haystack and dream. But out on the haystack you dreamed away your life saying never a word.

And here at Phillips, Daniel sat among a crowd of people. He made friends and talked. Here a fellow was compelled to use words in order to get along. And Daniel discovered he had a voice. So did all the masters and boys around him. Lord, he could talk people into a hypnotic spell with that musical voice of his. And what did he talk about? Why, nothing at all! Just words. Glittering golden words.

When he plodded toward the hills of Hanover to take his entrance examinations for Dartmouth College, he remembered the advice of his schoolmaster at Phillips Academy. "Bear a bold front, boy, bear a bold front. Your Latin is no great thing. Your Greek is worse. And your geography? Oh, fie! But you have the gift of the gab. You'll make a glib tongue carry a lame mind . . ." Such was the rough psychology handed down by a New England schoolteacher in the land of the cold East Wind.

II

"THE LESS he knows, the more he crows," the other students in their bowlers said of Dan'l. Jealousy! Their hats weren't nearly as large as his. They envied his gigantic cranium. By this time everybody knew it wasn't a case of rickets. They regarded him with envy mingled with contempt.

And they had reason for their envy. What a way he had with the ladies! How he could "catch" a pretty ankle!

Yet he was "thin as a weasel and swarthy as a crow." What was it, then, that so captivated the maidens of New Hampshire? It must have been his eyes. Those eyes of Dan'l Webster were "black as death." They seemed to penetrate every secret. They were the eyes of the Devil. That's what fascinated the women. The irresistible Devil in Dan'l Webster.

Yes, he was quite a character. They used to say in those days that Dartmouth had "four professors, three chapels, a college bell, a deficit— and Black Dan'l."

And now he was out of college and nothing to do. For a while he tried teaching school at Freyburg. And then he entered the office of the great Boston lawyer, Christopher Gore, in order to learn the "mysteries of legal procedure." Not that Daniel cared one grain of alfalfa for the law. It bored him. His head was too large and labyrinthine for the straight and precise technicalities of the courtroom; it ached for the surges of the wind, for the sweeping of a tropical tempest to stir up the great frozen chambers of his New England imagination.

He loved to talk, to sway a jury with a torrent of words. It was the hours of research, the painful agony of forming the legal brief, all the hateful contents of the green bag, that annoyed him. Well, Lawyer Gore knew that a strong haul of wine would help young Dan'l to forget his annoyance.

Finally the patient Mr. Gore made Daniel learned in the law and felt like an enchanter who had given away the gravest secrets of his magic. Now, with his new-found power, the fledgling lawyer could become a ruthless tyrant. Or a glowing prophet. "Make yourself useful to your friends,

Daniel," was Gore's final injunction. "And a little formidable to your enemies. And whatever bread you eat, let it be the bread of independence."

III

DANIEL put on his finest pearl-buttoned broadcloth from the lapels of which you could see the fringes of his sarsenet shirt. He put aside the brightly colored whip which he had carried to fairs in his student days and replaced it with a malacca cane. And he strode like a cavalier into the grim Puritan dinginess of the New England courtroom to commence his pleadings. The judges and the juries who heard him were men from the surrounding farm lands, neighbors who had known him and his father for many years. Ebenezer himself had been appointed lay judge for one of the county courts, and the old farmer sat proudly listening to his son's plea in a minor case. He looked around the courtroom, and his eyes grew dim as he saw the openmouthed astonishment of the spectators. Is this young Dan Webster, the little fellow with the big head who used to sit dreaming lazily by the roadside?

Numbers of people flocked to the new lawyer. He had such an uncanny power to sway juries. "It ain't what he says. But you can't keep from weepin' out loud when he says it."

"Yes, an' when he puts his mind to it, he can frighten you too. Sometimes it seems as if the Lord is shinin' in his eyes, an' sometimes the devil."

And Daniel threw back his shaggy head and laughed.

IV

LIKE the Pied Piper of Hamelin, who had cast a spell over the burghers' children, Daniel Webster was able to charm the moneybags away from the merchants of Boston. The coins, like the children, followed the piper wherever he went. As his legend grew, he felt it increasingly necessary to clothe himself in a vision of gold. A man who is thought to be godlike must be a god with a golden halo. "I never heard," observed Daniel, "what particular substance Archimedes wished his world-moving fulcrum to be . . . But if his design had been to move everything in the world, he would have wished it to be a fulcrum of hard cash . . ."

Cash! Money! Without it he was a New Hampshire peasant. With it he could be king.

To make money became the master motive of his life. He had entered the Temple of Justice as a humble suppliant. Soon he was established as a money-changer within its precincts. Here he did his business, boosted his stock for more clients and higher fees. Every thundering sentence was a price quotation, every forensic gesture an invitation to haggle.

A lawyer could get a good price for trying to outsmart the law, and a still better price for making a new and more suitable law. A lawyer who is ambitious should become a legislator. To the Congress, then, said Daniel Webster!

He went to Congress as the representative of the solid businessmen of New England. Their interests spoke through the massive sounding board of his oratory. He had become the voice of the Federalists. A young Demosthenes, fired with the ambition of Croesus. There was a war going on with England (1812) over the impressment of American seamen— "Mr. Madison's War." The merchants of New England wanted nothing to do with it. They were losing too much profitable business with the Empire on account of a "silly squabble over principles." They sent this young man to Washington as an obstructionist—a deep-browed, golden-voiced advocate of peace. Here comes Dan Webster—devilishly handsome, incredibly ambitious. "Warn the ladies, and tell that Southerner, Henry Clay, that a rival has entered the field."

He did a great deal of talking at Washington, and a great deal of drinking. That famous "Daniel Webster punch." The strong stimulants gave him moments of exaltation even though they slowly undermined his health. He lived in a world of enchantment and temptation and ever-accumulating riches. He owned a house in Boston, an estate at Marshfield, horses, yachts, hunting dogs, champagne-filled cellars. Was not the possession of things the very essence of the happy life?

He returned from Washington and strode again into the chambers of the law and pleaded his cases until even his enemies became his clients. His voice rose to pitches of agony and his face assumed a mask of suffering and he drew tears, this modern Orpheus, from the iron countenances of the learned justices of the Supreme Court.

And then, when Andrew Jackson became President, Webster was returned to the Senate and commenced his pleadings in behalf of the most powerful client in the United States. The Bank of Nicholas Biddle had "engaged" Webster, along with Henry Clay and a "select" group of other senators, to jockey through the Senate the bill for its recharter. Webster was high on the list of the men who received regular fees for his endeavors. And when the bank was slow in its "retainers," Webster did not hesitate to demand his usual "refreshments." Such were the legislative ethics of those days.

But it was exciting. You never knew who your next client would be. Daniel was intoxicated with his power. And he would accept all newcomers—those with a price to pay and those without a price provided the case fascinated him.

And then, in the midst of all this aimless splendor, a new client began to appear in the company of Daniel Webster. As he sat over his punch bowl and surveyed the glory and the vanity of his brilliant career, his mind reverted to some of the speeches he had read in his student days —the patriotic appeals of Pericles, of Cicero, of Edmund Burke. It was at such moments that this new client made his most insistent demands. And little by little he won Daniel Webster over to his cause. "The mere reading of the Constitution of the United States brings tears to my eyes." This overwhelmingly persuasive client refused to be denied. His country!

V

DAN WEBSTER made his first conspicuous appeal in behalf of his country on a cold January day in 1830, when the Senate gallery was aglow with the finery of the Washington aristocracy and the floor was jammed with angry, bickering legislators. General Hayne of South Carolina had risen, on the occasion of an unimportant matter of legislation, to introduce into his argument a doctrine of political philosophy that had grown notorious among certain Southern gentlemen through the course of thirty years. He had declared that his state had the right to decide for herself as to whether any law passed by Congress was constitutional and that, moreover, his state had the right to disobey any law which she regarded as unconstitutional. Hayne's argument, the alleged right of a state to nullify a federal law, was the virus of anarchy. For it meant the breaking up of the United States into a disunited jumble of antagonistic governments.

But Hayne went even further than that. If the federal government persisted in enforcing a law after the state legislature had nullified it, then the state had the right—declared Hayne—to secede from the Union. "For the Union is nothing but an agreement, a compact between the states from which any party may withdraw when dissatisfied."

Hayne's speech had struck Washington like a thunderbolt. Daniel Webster felt constrained to answer this speech—not only as an advocate of the North, but even more compellingly as a citizen of the United States. In the greatest defense of the Constitution ever heard in the Capitol, the senator from New Hampshire delivered an oration that was printed throughout the land and reached the heart of every patriot. Why, he asked, should any Southern state feel that the interests of the country as a whole are inimical to her? "Sir, we in New England do not reason thus. Our notion of things is entirely different. We do not impose geographical limits to our patriotic feeling or regard." If—he declared—he were to vote narrow-mindedly against any legislation that was partial to the South, his constituents would feel betrayed. "These . . . men would tell me that they had sent me to act for the whole country, and that anyone who possessed too little comprehension either of intellect or of feeling—one who was not large enough in mind and heart to embrace the whole—was not fit to be entrusted with the interest of any part."

The Constitution of the United States—he continued—was not a compact entered into by the states, but the law of the land as formulated and ratified by the American people. The law of the Constitution was superior to any legislation of the states. And any defiance of it was open rebellion, treason, "no matter what euphemistic name the Senator may choose to give it . . . The people, sir, erected this government . . . The people so willed it." Would the legislators of any one state presume to obstruct the will of the majority of the American people? It is folly to define liberty as the right to defy the sovereignty of the people. Such defiance is not liberty at all. There can be no such motto waving over America as "Liberty first and Union afterwards." There can only be "Liberty *and* Union, now and forever, one and inseparable."

When he had finished, a senator from the South who had supported Hayne walked over to him and declared: "Mr. Webster, I think you had better die now, and rest your fame on that speech."

But Webster was too busy to listen. He had already rushed off to other litigations. His interests were so manifold, always piling up. No wonder he drank so heavily. . . .

He needed money and more of it. He was adding acre upon acre to his dream farm at Marshfield. The upkeep of this farm was a constant drain upon his purse. Well, he could raise all the funds he needed now on the security of his reputation as the "Defender of the Constitution." He could get large loans from the most prominent men in the country. The finest investments were open to him. New England wasn't his only gold mine. He would travel West and speculate in land values out there. Throughout the country he was regarded as a "good risk." Every new honor that the press gave him was a gilt-edged security.

He took a trip to the West and mortgaged himself heavily and bowed to the thunderous applause. Why, he was popular enough to be President of the United States. He'd make a try for it. His sponsors would be the landowners of the West and the bankers of the East—an unbeatable combination. Could his rival Henry Clay, that insatiable aspirant for the presidency, play a better hand than that?

Yet Webster had reckoned without his political hosts. The Whig convention turned a deaf ear to him in 1836, and again in 1840. The harmless old soldier, General Harrison, was selected as the standard-bearer of the Whig party. He was guaranteed to be a faithful servant of Nicholas Biddle and his bank. No fear of him. As a good party member, Webster was bound to support him. And the people accepted him as their President. What a relief to the Whigs after those "barbarian" Democrats, Jackson and Van Buren! To be sure, his running mate, John Tyler, was a dark horse. Nobody knew what his principles were. But why worry about the principles of a mere Vice-President?

President Harrison made Daniel Webster a handsome offer—the office of Secretary of State. His political friends urged him to accept, and Daniel did. Now he was in a real position to serve.

Then the blow fell. One month after his inauguration, old General Harrison passed away. And Mr. Tyler, the "Great Unknown" became President of the United States. When the Unknown made his principles known, the entire Whig party was convulsed with fury. He had proved to be a traitor in their midst—a Jacksonian Democrat opposed to sound money, big business, tariffs! When the Whigs had once again brought up the bill to recharter Biddle's bank, Tyler had reacted exactly as Jackson and Van Buren had reacted before him. He had vetoed the bill. A horrible catastrophe had overtaken the Whig aspirations. There was nothing for the party to do now but to demand the resignation of all the Whig members of the Tyler Cabinet as a protest against his "treachery."

In the meantime Daniel Webster, in his new office, had been handling certain ticklish matters of foreign policy with the utmost skill. Trouble had been brewing between the United States and Great Britain over the Canadian boundaries. There had been border attacks, reprisals, arrests. The two nations were close to war. It would take the most delicate deliberation to keep the United States at peace.

It was in the midst of this deliberation that the crisis arose in the politics of the Whig party. The leaders of this party, with Biddle pulling the purse strings, ordered Webster to leave the Tyler Cabinet. One by one the other members of the Cabinet had handed in their resignations.

Daniel felt strangely old of a sudden. He was the last Whig still remaining in the Cabinet. They would expect his resignation tomorrow. Yet he was in the midst of negotiations more important than party politics.

He sat in his office with his head heavy and a terrible odor of liquor on his breath. Couldn't he ever give up this confounded habit of drinking? Well, he drank because he was sick. That was it. He drank to forget the effects of the opium which he took to relieve the chronic ailment of his stomach. The famous "Daniel Webster punch." Really it deserved company along with him to taste it. This blend of Medford rum, brandy, champagne, arrack, and maraschino. A base of strong tea laced with lemon . . . Really he should be drinking it along with someone.

He wasn't exactly sure but it *did* seem as though somebody had come in to help him drink his brew. He'd seen this company before.

"Mighty fine-tasting punch, Dan'l." And then, after a pause: "So you're going back to Boston tomorrow?"

"Yes, I'm through here."

"What about my business, Dan'l? Ain't you going to see my claim through? Have you forgotten me?"

"I worked for you in 1830 and won you a decision against General Hayne. And what did it get me? The hatred of my Southern friends." Confound this fellow! Always turning up at the most embarrassing moments.

Daniel rose abruptly to go to bed. But the voice detained him. "Then I'll go to other lawyers, Dan'l. There are plenty of them in this country who will want my business. And they'll be remembered in after years for what they've done. Isn't it time you settled down again to a job that'll be worthy of Dan'l Webster? Well, go off to bed now . . . Ah, you hesitate . . . Can we talk business?"

VI

DANIEL WEBSTER remained in the Cabinet of President Tyler and continued to arbitrate the boundary dispute between the United States and Canada. He insisted on the rights of the Americans to the high seas and demanded that the British Navy show respect for citizens sailing under the American flag.

But the entire Whig world was in a fury. When he returned to Boston and prepared to address her citizens in Faneuil Hall, he faced a sullen and unfriendly crowd. Who was this inconsistent politician? Was he still a Whig? When England on the high seas had interfered with a cargo of runaway slaves from the Southern plantations, he had demanded in the name of the Constitution that England return the slave property of the South. What was this Northerner, pro-slavery? Well, now, he would have to do some tall explaining.

"I give no pledges; I make no intimation one way or the other, and I will be as free when this day closes to act as duty calls as I was when the dawn of this day broke . . . Take it or leave it, Whigs of Massachusetts!"

They couldn't help cheering him. They admired his courage. Once more they knew him for their leader. But never again would he be, in the old sense, their idol as he once had been. From now on they would keep a shrewd weather eye upon the "shifting currents" of his sympathies.

He settled a few more incidents that had created friction between England and the United States; and then, when his business was finished and his presence in the Cabinet could be no longer advantageous to the country, he resigned.

And now they began whispering strange stories about him. They said he was drinking harder than ever to keep going, that he made many of his speeches in a drunken stupor. "During his address to the farmers at the Rochester Fair he could hardly keep his feet." "In his speech at the banquet of the economists he dug into his wallet and offered to pay the national debt." Pay the national debt! Why, he couldn't even pay his own debts. A curse had fastened itself upon his finances. He never had any cash. "His method of doing business is as impractical as that of a Hottentot." Always he was borrowing on notes to pay off other notes, always drafting on banks where he had friends but no funds. He was mortgaged to every moneylender in Massachusetts. "The Devil is snatching after him, determined to bring him to hell." He had sold his soul to old Beelzebub. Rich banquets and dazzling clothes and acres of estates—and hardly a penny of ready cash.

He went back to his law practice to recoup his finances. A case with the Goodrich Rubber Company and a claim for John Jacob Astor—and he paid off a good slice of his notes. And then again his notes began to pile higher and higher. It wasn't the Devil; it was the men in State Street who had a mortgage on his very life.

But not on his tongue. Perhaps if they sent him again to Washington, they mused, he wouldn't be so free with his speech. He would realize where his soul belonged. They hadn't wished to punish such a tongue too severely! Yet they must try to restrain it somehow.

And so a group of businessmen met and collected a fund to send Daniel Webster back to Washington. To ward off the ugly charge of "vested interests," they called it a memorial fund—a sort of token of affection and esteem presented by his friends. With the "token," Webster ran a handsome campaign and was re-elected to the Senate.

Brave old fellow, coming back to battle. And a battle royal it was! That same irresistible question that had split the Union for forty years had come up again in acute form. Should the South be allowed to extend her institution of slavery into any new territory incorporated into the Union? Would not this destroy the balance of political and financial power as between the North and the South, leaving the South finally in complete domination? But the Southerners, too, had their argument. When they moved into the new Western territory they insisted upon taking their slaves along with them. For a slave was property just as an article of household furniture or a covered van. The Constitution had declared this to be an established fact.

And thus the South was determined to force slavery upon the new land. The North, on the other hand, was equally determined that this new land be free. The South repeated the ominous arguments of General Hayne, justifying the right of secession from the Union whenever any state was dissatisfied with the federal laws as impinging upon its own sovereignty. And who was there to reply to this threat but Daniel Webster, who had made a reply on that famous earlier occasion? Again he loomed as the foremost spokesman of the Northern Whigs—of the reactionary capitalists who were implacable foes of cheap plantation labor, as well as of the fanatical idealists who insisted upon nothing short of abolition throughout the United States.

In the Congress of the United States the situation (in 1850) seemed beyond the power of words. Two systems of economics and ideology were deadlocked. Senators concealed pistols in their pockets as they rose to speak. It was rumored that the Southern militia was ready to march upon Washington. In the North the abolitionists invoked the lightning of heaven upon the heads of the transgressors.

And yet many men hoped that the words of one would win the day. Daniel Webster was a Northerner and a man of principle. And also a man of ambition. Didn't he have his eyes on the presidency in 1852? He had been turned down four times by his party. But he still nursed his ambition, they said. Alexander the Great had conquered the world at thirty; and here was Daniel Webster, sixty-eight and the most brilliant speaker in the land, and not President yet? This time he would make the grade with the right speech. "Show the South your fist, Dan'l, and we Northerners will put you over."

And then in the cold of March he rose to his feet and trembled. If people only knew how he trembled inwardly when he spoke! He looked at the gentlemen on the floor and at the ladies in the gallery. Yes, he had made a very important speech here twenty years earlier, on another winter day, to another gallery. That would be when his beloved son Edward was eleven years old. His youngest son, who was no more now than a picture on the bureau, a handful of dust in the soil of New England, a cypress tree above. Edward had died in the Mexican War—a war engineered by hotheads who were anxious to show their fists. And now once more there were hotheads in the North and the South who were eager to show their fists, to rush into another war, another killing of sons . . .

He spoke firmly and almost scornfully. He spoke in defense of the South's constitutional right to hold slaves. He hated slavery, but he was certain that it would die a natural death in the liberal progress of the world without fulmination from the North. It was ridiculous to assume in any controversy that all the goodness was on one side and all the wickedness on the other. He spoke for compromise and tolerance. And his eyes intermittently blackened with gloom and sparkled in exaltation. There could be only one alternative to a complete break—compromise, a gentle yielding of the extremists on both sides for the sake of the United Destiny of both, for the health and the liberty and the preservation of the Union. How could Daniel Webster be expected to make a stand on extreme Northern principles? Did they not remember the words he had once spoken? "One who is not large enough in mind and heart to embrace the whole . . . is not fit to be entrusted with the interest of any one part."

And when he had finished there was a chill silence—the first time that a speech of his had been received in chill silence. To keep the Union! For a moment he looked formidable and glowing—"like a transparent bronze statue brilliantly lighted from within."

Then he sat down, cold and extinguished.

VII

THE North was stunned. And then it rose to a fury unequaled. There was a "traitor" in her midst!

Liberty! "This word in Webster's mouth is like the word *love* in the mouth of a courtesan . . . Every drop of blood in that man's veins has eyes that look downward."

Silently Webster accepted the portfolio of Secretary of State in the Cabinet of Fillmore, "in preparation for the Presidency which he expects to get through the support of the South in 1852." He came to Boston for an address. But the board of aldermen refused him Faneuil Hall. In his ears, wherever he went, rang the challenging words of Seward's reply to his speech: "There is a higher law than the Constitution!"

1852. The Whig Convention. The man "who sold out to the South" is waiting for the Southern Whigs to swing over to his support. He is waiting in vain. The South distrusts him. New England deserts him— first, his native state of New Hampshire; then, Vermont . . .

He waits. The lines of Whittier run through his mind like a sword:

> *When faith is lost, when honor dies,*
> *The man is dead.*

There was nothing left for him to do but to return to Marshfield. "Go back to your farm, Dan'l. You have done enough work here," counseled the client who of late had kept him faithful company. "Go back to the oxen and the Punch Brook pasture. Get away from all the yelping voices. Lie down and listen to the sea breaking her heart for you. Isn't it time you wrote your hired man a letter, Daniel, telling him you're coming home? . . . Maybe there will come wise men after you who will find a way to continue in peace. Maybe war is bound to come in any case. Never fear. You have kept your hands from brothers' blood."

He wrote a letter to his hired man. "John Taylor, I am coming home. You and I are farmers; we never talk politics—our talk is of oxen. But remember this: that any man who attempts to excite one part of this country against another is just as wicked as he who should attempt to get up a quarrel between John Taylor and his neighbor, old Mr. John Sanborn . . . I think I never wrote you a word upon politics. I shall not do it again. I only say, love your country and your whole country, and when men attempt to persuade you to get into a quarrel with the laws of other states, tell them that you mean to mind your own business and tell them to do the same . . . John Taylor, thank God morning and evening that you were born in such a country . . . John Taylor, never write to me another word upon politics."

IMPORTANT DATES IN THE LIFE OF DANIEL WEBSTER

1782—Born, Salisbury, New Hampshire.

1797—Entered Dartmouth College.

1805—Admitted to the Massachusetts bar.

1813—Elected to Congress.

1818—Argued the Dartmouth College case.

1820—Delivered his oration on the Pilgrim Fathers.

1825—Delivered his Bunker Hill address.

1830—Made his famous reply to Hayne—an interpretation and defense of the American Constitution.

1840—Appointed Secretary of State in Harrison's Cabinet.

1842—Made treaty with Ashburton about the northeastern boundary of the United States.

1850—Delivered speech in favor of Clay's "Compromise" on slavery.

1852—Died, Marshfield, Massachusetts.

Sam Houston

[1793-1863]

SAM Houston came of a long line of fighting Irish—wild Ulster-
men who defied European tyranny and battled their way to the
new land of religious freedom, America. In his soul were the
poetry and the uncompromising honesty of the Gaelic bards—a
race of giants whose pride and courage earned them tragic ends.

At fourteen, when his father died, he was already a man. Well over six
feet he stood, with a voice and a will that matched his stature.

The widowed mother turned her back upon civilization. Taking her
nine strapping sons from Virginia, she marched them to the Tennessee
wilderness. There they cleared the soil and built a cabin—a task well to
the liking of their untamed spirit. Sam, tallest of these young Titans, was
especially pleased with the new life. His entire education had been confined to reading and writing. When a copy of Homer's *Iliad* found its way
across the Alleghenies into Sam's possession, he devoured its pages, all
athrill to the ringing verse. He read the book again and again until its
tattered leaves almost fell apart.

When he reached the age of fifteen, Sam's older brothers decided it was
time to discipline the youth. They apprenticed him to the village storekeeper. This confinement Sam endured for a few weeks, and then he ran
away to join a tribe of Cherokees. The brothers endeavored to persuade
the truant to return. But Sam was adamant. "I prefer measuring deer
tracks to measuring tape," he told them. "I can at least read a translation
from the Greek here in the woods, and read it in peace." The Indians
named him Colon-neh (the Rover).

Three years he dwelt among the Cherokees, their adopted darling.
From them he learned forest craft. The oratory of the chiefs around their
council fire satisfied his love for the dramatic. He absorbed their traits as
naturally as he breathed the clean forest air. Their implacable enmity in
the face of injustice, their remembrance of a favor bestowed, their fond-

ness for little children, their joy in bright colors, their stoic courage—all
these became integral parts of Sam's character.

His penchant for barbaric costumes and for bestowing gifts led him
oftentimes to the shops across the Tennessee River, boundary between
white and Indian territory. On these many excursions he incurred debts
which he was determined to pay off. Bidding his Cherokee family au
revoir, he left them with a promise to return as soon as his indebtedness
was discharged.

With absolute faith in his ability to succeed in any undertaking, Sam
opened a school. His fees were outrageously high by frontier standards.
Yet his little schoolhouse was crowded, and he was soon able to discharge
his obligations. The role of schoolmaster suited him. With flowered calico
shirt, a long queue hanging down his back, he strutted before the enthralled youngsters. A sourwood stick for disciplinary measures and Sam's
overwhelming personality kept the pupils on their toes. They studied well
and they paid well. His creditors appeased, Sam closed the doors of the
school. He had enjoyed himself immensely. Deciding now that teaching
was his natural bent, he entered the academy at Maryville to prepare himself the better for the job. A few short weeks of books and classrooms,
however, and Sam's enthusiasm had soured to distaste. Heading for the
woods again, he left to rejoin the Cherokees.

News of war, and Old Hickory Jackson's valiant struggle with only a
handful of men at his command. Sam halted his journey and enlisted as a
private. When his friends told him he was foolish not to have applied for
a commission, Sam retorted: "Go to with such stuff. I would rather honor
the ranks than disgrace an appointment."

Sam's mother approved of his act. Placing a rifle in his hand, she said:
"Never disgrace it, for I had rather all my sons fill one honorable grave
than that one of them should turn his back. My door is open to brave
men. It is eternally shut to cowards."

II

Joining Old Hickory's forces, Sam began immediately to distinguish
himself. Before long he was a sergeant. At Horseshoe Bend he displayed
the courage and the selfless disregard for his safety that were characteristic of his entire career. The Indians had thrown up earthen breastworks
that for a time appeared impregnable. Jackson could not bring himself to
order his men into certain slaughter, and the battle was at a standstill. But
Sam waited for no orders. His reckless daring and his long legs carried
him halfway up the defenses before an arrow in his thigh felled him. By
that time the others, fired by his courage, stormed past him and captured
the fort. Catching a hurrying soldier by the arm, Sam ordered him to pull
the arrow from his thigh. The effort expended was more considerate than
effective. Sam bellowed his rage. "Try it again. If you fail this time, I'll
smite you to earth!" Frightened, the soldier tugged. The arrow left the
flesh, but brought in its wake such a flow of blood that Sam had to be

carried behind the lines for medical treatment. Seeing the young man's
wound, Old Hickory ordered him to retire. Sam obeyed—just so long as
his superior officer was looking. Jackson's back was no sooner turned than
Sam was once more in the vanguard.

Only a few hundred of the Indians were left alive at the Bend. These
had barricaded themselves in a cave. Jackson demanded that they surrender. They shouted angry defiance. Again Jackson refused to order his men
to attack. The redskins had the advantage, could pick off the attackers at
their leisure. Another impasse, until Sam dashed headlong up toward the
cave, and the rest followed him. A slug in the shoulder laid Sam low—this
time, it seemed, past all rising. Swarming over and around him, his comrades captured the cave.

When the smoke of the battle had cleared, Sam's unconscious form was
discovered beneath a mound of corpses. So far beyond help did he appear
that the doctors refused to waste their time on him. But they had not
counted upon Sam's spirit—nor upon the resilience of that amazing body.
Though he lay without treatment through a day and a night, and then
received only improper care, he clung tenaciously to the shreds of life.
When at last he was carried on a litter through his mother's door, only his
eyes were recognizable in the emaciated and bloody frame. Sam had come
home a hero—a daredevil who could not be beaten save by his own
gigantic emotions.

For weeks he lay half dead, willing himself slowly back to life. And
then, still feeble from his unhealed wounds, he journeyed on horseback to
New York for further treatment. But the cure was never complete.
Throughout the rest of his life the wounds were to open under excessive
strain, bringing him great suffering. But not for Sam Houston to complain
of such little things.

His service had been rewarded with a lieutenant's commission. Everywhere he was hailed as the hero of Horseshoe Bend. A good man, the
general said of him, to break up the smuggling rings that abounded along
the shores of America. Among the smugglers who flaunted their evil trade
almost unhampered were the Blackbirders—a band of pirates who sold
black flesh captured in Africa. Against them Sam proceeded with impetuous ardor. He had nearly succeeded in stamping out this menace, when
the government called him to deal with the Cherokees, who were waxing
warlike over the unfair treaty that had been foisted upon them.

Sam had little heart for his new task. To persuade his Indian friends
to accept the terms of the treaty gave him no pleasure. But realizing that
defiance could only mean heartbreak and eventual annihilation for themselves, he counseled acceptance. Having perfect trust in their white
brother, and seeing the wisdom of his counsel, the Cherokees capitulated.
For a time there was peace between the white men and the red.

Sam now returned to his unfinished job against the Blackbirders. These
pirates had been backed by powerful interests who refused to take their
setback as final. In Washington they put in motion wheels that would
once more clear the way for their trade. Sam was the stumbling block in
their path, and so they concentrated all their venom upon him. The Secre-

tary of War called him to the capital to answer charges of misdealing. Between the secretary and the rough-and-ready soldier an immediate antagonism developed. And though Sam offered every proof of his innocence—was exonerated and received public apology—he remained infuriated at the injustice of his treatment. Coming back to Nashville, he resigned his commission in the army and turned his thoughts to law. A fit profession for a man whose passions were oratory and justice.

He presented himself at the offices of James Trimble, a friend whose advice was encouraging. "You have all the necessary qualities for the successful practice of law. But it will require eighteen months of study." This idea Sam laughed to scorn. He had neither the time nor the money for such a protracted scholastic program. "I will be ready in six months," he prophesied. Six months later Sam passed his bar examinations and hung out his shingle in the town of Lebanon, Tennessee.

Sam's resources were practically nonexistent; but from Isaac Golladay, a merchant of the town, he obtained unlimited credit. Just as Sam never forgave an affront, he never forgot a kindness. Though it took him thirty-five years to repay Isaac, he did so many times over, adding services that could not be measured in money. "The seed of generosity grows into a cluster of many-colored roses."

III

As a LAWYER Sam prospered from the first day of his practice. His classical speech and picturesque appearance, as well as his stalwart character, won universal admiration. It was not long before he was persuaded to enter politics. His rise in public life was fast and steady. Six feet six inches tall and weighing over two hundred pounds—his flamboyant attire in no way detracting from the picture—he dominated every group of which he was a part. At all times Sam remained a staunch admirer and follower of Jackson. They understood and appreciated each other, these two war horses, and their relationship was that of father and son.

Sam's adopted state sent him to Washington as senator. His farewell speech to Lebanon was typically half Homer, half Houston. "I was naked, and ye clothed me. I was hungry, and ye fed me." Overdramatic, perhaps, but the sincerity was absolute, and this sincerity conveyed itself to his listeners. They wept.

In the Senate, Sam strove to tone his speech and manners down to Washington standards, but without success. Gulliver could not make himself inconspicuous among the Lilliputians. His political career was punctuated by a single duel. Old Hickory's advice on that occasion was homely and to the point. "Keep a bullet between your teeth," Jackson said. "You'll find that the bite will steady you." Sam emerged from the duel victorious, but with a horror for the then popular means of settling arguments. Forever after he put challengers off with scorn or humor. To one opponent he said: "I will not fight downhill." And to another, who wished to avenge an insult, he replied: "I thought you were a friend. If a man can't abuse his friends, then who the hell can he abuse?"

Three terms he served in the Senate, then returned to Tennessee to run for governor. His victory was overwhelming, and he brought to the governorship all the fire and fight that had so far marked his headlong path. Tennessee adored its Sam. While in this office, he married young and beautiful Eliza Allen. For a time it seemed that Sam's colorful cup was full to overflowing. Planning to run for a second term, and expecting another great victory, Sam was struck by a tragedy that shocked the country and sent him into the depths of despair and degradation. The lovely Eliza betook herself from the gubernatorial mansion and Sam's life. The state rocked with the scandal, and speculation ran rife.

It was typical of Sam's generosity and reverence for women that he never uttered a word of reproach against his wife. Eliza, while loving another, had been forced by her ambitious parents into the marriage with Sam Houston. And now, suing for and obtaining a divorce which Sam refused to contest, she married the man of her choice. The blow to Sam's pride, however, had left its indelible mark. Resigning from the governorship, he prepared to leave public life forever. To the scandalmongers who made accusations uncomplimentary to both sides, Sam uttered threats only on behalf of Eliza. "If any wretch dares utter a word against the purity of Mrs. Houston," he threatened, "I will return and write the libel in his heart's blood."

He took a boat into the wilderness. A great depression had descended upon him. He felt he had betrayed the trust that Jackson had imposed upon him—that he had brought sorrow to the man he worshiped. He contemplated throwing himself overboard. At that moment a giant eagle swooped close to the deck, then flew screaming into the sunset. Sam's spirits rose; he felt that the bird's flight indicated a future for him in the West.

Once more Sam sought haven with the Cherokees, certain of a welcome. Chief John Jolly greeted him warmly, extending to him all the rights of citizenship in the tribe. "I heard that you were a great chief among your people," said the Indian. "I heard that a dark cloud had fallen on the white path you were walking. My wigwam is yours."

Taking again the name of Colon-neh, Sam gave himself up to drink with a wholeheartedness that would have killed a weaker man. For years the huge figure—blanketed and sprawled in drunken stupor—was a familiar sight on the streets of Fort Gibson. Yet such was the innate dignity of the man that no one ever dared to insult the "town drunk." The Indians sometimes nicknamed him Old Souse; but this was a term of affection, not of criticism. A half-breed squaw became his wife according to Indian custom. Tallahina lavished on her squaw man a deep and tender affection. Sam treated her always with thoughtful respect. And though in time their destinies separated them, Sam never considered himself at liberty to remarry until her death.

Sam's sense of justice and his love for the Indian finally proved the instruments that brought about his redemption. The Cherokees were in sad plight, due to the ravishing of their land at the hands of unprincipled white men. Chief Oo-loo-tee-kag (John Jolly) begged his White Brother to intercede in their behalf. Sam could not find it in his heart to let this plea go unheeded. With terrific effort he pulled himself from his sodden state and journeyed to Washington, shepherding his little flock of Cherokees.

He was granted an immediate audience; Old Hickory's interest enabled him to get justice for the Cherokees. It was a sad meeting between the two warriors. Jackson now President, and Sam a despised squaw man. Old Hickory urged his friend to take office, and thus to redeem himself. Sam refused. "I am through with the world of white men."

Into Texas, which at that time was a part of Mexico, Sam journeyed on a mission for his Indian friends. The ragged, unkempt giant, as he rode into the sunset, little guessed what glory and fulfillment awaited him in that bright land. Sam loved Texas. Texas loved Sam. A new chapter had begun in his crowded career. He had come to Texas on a short visit. He remained there for the rest of his life.

IV

IN TEXAS Sam's past met with no criticism. A man was judged there by his qualities alone. Old Drunk was soon known far and wide as Old Sam—a brave and honest man in a land where bravery and honesty were the order of the day. He warmed to the new life and threw himself into it with his old-time zest.

Among his first acquaintances in Texas was Stephen Austin, one of the earliest settlers and a firm believer in the future of that country. These two men, immediately drawn to each other, formed a friendship which lasted their lifetime. Texas was then entering into the throes of her heroic struggle against the power-thirsty Santa Anna. The handful of colonists, weary of his double-dealing and oppression, had decided to arm themselves against him. Into the fray Sam threw himself joyfully, and was soon commander in chief of the Texas forces. There were dreadful days ahead for the gallant Texans, when only a man of Sam's caliber could have led them through to final freedom. There were many who thought that conciliation with Santa Anna was possible. One of these conciliators was Austin. He made the journey to Mexico to put before the dictator a plea for the Texans. He found a drug-crazed tyrant who threw him into a dungeon. There he remained for two years. When finally he was released he returned to Texas to find it already overrun with Santa Anna's troops, who were destroying everything that lay in their path. He made his way to Sam Houston's side; Houston urged him to join in a revolt against the Mexicans. "There's no decency to be expected from them. We've got to meet force with force."

Attempting to whip the infuriated Texans into an orderly army was a colossal task. Most of the men in the ranks were loyal to Old Sam. But many of the officers, unused to discipline and eager for action, left in small bands, forming disorganized garrisons about the country and thus weakening the main body of the army.

But Sam did his best under the circumstances. And Sam's best was human endeavor pretty nearly at its best. His great soul understood the little soul of Santa Anna. He knew that he would need cunning against the blood-drunk dictator. Watching from afar the slaughter, as Santa Anna conquered first the garrison at the Alamo, then one by one the other isolated forts, Sam strengthened in his purpose. It was Sam's aim to entice Santa Anna into a trap where his own arrogance would prove his undoing.

At San Jacinto, Sam achieved his purpose. With Santa Anna and his army lured into a cul-de-sac and lulled into a sense of false security, Sam and his five hundred men descended on the unsuspecting Mexicans, shouting: "Remember the Alamo!" In a battle that lasted eighteen minutes the Texans killed, captured, or put to rout the entire force of the enemy with hardly a loss on their own side.

After a night of celebration, the Texans set out in search of whatever fugitives might have escaped into the forest. Above all, they wanted Santa Anna. Again Sam knew his man. "You will find the hero of Tampico," Sam told his soldiers, "making his retreat on all fours, dressed as an ordinary private." That was just how they found him. The meeting between the two generals was dramatic. Wounded in the leg, Sam sat propped against a huge tree. Santa Anna was brought before him. The blustering conqueror was now a sniveling bunch of rags, whining for the opium in his saddlebag. Sam ordered his men to administer the drug. His raw nerves soothed, Santa Anna regained some of his former swagger.

"I ask generosity for the vanquished," he demanded.

"You should have remembered that at the Alamo," was Sam's stern reply. . . .

And now, thanks to Sam Houston, Texas was free of Mexican tyranny. Yet she was still in an unenviable position. Although Texas wished to be annexed to the United States, the United States did not wish to annex Texas. The question as to the disposal of the infant republic became a political football in Washington. For years it was tossed around from administration to administration and nobody did anything about it. Finally Sam Houston, as governor of Texas, took the battered ball into his own strong hands. He entered into negotiations with France and England with a view to securing recognition for Texas as an independent empire. Yet this effort, too, came to naught. When it appeared that Texas was to remain forever suspended in the political void, a treaty was concluded under President Tyler (1844), and Texas became a part of the United States.

Sam served a second term as governor. And almost simultaneously with his re-election a great happiness came to him. At forty-seven he married Margaret Moffette Lea. His new bride was twenty-one. Their union proved perfect. For the first time he knew the companionship and the domestic comfort that his romantic soul had always craved. And his wife brought him the gift of robust sons and daughters to gladden his days and to receive the heritage that was his to bestow.

As senator from Texas, Sam once again trod the floor of the congressional chamber. More picturesque, more forceful than ever, he was a figure to fire the imagination. But new heartbreak awaited him. On the one side stood the abolitionists, whose cause—though he disliked the Northerners—he espoused. Ranged on the other side were the Southerners, threatening secession. In the center stood Old Sam Houston—alone. His clear vision showed him what war would mean for his beloved South. The Secessionists could only bring disaster upon themselves, he pointed out. His words fell on deaf ears. Fearful of what lay ahead for Texas in the event of her joining the Confederates, Sam left the Senate and tried to stem the tide of war sentiment that was sweeping his state. His farewell address to the Senate was impassioned, and without compromise. He prayed for unity, and for peace.

Only Sam Houston could influence Texas in the right direction, and he was determined to do his utmost. Though weary and depressed upon his return, he shook himself free of his lassitude when he saw the blind hatred into which Texas had fallen. Once more he plunged into the race for the governorship. He lashed the people with invective and insult. He caressed them with humor and affection. His campaign became a triumphal tour. Everywhere crowds cheered him, laughing or weeping at his words. "Texas will stand by the Union," he shouted. "It is all that can save us as a nation!" And the crowds shouted back their approval.

But their enthusiasm was for Old Sam, not for his cause. Though, as before, his election was a landslide, his efforts at maintaining peace were futile. There came a day—he had long expected it—when, walking into his office, he found his place filled by the lieutenant governor. Calmly he gathered his personal belongings. With head high he walked out, through a lane of jeering and insulting men. Texas had seceded, and Sam was no longer wanted. A Union army, with fifty thousand men massed at the border, was ready to enter Texas. They offered Sam a commission as major general. He refused. He loved the Union, had given thirty years of his life laboring in its behalf—but he was loyal to Texas even in the hour of her folly. A strange, twisted, chaotic tangle of destiny, this war of brother against brother, child against father. Sam Houston's son and namesake commanded a Texas regiment in the Confederate Army.

Sam's abolitionist sympathies had earned him in many places the name of traitor. As is the case with all great personalities, he had numerous enemies. By these he was as thoroughly hated as he was loved by his admirers. Among the most violent of the mudslingers was Judge Campbell. One day, when young Sam's regiment had asked Old Sam to review it, he appeared in the very uniform in which he had defeated Santa Anna and given Texas her freedom. The uniform was in rags now. At his side hung the old sword, fastened with the same buckskin thong. Throwing aside his cane, Old Sam hobbled forward, bellowing orders. Smartly the young soldiers responded, thrilled by the presence of their hero.

"Do you see Judge Campbell or his son here?" he demanded.

"No!" shouted the regiment.

"Do you see old and young Sam Houston here?" he roared.

The soldiers understood his point. The Houstons were loyal to their state—their life's blood, hers. Their answer was such an appreciative shout as to bring tears to the eyes of Old Sam. There were tears still in his eyes as he hobbled away. He foresaw only too clearly the fate of the brave young men, the flower of Texas.

Retiring to a small log cabin—and to poverty—Sam sat down to await the inevitable outcome of the war. Even the early victories for the South did not cheer him. He knew that these triumphs would be only momentary, that they must give way to the superior arms and man power of the Union forces.

When news of the fall of Vicksburg reached him, he realized that it was the beginning of the end. The emotional strain was too much. Taking to his bed, he rose no more. For weeks he lay, sometimes conscious, more often in a coma. In a lucid moment, just before the end, he was heard to murmur: "Texas, Texas."

IMPORTANT DATES IN THE LIFE OF SAM HOUSTON

1793—Born, Lexington, Virginia.

1806—Moved, with mother, to Tennessee.

1808—Left home to live with Indians.

1811—Returned home and opened a school.

1813—Enlisted in United States Army.

1814—Fought against Indians under General Jackson; severely wounded.

1817—Appointed Indian sub-agent.

1818—Settled in Nashville to study law.

1819—Elected district attorney.

1821—Appointed major general of militia.

1823—Elected to Congress.

1825—Elected governor of Tennessee.

1829—Married Eliza Allen. His wife left him. Retired to live among Indians.

1832—Went to Texas, appointed commander in chief of Texan Army.

1836—Defeated Santa Anna at San Jacinto. Elected president of the Republic of Texas.

1841—Re-elected president of Texas.

1845—Texas annexed to United States.

1848–59—Served as United States senator.

1859—Elected governor of Texas.

1863—Died, Huntsville, Texas.

Brigham Young

[1801-1877]

DOWN in the American backwoods, about a hundred and fifty years ago, there arose a tribe of minor prophets—*jerkers, groaners, revivalists.* And hordes of farming folk with the old Adam in them suddenly "got religion," kneeling at night by the moaning trees and following their leaders who had gone a-pioneering into the secrets of God. They found that they could handle a Bible as easily as a gun. They got baptized for their sins, built churches, stopped playing poker, and started adventuring over the countryside to "nudge their neighbors into the ways of the Lord."

One of the farmer lads who listened to these prophets was Brigham Young. An unvarnished soul, this Brigham—a Huckleberry Finn sort of fellow who believed that the age of miracles hadn't as yet departed, in spite of what the more sophisticated folk were saying. Out here in the woods of western New York it was miracle enough that folk lived and scraped together enough food and turned the wilderness into homesteads and the homesteads into cities. To the pioneer there's no miracle too miraculous to come true.

Brigham had been to school only eleven days in his life. He was too busy chopping the trees and plowing the fields. A life full of toil and hunger—and contentment. "If I had on a pair of pants that covered me, I thought I was doing pretty well." And when his legs grew longer and there was more of him to cover, he set to work the harder. He took up house painting and carpentry. And then, finding that he needed help, he married. For a wife is good at sewing scrap ends into coverings, and baking bread, and making beds. At harvest time he gathered the crops for the farmers at seventy-five cents a day. And all this time he was waiting for the miracle. Searching for the gold mine of the spirit that would make him rich.

Huckleberry Young has an angel within him. That's what makes the story epic. This young Brigham, who spits and swears with the rest of them, is looking for religion. A new kind of religion, and not a new label for an old creed. He is hungry for a personal revelation from God. He wants to find out what all this drudgery is for—this being born into a rough, unmannered body, leading the life of a lout in the semiwilderness that is furrowed with so many untimely graves. What is all this building and suffering and dreaming for? *Why* is the American pioneer? Isn't it time to receive a new word from God for His frontier people of Israel? How much farther must they drive their sweating caravans before they can reach the Promised Land?

Such were the crude questionings that went on in Huckleberry Young's mind. When he spoke of the matter years later, the words sounded somewhat more polished: "I felt . . . that if I could see the face of a prophet, such as had lived on the earth in former times, a man who had revelations, to whom the heavens were opened, who knew God and His character, I would freely circumscribe the earth on my hands and knees; I thought that there was no hardship but what I would undergo, if I could see one person that knew what God is and where He is, and what His character, and what eternity was . . ." Others cared only for whisky. But Brigham Young wanted a deep, long, cooling draught of eternity. And then he stumbled upon a fellow who knew how to prepare the drink. Not one of those sellers of nostrums, but a real prophet. An uncouth rough diamond of a Yankee from New England who had just founded a religion. He called it *Mormonism*—from the English word *more,* and the Egyptian word *mon,* which means *good.* He had a Bible, a revelation, a prophecy. He declared that he was the latest appointee of God. Brigham looked into the matter, read the *Book of Mormon,* and forever gave up chopping wood at eighteen cents a cord.

II

Brigham young had just turned thirty when he was baptized into the Church of the Latter-Day Saints, as the Mormons called themselves. Immediately he set out on a missionary journey over the eastern states. In all sorts of weather he knocked at the doors of the farmers; and as he dried his feet by their fireplaces and took their coffee, he told them the story of Joseph Smith, the modern prophet. Joseph was only an obscure lad of eighteen when the angel Moroni had descended from heaven to his bedside with a message from God. The angel informed him that in the fourth century the Lost Tribe of Israel had migrated to America, where they had prepared the Bible of a new religion for the Americans of the nineteenth century. This Bible—said the angel—was inscribed in Egyptian characters on plates of gold. And now the Lord God commanded Joseph Smith, as the prophet of the new religion, to unearth the Bible from its burial place on Cumorah Hill in Manchester, New York, and to translate it into English for the guidance of his own generation. To Cumorah Hill he went, and there—he declared—he found the Bible exactly as described in the vision. Together with the Bible, he said, he had also found a pair of "spiritual spectacles," Urim and Thummim; and when he put them on he automatically was able to translate the Egyptian hieroglyphics into English sentences. When the translation was completed, eight men testified that they had seen the gold plates in the original and that these plates had come truly from God. The Bible gained many converts who declared themselves the successors to the Lost Tribe—the Mormon tribe of the Latter-Day Saints.

Amazing how rapidly the movement grows. First the members of a family take the baptism. Then they baptize their immediate friends. And finally these friends go scurrying through the hinterlands with the *Book of Mormon* to convert more friends. The story of the magic spectacles does not stretch the credulity of these poor illiterates of the wilderness. There is scarcely a person among them who has not "seen God" and felt the wings of His angels brushing past his face. These Americans of the backwoods needed some emotional stimulant for their lives or they couldn't go on. And for these uncritical folk of the 1830s what was emotionally pleasant was literally true. "I knew this religion was true," declared Brigham Young, "as well as I knew that I could see with my eyes, or feel by the touch of my fingers, or be sensible of the demonstration of any sense."

He comes like a salesman with the book in his hand. He gets many free meals and lodgings and blessings—and discomforts. "I stayed overnight with Brother Atkinson, who lived in a very large frame house, said to have stood 150 years, which was so infested with bedbugs that we could not sleep. Brother George A. Smith gave it as his legal opinion that there were bedbugs there which had danced to the music at the battle of Trenton, as their heads were perfectly gray."

And thus a new religion sprang up in the American frontier. Joseph Smith, the prophet of this new religion, surrounded himself with a group of followers, and chose twelve apostles, of whom the leader was Brigham Young.

Inspired by their vision of a fuller, freer life, the apostles and their followers established their headquarters at Kirtland, Ohio. But here a charge of embezzlement was trumped up against Joseph Smith and Brigham Young. Together the prophet and his disciple escaped, not unlike Mohammed and Abu-Bekr, and made their way through the enemy lines to safety.

They organized a Mormon settlement in Missouri. For a time the people of the neighboring counties tolerated them and their peculiar ideas. But how can a new church grow except through persecution? Martyrdom is as indigenous to the climate of a new religion as the east wind is to New England. It wasn't long before the Missouri mobs attacked and stoned the Mormons and demanded that the legislature drive them out of the state.

And what was their crime? They refused to own slaves at a time when the entire South was inflamed with hatred against the abolitionists. Furthermore, "these people work too hard." They took no time off for loafing or pleasure. The result was that they became more prosperous than their neighbors. But most important of all was the instinctive aversion of old people to new ideas. "The religious tenets of the Mormons are so different from the present churches of the age, that they always have excited, and always will excite, deep prejudices against them, in any populous country where they may locate themselves . . ."

But the Mormons were not a bloodless people nursed on milk toast. They refused to leave their women and their children to the mercy of the mobs. They organized a secret band of "killers"—the Destroying Angels —who took an eye for an eye, a life for a life. Joseph Smith was arrested by the Missouri militia, and the following exchange of letters took place:

BRIGADIER-GENERAL DONIPHAN:

SIR—*You will take Joseph Smith and the other prisoners into the public square . . . and shoot them at 9 o'clock tomorrow morning.*
SAMUEL D. LUCAS, *Major-General Commanding.*

And the reply:

It is cold-blooded murder. I will not obey your order. My brigade will march for Liberty tomorrow morning at 8 o'clock; and if you execute these men, I will hold you responsible before an early tribunal, so help me God.
A. W. DONIPHAN, *Brigadier-General.*

Nevertheless the governor of Missouri issued an order that the "Mormons must leave Missouri in a body or be exterminated, unless they are willing to renounce their religion and live as other Missourians."

And Brigham Young, who had become the leader of his people after the imprisonment of Smith, answered for all his band. "Renounce our religion? No, sir, it is all that we have on this earth . . ."

There was nothing to do but to leave. And Brigham led his people out of their house of bondage. The exodus was attended with much misery. To Illinois trekked three thousand Mormons. And here they were joined by Joseph Smith, who had escaped from jail. They settled upon the east bank of the Mississippi and secured an entire township for the asking— "since this land is unhealthy, a fit place for an unwelcome tribe." They changed the name of the settlement from Commerce to Nauvoo, which in the secret language of the Mormons meant The City Beautiful.

III

ONCE AGAIN the Mormons prospered. "The Lord has showered manna upon our tribe." But the sons and the daughters of Modern Israel were still in exile. Nauvoo was still within the borders of Egypt and not in the Promised Land. Again the Pharaohs began to persecute them. For the Latter-Day Saints had established a custom which was most objectionable to their neighbors. They had begun to practice "plural marriages." Joseph

Smith had "received a momentous commandment from the Lord" to return to the days of Abraham and Isaac and Jacob and to take many wives
in order that they might beget many children. The Lord had revealed to
him, he maintained, that the soul of every human being exists not only
after death but before birth. Every soul must go through life in a human
body in order to be promoted to a higher stage of development after
death. There are millions of souls in heaven waiting to be born, pleading
for the men and the women below to provide them with a tabernacle of
flesh "in order that they may enter upon the final step in their journey to
the divine." And who—asked Joseph Smith—can deny them this right?
"It is the religious duty of every pious Mormon to bring to birth as many
of these souls, through the medium of as many wives, as possible."

When Brigham Young learned that he must enter upon a life "revolting
to his natural inclinations" or else "treat lightly of the things of God," he
decided to do his "divine duty." While he remained at Nauvoo he married eight women. Before he died he had taken twenty-seven wives and
had become the father of fifty-six children.

Yet he was not a lascivious man. On the contrary, he was unusually temperate in his appetites and methodical in his habits. In spite of the witticisms of the facetious, Brigham Young was able to prove in the United
States courts that polygamy with him was a religious commandment
rather than a licentious whim. He testified that he was personally opposed
to polygamy and that he had decided to enter upon it only after a long
and bitter struggle with his own conscience. And the impartial judges
who heard his testimony believed him.

But the public felt differently about the matter. When the news spread
that a "City of Venus" had been founded in the state of Illinois, an avalanche of invective descended upon the Mormons. A crusade was launched
to fight fire with fire, to meet the "immorality of polygamy" with the
equally outrageous immorality of persecution. And the flames of the
public hatred were fanned into greater fury when Joseph Smith announced himself as one of the candidates for the presidency of the United
States (in 1844).

And then the blow fell. Brigham Young was at the time campaigning
for his prophet in the New England states. One day, as he sat waiting for
a train in the Boston railway depot, the news reached him that his candidate was no more. The Illinois authorities had taken Joseph Smith into
custody—and then a mob had broken into the jail and shot him to death.

Brigham Young, as the chief of the twelve apostles, immediately returned to Nauvoo and claimed the leadership of the Mormon Church. A
few dissenters broke away from the community to organize churches of
their own. But the main body of the Mormons remained intact under the
new leader, who proceeded to prove that "when the half-gods go, the gods
arrive." The assassins of Joseph Smith had taken a man with very human
failings, had bestowed upon him the gift of martyrdom, and thereby had
raised him to the rank of an immortal legend. On the day on which Joseph
Smith was murdered, the Mormon religion did not die; it entered upon a
new life of irresistible adventure.

And the Moses of this new adventure was Brigham Young. He called his folk together and told them that they were ordered out of Illinois into the wilderness beyond. It was a bleak February morning in 1846 when the vanguard of the Mormon exiles crossed the Mississippi and began their final long pilgrimage. It was like the march of a conquering army rather than the flight of a dispossessed and poverty-stricken sect. Brigham had taken along a brass band so that his people might dance away the cold of the wilderness nights, and sing songs in their sickness, and play an entrance march into heaven for the multitudes of their loved ones who had dropped on the way. The March of the Twenty Thousand. An epic in sweat and prairie storms and desert suns. A mass migration blazing a trail through two fifths of the western United States—a pioneering feat for historians to marvel at. But they were not doing historians' work. They were doing God's work.

"You might see women sit in the open tents keeping the flies off their dead children, sometimes after decomposition had set in." You might see endless miles of prairies until your eyes watered, endless miles of monotony broken only here and there by cottonwood trees and a few marked graves of men who had set out before them and had only half finished their adventure. You might see Brigham Young moving everywhere about his party, helping the old women and the young wives as they poured their coffee for their menfolk, taking the driver's seat when a man grew sick and weary, huddling on sentinel duty by the shivering fires, planning every last detail of the heartening, heartbreaking voyage.

His organizing ability had brought order out of chaos. He had introduced a regular routine for eating, sleeping, playing, and marching; and everybody in the company was obliged to follow this routine to the minutest detail. Every morning, at five o'clock, the bugle gave the signal for rising. By seven o'clock breakfast had been eaten, the dishes had been scoured, and the caravan was on the march. At twelve o'clock, they stopped to eat and to rest, and two hours later they were again on the march. At six o'clock they settled down for the night, and within a few minutes the desert blossomed into a city. At eight the bugle announced that the hour for relaxation had arrived. It was an hour of band playing and singing and—for those who had the energy after the day's march— social dancing. At nine o'clock they went to sleep.

This routine was broken only on Sunday, when the entire camp rested and gathered physical and moral strength for the next week's march.

Such was the invariable procedure throughout the spring and the summer and the fall months. And then, when the snows came, Brigham set up the main body of his people in winter quarters and took along a select handful of stalwarts to seek for the final settlement in the Far West. Where would this settlement be? He studied maps and heard reports. An old scout, Jim Bridger, told him about the valley of the Great Salt Lake. Here was virgin country. It contained no settlements of people to drive the Mormons out as soon as they had made the land prosperous; no judges and juries to incite the mob against them in the name of civilization.

As the party approached the Great Salt Lake, Brigham Young took sick with mountain fever. This new Moses, like his ancient prototype, seemed destined to die before the very portals of the Promised Land. But he lived! In the heat of July, seventeen months after he had led his people across the Mississippi, he rode into the Blessed Valley. He lay convalescing from his long illness as his team and horses drove him through the cañon into the Land of the Heart's Desire. He looked, and he held his breath in adoration. Behind him, in the distance, a backdrop of snow-whipped mountains as glittering as the Alps; and beyond him, the blue stretches of the Salt Lake that sparkled with the magic of Italy.

But the level land of the valley before him looked arid and stony and severe. God's children would have to work very hard to provision this temple of beauty. Yet in spite of all the salt and the drought, the seeds would be sown. And Brigham Young raised himself from his bed with fire in his eye. "Here we can raise our own potatoes and eat them; and I calculate to stay here . . . The desert shall rejoice and blossom as the rose."

IV

IN UTAH the Mormons passed through the usual diseases that attack an infant colony—plagues of locusts that ate away their crops, winds that froze their bodies, quarrels that paralyzed their efforts. But slowly the settlement grew into vigorous maturity under the care of "Doctor" Brigham Young. For he knew how to treat men's bodies and minds and souls. He might have been a novelist or an actor if he had not been destined to be a statesman; for he felt keenly, as only the greatest artists have felt, the inner springs of human psychology. And his people followed him implicitly in his adventure of mutual understanding. For Brigham Young was not only their teacher but their prophet.

He was not a poet-prophet; he was a prose-prophet. His was a mind encircled in homilies, not in halos. He had no sublime imaginings. His fancy lay in the roughness of his hands; it was limited entirely to what those two hands might achieve. He scorned all theory. He simply could not conceive of his being obliged "to philosophize for ten years without erecting a building or founding a city." He took pride in the fact that his mind "was uncorrupted by books." And he spoke the gospel of the pioneer who had never had the time to realize the expediency of ideas as the material for building. "Education will not enable a youth to marry and to set up housekeeping in the Rocky Mountains."

A prosaic prophet for a prosaic race. Strong, eager, simple folk came from many dark corners of the world to set up housekeeping in Utah. The *Book of Mormon* had crossed the ocean to the farming settlements of Denmark and the mining districts of Britain. And Old World blood came flowing to mingle with the new. Forty-niners stopped at Utah on their way to the gold fields of California, forgot about the gold and became converted to the Mormon faith. Wheelwrights and carpenters, butchers and builders and woodcutters and sawyers and smiths—all sorts of men of brawny muscle and sturdy faith came to set up their adobe huts and to hew out new streets in Utah. Most of the immigrants were poor folk. For Brigham Young had nothing to offer to the rich. And most of them were *illiterate* folk. For Brigham Young had nothing to offer to the learned. "We take the poorest we can find on earth . . . We are trying to make ladies and gentlemen of them. We are trying to school their children, and to so train them that they may be able to gather around them the comforts of life, that they may pass their lives as the human family should do—that their days, weeks, and months may be pleasant to them."

Brigham took care that his desert settlement would not become a dead cemetery of reposeful faith watered by prayers and tears. He told his people that they must not pray to God to perform miracles for them, but to build and to act and to plan with their own good limbs and brains. "I do not feel disposed to ask the Lord to do for me what I can do for myself," he said.

As a result the Mormons trusted in God but kept their hands busy, traded shrewdly but honestly with the pioneers who were streaming toward the West, developed warehouses and banks and factories and printing presses and schools. They had no trouble with the Indians, for they dealt with them on the principle that it was cheaper to feed them than to fight them. They undertook—and completed—the first large-scale irrigation project in the country. They established co-operative enterprises. They gave the franchise to women. They denounced slavery. They contributed money toward the building of a Catholic church and a Jewish synagogue. And they instituted the tithing system—that is, the appropriation of one tenth of every man's earnings for the maintenance of the poor. The Mormon Church, in other words, was interested in the temporal as well as in the eternal welfare of its members. We may scoff at Joseph Smith's "discovery" of the Golden Book. But we cannot scoff at Brigham Young's application of the Golden Rule. The principle of Brigham Young, and of Mormonism at its best, may be summarized in a few words: *Try to serve your neighbor's need rather than your own greed.* "I have made no man poor," remarked Brigham Young proudly, "but I have made thousands rich."

And thus, adhering to the principle of tolerant interdependence, the Mormons dug out and scaffolded and gilded a prosperous city. Word spread throughout the vision-teeming United States, athrill with the stories of Paul Bunyan, that a new prodigious miracle of the American heart and muscle had been accomplished in Utah. Brigham Young had sown the teeth of Cadmus anew, and a race of giants was born in the American desert.

Finally Utah was admitted into the Union as one of the states. The theocracy of Brigham Young was merged with the democracy of America. But not before the federal government had compelled the Latter-Day Saints to give up their practice of polygamy.

And now, when this new chapter in the epic of Mormonism had begun, Brigham Young was no longer leader of his people. He had gone to his rest—with the serene confidence of a man who looks forward to a cool, refreshing rainfall in the desert. "I have done my work faithfully," he said. "Let me have a good sleep until the morning of the resurrection."

IMPORTANT DATES IN THE LIFE OF BRIGHAM YOUNG

1801—Born, Whittingham, Vermont.

1829—Moved to Mendon, New York.

1832—Joined Mormon Church, April 14.

1835—Appointed apostle of Mormon Church.
Led persecuted members of church to Illinois.

1844—At death of Joseph Smith, became head of church.

1846—Organized famous Exodus of Mormons from Illinois.

1847—Arrived in valley of Great Salt Lake.

1850—Appointed (by President Fillmore) governor of Territory of Utah.

1854—Reappointed governor.

1877—Died, Salt Lake City, August 29.

Ralph Waldo Emerson

[1803-1882]

O N JULY 15, 1838, Ralph Waldo Emerson delivered an address before the senior class of the Harvard Divinity School. In this address he pointed out "the simplicity and energy of the Highest Law—the oneness of mankind." He proclaimed the doctrine of individual liberty and universal tolerance—the New World principle of mutual collaboration between free men as against the Old World formula of mutual distrust between enslaved individuals and nations. He placed the ethical code of humanity upon a practical American basis—*to live, let live, and help live*.

This address marked the moral Declaration of Independence for the United States. "From now on," observed a member of the audience, "our young men will have a Fifth Gospel in their Testaments—the *American* Gospel."

What sort of man was this New England Isaiah who paraphrased the Bible into the Yankee dialect?

II

HE CAME of a pioneer stock—poor but self-reliant, unconquerable, free. "My American forebears"—Thomas Emerson had come to Concord in 1635—"had hard labor and spare diet, and off wooden trenchers, but they had peace and freedom. . . . The light struggled in through windows of oiled paper, but they read the word of God by it." One of his ancestors had prayed every evening that none of his descendants might ever be rich. His prayer was answered. The Emersons were born "not to be rich but to be educated." William Emerson, Waldo's father, was a clergyman—"the most liberal preacher who had yet appeared in Boston." But "those who supply the bread of life are often repaid with stones." He

died, like most of the Emerson tribe, a poor man. He left five children, all
boys, of whom Waldo was the second. At the time of his father's death
(1811) Waldo was eight years old.

His mother opened a boardinghouse in order to support the family.
From the very beginning, therefore, Waldo learned to know and to like
people. And he also learned to be cheerful in the face of poverty. In the
winter he and his older brother William had but a single overcoat between them, so that one of them was always compelled to stay indoors
when the other was out.

Waldo missed his play, but he made the best of his winter evenings—
listening to the conversation of the boarders and feasting voraciously
upon the books in his mother's library. In bed, covered to the chin with
his woolen blankets, he followed Plato in the breathless adventures of his
Dialogues; and during the Sunday sermon at church he dipped into the
Thoughts of Pascal, a copy of which he always carried in his pocket.

And thus his growing mind was nurtured upon Yankee common sense
and metaphysical philosophy—not a bad combination, thought his mother,
for a future minister of the Gospel. For that was the career—the Emerson
career—to which she was trying to dedicate him. In 1817 she sent him to
Harvard, where he added Shakespeare and Spinoza and Montaigne to the
intimate circle of his "beloved masters." Scholastically, however, his college career was undistinguished. He was appointed class poet only after
seven others had declined the honor. But he was barely eighteen at the
time of his graduation—tall and thin as a lamppost and with a lamplike
glow in his large and gentle eyes. He had fallen a prey to "the Emerson
plague"—consumption—which had destroyed his father and was soon to
carry off two of his brothers. For twelve years he lived "in the House of
Pain," fought desperately against death, and strove to find a financial as
well as a physical foothold on life. He tried teaching among the hills in
Roxbury, "where man in the bush with God may meet." He wrote poetry
that was a poor substitute for prose, and prose that was the very essence
of poetry—and failed to sell enough of either to make a living. He was
invited to "preach on trial" at various churches, where he was unable to
reap the harvest of a job but succeeded in planting many a seed of joy.
"O Sally!" wrote a woman in Northampton to her sister after she had
heard one of Emerson's "trial" sermons. "We thought to entertain 'a pious
indigent,' but lo! an angel unawares!"

Finally, however, a few of the New Englanders became aware of the
"angel in their midst." On March 11, 1829, Emerson was ordained minister of the Second (Unitarian) Church in Boston. He had a most remarkable voice, a soft and golden instrument that melted away the frosts of
New England Calvinism like an April sun.

But he preached a doctrine which was unpalatable to the reactionary
mind. He advocated a practical application of the Sermon on the Mount
rather than a conventional adherence to the ceremonials of the church.
Indeed, he definitely objected to some of these ceremonials—especially
the one dealing with the sacrament of the Lord's Supper. "The kingdom
of God," he said, "is not meat and drink but righteousness and peace."

The deacons of the church, while expressing their "undiminished regard for our pastor," nevertheless insisted upon the continuance of "the customary administration of the Supper." Whereupon Emerson resigned from his pastorate. His interpretation of religion, he explained, was too unorthodox for the rigid formulas of the established church. "Christianity, as I see it, has for its object simply to make men good and wise. Its institutions, then, should be as flexible as the wants of men."

In severing himself from his church, Emerson attacked no institution and no man. He merely observed that since he was unable to see eye to eye with his congregation it would be best for them to get another pastor. Thus, by a single simple act, he banished from his soul the idols of an ancient—and to him outmoded—tradition. But, as Oliver Wendell Holmes remarked, "here was an iconoclast without a hammer, who took down his idols from their pedestals so tenderly that it seemed like an act of worship."

Yet to many of the reactionaries his iconoclasm was anything but tender. Indeed, they maintained that he had enthroned the Devil in the place of God. He would be punished for his sins. "We are sorry for Mr. Emerson, but it certainly looks as if he is going to hell." "It does indeed look so," replied one of his friends. "But I am sure of one thing—if Emerson goes to hell, he will so change its climate that it will become a popular resort for all the good souls of heaven."

III

WHEN EMERSON left his pulpit he went out to search for the meaning of life. He took long walks in the country. He tried to attune his ear and his heart to the music of Nature. And before long he made a strange discovery. He learned that the heart of Nature was beating in unison with his own heart. He was an intimate part of a living world. His mind was an important cell in the world mind—or, as he called it, the World Soul or Oversoul. And this abstract discovery led him to a practical observation. He noticed, when he reflected upon the intimate relationship between himself and the rest of the world, that his whole being was electrified with a surge of power, an overmastering confidence in himself and in his fellow men. This power was infinite. He could draw upon it at will. *And he could teach others to draw upon this same power within themselves.* Each of us, he concluded, possesses the spiritual capital for developing an enormous business—the business of acquiring and exchanging beauty and joyousness and freedom and friendship and peace.

It was a doctrine admirably suited to the temperament and the genius of America. We are forever, he said, "on the verge of all that is great." Trust in yourself. Claim your share of the greatness of life. Assert your relationship to the divine. Surrender yourself to the power within you— not the power to enslave but the power to liberate, to help. Dare to become the master of your own fate and teach all and sundry to dare likewise.

And thus Emerson became a teacher of man, the immortal pupil—"a professor," to use his own expression, "of the Science of Joy."

His own life, however, was not a life of unmixed joy. He had fallen in love and married and lost his wife—all within eighteen months. For two years after her death he paid a daily visit to her grave. He himself expected to follow her shortly, for his painful cough was "like a sexton singing a funeral dirge" in his chest.

But Emerson was the philosopher of life. He refused to die. He took a trip to Europe in order to sit at the feet of the masters of the Old World. One evening he came to see Carlyle. The "hermit of Craigenputtock" gave his young American visitor a pipe and took one himself. In perfect silence —so the story goes—the two puffed away at their pipes until bedtime, when they shook hands and congratulated each other on the fruitful evening they had spent together. On his subsequent visits, however, when he had become more familiar with the philosophy of Carlyle, Emerson found him somewhat disappointing. Carlyle's eyes were fixed too intently upon the dead glory of the Old World and were insufficiently open to the living beauty of the New World. "Carlyle is too provincial and speaks not out of the celestial region." He was so eager to praise the *great* men, thought Emerson, that he failed to appraise the greatness of the *common* man.

Emerson found the same fault with many of the other celebrities of Europe. For these men were still encumbered with political beliefs and ethical dogmas which Emerson had long outgrown. "For a thousand years these poor men [of Europe] have sat before the gates of Paradise to catch a glimpse of the beauty within. And now that the gates have been opened, these men have fallen asleep."

Disappointed with his European trip, Emerson returned home. Europe had little to say to him, but he had much to say to America. He found a new kind of schoolroom, the village lyceum. Here, liberated from the shackles of conventional creeds, he expressed his independent thoughts on mice and men and angels and gods. The intellectual Brahmins of Boston and Cambridge didn't like his ideas. For he was too irreverent toward the old traditions and professions. Once they hooted him off the platform at Harvard College. But the common people, the men and the women with the homespun thoughts, understood his simple teaching even though they couldn't always follow his elegant phrases. For the lesson that he brought home to them was but an echo of the ambitions and the hopes that were stirring vaguely within their own minds. "We are simple folk here," said a Lexington woman after one of his lectures, "and we understand Mr. Emerson because he speaks directly to our hearts."

His lectures were, for those days, fairly remunerative. They brought him about eight hundred dollars a year. To this he was able to add an annual income of twelve hundred dollars, a legacy which he had inherited from his wife. He felt himself a rich man. He bought a "mansion" in Concord for thirty-five hundred dollars, married a second time, and settled down to cultivate the flowers in his garden and the friendship of his neighbors.

And his friends were among the richest personalities in the world. For some mysterious reason which the scientists have not as yet been able to explain, the gods occasionally select a single spot on earth and people it with the citizens of heaven. This happened in the Athens of the fifth century (B.C.), with its Aeschylus and Euripides and Phidias and Socrates and Plato; in the London of the Elizabethan period, with its Beaumont and Drayton and Fletcher and Jonson and Shakespeare; in the Germany of the early nineteenth century, with its Goethe and Schiller and Heine and Mozart and Schubert and Beethoven; and in the Russia of the latter part of the nineteenth century, with its Turgenev and Tchaikovsky and Chekhov and Dostoyevsky and Tolstoy. In a lesser sense the Concord of Emerson was the scene of another of those periodic flowerings of the divine mind on human soil. Among the intimates of Emerson were Nathaniel Hawthorne, the man who immortalized the struggle between the Puritan love of religion and the pagan religion of love; Margaret Fuller, a female Merlin whose eyes were "visible at night" and who could play with ideas as a juggler plays with colored balls; Bronson Alcott, the peddler-prophet whose personality was a combination of the wisdom of Plato and the wholesomeness of St. Francis; Henry Thoreau, the saintly vagabond whose capital was about twenty-five dollars a year and an infinity of love; Sarah Ripley, a Greek goddess in a Yankee wrapper, who washed the family clothes and scrubbed the floors and translated Klopstock and taught Homer and Virgil and Aristotle in her husband's school; and "Aunt Mary" Emerson, a living flame of four feet and three inches, who galloped over the fields of Concord dressed in her shroud and a scarlet shawl and whose wit could tear into shreds the conventions and pretensions of the day.

With these friends and many others, in Boston and in Cambridge as well as in Concord, Emerson exchanged ideas; and then he went into his study and transformed these ideas into the minted gold of his essays and lectures. He traveled over New England, into the South, and across the continent to California. He delivered talks to all sorts of people—sailors and blacksmiths and poets and teachers and farmers and shoemakers and politicians and pioneers. He took another trip to England—this time to bring the idea of Democracy, the message of the New World, to the inhabitants of the Old. Everywhere they listened in amazement to this New England apostle, "straight and thin as a birch tree in winter," whose keen strong face was like a block of granite chiseled out of Mount Monadnock and whose optimism was grounded upon a firm foundation of American faith. Faith in the justice of the American idea and in the heroism of the average American man.

IV

EMERSON had no cut-and-dried system of philosophy. There was no dogmatic consistency to his thought. And purposely so. "A foolish consistency," he observed, "is the hobgoblin of little minds." He did not pretend to know the truth. The truth, he said, is as hard to capture and bottle up as light. All that he tried to do was to pick out, here and there, a stray thread which to him seemed to be part of an intricately woven yet definite design of a benevolent Providence. These threads may be briefly pieced together into the following pattern:

All men are vital parts of one organism—mankind. This philosophy, to distinguish it from pantheism, may be called panhumanism. In "The American Scholar" Emerson repeats "one of those fables which out of an unknown antiquity convey an unlooked-for wisdom—that the gods, in the beginning, divided Man into men, that he might be more helpful to himself; just as the hand was divided into fingers, the better to answer its end." But unfortunately, continues Emerson, the individual units which compose this united human organism have allowed themselves to be "peddled out," to be "spilled into drops," so that our present-day society is one in which "the members have suffered amputation from the trunk and strut about so many walking monsters—a good finger, a neck, a stomach, an elbow, but never a man."

It is our business, therefore, to reaffirm the "oneness of mankind." Indeed, we must not only reaffirm this fact but we must actively dedicate ourselves to it. American philosophy is a philosophy of action. "Good thoughts are no better than good dreams, unless they are executed." The prophets of the East had preached the passive doctrine that God is One. But now came the prophet of the West with the added active doctrine that Man, too, is One. Man is one, declares Emerson, because his soul is "part and parcel of God. . . . Let us stun and astonish the intruding rabble of men and books and institutions by a simple declaration of [this] fact. Bid the invaders take the shoes from off their feet"; for every man, every human part of that divine entity known as mankind, is a god in the making.

Emerson applied the term *transcendentalism* to this idea of the oneness of man through relationship with God. It is an unfortunate term, for it obscures a simple idea with a difficult name. Many of Emerson's contemporaries sneered at this exotic name and failed to understand that it encompassed a vital American thought. One of Emerson's critics, Dr. Burnap of Baltimore, characterized transcendentalism as "the new philosophy which maintains that nothing is everything in general and everything is nothing in particular"—a definition which is as false as it is facetious. For, properly understood, the philosophy of Emerson is but the ethical foundation for the political doctrine of American Democracy.

And this brings us to the second point in Emerson's philosophy—his insistence upon the dignity of the common man. "In all my lectures I have taught one doctrine, namely, the infinitude of the private man." With the annunciation of this principle Emerson turned his back completely upon the European institutions with their superficial nobilities and their artificial class distinctions. Come out of the cemeteries of the past! Look forward into the woodlands of the future! "The eyes of man are set in his forehead, not in his hindhead." We have outlived the despotic traditions of the old. "There are new lands, new men, new thoughts." Let us stop imitating our brothers of the Old World. For "what is imitation but the [backward] traveling of the mind? Our houses are built with foreign taste; our shelves are garnished with foreign ornaments; our opinions, our tastes, our faculties lean and follow the Past and the Distant." Stop being followers and leaners; become founders and leaders. "Build your own world." Build your own life. "The private life of one man" can be made "more illustrious than any kingdom in history."

And it is the business of the American thinkers, the American scholars, to teach their fellow citizens how to build. "Let each one of us begin at home." Here in Concord, observed Emerson, there are no manufacturing industries. "Well, then, let us manufacture schoolteachers and make them the best in the world." *American* teachers—teachers of the American Way.

But what is the American Way? The recognition of the importance of each in the summation of the whole. Size doesn't matter; neither does pomposity nor blatancy nor fame matter. The gods descend upon the earth in lowly disguises. In the folklore of many nations the most powerful creatures are the smallest. Let each man attend to his own work, and let every man respect the work of his fellows. What, the blacksmith is unable to write a poem? Well, but the poet is unable to hammer out a horseshoe. "If I cannot carry forests on my back," declares the squirrel to the mountain, "neither can you crack a nut."

Emerson's philosophy pointed out the nobility of the commonplace. "Know, whoever you are, that the world exists for you." In each and every man "there is an angel in disguise who plays the fool." It was to these "angels in disguise" that Emerson spoke when he addressed his audiences, exhorting them to cast off their foolish outer garments of servitude and sycophancy and humiliation and prejudice and hate and to stand forth in all their divine splendor as free men. He told them to liberate themselves from the European philosophy of resignation and to accept the American Gospel of aspiration. He urged every man to assert himself—not his isolated self but his *inclusive* self. Strengthen your heart with the knowledge of this inclusive self, this social individualism which is yours by right of birth, and you have mastered the secret of all power. "All that Adam had, all that Caesar could, you have and can do." Unshackle your mind from its chains and learn to know yourself for the man that you are destined to become. "There are no bounds to the possibilities of man."

Emerson's was the voice which, as he remarked in a letter to a friend, he had sought in vain among other philosophers—"that profound voice which might speak to the American heart, cheering timid good men, animating the youth, consoling the defeated and intelligently announcing duties which clothe life with joy and endear the land and sea to men." America, he said, needs a new kind of virtue—virtue "with guts in it." Pride in our work and justice for our workers. For the workers are the channels through which aspiration flows into creation. This is to be a country of great deeds and of great ideas. Free, dynamic, and daring ideas. America "shall be the asylum and patron of every new thought, every unproven opinion, every untried project which proceeds out of good will and honest seeking."

America is to be the Great Experiment. It is to be dominated by the strong courageous will of the pioneers and guided by the wise and gentle counsel of the scholars. And the goal of the Experiment? Complete Democracy, social, political, economic. A future hope, founded upon past mistakes. Keep on trying and blundering and failing—and trying again. Do not despair. In spite of your failures, in spite of your sufferings, in spite of your discouragements, keep "antagonizing on." The race is not to the swift but to the resolute. Have you been pushed aside? Have you stumbled? Never mind the ridicule, never mind the defeat. Up again, old heart! "Be of good cheer. . . . Patience and patience, we shall win at last."

Be of good cheer! "This world belongs to the cheerful, the energetic, the daring." Dare to assert yourself as an accredited citizen in the great Republic of Mankind. Your birth into this world has been no mistake. You are an invited guest to the banquet of life. And He who has sent you the invitation is no niggardly host. Divine generosity is hidden somewhere behind the mystery of creation. "There is intelligence and good will at the heart of things."

And—here Emerson stresses again the idea which dominates his entire thought—this divine intelligence has created individual men as the vital component parts of a united mankind. One for all, all for one. "The heart in thee is the heart of all. Not a valve, not a wall, not an intersection is there anywhere in nature, but one blood rolls uninterruptedly an endless circulation through all men, as the water of the globe is all one sea, and, truly seen, its tide is one."

Again and again Emerson appeals to this one tide of humanity which flows in the hearts of all living men. Indeed, Emerson may be said to have written the final clause to the American Declaration of Independence. For his brave and gentle philosophy represents the Universal Declaration of *Interdependence.*

This philosophy of interdependence receives perhaps its highest utterance in Emerson's essay on *Friendship.* The beauty of friendship lies in the recognition of the ultimate relationship that exists between man and man. "The essence of friendship is entireness," the intuitive knowledge that you and I are an undivided unit. When we are in the presence of our friends "let us be silent—so that we may hear the whisper of the gods." And in the music of that whisper we can feel "the flowing of two souls into one." Wherever two friends engage in conversation there is a third party present—God. "Shall I not call God the Beautiful, who daily showeth Himself to me in His gift of friendship?" When I encounter my friends "it is not I but the Deity in me and in them" which "derides and cancels the thick walls of individual character . . . and now makes many one."

The life of man is a quest for friendship, a striving for the class reunion of the human soul. But true friendship is not merely a passion but it is also an action of the soul. It is a divine game of give and take. "The only way to have a friend is to be one." We must learn to "grasp heroic hands in heroic hands." This active and heroic conception of friendship is to Emerson the one solid thing in a world of shadows. It is a substance of such reality and duration that compared to it "the Alps and the Andes come and go as rainbows."

Cultivate the art of friendship and you come close to the heart of reality. You stop looking at the rainbows and you begin to see the true source of light. "If man could be inspired with a tender kindness to the souls of men and should come to feel that every man was another self . . . this feeling would cause the most striking changes of external things: the tents would be struck; the cannon would become street posts; the pikes, a fisher's harpoon; the aggressors would be disenthroned; and the marching regiment would be a caravan of emigrants, peaceful pioneers."

Peaceful pioneers. This was the philosophical dream of Emerson—a warless world of courageous, independent, joyous, loving, and adventuring friends.

V

HAWTHORNE gives us a gracious picture of the serene and friendly sage of Concord as he met him on his daily walks. "It was good to encounter him in the wood paths, or sometimes in our avenue, with that pure intellectual gleam diffused about his presence like the garment of a shining one; and he, so quiet, so simple, so without pretensions, encountering each man alive as if expecting to receive more than he could impart. But it was impossible to dwell in his vicinity without inhaling the mountain atmosphere of his lofty thoughts."

There was in his make-up no hatred, no rancor, no disdain, only an infinite forgiveness and love. When he lost his son Waldo, a Unitarian preacher attributed the loss to Emerson's "lack of faith." Emerson merely replied: "Neither my friend nor I can understand the ways of life and faith and death." Once, when he had concluded a lecture at Middlebury College, the presiding minister offered up a prayer as an antidote. "We beseech Thee, O Lord, to deliver us from ever hearing any more such transcendental nonsense as we have just listened to from this sacred desk." Asked to comment on this public insult, Emerson remarked: "The minister seems a very conscientious, plain-spoken gentleman."

He failed to get excited at the foolishness of men. One day a "Millerite" came to him with alarming news. "Mr. Emerson," he cried, "do you know that tonight the world is coming to an end?" "I'm glad to hear it," smiled Emerson. "Man will get along better without it."

Yet on occasion his voice could grow sharp—especially when he cried out against injustice. On November 7, 1837, when opposition to slavery was still regarded as a crime in the intellectual circles of Boston, he dared at a public lecture to express his admiration for the abolitionist martyr, Elijah P. Lovejoy. "The brave Lovejoy gave his breast to the bullets of a mob for the right of free speech and opinion and died when it was better not to live." One of Emerson's friends, who was present at the lecture, remarked that "a sort of cold shudder ran through the audience at this calm braving of the public opinion."

Emerson was fearless not only in braving the opinions of others but in changing his own opinions whenever he found himself to be in the wrong. The one great hero of his early youth had been Daniel Webster. "There is the Bunker Hill Monument, and there is Webster," he once wrote, referring to the "two wonders of the New England world." Yet when his hero surrendered to slavery Emerson was one of the first to stigmatize his conduct in public. At a political rally in Cambridge—one of the few in which Emerson ever took an active part—he pictured "the car of slavery and its abominations," with Webster as the leading horse. His words were greeted with a storm of hisses. Emerson waited patiently until the noise subsided, and then he went on: "Every drop of Webster's blood has eyes that look downward. He knows the heroes of 1776, but he cannot see the heroes of 1851 when he meets them on the street."

When Webster died he received perhaps his most fitting epitaph in the paradoxical tribute of Emerson: "He had honor enough to feel degraded."

In the tragic days preceding the Civil War, and throughout the war, Emerson always spoke "the best and bravest word." Several of his close friends were killed in the war, and his only living son was wounded. In spite of his advanced age and his always precarious health, he was tireless in his advocacy of the black man's cause. He had the highest admiration for Lincoln, "the Protector of American Freedom"; and Lincoln returned this admiration for Emerson, "the Prophet of American Faith." At the conclusion of the war Emerson proclaimed this faith in one of his most inspired lectures. "America means opportunity, freedom, power. The genius of this country has marked out her true policy: opportunity—doors wide open—every port open. If I could, I would have free trade with all the world, without toll or customhouse. Let us invite every nation, every race, every skin; white man, black man, red man, yellow man. Let us offer hospitality, a fair field, and equal justice to all."

VI

"LIFE," said Emerson in one of his lectures, "is unnecessarily long." He had always hoped that he might not outlive the decay of his mental faculties. This hope was not completely fulfilled. In 1872 his house burned down. "The morning after the fire," he said, "I felt something snap in my brain." From that day onward his "naughty memory" gave him "but fitful service." One evening his daughter read to him a passage from his lecture on *Nature.* "I don't know who wrote this," said Emerson, "but he must have been a great man."

Yet there were moments when his former greatness broke through like a flash of lightning in the gathering dusk. One day, as he was walking through his garden with his friend Moncure Conway, he handed the young man a plum. "Take this," he said. "At its best it is the fruit of Paradise."

These words were symbolical of Emerson's attitude not only toward the humblest of fruits but also toward the humblest of men. "At his best he is the child of Paradise."

IMPORTANT DATES IN THE LIFE OF
RALPH WALDO EMERSON

1803—Born, Boston.

1821—Graduated from Harvard College.

1825—Entered the Divinity School in Cambridge.

1829—Appointed minister of Old North Church, Boston.

1832—Made first visit to England and met Carlyle.

1836—Published essays on *Nature*.

1837—Delivered Phi Beta Kappa oration on "The American Scholar."

1847—Visited England for a second time.

1850—Published *Representative Men*.

1856—Published *English Traits*.

1866—Received degree of Doctor of Literature from Harvard.

1872—Went on third foreign tour.

1882—Died, Concord, Massachusetts.

Robert Edward Lee

[1807-1870]

THE tide of the Civil War was turning against the South. Inadequate forces, imperfect equipment, unfavorable weather, incompetent generalship on the part of Lee's subordinates—all these factors were proving too much for the almost superhuman efforts of General Lee. The newspapers accused him of poor leadership, demanded his removal from the high command, sneered at his "West Point tactics," insinuated that he had won his post merely through his family connections—his wife was the stepgranddaughter of George Washington. "A pretty coxcomb in the saddle," was the comment of one of the editors, "and a dismal failure on the battlefield."

The storm of abuse was growing daily more intense. The President of the Confederacy, Jefferson Davis, tried to defend him: "Lee came back [from the campaign in West Virginia], carrying the weight of defeat, and unappreciated by the people whom he served; for they could not know, as I knew, that if his orders and plans had been carried out, the result would have been victory rather than defeat."

In addition to Jefferson Davis, one other man came to the rescue. "General Lee," said Stonewall Jackson, "is a phenomenon. He is the only man I would follow blindfold."

For a while the storm of abuse had abated. The South had met with the dawning flush of victory. And then another series of defeats, and the editors lashed themselves once more into a fury of vituperation. "The retreating General." "All we can see is his back." "Underground Lee, digger of entrenchments."

The Battle of Gettysburg. Lee had ordered General Longstreet to take the initiative. "The enemy is here, and if we don't attack him, he will attack us—and whip us."

But Longstreet disobeyed the order. Instead of attacking, he sat like

Achilles sulking in his tent. And then, when the battle was over and lost, he added insult to injury. He wrote an article to excuse his own mistake by "informing the public of eleven mistakes Lee made at Gettysburg."

And how did General Lee meet this "last unkindest" cut of all? In his report to President Davis about the loss of the battle, he wrote: "I find no fault with any one but myself."

II

GENERAL LEE, the perfect cavalier. An iron-gray man on an iron-gray horse, firmness mounted on grace, the most chivalrous soldier in the South on the most thoroughbred horse in Virginia—Robert E. Lee and his Traveler.

Lincoln stood for integrity; Davis represented fortitude; Lee symbolized duty. When the Civil War broke out, Lincoln offered him the supreme command of the Union Army. But Lee was a Virginian. He felt it his duty to stick by his state. He was ready, if necessary, to enlist as a private in the army of the South.

Yet he hated secession. "I can anticipate no greater calamity for this country," he wrote, "than the dissolution of the Union . . . Secession is nothing but revolution."

And he hated war. He dreaded to see the day on which "strife and civil war are to take the place of brotherly love." And when the war came, he repeatedly expressed his horror at the unnecessary carnage. "My heart bleeds for the people," he wrote to his wife after one of his victorious battles. "You can have no idea how ghastly the sight of a battlefield is."

And, above all, he hated slavery. He condemned it in words that were almost as vehement as those of Abraham Lincoln. "Slavery as an institution," he said, "is a moral and political evil. I regard it as a greater evil for the whites than for the blacks." His attitude toward slavery went beyond the mere expression of his hatred for it. In 1861 he freed all the slaves that he owned himself, and in 1862 he freed all those that belonged to his wife.

Yet this lover of unity and freedom deliberately chose the side of disunity and slavery. "I shall draw the sword," he had said before the war, "only in defense of my home." It was only after long and heart-searching deliberation that he had decided upon this step. And he based his final decision upon his sense of honor, his duty, his integrity, his affection, and his faith in the word of God. Did not the Holy Scriptures point the way? There it was, the injunction of the Apostle Paul in his First Letter to Timothy: "But if any provide not for his own, and especially for those of his own house, he hath denied the faith, and is worse than an infidel."

His allegiance to his home, his children, his invalid wife—this was the path of his duty. A path paved with tragedy, leading out of heartbreak house into a future of tears and blood.

He must repel the invader at all cost, yet with no rancor in his heart. He had nothing but words of sorrow for the soldiers on the other side. When he was retreating from Gettysburg, he chanced upon a wounded enemy. "I recognized him," wrote this wounded soldier later on, "and though faint from loss of blood, I raised my hands, looked Lee in the face, and shouted—'Hurrah for the Union!'

"The general heard me, dismounted, and came toward me . . . I thought he meant to kill me . . . But he extended his hand to me, grasping mine firmly, and looking right into my eyes, said—'My son, I hope you will soon be well.' "

III

TENDER TO MEN, and to beasts. One day as he mounted his horse Traveler, while taking leave of several ladies, one of them reached out to pluck a gray hair from the horse's mane. "I want it as a memento, General." Whereupon Lee took off his hat, bowed his gray head with a courteous smile, and said, "If you please, madam, I would prefer that you tear out one of my own hairs."

IV

THE LEES were the aristocrats of the Southern aristocracy. On both sides of the family Robert was the heir to some of the most illustrious of the Virginia councilors and governors. Two of the Lees had been among the signers of the Declaration of Independence. Another had served as the European fiscal agent of the Colonies during the Revolution. And it was Robert's father, "Light-Horse Harry" Lee, who had coined that famous epigram about Washington: "First in war, first in peace, and first in the hearts of his countrymen."

Yet the Lees were none too well off in the goods of the world. Theirs was an aristocracy of breeding rather than of wealth. Indeed, in 1807 the Lee family was decidedly on the ragged edge of prosperity; and when Robert came, on January 19, he was an unwanted child.

Robert lost his father when he was only eleven. Upon the competent shoulders of the little fellow descended the direction of the household and the care of his invalid mother. Every day, after school, he took his mother out for a drive. And he made it his special business to fasten the curtains in the carriage in order to protect his mother from the drafts. This sort of thoughtfulness was characteristic of him throughout his life.

His mother had received as her wedding portion a sufficient fund to keep the wolf from the door and to give the children an adequate education. Following in the footsteps of his father, Robert decided upon a military career. He entered West Point at eighteen and graduated second in his class.

His mother lived just long enough to enjoy his graduation. Her unwanted child had become her favorite. Proudly she looked upon her handsome young lieutenant in his resplendent uniform, and then she closed her tired eyes.

Lee's first assignment was at Fortress Monroe, a station not far from Arlington Heights—and Mary Ann Custis. This prepossessing young lady was the only child of George Custis, the adopted son of George Washington. She had met Lee at a dance while he was still a cadet at West Point. They were married on June 30, 1831; and when George Custis died, the entire estate of Arlington passed into their hands. From that day on poverty and Robert Lee were no longer on intimate terms.

Young as he was, Lee had already gained the reputation of being the most resourceful engineer in the American Army. The Mississippi River was threatening the city of St. Louis. To save the city required a feat of unusual engineering skill. There was but one man in the army, said General Scott, who was equal to the task, and that man was Brevet Captain Lee. "He is young," reported the general, "but if the work can be done, he can do it."

Lee was appointed to the job, and he did it. He put "the Father of Waters into a strait jacket," diverted its course, and thus not only removed the danger of floods from St. Louis but improved the navigation of the entire stretch of the Upper Mississippi.

His next job was in the Mexican War. Referring to his services in that war, General Scott declared that Lee was "the very best soldier I have ever seen in the field." In overcoming the passes of apparently impassable mountains, he displayed the resourcefulness of a Hannibal. Perhaps the most important feat in his Mexican campaign was his march, through a pelting tropical storm, across the lava peaks of the Pedregal. General Henry J. Hunt, who had unsuccessfully attempted the same march, had this to say of Lee's achievement: "I would not believe that it could have been made, that passage of the Pedregal, if he had not made it." It was this maneuver of Captain Lee's that enabled the American Army to occupy Mexico City and to end the war.

Yet Lee himself recalled an altogether different scene as the most memorable incident of the war—the scene of a little Mexican girl bending over a dying drummer boy. Of all the soldiers in history, Lee had the most unsoldierlike soul. Why a man of such gentle sympathies should have chosen a military career is one of God's unsolved mysteries.

Lee was not by nature a happy warrior. He loved his own family too well to take delight in breaking up other families. His thoughts were centered on saving and not on destroying. After the Battle of Contreras he wrote to his son Custis, who was then at school: "I wondered when the musket balls and grape were whistling over my head in a perfect shower, where I could put you, if with me, to be safe." In the middle of another battle he picked up a bird that had fallen out of its nest and placed it behind a rock where it might be sheltered from the bullets. He found the fireside of his home more congenial to his nature than the campfire of the battlefield. Indeed, he hoped that after his Mexican campaign he would be able to spend the rest of his days with his family. "I pray that this shall be the last time"—he wrote to his wife from Mexico—"that I shall be absent from you in my life."

But the call of his duty would not let him rest. In 1859 he was ordered to put down the threatened rebellion of the slaves under John Brown. It was Colonel Lee who captured Brown and handed him over to justice. And in 1861 he followed the call of duty once more into the ranks of the invaded South. "Duty," he wrote in a letter to his eldest son, "is the sublimest word in our language."

V

THE OUTCOME of the Civil War was decided even before the war began. From first to last the South had about a million men on her muster rolls. The north had three million. The taxable property in the South was worth five billion dollars; in the North, eleven billion. The Southern navy was practically nonexistent; the Northern navy numbered almost two hundred thousand men. The South, in other words, was conquered by arithmetic. And it was only the military genius of Lee that kept the unequal contest in the balance for four years.

There are those who think that Lee might have even won the war if Stonewall Jackson, the ablest and bravest of his lieutenants, had not been killed at Chancellorsville. But let the poets and the novelists deal with the problems of the historical might-have-beens. To the scientific historian the ultimate defeat of General Lee was as inevitable as the destruction of a glass ball coming into collision with a cannon ball.

Yet the resiliency of Lee's army was one of the amazing miracles in history. He met the superior forces of Pope, of McClellan, of Burnside, of Hooker, and in every case he rebounded with new energy and with new determination. The North had adopted a policy of "attrition"—that is, an endless and relentless slaughter of both sides in the expectation that the side having the lesser number of men would be the first to become exhausted. And yet in the face of this obvious fact, Lee dared again and again to take the offensive. And in these tactics there was more of method than of madness. For Lee generally managed to maneuver his army into the more advantageous position, and in this way he lost considerably fewer men than his opponents.

Following these tactics, he pushed the bewildered Union generals from one dangerous position into another. He routed them at Manassas; he swept them away from Richmond; he even planned to march upon Washington. But his plan was frustrated by one of those insignificant instances that produce some of the most significant events in history. One of Lee's officers, in gathering up his effects as he was moving from one camp into another, forgot a single trifling item—a package of cigars wrapped in a piece of paper. But this wrapping paper happened to be a copy of Lee's plan for the capture of Washington. It fell into the hands of a Union officer, who promptly turned it over to McClellan. And thus Washington was saved from Lee's invasion by a handful of cigars.

But Lee's soldiers were not discouraged. "Uncle Robert will get us into Washington yet," they cried. "You bet he will!" For he was their idol. Unaware of the tremendous odds against him, they hadn't the slightest suspicion of ultimate failure. Not with Uncle Robert at their head. Hadn't General Scott himself admitted that Lee was worth an entire army? How, then, could the North expect to win, with two armies arrayed against it?

And so they cheered Uncle Robert, and sang "Maryland, My Maryland," and marched hopefully into the fields of Antietam—forty thousand men against eighty-seven thousand.

It was the deadliest battle of the war. The plain of Antietam became transformed into a gigantic altar—an altar of flame, on which twenty-five thousand lives were offered up.

The military tacticians called it a drawn battle. But it was not. Antietam was a severe blow to the Southern cause. It ended Lee's first offensive against the North. It placed Maryland definitely out of the Confederacy and on the side of the Union. And most important of all, it gave Lincoln the psychological moment for the Emancipation Proclamation.

But Lee was not defeated. Not yet. At Fredericksburg he beat off a host of a hundred and thirteen thousand men with an ill-fed, ill-shod, and ill-armed force of seventy-eight thousand. At Chancellorsville, with sixty-two thousand men, he outflanked an array of one hundred and twenty thousand and "rolled them up like a scroll." And then, with a daring that far overbalanced his strength, he entered upon a second invasion of the North.

VI

LEE was an excellent strategist, but a poor aggressor. He lacked the beastliness necessary to a successful commander. He was too human for the inhumanity of war. He played the game according to the rules; and this, from a military standpoint, was a fatal error. He fought only against men, and not against women and children. General Sherman, on the other hand, was more realistic. He understood war for what it was—a relentless struggle to crush the enemy at whatever cost. Everything to him was fair in war. Every weapon that could prostrate the enemy was, in his eyes, a legitimate weapon. To win a war, he maintained, you must kill the men and terrify the women and starve the children. Fighting against women and children is ungallant and savage, to be sure. But war—Sherman was frank enough to insist—is murder; and it is ridiculous to talk of committing murder in a gallant and gentlemanly manner. Lee was mentally and morally attuned to peace. Sherman was logically and psychologically attuned to war. When Lee invaded the North he ordered his troops to refrain from "barbarous outrages against the innocent and the defenceless." His soldiers, he demanded, must "fight like Christian gentlemen." What a naïve demand! As if there could be anything in common between the gentleness of Christianity and the savagery of war! Sherman knew better than that. "War is hell," he asserted, and then he proceeded to make his assertion true. When he marched into Georgia he wrote coldly, "I would not restrain the army, lest its vigor and energy should be impaired." And to the commander of one of his divisions he sent the all-inclusive order "to spare nothing."

Lee, if the truth must be told, didn't have his heart in the war. He "pulled" his punches, because he was temperamentally not a fighter. Sherman, by contrast, was a two-fisted killer. In his march to the sea he cut a swath of devastation sixty miles wide. He "swept the country clean" with as much thoroughness and with as little regard for human suffering as a prairie fire.

And so at last the strength of the South gave out. It was a pitiable but courageous defeat. "What will history say of our surrender?" asked one of Lee's staff officers in a passion of grief.

"Yes," replied Lee. "I know they will say hard things of us . . . But at least we are conscious that we have humbly tried to do our duty."

VII

AFTER HIS SURRENDER, Lee mounted his horse and rode away. But not to his home. His home had been burned down by the Union soldiers. There was sadness in his heart, but no bitterness. One Sunday at church he heard a preacher scathingly denounce the North. "Doctor," he said after the sermon, "I remember to have read in the Good Book that we must love our enemies."

"These words from you?" exclaimed the astonished preacher.

"Yes, Doctor. I have fought against the Union soldiers, but I have never cherished any vindictive feelings . . . I have never seen the day when I did not pray for them."

Yet the North neither prayed nor cherished any friendly feeling for Lee. At the order of President Johnson, he was disfranchised.

A man without a country. But even then there was in the soul of General Lee no surrender to despair. "Human virtue," he had once remarked, "ought to be equal to human calamity." And strangely enough, it was after all his defeats and his sufferings that he found his true virtue, his real vocation. He was appointed president of Washington College, in Virginia, and there at last he enjoyed the satisfaction of a fulfilled life. For, in the final analysis, his genius was not military but inspirational. With all his greatness as a tactician, he was a misfit on the battlefield. He never was quite in his element when he led men to their death. He felt much more at home when he taught them how to live.

To live as brothers in a common country for a common cause. "Madam," he said to the mother of one of his students when she spoke disparagingly of the North, "don't bring up your sons to detest the United States. Remember that we form one country now. Let us abandon all these local animosities, and *make our sons Americans.*"

IMPORTANT DATES IN THE LIFE OF
ROBERT EDWARD LEE

1807—Born, Stratford, Virginia.

1818—Lost father.

1825—Entered West Point.

1829—Graduated second in his class.

1831—Married Mary Randolph Custis.

1834—Became assistant to chief engineer of United States Army.

1847—Made lieutenant colonel in Mexican War.

1849-52—Employed in construction of harbor defenses at Baltimore.

1852—Became superintendent of West Point.

1855—Left to serve as lieutenant colonel of 2nd Cavalry.

1859—Captured John Brown at Harpers Ferry.

1861—Appointed commander in chief of Virginia forces.

1862—Made military adviser to Jefferson Davis.

1865—Appointed commander in chief of all Confederate armies.
Surrendered to General Grant.
Elected president of Washington College.

1870—Died, Lexington, Virginia.

Edgar Allan Poe

[1809-1849]

IN LOOKING back through history," wrote Edgar Allan Poe, "we should pass over the biographies of 'the good and the great,' while we search carefully for the records of wretches who died in prison, in Bedlam, or upon the gallows." Poe had a tender fellow feeling for the picturesque denizens of the dump.

Poe's own life, to be sure, began in Boston—the most "proper" of American cities. A man born here could not be destined for the scrap heap if given half a chance. But Poe was given somewhat less than half a chance. He was born of a pair of strolling players, and he lost them both in his earliest years. As a compensation for the loss of his parents, the fates presented him with a couple of foster parents. The wealthy and aristocratic Allans of Virginia, who adopted Edgar Poe, gave him their name and their affection but not their comprehension. They could never quite make out this wayward little bohemian who had come to them from an alien world. They tried their best to prepare him for their own world of exclusive snobbery and conventional culture—and they failed. It was not in his blood.

As the first step in their effort to turn him into a Southern gentleman, they sent him to an English boarding school. He returned to the States with an exterior polish, a dashing manner, and a drawing-room etiquette. But he had also picked up the besettting vice of the English aristocrat— a passion for cards and for wine. And he had neither the purse nor the constitution necessary for the lavish indulgence of this vice.

Add to this a fiery but morbid imagination, a supersensitive heart, a feeble will, and an impetuous tongue, and you have a young poet hardly suited to pass unscathed through the battles of life.

And, sure enough, his troubles began early. Shortly after he entered the University of Virginia he confronted his foster father with a gambling debt that sent the old gentleman into a fury. Poe was taken out of college and put into the countinghouse.

His career among the money-changers was as brief as it was distasteful. He ran away from his desk and enlisted in the army. He gave his name as Edgar A. Perry. Within two years he rose to the rank of sergeant major. And then he escaped.

His guardian had traced him in his flight. He was bitterly disappointed in "this good-for-nothing son of those good-for-nothing actors." But he decided to give him another chance. He secured for him a congressional recommendation to West Point.

Poe entered the military academy at the age of twenty. But it soon became apparent that he was not fitted for the life of a commissioned officer. He could brook no discipline. He had become unruly. He showed an utter contempt for his duties. He was discharged in disgrace.

No one could make head or tail of him. Mr. Allan threw up his hands in despair. He had committed the terrible error of taking under his wing no ordinary personality. Of all the lovely babies he might have adopted, he remarked bitterly, the rulers of the world in their jest had given him the one incomprehensible problem child of the generation!

II

THE CHARACTER OF POE was indeed beyond the comprehension of Mr. Allan, who, for all his wealth and aristocracy, was a simple-minded man. He never dreamt that his foster son was endowed with poetic genius. Nor did any of Poe's companions suspect the feverish activity that went on inside his head. For all his pleasant intercourse, Poe had as yet shared his heart with no one. In fact, it was said that he lacked the power of making intimate friends. There was a strange reserve about him, people remarked. Even at the university, where he had often acted as a ringleader in the frolics, "no one knew him at all." What was the reason for this inner aloofness? his companions asked themselves. And a few of them suggested that perhaps it was due to his inherent loneliness. He lived out of his environment, like a fish out of water. He was a miscast and unhappy actor—a child of the gutter compelled to assume the role of an aristocrat. And in a sense they were right. He found no warmth in his uncongenial environment, no tribal sympathy, no parental love. Once, indeed, when a mere boy at school, he had known for an instant the tenderness of an older woman's understanding. She was the mother of a school chum. And she had spoken words of affection with a voice he had never heard before! But then she had died, and the few words of love he had known in his childhood remained nothing but an echo and a memory.

He lived alone in his memories and his dreams. And passing these memories and dreams through the filter of his morbid imagination, he transmuted them into poetry the like of which had never yet been heard in America.

When he was discharged from West Point he submitted these dream poems to the Baltimore papers. The editors of these papers looked quizzically at the author. He had written sheer nonsense, they thought. But it was such exquisite nonsense!

Penniless and out of tune with the world, Poe went on with his bizarre poetry—"Tamerlane," the story of the man who conquered the world for his beloved and returned to lay it at her feet, only to find that in his absence she had died of a lonely heart; "Al Aaraaf," the outlandish tale of another world; poems and stories that were no tales at all but fantastic visions set to a new music. Of course nobody could understand these poems. Yet all those who read them could hear the strange and haunting echo of a new music.

He published a slender volume of his verse—written during his student days among the cadets. The press reviewed the book favorably. It was a good beginning. The author might write a beautiful if not a magnificent poem once he had mastered his material. "I am certain that as yet I have written neither a beautiful nor a magnificent poem. But I will do so—I take my oath upon it—if only they will give me time!"

III

MEANWHILE he turned his attention to prose. He had decided upon a literary career and he realized that the way to fame and fortune lay over the adventurous highways of fiction. He submitted a weird thriller—the fantastic story of a shipwreck—in a prize competition and succeeded in winning the first prize. When the editors of the *Baltimore Saturday Visitor* expressed a desire to dine with the man to whom they had awarded the money Poe sent them the following reply: "Your invitation to dinner has wounded me to the quick. I cannot come, for reasons of the most humiliating nature. I haven't a decent suit of clothes to wear."

His foster father had broken off intercourse with him. One day Poe heard that Mr. Allan was dangerously ill. He rushed to his bedside. But Allan, summoning his last flicker of strength, rose from his bed, grasped his cane and waved it menacingly, demanding that Poe leave the house at once. Shortly thereafter Allan died. By the terms of the will Poe was left not a single penny.

Yet he seemed to be on the way to success. The literary gentry in Baltimore were wagging their tongues about him. There were rumors that he was about to publish a volume of bizarre tales. "The young fellow is highly imaginative, though slightly given to the terrific."

They were willing to help him to a start. Thanks to their recommendation, he received an offer for an editorial position on the *Southern Literary Messenger* in Richmond, Virginia. He accepted the offer. Encouraged by the prospect of a steady income—ten dollars a week—Poe felt that he could now publicly announce his marriage which had taken place privately sometime earlier. He had wedded his thirteen-year-old cousin, Virginia Clemm, despite the endeavors of her relatives to postpone the match until the girl was older. They had braved the conventional opinion of the folk around them. Conventional opinions, conventional acts—these were but the passing shadows of the unimaginative world in which most men lived. Of what interest were they to Poe, who lived in the comforting solidity of his own fantastic world?

He was entirely unorthodox. He couldn't be fathomed. No sooner did he find himself more or less settled in life, with a growing reputation and a future, than he drank himself out of his security. He had a queer sense of humor. It was hollow and mocking. There was no laughter to it. Mr. White, in dismissing him from his editorial job, wrote a cordial enough letter. "I cannot address you in such language as this occasion and my feelings demand. . . . When you once again tread these streets I have my fears . . . that you will again drink till your senses are lost. Unless you look to your Maker for help you will not be safe. . . . If you would make yourself contented with quarters in my house, or with any other private family, where liquor is not used, I should think there was some hope for you. But if you go to a tavern or to any place where it is used at table, you are not safe."

He left Baltimore to seek his fortune in Philadelphia. To seek his fortune and to find new misfortunes. For wherever he went he took his sensitiveness and his weakness along with him.

Yet his weakness, he insisted, was the direct result of his sensitiveness. It wasn't that he drank excessively, he explained, but that he couldn't drink at all. Physically as well as mentally he was different from other people. His nerves were so tense that the slightest stimulus moved him to the greatest excitement. "I pledge, before God, the solemn word of a gentleman that I am temperate even to rigor." If he took a single glass of weak wine or beer, he declared, it almost always ended in severe illness. His own excess was the average man's daily stint.

Thus he argued before the world. He couldn't drink much, yet he was compelled to drink a little. He appealed to "all the physicians in the world" that it required something stronger than water to translate his glowing fancies into living words.

But he had little opportunity to indulge his fancies. Occasionally the editors offered him a job as a book reviewer—a chore he heartily detested. "They want me to make myself the shifting toady of the hour and bow and cringe and sound the glory of third-rate ability with a penny trumpet! Then I would be feted alive. And then *perhaps* I would be praised when dead." But he couldn't be connected permanently with any publication not his own. He couldn't go on forever writing reviews in other people's magazines, compelled to express opinions backed by financial investment, required to shout "amen" along with the public to the "microscopical literary efforts of a hundred animalcula who call themselves authors."

Someday he would start a magazine of his own and work only for himself. And *then* he would give free wing to his fantasies. This was the subject of his hope and his despair. For there were times when he doubted whether he could ever find the proper channel to communicate to the mass of mankind the images that came to him in that borderline interval between his sleeping and his waking moments. Perhaps there was no one who had ever gone through his own strange mental experiences. Perhaps, indeed, there were no human words to express such experiences. "They are not ideas in my brain. They are not dreams. They arise from the soul in its utmost tranquillity. They are not born of a waking state; they come not to one in sleep. They take shape at those mere points in time when the waking world blends with the world of sleep—at the split second when my mind hovers between dreams and consciousness—and who can say whether the human being is at that absolutely psychical moment awake or asleep?" Such a moment of exquisite delicacy can scarcely be experienced by the normal five senses. It lies in the province of an infinity of supersenses entirely alien to the physical state. "Is not such a moment the very origin of my life, the very essence of my genius? And, if so, is such an experience common to every man or is it confined only to my individual self?"

Lost in this haunted borderland, the poet tried to find an answer to his questions. He must transfer his own fluid moment into the frozen store of memory and survey his dreams with a practical eye. He must have faith in the power of words. He must demonstrate the fact that fantasies as well as thoughts could survive within the province of precise language. Otherwise he would be lost, like a ghost haunting the house of life and vainly trying to take his place in the reality of his fellow men.

"I must make my fantasies worthy of belief." He would introduce his readers into the highest reaches of impossible imaginings, leading them subtly and imperceptibly to accept the ghost for the substance, the myth for the truth, hardly aware of the point where they had overstepped the bounds of the solid world into the land of somber hues and twilight landscapes whose secrets were known to only one man.

And so he tried to capture the moments between his sleeping and his waking and translated them into pseudorealistic visions that seemed more real than reality. He published a book of these stories—"Ligeia," "The Fall of the House of Usher," "William Wilson." . . . The public read them and understood. Now at last he would be able to enjoy all the good things to which a man of genius was entitled—love, fame, the dominion of the intellect, the consciousness of power, the thrilling sense of beauty, the free air of heaven. His troubles, he thought, were over at last!

IV

BUT HIS TROUBLES had only begun. He was slandered by his fellow crafts-men—critics who were jealous of his success as a writer, writers who were incensed at his honesty as a critic. And climaxing all these difficulties came the discouraging succession of cant-ridden letters from the editors dispensing with his services. They would be glad to take him back, they always advised him patronizingly, if only he would stop drinking. They might as well have worded it, if only he would stop writing!

And then a still greater evil befell him. Virginia, his child wife whom he loved "as no man ever loved before," had ruptured a blood vessel while

singing. Her life was despaired of. "I took leave of her forever and underwent the agonies of her death. She recovered partially, and I again hoped.
At the end of a year the vessel broke again." Then again—again. "I
became insane with long intervals of horrible sanity. During those fits
of absolute unconsciousness I drank—God only knows how often or how
much." And then he found a temporary cure for himself—found it in the
definite verdict of the doctors that an early death awaited her. This certain tragedy he could bear like a man. It was the horrible oscillation
between hope and despair that he could not have endured much longer.

But it was six years before she died—a slow and agonizing death for
them both. He hovered around her couch with tender anxiety, and a shudder seized him like a convulsion at her slightest cough. There were nights
when no one dared to speak to him. When the warm weather came he
rode out with her in the twilight, and his watchful eyes eagerly searched
her pallid face for the slightest change of expression.

"Dear Griswold," the man of pride was finally compelled to write to
one of his friends, "can you not send me five dollars? I am sick and Virginia is almost gone."

Once more he had lost his editorial job, this time on *Graham's Magazine*. Together with his invalid wife he left Philadelphia to try his luck
in New York. He had ten dollars in his pocket. Upon his arrival in the
City of New Hope he wrote a letter to Virginia's mother:

"My Dear Muddy, we arrived safe at the Walnut Street Wharf. . . . I
took Sis to the Depôt Hotel. . . . Last night for supper we had the nicest
tea you ever drank, strong and hot—wheat bread and rye bread—cheese
—teacakes (elegant), a great dish (two dishes) of elegant ham and two
of cold veal, piled up like a mountain in large slices—three dishes of the
cakes and everything in the greatest profusion. . . . Sis is delighted.
. . . She has coughed hardly any and has had no night sweats. She is now
busy mending my pants which I tore against a nail. . . . We have got
four dollars and a half left. . . . I feel in excellent spirits and haven't
taken a drop—so that I hope soon to get out of trouble."

It was but a faint beam of happiness in the black vigil of their despair.
Soon the winter came—and with it the coughing and the fevers and the
sweats. Virginia lay on a bed that had no mattress or any other bedding
except straw and a white counterpane and sheets. She was wrapped in
the coat of her husband and she held a large furry kitten to her bosom
for warmth. Her husband clasped her hands. This contact helped the
circulation somewhat. Her mother rubbed her feet to keep them from
frostbite.

She passed into eternity on the Lord's Day, while the church bells were
ringing and the faithful were at worship. He escorted her poor little body
to the grave in the black military coat that had kept her warm in her last
moments. And as they lowered her to her rest he recalled the words he
had written in his despair: "The star-shaped flowers shrank into the
stems of the trees and appeared no more. . . . And Life departed from
our paths; for the tall flamingo flaunted no more his scarlet plumage
before us, but flew sadly from the vale into the hills. . . . And the golden

and silver fish swam down through the gorge at the lower end of our
domain and bedecked the sweet river never again. . . . And the lulling
melody . . . died little by little away, in murmurs growing lower and
lower. . . ."

V

AT LAST Poe had become famous as a writer of the bizarre. Famous but
not prosperous. The entire literary world had been startled into recognition of his genius when he won the first prize for "The Gold Bug," the
short story of ciphers and secrets. But the prize brought him only one
hundred dollars and an infinity of trouble. For the story had started a
"cipher" fad. A host of admirers sent him cryptograms and challenged
him to solve them. "I have lost in time, which to me is money, more than
a thousand dollars, solving secret messages" with no other purpose than
to demonstrate his analytical powers before so large an audience. And
his audience grew even larger when he startled the world with "The
Raven." Yet with all his fame he remained as poor as ever—he had sold
"The Raven" for ten dollars. And so he slunk through the world, a sad,
solitary, hungry celebrity robed in black, meeting people with a cynical
smile on his lips and "dreaming dreams no mortal ever dreamed before."

And in spite of his sadness and his hunger he kept on creating his
strange visions and—let it be admitted—plagiarizing freely when the fire
of his creation burned low. When other writers stooped to this sort of
unpermitted borrowing he called it downright theft. When he himself
did it—well, he did it, and that was that! For he lived in a world whose
laws, whose customs, and whose demands, he insisted, were quite beyond
the sympathetic understanding of the average human mind. His cryptograms, his hoaxes, his pseudoscientific accounts of journeys in a balloon,
and his supernatural reports of conversations with the dead and of corpses
come to life—all these were part and parcel of the phantasmagoria in
which his spirit habitually dwelt. Wasn't all life a hoax, a fantastic vision
plagiarized by some Divine Poet out of the epic nightmare of a diabolical
mind? Then why should not he, a human poet, plagiarize the fantastic
visions of other human minds?

He therefore felt no compunction when it was pointed out that his sea
narrative of Arthur Gordon Pym was copied largely from an account of
Morell's *Voyages* and that his startling essay on conchology (shells)—a
subject on which he hadn't the slightest training—was an almost exact
reproduction of a book written by Captain Thomas Brown.

Always posing, always pretending to a knowledge he didn't possess,
always coloring his imposture with verisimilitude, living in a world of
subjective fancies and self-made laws. Again and again in his stories and
his articles he referred to foreign books which, upon investigation, were
found never to have existed. Like other writers handicapped by insuffi-
cient education, he loved to show off his pseudo scholarship through the
"quotations" of passages from languages he knew nothing about.

But he did not regard his fictitious quotations as impostures. He was an artist. He sought no facts; he sought only effects. He was a painter of the grotesque and the arabesque. He was interested not so much in the true as in the beautiful. "The sense of beauty," he wrote, "is an immortal instinct deep within the spirit of man."

To evoke beauty through the music of words—that, and that alone, was the purpose of his art. He called music "the most entrancing of poetic moods." In order to create these entrancing moods, these musical pictures of the grotesque and the arabesque, he employed the entire repertory of the literary magician's tricks—"novelty, quotation, repetition, unexpected phrases, quaintnesses . . . sentences and sentiments of sweet sounds" that were "simply beyond the reach of analysis." He maintained that those who persist in reconciling "the obstinate oils of poetry and truth" are "mad beyond redemption." No work of art, he declared, should ever point a moral or embody a truth.

What he tried to create, therefore, was *artistic* rather than *scientific* reality, *verisimilitude* rather than *verity,* a mere *semblance* of the truth rather than the *actual* truth. And this, he explained, was the justification for his artifices and his hoaxes and his pseudoscientific "discoveries" and his fictitious quotations. He was, in his poetry as well as in his prose, a writer of fiction. But he was also a creator, and therefore his fiction appeared at times to be even truer than the truth.

VI

AFTER THE DEATH OF HIS WIFE he continued to live in his rented cottage at Fordham. He underwent a critical illness during these "lonesome latter years." And then, as he slowly recuperated among his pet tropical songbirds and his dahlias and his heliotropes, his mind became wrapped in the clouds of mysticism. He began to lecture on the universe and planned the prospectus of a philosophy compared to which "Newton's discovery of gravitation would be a mere incident." He wrote the book and called it *Eureka—I Have Made the Discovery!* He regarded this as the greatest of his works. It was not enough that he had taken his place among the masters of poetry and fiction; he had now become—he believed—the leading philosopher of the century. But the critics thought otherwise. They regarded the book as the sad outpouring of a pompous obscurity, the pathetic attempt of a mortal failure to find an immortal soul.

But Poe was not yet ready to confess himself a failure. He still clung to the hope of starting his own magazine and of "generally re-establishing myself in the literary world." He made a speaking tour of New England. "Those clear, sad eyes," wrote a reviewer of one of his lectures, "seemed to look down upon us from an eminence. . . . He smiled, but seldom laughed or said anything to excite mirth in others."

At a lecture on poetry which he delivered in Providence he met Mrs. Whitman, a fellow poet to whom he became deeply attached. They were engaged to be married. But his conduct repelled her. Often he was found unconscious on the streets—a victim of laudanum or of alcohol. He was a pitiable object when in his cups. Staggering along the gutter, his eyes bleary and his clothes a bundle of mud-stained rags, he would lose himself in "sublime rhapsodies on the evolution of the universe," speaking as from some imaginary platform to multitudinous dream audiences of "vast and attentive visitors."

Finally, when he had drunk and drugged himself into popular discredit, Mrs. Whitman broke the engagement.

But he still entertained the dream of that magazine he was going to start. In 1849 he left Fordham for Richmond to work out the plans for the project. And then this hope, too, was shattered—not through any external opposition but through the inadequacy of his own will. His mind had become tormented with the suspicion of some dreadful conspiracy against his life. He begged an acquaintance for a razor so that he might remove his mustache and thus effect a disguise against his pursuers. His friends feared for his sanity unless he could find a companion to watch over him. They were much relieved when he renewed his courtship for an old childhood sweetheart, now a wealthy widow. Once again an engagement was announced. Poe wound up his affairs and then left for his wedding in the South.

But he never reached his destination. They found him in Baltimore—in one of the election polls of the fourth ward—out of his mind, his traveling bag missing, all his money gone. It was believed that, under the influence of liquor, he had fallen into the hands of a band of electioneering ruffians who had drugged him and kept him prisoner until the day of election and who had then led him stupefied from one ward to the next to vote under various names.

They took him to the hospital. His face was drenched with perspiration. He talked deliriously for hours. And then his mind became somewhat clearer. He mumbled a few coherent phrases just before he died.

> O God! . . . Is all we see or seem
> But a dream within a dream?

IMPORTANT DATES IN THE LIFE OF
EDGAR ALLAN POE

1809—Born, Boston.
1811—Lost his mother.
    Adopted by Mrs. Allan.
1826—Entered University of Virginia.
1827—Published *Tamerlane*.
1827-31—Served as volunteer in United States Army.

1831—Published collection of *Poems*.
1832—Started writing prose tales.
1836—Married Virginia Clemm.
1847—His wife died.
1849—Died, Baltimore.

Abraham Lincoln
[1809-1865]

ON THE night of November 13, 1861, President Lincoln paid a visit to the home of George B. McClellan, general in chief of the Union Army. The servant at the door said the general was out but would soon return. "Very well," nodded Lincoln, "I will wait."

An hour later McClellan came in at the front door. "General," said the servant, "the President is waiting for you in the parlor."

"Is that so?" And without stopping to greet the President, McClellan walked upstairs.

Another half hour of waiting, and Lincoln became somewhat impatient. "Will you please inform the general," he said to the servant, "that I am still here?"

The servant went up to McClellan's room—and returned without his master. "Sorry, Mr. President, but the general asked me to tell you he's gone to bed."

McClellan was a strutting little cockerel of an officer whose bluster was far in excess of his ability. "What this fellow needs," observed Lincoln's friends, "is a good spanking with the flat of his own sword." But Lincoln only smiled. "I am ready to hold McClellan's stirrup for him, if he will only win us victories."

Such was Abe Lincoln—a rare combination of humor and humility that made him the beloved of men.

II

No PLAYWRIGHT has ever created a more dramatic plot than the life of Lincoln. Like the hero in an ancient Greek tragedy, he failed in almost everything he undertook; and when he did succeed, he found success more bitter than failure. He lost the only woman he loved; and the woman he married was more anxious to see him famous than to see him happy. He entered business, and failed. He ran for the United States Senate, and was defeated. He applied for an appointment to the United States Land Office, and was rejected. He ran for the vice-presidency, and lost. When finally he was elected to the presidency, it was in sorrow rather than in triumph that he rode into the White House. For, though passionately devoted to peace, he found himself compelled to plunge into war. Tenderest of fathers, he twice had to bow his head in mourning over the untimely graves of his children. Gentle toward every living thing, he was again and again called upon to sign the death warrants of runaway soldiers who were afraid to die. He was a soul attuned to the daylight yet forced to live in the night. And at last, when the dawn of victory arrived after the night of despair, Lincoln did not survive to see the day. His assassination came less than a week after the surrender of General Lee.

In the life of Lincoln the Great Dramatist of Heaven showed the little dramatists of the earth how to write a perfect tragedy.

III

THE DAY after Lincoln was born his nine-year-old cousin, Dennis Hanks, looked at him. "His skin makes me think of cherry pulp squeezed dry." The baby began to wail. "Aw, take him away!" exclaimed Dennis Hanks in disgust. "I guess he'll never come to much."

And indeed there was no reason for anyone to think otherwise. Lincoln's parents and three of his grandparents were uneducated and unambitious. But his fourth grandparent, the father of Nancy Hanks, was a "mysterious stranger from the South." Lincoln's mother, in other words, was a "natural" child. Lincoln thought that his poetical and political genius came from this unknown Southern grandfather. But his never-say-die spirit in the face of failure came to him from a whole line of pioneering ancestors. It took supreme courage to survive in the adventures of the American frontier. There was a concise and picturesque proverb that summarized the epic of America's migration to the Middle West: "The cowards never started and the weak ones died by the way."

Lincoln was descended from those who had the courage to start and the hardihood to survive. A poet born out of a race of pioneers. Lincoln's entire political career was a great epic poem in action.

As a young man he wanted to be a writer. He had drunk deep of the sap of the earth and the sweetness of the air. He had caught the rhythm of the swinging ax and the music of the growing grass. And he reproduced this rhythm and this music in a number of juvenile poems. He could work hard when he had to. But he preferred to *think* hard. "Abe Lincoln worked for me," remarked a neighbor, John Romine, "but he was always reading and thinking instead of attending to his job . . . He said to me one day that his father taught him to work, but he never taught him to love it."

When the day's work was over, he sat around swapping stories and "just learning to be friendly with people." One evening a farmer's wife upbraided him for his laziness. "What's going to become of you, Abe?"

"Me?" drawled Lincoln. "I'm going to be President of the United States."

Lincoln, of course, was spoofing when he said this. At the time he hadn't the slightest idea that he would attain to political distinction. But he had decided to go into politics. For he was not only a poetical pioneer but a practical Yankee as well. At an early age he had dedicated himself to a life of concrete usefulness. Instead of combining words into a great poem, he would help unite men into a great nation.

And so he announced himself as a candidate for public service. He canvassed his neighbors with humorous anecdotes and homely parables. These speeches were honest and unassuming prose poems. And his neighbors understood them just as readily as they understood the solid earth under their feet and the simple stars overhead. They trusted his uncouth ruggedness, his open smile, and his generous heart. He was so much like them and yet so very much above them. Like an oak tree in a forest of saplings. "There's suthin' peculiarsome about Abe," they said, "yes, an' suthin' kindlike an' strong." He could split a rail and pull a boat faster than any other man in Sangamon County; he could floor the strongest "rassler" in the state of Illinois; he could lift an ax by the tip of the handle between the forefinger and the thumb; and he could talk like an apostle out of the Bible. He was quite the homeliest man in the state, and just as lovable as he was homely, was this awkward Honest Abe, with his big gnarled hands, and his ill-fitting clothes, and his furrowed face and sensitive mouth and gentle eyes. A first-rate man to look after their interests. "If elected, I shall consider the whole people of Sangamon my constituents, as well those that oppose as those that support me." They elected him to the State Assembly.

He was a young man of little learning and much wisdom. For he had touched life at many points. He had been field hand and ferryman, wood chopper and butcher boy, tanner and storekeeper and surveyor. And letter writer for all the inarticulate folk of the neighborhood. He had learned to understand and to reproduce in his own simple honest phrases the innermost yearnings of his fellows—men who toiled and suffered and lost their loved ones and kept toiling on. He, too, had loved and suffered. He had lost his only sister, his mother, and the girl he was about to marry. For several weeks following the death of Ann Rutledge he was almost out of his mind with grief. One night in a thunderstorm he rushed to the door of his house and cried: "I can't bear to think of her lying out there alone, with the rain and the storm beating on her grave!"

But he pulled himself together and carried on.

IV

As a child he had written in his notebook: "Abraham Lincoln his hand and pen he will be good but god knows when." And now he had made good much sooner than he, or anybody else, had expected. At a dinner given by his constituents in his honor the toastmaster referred to him as a young man "who has fulfilled the expectations of his friends and disappointed the hopes of his enemies."

Such was the verdict of the common people. But not of the expert politicians. When Lincoln took his seat in the Assembly, one of the other members gave him a quick and appraising glance. It was his custom to do this whenever a new member arrived. He wanted to size up the men who might become his possible rivals in the future. For, though short in stature, this young assemblyman had a tall ambition. His brilliant mind was occupied with nothing less than senatorial and presidential dreams. His name was Stephen A. Douglas.

His quick appraisal of Lincoln apparently satisfied him that there was nothing to be feared from that quarter. Great statesmen, he concluded, were not hewn out of such unpromising timber. For a time he didn't even take the trouble to make Lincoln's acquaintance. And Lincoln, on his part, paid no attention to Douglas. Neither of them suspected how closely their lives were to be intertwined and how vital a role their own destiny was to play in the destiny of America. The clash in their characters, in their ambitions, in their very appearance was but another manifestation of the perfect drama woven around the life of Lincoln.

And now there appeared upon the scene a person who was to bring about the first complication in the plot. One evening the two assemblymen met an aristocratic young lady from the South—a Becky Sharp type of character who was visiting her married sister in Springfield. Mary Todd was a buxom and beautiful and superficial little creature, whose mind was as bright as a bubble—and as empty. Puffed up with a superabundance of vanity, she was determined to become "the empress of all she surveyed." An exquisite dancer, she meant to dance her way into the heart of the most promising young man in America. When she met the suave Douglas and the uncouth Lincoln, she sized them up immediately. Crude power was nearer to the heart of America than cultivated splendor. Though Mary Todd's mind was shallow, her instinct was sound. She chose Lincoln as the more likely candidate for supreme honors. And so, much to the chagrin of Douglas—a feeling that was to play no little part in his future antagonism to the "homely interloper from the backwoods" —the elegant young lady gave her hand to Lincoln. Or, to be more exact, she took Lincoln's reluctant hand into her own and led him to the altar.

After his marriage Lincoln settled down to the business of making a living. He entered into a law partnership with William A. Herndon, bought a rickety, leather-covered sofa on which he could stretch out his full length of six feet four and dream away his time, allowing the papers to pile up on the desk and the dust to accumulate on the floor until the grass began to sprout in the cracks. He was set down as the untidiest and most eccentric young man in Illinois. He steadfastly refused to represent unethical clients. "I shall not take your case," he said to a man who had pointed out how, by a legal technicality, he could win six hundred dollars. "You may be legally right, but you are morally wrong . . . And by the way," he added as the disgruntled client turned to leave, "you look like a pretty energetic fellow. Why not try an *honest* way of making six hundred dollars?"

As for Lincoln himself, he made a fairly satisfactory living in spite of his scruples. Perhaps *because* of his scruples. For his clients appreciated his candor, and the judges admired his common sense. What he lacked in good manners he made up in goodness. And *that,* to the simple folk of Illinois, was the yardstick by which they measured a man's character.

He was popular with everybody—except his own wife. Theirs was not a happy marriage. Lincoln's unrefined manners clashed all too frequently with Mary's ungovernable temper. She treated him like a precocious but ill-behaved schoolboy. She nagged him because he sat down to dinner in his shirt sleeves, and went out to milk the cow in his shuffling slippers, and held up his trousers with one suspender, and ran ahead of the maid to open the door when guests arrived, and spoke to his fashionable visitors about pigs and chickens and turnips and horses, "just like the vulgar yokels from whom he had sprung." She was ashamed of his kind, she reminded him, and she never invited any of his kinsfolk to her house. He was fit to associate only with workingmen and plowmen, she told him contemptuously. In short, he was merely one of the "common people."

Lincoln listened to these accusations and smiled—drat that irritating smile of his! she stormed—and he pleaded guilty. He loved the common people, he confessed. "God too must love them, I guess, or He wouldn't have made so many of them."

For Lincoln was not ashamed of his lowly origin. On the contrary, he wore it like a badge of pride. His heart went out to the underprivileged because he was one of them. Intent upon their investigation of Lincoln's attitude toward the black slaves, many students of history have overlooked his attitude toward the white toilers. Lincoln abhorred wage slavery as intensely as he abhorred black slavery. "Inasmuch as most good things are produced by labor," he said in one of his early campaign speeches, "it follows that all such things of right belong to those whose labor has produced them . . . To secure to each laborer the whole product of his labor . . . is a worthy object of any government."

Lincoln was a friend of labor and an apostle of liberty. But he took care to distinguish between two kinds of liberty—liberty from exploitation, and liberty to exploit. In one of his speeches he pointed out this distinction by means of a parable. "A shepherd drives the wolf from the throat of his sheep . . . and the sheep of course thanks the shepherd . . . but the wolf denounces him." To the sheep the shepherd has given liberty from exploitation; but from the wolf he has taken away the liberty to exploit. "Let not the wolves cry *liberty,* when the word that they really mean is *tyranny."*

In every controversy between the so-called upper and lower classes, Lincoln was on the side of the underdog. He was not only the champion of the laborer but the friend of the immigrant as well. He laughed at the pretensions of those who referred to themselves as *Americans* and to their immigrant neighbors as *foreigners*. All of us, he said, are foreigners. The only native Americans are those who "wear the breechclout and carry the tomahawk." Our forefathers were immigrants when "they drove these Indians from their homes." How stupid, therefore, of us to look down upon "those not fortunate enough to come over so early as we or our forefathers."

Such was the ugly duckling with the strange figure and the unconventional ideas who walked through the streets of Springfield in the 1850s. So absorbed was he in his "peculiarsome" thoughts that he frequently passed by his friends without noticing them. One day he strolled along the sidewalk near his house, trundling behind him a cart in which his little son Willie was riding. The child fell out and lay crying on the street; but his father, unaware of what had happened, kept calmly pulling at the empty cart.

Yet he loved his children with the tenderness of a man whose own childhood had had more than its share of suffering. He allowed them to make his office their playground. "The boys," writes Herndon, "were absolutely unrestrained . . . They pulled down the books from the shelves, bent the points of the pens, overturned the spittoon—but it never disturbed the serenity of their father's good nature." To all of Herndon's suggestions that Lincoln "wring their little necks" the father had but a single reply: "Let them play. Time enough for trouble when they grow up."

We see Lincoln in one of his most revealing moments on a midsummer afternoon when Willie is about four years old. His mother has been trying to give the child a bath. Willie has wriggled out of the tub and scampered naked into the street. His father, sitting on the porch, is holding his sides with laughter at the sight of his pink-and-white little "monkey" who has slipped under a fence and is scurrying across a field. His wife stalks angrily up to Lincoln. "Stop that stupid hilarity and go fetch your son!" Still laughing, Lincoln starts after Willie. He catches him halfway across the field, gathers him up in his long gentle arms, covers his wet little body with kisses, and then mounts him on his shoulders to bring him back to his outraged mother.

Lincoln's tenderness toward his children extended to the entire human race. His was one of those rarely attuned organisms that rejoiced with the joys and suffered with the sufferings of his fellows. His universal sympathy included not only the whites but the blacks. From the very beginning he was interested in the emancipation of the slaves. As a young man he had taken a trip to New Orleans. There he saw the slave market where the Negroes were being auctioned off to the highest bidders. He saw a young girl driven like an animal up and down the platform in order that the prospective purchasers might look her over. "If ever I get a chance to hit that thing," he exclaimed, "I'll hit it hard!" To this end he dedi-

cated his entire life. When he was elected to Congress he drafted a Bill
to Abolish Slavery in the District of Columbia. The bill was defeated,
but Lincoln refused to bow to his defeat. He returned to the fight again
and again. During the Kansas controversy on slavery he raised his voice
in behalf of the black men. When the Republican party was formed
(1854) on the Jeffersonian principle of democratic equality, Lincoln was
one of its most active organizers. And when Douglas, in his ambition
for the presidency, was ready to encourage the extension of slavery in the
South, Lincoln challenged him to a series of debates on the subject.

These debates between Lincoln and Douglas were something new in
American politics. They were mental duels fought before a tribunal of
the American people. And the weapons that the fighters used were the
two sharpest tongues in the United States.

But in Lincoln's speeches there was something more than brilliance.
To paraphrase his own words, it was out of the abundance of his heart
that his mouth continued to speak.

It was during his debates with Douglas that his eyes began to fail him
—the result of the continuous reading of historical and legal documents.
To strengthen his physical vision he went into a jewelry store and
bought a pair of eyeglasses—for thirty-eight cents. He fitted the glasses
to his eyes by the then common method of trying on all kinds until he
found the kind that enabled him to see well. And to strengthen his
mental vision he used the selfsame method. He examined all kinds of
human relationships until he found the kind that enabled men to get
along well. And this relationship he summarized in the following words:
"Stand with anybody that stands right."

As a result of this application of ethics to politics, Lincoln became a
national figure. There had been talk of secession in the South, but Lincoln
declared that America must remain united. "United and right." A house
divided against itself cannot stand. And America must become not partially but completely free. "This government cannot endure permanently
half slave and half free."

Douglas tried to belittle the significance of these words and the importance of Lincoln. "Mr. Lincoln," he said, "is a kind, amiable, intelligent gentleman, but not a national leader." But the common folk felt
otherwise. He was just exactly the sort of leader they wanted in the
national crisis of 1860. And so they rejected Douglas and elected Lincoln
to the presidency.

Between his election and his inauguration his friends came by the
hundreds to wish him Godspeed. And in spite of his busy hours he found
the time to exchange a kind word with every one of them. Among his
visitors was an old lady he had known when he kept store in New
Salem. Lincoln was talking to a group of distinguished politicians when
she arrived. But as soon as he saw her he left the group and walked over
to her with a cordial greeting. Timidly she opened a package wrapped
in brown paper and handed him a pair of coarse woolen socks. "Take
them socks to the White House, Abe. I spun the yarn an' did the knittin'
all by myself." Lincoln thanked her warmly, took the socks and held

them by the toes, one in each hand. "Gentlemen," he said to the astonished bigwigs, "the lady seems to have got my latitude and longitude just about right, don't you think?"

Yes, his friends had got his latitude and longitude—moral as well as physical—just about right.

V

LINCOLN'S ELECTION to the presidency meant the fulfillment of Mary's ambition. But it also meant the end of Lincoln's peace of mind. The planters of the South had clamored for the election of Douglas. They had threatened to revolt in the event of a Republican victory. While still a candidate Lincoln had clearly understood the issue. His own election would result in a personal triumph and probably a national disaster. The election of Douglas, on the other hand, would bring obscurity to Lincoln, but it might possibly avert the tragedy of a war. But would it? Could any power on earth at this stage divert the sweeping tide of hatred that had descended upon the country? And if war must come, would Douglas be the man to steer his nation safely through the storm? Wasn't he too self-centered, too devoid of moral backbone, to take a positive stand for freedom and unity? Was not his heart, as a matter of fact, on the side of the rebels, the seceders, the slaveholders? Would Lincoln be morally justified, therefore, in stepping out of the contest? Did not the presidency need Lincoln more than Lincoln needed the presidency?

Such were the thoughts that tormented him during his campaign and immediately after his election. Rarely in history did a man experience a more bitter triumph. He hated strife. When war had been declared against Mexico (1846), he had raised his voice in protest. It had sickened him to see his country embarked upon a course of military conquest— "that attractive rainbow that rises in showers of blood." And now here he was, the most peaceful of men, compelled to lead his people into another deluge of blood.

Yet even at this late date the war might have been avoided or at least postponed if Buchanan, the outgoing President, had possessed a character of greater firmness. Buchanan saw the gathering storm immediately after the election of Lincoln. But he did nothing to stop it. Let his successor worry about it—if indeed there would be any successor. Again and again he remarked lugubriously, "I am the last President of the United States."

And so he sat irresolutely in the White House while South Carolina seceded two and a half months before the inauguration of Lincoln. Had Buchanan taken a prompt and decided stand against the secession of this state in 1860, just as Jackson had done in 1833, the Civil War might have been nipped in the bud. But instead of discouraging South Carolina, Buchanan actually encouraged it. He not only retained in his Cabinet such men as Jacob Thompson, who had helped South Carolina to secede, but he permitted the transfer of arms from the North to the South. And he sat impassively by when six other states—Mississippi, Florida, Alabama,

Georgia, Louisiana, and Texas—seceded between the election and the inauguration of Lincoln. When Lincoln was sworn into office on March 4, 1861, Buchanan gave him the Civil War as an inauguration present.

VI

THROUGHOUT THE WAR, Abraham Lincoln had a double danger to fight against—invasion from without, disloyalty from within. The Copperheads —a copperhead is a "venomous snake that strikes without warning"— were beclouding the issues of the war with the propaganda of racial hatred. But Lincoln faced the rebellion of the South and the obstruction- ism of the North with a single courageous purpose—to keep the states united. "My paramount object in this struggle," he said, "is to save the Union . . . If I could save the Union without freeing any slave, I would do it; and if I could do it by freeing all the slaves, I would do it; and if I could do it by freeing some and leaving others alone, I would do that. What I do about slavery and the colored race, I do because I believe it helps to save the Union."

Here we see Lincoln thinking aloud. And, as a result of his clear and logical thinking, he came to the conclusion that the only way in which he could save the Union was to free the slaves. The Emancipation Proc- lamation was the inevitable final paragraph in the thesis of Lincoln's philosophy.

And Lincoln's entire philosophy may be summarized in a few simple words—impartial love for the united family of America. His attitude even toward the South was one of tenderness and pity. He always spoke of the rebels as "these Southern gentlemen." He had an intense hatred against slavery but no hatred against those who believed in it. "They are just what we would be in their situation." He regarded the slaveowners, no less than the slaves, as the victims of a diseased institution that must be purged out of society if the nation was to be healed. He wanted to bring about a twofold freedom—to free the black man from the slavery of his body and the white man from the slavery of his soul.

He was a man of infinite patience. He bore not only with the insults of McClellan but with those of his official family as well. When Seward and Chase reviled him, and Stanton referred to him as "that damned, gawky, long-armed gorilla," he neither rebuked them nor dismissed them from the Cabinet. "It is a dangerous thing to swap horses in the middle of the stream." And when the swivel-chair patriots—the men who did all the inciting and none of the fighting—accused him of incompetence, he let them talk and went quietly on with his work.

The vituperations against Lincoln continued throughout his life. Every- thing he did, insisted his obstreperous opponents, was wrong. Even his Gettysburg Address was denounced in the hostile papers as "silly and sentimental and unworthy of the occasion." It was not until after his assassination that America awoke to his greatness. Destiny, it seemed, had deliberately injected a melodramatic climax in order to emphasize the beautiful drama of his life. For now, at last, Lincoln stood forth as a man among a nation of children. Father Abraham . . . with malice toward none, with charity for all.

IMPORTANT DATES IN THE LIFE OF ABRAHAM LINCOLN

1809—Born, Kentucky.

1831—Employed as clerk in general store at New Salem, Illinois.

1834—Elected to the Illinois state legislature.

1835—Death of his betrothed, Ann Rutledge.

1837—Began practice of law.

1842—Married Mary Todd.

1847-49—Served in the House of Representatives.

1854—Delivered (in Peoria) speech against the extension of slavery.

1856—Joined the new Republican party.

1858—Debated with Stephen A. Douglas on the question of slavery.

1860—Delivered address at Cooper Union.

Elected the sixteenth President of the United States.

1861—As commander in chief of the Union Army, assumed burden of Civil War.

1863—Issued Emancipation Proclamation.

Delivered Gettysburg Address.

1864—Re-elected President.

1865—Assassinated, Ford's Theater, Washington.

Walt Whitman

[1819–1892]

A NAVY Yard horsecar is lumbering over the cobblestones at the foot of Capitol Hill in Washington. It is near sundown on a stifling July day. The air is rancid with the midsummer perspiration of a packed carful of laborers returning home from their work. Inside the car, near the door, stands a young woman holding one child by the hand and another—a babe of about eleven months—against her breast. The infant is hot and fretful. Its interminable howling annoys the passengers and drives the mother to the verge of distraction.

The car stops to let on a number of new passengers. One of them, a middle-aged, bearded, and florid-faced giant of a man, swings with an awkward but agile step onto the rear platform. He stops near the conductor and begins to talk to him in a low voice. Evidently these two men are intimate friends.

There is something fresh and fragrant about the bearded passenger. "He has the look of a man who has just taken a sea bath." He is dressed in workingman's clothes, but his shirt, though open at the throat, is spotlessly white. His head is covered with a broad-brimmed white hat. His face is "suffused with serenity and goodness and physical and mental health." He looks calm and cheerful and cool in this suffocating caldron of human fretfulness.

The car, with its grumbling workers and howling infant, is tugging slowly toward the top of Capitol Hill. The atmosphere inside has become unbearable. The flushed and exhausted mother is ready to burst into tears. The car stops at a street corner to let off several of the passengers. The rear platform is almost empty now. The bearded man reaches inside and, in spite of the mother's protests, takes the infant out of her sweltering arms and into the open air of the platform. The child, astonished at its sudden adventure, stops its screaming. With its chubby fists planted against the stranger's breast, it throws its little head back and gazes into the man's face. The result of the examination is apparently satisfactory. For the child snuggles up against the stranger's shoulder and within a few moments is fast asleep.

Another stop. The conductor gets off for his supper and a bit of rest. "Pick you up on the way back, Pete!" shouts the bearded man as, with the sleeping babe in his arms, he assumes the duties of the conductor. Leaning against the dashboard on the rear platform, he keeps an eye on the passengers, pulls the bell to leave them off the car, and exchanges a parting good word with each and every one of them as they step down from the platform.

"Queer chap," remarks one of the passengers to another as they leave the car together.

"Yeah, queer chap and the author of a queer book."

"What's the name of the book?"

"*Leaves of Grass.*"

II

THE TITLE of his poems, *Leaves of Grass,* was one of the happiest of Walt Whitman's inspirations. For this title represents the perfect symbol for the Poetry of Democracy. The leaves of grass, like the common people, are the simplest and the sturdiest of growing things. Disregarded, trampled underfoot, and flourishing best in the obscurest places, the grass bows but never breaks under the lash of the angry winds. While the higher and the hardier plants break down, the lowly grass keeps growing and spreading everywhere. Walt Whitman might have paraphrased the words of Abraham Lincoln: "God must love the blades of grass and the common people, or he wouldn't have made so many of them."

Leaves of Grass could have been written only by an American son of poverty—the obscure member of a democratic race. Walt Whitman boasted an ancestry that was both poor and obscure. He got his blunt and sturdy honesty from his American father, his Quaker gentleness from his Dutch mother, and his rebellious hunger for justice from both branches of the family. His paternal as well as his maternal ancestors had served in Washington's army. And there seemed to be a rebellious strain even in the women of the Whitman family. His great-grandmother on his father's side was quite a legend among her neighbors. Smoking a pipe and swearing like a trooper, she had been the terror of the village hoodlums and the guardian angel of the Negro slaves' children. It was from her that Whitman inherited his stubbornness as well as his kindness and his fellow feeling for the underdog.

The second of nine children, Walt Whitman was born (May 31, 1819) at West Hills, Long Island—or, as Whitman preferred to call it, Paumanok, "the island with its breast against the sea." In his infancy he was rocked to sleep by the beating of the sea surf on the headlands near his home. This irregular rhythm of the wind and the waves got into his blood stream and found an echo many years later in the unmetrical cadences of his poetry.

When Walt was four years old the Whitmans moved to Brooklyn. For his father had decided to give up farming in favor of carpentry as a better means of livelihood. But the children were sent to spend their summer vacations with their grandparents at West Hills. Here Walt "adventured" for hours at a stretch and became intimately acquainted with the rivers and the fields and the forests and that most beloved of all his comrades, the everlastingly resounding sea.

In the skimpy school hours of the winter months young Whitman applied himself to the four Rs—readin', 'ritin', 'rithmetic, and restin'. Especially the fourth. "This boy is so idle," said his schoolteacher, Benjamin Halleck, "I am sure he will never amount to anything."

Walt's father agreed with Mr. Halleck. It was useless for the boy to continue with his education. Let him rub shoulders with people and learn to do an honest day's labor. And so, at thirteen, he took Walt out of school and apprenticed him to a printer.

But in the printing shop, as in the classroom, the youngster continued to devote himself to the fine art of doing nothing. "If the boy caught an ague," his employer once remarked, "he would be too lazy to shake."

It was not mere laziness, however, that kept him wrapped up in the perpetual enchantment of his daydreams. "I loafe and invite my soul." While his body was quiescent, his mind was active. "I lean and loafe at my ease observing a spear of summer grass." His eye and his heart were constantly open to the world about him. Though he had left school, he was still educating himself. Indeed, he had entered upon a higher course of education—higher than any of the courses to be found in the colleges. The antennae of his mind were reaching out to come into contact with reality. The *real* reality. He was trying, subconsciously perhaps at the start, to find a clear way "through the dimness" called *the mystery of life.* What is the grass? What are the stars? And what am I?

And for the present there was a definite and insistent answer at least to the last of these questions. I am a creature that must be fed and clothed and sheltered. In other words, he must make a living for himself. For a time he tried carpentry and disliked it. He then turned to schoolteaching, and this too he found distasteful. Finally he drifted into literature and knew at once that this was where he belonged.

He was only twenty-two when he wrote his first book—a melodramatic temperance novel. And it almost proved to be his artistic undoing, for it was a financial success. Within a short time the publishers had disposed of twenty thousand copies. A reception such as this, at so early an age, was enough to turn the head of any young author. Walt Whitman seemed destined for popular mediocrity as a scribbler of sermons in fiction. His sense of humor saved him, however. He gave a beer party to his friends in order to celebrate the success of his temperance story and then entered upon the slow steps of his development from a second-rate novelist into a first-rate poet.

III

IN ORDER to solve the bread-and-butter problem during the years of his apprenticeship to the Muse he accepted an editorial job on the *Brooklyn Daily Eagle*. The pay was good and the work congenial. "There is a curious kind of sympathy," he wrote in one of his editorials, "between the editor and his public. . . . Daily communion creates a sort of brotherhood . . . between the two parties. As for us, we like it."

He liked his work, but he liked his leisure even more. Again and again he would urge his readers to relax. "Let us enjoy life a little. Has God made this beautiful earth . . . all for nothing? Let us go forth awhile and get better air in our lungs." He loved to be out in the air wherever possible. Though not athletic himself—"I am more of a floater than a swimmer"—he enjoyed watching the athletic games of other people. Indeed, he enjoyed watching anything and everything about him. Watching and absorbing—slowly, methodically, thoroughly. He was never in a hurry. He couldn't understand why people should "run after ferries with hats flying off and skirts flying behind." His favorite pastime when he crossed the ferry from Brooklyn to New York was to stand aside and look at the people. "Crowds of men and women attired in the usual costumes, how curious you are to me! . . . I, too, am one of the crowd. . . . The men and the women I see are all near to me."

This was the thought that kept recurring to him again and again. The united kinship of human life. All men draw their sustenance from the one spiritual fountain which is God, just as all plants derive their strength from the one common breast of Mother Earth.

All men are interrelated members of one body—mankind. White men, red men, yellow men, black men—all are brothers under their skin. It was this thought that he tried to emphasize in the editorial pages of the *Eagle*. And it was because of this thought that he lost his position on the paper. One day he had become involved in an argument with an influential politician on the question of slavery. Rumor had it that he had kicked the proslavery gentleman down the steps. At any rate, Whitman was told to look for another job.

He found his new job in New Orleans. And when he came to this Queen City of the South he entered upon "the most interesting episode" of his life. Unfortunately we can only guess as to the nature of this episode, since he has drawn the veil of silence over it. But one thing seems certain—that he became "intimately acquainted with a woman of a different social rank" from his own. He met her, apparently at a ball in the suburb known as Lafayette. It was an evening in May. Walt Whitman, at the insistence of his friends, had put on formal clothes—probably for the first time in his life. As he drew the white kid gloves over his large hands he burst them, so that they looked like "cracked dumplings." Folding his hands "nonchalantly" behind his back, he watched "the Creole beauties, the free women of color, the graceful forms and lovely faces in plain, fancy, and mask dresses." As he looked at these women, "each one lovelier than the other," he caught a glimpse of "what I conceived the very pink of perfection, in form, grace, and movement, in fancy dress." He managed to get an introduction to her. . . .

And this is all we know with regard to the entire episode. Walt Whitman had written a full account of his visit to New Orleans, but he later destroyed all the pages in which he had referred to this "solitary romance" of his life. This romance resulted in no marriage, either because the lady in question was already married to another man or else because her family objected to Walt for financial or for social reasons. But he became the father of at least one of her children. Many years later he wrote to John Addington Symonds about this episode and mentioned a grandson with whom he kept in constant touch. But he begged Symonds never to "disclose the secret" to anybody else. To do so, he said, "would indisputably do a great injury to someone."

This, then, is all we know of his "one brief hour of madness and joy" —this, and a poem or two in which he hinted about his New Orleans experience.

> Out of the rolling ocean, the crowd, came a drop gently to me,
> Whispering I love you, before long I die,
> I have travel'd a long way merely to look on you, to touch you,
> For I could not die till I once looked on you.

> .　　.　　.　　.　　.　　.　　.

> Again we wander—we love—we separate again,
> Again she holds me by the hand—I must not go!
> I see her close beside me, with silent lips, sad and tremulous.

> .　　.　　.　　.　　.　　.

> Return in peace to the ocean, my love,
> I too am part of that ocean, my love. . . .

And that ocean is one indivisible stream of inseparable life. For a brief space it may "carry us diverse, yet [it] cannot carry us diverse forever."

Be not impatient—a little space—— And in the meantime, "I salute the air, the ocean, and the land every day at sundown for your dear sake, my love. . . ."

His mysterious romance at New Orleans proved to be the final ingredient of sunlight and sadness necessary for the flowering of his poetical genius. It was shortly after his return from New Orleans that he began to write his *Leaves of Grass*.

IV

THE FIRST EDITION of *Leaves of Grass* came out in 1855. It fell like a feather upon a sea of contemptuous silence. There was only one man in America

—Ralph Waldo Emerson—who recognized something of its greatness. Having come across a copy of the book, Emerson wrote to its unknown author: "I am not blind to the worth of the wonderful gift of the *Leaves of Grass*. I find it the most extraordinary piece of wit and wisdom that America has yet contributed. . . . I find incomparable things, said incomparably well. . . . I greet you at the beginning of a great career. . . ."

While Emerson was still under the enchantment of his first reading of the *Leaves of Grass* he sent one of his own admirers to visit Walt Whitman in Brooklyn. "*There* you will see a poet you can *really* admire. . . . Americans abroad may now come home: unto us a man is born."

Later, however, Emerson found the language of Whitman a little too pungent for his delicate New England palate. He could stand Whitman's doctrine of equality; he himself had advanced it, with a somewhat dainty timidity, in his democratic poem *The Mountain and the Squirrel*. But what he could not tolerate was Whitman's disconcerting frankness. The Sage of Concord was too cultured a gentleman "to expose the unexposable and to mention the unmentionable"—at least in the open pages of a book. There was no need, he felt, to emphasize bluntly the obvious fact that there are puddles on the earth as well as stars in the heavens. When Emerson reread some of Whitman's outspoken sex poems he repented of his earlier wholehearted endorsement. He advised Whitman to omit these poems from the next edition, pointing out to him the danger that the "unnecessary inclusion of the sex element" might attract the wrong readers and repel the right readers. To all of which criticism the younger poet replied that there was no unnecessary element in his book, that every poem was just as important to the book as every organ is important to the body, and that in spite of Emerson's advice—which he most deeply respected—he remained "more convinced than ever to adhere to my own theory."

Emerson gently decided to leave Whitman to his own theory. But he was now inclined to agree with the editor of one of the literary journals (the *Boston Intelligence*) that Whitman was an escaped lunatic. He failed to realize, as at first the entire world failed to realize, that here was no prurient dabbler in forbidden things, but a poet of universal sympathy. Whitman spoke of the various parts of the body in the same spirit in which God had created them. Whitman's poems are a glorification of life —of every phase of it. To the pure all things are pure. Whitman found beauty and holiness everywhere because he examined everything with an attitude of holiness and beauty. A hasty stroll over the *Leaves of Grass* should demonstrate this fact.

This book of Whitman's poems is, like the life of its author, foursquare. It is founded upon the principles of *equality, pity, religion,* and *love.*

We have already referred to Whitman's doctrine of equality. He worships the "divine average"—that is, he reveals the divine essence that inheres in the everyday life of the average man. His aim is "to teach the average man the glory of his daily walk and trade." No one, however lowly, need fear that he is unworthy to live and to enjoy life. Let no one presume to lord it over others and let no one allow others to lord it over

him. "Resist much, obey little." Do not bow to superiors, for no one is
your superior. You are the equal of any. All are the children of the earth,
and in the final reckoning the impartial mother plays no favorites. All
things are the related parts of God. They are the leaves of the undying
tree of life. The selfsame immortal sap flows through the veins of the
entire universe. "I know that the spirit of God is the brother of my own
and that all the men ever born are also my brothers and the women my
sisters and lovers." The greatest and the least are tending toward the
same goal, and all alike will reach it in the end. Have you outstripped
the rest? Are you the President? It is a trifle; they will more than arrive
there, every one, and still pass on." Whitman believes in the evolution
of the individual as well as of the race. Each human soul undergoes a
lengthy process of education—before its appearance upon this earth,
throughout its earthly existence, and after its passage into the next
world. Each soul must pass through every grade of this education. Those
who during their lifetime upon earth appear to belong to the humbler
classes are merely, for the time being, going through a lower grade than
their fellow pupils in the democratic school of eternal life. But in the
long run every human soul will reach the highest grade in this universal
school and graduate into the presence of God. Walt Whitman's democracy is not merely a political or a social doctrine. It is a religious faith—
a supreme conviction that each and every one of us will attain to perfection in the end. Just what this "perfection" may be, Whitman does not
pretend to know. "But I know that it will in its turn prove sufficient and
cannot fail."

It cannot fail the young man who died and was buried,
Nor the young woman who died and was put by his side,
Nor the little child that peeped in at the door, and then drew back and
*   was never seen again,*
Nor the old man who has lived without purpose, and feels it with bit-
*   terness worse than gall. . . .*

The glory of an immortal life awaits them all. "I do not call one greater
and one smaller. That which fills its period and space is equal to any."
The great Camerado will be there to greet us all with His kindly smile
of infinite love.

Whitman's doctrine of equality is due to his great sense of pity. He
feels akin to all the sufferers of the world. "Whoever walks a furlong
without sympathy," he writes, "walks to his own funeral dressed in his
own shroud." Unable to injure any living creature, Walt Whitman cannot conceive of a Creator whose sense of pity is less than his own. He
salutes all the inhabitants of the earth. His good will extends to all things
created. "Health to you, good will to you all . . . in America's name!"

Walt Whitman was perhaps the most compassionate of modern poets.
And because of his compassion he was constantly preoccupied with the
problem of death. Always he spoke in its praise. Death, he said, is the
great Physician whose white hand brushes away the last vestige of human
pain. Whatever may be our burden in the glare and the turmoil of

the world, the poet comforts us all alike with the lovely and soothing promise of "night, sleep, death, and the stars." Do you weep at the brevity of your life and the intensity of your suffering? "Weep not, child, weep not, my darling; something there is more immortal even than the stars, something that shall endure longer even than lustrous Jupiter, longer than sun or any revolving satellite or the radiant sisters the Pleiades." And what is that something? Your ultimate happiness, your triumphant destiny, your undying soul.

Walt Whitman rarely went to church, but he was one of the most religious of poets. As we have already noted, he made a religion of Democracy. He transplanted the pantheism of Spinoza into the soil of American republicanism. The United States of America—the United Body of Mankind—the United Soul of the Universe. The body and the soul, he said, are one; and death is merely an extension of life. "I laugh at what you call dissolution," for "I know I am deathless." This conviction that all men are deathless, and that all human lives are equally important ripples that play upon the surface of the universal ocean of life, is everywhere expressed with a finality that becomes a gospel in his *Leaves of Grass*. This new Gospel of American Democracy glorifies the dignity of man. Every human creature is a high priest who can, if he will, speak face to face with God. A new era will begin when the human race becomes aware of this fact. A new religion, greater and more inclusive than the old, will flush the world with love. For each individual life will then recognize its kinship with the whole. Walt Whitman sings the song of a new world, a new race, a new devotion, a new faith. "I say no man has ever yet been half devout enough, none has ever yet adored or worship'd half enough, none has begun to think how divine he himself is and how certain the future is."

With this faith implanted in his heart Walt Whitman offers the hand of friendship to all men. He sings to them "the evangel poem" of comrades and of love. "For who but I should understand love with all its sorrow and joy? And who but I should be the poet of comrades?"

Love, to Whitman, is a reunion—a meeting again with those to whom we have been united in a remote past. "Passing stranger, you do not know how longingly I look upon you. You must be he I was seeking or she I was seeking (it comes to me as of a dream). I have somewhere surely lived a life of joy with you."

In his communion with other people Walt Whitman found a joy that passes understanding. He did not merely *sing* of comradeship. He was one of those very rare men who actually *lived* it. He identified himself with the whole world and tried to give of himself to everybody. He had a passion for cultivating the friendship of the humble. He extended the comradely hand to those who couldn't "get on" in the competitive struggle of life. He drove a coach during an entire winter for a coachman who was ill. Following his own prescription as set forth in the preface to the 1855 edition of *Leaves of Grass,* he loved the earth and sun and the animals, despised riches, gave alms to everybody that asked, stood up for the stupid and the weak, took off his hat to nothing known or unknown, and entered into close fellowship with all those who were poor in the possession of friends.

His was the American Gospel at its best.

V

DURING THE CIVIL WAR he offered his life to the service of humanity—not on the battlefields but in the hospitals. His brother George, who had enlisted in the 51st New York Volunteers, was wounded at the Battle of Fredericksburg. Walt went down to nurse him at the Soldiers' Hospital in Washington. When he arrived there George was already well. But Walt remained in Washington to look after the other wounded and dying soldiers. This was his daily occupation to the end of the war. Never was nurse more skillful or minister more tender. Walt became the companion of the sick soldiers, their secretary, their attendant, their comforter, their friend. We have a picture of the "Good Gray Poet" from the pen of a man who accompanied Walt on one of his hospital visits:

"Never shall I forget that visit. . . . There were three rows of cots, and each cot bore its man. When he appeared, in passing along, there was a smile of affection and welcome on every face, however wan, and his presence seemed to light up the place as it might be lit by the presence of the Son of Love. From cot to cot they called him, often in tremulous tones or in whispers; they embraced him, they touched his hand, they gazed at him. To one he gave a few words of cheer, for another he wrote a letter home, to others he gave an orange, a few comfits, a cigar, a pipe and tobacco, a sheet of paper or a postage stamp, all of which and many other things were in his capacious haversack. From another he would receive a dying message for mother, wife, or sweetheart; for another he would promise to go on an errand; to another, some special friend, very low, he would give a manly farewell kiss. He did the things for them which no nurse or doctor could do, and he seemed to leave a benediction at every cot as he passed along. . . ."

He performed miracles, the doctors said—miracles of healing. A few courageous words, spoken in his gentle voice, would at times bring back to life those who had resigned themselves to death and whom even the doctors had given up. Many of the soldiers remembered him years later as "the man with the face of the Saviour."

In his work among the wounded soldiers he made no distinction between friend and foe. All the stricken men, whether of the North or of the South, were his "brothers in distress." One of the most beautiful of the poems which he wrote during the Civil War describes his feeling at the sight of a slain enemy:

Word over all, beautiful as the sky,
Beautiful that war and all its carnage must in time be utterly lost,
That the hands of the sisters Death and Night incessantly softly wash
*   again, and ever again, this soil'd world;*

For my enemy is dead, a man divine as myself is dead;
I look where he lies white-faced and stiff in the coffin—I draw near,
Bend down and touch lightly with my lips the white face in the coffin.

Whitman received no pay for his ministration to the sick and the dying soldiers. In order to support himself during this period he secured a clerical post in the Indian Bureau of the Department of the Interior. Some busybody, however, called the attention of James Harlan, the Secretary of the Interior, to Walt Whitman's "pernicious poetry." One evening, while Walt was making his usual rounds of the hospitals, the curious Mr. Harlan walked into the poet's office, found a copy of *Leaves of Grass* on the desk, and read enough of it to shut the book with a complete miscomprehension of the poems and with a muddle-witted prejudice against their author. The next morning, when the poet arrived at his desk, he found the following note awaiting him:

"The service of Walter Whitman will be dispensed with from and after this date."

The gods, wrote an Eastern sage, are forever walking through the cities of men. But the eyes of men are too blind to see them.

VI

In 1873 Walt Whitman suffered a paralytic stroke. The seeds of this illness, said his doctor, had been planted in his body during the long vigils and the laborious sacrifices in the soldiers' hospitals. He recovered partially from his paralysis, but he was never himself again. His body remained broken to the end of his days. He limped his painful way through the cities of men, an obscure, lonely, and at times hungry god. With a basket over his arm he peddled his books from door to door. One winter day, as he was thus trying to exchange nuggets of gold for crusts of bread, an elderly widow, Mrs. Mary Davis, took pity on him. She invited him into her cottage, offered him a warm breakfast, and decided then and there to take care of him for the rest of his life. A few of his admirers bought him a little box of a house in Camden, New Jersey, the town in which his mother had died and in which he was anxious to end his own days. The furniture was of the scantiest—a bed, a dry-goods case to write on, a couple of chairs, a table on which stood an oilstove to cook his food, nothing more. After a while, however, Mrs. Davis moved in as his housekeeper and brought her own furniture along with her. He now lived "like a prince in his own domain."

A prince in a ramshackle hovel. The house was "on the other side of the railroad tracks." The street was shabby, noise-ridden, and infested with the offensive odors of a near-by guano factory. But in the back yard there was a pear tree under which he would sit on summer evenings. And on the front doorstep the children would come to play and to wait for the pennies that he tossed them—whenever he could spare them—out of the window.

Thus he spent the last few years of his life—receiving his friends in the downstairs "parlor" as long as he was able to move around and in his upstairs "study" when his strength had given out. Both "parlor" and "study" were cluttered—chairs, tables, mantelpieces, floor—with hundreds of copies of his unsold books.

On his seventy-second birthday (May 31, 1891) a group of his friends hired a caterer and gave the poet a "banquet" in his home. "We had a capital supper," he wrote, "chicken soup, salmon, roast lamb, etc., etc., etc. I had been under a horrible spell from 5 to 6, but Warry got me dress'd and down (like carrying down a great log) . . ."

This was his last birthday on earth. A few months later they got him dressed and carried him—to his first birthday in heaven? Speaking of the afterlife to the agnostic Robert G. Ingersoll, Walt Whitman had once declared, "Well, Bob, I don't know—for anybody but *myself*. But for *myself* —I am as certain of it as I am that we are all here!"

IMPORTANT DATES IN THE LIFE OF
WALT WHITMAN

1819—Born, West Hills, Long Island.

1824—Family moved to Brooklyn.

1846–48—Worked on *Brooklyn Daily Eagle*.

1855—Published first edition of *Leaves of Grass*.

1862–65—Ministered to wounded soldiers in Civil War.

1865—Published *Drum Taps*.

1865–73—Served as government clerk in Washington.

1870—Published *Democratic Vistas*.

1873—Stricken with partial paralysis.

Moved to Camden, New Jersey.

1888—Published *Sands at Seventy*.

1892—Died, Camden, New Jersey.

Susan B. Anthony

[1820-1906]

SHE was not like other children. "The girls of the nineteenth century," said her teacher, Miss Deborah Moulson, "must behave precisely as the girls have behaved in all the other centuries ... The sanctity of tradition must be always upheld." But Susan believed neither in precision nor in tradition. She had a mind of her own—an unheard-of crime in Miss Moulson's Select Seminary for Females. The curriculum at the seminary was based upon the time-honored triangle of Morality, Love of Virtue, and—above all—Humility. Susan couldn't be humble. She tried her best, but in vain. Children, insisted Deborah, must rarely be seen and never heard. But Susan liked to be heard as well as seen. One day she laughed in class out of turn. "Traitor," snapped Deborah, "remember the fate of Judas Iscariot!" All letters written by the students to their parents, declared Deborah, must first be submitted to her censorial scrutiny. Susan prepared a letter containing some "private" information and tried to send it off to her father uncensored. Deborah intercepted the letter. The memory of the scene that followed brought tears to Susan's eyes years afterward.

But the climax of her "unregenerate conduct" came on the day of the spring house cleaning at the seminary. In her eagerness to sweep a cobweb off the ceiling, Susan jumped upon Deborah's desk—and broke it! This was a misdemeanor that demanded nothing less than a public scolding before the entire school. Miss Moulson assembled the school and, after the solemn reading of a chapter from the Scriptures, consigned Susan to those regions where "the worm dieth not and the fire is not quenched." Miss Deborah's homilies, wrote Susan in her diary, "made me indeed feel like a worm ... But there were times when I preferred to be a worm rather than a girl. For then I could do my wriggling without the eternal scrutiny of my fellow worms."

II

HER ATTENDANCE at Miss Moulson's Seminary gave Susan two things: a stiff literary style—"whenever I take my pen in hand I seem to be mounted on stilts"—and a wholesome disrespect for the "conventions of the ant-hill." She came by her rebellion from her father, who, though himself a Quaker, had defied the rules of his order by marrying a Baptist. And his young bride, Lucy Read, was not an orthodox Baptist at that. She was fond of pretty compliments and pretty clothes, she sang at her spinning wheel—a frivolous indiscretion in the second decade of the nineteenth century—and she danced until four o'clock in the morning just a few days before her marriage—an *unpardonable sin* in the second decade of the nineteenth century. She developed, however, into a sensible wife and sensitive mother. And her eight children—of whom Susan was the second —inherited their mother's sensitiveness as well as their father's rebellion.

Susan's early years were spent in an atmosphere of "comfortable hard-ship." Her father was the owner of a small cotton mill. The older children had their hands full in helping their mother to take care not only of the younger children but of the mill hands who boarded in their house. During one summer, with a nursing baby in her arms, Mrs. Anthony was obliged to board eleven "guests." No time now for the mother to sing at her spinning wheel. Or for the children to play. Too many hours to spend in washing, ironing, weaving, sewing, cooking, baking. On one of the pages of her diary Susan makes the following casual entry—"Made twenty-one loaves of bread today." Recreation was not meant for the womenfolk of the world. Theirs was the business "to attend to the house-hold work, to fear the Lord, and to hold their tongues."

But Susan was not one to hold her tongue. Her father having lost his mill in the panic of 1838, she was obliged to help out the family budget with the two dollars a week she earned as a schoolteacher. Her contract, however, was not renewed after the first term. Her acts and her speech were too free. Warned again and again that she must not jeopardize her position through her association with the "niggers" of the community, she finally answered the warnings with this rifleshot of defiance: "Since school today I have had the unspeakable satisfaction of visiting four col-ored people and drinking tea with them."

Though she felt pity for the black sheep of the human family, she had nothing but contempt for the white bullies. She was now teaching in another school, a whirlpool of ruffianism from which the male teacher had just been dismissed for his failure as a disciplinarian. The farm louts who attended that school had enrolled there not for study but for sport —the hoodlum sport of teacher-baiting. They soon found, to their sor-row, that Miss Anthony was a teacher not to be baited. Cutting a heavy stick from a birch tree, she trounced the leader of the rowdies into so abject a state of submission that from that day on the entire school treated her with the proper respect. "By gosh, this woman's got the nerve of a man!"

And the *brains* of a man. Appointed as the principal of the girls' department of the Canajoharie (New York) Academy, she made a profound impression upon the citizens of that village. "This woman," said one of the trustees of the school, "is the smartest man that ever came to Canajoharie."

Several of the local "magnates" proposed marriage to her. These men, however, were attracted not so much by her wisdom as by her vigor. "A fine figure of a woman," said one of them—the owner of a sixty-cow dairy. "She'll do a good job milking those sixty cows." Susan politely but emphatically refused this man as well as her other suitors. "No, thank you, I don't want to be any man's legalized servant."

She preferred to stick to her independence. Her shoulders were sturdy enough and her heart stout enough to sustain the burden of her livelihood. But what of those millions of women who were neither strong enough nor courageous enough to stand up against the injustices of a man-made world? One day in the summer of 1848 she read about a convention of women that had been held in Seneca Falls, New York, for the purpose of discussing their "social, civil, and religious rights." The idea intrigued her. She began to study the social, civil, and religious status of women in the United States—and was appalled at the revelation. The legal code of America, like that of every other country in the world, had relegated the women to a position of undignified inferiority. In accordance with this code, every woman was a perpetual minor. She could never grow up to legal maturity. If she married, she became the property of her husband. And if she remained a spinster, she was obliged to assign her property to a male guardian. No married woman was allowed to sue for breach of contract, to retain the wages that she earned for her work, or to receive damages for injury done to her person or character. In every case the husband was the beneficiary. He was not only the arbiter of her fate and fortune but the owner of her children. He could give or will away the children without the mother's consent; and even though he were proved to be a degenerate or a drunkard, he became the children's sole custodian in the event of divorce. A man was allowed to beat his wife, his children, and his dog; and a woman was not allowed to divorce her husband even on the ground of cruelty. Every American woman, in short, was a slave.

When the women attempted to break the chains of their slavery, they were met everywhere with a howl of derision. The delegates to the Seneca Falls Convention were characterized as "atheists, hermaphrodites, hyenas in petticoats." A few courageous voices, however, had dared to approve of the women's Declaration of Independence. One of the approving voices was that of Susan's father, Daniel Anthony. In his own cotton mills he had regarded his workers like human beings. But in *most* of the cotton mills, he learned from the speeches of the convention, the workers were treated merely like so many mechanical hands. Especially the women. For a working day of fourteen hours they received thirty-one cents. The same situation held true in all the other trades open to women. For sewing a coat, a woman received forty cents; for a pair of trousers, twelve cents. But—most deplorable of all—these working women, if married, had no claim to their own wages, but were compelled by law to turn every cent over to their husbands. And many of these husbands, it was pointed out, wasted their women's earnings on drink or on other women.

The Anthonys discussed these matters around the dinner table. Daniel Anthony told Susan about another woman's rights convention, held at Rochester, which he had personally attended. He related an amusing anecdote about that convention. One of the speakers, Mrs. Elizabeth Cady Stanton, had been taken to task by a married clergyman. "The Apostle Paul," the clergyman scolded her, "recommends silence to women. Why don't you mind him?" Whereupon Mrs. Stanton retorted, "The Apostle Paul also recommends celibacy to clergymen. Why don't *you* mind him?"

Susan laughed when she heard this story. "Mrs. Stanton," she said, "is a woman after my own heart. I should like to meet her."

III

It was some years before Susan Anthony met Elizabeth Cady Stanton. For at the time of the Seneca Falls Convention, Miss Anthony was interested in reforming the men rather than in liberating the women. An ardent rebel like her father, she had allied herself not only with the abolitionists but also—and especially—with the prohibitionists. Equally pernicious with the curse of slavery, it seemed to her, was the curse of drink. For drinking, in those days, was a serious matter. The pioneers were men of leathery throats and fireproof stomachs. Everybody drank, and almost everybody drank to excess. At a banquet given in honor of Daniel Webster, at which there were twelve hundred invited guests, the champagne consumed amounted to exactly twenty-four hundred bottles—two bottles to every guest. And this was merely the appetizer for the stronger drinks.

The excessive taste for alcohol was a reaction against the puritanism of the age. The conscience of America forbade the people to play; and the people, out of revenge, decided to drown their conscience in a deluge of whisky. Almost the entire male population, from the workingman in the factory to the judge on the bench, went about their business in a perpetual fog of intoxication.

Such was the state of affairs when Miss Anthony joined the Temperance movement. At that period she hadn't the slightest interest in votes for women. Or in votes for men, either. For she had been brought up in a Quaker community, and the Quakers were philosophical anarchists who did not believe in voting. But the Anthonys did believe in speaking their minds. Especially Susan. One day, when she was attending a Temperance Convention in Albany (1852), she stood up and tried to make a speech. Whereupon the chairman promptly silenced her. Women, he declared bluntly, must listen and learn but they must never talk. Furious over the ungallantry of the dominant sex, she stalked out of the room. If the men refused to give the women equal courtesy, the women would begin to demand equal rights. On that day Militant Feminism was born.

As soon as she joined the Feminist movement Susan became one of its leaders. For everybody recognized her dynamic personality and her extraordinary intellect. Yet she knew her own limitations. She was a great organizer, but she was not a great writer or speaker. And so she supplemented her own talents with those of the two other leading Feminists of the day—Elizabeth Cady Stanton and Ernestine Rose. These "three musketeers" organized themselves into what may be called the first "female triumvirate" in history. Susan Anthony, who was the most practical member of the triumvirate, supplied the plans for the campaign. Elizabeth Stanton, who had a feeling for poetical phrases, put the plans into winged words. And Ernestine Rose, whose eloquent tongue had distinguished her as "the Queen of the Platform," delivered the speeches. These three women were socially and economically so far apart that only in America could an intimate alliance have been possible between them. Susan Anthony was the daughter of a poor Quaker. Elizabeth Stanton was the wife of a wealthy attorney. Ernestine Rose was a Jewish immigrant.

Together the three went traveling over the country, organizing meetings, encouraging the women, and upbraiding the men. It was a long and uphill fight, at first without the benefit of publicity from the press. "Who would be interested in reading about these crazy female ranters?" But little by little the editors became scurrilously interested. They tried to drown out the movement in a deluge of Rabelaisian innuendo. "What do the leaders of the woman's rights organization want?" asked the elder Mr. Bennett in the *New York Herald* (September 12, 1852). "They want to fill all the posts which men are ambitious to occupy, to be lawyers, doctors, captains of vessels, and generals in the field. How funny it would sound in the newspapers that Lucy Stone, pleading a case, took suddenly ill in the pains of parturition . . . Or that the Reverend Antoinette Brown was arrested in the pulpit in the middle of her sermon from the same cause . . . Or that Dr. Harriot K. Hunt, while attending a gentleman patient for a fistula in ano, found it necessary to send for a doctor, there and then, to be delivered of twins."

And then, when they saw that the Feminist movement was gaining adherents, the editors descended from derision to denunciation. The Feminist triumvirate had advocated, among other things, divorce for drunkenness and birth control for drunkards' wives. "Such heresies," wrote the *Syracuse Star,* "would make demons of the pit shudder to head." Even those who sympathized with the principles of Feminism were aghast at the spectacle of a woman speaking in public. "That was a magnificent address," said a prominent journalist after one of Ernestine Rose's speeches. "But . . . I would rather see my wife or my daughter in her coffin than hear her speaking . . . before a public assembly."

Allied with the journalists in their denunciation of the Feminist movement were the politicians. When Susan Anthony presented a petition for woman's rights to the New York Legislature, the anti-Feminist lobbyists began to quote Scripture for their purpose. "Are we, sir," cried Assemblyman Burnett, "to give the least countenance to claims so preposterous, disgraceful, and criminal as are embodied in this petition? . . . Are we to put the stamp of truth upon the libel here set forth that men and women . . . are to be equal? We *know* that God created man as the representative of the race; that after His creation the Creator took from His side the material for woman's creation . . . and that they thus became one flesh and one being, the man being the head." And if the women persisted in demanding their rights, continued Mr. Burnett, "there would be no way of preserving men's honor except by locking their wives behind bolts and bars."

But the women refused, mentally as well as physically, to be locked behind bolts and bars. Little by little the flower of American womanhood —Lucy Stone Blackwell, Lucretia Mott, Isabella Beecher (the sister of Harriet Beecher Stowe), Antoinette Brown, Anna Shaw, and Carrie Chapman Catt—added their brains and their determination to the cause. For a time, in order to "sensationalize" the menfolk out of their "fossilized prejudices," the leaders of the movement cut their hair short and dressed themselves in bloomers. "There's no publicity like a shock." And the male population of America was shocked indeed. What? Release the women from their seven layers of underwear, their starched and quilted petticoats, their tight corsets, their long and dust-sweeping skirts? How preposterous! Why, dressed in her bloomers, a woman was almost as free as a man!

Before long, however, the women gave up their bloomers. But not their fight for freedom. They went on with their endless and tireless crusade for the "right of women to their earnings and their children." And the most tireless crusader of them all was Susan B. Anthony. They called her the Napoleon of the Feminist movement. Though she had none of the cruelty of Napoleon, she had much of his genius—his ability to organize, his power to command, his insensibility to pain, and his persistency in the face of defeat. The harder the odds against her, the more eager she was for the fight. Through dint of constant practice, she had become a competent speaker. And now she went about the country, agitating and educating and organizing all by herself. Elizabeth Stanton and Ernestine Rose had fallen by the wayside. They were glad to rest from their labors. But Susan Anthony knew no rest. Her physical endurance was one of the miracles of the century. Her tall, spare frame had become a legend as it sloshed its way through the sleet and the rain, hurrying, hurrying, fighting against time and the weather, plunging through the snowdrifts and breasting the wind, always anxious to bring her message to the women of the next village or town. On one occasion, she wrote to her "good folks at home," the train on which she was traveling over the Rocky Mountains had become "stuck in a snowdrift eleven feet deep." But she managed, somehow, to keep her appointment for the next lecture. Again and again her health broke down. There were times when she stood on the platform with frostbitten feet, or with her back almost bent double with pain. Once in the dead of winter she was obliged to take the "water cure." It was a heroic measure for Spartan souls—wet sheets, ice packs, sitz baths followed by cold showers and heart-straining gymnastics, all this self-inflicted torture repeated four times a day. And she survived the ordeal. For more than half a century she was in the forefront of the Feminist Revolution—

shuttling back and forth over the country, raising hundreds of thousands of dollars for the cause, accepting a wage of only twelve dollars a week for herself. Her amazed friends began to look upon her as an immortal goddess—a poverty-stricken goddess with a rheumatic body and a flaming soul.

And through all her poverty and her hardship and her pain, she retained her saving sense of humor. Her tongue, though never deliberately cruel, could on occasion administer a vigorous thrust. "Miss Anthony," mocked Horace Greeley during one of her interviews, "you are aware, are you not, that the ballot and the bullet go together? If you get the vote, are you also prepared to fight?"

"Why, certainly, Mr. Greeley," came the instant reply. "Just as *you* fought in the Civil War—at the point of a goose quill."

IV

Miss ANTHONY lived to see the flower, but not the fruit, of her labor. Once, for trying to vote, she had been arrested and sent to jail. But now she was no longer an object of ridicule. The women of the nation had learned to worship her, and even the men had come to look upon her as one of the makers of American history. And she had indeed made history. Largely as the result of her agitation, the women of America had crowded the progress of a thousand years into the short span of a half century. In 1865, Vassar opened its doors to higher education for women with a curriculum equal to that of the best colleges for men. Within the next decade no less than fourteen state universities adopted the system of indiscriminate co-education. By 1880 the number of colleges admitting both sexes had grown to one hundred and fifty-four.

Fortified by their higher education, the women had begun to enter the professions. In 1850 there were only a few women who taught school. In 1900 two thirds of the schoolteachers in the United States were women. In art, in medicine, in literature, in theology, and in law the women were rapidly taking their place side by side with the men. In 1879 the first woman was allowed to plead before the Supreme Court—a landmark in American history.

Most important of all was the civil emancipation of the women. By the end of the nineteenth century nearly every state in the Union had abolished the old legal disabilities against married women. They now were given the right to own and to control their property, to sue and to be sued, to retain their earnings, to make contracts, and to exercise a joint guardianship over their children. Marriage was no longer an enslavement, but an agreement—a mutual compact between equal partners.

All these radical reforms Miss Anthony lived to see as the flowering of her life's work. But the fruition of her life's work she did not live to see. Although a few isolated states had enacted a law to allow votes for women, the national amendment for woman suffrage was not passed until 1920, fourteen years after her death.

But to the last day of her life she labored to bring the final victory nearer. Her vitality remained undiminished to the end. Especially her *mental* vitality. "Miss Anthony," wrote the *Chicago Herald* in 1895, "has grown slightly thinner and more spiritual looking . . . With her transparent hands, her thin face, and her keen eyes flashing white, she looks like Pope Leo XIII. The whole physical being is as nearly submerged as possible in a great mentality."

Yet her "submerged" physical strength enabled her, as a climax to the labors of a lifetime, to take a trip to Europe and to climb Mount Vesuvius. And then, at the age of eighty-four, she attended a Feminist convention in Germany, lecturing, writing, entertaining, arguing—an inexhaustible fountain of perpetual youth. "How do you manage to keep your energy?" asked an admiring friend. "By being the leader of an unpopular cause," she replied.

Her stay in Germany was marked by an incident which served to illustrate the backward-looking mentality of the Prussian Government. To while away her time during a rainy spell, she wrote a number of letters to her friends in America. All these letters were interspersed with her customary slogans—"no just government can be formed without the consent of the governed"—"taxation without representation is tyranny." The entire batch of these letters was returned to her hotel with the following official notation: "Such sentiments cannot pass through the post office in Germany."

V

SHE DIED at the age of eighty-six—and in harness. There was to be a birthday celebration in her honor at Washington. She had recently suffered a paralytic stroke, and the doctors ordered her to stay in bed. But "Aunt Susan" laughed at the doctors. "If the hammer must fall," she said, "let it fall while I'm on my feet."

And it was practically while on her feet that she received the blow. She went to the birthday dinner and, in answer to the ovation, stood up to make her final fiery speech. "What I ask is not praise, but justice." And justice, she declared, was bound to come in the end. "Failure is impossible!"

She collapsed immediately on her return home. They buried her in a blizzard—a fitting exit for a heroine who all her life had plowed her way through the snowdrifts.

IMPORTANT DATES IN THE LIFE OF
SUSAN B. ANTHONY

1820—Born, Adams, Massachusetts.

1852—Organized first woman's state temperance society in America.

1854—Began her lifelong career of agitation for woman's rights.

1856—Assumed active part in American Anti-Slavery Society.

1868—Started a weekly woman's rights paper, *The Revolution*.

1869—Became vice-president of the National Woman Suffrage Association.

1872—Arrested for casting vote in the presidential election.

1884-87—Collaborated on a four-volume *History of Woman Suffrage*.

1899—Her last public appearance as a delegate to the International Council of Women (London, England).

1900—Public celebration of her eightieth birthday.

1906—Died, Rochester, New York.

Stephen Collins Foster
[1826-1864]

JULY 4, 1826—a memorable day in American history. For that day witnessed the death of Thomas Jefferson and the birth of Stephen Foster. The author of American independence and the creator of America's songs.

Stephen was the last of seven children, the oldest of whom, Charlotte, was sixteen at the time of Stephen's birth. Sixteen, fourteen, ten, seven, five, three, and now the baby. A stairway of tousled heads that led the way down into the Valley of Poverty. Their father, William Foster, had the virility to produce a large family, but he lacked the ability to provide for them. Stephen's childhood was a continual succession of migrations—from Lawrenceville (Pennsylvania) to Harmony, from Harmony to Pittsburgh, from Pittsburgh to Allegheny, from Allegheny to Poland (Ohio), from Poland to Youngstown, and so on and on. Always they went in quest of a better job for Father Foster, and always the quest ended in disappointment.

Schooling for the Foster children was, under the circumstances, intermittent—to the sorrow of Mr. and Mrs. Foster and to the delight of young Stephen. On the first day that he attended school his teacher set him to studying the alphabet through a series of silly jingles. She began with the letter A:

> *In Adam's fall*
> *We sinnèd all.*

And then she went on, from absurdity to absurdity, until she came to the letter Z:

> *Zaccheus he*
> *Did climb a tree*
> *His Lord to see.*

One by one she made the boys recite the jingles after her. Finally it was Stephen's turn. He stood up, clenched his little fists, opened his mouth, "and"—we are quoting his brother Morrison—"with a yell like that of a Comanche Indian, he bounded bareheaded out of the schoolroom and into the open fields."

There was so much nonsense in the schoolbooks, and so much that was sensible in the fields and along the riverbanks. Great fun to play truant from school and to watch the gaily painted boats drifting down the stream. Listen to those boatmen singing:

> *There is a wild boar in the wood,*
> *Dillum dan diddly, dillum dan diddle.*
> *He eats our flesh and drinks our blood,*
> *Tun-a-qui quiddle-quo-quum.*

And even better is the song of the black folk, on that flat-bottom boat with the paddle wheels:

> *Lis'en to de lam's—all a-cryin',*
> *Lis'en to de lam's—all a-cryin',*
> *Lis'en to de lam's—all a-cryin',*
> *I wanta go to heaben when I die.*

A great problem to his parents, this youngest son of theirs. Neglected his books and wasted all his time on those silly songs. From infancy he had loved to hum and to drum. One day he sent a letter to his father— Mr. Foster was working in Pittsburgh while the family lived at Youngstown. "My dear father," he wrote, "I wish you to send me a commic songster, for you promised to. if I had my pensyl I could rule my paper. or if I had the money to by Black ink But if I had a whistle I would be so taken with it I do not think I would writ atall . . ."

When Stephen expressed this desire to give up his writing for a whistle, he was a "hopeless little rebel" of ten.

II

HE GOT HIS WHISTLE. But he didn't give up his writing. At last he found a congenial teacher, Mr. John Kelly, who taught at the Stockton Academy and whose Irish sense of humor saw nothing wrong in a boy who preferred his music to his books. He encouraged Stephen in his *musical* education, and thereby he inspired him with a respect for *all* education. Under the tolerant eye of Mr. Kelly, Stephen learned to play several instruments, to read and to write music, and to compose verses for his own tunes.

Haunting tunes. Memories of snatches he had heard on his riverside excursions. Songs of sailors heaving at their ropes; of darkies unloading bales of cotton at the wharves; of pioneers facing toward the West, their eyes aflame with the dreams of new adventures and new hopes. Songs of poverty—"hard times, come again no more"; of joyous nonsense—"ain't it dinner? ho, ho! ain't it dinner? tell me so"; of buck-and-wing dances —"lef' foot dance, right foot res', ah shakes mah shoulders an' grins mah bes'"; happy-go-lucky tunes of the riverman—"hi-O, away we go, floating down the river on the O-hi-O." The scattered syllables of many tongues gathered together from many lands. The fusing rivulets of sound that were to merge into the great Folk Song of America.

And then, an exciting adventure for Stephen Foster. "The minstrels are in town!"

Stephen had never been to a minstrel show. His first experience of the blackface comedians was like the opening of a new door in his life. The racket, the abandon, the rhythm, the music, the gaiety of it all—*this* was America singing! If only someday *he* could write a song for these minstrels!

But he was too young as yet—only thirteen. And he knew too little of the lives of the Negroes, of life in general. And, worst of all, his parents disapproved of his "song-scribbling." He was no longer under the tutelage of Mr. Kelly. A friend of the Fosters—they called him "Brother William" —offered to pay his tuition at Athens Academy. A sleigh ride of four hundred miles, a great loneliness, and a promise, exacted by Brother William, that he would neglect his music in favor of his other studies. "My dear Brother," he wrote, "I will promise not to be seen out of doors between the hours of nine and twelve A.M. and one and four P.M. Which hours I will attribute to study . . . I will also promise not to pay any attention to my music untill after eight o'clock in the evening . . ."

He had yielded to the pressure of his elders. But the artistic urge was too strong within him. Before he left school he composed (in 1841) his first important piece, the "Tioga Waltz" for flutes. "A pretty good musician," said the headmaster, "but a poor student." Stephen was sent home without a diploma.

For five years he remained at home, the "dunce" of the family; and then he was sent to Jefferson College—and stayed there exactly seven days. He returned to his idleness and his music. Private tutoring for a while in mathematics, French, and German—and constant improvisation on his flute. During his leisure hours he took to browsing about the music stores of Pittsburgh. In one of these stores he met an immigrant German musician, Henry Kleber, who introduced him to the songs of Schubert. "Gosh, I didn't know there was so much beauty in the world!"

"You would like to write like Schubert, yes?"

"I'd give my right hand to do it!"

"Nonsense, *mein Freund,* you need both your hands for practicing your compositions on the piano. Here, let me teach you how."

And Kleber proceeded to teach Foster not only how to harmonize but how to play his own compositions. "Someday, my boy, you may be perhaps the American Schubert, yes?"

"Please don't make fun of me, Mr. Kleber!"

"I'm not making fun of you. Heaven has gifted you with a strange sacred talent. Be faithful to this talent, *mein Knabe."*

And faithful he remained to it, under the kindly tutelage of Mr. Kleber. "He would sit in the evening at the piano," writes his brother Morrison, "and improvise by the hour beautiful strains and harmonies which he did not preserve, but let them float away like fragrant flowers cast upon the flowing water . . . At times tears could be seen on his cheeks . . ."

And thus, wrapped in his music and his dreams, he drifted idly along through his adolescent years. He hated formal society. Once a lady invited him to a party. "Bring Stephen," she said to his brother, "but not without his flute."

"Tell the lady," retorted the young musician, "that you can bring the flute, but without Stephen."

A morose, unsocial, impractical loafer, thought his parents. He would dream his days away on the side lines while the stream of life rushed by.

Yet Stephen Foster was not a recluse. He loved the companionship of cheerful, singing spirits like himself. He joined a club of youngsters who picnicked in the summer and skated in the winter. And sang. Folk tunes, sentimental ballads, roisterous love songs. "Our repertory is getting rather thin," complained one of the members. "I wish we had something new."

"I've just written something," said Foster hesitantly. "Would you like to try it?" He took a sheet out of his pocket. "The name of the song is 'Lou'siana Belle.'"

This was the beginning of a flood of tunes that came pouring out of his heart for his boon companions. And then, one day at twenty, he composed a piece—"just another of my silly trifles"—which marked a departure in American folk music: "Old Uncle Ned." America caught up the song, and critics and public alike realized that a new voice had come upon the scene. "There is something in the melody of 'Uncle Ned,'" reported the *Albany State Register,* "that goes directly to the heart, and makes Italian trills seem tame."

Stephen Foster had joined the stream of life—in his own unique way.

III

BUT NOT in his parents' way. They still persisted in making a practical businessman out of him. They secured him a job as bookkeeper in Cincinnati.

A dismal ride on a steamboat, a dismal prospect ahead of him. To while away the time, he composed one of his songs. A rollicking song of adventure and love, yet with a catch in the throat. It sang its way into the hearts of the passengers, the sailors, the dark and the white folk throughout the country. Within a short time it became an American classic. "Oh, Susanna, oh don't you cry for me; I've come from Alabama wid my banjo on my knee."

And Foster sat in the countinghouse, and added and subtracted figures, and dreamed of the day when he could devote all his time to his music. He secured a publisher for two of his songs. Net result—the publisher made ten thousand dollars, the composer made nothing.

More dreary days in the countinghouse. A brief vacation, a trip to the South, new scenes, new music—the Negroes at their toil, in their prayers, at their play. "Away Down Souf'," "My Old Kentucky Home," "Old Black Joe."

He gave up his bookkeeping and signed a contract with a publisher. A very unbusinesslike contract, but promising enough to marry on—with the wolf at the door as a lifelong companion. He married a boyhood sweetheart of his, Jane McDowell—Jeanie with the light brown hair. A rapturous honeymoon, and then they lived unhappily ever after. Stephen Foster was too poor in worldly goods and too rich in boon companionship to make a satisfactory husband. In an effort to patch up their troubles, they took a trip to the South together; and then for a while they tried to go their separate ways. But they were too fond of each other to live apart, and too irritable toward each other to live together. They moved to New York, to Pittsburgh, to Allegheny City, seeking everywhere for that peace which nowhere could be found. He took to excessive drink—"drink is an effort to fill an aching void"—and this was another cause for friction. He smoked until his throat swelled almost shut and for a time his life was given up.

But he recovered—for further suffering and further creation. His creation came out of his suffering. One day he sat in the park, playing with his dog—an Irish setter he had received as a present shortly after his marriage. It was rarely he received presents now, or ever saw his friends. They had deserted him, one by one. Two stray dogs, with nary a one to greet them with a pleasant word. Stephen Foster smiled a bitter smile, and then a thought struck him. Snatching a piece of paper out of his pocket, he jotted down a tribute to his dog—a sentimental song, yet inspired with the emotion of a universal experience:

> *Old Dog Tray's ever faithful,*
> *Grief cannot drive him away;*
> * He's gentle, he is kind,*
> * I'll never, never find*
> *A better friend than Old Dog Tray.*

Another household song for America, another period of heartaches for its creator. He was too sensitive to suffering and to song. The source of his genius was the cause of his affliction. Occasionally he tried to compose a song full of gaiety and laughter, as an antidote to his own sad spirit:

> *Some folks like to sigh,*
> * Some folks do, some folks do;*
> *Some folks long to die,*
> * But that's not me nor you.*

Several stanzas of this rollicking make-believe at merriment, and then he reveals the true picture of his heart. People toil and save—yes they do, yes they do—to what end? "To buy themselves a grave."

More and more attempts at forgetfulness in drink, nightlong serenades along the streets of Allegheny, and days of stupor illumined by flashes of creation. At last his wife left him for good. He lived now literally in the gutter, peddling out his songs for the price of a drink. Shabby, hungry, and unkempt—there were days when he had only an apple for dinner—he was taken to task by his brother Morrison. "Stevie, why do you go around looking so bedraggled? Aren't you afraid of being insulted?"

"Don't worry about me," retorted Stephen. "No gentleman *will* insult me, and no other man *can*."

And the summer days passed, and the autumn, and then came the winter snows. One day he set out in a blizzard to sell his latest song, "Willie Has Gone to the War." He had no overcoat. His shoes were cracked. The snow slushed through his raggedy covering and soaked him to the skin. Sometime later an acquaintance discovered him in a dingy basement that Foster occupied rent free. The composer's face was bleeding. He had cut himself on a broken pitcher.

"How long have you been like this?"

"Oh, I don't know. Days, weeks, months, maybe years." Foster was almost delirious.

They took him to a charity ward in the hospital. And there, on January 13, 1864, he jotted down on a piece of paper his farewell to the world. "Dear friends and gentle hearts."

He was thirty-eight years old when he died. In his pocket after his death they found exactly thirty-eight cents.

IMPORTANT DATES IN THE LIFE OF STEPHEN COLLINS FOSTER

1826—Born, Pittsburgh, Pennsylvania.

1840—Composed "Tioga Waltz."

1846–50—Employed as bookkeeper in Cincinnati.

1848—Composed "Nelly Bly."

1850—Returned from Cincinnati to Pittsburgh.

1851—Composed "Swanee River."

1852—Decided to establish his name "as the best Ethiopian song writer."
Composed "Massa's in the Cold, Cold Ground."

1853—Composed "My Old Kentucky Home" and "Old Dog Tray."

1860—Composed "Old Black Joe." Settled in New York.

1864—Died, New York.

James Abbott McNeill Whistler

[1834-1903]

WHEN James Abbott McNeill Whistler was a cadet at West Point he was very poor in chemistry. One day, at an oral examination, his professor asked him to discuss the properties of silicon.

"Silicon," began Whistler, "is a gas——"

"That will do, Mr. Whistler," barked his examiner.

It was with no feeling of regret that Whistler was dismissed from the military academy for failure in chemistry. "Just think of it," he said many years later. "Had silicon been a gas, I would be a major general."

Imagine Whistler confined within the discipline of a military unit! Imagine the hurricane bottled up in a glass jar. The life of a soldier would have been the very last career in the world for this undisciplined, irrepressible, self-assertive, and iconoclastic citizen of half a dozen countries. Born in America and educated in Russia, he lived at various periods in Italy and in the Netherlands and for the greater part of his life in France and in England.

His father, at the time of Whistler's birth (on July 10, 1834), was a civil engineer living in Lowell, Massachusetts. The nature of his work had turned his family into a tribe of gypsies. They were always on the go—from Lowell, Massachusetts, to Stonington, Connecticut; from Stonington, Connecticut, to Springfield, Massachusetts; and from Springfield, Massachusetts, to St. Petersburg, Russia. James was eight years old when his family arrived in this imperial city of vanity, vodka, and vice. Here he absorbed the elements of religion from his mother, who began the daily routine for her children with a recitation from the Psalms, and the rudiments of art from the teachers of the Imperial Academy. Throughout his life, religion and art remained his two absorbing passions. Though rarely a churchgoer, he was always a profound worshiper. His studio was his shrine, and his canvases were devout prayers of the brush—hymns of adoration to the glory and the beauty of the world.

His religion, however, unlike that of his mother, was pagan rather than Puritan. It was a religion of gaiety. In fair weather or foul, in the brief moments of his prosperity as well as in the long days of his hunger, he wore this gaiety of his like a boutonniere. His gaiety and his profoundity. A symphony in white and black. Like so many of his paintings. Whistler was one of the supreme jesters and at the time one of the most observant philosophers of the nineteenth century. Jesters, as Gilbert K. Chesterton reminds us, are the most serious people in the world.

The most serious and the most unpopular. Even as a child he shocked the Russian officials and caused his mother no end of anxiety with his double-edged tongue and his cynical laughter—a crackling *ha! ha!* that struck at the vanity of his listeners like the sudden explosion of two fire-crackers. His mother warned him that he would lose his friends with this too effervescent cynicism of his. "Who cares for such friends?" he retorted, and his mother shook her head. There was no stopping her little Jamie's overbubbling spirit.

This overbubbling spirit was his most striking characteristic at the Pomfret School in Connecticut, whither his family had returned after the death of his father in 1849. It was his outstanding characteristic at West Point. "What!" cried his history professor. "Do you mean to tell me you don't know the date of the Battle of Buena Vista? Suppose you went out to dinner and the talk drifted to the Mexican War, and suppose someone asked you, a West Pointer, the date of the Battle of Buena Vista? What would you do?"

"Do?" replied Whistler. "Why, I'd have *nothing* to do with people who could talk of such things at the dinner table."

Good riddance, cried the authorities at West Point when Whistler was dismissed from the academy. No use trying to make a soldier out of a youngster with a sense of humor like that!

II

FOR A SHORT TIME he worked as an engraver of maps at the United States Geodetic Office. But he interspersed his geographical sketches with the caricatures of his superiors. He was told to go. The United States, he was advised, was no place for him. There was only one fitting spot for a queer fellow like him—the city of Paris.

And to Paris he went. He took his gaiety to the gayest of all places, the Latin Quarter, and soon became its guiding spirit—the unceremonious master of ceremonies to the bohemian vagabondia, the "no-shirt brigade." Taking a room up six flights of stairs, he "pawned his coat and ate his washstand and his wardrobe," as he explained to a solicitous friend, dressed like nobody else, flirted with the grisettes, led the dances at the students' balls, and won the reputation of being the "Idle Apprentice of the Parisian Loafers." But this reputation was undeserved, for Whistler loved to paint as well as to play. Dressed in his loose black blouse, his broad-brimmed felt hat in his hand, he would sit for hours in the Louvre before a painting by Velasquez: studying, absorbing, measuring every line, analyzing every tint, memorizing beauty. It was during these years that Whistler acquired his prodigious visual memory. He knew a Velasquez painting by heart just as thoroughly as Toscanini knows a Beethoven symphony by heart. He learned to transcribe from memory every last technical nicety and tonal gradation of the pictures that he studied at the Louvre. And he made perfect copies of some of these pictures—copies that it was hard to distinguish from the original.

It was not, however, as a copyist that Whistler was eager to excel. For his genius was individual, unconventional, unique. Even in his earliest pictures, At the Piano and The Little White Girl, for example, we find this individualistic note that makes a Whistler so unlike any other painting in the world. At the piano is the picture of a woman in black, who plays at the piano, and of a little girl in white, who listens to the playing —a semiscientific, semimystical study in contrasts, a symphony of music in color. We find the same color symphony in The Little White Girl. This, too, is the half-realistic, half-poetic portrait of a woman, "Jo" Heffernan, the Irish girl who served him as a model and faithful companion for a number of years. In this picture the girl is seen in profile, with loosened hair, leaning languidly against a mantelpiece in front of a mirror, from which the reflection of her face looks back at the spectator. It is a study in white and red—the white muslin dress and the sad white face of the girl, the white mantel, the red hair, the red lacquer box on the mantelpiece, and a spray of reddish-pink azaleas that serve as a decorative arrangement on the canvas. There are bits of other colors, too, in the picture—a blue-and-white vase on the mantel and a Japanese fan of various tints that the girl holds at her side. But the white and the red predominate. When Swinburne saw The Little White Girl for the first time he was moved to translate into words the haunting effect of this picture:

> *Come snow, come wind or thunder,*
> *High up in the air*
> *I watch my face and wonder*
> *At my bright hair.*
> *Naught else exalts or grieves*
> *The rose at heart that heaves*
> *With love of our own leaves, and lips that pair.*
>
> *I cannot tell what pleasures*
> *Or what pains were,*
> *What pale new loves and treasures*
> *New years will bear,*
> *What beam will fall, what shower*
> *With grief or joy for dower.*
> *But one thing knows the flower, the flower is fair.*

Whistler was deeply touched at this tribute, and he had the verses inscribed upon the frame of the picture. "I watch my face and wonder at my

bright hair." This, in a sentence, is the keynote to the art of Whistler—
Nature contemplating itself in the mirror and holding its breath at the
reflection of its own beauty.

III

THE ACADEMIC WORLD was slow to recognize the genius of Whistler. Rejected by the Paris Salon, he was obliged at first to exhibit his pictures at
the Salon des Refusés. Here he was in good company. For side by side
with his own pictures hung the paintings of some of the greatest French
artists whose work the academicians didn't possess the necessary stature
to understand. The exhibition of the Refused was artistically if not financially successful. Napoleon III sponsored it, and the Empress Eugénie and
the entire court came to see it.

Whistler was now becoming recognized in Paris as an unusual though
incomprehensible painter. But, while his ears were filled with praises, his
pockets still remained empty of money. He decided to seek his fortune in
London.

His arrival in England was a bombshell. His gaiety scattered the fogs of
London—and frightened the Londoners. They could understand neither
his art nor his personality nor his clothes. They were scandalized one summer morning when he appeared on the streets with two umbrellas in his
hands—a white and a black. When asked for an explanation, he said that
in the treacherous weather of London he wanted to be protected both
against possible sunshine and probable rain. They called him a mounte-
bank, a charlatan, a poseur. He was all of these things, but he was also a
superb painter. And in his painting there was nothing of the charlatan.
Indeed, those who knew him most intimately insisted that he assumed an
insincerity in his behavior in order to startle an indifferent world into an
appreciation for the sincerity of his art.

And after a time he succeeded. At first the people laughed at his eccentricities. They pointed him out as one of the "characters" of London—a
character that seemed to have stepped out of the pages of a Dickens novel.
They sniggered at his oversize topcoat, his long bamboo cane that looked
like a fishing pole, his tieless but otherwise immaculate evening dress at
the theater, the white lock of hair which he had combed and twisted into
an exaggerated prominence. They came to his exhibitions, at which he
strutted about with an impish pomposity, half king and half clown. And
little by little they turned their gaze from the amazing artist to his amazing art. Amazing but sincere. *Amazingly* sincere. Genuine as a coin of the
purest gold. Nothing of the poseur in that inspired priest who had sat
worshiping upon the banks of the Thames, memorizing beauty, etching
into his soul the very essence of the night, the starlight throwing a shimmer of blue and silver magic over the Battersea Bridge, the Wharf at
Wapping, or the Black Lion Wharf. Silent symphonies and sonatas, out of
which the Earth speaks her secrets to the understanding heart. Not a
single wasted line or false color or dishonest thought in these painted

fragments of the Psalm of Life. If ever there was a serious and sincere painter, that painter was the Whistler of the Nocturnes. Or the Whistler of those other new glimpses into the human soul—the portraits which he called his Symphonies in White, in Gray and Green, in Rose and Purple, in Black and Gold, and those two supreme achievements in portraiture, the Arrangements in Black and Gray. These two Arrangements are the famous portraits of Carlyle and of Whistler's mother. Impatience and Serenity in old age. The man of the world, weary, disillusioned, cynical, disgusted with a life that promises so much and gives so little; and the woman in the home, tireless, hopeful, devout, contented with a life that brings the bitterness of mortality and the joys of motherhood. Philosophers, both of them. The one an apostle of mystical wisdom, the other a purveyor of homespun common sense. Carlyle, the worshiper of heroes; Matilda Whistler, the lover of children.

These two portraits, like most of the other paintings of Whistler, are so simple that they seem to have been dashed off with a few inspired strokes of the brush. But they are the result of long and painstaking labor. Tennyson, the master of the facile phrase, was once asked how he managed to round off such perfect expressions with such unpremeditated ease. "Unpremeditated?" said the poet of the Round Table as he puffed away at his pipe. "Why, man"—pointing to the first line in his *Crossing the Bar,* with its almost childlike simplicity—"it took me twenty pipefuls of tobacco to write this single phrase."

There is the simplicity of ignorance and the simplicity of genius. It took Whistler many anxious hours to acquire the "easy effortlessness" of his style. During the time that he was painting the portrait of Carlyle he was also engaged upon the portrait of a child, Miss Alexander. One day the old man and the little girl met at the door of the studio. Carlyle had just got through with a sitting, and Henrietta Alexander was coming in for one. The aged philosopher looked at the child, shook his head, and murmured: "Puir lassie! Puir lassie!" And no wonder he sympathized with her. For the child was compelled to have seventy sittings before Whistler was completely satisfied with his job.

And yet there were times when, in spite of all his labor, he was unable to please his disgruntled sitters. He possessed too uncanny a faculty for bringing out their true character. To such people, whenever they presumed to criticize his work, his tongue was no more flattering than his brush. "Do you call this a good piece of art?" asked one of his sitters insolently. "Well," replied Whistler with a diabolical grin, "do you call yourself a good piece of nature?"

IV

Whistler fought hard, just as he played hard and worked hard. He was merciless to his critics, especially to those whose criticism he considered either stupid or unfair. The dean of the British art critics, P. G. Hamerton, wrote a caustic review about one of his paintings, Symphony in White

No. III. "A Symphony in White indeed! . . . Why, one of the girls has a yellowish dress and a bit of blue ribbon . . . She has reddish hair, and, of course, there is the flesh color of the complexion." This sort of unenlightened judgment was more than Whistler could bear. *"Bon Dieu!"* he wrote to the editor of the *Saturday Review.* "Did this wise person expect white hair and chalked faces? And does he then, in his astounding consequence, believe that a Symphony in F contains no other note, but shall be a continued repetition of F F F? . . . Fool!"

He never started a fight. But he never avoided one if somebody else started it. He hated salaciousness. But he also hated prudery. One of the Anthony Comstocks of the London Academy, a man by the name of Horsley, had attacked the practice of painting nude models from life. Whereupon Whistler painted a nude and sent it to the British Artists' Exhibition. Underneath the picture he wrote the words: *"Horsley soit qui mal y pense."*

He ridiculed stupidity wherever he found it—among his students as well as among his critics. Some of his students came to him not because they had talent to paint but because they wanted their friends to admire their paintings. For these insincere worshipers in the temple of art he saved some of the keenest shafts of his wit. One of his students persisted in smoking a pipe while he painted. "Young man," said Whistler, "you had better stop painting. For you might get interested in your work and then your pipe would go out." Another student, a young lady, took exception to his criticism of her work. "Mr. Whistler," she said, "I paint what I see." "Yes," he replied, "but wait till you see what you paint!"

Sometimes he turned the defense of his sarcasm into the weapons of a counterattack. This was especially true when his critics became abusive as well as destructive. When he exhibited his now famous Nocturne in Black and Gold—the picture of a skyrocket bursting through the night—he set upon it a price of two hundred guineas. Whereupon John Ruskin, usually so fair in his criticism, published the following injudicious attack upon this painting:

"For Mr. Whistler's sake, no less than for the protection of the purchasers, Sir Coutts Lindsey ought not to have admitted works into the gallery in which the ill-educated conceit of the artist so nearly approached the aspect of the wilful imposture. I have seen, and heard, much of cockney impudence before now; but never expected to hear a coxcomb ask two hundred guineas for flinging a pot of paint into the public's face."

Enraged, and justly so, at this uncalled-for stab in the back, Whistler sued Ruskin for libel. During the cross-examination at the trial the attorney general, counsel for the defendant, tried to badger Whistler. It was a battle of wits.

Attorney General: Can you tell me how long it took you to knock off that Nocturne?

Whistler: I beg your pardon?

Attorney General: I am afraid that I am using a term that applies rather perhaps to my own work . . .

Whistler: As well as I remember, it took me about a day . . . I may have still put a few more touches to it the next day if the painting were not dry. I had better say, then, that I was two days at work on it.

Attorney General: The labor of two days, then, is that for which you ask two hundred guineas?

Whistler: No, I ask it for the knowledge of a lifetime.

Whistler won the case, but it was merely a moral victory. The judge ordered Ruskin to pay Whistler the compliment of an apology and nothing more.

V

WHISTLER made friends easily and easily lost them. "I'm always being asked out to dinner," he said, "but I'm never asked to the same house twice." One of the men with whom he dined frequently, however, was Oscar Wilde. Whenever they got together their associates knew that they were going to be treated to a duel of wits. For Jimmie Whistler and Oscar Wilde had the two sharpest tongues in the British Isles. A critic in the London *Times* wrote a striking if not altogether accurate summary of the difference between the two men: "With a mind not a jot less keen than Whistler's, Oscar Wilde had none of the convictions, the high faith for which Whistler found it worth while to defy the crowd. Wilde had posed to attract the crowd. And the difference was this, that, while Whistler was a prophet who liked to play Pierrot, Wilde grew into Pierrot who liked to play the prophet."

Whistler was not quite so saintly nor Wilde quite so devilish as they are painted in this clever little study in contrasts. In reality they were both very human individuals who heartily enjoyed a laugh at each other's expense. And, more often than not, it was Whistler who got in the last laugh. His humor was more spontaneous, less polished, more explosive, and more original than that of Oscar Wilde, who frequently borrowed his best bons mots from his friends. "Heavens," cried Oscar Wilde at one of Whistler's most effective epigrams, "I wish I had invented that!" "You will," replied Whistler dryly.

Once, in a heated argument, Oscar remarked, "As for me, I take my good where I find it." "Excellent," retorted Whistler. "This epigram needs but the change of a single word to make it perfect. What you ought to have said is this: 'I take *his* good where I find it.'"

A writer in *Punch* once referred to the wide range of the subjects discussed in the conversations of these two foremost London wits. Oscar, who was in Exeter at the time, sent the following wire to Whistler: "*Punch* too ridiculous—when you and I are together we never talk about anything except ourselves." Whereupon Whistler wired back: "No, no, Oscar, you forget—when you and I are together we never talk about anything except me."

Whistler's thrusts at Oscar, though sharp, were good-natured as a rule. They tickled rather than stabbed. But Oscar's sallies at Whistler were frequently ill-tempered as well as sharp. His arrows had poison at their tip. Whistler could never forgive that insulting epigram of Wilde's which all

London was only too happy to adopt as its own: "With our James," said Wilde, "vulgarity begins at home; would that it might stop there."

Cut to the quick by this clumsy stab, Whistler parried the blow with another of his pungent thrusts: "A poor thing, Oscar, but for once, I suppose, your own."

The friendship between Whistler and Oscar Wilde, like most of the other friendships of Whistler, broke up in the end. To a lady who complained of the trouble that her friends gave her Whistler remarked: "Do as I do, madame, lose them."

No other man in England, indeed, had so perfect a talent for losing friends. He suffered from the consequences of an excessive honesty. "Suffered," however, is hardly the word. He actually *enjoyed* the consequences of his honest frankness. One of the gayest satires of the nineteenth century is his little pamphlet entitled *The Gentle Art of Making Enemies*.

VI

AND SO HE PAINTED, and exhibited, and entertained, and won friends and lost them, and defied the critics, and lived now in London and now in Paris, and attracted a small but enthusiastic school of artists who were blessed with "musical eyes," and began to make a comfortable though far from lavish livelihood, and at last, at the age of fifty-three, he took a wife. He married her on August 11, 1888.

The marriage was very happy but all too brief. His wife died of cancer just three months before their tenth wedding anniversary.

Whistler was never the same after the death of his wife. Gone was the old gaiety. Rarely now did he fling his head back in that cynical staccato laughter. It was a sadder and wiser man who gazed at the Thames out of the windows of his lodgings at the Savoy. He rarely sought the company of his fellows now, but sat painting and etching the restless river as it drifted back and forth before his eyes. The Thames was a screen upon which the procession of life passed in constant review, and Whistler recorded the most arresting moments of that eternal procession. To the end he remained true to his calling—the calling of the painter prophet—to turn science into an art and art into a science. All art, he said, ought to be treated as a science, "the science of the beautiful." It was but another way of formulating the immortal idea of John Keats: "Beauty is truth, truth beauty." That is all, said Whistler, that any artist needs to know.

And now that he was drawing toward his own twilight Whistler became more than ever enamored of the night. He expressed this deep emotion that he felt for the night in words that are almost as supreme as his paintings:

"And when the evening mist clothes the riverside with poetry, as with a veil, and the poor buildings lose themselves in the dim sky, and the tall chimneys become campanili, and the warehouses are palaces in the night, and the whole city hangs in the heavens, and fairyland is before us—then the wayfarer hastens home; the workingman and the cultured one, the wise man and the one of pleasure, cease to understand, as they have ceased to see, and Nature, who, for once, has sung in tune, sings her exquisite song to the artist alone, her son and her master—her son in that he loves her, her master in that he knows her."

VII

HE SPENT the last few years of his life in a hopeless search for health. He went to Bath, to Corsica, to Holland; he took an occasional sea voyage; but his lost youth was nowhere to be found. Occasionally a flicker of the old fire would break through the ashes of his waning life. One day, at a lecture, he met a critic who in the past had done his best to keep him down. "Come now, Mr. Whistler," said the critic, "be a gentleman and shake hands with me." Whistler drew himself up and with the old sarcastic ring in his voice replied: "It is because I am a gentleman that I refuse to shake hands with you."

But these outbursts became more and more sporadic. The fire was dying out. He who had never been afraid of life was now terribly afraid of death. He couldn't reconcile himself to the thought that so much of his remembered beauty must remain unrecorded. More and more his painting was now being interrupted by long sieges in bed. He was at work on a picture called the Daughter of Eve. He had felt ill for some time. For the spring of 1903 was cold, and the fogs of London had penetrated to his very marrow. But as the month of July brought summer days he rallied. On the seventeenth he ordered a cab for a drive. When he returned he sat down to work. A few minutes later the brush fell out of his hand.

He was refused the honor of a burial at Westminster Abbey. But he received a greater honor. For his body was laid to rest at the Old Chiswick Graveyard, the same burial ground which holds the remains of William Hogarth. And Hogarth was the man whom Whistler had always worshiped as the supreme painter of England.

IMPORTANT DATES IN THE LIFE OF
JAMES ABBOTT McNEILL WHISTLER

1834—Born, Lowell, Massachusetts.

1851—Appointed to West Point.

1854-55—Draughtsman in Coast and Geodetic Survey.

1855-57—Studied art in Paris.

1863—Settled in London.

1871—Published etchings, The Thames Set.

1872—Painted Arrangement in Gray and Black (better known as Whistler's Mother).

1878—Famous quarrel with Ruskin about his painting, Nocturne.

1880-86—Exhibitions of his paintings at Fine Arts Society, London.

1884—Elected member of Royal Society of British Artists.

1886—Elected president of Royal Society.

1900—Received gold medal in Paris for etchings and paintings.

1902—Received gold medal at Pennsylvania Academy of Fine Arts.

1903—Died, London.

Mark Twain
(Samuel Langhorne Clemens)
[1835-1910]

MARK Twain, we suspect, has not as yet received his full measure of recognition. His work has been crowned with every honor save one—an appreciative understanding. We have allowed his reputation to rest upon his second-best work. We admire him as America's greatest jester and we ignore him as one of America's profoundest philosophers. In our laughter over his jokes we forget the lash that lies hidden in many of them. Centering our attention upon his cap and bells, we have failed to see the prophet under the disguise of the clown.

To be sure, Mark Twain was a jester. But jesters of this type are men with a grin upon their faces and acid in their hearts. They laugh, as that other humorous pessimist, Voltaire, has pointed out, in order to keep from hanging themselves. Having looked deeply into the heart of things, they are overwhelmed with the pitiful stupidity of the "damned human race." And so they put on the comic mask as a means for concealing the tears that lurk behind it.

Those who have suffered most have learned to laugh best. The humorists, the satirists, the cynics—these naughty urchins of literature are the defeated rebels of life. They thumb their noses at fate because they realize, in their impotence, that there is no other gesture left to them.

Mark Twain was one of these defeated rebels. He believed that all human striving is an aimless farce—"a tale told by an idiot, full of sound and fury, signifying nothing." We scramble toward the rainbow and are drowned in the gutter. We reach for the moon and we break our bones. Our persistent aspiration in the face of our persistent defeat is a spectacle for the amusement of the gods. But we too—believed Mark Twain—can be amused if we mitigate the pangs of our defeat with the anodyne of our laughter. We can detach ourselves sufficiently to enjoy the spectacle of our own suffering. "Learn to agonize as an actor in the drama of life; but learn also, as an onlooker, to smile at your own agony."

II

SAMUEL CLEMENS was a product of his time and place. A child of the border, he met life like all pioneers—with a grim sense of humor. This type of humor, writes his biographer Albert Bigelow Paine, "grew out of a distinct condition—the battle with the frontier. The fight was so desperate, to take it seriously was to surrender. Women laughed that they might not weep; men, when they could no longer swear. *Western humor* was the result. It is the freshest, wildest humor in the world, but there is tragedy behind it."

Even as a child Samuel Clemens was acquainted with many of the tragedies of life. Brought up in a Midwestern village of poor whites, he saw slaves flogged and men shot down in the streets. His parents led a migratory life of hopeless and loveless privation. They were always "on the westward wing"—trekking from the seaboard to Kentucky, from Kentucky to Tennessee, and from Tennessee to Missouri. It was in Missouri that Samuel was born (November 30, 1835).

His father, a morose and discouraged derelict, hardly ever played with his children or showed them any affection. In the winter of 1847 he died; and Samuel, an unruly, ragged, undersized, sickly, and neurotic little roughneck of eleven, found himself thrust upon the untender mercies of the world. Taken out of school, he was put to work as a "printer's devil." His employer described him as a youngster with a huge head, an ink-smudged face, and an infinite capacity for laziness. He fell in with the idlers of the village and became acquainted with every phase of human aberration. And of human sorrow. In his early teens he witnessed the death of a sister and a brother. At twenty-three his hair turned gray when another of his brothers was burned to death in a steamboat explosion on the Mississippi. At thirty he was so disgusted with life that "he put a loaded pistol to his head, but found he lacked courage to pull the trigger." He decided to live and to translate his sorrow into laughter. Yet his later experiences, though they brought him many honors, afforded him but little occasion for laughter. His first child died soon after its birth. A second succumbed to pneumonia as a result of Mark Twain's absent-minded carelessness. He had been out driving with the child on a snowy day and, wrapped in his own dreams, he had forgotten to cover the child sufficiently against the cold. Another of his children barely escaped death when Mark Twain heedlessly let go of the perambulator at the summit of a steep hill. "I shouldn't have been entrusted with the job," he said when the child, with bleeding head, was picked up from the stones at the bottom of the hill. "I was not qualified for any such responsibility as that. Someone should have gone who had at least the rudiments of a mind.

Necessarily I would lose myself in woolgathering." Several years later, when he returned from a triumphant lecture tour that had taken him around the world, he learned that Susy, the most gifted of his children, had died in his absence. And then came the bitterest tragedy of them all. On December 23, 1909, his daughter Jean had worked hard all day preparing for the Christmas celebration. The tree was set, the presents were neatly wrapped and addressed, and everything was ready for the holiday. Jean kissed her father good night, as usual, and went to bed. The next morning word was brought to Mark Twain that Jean was dead. She had suffered an epileptic stroke while taking a bath.

Very few men have been more famous than Mark Twain. And very few men have been more unhappy. He knew how to laugh uproariously. But there was tragedy in his laughter.

III

MARK TWAIN was a true son of the frontier—the frontier between human hope and human disappointment. Wherever he traveled—as a pilot on the Mississippi, as a mining prospector in Nevada, as a reporter in San Francisco—he became "personally and familiarly acquainted" with the struggles and the rebuffs and the renewed struggles of his "fellow-damned human brothers." Everywhere he became saturated with the life and the humor of the border. It was a boisterous life and an exuberant humor. The pioneers lived on the boundary between bitter fact and extravagant fancy. Their stories, created in the mirage of the desert, were coarse and vivid and hilarious tales of gigantic heroes and superhuman adventures. Tales of legendary American Samsons like Paul Bunyan, whose perspiration, as he toiled on the mountainside, flowed down into the valley and formed the Great Salt Lake. Sagas of American Munchausens like Jim Bridger, who lost his way in the Petrified Forest while trying to escape from the Indians, and who was himself turned into stone in mid-air as he leaped across a canyon, since in that forest the very law of gravity had become petrified. Fantastic extravaganzas about a grasshopper from whose rump an enormous steak had been cut to be served to all the guests in a restaurant; about a turnip whose roots reached so far down into the earth that when you pulled it up an artesian well spurted into your face and flung you into the air; about a needle which a little girl accidentally thrust into her foot and which two generations later came out through the head of her granddaughter. And—what the men of the frontier loved to hear most frequently—preposterous burlesques about the newly made American millionaires. One of these millionaires, the owner of a silver mine in Nevada, was sleeping in the upper bunk of an inn. In the lower bunk—so ran the story—slept an ordinary workingman. In the morning the workingman awoke with excruciating aches and pains all over him. No medicine could cure him of his torture until he went to a Turkish bath—and sweated out of his pores a pile of silver dust amounting to $417.92, which he had absorbed from the millionaire who had slept above him.

Such were the folk tales that delighted the pioneers in the middle of the nineteenth century. They formed much of the early literary fare of Mark Twain.

But added to the laughter of a boisterous people overbubbling with life was the sadness of a gentle personality contending with death. Mark Twain was a pessimist. "A man who doesn't become a pessimist," he observed, "knows too little about the world." He himself knew too much about the world to regard it as anything more than a "football of the gods." The greatest gift that life can give us, he said, is death. "I have never greatly envied anyone but the dead. I always envy the dead." In the first outburst of his sorrow after the death of Jean, he expressed his conviction that he would not bring her back to life even if he could. "In her loss I am almost bankrupt, and my life is a bitterness, but I am content; for she has been enriched with the most precious of all gifts—that gift which makes all other gifts mean and poor—death. I have never wanted any released friend of mine restored to life since I reached manhood."

With the ancient Greek philosopher Solon, Mark Twain believed that no man ought to be accounted happy until he is dead. This epitome of human wisdom, born of human suffering, finds a continual echo in the works of Mark Twain. "Whoever has lived long enough to find out what life is," he writes in *Pudd'nhead Wilson,* "knows how deep a debt of gratitude we owe to Adam, the first great benefactor of our race. He brought death into the world." And again, "All say, how hard it is that we have to die—a strange complaint to come from the mouths of people who have had to live." In *The Mysterious Stranger* the Devil makes the following comment on human happiness: "No sane man can be happy, for to him life is real, and he sees what a fearful thing it is. Only the mad can be happy . . ."

All this was more than a mere pose on the part of Mark Twain. His words about life and death had the ring of sincerity about them. They had been minted out of his own experience. He had proved, to his own bitter satisfaction, the validity of the old Horatian advice to poets: No writer can make others weep who has not himself wept. "Words," remarks the Connecticut Yankee, "realize nothing, vivify nothing to you, unless you have suffered in your own person the thing which the words try to describe." Mark Twain, like that other great unappreciated thinker of the nineteenth century, Walt Whitman, knew whereof he spoke when he greeted "Death, blessed Death" as the gentle physician that liberates us from that most dreadful of all diseases—Life.

IV

IN ALL GREAT IRONY there is a vein of pity. Mark Twain's irony grew out of his pity—and his scorn. He had pity for the helplessness of the weak and scorn for the ruthlessness of the strong. Anatole France tells us that the entire history of the human race may be summarized in a few words—

men are born, they suffer, they die. Mark Twain would have emended these words to read—men are born, *they compel one another to suffer,* they die. Although he loved human beings as harassed individuals, he detested them as a harassing pack of wolves. As a young journalist with a clear eye and a caustic pen, he was obliged to flee from San Francisco because he criticized the dishonesty of its business and the corruption of its politics. He came East, where his vision grew even clearer and his pen more caustic. The East, and New England in particular, had "an instinctive preference," to quote the apt phrase of Mr. Bernard De Voto, "for the second rate." The "nice people" were unable to understand this redheaded anarchist from the West. But the redheaded anarchist understood the "nice people" and he found them, whether in Hartford or in Boston or in Cambridge or anywhere else, not quite so nice. Taken as a whole, he looked upon mankind—including in all fairness himself—as among the lowest of the animals. When asked whether he dared to put a man on a level with a rat, he replied in all seriousness, "I don't . . . That would be unfair to the rat." The principal difference between a man and a dog, he observed in *Pudd'nhead Wilson,* is this—"If you pick a starving dog and make him prosperous, he will not bite you." He was preoccupied with this idea for the greater part of his life. A few days before his death he wrote in that caustic-humorous vein of his: "When you reach the gate of Heaven, leave your dog outside. Heaven goes by favor. If it went by merit, you would stay out and the dog would go in."

Man is an animal, declared Mark Twain, but he is not a brute. He has not as yet reached up to the moral level of the brute. A brute kills out of hunger. A man kills out of spite. In *The Mysterious Stranger* the Devil points out to a little boy how a heretic is being tortured by his executioners. The boy, sickened by the spectacle, remarks to the Devil that it is a brutal thing. "No," replies the Devil, "it is a *human* thing."

No self-respecting animal, observed Mark Twain, would choose to live with humans if he could help it. In *A Horse's Tale* two philosophical horses, Sage-Brush and Mongrel, are discussing the ways of the gods and the wiles of men:

Sage-Brush: I've seen a good many human beings in my time. They are created as they are; they cannot help it. They are only brutal because it is their make; brutes would be brutal if it was *their* make.

Mongrel: To me, Sage-Brush, man is most strange and unaccountable. Why should he treat dumb animals cruelly? . . . (*A reflective pause, lasting some moments. And then:*) When we die, Sage-Brush, do we go to heaven and dwell with men?

Sage-Brush: My father thought not. He believed we do not have to dwell with men in heaven unless we deserve it.

V

MARK TWAIN'S INDICTMENT against the human race is not merely abstract. Time and again, even in his most playful books, he cites concrete instances of man's inhumanity to man. He holds up to ridicule every phase of oppression, of corruption, of exploitation, of bribery, of hypocrisy, of coercion, of hatred, and of greed. He tries to drown injustice in a deluge of derision. He washes away the superficial gilding of the Gilded Age, and he exposes the coarse and undecorated ugliness of the politicians and the profiteers who batten upon the misfortunes of their fellows. He tears away the trappings of the dictators and the emperors, and he shows them to be nothing but "hollow artificialities" underneath. The Connecticut Yankee and King Arthur, traveling in disguise, are taken for a couple of country bumpkins and sold into slavery. The Connecticut Yankee fetches a price of nine dollars, but the king is adjudged to be worth not a cent more than seven dollars.

Kings, observes Mark Twain, are a dangerous luxury. If the world *must* have something to adore, let them enthrone a royal family of cats. "As a rule, the character of these cats would be considerably above the character of the average king . . . It would . . . be noticed that they hanged nobody, beheaded nobody, imprisoned nobody, inflicted no cruelties or injustices of any sort, and so must be worthy of a deeper love and reverence than the customary human monarch . . . The eyes of the whole harried world would soon be fixed upon this humane and gentle system, and royal butchers would presently begin to disappear."

Mark Twain had no quarrel with the *peaceful* rulers. His quarrel was merely with the royal *butchers*. These ill-behaved and dictatorial children of the human family, dissatisfied with the slice of earth that has been allotted to them, clamor for more than their share—and ever more. Mark Twain detested the spirit of military aggressiveness more than he detested anything else in the world. He had seen so much brawling as a youngster that he had become utterly cured of it for the rest of his life. When a bully wants to fight you, he once declared, take off your coat, slowly and deliberately, and look him straight in the eye. Then, still slowly and deliberately, take off your vest. Then roll up your sleeves and keep on looking him straight in the eye. And if by this time your opponent hasn't run away, you'd better run yourself.

This isn't to say that Mark Twain was either an appeaser or a coward. On the contrary, when the Civil War broke out, he enlisted in the Union Army and served until he was honorably discharged. He wasn't afraid of an honest fight, but he had a horror of dishonest brigandage. And the history of the human race, he said, is full of these examples of dishonest brigandage—always under the cloak of a noble cause. "The story of mankind is little more than a summary of human bloodshed. First came a long series of unknown wars, murders, and massacres . . . Next came the Assyrian wars . . . Next we had Egyptian wars, Greek wars, Roman wars, hideous drenchings of the earth with blood . . . And always we had wars, and more wars—all over Europe, all over the world. Sometimes in the private interest of royal families, sometimes to crush a weak nation; *but never a war started by an aggressor for any clean purpose*—there is no such war in the history of the race."

But the most scathing indictment against the brutality of aggression ever penned by Mark Twain, ever penned by any American writer, is his ironical *Soldier's Prayer*. This "imaginary" prayer is in reality a concrete picture of the Napoleonic—were Mark Twain alive today, he would call it the Hitlerian—type of mind:

"O Lord our God, help us to tear their soldiers to bloody shreds with our shells; help us to cover their smiling fields with the pale forms of their patriot dead; help us to drown the thunder of the guns with the cries of their wounded, writhing in pain; help us to lay waste their humble homes with a hurricane of fire; help us to wring the hearts of their unoffending widows with unavailing grief; help us to turn them out roofless with their little children to wander unfriended through wastes of their desolated land in rags and hunger and thirst, sport of the sun-flames of summer and the icy winds of winter, broken in spirit, worn with travail, imploring Thee for the refuge of the grave and denied it—for our sakes who adore Thee, Lord, blast their hopes, blight their lives, protract their bitter pilgrimage, make heavy their steps, water their way with tears, stain the white snow with the blood of their wounded feet! Grant our prayer, O Lord, and Thine shall be the praise and glory now and forever, Amen."

VI

MARK TWAIN HATED HATRED. At times this feeling within him became so intense that, as he asserted, "I have to take the pen and put my thoughts out on paper to keep them from setting me afire inside." At his best, Mark Twain belonged to the company of the prophets. Yet, by his own admission, he did not always offer his best to the world. He was too fond of luxury, and too hungry for fame, to have his full say in any of his earlier books. He tried to cover with a cloak of respectability the rebelliousness within his own soul. His one serious excursion into open rebellion—when he attempted to "clean up" the politics of San Francisco—had cleaned him out of a job and a home. Thereafter he decided that "it doesn't pay to swim against the tide." He had found that in order to be successful, you must attach yourself to those that are in power. Anson Burlingame, the American minister to China, had once said to him: "Never affiliate with inferiors; always climb." This advice, writes Albert Bigelow Paine, was to Mark Twain "a gospel which he would never forget."

For the greater part of his life Mark Twain was chiefly interested in climbing. He didn't care to write any book "unless," to use his own words, "there was *money* in it, and a good deal of it." He therefore expurgated, or allowed his friends to expurgate, much of the bitterness in those books which he wrote during his "climbing" period. His public would neither understand nor pay for serious thinking. "Irony," he wrote in *Pudd'nhead Wilson*, "was not for those people; their mental vision was not focussed for it." And so he gave them a series of books—*The Innocents Abroad, Tom Sawyer, Huckleberry Finn, The Prince and the Pauper*, and a harvest of short stories—in which there was a minimum of wormwood sweetened with a maximum of honey. His own taste was ever so much superior to the taste of many of his readers. He was amazed at the naïve mentality that could laugh over such an insipid story as *The Jumping Frog*. Nor was he particularly proud even of *Huckleberry Finn,* the best of his stories which fell into this group. The appeal of these stories, he agreed with Henry James, was "an appeal to rudimentary minds." He wrote for a large public because he cared for his money more than he cared for his art. He was ashamed of his enormous public. "You have a mongrel perception of humor, nothing more; a multitude of you possess that. This multitude see the comic side of a thousand low-grade and trivial things—broad incongruities, mainly; grotesqueries, absurdities, evokers of the horselaugh."

He was ashamed of his enormous and uncritical public—and he was ashamed of himself because he hadn't the courage to write for a smaller and more exacting audience. "You observe," he once remarked, "that under a cheerful exterior I have got a spirit that is angry with me and gives me freely its contempt."

He confessed that he was carried away by the glitter of gold. His unexpected rise to fame and prosperity was like a fairy tale out of the *Arabian Nights,* and he could never quite get over the wonder of it. A printer's apprentice, a pilot on a Mississippi steamboat, an unsuccessful prospector in Nevada, and an obscure reporter in San Francisco, he suddenly found himself the wealthy author of a celebrated book—he made three hundred thousand dollars out of *The Innocents Abroad*—and the son-in-law of a millionaire coal baron. His head was completely turned. He began, like so many of his contemporaries, to aim at the rainbow, to reach for the moon. Literature had become a business with him. He was anxious to show his father-in-law, Mr. Rogers, that there was as much money in writing books as in selling coal. All you had to do was to give the public what the public wanted.

And so he sold laughter for gold, and the gold turned into ashes in his hands. For he was a dual personality. He had the money-grubbing body of Samuel Clemens and the freedom-loving soul of Mark Twain. It was his regular habit to write two letters when he addressed people on vital subjects. The one in which he expressed his own views he put away in his desk. The other, in which he expressed the *popular* view, he mailed. "I have a family to support," he explained, "and I can't afford to tell the whole truth."

But in spite of his indecision he was mentally—if not morally—a pioneer. It was this pioneer soul of Mark Twain that ventured forth hesitantly in *Tom Sawyer,* in *The Prince and the Pauper,* in *Captain Stormfield's Visit to Heaven,* in *Pudd'nhead Wilson,* in *A Connecticut Yankee,* in *The Man that Corrupted Hadleyburg,* in *Huckleberry Finn.* These books came like a succession of midsummer days full of a lazy sunlight and laughter but interrupted occasionally by the crashing of ironic thunder in the distance. And it was this same pioneer soul that at last spoke out fearlessly in *The Mysterious Stranger.* In this book—at his wife's request it was not published till after his death—he finally told the truth as he saw it. He had aimed at the rainbow and had found it nothing but a passing mirage. Having made several fortunes and lost them, having tasted the "sad satiety" of friendship and of fame, and having experienced the blessedness of loving and the bitterness of losing those that he loved, he gathered all the threads of his wisdom and his suffering and wove them into a single masterpiece—*The Mysterious Stranger*. The idea of this book had grown in his mind for several years. "I have been intending for a long time," he told William Dean Howells, "to write [such] a book without reserve—a book which should take account of no one's feelings, and no one's prejudices, opinions, beliefs, hopes, illusions, delusions: a book which should say my say, right out of my heart, in the plainest language and without a limitation of any sort."

The Mysterious Stranger is the only book of Mark Twain's in which he said his whole say. Artistically it may be inferior to *Huckleberry Finn*. Philosophically, however, this is his outstanding work. It is, we believe, the one book which places him on a level with the world's great satirists— Juvenal, Cervantes, Swift, Voltaire, Anatole France. *The Mysterious Stranger* is the story of Satan's visit to Eseldorf (Assville), a medieval town in Austria. Eseldorf is a miniature of the world, and its inhabitants are a cross section of the human race. Satan in this story is interested neither in helping nor in corrupting humanity. He merely watches our struggle occasionally, as an amused spectator, when he has nothing better to do. When he comes to Eseldorf he makes himself known to three children—in the eyes of Satan we are *all* children—and for a short time he enables them to see life just as he, in his superior wisdom, sees it. He shows them what an ugly dung heap we have made out of the beautiful garden into which we have been born. An old priest, Father Peter, is suspended from his church because he dares to assert the doctrine that God is all goodness. What will become of the fear of hell, the inhabitants of Eseldorf ask themselves, if such men are allowed to remain in the pulpit?

And the magistrates of Eseldorf are only too eager to lead the people in their persecution of Father Peter. A priest who maintains that God will not eternally torture the sinners, conclude the magistrates, must be a sinner himself. And so they accuse Father Peter of theft and lock him in a cell to await his trial.

The three boys, who love Father Peter, are aghast at the spectacle of his suffering. But Satan assures them that everything will turn out for the best.

While the priest is awaiting trial, Satan amuses two of the boys by giving them a glimpse into the heart of things. It is not a pretty spectacle. As for the third boy, Satan reserves for him a treat of another sort. He drowns him. This, he explains to the two heartbroken playmates of the dead boy, is the greatest good fortune that can happen to any living creature.

Father Peter is put on trial at last. His chances for acquittal appear to be very slim. For the magistrates have trumped up an airtight case against him. But Satan tells the boys not to worry, "Everything will turn out for the best."

And sure enough, the Devil proves to be as "good" as his word. He not only establishes the innocence of the gentle old priest, but he makes him supremely happy for the rest of his life. The manner in which he brings about Father Peter's happiness is devilishly simple. He brings to the old prisoner in his cell a false report of the verdict. "The trial is over, and you stand forever disgraced as a thief!"

The old man, hearing this, loses his mind and becomes "as happy as a bird." From now on he imagines that he is the Emperor of the World. He enjoys all the glory, but none of the worry, of an absolute monarch. The friends of Father Peter are struck dumb with horror. But the Devil reassures them. Next to death, he explains, insanity is the greatest gift which the gods can bestow upon mankind. The only way in which they can make a human being supremely happy is to make him supremely mad.

For the world, concludes Mark Twain, is a madhouse, and life is an insane nightmare between a sleep and a sleep. "Strange," he declares, "that you should not have suspected that your universe and its content were only dreams, visions, fiction! Strange, because they are so frankly and hysterically insane—like all dreams: a God who could make good children as easily as bad, yet preferred to make bad ones; who could have made every one of them happy, yet never made a single happy one; who made them prize their bitter life, yet stingily cut it short; who gave his angels eternal happiness unearned, yet required his other children to earn it; who gave his angels painless lives, yet cursed his other children with biting miseries and maladies of mind and body; who mouths justice and invented hell—mouths mercy and invented hell—mouths Golden Rules and forgiveness multiplied by seventy times seven, and invented hell . . . who created man without invitation, then tries to shuffle the responsibility for man's acts upon man . . .

". . . It is true, that which I have revealed to you; there is no universe, no human race, no earthly life, no heaven, no hell. It is all a dream—a grotesque and foolish dream. Nothing exists but you. And you are but a *thought*—a vagrant thought, a useless thought, a homeless thought, wandering forlorn among the empty centuries!"

And then, having at last declared what he sincerely believed, the great sad satirist son of the pioneers passed beyond the frontier and into—who knows?—perhaps a fairer and truer dream.

IMPORTANT DATES IN THE LIFE OF
MARK TWAIN

1835—Born, Florida, Missouri.

1857—Became a pilot on the Mississippi River.

1867—Published first book, *The Celebrated Jumping Frog of Calaveras County*.

1869—Published *Innocents Abroad*.

1870—Married Olivia L. Langdon.

1875—Wrote *The Adventures of Tom Sawyer*.

1881—Issued *The Prince and the Pauper*.

1884—Wrote *The Adventures of Huckleberry Finn*.

1906—Built country house, Stormfield, in Connecticut.

1907—Received degree of Doctor of Literature from Oxford.

1910—Died, Redding, Connecticut.

Andrew Carnegie

[1835-1919]

A GENEALOGIST told Andrew Carnegie that he could trace his descent from Scottish kings. "My wife," replied Carnegie, "will be sorry to hear that. She married me under the impression that I was descended from Scottish weavers."
        His father, his grandfather, and his great-grandfather had been common laborers, and Carnegie never outgrew his fondness for the common man.

Willie Carnegie was "a saint"—to quote Andrew's description of his father—"not much of a man for the world, but a man all over for heaven." He kept weaving at his loom in Dunfermline, and dreaming of a better day for mankind, until his poverty compelled him to seek elsewhere for a change of luck. "Why not America?" suggested his practical wife, Margaret.

"Very well," said Willie reluctantly, "let it be America."

And so they set sail, on borrowed money, in the spring of 1848. Andy was twelve years old at the time. A towheaded, blue-eyed "little rebel of a Scotchie," brought up on the "rights of labor" and Bobbie Burns. What though his father was a weaver and his uncle Tammy a shoemaker? "A man's a man for a' that." Andy had often recited the "plowman's" poems—to the delight of his elders. "I gloated over the gems of Burns," he wrote many years later, "like a Prince of Ind over his jewels." He had learned, from this master, to despise all royalty save "the royalty of man." He was proud of the fact that his family had had "an uncle in jail for holding a prohibited meeting" of workingmen. "My childhood's desire was to get to be a man and kill a king."

Such was the background of the child who sailed with his family "to get to be a man" in America.

II

"IF I HAD REMAINED in Dunfermline," wrote Carnegie to one of his relatives in Scotland, "it is very likely I would have been a poor weaver all my days. But here I can surely do something better."

Not, however, at the beginning. His family settled at Allegheny, Pennsylvania—a city of mud, flood, fire, and cholera. Here his father exchanged a British for an American loom and remained, as before, a poor and unambitious dreamer. And Andy, for whom a formal education was out of the question, went to work as bobbin boy in a cotton mill. His pay was $1.20 a week. Hardly a promising start for "something better." Twelve hours a day—from six to six—and a damp hovel in the mud flats to return to in the evening.

But a father with a gentle heart, and a mother with a tenacity of purpose engendered in the Scottish Highlands. "Keep persisting, Andy, and someday you'll be a great mon!" His wages rose from $1.20 to $1.65 a week. The other boys in the mill made fun of his diminutive body and his foreign accent. "Scotchie! Scotchie! Scotchie!" they used to taunt him. And he would taunt back, "Aye, and I'm prood o' the name!"

He gradually lost his accent, but he never grew up. Lilliputian body, titanic energy, irresistible charm. A job as messenger boy at the telegraph office in Pittsburgh, and a salary of $2.50 a week. "I'm on the way to becoming rich!" An excellent job for an ambitious youngster, for it enabled him to meet all sorts of influential people. One of his "customers" was the manager of the Pittsburgh Theater, where Shakespeare was the perennial favorite. Young Andy got a free pass to the top gallery and thus added another divinity to the pantheon of his literary adorations, Bobbie Burns and William Shakespeare. To the end of his life he retained a passionate love for these two poets. And—so retentive was his memory—he could quote entire poems or scenes, and on occasion almost an entire play, to the amazement of his friends.

In addition to his literary attachments, young Andy became imbued with two other enthusiasms—for American Democracy and International Peace. He inherited these enthusiasms from a long line of ancestors—lovers of freedom and men of good will. "If I had not gone into business," he remarked late in life, "I would have become a journalist or a pamphleteer." Even as a youngster he wrote numerous letters to the newspapers and to his relatives in Scotland—excoriating war, denouncing slavery, and extolling the United States. "The two most prominent candidates for the Presidency," he writes to his uncle (1852), "I am sorry to say are warriors." Two years later the young pacifist urges the editor of a Sunday-school paper to initiate a campaign against war. "If each one was educated to look upon the machines made expressly for the destruction of their fellow men with the same horror that they behold the Scaffold and the Guillotine; if they could be seen only in the Museum, as relics of a barbarous age; if war could be shown to the young men in its true light . . . all would be well."

That is, if mankind would abolish slavery along with the abolition of war. "Slavery, I hope, will soon be a thing of the past." In politics, though he was far too young to vote, he was a free-soil Democrat. "Free-soilers," he explains in one of his letters, "get that name from their hatred of slavery and slave labor."

Yet in spite of the blot of slavery—"a blot which will soon be erased"— he worshiped the American idea. "In this country," he wrote to a cousin in Scotland, "there is no class of drones feasting upon the industry of the hive and protected by 'the divine right of kings.' Here the workers find no royal family to squander their hard-made earnings, no aristocracy to support . . . No primogeniture to curse the land and stop improvements in the soil . . . And all our great reforms are gained without the threat of revolution . . . For our politicians are accountable to the people, and hence our government is founded upon justice."

An astute mind—not only in the contemplation of politics but in the preparation for business. "Let those ruling 'by divine right' quarrel about succession and protectorates while we clear the forests and build school-houses and prepare homes for the working bees compelled to leave the old hives for the new."

A young man with an instinct for building and a passion for peace.

III

HE MADE AMAZING STRIDES in the building of his own career. At fifteen his annual earnings were about eighty-six dollars; at twenty-seven he made fifty thousand dollars in a single year. An open eye, a nimble tongue, and a ready smile—these were among the assets that enabled him to climb so rapidly to the top. These, and an audacity for taking chances where others hesitated. Like Emerson, he believed in attaching his wagon to a star. This propensity for making friends in high places secured him a job as telegraph operator on the Pennsylvania Railroad. "I had become acquainted with the superintendent of this road, Mr. Thomas A. Scott, while working as messenger boy." Though only eighteen when he entered this new job, he assumed his duties with an assurance that delighted and at times rather awed his employer. One day a serious accident tied up the Pennsylvania system. The freight trains were standing on the sidings all along the line. They could be moved only by telegraphic orders from the superintendent's office. But the superintendent was not in his office that morning. No telling when he might arrive. And so Carnegie took the responsibility upon his own shoulders. The slightest mistake might mean his job. "But the traffic must be kept on the move."

That evening Mr. Scott related the incident to one of his friends:

"Do you know what that white-haired little Scotch devil of mine did this morning?"

"No."

"Damned if he didn't run every train on the division *in my name,* and without the slightest authority . . . And he did it as well as I could have done it myself!"

A youngster to whom you could safely delegate your most important duties. He was not yet twenty-one when he became manager of the Western Division of the Railroad. And it was only a few months later that he made his first investment—ten shares of stock in the Adams Express Company. He raised the money for this investment through the mortgaging of his mother's five-hundred-and-fifty-dollar home—his father was now dead, and Andrew was the business head of the family.

His next—and far more profitable—investment didn't cost him a cent. He had become interested in a new invention—a sleeping car, the parent of the modern Pullman—and he had induced Mr. Scott to build a few of these cars for his Pennsylvania Railroad. The grateful inventor of the car, Mr. Theodore T. Woodruff, presented Carnegie with a one-eighth interest in his newly organized company.

This eighth interest was the cornerstone in the building of the Carnegie fortune. "The first considerable sum I ever made was from this source." Such were the investments, the results of an audacity seasoned with shrewdness, that brought his total earnings for 1863 to $47,860. Of this sum, his salary represented only twenty-four hundred dollars. "I believe in devoting my time to planning and to playing. Let the other fellows do the work." Throughout his mature life Carnegie gave only six months a year to his job. The rest of the time he spent in strengthening his body and developing his mind. Though far from a scholar, he acquired a general education and a facility of expression that enabled him to stand out even among the intellectually elite.

IV

BUT HIS MATURING GENIUS kept ever groping toward the promise of greater things. From telegraphy to transportation. From transportation to construction. The building of a fortune. More important yet—for the piling up of a fortune was but subsidiary to a nobler aim—the building of a material structure for the civilization of a new day. It was no mere accident that his mind was attracted to iron as the magnet of his life's work. During the Civil War—a war which he justified in spite of his pacific creed—he was put in charge of the reconstruction of the demolished bridges and railroads which linked Washington to the loyal states. In the course of this work he became deeply impressed with a fact which he had noted again and again. To fortify the trains and the bridges against fire and flood, it was necessary to use something more durable than wood for their construction. Frames of iron. (Steel had not as yet been invented.) Moreover, the rapid expansion of the country after the Civil War meant the building of more bridges, more railroads, the laying of a network of tracks over tens of thousands of miles. An important and profitable job, the supplying of the iron for all this impending work. Just the sort of business for a young fellow with a vision.

At this time Carnegie met "Old Pipe" (J. L. Piper), the inventor of an iron bridge. "With your inventive skill and my intimate knowledge of railroads," said Carnegie, "I believe we could do something worth while." Piper listened to Carnegie's persuasive logic, and a new firm was organized: the Keystone Bridge Company. Piper and his fellow mechanics produced the work, and Carnegie supplied the energy and the enthusiasm and the brains. "His presence is like the sun, which causes everything to spring into life." Whether in the factory or on the road—for he was constantly taking "drumming" trips—he made everybody "bridge-conscious." New bridges for old. The tearing down of the Age of Wood. The building up of the Age of Iron. "And I take pride in the fact that not one of our structures has ever collapsed."

The widening of America's horizons, and the expansion of Carnegie's mind. His brother Thomas, somewhat younger than Andrew and almost equally ambitious, had organized a rival iron company. But Andrew "absorbed" his brother's business and took him as a partner into his own growing concerns. Four of them by now—the Keystone Bridge Company, the Union Iron Mills, the Superior Rail Mill, and the Pittsburgh Locomotive Works. Only thirty years old, and already one of the most talked-about businessmen in America.

Time now to turn away from business for a while. Carnegie took his first extended vacation—a six months' trip to Europe. England, France, Germany, Switzerland, Rome. Reading books, attending operas, visiting museums, meeting people, making friends. "The man isn't worth his salt who cannot have his affairs so efficiently organized that he can drop them at a moment's notice."

And leave them in expert hands. This was one of the secrets of Carnegie's success—his genius for finding and training experts to assist him in his work. "The able executive is the man who can train assistants more capable than himself."

V

AT THIRTY-THREE it was his intention to retire from business within two years. With this in mind, he drew up a program for the remainder of his life. "Make no effort to increase fortune beyond $50,000 per annum . . . Spend the surplus each year for benevolent purposes . . . Get a thorough education . . . pay especial attention to speaking in public . . . Take a part in public matters, especially those connected with education and improvement of the poorer classes . . ."

This program Carnegie carried out almost to the letter. But it was considerably more than two years before he felt justified in retiring from business and devoting himself to the public good. For the country was growing too rapidly for a young man to sit still. There was a new transformation in the building material of America. Just as wood had given place to iron, iron was now giving place to steel.

And, as usual, it was Carnegie who was among the first to see the new trend. A "crazy young Frenchman," Henry Bessemer, had discovered—so he declared to an unbelieving world—a method for burning out the impurities of iron and converting it into a metal of infinitely greater elasticity and strength. In 1872, Carnegie met Bessemer, witnessed his invention, and immediately leaped to the most important of his many audacious decisions. He would enter upon the manufacture of steel and build a new framework for the structure of American prosperity. His imagination had become aflame with the possibilities of the plan—steel railways, steel bridges, steel buildings, steel instruments for the farm and the factory and the home, steel ships. An entire new world based upon a foundation of steel. The purification of the commonest metal and its transmutation into the substance of the greatest service to man.

"I must start with the manufacture of steel rails, and start at once!" To get the machinery of the world into motion toward the new day. The world looked on with a skeptical smile. "This time the daredevil of a Scotchman's gone completely out of his mind!" The Bessemer process had thus far met with more failure than success. But Carnegie's uncanny intuition told him that the promise was greater than the risk. "It was not a task for timid men. But I had some faith in my star."

And so, surrounding himself with a handful of partners who were willing to follow a reckless lead, he organized the Carnegie, McCandless and Company for the rolling of steel rails. And immediately he ran into one of the most terrible depressions (1873) in the history of the United States.

But even this panic served only as a stimulus to Carnegie's imagination. "The best time to expand is when others are lying low." While business after business went into bankruptcy, Carnegie kept improving his new mill, installing the most up-to-date machinery, and preparing himself for the orders that were "bound to come" in the rebuilding after the storm.

And his optimism proved to be right. When the panic was over and the reconstruction began, Carnegie was the one man fully equipped to supply the demand. This was a principle which Carnegie followed throughout his life—a principle which his rivals never seemed to understand. His rivals built in boom times, at a high cost; and when the building was completed, the boom times were over. But Carnegie built in periods of depression, at a low cost; and when *his* building was completed, a new boom was on. His theory was simple: "Have faith in America. Every financial flurry is but the prelude to a prosperity greater than ever before."

A sound theory, accompanied by a solid purse. Carnegie was able to build in times of depression because he always had the ready cash. For he never operated on borrowed money or invested on margin. "I always pay dollar for dollar for every share. And thus I can always raise enough money for any emergency that may arise."

A reckless imagination, guided by a sagacious mind.

VI

AND NOW, as he foresaw the needs of a rapidly growing nation, he poured his every dollar into his steelworks. And his every ounce of energy into this single objective of his industrial plan. "Invest in no other business but your own. For yours is the only business you know anything about."

And thus he added another unorthodox commandment to the gospel of business success: "Put all your eggs into one basket, and then watch the basket."

His concentration upon his own business, building when others lagged behind and saving his money when others wasted it, enabled Carnegie not only to *outproduce* his competitors but to *undersell* them. "When we first commenced the manufacture of steel, our competitors did not believe that we would be ready to make it for another year . . . And then we went out to the various railroads and persuaded them to give us orders at $65 a ton . . . $5 a ton less than our competitors were charging."

An eager competitor against his rivals, he compelled his workers to become eager competitors against one another. His single demand— more and better steel. Once, when he was vacationing in Scotland, he received a cable from his foreman, Bill Jones: "No. 8 Furnace broke all records today." Whereupon Carnegie cabled back: "Good! But what were the other ten furnaces doing?"

He expected much from his assistants, and he paid them well when they lived up to his expectations. One day he commended the work of his foreman. "Bill, you deserve something for what you've done. What do you suggest?"

"Well," said Jones, "you might pay me a hell of a big salary."

He had spoken this in jest, but Carnegie took him up. "I'll do it! From now on your salary will be equal to that of the President of the United States." And Carnegie was true to his word.

But he saw to it that Bill Jones, like all his other co-workers, was worthy of his salary. As he was preparing to sail on one of his annual trips to Europe, he called his foreman into his office. "Oh, Bill, when once I see the steamer rounding Sandy Hook, with the long vacation ahead, you don't know what a relief it will be to me!"

"And you, Mr. Carnegie," replied Jones, "don't know what a relief it will be to all of us!"

VII

IN 1881, Carnegie had become the undisputed head of the American steel industry. He had built up a fabulous fortune, and he now began to use it in the manner he had planned several years earlier. "Spend the surplus each year for benevolent purposes . . . especially those connected with education and improvement of the poorer classes."

His first expenditure of that nature was for the endowment of a public library in his native city of Dunfermline. This was the parent of several thousand similar free institutions which he donated to the improvement of the human mind. In the distribution of his fortune, as well as in its accumulation, he displayed an imagination based upon common sense. He built his libraries in no other communities save those that were willing to supply the buildings with books at their own expense. Help those alone who are willing to help themselves. Prepare a congenial atmosphere for the introduction of the little minds to the great. But the little minds must give proof of their eagerness to *meet* the great.

Even as Carnegie himself was eager to meet them. He spent much of his leisure time in reading the books of the wisest men—and, whenever possible, in corresponding with them or talking to them in person. He thus made the acquaintance of statesmen like Gladstone, historians like Morley, philosophers like Herbert Spencer, poets like Matthew Arnold, educators like Booker T. Washington—Carnegie drew no color line in his human contacts—college presidents, painters, musicians, novelists, editors—distinguished men and women from every walk of life. And he sought out these men not for their material fame but for their spiritual worth. With some of these intellectually and esthetically elect he formed lifelong friendships. His correspondence with Gladstone and Morley, for example, forms a beautiful chapter in the history of human devotion.

But he didn't confine his friendships to the elect. His Skibo Castle— a home he had bought in Scotland—was the rendezvous of many a dear attachment he had formed in his darker days. Men and women of humble means whom he invited from England, and even from America, and whose expenses he paid from the moment they left home to the moment they returned. Teachers, librarians, lawyers, unsuccessful tradesmen, and even workers from his mills.

In general, Carnegie's attitude toward his workers was that of an understanding friend. To many of them he was neither "A. C." nor "the Boss," but simply "Andy." He had the knack of living happily with his men. "Labor," he repeated again and again, "has a right to a fair share of the profits of industry." The best way to guarantee the distribution of the workers' share, he believed, was to adopt a sliding wage scale. That is, a scale which slid indefinitely *up* with *increasing* profits, but did not slide indefinitely *down* with *diminishing* profits. In other words, he advocated a minimum below which the wages should never go.

Time and again, when workers were striking in other industries, his sympathies were on the side of the strikers. Yet most strikes, he felt, could be avoided if both sides would be willing to resort to arbitration. "But if arbitration fails and a strike is called, the employer must *never* hire scabs to break the strike . . . There is an unwritten law among the best workmen: 'Thou shalt not take thy neighbor's job.'"

This was the principle he applied whenever his own workers threatened to strike. First he tried arbitration. And if arbitration failed, he shut down the mill until such time as both sides would "see the light" and come to mutual terms. And throughout the idle period he held personal conferences with the workers' representatives in an honest attempt to enable each side to see the other's point of view.

During these personal conferences with the workers' representatives, Carnegie displayed a humane understanding that generally won the workers' good will even though they might disagree with his terms. On one such occasion he explained his problems, and then he asked any man who had a grievance to stand up and present it.

"Well, Mr. Carnegie," began a worker in an angry tone, "you take my job——"

Whereupon Carnegie retorted, "Mr. Carnegie takes no man's job!"

Roars of laughter, cheers, and within a couple of hours the dispute was adjusted. For Carnegie possessed the human touch that turned would-be enemies into ardent friends.

But when Carnegie was absent from his mills, the disputes between the workers' representatives and his own were not so easy to adjust. One of the disputes led to a tragedy that culminated in the shedding of blood. It was during the famous Homestead Strike (1892). The workers at the Carnegie Homestead plant wanted a renewal of the then existing wage contract. The management insisted upon a reduction in wages. Had Carnegie been in the country at the time, all might have been well. For he knew how to effect a compromise. Unfortunately, however, he had put Henry C. Frick in complete charge of his business interests. The appointment of Frick was the one great flaw in the general excellence of Carnegie's business acumen. "Mr. Frick"—we are quoting from a Congressional Committee report made after the strike—"seemed to have been too stern, brusque, and somewhat autocratic . . . We do not think he exercised that degree of patience, indulgence, and solicitude which he should have done."

Or, they might have added, which Carnegie would have done. When the strike broke out, Carnegie was vacationing in Europe. He was unaware of Frick's action against the striking men. And this action was unnecessarily precipitate and severe. He barricaded the plant like a military camp—high wooden fence, portholes for guns, barbed wire strung along the top of the fortifications, and elevated platforms with searchlights at strategic points. And then, to cap the climax, he imported a "private army" of strikebreakers—the hated "Pinkerton men."

The result was inevitable. A pitched battle between the strikers and the Pinkertons—eight men killed and more than a score wounded. All this on the property of a man consumed with a passionate hatred against war.

And yet when the news of the bloodshed reached Carnegie in Europe, he upheld Frick against the world. A strange commentary on the human struggle for material success!

VIII

A storm of editorial censure descended upon Carnegie's head for his refusal to denounce Frick in public. In his heart of hearts, however, he must have been thoroughly ashamed of his partner's stubborn cruelty.

For a number of years he continued the partnership, and then they went their different ways. "Divorce under incompatibility of temper."

Exit Henry C. Frick. Enter Charles M. Schwab. And the drama goes on.

Schwab had come to Carnegie as a rail worker and he wound up as the most efficient of his managers. An expert driver of stakes, an expert driver of bargains. A man of glib tongue, bubbling wit, uncanny foresight, abounding sympathy, compelling ambition. An alter ego of Carnegie himself. The two personalities melted together like two drops of water. Carnegie came to trust "Charlie's" intuitions just as he trusted his own. During one of the national depressions—Carnegie's building times— Schwab informed Carnegie that he could save him fifty cents a ton in the making of steel if he were allowed to build a new mill.

"Go ahead, Charlie," said Carnegie. And Charlie went ahead.

The mill was completed and put into operation. Carnegie came out from New York—where he was living at the time—to look at the new structure. As Schwab showed him around, Carnegie watched him out of the corner of his eye. Suddenly he said, "What's wrong, Charlie?"

"Well, Andy, the mill is doing all I promised. But if I were to build it over again, I could save a dollar instead of fifty cents a ton."

"Couldn't you remodel *this* mill?"

"No, I'd have to tear it down."

"Go ahead, then, and tear it down."

Such was the understanding cameraderie of these two daring builders in steel.

IX

FOR A LONG TIME Carnegie was the richest bachelor in the world. He was too busy to think of marriage. But finally, at the age of fifty-one, he took a wife—Miss Louise Whitfield, the thirty-year-old daughter of a New York businessman. And eleven years later—at sixty-two—he experienced for the first time the happiness of fatherhood. His family life was as successful as his business career. Mrs. Carnegie was a woman of great understanding and charm. And his daughter Margaret, named after his mother, was—to quote his own words—"a wonderful wean . . . Her chief work is making up parties who never had a motor ride and taking them as her guests. Already the young socialist crops out. Why—she wants to know—should some people be rich and others poor?"

And Carnegie, though unable to answer the question, became richer from day to day. In 1900 his property was worth four hundred million dollars. A golden kingdom ruled by a benevolent despot. His partners had their say, to be sure; but after they had had their say, Carnegie had his way. "We are all a happy and harmonious family here," he remarked at a directors' meeting. "Nothing important is done except by unanimous vote." Whereupon one of the directors retorted in a stage whisper: "God help the man who isn't unanimous!"

And now, at last, time to lay down his scepter. The turn of the century. A tempting offer has been made for the Carnegie business. The Morgan interests are eager to take it over. A grand opportunity to devote himself to the *real* business of his life—the *giving away* of his fortune. "It's going to be a much harder job than the *amassing* of it."

He disposed of his holdings to Morgan—the greatest commercial transaction in history. "And now, Pierpont, I am the happiest man in the world. I've unloaded this burden on your back and I'm off to Europe to play."

But he played—as before—only half the time. The rest of the time he devoted to the distribution of his wealth. A sort of terrestrial deity, dispersing showers of gold for the blossoming of a better race. A race with less contentiousness and greater content. Peace foundations, educational endowments, astronomical observatories, funds for scientific research—to Madame Curie for her experiments on radium, to Koch for his studies in bacteriology—parks for "the bringing of more sweetness and light into the monotonous lives of the toiling masses," organs for cathedrals, auditoriums for orchestras, the Carnegie School of Technology and the Carnegie Museum of Art—these are but a few of his contributions "to the fitting of the new generation to cope more successfully with life." These, and the many pensions to private individuals of slender means. "When I lie awake at night and get to thinking about my gifts, my pension list is the thing that comes closest to my heart." These benefactions were bestowed upon a great number of famous men—poets, scholars, novelists, musicians, painters, priests—and upon an even greater number of the poor and the obscure. Every day he received stacks of mail from thousands of people imploring his aid. "The Lord has got tired of beggars, and He has sent them all to me." With the help of his secretaries, Carnegie sifted the mail and never allowed a "deserving" request to go unanswered. Old friends of his childhood, a woman who had rocked him in his cradle, a schoolmate who had "held your books while you ran a race," a daughter of the manufacturer who had given him his first job at $1.20 a week, two maiden sisters who had danced with him as a young man, and many of the retired workers from his various mills.

Including even those who had rebelled against him. One day he received a letter from his friend Dr. Van Dyke, who informed him that on the Mexican desert he had come across a derelict by the name of McLuckie. "The man, I understand, was one of the leaders in the Homestead Strike." At once Carnegie replied: "Give McLuckie all the money he needs, but don't mention my name." A year later Dr. Van Dyke ran across this man again. But he had a job now and declined the help. "I want you to know," said Dr. Van Dyke, "that this offer was not mine but Andrew Carnegie's."

"Well," gasped the astonished McLuckie. "That was damned white of Andy, wasn't it?"

When Carnegie heard of this he said: "I'd rather have McLuckie's words on my tombstone than any other inscription. And," he added, "I wouldn't want any dash between the *d*s."

X

A NEW MANSION at Number 2 East Ninety-first Street, New York. And at his desk a very tired old man busily engaged in dispensing $325,000,000 for the "improvement of mankind."

A very tired, and very busy, and very sad old man. For the world was drifting toward war. He had seen the conflict coming as early as 1907, and he knew where the responsibility lay. In the hands of Kaiser William. He paid a futile visit to the Kaiser in an effort to convert him to the Gospel of Peace. "If you make war, you may be great as Napoleon—but great only as a monster . . . But if you remain at peace . . . *and organize the world for peace* . . . you have it in your power to become *the supreme leader* of history . . ."

The emperor thanked Carnegie for his "kindly wisdom," declared himself for peace—and plunged promptly into war.

Yet Carnegie refused even now to lose faith in mankind. "The day of peace may be a little deferred, but it is sure to come." An organizer of industry on a gigantic scale, he saw everything in the large. There is bound to be universal peace, he believed, through the final interlocking of the national interests throughout the world. At first a coalition of America and England—a union of the *English-speaking* race. Then a United States of Europe. And finally a unification of the entire *human* race.

IMPORTANT DATES IN THE LIFE OF
ANDREW CARNEGIE

1835—Born, Dunfermline, Scotland.

1848—Came to America.
Started as bobbin boy in mill at Allegheny, Pennsylvania.

1860—Became superintendent of Western Division of Pennsylvania Railroad.

1861-65—Served as superintendent of military railroads and government telegraph lines in the East.

1865-1901—Actively engaged in iron and steel business.

1872—Introduced Bessemer process into the United States.

1886—Married Louise Whitfield.

1888—Principal owner of Homestead Steel Works.

1892—Homestead steelworkers' strike.

1898—Combined his interests into Carnegie Steel Company.

1901—Sold his steel interests to J. P. Morgan interests.
Retired from business.

1901-19—Endowed libraries, schools, museums, et cetera.

1919—Died, Shadowbrook, Massachusetts.

John Wanamaker

[1838-1922]

THROUGHOUT his life John Wanamaker was guided by a simple rule. All the different religions, he believed, are but different highways to God; and all men are entitled to travel their own way without jostling or interference from other men. His career was in a sense paradoxical—the role of a minister miscast as a merchant. Yet the very paradox gave rise to a new trend in history. John Wanamaker introduced the gospel of goodness into the selling of goods.

This idea of business for service is today—in theory at least—an accepted fact. In Wanamaker's day it was regarded as the conception of a madman intent upon commercial suicide. In the competitive jungle of that period a customer was somebody to exploit. The more completely you fooled him, the more successful your deal. But Wanamaker proved that the most profitable way to do business is to satisfy your customer's need rather than your own greed.

The story of Wanamaker's life, therefore, is one of the most unusual among the biographies of great men. It is the history of a business built upon the literal application of the Golden Rule.

II

FROM EARLY CHILDHOOD John Wanamaker was brought up in the belief that "religion is the best thing in the world to live by." *Any* religion, so long as you adhere to it with sincerity and tolerance and love. In the formative period of his life he went through a mixture of creeds. Born a Methodist, he attended the Lutheran Sunday school, and at twelve became—of his own volition—a member of the Presbyterian Church. And thus, having sought salvation through various paths, he found at the end of them all the selfsame guidance of God.

The Father of us all. The image of his own father—strong, steady, watchful, insistent, just. A stern and tender spirit, forever exacting obedience and forever dispensing love.

And Wanamaker's mother—"such little hands . . . and so cool on a boy's face when he was sick . . . Leaning little arms upon her knees, I learned my first prayers . . ."

Old-fashioned parents, old-fashioned home, old-fashioned faith in the goodness of God and the dignity of his fellow men.

John Wanamaker was the eldest of seven children. Not much time for schooling when you've got to help your father—a poorly paid brick-maker—to support so large a family. Up every day at four—a habit that John retained to the end of his life—family prayers before breakfast—and work until well into the evening. Helping his father at the brickyard— "I would turn the bricks on their edge to let them dry." The first pay he received for this work, seven copper cents. "Never was I so proud of any other sum I earned, however great."

His only recreation, reading books. *Robinson Crusoe, Benjamin Franklin, Pilgrim's Progress,* and the Bible. "People who saw me when a boy must have thought I had a tumor . . . where my pockets were—they were so stuffed out with books I had put there to study in my spare moments."

Only nineteen months of regular schooling, but a lifetime of activity in the Sunday school. Not that he was a priggish sort of youngster—he was merely a child with a heart full of devotion that sought for an adequate outlet. He organized his first Sunday-school class and began to teach it at twelve. "This boy," said everybody, "will surely become a preacher."

But when the time came for him to choose a vocation, he decided upon storekeeping rather than preaching. For in the mosaic of his old-fashioned ideas there was a pattern of practical genius. And, perhaps, of material shrewdness as well. Instead of advancing the earth toward heaven, he would bring heaven a little nearer to earth. "It was the interest in the wants of a community that led me to try . . . to make things easier and better."

To sell honest goods at an honest price.

He started his business at a bad time—the outbreak of the Civil War. And under risky conditions—he had just married and could hardly spare the nineteen hundred dollars he had saved up at various jobs. But Wanamaker was always a man to take risks. "I didn't think much about conditions; I thought only of my desire to make good." He had volunteered for military duty, but was turned down for a "congenital weakness of the lungs." Why sit and mope over the fact that he was physically unfit? Why not open his store right now and sink his worries in the forgetfulness of work?

And so he induced his brother-in-law, Nathan Brown, to invest sixteen hundred dollars along with his own nineteen hundred, and opened the Oak Hall Clothing Bazaar at the corner of Sixth and Market streets, in Philadelphia. A small advertisement, inserted in the *Philadelphia Ledger* (April 8, 1861), informed the public that "Wanamaker and Brown . . ."

having purchased their goods under the pressure of the times at very low rates, will sell them accordingly."

This was to be the tenor of the Wanamaker publicity throughout his life. No flaring headlines, no flamboyant displays, but just a simple statement of what he had to sell. A little better goods, at a little lower price, than could be gotten elsewhere. In this sort of publicity there was no effort at crushing competition. "I invite the public to look at my goods, and I invite my competitors to offer equal values at an equal price."

III

But here was something revolutionary in the commercial world. *One price to all*. No haggling, no favoritism, no connivance for one customer's gain to be paid out of another customer's loss. The equality of all in the buying of goods. Applied Democracy in the ethics of business.

And now came an idea that was even more revolutionary. One day the following notice appeared in the Philadelphia papers: "Wanamaker and Brown desire to say that the quality of all the goods sold at their Clothing Bazaar will be guaranteed."

What a strange idea—a published guarantee to customers who had always been subjected to the maxim *caveat emptor,* let the buyer beware. Here was a seller who actually had the buyer's interest at heart. But how, asked the business world, could Wanamaker protect that interest? The answer appeared in the next day's advertisement:

"Any article that does not fit well, is not the proper color or quality, does not please the folks at home, or for any other reason is not perfectly satisfactory, should be brought back at once, and if it is returned as purchased within ten days, we will refund the money. It is our intention always to give value for value in every sale we make, and those who are not pleased with what they buy will do us a positive favor to return the goods and get the money back."

This announcement amazed not only the merchants of Philadelphia but the general public as well. "But," inquired a skeptical customer, "suppose I returned a yard of dry goods cut from the piece, would you take that back too?"

"Yes," replied Wanamaker, "I would take that too."

A peculiar merchant, with peculiar ideas. Wouldn't take long before he's pushed to the wall. "With this method of yours," asked an anxious friend, "what in the world do you ever expect to sell?"

Quick as a flash came the reply: "Satisfaction."

IV

They called it the *foolish store,* but before long it began to pile up profits more rapidly than the stores of the *wise*.

For Wanamaker's business was built upon the principle of fair play.

It was an incident in his life as a boy that "created the foundation" for this sort of business. He had gone into a jewelry store to buy his mother a Christmas present. He had only a few dollars in his pocket. Anxious to spend the money to the best possible advantage, he carefully examined the various articles in the showcase. "The jeweler was growing impatient. Finally I said, 'I'll take that,' indicating a piece—just what it was I don't recall.

"The jeweler began wrapping it up. Suddenly I saw another piece that I thought would better please my mother. 'Excuse me, sir,' I said, 'but I've changed my mind. I'll take *that* piece instead.'

" 'Too late to change, young feller,' said the jeweler. 'You've already bought *this* piece, and you've got to keep it.' "

As a result of this humiliating incident, Wanamaker made it his life-long principle to give people what they wanted. For, in so doing, he made them want to come back. "The best way to keep your customers is to keep them satisfied. And the surest way to profit from your sales is to make them profitable to both sides."

V

HIS PARTNER, Nathan Brown, died in 1868. Wanamaker bought his interest in the store and became the sole owner. The Oak Hall Clothing Bazaar had now outgrown its space. Time to expand—a phrase that was to recur again and again in Wanamaker's career. He rented some buildings adjoining the store, increased the floor space of Oak Hall to two acres, and opened an additional store—on Chestnut Street—for the sale of "a finer grade of men's and boys' clothing."

Again everybody predicted failure. For Chestnut Street was too "smart" a location, and its patrons were too conservative in their ways, for a "sensational" store of this kind. But again Wanamaker proved that his new business policy—equal values received for equal prices paid—was as appealing to the rich as it was to the poor.

And to the customers of other cities as well as to those of Philadelphia. In 1872, Wanamaker opened branch stores in Baltimore, Richmond, Memphis, St. Louis, Louisville, and Pittsburgh. The Wanamaker stores had now become the largest retail clothing business in America. The Oak Hall Bazaar alone had advanced from a sales total of less than twenty-five thousand dollars in 1861 to more than two million dollars in 1871. And this growth was largely due to the fact that "the customers"—as Wanamaker himself expressed it—"are respected and protected at every point."

It was this solid foundation of mutual trust that enabled Wanamaker to weather the panic of 1873. At a time when money was scarce and credit almost impossible to find, the Wanamaker stores threw another bombshell into the business world. On October 1, 1873, the Philadelphia papers carried the following terse announcement under the Wanamaker heading:

"Checks taken from buyers. Change given in cash."

He *gave* and he *received* credit. Unable to meet his notes to a woolen factory owned by A. T. Stewart and Company, he asked for an extension of time. The extension was readily granted, in spite of the many malicious rumors that Wanamaker was about to fail. "In regard to your obligations," wrote William Libbey, an officer of the company, "I do not know whether you owe us six thousand or sixteen thousand, it makes no difference which . . . Your credit is good enough, and you are able to take care of it in spite of all the lies that the devil may get into line to do their dirty work under his generalship."

And thus Wanamaker rode safely into port, and the business world began to look with greater respect upon his revolutionary methods. One by one they began to adopt these methods—"a fixed price marked in plain figures on each article, purchase money returned if goods are brought back unworn and uninjured, description and quality of the goods attached to each article so that the customer knows exactly what he buys." A new era of honest storekeeping had dawned upon the world.

VI

A TRIP TO EUROPE (1875), and Wanamaker came back with another new idea. A store in which you can sell everything that a customer may need. The origin of the modern department store. It was the time of the Centennial Exposition in Philadelphia. Organize a business that will become a permanent national exposition—a center, insofar as humanly possible, for all the material goods of the world.

"But," objected his friends, "why take in articles that are not in your line?"

"Why not?" he retorted. "Who has a patent on merchandising? . . . If we were just starting in business, who would consider it proper to question what business we chose to follow?"

On the opening day of this "new kind of store" there were seventy thousand visitors. A few days prior to the formal opening General Grant had visited the store. "It requires as much generalship to organize a business like this," he had observed, "as to organize an army." John Wanamaker had taken the old philosophic theory—"the greatest good to the greatest number"—and turned it into a practical fact—the greatest collection of goods to the greatest number of customers.

The idea was burlesqued in some of the cheaper newspapers. One of them, the *Philadelphia Sunday Gazette,* printed a mock "advertisement" for this "new kind of store":

> *Billions of Millions!*
> more or less, of Ladies and Gentlemen, Boys and Girls, Spitzdogs and Poodles, have visited our Immense Emporium during the first week of its existence and the mammoth headquarters of Monopoly is now an established fact, and must remain a monument to the Gullibility of the Public as long as there is a Public to be gulled.

But Wanamaker proceeded quietly to point out—and, as time went on, to prove—the fact that "this new kind of store-keeping . . . performs a public service in retiring middlemen . . . that the profit therefrom to the owners is insignificant compared to the people benefited by the cheapening of the comforts of life . . . that its principal claim to favor is that it distributes to the consumer in substance or cash the compounded earnings hitherto wasted on commission men, importers, jobbers, wholesalers, and commercial travelers . . ."

From the manufacturer, through the retailer, direct to the customer—this, in substance, was Wanamaker's principal aim in the continual expansion of his business. While he was not averse to his profits—Wanamaker never pretended he was a saint—he always had the public as well as his own interest at heart. He had a flair for showmanship, but he insisted upon putting on a good show. And at a reasonable price. In addition to the goods he sold, he entertained the public with art exhibits and free concerts at his stores. "My business is not only commercial, it is also educational." He often referred to his store as a *school*. "A school of progress." He established classes for his salesfolk in order that "those compelled to work for a living might enjoy the privileges of the leisure class."

He regarded his employees as his second family. For he had, as he expressed it, two homes—"my old home where I sleep, and this new home where I work." And in both homes he made it his business to treat his "co-familiars" with the utmost consideration and courtesy. "If I have said anything to hurt anyone's feelings," he said in a public address to his people, "forgive me for I never intended it. If I have been misunderstood, I hope you will take the liberty of writing me about it."

And his employees trusted him, and confided in him, and repaid him with a devotion equal to his own. On the fiftieth anniversary of his Philadelphia store his "business family" presented him with a deed to his birthplace. They had bought this home for him, out of their own savings, as a token of "our Loyalty, our Honor, and our Love."

Yet in spite of his devotion to his employees, he believed in the gospel of hard work. For himself as well as for others. When he opened his store in New York he traveled there from Philadelphia at least twice a week. And he continued this practice until the very end of his long life. He generally took an early train out of Philadelphia and was at his New York desk promptly at nine.

At times, however, he strayed from his desk in the morning and took his place at the entrance to the store. And when the heads of the departments happened to come late, he would merely smile and say, "Good morning." A single affable greeting of this nature was enough to cure most of them of their tardiness.

For, throughout his life, he worked on a single plan: "My success is your success. I don't want to fail you. I don't want you to fail me."

VII

To WHILE AWAY HIS TIME on the train between Philadelphia and New York, he began to write—at the suggestion of his son Rodman—a series of business editorials. Some of these editorials, in their lucidity and their tang, are reminiscent of *Poor Richard's Almanack*. "Some men have to be put into a quart measure and then ladled out to see how much of them is froth." "We have no one to fear except ourselves." "Where there are faults on both sides, forgive and forget." "Nobility is elective and not hereditary." "No man can dream character into himself—he must hammer and forge himself into a man." "Neither nations nor individuals have an unchallengeable right to walk over each other." "Spend yourself in courtesy, and the more courtesy you spend the more you will have left." "Mankind is one family."

All in all, he wrote about five thousand of these "editorials"—most of them on the backs of envelopes. They were incorporated into advertising copy. He composed all his advertisements himself. Though seventy-four now, he still held the reins of the business in his own hands. Of the two sons—Thomas and Rodman—whom he had taken into his stores, the first had died early and the second had become his European representative. So long as he remained actively at work he remained perpetually young. "To suffer oneself to being talked into feeling old, and therefore to lay aside one's occupation and to settle down into ease and inactivity, is to hasten the years and to hurry forward the end of life."

Wanamaker was in no hurry to quit. "To judge from your vitality," observed a friend, "you will live to be a hundred."

"Why stop at a hundred?" retorted Wanamaker. "I shall then be only at the beginning of my work."

This from the man who had already accomplished the work of ten men. In addition to his manifold activities in the department stores, he had served as Postmaster General under President Harrison, had organized the largest group of Sunday schools in the world, and now, at the outbreak of World War I, was throwing all his energy and resources into the struggle to make the world a better place to live in.

Always he was in the forefront of human endeavor. A list of "Wanamaker firsts" would cover several pages. Here are just a few of them:

He was the first to offer vacations, with pay, to all his employees; the first to introduce electricity and the telephone into a business firm; to insert a full-page advertisement in a newspaper; to open reading and resting rooms for his customers; to establish a Penny Savings Bank; to build a hotel for his women employees; to give liberal Christmas gifts, in the form of bonuses, to all his salespeople; to open a seashore camp for the boys who worked at the store; to inaugurate a students' art exhibition; to install—in the Philadelphia store—the largest organ in the world; to urge the establishment of a United States Parcel Post; to designate all Saturdays in July and August as full holidays with full pay; and to establish medical service—with hospital, nurses, and doctors—free to his employees.

VIII

EIGHTY-FOUR NOW, and still a young man. Nearly six feet of erect and vigorous manhood; ruddy complexion, blue-gray eyes, fine tawny hair with only an occasional suggestion of white, high forehead, fairly large nose, strong chin, and a whimsical mouth full of laughter and life. The reflected good will of a life devoted to building "with the plumb of Honor, the level of Truth, and the square of Integrity, Education, Courtesy, and Mutuality."

These words, cut into the rock of the capstone of his Philadelphia store, were meant to serve as his monument.

But even now he was not yet ready for the end. On September 19, 1922, he traveled as usual to his New York store, held conferences with three of his assistants, returned to Philadelphia on the four o'clock train, attended prayer meeting at Bethany Church, went to a lodge meeting at the Masonic Temple, and returned home at midnight.

He felt, as he expressed it, "just a bit tired. But I'll be all right tomorrow."

The next day, however, he was unable to go to his office. A heavy cold. Nothing to do but to read, to write his editorials, and to wait patiently until he got well.

On the morning of December twelfth he knew that he was dying. But he was not afraid. "I'm getting well at last . . . I have served my apprenticeship . . . I shall now begin my work."

IX

ONCE, when asked to write his autobiography, Wanamaker replied: "I can summarize my life in a very few words—thinking, trying, toiling, and trusting in God."

IMPORTANT DATES IN THE LIFE OF JOHN WANAMAKER

1838—Born, Philadelphia.

1858—Organized Bethany Sunday School.

1861—Opened clothing house of Wanamaker and Brown in Philadelphia.

1869—Founded store of John Wanamaker and Company.

1876—Transformed Pennsylvania Railroad freight depot into a department store.

1889–93—Served as Postmaster General under President Harrison.

1896—Bought A. T. Stewart store in New York City.

1903—Built "skyscraper" annex to Wanamaker store in New York.

1922—Died, Philadelphia.

John Davison Rockefeller

[1839-1937]

ROCKEFELLER was one of the most self-centered individuals in all history. He was a man with a single passion—gold. Even the most ardent of his admirers, Mark Hanna, observed that "Rockefeller is sane in every respect save one: he is money-mad!"

Rockefeller came by his money-madness from his German ancestry, the Rockenfellers of Sagendorf. "Away back in the money age," a genealogist who had investigated the family history reported, "the Rockenfellers had money—coins—bearing their name."

From his infancy Johnny was taught to worship the golden-calf god of his ancestors. His father took special pains to inspire his children with a genius for enticing the coins from other people's pockets into their own. A quack doctor who claimed to cure everything, from chilblains to cancer, Bill Rockefeller believed that the Lord had created the many to serve as suckers for the few. And he transmitted this belief to his children by many a concrete example. "I cheat my boys every chance I get," he boasted. "I want to make 'em sharp. I trade with the boys and skin 'em and I just beat 'em every time I can. I want to make 'em sharp."

And Johnny grew up sharp and ruthless as a razor's edge. He was only ten (1849) when he discovered the important fact that money is like a fruit-bearing tree. Out of the seed of a loan it produces the fruit of interest. For some years past he had been saving his pennies in a little blue bowl. One day he heard that a neighbor wanted to borrow fifty dollars. The neighbor was willing to pay an interest of 7 per cent. Johnny ran to his father and asked him to explain the whole thing. "What is interest? What do you mean by 7 per cent? How much will that make on fifty dollars?" And with the magic of the explanation singing in his ears, he took fifty dollars out of his bowl and loaned it to the neighbor. A year later he received his principal of fifty dollars and his interest of three dollars and a half. "Gee whiz," he cried, "I never knew you could make money without working for it!" And from that day on, as he declared many years later, he was "determined to make money work for me."

II

OF THE THREE Rs in his school curriculum, he cared only for 'rithmetic. "Reading and writing are a waste of time." In the Rockefeller household there were no books. But there was a good deal of figuring. Bill Rockefeller loved to explain, by facts and figures, how he had outsmarted everybody with whom he had had any dealings. "When I grow up," said John, "I'll be smart like my father. And I'll make a lot of money. *A hundred thousand dollars!*"

"And God willing," said his mother, "you will make it, my son."

His mother was a pious woman. She believed in God. Not in the God of the Prophets who required justice and mercy, but in the God of the Patriarchs who encouraged enterprise and wealth. Rockefeller grew up with the conviction that the Lord had elected him, as He had elected Jacob, to outsmart the Labans of the world and to become the guardian of His wealth for the less astute members of the human race. "Seest thou a man diligent in his business? He shall stand before kings." Throughout his life Rockefeller suffered from an atrophied conscience. He never felt that he had deprived others of their rights. It was God's doing. "God gave me my money," he once declared to a representative of the *Woman's Home Companion*. He was God's favorite, he believed, not only because he was *smarter,* but also because he was *better* than his fellows. When he cornered the oil distribution of America, he was but following in the footsteps of Joseph who had cornered the grain distribution of Egypt.

Rockefeller found nothing inconsistent between his religious beliefs and his business practices. He regarded his wealth as a reward for his virtue. The entire philosophy of his life—a philosophy which he had acquired in the home environment of his childhood—could be summed up in a few words: "Serve the Lord and exploit thy neighbors."

III

EVEN AS A YOUNGSTER he delighted his father with his ability to drive a bargain. "The boy," said the elder Rockefeller, "has a magical tongue. He bewitches people into thinking he does them a favor when he fleeces them."

He sent John to a commercial school (in Cleveland) to study "facts and figures; all other learning is useless if you want to make money." John D. took this lesson to heart. He became an expert bookkeeper; and when he left the commercial school (in 1855) he was a devout believer in two sacred entities—the Ledger and the Lord. Broad-shouldered, blue-eyed, and straight-lipped, he faced the world confidently. His voice was soft and low and pleasant to the ear. And it was always ready with some pious platitude. His schoolmates had called him Deacon. He joined the Erie Baptist Church and offered his clerical services, free, to the board of trustees. "If I help the Lord, the Lord will help me." He was eager to hire God as his official guide to the gold fields of the earth.

"A very exemplary young man," said the minister of the Baptist Church. "Attends strictly to his business." Armed with this flattering recommendation from his spiritual adviser, young Rockefeller applied for a job at the warehouse of Hewitt and Tuttle. He got the job, and devoted himself to his work, and regularly gave his tithe to the church—and within two years he rose from the position of errand boy to that of head bookkeeper.

And then, at eighteen, he felt that he had worked enough for other people. He wanted to go into business for himself. And so he borrowed one thousand dollars from his father—"the interest, son, will be 10%, not a whit less"—and formed a "Produce and Commission Brokerage" with a young partner by the name of Maurice B. Clark. That night he knelt and prayed for guidance and success—to the partnership, if possible, but at any rate to John D.

Before long John D. had outstripped his partner. He was now the sole owner of the brokerage. Young Clark had wanted to mix a little pleasure into his business. He had asked Rockefeller to take an afternoon off occasionally to go sailing with him. And when Rockefeller had refused, Clark had warned him that all work and no play would make Jack a dull boy. "Yes," replied Rockefeller, "but it will also make Jack a *rich* boy."

IV

ROCKEFELLER attended to his business, saved his money, and waited for the big opportunity. It came in the oil rush of the early sixties. New lamps for old. Genii of petroleum spouting out of the earth and towering into clouds. Aladdin cities springing up overnight—cities of grease and gambling and filth, whirlpools of bad whisky and bad women and bad faith. Geysers of liquid gold.

This liquid gold attracted Rockefeller like a magnet. He packed up his belongings and went to Oil Creek. But he kept his head. Instead of joining the crazy merry-go-round of gaiety and gambling, he read his Bible and scratched long lines of figures on his carefully ruled sheets of paper. You buy a barrel of crude oil for a dollar. You refine it and sell it for twenty dollars. Multiply this barrel by a hundred, a thousand, a million, ten million, a hundred million! . . . Another man might have become intoxicated with the daring magnitude of these figures. But not Rockefeller. He proceeded methodically to translate the figures into facts. He must gather all the oil business, if possible, into his own hands. And so he purchased his own crude oil, built his own refinery, made his own barrels, put up his own storage tanks, and acted as his own middleman. He was only twenty-six years old; yet he was already, to quote the felicitous phrase of John K. Winkler, America's outstanding "Portrait in Oil." A rather enticing portrait, in spite of his self-centered philosophy. Small glittering eyes that twinkled with humor—especially when he closed a "smart" deal; a firm, respect-compelling jaw; a mouth whose callous lines could melt into an ingratiating smile when he wanted to gain your good will; a fringe of reddish silk side whiskers that gave him the look of a holy man; and long bony fingers trained to caress the unsuspecting little flies into the web of his commercial genius. A skillful, fascinating, determined, and voracious spider of a man.

V

HE WAS PERHAPS the hardest-working businessman in the country. Yet he found time to court and to win the hand of Laura C. Spelman.

On his wedding day he worked several hours at the office. Before he left he treated his employees to a good dinner. At the end of the dinner he turned to the foreman.

"Treat them well," he said, *"but see that they work."*

Rockefeller was fortunate in his marriage. Miss Spelman had been a schoolteacher; but, like her fiancé, she possessed a most unscholarly affection for business. Together they enjoyed a happy companionship of commercial and domestic harmony.

His growing family—they had five children in all—drove him more passionately than ever to become the richest man in America. Bent upon his single purpose, he made no friends. As his business expanded and he found himself in need of new capital, he began to take in partners. But he looked upon these partners not as friends or even as business companions. He reduced them to the ranks of subordinates. His personality and his genius dominated them all. Andrews, Flagler, Rogers, Archbold, Clark—all these men are remembered not as his associates but as his agents. The agents of his dictatorial and unbreakable will. He had a way of bending everybody to his demands. He never argued with people. He either got them to agree with him or he crushed them. "There are too many people in the oil business. Drive them out." And one by one he drove out—that is, he bought out or squeezed out—his competitors. Those of them whose talents he needed in his monopolistic plans he absorbed into his organization. The rest he dropped by the wayside.

And he did all this with a clear conscience. "It was right between me and my God. If I had to do it tomorrow I would do it again . . . do it a hundred times."

The method which he used in outwitting his competitors was as ingenious as it was vicious. He killed them with a double-edged weapon of rebates. He made secret arrangements with the railroads to carry his own oil at ten cents a barrel and his competitors' oil at thirty-five cents a barrel. But that was only half the story. He made further arrangements whereby the railroads paid back to him the extra twenty-five cents which they charged to his competitors. In the face of such competition his business rivals were helpless. It was like a duel in which only one of the men is armed, and in which the armed man strikes from the back. When asked what he thought of the morality of his rebates, Rockefeller laughingly retorted: "Laddie, I'm agin 'em—unless I'm in 'em."

And thus he went on merging and submerging, until in 1870 nearly all his rivals were killed off and the first of the oil trusts, the Standard Oil Company, was born.

<h1 style="text-align:center">VI</h1>

ROCKEFELLER was now thirty-one years old. To add dignity to his years, he had grown a full beard. He still retained his honored position in the church. He was as sincerely pious as he was sincerely predatory. It paid him good dividends to be devout and clever and ruthless. It provided him with great comforts in this world and prepared the way—so he believed—for still greater comforts in the next. He never for a moment suspected that what he was doing was not good in the eyes of the Lord. It was with a perfectly clear conscience that he accumulated his vast reservoir of oil and then parceled it out, at his own price, for the lamps of the poor. And, as his monopoly kept growing, he kept raising the price more and more. Desperate men began to send him threats against his life, newspaper editors bespattered him with showers of uncomplimentary ink, and a grand jury indicted him as "a cheat, conspirator, and business fraud." But he sat serenely in his office and manipulated his figures and praised the Lord and defied the world. Nothing, he was determined, would stop him from becoming the richest man in America.

And the richer he grew, the lonelier he grew. "Open yourself up to no one, and allow no one to open himself up to you." One day he observed a clerk talking to a stranger. "What did the man want here?" he asked the clerk when the stranger had left.

"Nothing, sir. The man is a friend of mine."

"Why didn't you keep your mouth shut when he was here?"

"But, sir, he is just a friend."

"Friend or no friend, be careful. Keep your mouth shut. You never can tell what they're trying to find out."

He was uncommunicative even toward his own partners. When they asked him about his plans for their mutual interests, he would say:

"You'd better not know. If you don't know anything, you won't tell anything."

He suffered from social blindness, a disease common to military aggressors and financial conquerors. And being socially blind, he was ethically obtuse. He was unable to distinguish between right and wrong. Justice was as vague a quality to him as light is to a man physically blind. He lacked the moral vision to see himself in relation to other people. The world, as he imagined it, consisted of one man—himself—surrounded by millions of worms. He used them as bait or stepped upon them with equal indifference. Their wrigglings served merely as a source of amusement to him. "People are so easily fooled." Once, when he managed to fool the people, relates his biographer, Ida Tarbell, "he was so overjoyed he kicked his heels and hugged himself and said: 'I'm bound to be rich! *Bound to be rich!* BOUND TO BE RICH!' "

In his quest for riches he stifled his affection for everybody outside of his family circle. He still indulged in his charities, to be sure, but even in his charity he was cold and calculating and economical. When one of his acquaintances was down in his luck, Rockefeller sent him a pair of old shoes. "Have these shoes recobbled," said the accompanying note, "and they will last another year."

And the Standard Oil Company, the child of Rockefeller's extraordinary brain, kept growing bigger and bigger. It monopolized not only the land but tried even to monopolize the laws of the country. One day in the fall of 1872 a circular went out from the Standard Oil Company to all its employees. This circular, labeled "Order No. 1," began as follows: "We deem the election of ——" (a man charged with being a professional lobbyist) "vital to our interests as well as yours." The Standard Oil was now launched upon a campaign to dominate the politics as well as the economics of the country. "Politics in the latter half of the nineteenth century," a cynic has remarked, "consisted in the passing of laws to help the strong against the weak."

And so, by means of bullying and bribery—in those days a *bribe* was conveniently labeled as a *loan*—the Standard Oil Company had by 1900 become a world-wide Empire of Greed. And the Oil King of the World, though personally Rockefeller kept aloof from the political activities of his company, could now enjoy the distinction of being one of the richest men in history.

And one of the most detested. As he grew old he confided to an acquaintance that he wanted desperately to be loved. Yet "wherever he turned," writes his biographer John T. Flynn, "he saw the evidences of hate." His face, like his heart, had become gray and shriveled and pinched. Rockefeller was turning into a dried-up image of emotional starvation. A sad old King Midas of the Industrial Age, he was unable to feel anything warmer than the touch of gold.

VII

AND THEN he entered upon a new ambition: he began to buy esteem. His conscience, which had been serenely asleep all his life, was now awakened at last. Perhaps there was some grain of truth, he concluded, in what people were saying of him. It wouldn't be a bad idea to throw a generous measure of oil upon the troubled waters of public opinion. He opened up his purse strings in a flood of charity. He donated one hundred thousand dollars to a church organization. The gift was roundly condemned in the public press. A clergyman delivered a sermon against Rockefeller in which he referred to his donations as *tainted money*. This phrase was taken up on the vaudeville stage. "Sure his money is tainted! 'Tain't for you and 'tain't for me!"

But the public soon got over its scruples. Churches, hospitals, and colleges began eagerly to accept his benefactions. And to glorify the bene-factor. "John D. Rockefeller," declared a professor at Chicago University, "is superior in creative genius to Shakespeare, Homer, and Dante."

And thus, with a flourish of the pen, one of the most hated had be-come one of the most respected men in America. Rockefeller now went about with an oil-burning halo around his head.

His charities mounted from day to day. To him they meant no sacrifice. They represented merely a handful of cold figures subtracted from his fabulous sums of gold. Some of his charities, to be sure, have performed a great service. The Rockefeller Institute for Medical Research, for example, has resulted in the saving of many lives. But what of the many lives stunted and crushed in Rockefeller's relentless reaping of the harvest of his wealth?

Yet we must not be unfair to Rockefeller. He was no worse than the other monopolists of his day. He was merely one of a type. It was an age of unprecedented expansion. The economic atmosphere of the country was breeding a race of Titans; and such men as Rockefeller and Carnegie and Morgan and Hill and Armour and Huntington happened to be the best adapted for growth in such an atmosphere. They were not men of high ethical standards. But high ethical standards produce martyrs and not masters. It is just as foolish to blame a Rockefeller for not being a Lincoln as it would be to blame an oak tree for not being a rosebush. The founders of the big American trusts played an inevitable and important part in the economic development of the United States. It was a dramatic but futile gesture when the government, in 1911, officially "busted" the Standard Oil Trust. In accordance with this official decree, the Standard Oil Company was to be thenceforth divided into several small concerns. It was like dividing the Atlantic Ocean with a carving knife. Both histori-cally and economically Rockefeller was right when he said: "If we limit opportunity we will have to put the brakes on our national development . . . We must build up, build up for years to come . . . We are too young a nation for this tearing down."

Rockefeller was brilliant enough to realize that the tendency of Ameri-can progress, of *all* progress, is not toward division but toward unification. Individuals are united into families, families into states, states into na-tions. The same is true of economic development. Individuals combine into partnerships, partnerships into corporations, corporations into trusts. Large-scale production is vital to a nation that has learned to live in a large way. But we have not as yet learned how to *regulate* this producing on a large scale so that it may redound to the greatest interest of the greatest number. We have allowed it to become an instrument of selfish exploitation instead of mutual co-operation.

And Rockefeller, a selfish yet sincere exploiter, felt that he was acting within his moral rights. A man is but the measure of his day. Rockefeller lived in a money-making day, and he felt it his duty to make as much money as he could. "God gave me my money," he said. "I believe the power to make money is a gift from Heaven . . . Having been endowed with the gift I possess, I believe it is my duty to make money and still more money, and to use the money I make for the good of my fellow man according to the dictates of my conscience."

And thus, believing in his own righteousness, he selfishly and serenely waited for the end. "His daily life," observed a friend shortly before his death, "is a round of work, play, and, above all, gratitude."

IMPORTANT DATES IN THE LIFE OF JOHN DAVISON ROCKEFELLER

1839—Born, Richford, New York.

1853—Family moved to Cleveland.

1858—Formed business partnership of Clark and Rockefeller.

1860—Entered oil business.

1865—Built Standard Oil Works at Cleveland.

1867—Incorporated Standard Oil Company.

1881—Standard Oil Company became a trust.

1892—Standard Oil Company declared illegal by courts. Rockefeller worth a billion dollars.

1900—Began to withdraw from business to devote self to charity.

1901—Founded Rockefeller Institute for Medical Research.

1911—Resigned from presidency of Standard Oil Company. Standard Oil Company "dissolved."

1913—Started Rockefeller Foundation.

1937—Died, Ormond Beach, Florida.

Oliver Wendell Holmes
[1841-1935]

OLIVER Holmes the boy was a mixture of all that was New England. Wendell the youth absorbed all that was America in the period of her transition. When he reached manhood these qualities had blended into a well-rounded being—a man of wisdom and honesty and a passionate love for fair play. American to the core—Justice Oliver Wendell Holmes, the great dissenter.

Quiet and reserved, Wendell might well have been thought shy. In a family dominated by the elder Holmes, loquacious Autocrat of the Breakfast Table, young Wendell's reticence was particularly noticeable. Amid the chattering, bustling women of the family, Wendell's slow smile and deliberate speech produced upon the newcomer the impression of aloofness. A glance at the alert eyes, however, would have revealed the keen intellectual fire that burned behind the calm exterior. As he winced at his father's dreadful puns, he gave people the impression that he was lacking in humor. And as he listened, sometimes ungraciously, to the doctor's too-oft-repeated anecdotes, he acquired a reputation for being supercilious. Yet his mind was developing a sense of humor richer and more kindly than that of the father, under whose shadow he reached adulthood and under whose disapproval his own personality remained for a number of years subdued.

At sixteen, when he entered Harvard, Wendell towered physically above the Autocrat. With a slightly guilty feeling, he admitted to himself that he enjoyed being away from home. With a shock of unruly hair, a gentle manner, and a pair of dreamy eyes, Wendell possessed a romantic charm that caused young feminine heads to turn and young feminine hearts to flutter. He was unaware of the stir he created; and though he called on many young ladies, he felt no interest other than friendship for any of them. Avoiding the homes where he would be welcomed as his father's son, he became a part of the gay younger set of Boston. While Wendell Senior berated the lack of competitive sports at Harvard, Wendell Junior pursued sports of the non-competitive type. Skating for hours with a group of students, he would repair afterward to some tavern, to consume quantities of beer and oysters. Then, late into the night, a few kindred souls would revel in an orgy of intellectual shuttlecock—tossing some obscure theory back and forth until they had worn it into non-existence.

As Wendell's tastes and personality matured, the breach between father and son widened. He was embarrassed by his father's crusading—it seemed that nothing was sacred to the doctor; he found his fishing for praise a trifle vulgar, his self-admiration distasteful. He turned to his uncle John for advice. Uncle John smiled tolerantly. "You will get used to your father, Wendell. I did."

Wendell was not a brilliant student. He acquitted himself tolerably well, and he liked his studies; but thus far he had not given himself wholly to scholarship. The subject that might really interest him had not as yet presented itself. His restless, inquiring mind ached for some outlet that would challenge his intellect to the fullness of its capacity. Science and language he examined and dismissed. Law, he decided, was the field in which his ability would be put to the test. And yet, as an undergraduate, he felt no compelling urge even in that direction. Unable to understand his son's mind and its needs, the doctor viewed his "laziness" with increasing irritation. Wendell had become practically inarticulate under his father's continual nagging. Spending as much time away from home as possible, he was scorned as an outsider, a disgrace to the Holmes tradition. He took to tiptoeing softly down the back stairs, in order to avoid an answer to his father's "Where are you going, Wendell?" followed by some derogatory remark.

II

WENDELL READ VORACIOUSLY, particularly in the field of philosophy; but his reading lacked direction. It was an unforeseen incident that supplied the impetus for which he had been seeking. Somewhat shocked by the fact that his fellow students read only for the sake of saying they were "on speaking terms" with a renowned author, he wrote an article for the college paper: "Read for Ideas, not for Authors." The article stimulated much comment and brought him a barrage of books at Christmas time. Everybody sought to make Wendell's yuletide complete with a feast of print. Among the gifts was Plato's *Republic*. He read and liked much of what Plato said. But there was a great deal that he found to quarrel with. Writing an essay in which he debated many of Plato's theories, he took it to his friend Emerson for comment. Sitting tensely on the edge of a chair, he waited for the verdict of the Sage of Concord. Emerson handed back the manuscript, shaking his head slowly. "When you shoot at a king, you must kill him," he said. Wendell understood the cryptic sentence. He had been skimming over the surface of things intellectual. Tearing the manuscript into shreds, he applied himself to his studies with all the energy at his command. The floodgates were down, the incentive had won. His aim now was to pursue a theory to its very source, to prove it either false or true. Night after night, often until dawn dimmed the lamplight, Wendell plunged into the depths of philosophy. To the exclusion of all else, he gave himself up to the scholar's life. He grew gaunt and absent-minded, but completely alive at last.

With all the intellectual food that Wendell absorbed, he was generating energy which needed an outlet. He found the outlet in the *Harvard Magazine*. Appointed editor of this paper, he used its pages as the testing ground for his ideas. His self-esteem began to rise. A slight pompousness marked his discourse—somewhat to the amusement of Fanny Dixwell, daughter of one of his former teachers. Fanny's sprightly wit and penetrating mind stimulated and charmed him. Amid the acclamations that now began to pour in on him, Fanny's criticism was refreshing. When Wendell received the coveted undergraduate prize for writing, Fanny's slender fingers pricked the bubble that threatened to carry him away. Wendell came down to earth. His article was brilliant, she said, but the author was inclined to be superficial and self-satisfied. This rebuke delighted him, and he found Fanny more enchanting than ever. "You attack a man's vanity like a she-wolf," he laughed. "You are a witch. And something in that gray-green eye of yours tells me you were born on a Friday night, with the moon at the quarter."

Wendell continued to seek her out, to have his cloud castle anchored to the earth. He failed to notice that a sadness was creeping into the green eyes, a gauntness attacking the smooth cheek. That Fanny was desperately in love with him never occurred to Wendell. That the witch longed to mother him, to make a home and surround him with affectionate encouragement—these were thoughts that never entered the realm of pure intellect in which he was dwelling.

Outside pressures were at work, forces that were to shatter the small contented world that Wendell had built for himself. North Carolina had seceded from the Union. President Lincoln had sent a call for men to rally to the Union Standard. Wendell recalled some of the scenes of his childhood, when escaped slaves had sought haven in Boston—the riots, the bonfires, the sight of black men chained and put aboard a vessel to be returned to their owners. These memories stirred up a restlessness in his mind. The recurring pictures obtruded themselves before the pages to which he had been so passionately devoted. A greater passion took hold of him. Wendell joined the Fourth Battalion of the New England Guard. In blue Zouave trousers and red cap, he looked more romantic than ever. He applied for a three-year commission; and while waiting for this commission he was graduated from Harvard. At commencement he read an original poem. Attending the exercises, the doctor for once took a back seat, listening while his son held the center of the stage.

That evening young Wendell strolled over the college grounds and watched the dancing. Seeing Fanny in the arms of a graduate, and moved by her grace, he plucked a rose and tossed it to her. Fanny's heart leaped at this first token of his interest. But there was no sequence to the gesture, and Lieutenant Holmes departed for the wars—leaving Fanny to grow a little thinner, a shade less sprightly as the months dragged on.

III

WITH OTHER VOLUNTEERS, the young lieutenant chafed at the enforced inactivity which kept him in Massachusetts during his training period. And again in Virginia he fretted, longing for actual combat. When it did come, it was like a thunderbolt. Surprised by the enemy at Ball's Bluff, his outfit suffered heavy losses and inglorious defeat. Wendell's part in the battle was short and tragic. In the first five minutes of fighting a bullet pierced his chest, barely missing his lungs and heart. Invalided home, Wendell was morose. He resented the ministrations of the doctors and refused to talk. The days of suffering among the sick and the near dead had left their mark. Only to Fanny could he open his heart. Her clear mind and realistic viewpoint brought him gradually back to the world.

Restored again to health, and the possessor of a captain's commission, Wendell was ordered back to Virginia. Months of guerrilla warfare, stalking unseen enemies through swamp and forest. Half-starved, ragged, sleepless men dragging out a nightmare existence. At times Wendell was not sure that he actually lived. The horrors of the campaign stood out as something apart from himself, while he moved as an automaton through the ghastly days and nights. It seemed to be Wendell's fate never to participate fully in a battle. At the very next open contact with the foe, a bullet through his neck brought quick oblivion. As he lay among the wounded on the field, the surgeons refused to treat him. They considered him too far beyond help. It was only the persistence of a friend, aided by a farmer's boy, that saved Captain Holmes. Together they carried him to a farmhouse and insisted on his receiving treatment before his life gave out.

Once more in Boston, in the neat white bed, Wendell's lips were forever sealed upon the horror he had witnessed. Not even Fanny could reach him now. To visitors he had but one comment. "War is an organized bore," he said. True to form, Dr. Holmes had written an article in which he described his search for his son among the wounded. His photographic mind had reconstructed in minute detail the after-battle scenes. Wendell fumed inwardly at this indignity, making apology to his soldier friends. Most of all he resented the fact that his father had pictured him as a hero. He felt very far from heroic, and he knew that his companions-in-arms would feel a like resentment at their being paraded before the public view. Back with his regiment once more, Wendell kept his troubles and his thoughts to himself. The doctor's hurt was sore. Wendell never wrote to him. The rift between father and son had widened, past all bridging.

A lieutenant colonel now, Wendell had the bearing of an officer. His voice had gained that authority which causes men to obey instinctively. At Alexandria, on the eve of a decisive battle, President Lincoln stood viewing the field, a tempting target. "Get down, you fool!" Wendell shouted. The President threw himself down without a moment's delay. Later he congratulated Wendell. "I'm glad you know how to talk to a civilian," he said, a smile playing about the thin lips.

His three-year enlistment over, Wendell wandered disconsolately about the house. Now he could return to his studies, devoting himself to the law. But did he really want to? He felt no great urge; and to return to the classroom after the smoke of the battlefield seemed remote and somewhat childish. To his father he said definitely that he had decided on the law school. "It's no use," the doctor replied. "A lawyer can never be a great man." But Wendell's mind was made up. If being a lawyer precluded the possibility of being a great man in the doctor's eyes, Wendell would be a lawyer. Turning on his heel, he strode over to the registrar's office.

IV

LAW, as taught at the time, proved to be a dull study for Wendell. The courses were inadequate and not at all stimulating. But the teachers themselves were an inspiration. Men were so much more alive than books. Men, and places. With the approach of the summer vacation, Wendell decided to take a trip to England. He talked to Fanny of the proposed journey. She listened quietly and hoped that England would not change him. Puzzling remark; Wendell repeated it to the assembled family. His young brother Neddy and his mother eyed him quizzically. "You are most undiscerning where Fanny is concerned," Neddy said.

Wendell was apprehensive as to his reception in England. The Englishmen's reserve and their belief that all Americans were half savage made him somewhat unsure of himself. At his first large dinner party in London he was seated near a general. The general fixed him with a cold eye and asked in his most British manner: "Can you train your men to fight in a line?" Wendell smiled pleasantly. "Why, General," he replied, "you can train monkeys to fight in a line." From that moment his social success was assured.

It was with a new vigor that Wendell, upon his return, took up life in Boston. He found New England, and especially his family, rather provincial after the continent. But the provincialism was comfortable and full of good will. For the time Wendell enjoyed the bustling atmosphere of his home. Even the doctor no longer irritated him. Wendell had gained in poise, and could outtalk his father, could even poke sly fun at the doctor's repetitiousness.

Wendell received his degree and in due course, on a rainy Monday morning, was sworn in to the bar. To his father's disparaging remarks he replied calmly, "To know is not less than to feel." Thus far to Wendell the object of life was to know—he had not yet begun to feel. And he found plenty of time in which to extend his knowledge. Though he attended the office regularly, he worked little at his profession. There were few clients; and his interest lay not in the practice of law, but in the theory and history of jurisprudence. He plunged into a treatise on the

Common Law, isolating himself more and more from his fellow men. He neglected even his most intimate friends, seeing hardly anyone but Fanny and Uncle John. Fanny scolded him for his failure to write to his closest friend, William James, then desperately ill. Wendell replied that he did not have sufficient facts to answer some abstract theory that James had propounded. Fanny turned impatiently to Uncle John. "Has your nephew, all his life, professed to care more for ideas than he cares for people?" she asked. The significance of her question passed over his head, and he continued to bury himself ever deeper in Kent's *Commentaries*—a work he had undertaken to bring up to date. Living in a world of his own fabrication, Wendell lost contact with the real world. Opinionated and didactic, he alienated all but his most intimate acquaintances. Invited to deliver a series of twelve lectures at Harvard, he strode about the halls and the grounds with the air of the president himself. So absorbed in his work had he become that he always carried his manuscript with him. Not even in the lavatory or at the dinner table would he be without his precious brief case. Wound up tight like a spring, he grew thin and pale. Nor did he hear the jokes that were made at the expense of the ever-present brief case.

A change in the family status suddenly jerked Wendell out of his self-sufficient world. Two weddings—his brother Neddy and his sister Amelia. Without them the house had become lonely and still. Fanny, who no longer had the excuse of visiting Amelia, came no more. And Wendell missed her. One Sunday Uncle John insisted that Wendell come with him to the Dixwells for tea. Wendell looked at Fanny wistfully. "I have not seen you for a whole week," he said.

"A week, Wendell? It is three weeks."

Uncle John took Wendell into another room and spoke to him sternly. Didn't he realize that Fanny was desperately in love with him? That they were both nearly thirty? That Fanny was pining into illness? Wendell, shocked, could not answer. For hours that night he paced the floor of his room. And then he strode, distracted, about the dark streets. When he returned home, his mind was made up. He would ask Fanny to be his wife. They were married a few weeks later.

The young couple occupied the third floor of the family home on Beacon Street. Laughter and gaiety returned with Fanny's coming. And, for Wendell, a new sense of comfort. Fanny's unfailing tact smoothed over many a rough scene between father and son. Yet husband and wife both realized that there could be no permanent harmony between the two clashing personalities and that a home of their own was imperative. At the first possible moment, therefore, they left the parental roof and started housekeeping in a small flat over a drugstore. An unpretentious and somewhat inconvenient home—but to the young couple, nothing short of Paradise.

With the new contentment, a greater capacity for work came to Wendell. Pleasantly the fruitful years slipped away, and more and more Wendell came to be accepted as an intellect to be reckoned with. Recognition in the world, peace within the household. In each other's presence, the Holmeses found completion. To Wendell, Fanny was perfection itself. To Fanny, the world revolved around one focal point—Wendell.

V

WENDELL'S FORTIETH BIRTHDAY—and the publication of his book, *Common Law*. Their friends celebrated the double event with champagne. Feeling that the occasion demanded a special gesture, Wendell kept the champagne cork as a memento, remarking: "The only reward which I have promised myself is that a few men will say, *well done*." His reward was greater than he had hoped. Not only in America, but in England as well, the reviewers heaped lavish praise upon his book.

As though forty had been a turning point, he now began to harvest the fruits of his long years of labor. He was appointed to a professorship at Harvard under the progressive President Eliot. Wendell enjoyed his work, introducing a new method of instruction to replace the old. Instead of lecturing to the students, he encouraged them to discuss their subject. The students responded to the stimulating system, and they adored Professor Holmes. His life seemed to have been set in an enduring pattern now, and he was content. He pictured himself as spending the rest of his days in quiet routine. But three months saw the termination of his professorship. In December there occurred a vacancy in the Supreme Court of Massachusetts, and Wendell was offered the appointment. With one hour in which to decide the course of his future life, Wendell took advantage of the resignation clause in his Harvard contract. From Professor Holmes to Justice Holmes.

It was an auspicious moment for the youngest judge to take his seat. America was growing, industry was expanding, trusts were being formed, and labor disputes were bringing restlessness to the country. It was a time when law was emerging from the disrespect with which it had been viewed. America was busy with the shaping of a new civilization. Men of vision were needed at the helm—jurists like Oliver Wendell Holmes. He argued that law was not precedent—a doctrine that shocked many of the old-school lawyers—but a developing process of history. "The Constitution is an experiment," he said, "as all life is an experiment."

The Holmeses no longer lived in the rooms above the drugstore. There was a house now near the river, with a cook and a maid in attendance. Fanny kept the place filled with birds, which she fed and scolded constantly. In Wendell's eyes the years had but added to her perfection. Wendell often lingered late to watch her at her tasks.

"Wendell, you will be late for court," Fanny oftentimes admonished him.

"I want to watch you feed the birds first," Wendell replied.

Wendell had developed into an accomplished public speaker; he was in demand everywhere. He could chuckle now at his father's prediction. "Wendell will never be a speaker," the doctor had said. "His neck is too thin."

In addition to his work in the chambers, Wendell had many other duties. Riding circuit, he was away from home for weeks at a time. He worked so hard that Fanny grew afraid for his health. But always she sensed the point where he had reached the end of his strength. Interrupting with some amusing story, she brought a smile and relaxation to Wendell.

And then—an interruption to their happiness. Death. At the passing of the elder Mrs. Holmes, it was necessary for one of the children to return and live with the father. This Amelia did, much to the relief of Wendell and Fanny. But shortly after her arrival Amelia died suddenly, and the young Holmeses faced the inevitable. They must go and care for the aged Autocrat. Wendell watched sadly as his wife bustled about packing. "Fanny, you will take your birds with you, of course," he said quietly. Fanny nodded.

Once more under the doctor's roof, Fanny bled inwardly to see all the dignity and assurance slip from Wendell's shoulders. Once more he had become the awkward, almost surly boy. When the older man died quietly, sitting in a chair, it was with relief that Fanny saw Wendell's shoulders straighten, heard him laugh again.

Wendell was keeping up with the world. Doggedly he rode the new-fangled two-wheel bicycle through the streets of Boston. With great persistence he learned to steer with one hand, the other free to wave at passing acquaintances. Justice Holmes startled staid Boston in other ways. In a public address he spoke of his city as "this smug, oversafe corner of the world . . ." Boston gasped. But these, and other words of Wendell's, reached the White House, where Theodore Roosevelt was busy deflating stuffed shirts and warring on trusts. An invitation to the Supreme Court of the United States, and for the first time in his life Wendell was afraid. Inwardly as apprehensive as her husband, Fanny urged acceptance. "We shall have to dine with the President, in tails and white satin, Fanny," he protested. Fanny turned to her Japanese robin. "The judge is frightened, Koko," she confided. Wendell accepted.

Their first White House dinner was in honor of the new justice. They entered timidly. But their timidity was not long-lived. Roosevelt at once took Fanny under his wing. "How do you like Washington?" he asked.

"Washington," Fanny replied, "is full of famous men, and the women they married when they were young." The President's roar of laughter caused all heads to turn. Watching her, Wendell was proud and happy. Both of them, he realized, fitted easily into the life of the capital. They were more at home here than they had been in the conventional confines of Boston. Wendell entered into the brilliant life of Washington with the zest of a schoolboy, enjoying at long last the youth which he had never had.

Life was widening in many ways as Wendell's youthfulness increased with his years. The house was always full of young people, aglow with life and laughter until the early morning hours. His secretaries were numerous. Every year the pick of the Harvard graduating class was sent to him. Calling them "Idiot," and "Sonny Boy," Wendell taught them not only what he knew of law but also what he knew of history and philosophy. "Holmes's Annuals," Washington called them. Dawn often found the I Street house still echoing to the sounds of discussion under the animated leadership of Justice Holmes. Whenever he came home to find some argument in progress, he would inquire joyfully, "What is it? I will take the opposite view." And, as the discussion progressed, Fanny served as the gracious hostess to them all.

Wendell did not care for the reputation he gained as dissenter. But for the truth as he saw it he must fight; he could not do otherwise. Free speech was one of the rights granted us in our Constitution, and that right he must defend—no matter against what power and at what price. The Supreme Court of America must be a reflection of the Supreme Law of God.

Eighty now, and his enjoyment of living keener than ever. Of course there would be a birthday party as always. But the house was dark. The cook, Fanny said, was sick, and they must celebrate at a hotel. Grumbling, Wendell dressed. Prohibition was in full swing. The prospect of a dry birthday was not alluring, but better than nothing at all. "Child of Hell, Black Satan, where are my cigars?" he roared at the houseboy, who answered with a grin. The dining-room doors were flung open. Lights, laughter, and a half score of his secretaries greeted him. Wendell smiled. "I knew that she-devil was up to something," he said, smiling at Fanny. And there was champagne. "Close the shutters," Wendell commanded. "My father always said I would die a drunkard."

The years had slipped quietly away. Fanny was dead. Somehow, Wendell kept on. For six years he had visited the grave regularly, first placing flowers at the foot of the stone, then walking wordlessly around, tapping it gently. Wendell's legs were weak, his step was slow, but he had not missed a day on the bench. His decisions were still as quick and penetrating as ever. He was still impatient with the long-winded oldsters, for his point of view was always focused along with the younger men. Every year the papers asked when Justice Holmes would retire. "I shall not retire," he answered, "until the Almighty Himself requests it."

Ninety—and the nation toasted one of its favorites. But he missed the most lovable toast of them all—the voice that would have teased: "Wendell, I see by the papers that you are almost as famous as your father."

Next day a cheer swept the continent as Justice Holmes again took his seat. But the years had begun to claim their own. In the mornings Wendell was as keen as ever—*alert* was the phrase he liked to apply to himself. But the afternoons brought a heaviness he could not fight off. Justice Holmes sat with his forehead against his fingertips, in the attitude of The Thinker, resting. A day came when he dozed off completely. Justice Hughes tapped his leg. Wendell's head jerked up. Later he dozed again. When court adjourned at four-thirty, he walked over to the clerk's desk. "I won't be down tomorrow," he said quietly. That night he wrote his resignation to the President, beginning: "The time has come, and I bow to the inevitable."

Several more years of useful thinking. Franklin Roosevelt visited him one day and found him reading Plato. "Why Plato?" he asked. "To improve my mind, Mr. President," Wendell answered. But the time was approaching when once again he must bow to the inevitable. "Why should I fear death?" he remarked to his secretary. "When he comes, he will look like an old friend." A chill, which quickly developed into pneumonia, and the nation knew that his days were numbered. "To have done what lay in you to do, to say that you have lived, and to be ready for the end," he said. He waited calmly. When an oxygen tent was placed above him, he said: "A lot of damfoolery."

At two o'clock in the morning, March 4, 1935, Justice Holmes greeted death quietly. Ninety-four years young.

IMPORTANT DATES IN THE LIFE OF OLIVER WENDELL HOLMES

1841—Born, Boston.
1861–64—Served in the Civil War.
1866—Graduated, Harvard Law School.
1870–73—Edited the American Law Review.
1872—Married Fanny Dixwell.
1882—Became professor at Harvard Law School.
Appointed justice of Supreme Court of Massachusetts.

1899—Became chief justice of Supreme Court of Massachusetts.
1902—Appointed member of Supreme Court of United States.
1929—Lost his wife.
1932—Retired from Supreme Court.
1935—Died, Washington, D. C.

William James

[1842-1910]

HIS grandfather, an Irish immigrant, was a practical man of the world. His father, an intimate of Emerson, was a free-thinking mystic. Take the practicality of the grandfather and the mysticism of the father, add to them a pinch of Irish humor and a generous dose of American forthrightness, and you have the combination that was the personality of William James.

He was born (January 11, 1842) at the Astor House in New York City, and he lived in or near big cities for the greater part of his life. His attitude toward the world, therefore, was colored by his conception of the earth as a "parcel of nature crowded with company."

He loved company from his earliest childhood. And in spite of the easy circumstances of his family, he was not snobbish in his attitude toward his companions. To a youngster who boasted about the exclusiveness of his playmates he declared, *"I play with boys who curse and swear!"*

He was an active youngster—in sharp contrast with his brother Henry, who was a quiet and contemplative little fellow. Since both of them showed an early aptitude for literature, the friends of the family predicted that William would take up fiction as his field and that Henry would choose philosophy. It turned out just the other way around. To some extent, however, the prophets were correct. William James developed into a philosopher who wrote like a novelist, and Henry James developed into a novelist who wrote like a philosopher.

As to their early preparation for their respective careers, both William and Henry regarded it as a waste of time. In their effort to provide their children with the best education available, their parents took them to Europe and enrolled them in one school after another—in London, Paris, Boulogne-sur-Mer, Geneva, Bonn. Always they sought for "the one perfect channel of truth" in which to bathe the precocious minds of the two youngsters. The result of this eclectic education was that the boys learned "a little of everything and not much of anything."

They did, however, acquire a facility in language which enabled them to devour all sorts of books on every conceivable subject. Thus their minds were trained to resemble long-distance swimmers rather than skill-ful divers. They were able to cover wide horizons of experience though they were incapable of plunging into the depths of the world's mysteries.

The mind of William James especially was ever restless, ever eager for adventure, ever curious for the new landscape before it had become thor-oughly familiar with the old. His interests were so manifold that he found it difficult to make a final choice among them. And so he sampled every intellectual and artistic dish that was offered to his healthy appetite, dab-bling in biology, anatomy, philosophy, chemistry, physics, natural history, and even painting. And in spite of his intellectual pursuits—or rather be-cause of his intellectual curiosity—he managed always to find plenty of time for his social activities. In 1860 he joined the Swiss students' club, Société de Zoffingue, where he showed an active interest in its debates and a somewhat more passive though no less fascinated interest in its de-baucheries. In the social parlance of the day, William James was "a hail-fellow-well-met" young specimen of the dynamic nineteenth century.

His dynamic versatility, however, must somehow be co-ordinated into a unified profession. It wasn't in his nature to drift aimlessly through life. He must now choose definitely between art and science. He chose science, entering the Lawrence Scientific School (Harvard University) in 1861.

But he had given up his brush only to become a painter with the pen. For few writers in the history of philosophy have been blessed with a more colorful style.

II

Though he had decided upon a scientific career, William James was still uncertain as to the particular branch of science that he wanted to adopt as his life's work. For a time he thought of chemistry. But then his inter-est shifted to medicine. He entered the Harvard Medical School, took his degree, and then quit medicine for natural history. He joined the Brazil-ian expedition of Professor Louis Agassiz, a man whom he admired more than any other of his teachers. "Since Benjamin Franklin," he wrote many years later, "we had never had among us a person of more popularly im-pressive type."

Together with Agassiz he studied the fishes of the Amazon. And under the influence of Agassiz he learned to regard the objects of natural history as the "translation into human language of the thoughts of the Creator." The philosophic scientist of Harvard had transformed the young natural-ist into a scientific philosopher.

When he returned to the United States, William James had a pretty clear idea as to the future course of his life. He would write and, if pos-sible, teach philosophy. He attended a philosophical lecture by Charles S. Peirce, a man who was trying to introduce a new system of thought called *pragmatism.* "I couldn't understand a word of the lecture," said James, "but I felt that it had a definite message for me." He was to spend the rest of his life in the effort to understand and to interpret this "definite message" of pragmatism.

Before he entered upon this work, however, he underwent a physical breakdown and a siege of mental depression. For a time he thought of committing suicide. "No man," he said in later life, "is psychologically complete unless he has at least once in his life meditated on self-destruction." He took a trip to Europe for his physical and his mental health, and within a few months was so completely recovered that he was able to "flirt in Bohemian" with his landlady's daughter. He had brought along with him his American democracy—or was it his Irish sense of humor?— for he accepted a "social" invitation to dine with an innkeeper's family. The talk, he said, was salty enough, but the soup tasted like the "perspiration of pigs."

On his return to America he was appointed instructor of physiology at Harvard College. From physiology he moved to psychology, and from psychology to philosophy. These successive steps from one academic department to another were quite in keeping with the steps of his own mental development. For his intellectual progress was not "from the sky down, but from the ground up." Like Socrates, he was more interested in the problems of men than he was in the Providence of God. Not that he was skeptical about God. On the contrary, he found himself "less and less able," as he wrote to his friend Thomas Davidson, "to get along without Him." His main preoccupation, however, was with the Here rather than with the Hereafter. His philosophy grew out of his own needs. He had suffered a serious illness and he had "pulled himself back" into health. Man's salvation depended upon his own will. In the course of his reading during his sickness he had come upon the *Essais* of Renouvier, and he had been struck with the French thinker's definition of Free Will—"the sustaining of a thought because one *actively chooses* to sustain it when he might have other thoughts." William James had chosen to sustain the thought of becoming well. He had *willed* himself out of sickness. "From now on I will abstain from speculation and depend upon action." For action is the human will transformed into life.

This was but a continuation of Emerson's philosophy of optimism. But James added something to it. Or rather he modified it. He transformed the somewhat impractical idea of optimism, the theory that all's well with the world, into the more practical idea of *meliorism,* the theory that all's *not* well with the world but that we can make things better *if we will.* It was an excellent philosophy for America at that period (1872), for the country had just entered upon its Golden Era of Expansion. It was the industrial age of Rockefeller, Carnegie, Gould, Harriman, Drew, Cook, and J. P. Morgan. William James was one of those fortunate children of destiny—the right man born into the right time. He came as the prophet of the Free Will to a free nation.

Thus far, however, his philosophy was still in its seedling stage. He had no opportunity to develop it further at this time because he was asked to write a textbook on psychology for Henry Holt's American Science Series. He expected to produce the book within two years. It was twelve years before the manuscript was finished.

In the meantime he met, wooed, and married Miss Alice Gibbens. Legend has it that his father, Henry James the elder, had first seen her at the Radical Club in Boston and had exclaimed upon his return home, "William, I have just met the woman you're going to marry!" Whereupon the young philosopher, resenting his father's interference in his private affairs, replied, "I shall refuse to see that woman." "I don't care whether or not you *see* her," retorted his father. "All I want you to do is to *marry* her."

In spite of his rebellious rejoinder to his father's suggestion, James did manage to see Miss Gibbens. And he fell a willing prey to "the great dark luminous eyes, soft brown hair, wild-rose complexion . . . and especially the smile which lit up her face and seemed to light up the world."

His marriage worked a miracle in his health—and in his habits. "She saved me from my *Zerrissenheit* (torn-to-pieces-ness) and gave me back to myself all in one piece." He had now found his mate and his métier. He settled down in Cambridge and devoted himself for the rest of his life to the cultivation of his philosophy.

III

His FIRST BOOK, *The Principles of Psychology* marks the formal transition from William James the scientist to William James the philosopher. For this book is more valuable as a masterpiece of literary abstractions than as a repository of concrete facts. James cared very little for the objective phenomena of the mind, but he cared very much for the subjective personality to whom the mind belonged. His psychology, therefore, is a study of persons and not of data. Human thought, to William James, was not a mechanically connected series of separate ideas—a doctrine of the European psychologists—but a continuously flowing stream of consciousness analogous to the blood stream that flows continuously through the body.

Furthermore, said James, the study of human consciousness must be subordinated to the study of human conduct. Psychology is a preface to morality. "The physiological study of mental conditions is . . . the most powerful ally of hortatory ethics."

The mind, in brief, is not a material but a spiritual instrument. It is not a recorder but a prompter of our ideas. It is our teacher and guide toward a freer, juster, and better world.

And this brings James back to his philosophy of *betterment* or *meliorism*. Let us at the outset, he said, admit the fact that the world is full of evil. But precisely because of this fact we find our life worth while. For the presence of evil has given us our most precious possession—hope. Hope is that moral activity which prompts us to challenge and to conquer evil. It gives us the courage "to take life strivingly." The philosophers who declare that the world is growing better *regardless* of our will are equally wrong with those who maintain that the world will remain bad *in spite* of our will. We alone can improve the world, and we can do it *because* of our will.

For this world is not a finished unit but "an aggregation of separate and contradictory elements." And here we come to the second point in James's philosophy—his *pluralism*. The world is not a *uni-verse* but a *multi-verse*—a conflict of currents, some good, some evil. We must all of us try to conquer the evil and to establish the good. Is success certain? No. Is it possible? Decidedly yes. But if success is only possible at best, what is the good of striving? To this question James gives an answer which is not unlike that of the ancient Stoics. The mere chance of succeeding ennobles the struggle and makes it worth while. "Suppose," writes James, "that the world's author put the case to you before creation, saying: 'I am going to make a world not certain to be saved, a world the perfection of which shall be conditioned merely, the condition being that each several agent does its own *level best*. I offer you the chance of taking part in such a world. Its safety, you see, is unwarranted. It is a real adventure, with real danger, yet it may win through. . . . Will you join the procession? Will you trust yourself and trust the other agents enough to face the risk?'

"Should you in all seriousness . . . feel bound to reject the offer as not safe enough? . . . If you are normally constituted, you would do nothing of the sort. There is a healthy-minded buoyancy in most of us which such a universe would exactly fit. . . . It would be just like the world we practically live in, and loyalty to our old nurse Nature would forbid us to say no."

This is the old Stoic doctrine plus the modern American spirit. It is joy to fight the good fight even though the outcome may be in doubt. And after all, though the issue may be uncertain for the individual, it is pretty certain to be victorious for the race. For we have an efficient ally on our side—God. In the pluralistic philosophy of James, God is not supreme. He is merely one among many divine forces, "one helper . . . in the midst of all the shapers of the great world's fate." But he is *"primus inter pares,"* first among equals. He is our teacher, our leader, our friend in the glorious struggle for a better world.

Let us then, with God's help, struggle gallantly on. Let us shape the world to our needs. Let us, in other words, live a *practical* life. And this is the third and cardinal point in James's philosophy—his *pragmatism*. The world we live in is not a theory but a fact. Indeed, it is a conglomeration of many facts. There is no such thing as *the* truth. What we call a truth is merely a working hypothesis, a temporary tool that enables us to transform a bit of chaos into a bit of order. What was true yesterday—that is, what was *helpful* yesterday—may not be true today. Old truths, like old weapons, tend to grow rusty and to become useless.

It is therefore impractical to try to reduce the universe to an "absolutely single fact." Truth is relative. Everything depends upon our individual point of view, and none of us has the right to say that *his* point of view is the only correct one. "Neither the whole of truth nor the whole of good is revealed to any single observer, although each observer gains a partial superiority of insight from the peculiar position in which he stands." And that superiority of insight which every individual has gained for himself is his own best tool in the struggle for the betterment of the world. Each man's faith, each man's church, each man's God is for him true if it enables him to cope with his legitimate daily problems.

That alone, therefore, is true which is expedient in practice. An idea is good only if it has a "cash value." Let us not, however, confuse the "cash value" pragmatism of William James with the crass materialism of our modern business life. The coinage of James's philosophical capital was not financial but moral. He looked down upon the mad scramble of his contemporaries for the accumulation of mere wealth. He scolded his fellow Americans for their worship of "that bitch goddess, success." His pragmatism was an ethical and therefore a practical urge to co-operation among the free members of a democratic society. The meaning of life, he believed, lies not in an isolated struggle as between man and man but in a united struggle of mankind against the forces of evil.

Pragmatism, said James, has no use for abstractions. It deals only with "concrete realities." It is not, strictly speaking, a system of philosophy. It is rather a "method for getting at the practical consequences" of all the philosophical systems. To quote the Italian philosopher Papini, James's pragmatism is "a collection of attitudes, and its chief characteristic is its armed neutrality in the midst of doctrines. It is like a corridor in a hotel, from which a hundred doors open into a hundred chambers. In one you may see a man on his knees praying to regain his faith; in another, a desk at which sits someone eager to destroy all metaphysics; in a third, a laboratory with an investigator looking for new footholds by which to advance toward wider horizons. But the corridor belongs to all."

IV

The corridor belongs to all. This is the very heart of James's philosophy. It was not his purpose to set himself up as the founder of a new school but as a guide for the practical interpretation of the old schools. He didn't want to be a master, and he asked for no disciples. Again and again he quoted to his students the passage from Ezekiel: "Son of man, stand upon thy feet, and I will speak unto thee." Let each man live upon his own spiritual capital. Let each one abide by his own truth. All that James was interested in doing was to stimulate man's mind, to release man's will, and to encourage man's action. Above all, he wanted to widen man's interests. For he himself was a man of wide interests. His own stream of consciousness embraced a large part of the general stream of life. He raised his voice against the unjust oppression of Dreyfus; he advocated a more equitable distribution of wealth; he threw himself actively into every sort of movement for human welfare; and he was foremost in urging a moral equivalent for war—that is, a concerted effort to abolish disease, to drain marshes, to irrigate canals, and to reclaim wastelands instead of an organized fight to kill men. In short, he wanted to open to others, as he had opened to himself, "the entire universe as an adventure." And he made the universe a familiar landscape, illuminating it to his students with the sudden flash of understanding, the happy phrase, the Socratic jest. "This universe," he said in one of his lectures, "will never be completely good as long as one being is unhappy, as long as one poor cockroach suffers the pangs of unrequited love."

He always tried to make his ideas picturesque, concrete, alive. He classified them in such a manner that his hearers might tuck them away in their minds like the neatly folded articles of clothing in a wardrobe, to be taken out for use at a moment's notice without any confusion or fumbling. For example, in describing the attitude of various types of people toward the world he divided them into the *tough-minded* and the *tender-minded*. The tough-minded, he said, are the hardheaded businessmen, the builders, the political leaders, the realists, the men who act. The tender-minded, on the other hand, are the softhearted visionaries, the dreamers, the poets, the artists, the idealists, the men who think. James himself was an example of neither one of these extreme types. Instead he was an admirable synthesis of the two. He was *healthy-minded*.

He had a healthy mind but not in a healthy body. Throughout his adult life he suffered from a weak heart. During one of his summer vacations he lost his way in the Adirondacks. He overexerted himself in his effort to find the road, and when he finally arrived home he collapsed.

Although he recovered from this illness, he was never himself again. In 1907 he resigned from the Harvard faculty owing to his poor health. He lived just long enough to make a tour of Europe. He meant this to be a quiet and undisturbed health trip, but it turned out to be an exciting procession of triumph.

The ordeal proved too much for his weakened heart. When he boarded the boat to return to America (in the summer of 1910) everybody knew that his days were numbered.

As he neared the end of his journey he sank back into his steamer chair and whispered, "It is so good to get home!"

IMPORTANT DATES IN THE LIFE OF WILLIAM JAMES

1842—Born, New York City.

1861—Entered Harvard University.

1869—Received degree from Harvard Medical School.

1872—Appointed instructor in physiology in Harvard College.

1878—Married Miss Alice H. Gibbens of Cambridge.

1884—Founded the American Society for Psychological Research.

1891—Published *The Principles of Psychology*.

1901–02—Delivered lectures on natural religion at the University of Edinburgh.

1902—Issued *The Varieties of Religious Experience*.

1907—Retired from faculty of Harvard College.

1910—Died, Chocorua, New Hampshire.

Joseph Pulitzer

[1847-1911]

LIEUTENANT William N. King, a writer of naval stories, was invited to contribute an article to the *New York World*. King asked for instructions as to the proper "slant" for the article in order to meet Mr. Pulitzer's policy. "Say what you believe to be right," replied Colonel John H. Cockerill, editor of the *World*. "Mr. Pulitzer has no friends and no enemies. He has no policy that interferes with facts."

Joseph Pulitzer, owner and publisher of the *New York World,* had a single devotion to the truth. And the men who worked on his paper had a single devotion to Joseph Pulitzer. One of his reporters was assigned to cover a revival meeting. As he was listening to the sermon, an "exhorter" whispered to him: "Won't you come forward?"

"I'm sorry, but I'm a reporter, and I'm here only on business."

"There is no business," declared the revivalist, "so momentous as the Lord's."

"Ah," smiled the reporter, "but you don't know Mr. Pulitzer!"

II

ONE of the most compelling factors in American history during the nineteenth century was the power of the press. With the spread of popular education, the masses began to look upon the newspaper as their daily teacher and guide. "The press," wrote Benjamin Constant, "is the mistress of intelligence, and intelligence is the mistress of the world." The real rulers in a democracy are not the congressmen who make the laws, but the journalists who mold the opinions that make the laws. The editorial page is the political pulpit in the religion of modern Republicanism.

The great journalists of the nineteenth century regarded themselves as being, in the best sense, politicians. "Politics," said Joseph Pulitzer, "is my passion . . . not politics in the general, selfish sense, but politics in the sense of liberty and freedom and ideals of justice."

The quest for liberty was a passion with Joseph Pulitzer. For he was an immigrant. He had escaped from oppression in Europe to find freedom in America. The so-called "foreigners" in our midst have played no little part in upholding the best of our institutions. It takes a man who has smarted under the lash of Autocracy to appraise the true blessings of Democracy.

Joseph Pulitzer's father was Hungarian; his mother was German. Educated at a private school in Budapest, he came to America at the age of seventeen (in 1864) and promptly enlisted in the Union Army. At the end of the war he drifted from one place to another, in search of work, and finally found his way to St. Louis. Excessively tall (six feet, two and a half inches) and excessively thin, he looked like a strange alien animal with his bulbous head, his small pointed chin, and his big elliptical nose. Added to his outlandish appearance was his foreign accent. He studied law and passed the bar; but, owing to the handicap of his figure and his speech, he was unable to get enough clients for a living.

Fortunately at this time (1868) there was an opening on a German paper in St. Louis—the *Westliche Post*. Young Pulitzer became a reporter. The other reporters of the local papers made sport of him and regarded him as the ugly duckling of their journalistic family. Yet in spite of his gawkiness and his gutturals, he generally managed to get the best "beats" for his paper. And the reason for this was simple—he possessed a keen scent for news and a voracious appetite for work. He was on the job every day from 10 A.M. to 2 A.M. It was not long before he became, with Carl Schurz, co-editor of the *Westliche Post*.

Joseph Pulitzer had found himself. Newspaper work was not only his bread and butter, it was the very lifeblood of his existence. From now on he had a definite purpose—to depict the contemporary scene and to uproot the contemporary evils. Every reporter, he felt, must be a reformer. Journalism must no longer be a trade. It must become a profession—one of the most important professions in the world.

III

PULITZER'S INTEREST in politics led to his election, in 1869, to the Missouri State Assembly. Here he served not only as a legislator but as a reporter. He reported corruption wherever he saw it, he got himself mixed up in a duel, and he finally succeeded in cleaning the bosses and the lobbyists out of the local government.

His success in exposing "the politicians without principle" brought him an unexpected honor at the early age of twenty-three. He was appointed one of the three police commissioners of St. Louis. Possessing a perfect instinct for phrasemaking, he declared that his principle as a public official was to "cater to the welfare of the millions rather than to the wealth of the millionaires." He therefore made it his business to prosecute the big scoundrels as well as the petty thieves. The young immigrant had now become one of the important figures in the Middle West. "Joseph Pulitzer," said Carl Schurz, "is going to be heard from."

His political allegiance was not to any one party or to any one section, but to the entire nation as a family of united interests. True to the spirit of Lincoln, he tried to "bind up" the wounds that were still festering as a result of the Civil War. "I stand here," he declared at Cooper Union (October 31, 1876), "to say that the Civil War is over, and it is time that it should be. When the South was wrong, I did not hesitate to enlist against it; but today, when the South is not wrong, I do not hesitate to enlist for it . . . The Southern people belong to us, and we belong to them. Their interests are our interests; their rights should be our rights; their wrongs should be our wrongs. Their prosperity is our prosperity; their poverty is our poverty. We are one people, one country, and one government; and whoever endeavors to array one section against another and endeavors to make the union of all people impossible is a traitor to his country."

Had he remained in politics, Joseph Pulitzer might have become another Carl Schurz. But he preferred the editorial sanctum to the senate chamber. He decided to give up politics and return to journalism.

For a time, however, it looked as if both his political and his journalistic careers would come to a precipitous end. His hard work had exacted its price. He began to spit blood, and the doctors shook their heads. But he fought off his weakness, went to Washington, and saw and conquered the beautiful Kate Davis, a distant cousin of Jefferson Davis, and took her on a honeymoon trip to Europe.

His renewed contact with European monarchy made him all the more attached to American democracy. "The people of Germany," he wrote in a letter to the *New York Sun,* "while they have to pay heavily for their princes and their rulers, do not profit by them. They pay for their fiddlers, but have execrable music. The more princes, the less principles . . . It would be bad enough if it only affected the pockets of the people. But it becomes worse by affecting their manhood and freedom." Even at that period (1878) he was keen enough to foresee the drift toward dictatorship, and he expressed his abhorrence against the idea of a one-man rule. "If that man were an angel from heaven, I should object."

Equally abhorrent to him was the European idea of aristocracy. Writing from England, he described that country as an unhappy place to live in because of its veneration for inherited aristocracy and inherited wealth. "Great wealth and great pauperism," he observed, "are the dominating features of the land."

As a result of his vacation in Europe, he came back to this country a better American. He was more determined than ever to exert a democratic influence through the press. Scraping together the sum of twenty-five hundred dollars, he bought at auction a paper that had just gone into bankruptcy—the *St. Louis Dispatch.* It was a reckless adventure, his skeptical friends told him. But Pulitzer knew better. He possessed that rarest of human senses—the sense of foresight. The tangible assets of the *Dispatch* were worth practically nothing. But there was an intangible asset which was worth many thousands of dollars. The *Dispatch* was one of the few papers in St. Louis with an Associated Press franchise. This meant a facility for obtaining national and international news in advance of those papers that were not members of the Associated Press. Pulitzer recognized this asset and was quick to take advantage of it. He suggested a merger between the *Dispatch* and the *Post,* a St. Louis paper which was much more prosperous but which did not possess a Press franchise. Pulitzer's suggestion was accepted; and the new paper, the *Post-Dispatch,* leaped into sudden life under the magic of his personality.

The *Post-Dispatch* was the first of the modern newspapers. It espoused the cause of the wage earners and it was written to appeal to their interests. The policy of this paper was to refrain from distinguishing any individual by his nationality. To Pulitzer and his associates the citizens of this country were not Italians or Frenchmen or Germans or Englishmen or Russians or Jews, but Americans. The *Post-Dispatch* insisted upon equal respect and equal justice toward all Americans, whether native- or foreign-born, whether rich or poor. It was the business of his newspaper, wrote Pulitzer, to "advocate those principles and ideas . . . upon which our government was originally founded." One of the first tasks he set himself when he became part owner of the *Post-Dispatch* was to expose special privilege and to insist upon equal opportunity. As commissioner of police he had noticed the systematic tax dodging on the part of the well-to-do. And now, as newspaper publisher, he began to call the attention of the people to these tax dodgers. In parallel columns he printed the returns from the rich and the poor. The popular clamor was such as to bring about the necessary reform in the unequal tax laws.

Such was the positive side of his popular journalism. On the negative side it was open to a great deal of criticism, and not all of it unjustified. In his effort to appeal to the interests of the wage earners—or, as his enemies maintained, in his eagerness to build up circulation and to make money—he catered not only to the needs, but to the vulgarity, of his readers. He introduced sensationalism into the daily press. He began to fill his columns with the most exciting rather than with the most important news—murders, suicides, divorces, fires, sports, and the like.

Pulitzer strenuously defended this phase of his journalism. He was publishing his paper, he said, not for the "high-brows" but for the "low-brows." The masses had just become literate, and their mentality needed the spur of sensationalism in order to make them think. He believed in feeding his public on meat, but the meat must be highly spiced with "tasty" incidents and with short and pungent phrases. Far better to do this, he said, than to spoil the appetite of the reading public with the polysyllabic vacuity of the so-called "intellectual" papers. He was catering, in short, to human beings, he said, and his stories must therefore have "human interest."

This infusion of the "human interest" element into the *Post-Dispatch* proved to be highly remunerative. The profits ranged from forty thousand to eighty-five thousand dollars a year. The success of his St. Louis experiment encouraged Pulitzer to try the same formula on a larger scale.

Accordingly, in 1883, he took a trip to New York; and on May 10 the following editorial announcement appeared in the *New York World*:

"The entire *World* newspaper property has been purchased by the undersigned [Joseph Pulitzer], and will from this day be under different management—different in men, measures, and methods—different in purpose, policy, and principle—different in objects and interests—different in sympathies and convictions—different in head and heart . . .

"There is room in this great and growing city for a journal . . . dedicated to the cause of the people rather than that of the purse potentates—devoted more to the news of the new than the old world, that will expose all fraud and sham, fight all public evils and abuses—that will serve and battle for the people with earnest sincerity."

Whatever mistakes Pulitzer made later, he rarely departed from the ideal which he had set himself in that editorial. He remained for the greater part of his life an earnest soldier in the battle for the rights of the people.

IV

On the sunday following his purchase of the *World*, Pulitzer announced that his paper was the organ of a new aristocracy—"the Aristocracy of Labor." It was a popular formula. Within three months the circulation of the *World* rose from twenty-two thousand to thirty-nine thousand. From this point it grew like a plant under the fingers of an oriental magician—from thirty-nine thousand to one hundred thousand; from one hundred thousand to two hundred and seventy-five thousand; from two hundred and seventy-five thousand to its highest peak of six hundred and twenty-three thousand.

The *World* under Pulitzer, like the *Post-Dispatch* and the other so-called "yellow journals" of the day, had its serious faults. But it had one consistent virtue—a tenacious and sincere adherence to the cause of the underdog. It took the side of the laborers in the Homestead Strike, when the Carnegie Steel Company hired three hundred armed Pinkerton detectives to break the strike. It demanded a tax on luxuries, on large incomes, on inheritances, and on corporations and monopolies—all of which demands subsequently became federal laws. It fumigated the political and the financial parasites out of City Hall and the State Capitol. It averted a threatened war between the United States and England over a disputed border in Venezuela. It protected the public against the more unprincipled speculators of Wall Street. And, with the help of Charles Evans Hughes, it exposed the illegal system whereby a number of insurance companies, by reaching their tentacles into various banks and other business establishments, controlled practically all the savings of the American people.

One of the most characteristic of Pulitzer's activities, through the columns of the *World*, was the raising of the fund in connection with the Statue of Liberty. This statue, the work of Auguste Bartholdi, was built at the expense of the French people and was a present to the people of America. It was to stand at the entrance of New York Harbor as "a welcome to the refugees of all the world." The statue was finished and boxed and ready for shipment from France to America. But America was unable to receive it. For it required one hundred thousand dollars to erect a pedestal that would raise the statue a hundred feet above the level of the sea. The American Government was asked to appropriate the necessary fund and refused. Whereupon Pulitzer took it upon himself to raise the money. He wrote an editorial, appealing "not to the millionaires, but to the masses" to adorn the threshold of America with "Liberty Enlightening the World."

The response was instantaneous. Thousands of people contributed their grain of sand toward the building of the mass of granite. "Inclosed," wrote one of the contributors, "please find five cents as a poor office boy's mite to the pedestal fund." A group of young men sent in its contribution with the following comment: "A few poor fellows, whose pockets are not as deep as a well but whose love of liberty is wider than a church door, hand you the inclosed $7.25 as their mite toward the Bartholdi fund." Much of the money came from people of foreign birth. "I have seen enough of monarchical governments," wrote one of them, "to worship this free Republic. Inclosed please find $2.00 for the Bartholdi statue."

Within less than five months Pulitzer was able to announce (August 11, 1888) that the one hundred thousand dollars had been raised. No other incident in his life gave him greater satisfaction. He had helped his people to set up a shrine to the Goddess of Liberty. And Liberty was to him the one true religion.

V

PULITZER was not only a worshiper of freedom but a lover of peace. "The danger of war," he declared in 1895, "lies not in any particular dispute, but in the irritation of the public mind which all the [war] talk creates . . . Let the war idea once dominate the minds of the American people and war will come whether there is cause for it or not."

True Americanism, he said on another occasion, "means arbitration . . . the reign of reason as opposed to the reign of force." He believed that every international dispute could be peacefully adjusted by a frank and honest discussion of mutual grievances. And thus he stood "for argument and lawful understanding as opposed to passion and war."

Yet he suffered one serious lapse from his pacific ideal. It was in 1898, when America was balancing on the tightrope between peace and war with Spain. Pulitzer supplied the sudden gust of propaganda that caused America to lose her balance and to plunge into war. His detractors asserted that he "created" the excitement of the war in order to increase the circulation of his paper. To a certain extent this was probably true. His bright character, unfortunately, was not without its black spots. But one of the chief motives for his warlike attitude was his desire to see a free Cuba. He wanted a swift and decisive war—a war without much expenditure of money or loss of life. But it was a pity that he should have urged any kind of war at all against Spain. Several years later he admitted that an antitoxin of common sense might have averted the epidemic of passion that had precipitated the war. Spain had been ready to meet Cuba's demands, and all that was needed was a little cool reflection on the part of America. But America had lost her wits. And Pulitzer was honest enough to place the blame where it belonged—largely upon his own shoulders. It was the duty of the editor, he confessed, to do the thinking when the rest of the country was muddled. And, outside of this one mistake, he thought often and clearly upon the issues of peace and war. On numerous occasions he fought editorially against the "crime of jingoism." He never wanted another war. He was ready, after his lapse in the Spainsh war, to stand alone, if necessary, in his desire for peace. "I would rather be the only man in the United States to protest against the jingoes," he wrote in his instructions to one of his editors, "than to echo without conviction the general feeling of the unthinking." America, he believed, is the one country which, because of its isolation and its strength, can afford to lead the rest of the world on the way to peace. "This, indeed, is America's principal job."

VI

PULITZER had amassed a great fortune as the publisher of the *World*. He spent much of it in a futile search for health. He traveled everywhere, but nowhere found relief. His nerves were so shattered that he couldn't bear the slightest noise. The old weakness of his lungs had returned, and the slightest change of air would bring on a heavy chest cold. Added to all this trouble, his eyes began to give out. One day, as he was sailing on the Mediterranean, he turned to his secretary: "How dark it's suddenly getting!"

"It's not dark at all," said the secretary.

"Well, it's dark to me."

And from that day on the world was dark to Pulitzer. Long before he died he became totally blind.

But his intellect and his interest in his work remained bright to the end. Wherever he happened to be, he kept in touch, by telephone or by cable, with the editorial policy of his paper. And this policy, from first to last, was "on the side of the people."

And, whatever the provocation, he never lost his editorial temper. Again and again he cautioned his editors to treat his critics "with courtesy and absence of violent language." On one occasion Rollo Ogden, editor of the *New York Evening Post,* wrote a scathing article about Pulitzer and the *World*. In his instructions to his own editor as to how to answer this attack, Pulitzer wrote from Carlsbad (May 15, 1907): "Treat Mr. Ogden with *exquisite* politeness, assuming that he did not intentionally mislead his readers but was probably misled himself."

Yet, on the other hand, he was as fair in criticizing his friends as in forgiving his enemies. When Charles Evans Hughes was governor of New York he was a little slow—as Pulitzer thought—in the "completion of the insurance clean-up" which he had started before his election to the governorship. "I am simply crazy about Hughes," wrote Pulitzer to his editor, "so vitally important do I regard his work . . . But be independent even about him. I would not go through thick and thin for anybody—not even myself. Your friends must be criticized when they are mistaken, like other people. It is difficult to see the truth when you are prejudiced, but try always to see the truth about friend or foe."

Try to see the truth about friend or foe. These words may be taken as a summary of his entire career.

VII

WHEN HE DIED he left three important monuments behind him: the Pulitzer School of Journalism, to perpetuate a Democratic Press; the Pulitzer prizes for prose and poetry, to encourage a Democratic Literature; and the Pulitzer Fund for a statue to Thomas Jefferson to point out the greatest exponent of the Democratic Idea.

IMPORTANT DATES IN THE LIFE OF JOSEPH PULITZER

1847—Born, Mako, Hungary.

1864—Came to the United States. Enlisted in the Federal Cavalry, Civil War.

1865—Employed as reporter on *Westliche Post,* St. Louis.

1869—Elected to Missouri legislature.

1874—Served on Missouri state constitutional convention.

1876-77—Washington correspondent for *New York Sun.*

1878—Married Kate Davis. Bought *St. Louis Dispatch.* Combined *Dispatch* with *Evening Post* into *Post-Dispatch.*

1883—Bought *New York World.*

1884—Elected to Congress.

1887—Began to lose eyesight.

1892—Took side of striking steelworkers at Homestead, Pennsylvania.

1896—Reduced price of *World* to one cent.

1903—Endowed Pulitzer School of Journalism at Columbia University.

1911—Died on his yacht, Charleston Harbor, South Carolina.

Alexander Graham Bell

[1847-1922]

BELL succeeded as an inventor because he was ignorant of electricity. "If he had known anything about electricity," wrote Moses G. Farmer, "he would never have invented the telephone."

When he told the leading scientists that he was trying to transmit human speech over an electric wire, they laughed at him. "It can't be done," they insisted. For it was impossible, they said, to send the continuous vibration of inflected speech over a make-and-break current of electricity.

"In that case," said Bell, "I shall make a continuous current of electricity to vibrate with words and music just as the air vibrates with them."

Whereupon the scientific world shook its learned head. "Crazy Bell."

But Bell was determined. He knew very little about the science of electricity, but he knew a great deal about the mechanics of speech. He was a teacher of elocution—"professor of vocal physiology"—at Boston University. "I *know* the thing can be done, and I'm going to *find the way.*"

And so he "foolishly" rushed into the precincts of the unknown where the "angels" of science feared to tread.

But he explored the field with the persistency of a Scotsman and the imagination of a sage.

II

ALEXANDER BELL—he was eleven when he adopted the middle name, Graham, after an admired friend—was descended from a family of scholars and adventurers into unfamiliar fields of thought. He was the third Bell, in direct line, to investigate the mystery of human speech. His grandfather, Alexander Bell, had begun life as a shoemaker and ended it as the most famous teacher of elocution and reader of Shakespeare in

Scotland. His specialty was to "correct defective utterance"—a method
of his own invention—through the manipulation of the vocal cords. His
father, Melville Bell, was a "professor of English diction," public reader
—he was expelled from his church for a reading from "the flippant
works of Mr. Charles Dickens"—and inventor of the famous system of
elocution known as "Visible Speech." This system, employed by Bernard
Shaw in his play *Pygmalion,* reduces to a series of "visible reproductions"
or sketches the various positions of the lips, the palate, the larynx, the
nose, and the tongue in the production of the various linguistic sounds.
In this way the pupil, even though he be deaf, can reproduce any required
sound by imitating the speech organs of the sketch with his own organs
of speech. For example, when the pupil closes his lips and passes his voice
through his nose, the resulting sound is *m*—no matter what the language.

This method of visible speech produced a great impression upon the
world. It was hailed as "the foundation of that dream of the philologists
—a universal language." Though it fell short of this goal, the science of
visible speech was instrumental in teaching young Alexander the anatomy
of the human voice and—years later—the application of this anatomy to
the transmitting and receiving "anatomy" of the electric telephone.

III

As a youngster Alexander Bell—his family called him "Aleck"—wanted
to be a musician. For he had inherited an ear of unusual sensitivity from
his musical mother. At home much of the talk centered on musical instruments, acoustics, and especially the mechanism of the human voice.
There were three boys in the family, and all three of them were profoundly interested in the universe of sound.

Especially Aleck. It wasn't difficult for his father to persuade him that
the teaching of speech would be—for him, at least—a worthier profession than the making of music. At school he devoted his interests to
but one of the three Rs—reading. In all other subjects he was, by his own
account, a rather "indolent and mediocre" student.

His formal schooling amounted, in all, to five years. But his informal
education—at home—continued for several years longer. His father's
insistence upon speech without an accent resulted in a strange phenomenon—an Edinburgh family that spoke a pure and unadulterated English.

"And it is your business, Aleck, to bring this purity of language unde-
filed to your fellow men."

Alexander Bell, by his father's wish and his own consent, was to become
a teacher of English speech. Like his grandfather and his father, both
of whom were now teaching in London. He would become their assistant,
after a course of study at London University.

But his plans received a serious jolt. His younger brother died of
tuberculosis. And then his older brother died of the same disease. Aleck,
too, was threatened with an early death. "Perhaps the climate of America
will save him," thought his distracted parents.

And so, to America (August 1870), "to give the climate of Ontario a two-year trial." The climate proved satisfactory beyond their dearest hopes. They never went back to England.

IV

FOR A YEAR Graham Bell—as he now called himself—worked on a Canadian farm to build up his health. And then, completely recovered, he began to substitute as a teacher when his father was called away to lecture out of town.

His immediate success as a teacher encouraged his father to recommend him as a lecturer to his own audiences. And so, at twenty-four, Graham Bell was invited to lecture in Boston on the Science of Visible Speech.

A stiff and formal audience in a stiff and formal city. A city to which a "correct" florist returned hastily from a holiday at the news of the death of a "correct" citizen because it was the "correct" thing for the family "to order from the proprietor rather than from a clerk the flowers for the funeral." A city in which the ladies minded their manners, the gentlemen parted their hair in the back, and everybody gazed longingly backward to "the virtues and the traditions" of their ancestors.

Yet Graham Bell created somewhat of a sensation in this backward-looking city with his forward-looking ideas. A pleasing personality to look at, even though you didn't agree with everything he said. Tall, slender, jet-black hair and olive face and flashing eyes, he looked like a foreign nobleman amid the nobility-worshiping Bostonians. But listen to his fancies! Visible speech . . . trying to teach the deaf to talk . . . undoing the work of the Creator, who in His wisdom made these creatures deaf because He wanted them to be mute. . . .

But here and there a nod of sympathetic approval in the audience. Note, for example, the man with the long white beard and the kindly look in his eyes. He seems to be drinking in every word. At the end of the lecture he introduces himself to Graham Bell. Mr. Hubbard, a prominent Boston lawyer. His daughter has lost her hearing from scarlet fever at the age of four. "Your plan, Mr. Bell, would be a godsend if it could succeed."

Another listener at the lecture, Mr. Thomas Sanders. His little son, George, has been born deaf. "I'd like to try your method on my child, Mr. Bell."

With the help of these men—whose children have become his private pupils—Graham Bell opens a "School for the Deaf" in Boston.

In addition to his work at this school, he secured a job as teacher of vocal physiology at Boston University.

His residence, however, was not in Boston but in the neighboring city of Salem—at the home of his patron, Thomas Sanders. Here he was graciously permitted to take over the basement and the attic for his "amusing" experiments in the "mechanics of speech." A jumble of wires, batteries, tuning forks, and other "outlandish" instruments—and in the midst of these, a tired and often hungry and sleepless Merlin, working for days on end without going out for a breath of air. Often, when Mrs. Sanders' call to dinner remained unheeded, she would slip the food on a tray inside his door. And now and then she would deliberately cut his candle short so that he would have to go to bed when it burned out.

At last his health broke down once more, and he was obliged to go to Canada for a complete rest. "No more thought of inventions, young man!" warned his doctor. "You're not built for that sort of thing."

But Bell's recuperative power was as amazing as his ability to concentrate on his work. Before long he was back to his classes and his laboratory and his dreams.

And foremost among these dreams was to make the world a happier place for the crippled children of the human family. All his scientific endeavors were the result of this single aim of his life. He started his inventive career with "a machine"—we are quoting his own words—"that should render visible to the eyes of the deaf the vibrations of the air that affect our ears as sound." From the vibrations of the air it was but a natural step to the vibrations of the electric wire. "That machine [for the deaf] became, in the process of time, the telephone of today . . . It is only right that it should be known that the telephone is one of the products of my work at the School [for the Deaf], and resulted from my attempts to benefit the children at this School."

V

BELL's FIRST ATTEMPT at invention resulted in the improved *phonauto-graph,* or *sound transcriber.* This apparatus contained an earlike membrane that intercepted sound and transmitted it into graphic waves or symbols on a surface covered with lampblack. As he continued his experiments with this instrument, he was struck—he said—"by the likeness between the mechanism of the phonautograph and the human ear."

And thus he began to study the anatomy of the ear. Through the assistance of a friend, Dr. Clarence J. Blake, surgeon at the Massachusetts Eye and Ear Infirmary, he secured the ear of a dead man and carefully examined its structure.

He took this ear on his vacation to his father's home in Canada; and there, in the summer of 1874, he began his experiments that were to culminate in the invention of the telephone.

But he was confronted with one great—the scientists insisted it was an *insurmountable*—difficulty. He was trying to transmit *continuous* sounds by a *make-and-break* current of electricity. And at this point, fortunately, it was his comparative ignorance of electricity that enabled him to persist where an expert electrician would have given up. His reason for his persistence was very simple—too simple for the complicated logic of the experts. "While I was experimenting with the human ear, I was at work . . . on the problem of transmitting musical sounds by an intermittent current . . . and I had dreams that we might transmit the quality of a sound if we could find in the electrical current any undulations of form like the undulations we observe in the air."

Such continuous undulations, declared the academic scientists, are not to be found in electricity. But Bell, in his "sublime ignorance" of academic subtleties, believed he could find them—*and he did find them.* "I had obtained the idea that theoretically you might, by magneto electricity, create such a [continuous] current. If you could only take a piece of steel, a good chunk of magnetized steel, and vibrate it in front of the pole of an electromagnet, you would get the kind of current we wanted.

"And thus," he concluded modestly, "the telephone was conceived."

Two simple ideas—an uninterrupted current to transcribe the modulations of sound, an earlike membrane to intercept the subtleties of these modulations—and the world is encircled with the sound of the human voice.

VI

To ASSIST HIM in his experiments—for Bell was clumsy with his fingers—he hired a young mechanic, Thomas A. Watson, on a part-time basis. A partnership of mutual profit—not, at first, financially, but spiritually. Bell acquired from Watson a working knowledge of electricity, and Watson acquired from Bell a general knowledge of the world. The world of science, of literature, of art. And of music. "The best thing Bell did for me was to emphasize my love of the music of the speaking voice. He was himself a master of expressive speech."

A master, a teacher, and a transmitter of speech. Out of his scant earnings, he offered Watson a full-time job. But Watson, who was regularly employed as an electrician, turned down the offer. "Sorry, but I can't afford to give up my eighteen-dollar-a-week job. I'll give you all the time I can spare, though."

This "spare" time sometimes lengthened into an entire sleepless night. Stringing wires, rushing up and down the steps—they now roomed in the same lodginghouse—waking their neighbors with their "tramping and their shouting," and trying to pacify the landlady, who threatened again and again to evict them unless they stopped their noise. And paid their rent.

For their experiments had so eaten into their earnings that they were far behind in their rent. Bell had made a financial arrangement with his two patrons, Mr. Hubbard and Mr. Sanders, to back him in his inventions. But thus far their backing had taken the form of encouragement rather than cash. And his own cash kept dwindling more and more. He had given up his teaching in order to devote all his time to his experiments. "I am now," he wrote to his parents (March 18, 1875), "beginning to realize the cares and anxieties of being an inventor . . . Flesh and blood could not stand much longer such a strain as I have had upon me."

He was now, to use his own expression, "in real want." His friends urged him to give up his "crazy experiments" and to go back to his teaching. But he refused to "quit." For, as he wrote in another letter to his parents (May 24, 1875), "I think that the transmission of the human voice is much more nearly at hand than I had supposed."

"A stubborn and reckless fool." And, on top of all this, he did another reckless thing. He proposed to Mabel Hubbard, the beautiful and—in spite of her deafness—accomplished daughter of Mr. Hubbard. Her father strenuously objected to their marriage. "You can't support her on magnetism and electric wires."

"This, sir, is precisely how I intend to support her." And he persisted in his wiring and his wooing until he had completed his invention and turned it into cash.

The first intimation of success came on June 2, 1875. Bell and his assistant were "tinkering around" at the Boston shop of Charles Williams, where Watson was employed at his eighteen-dollar-a-week job. Bell was pressing the receiving springs to his ear. In another room, about sixty feet away, Watson was plucking the transmitting spring. Suddenly Bell jumped into the air. The "impossible" had come to pass. Bell had generated, by means of his magnetized steel, the continuous current of electricity that vibrated, like the air, to the various vibrations of the human voice. "At that moment the telephone was born."

He tried to interest the British in his new invention before he took out an American patent. But the British dismissed the telephone as "the latest American humbug." Bell kept waiting and hoping for a change of mind in England, and neglected his application for an American patent, until he came near to losing the entire fruits of his invention. It was only a miracle that saved him.

A miracle—and the astuteness of his prospective father-in-law, Mr. Hubbard. On the morning of February 14, 1876, Hubbard decided to take matters into his own hands. Without consulting Bell—"He may be a great inventor, but he's an obdurate Scotchman"—he filed an application for a patent on the telephone, in Bell's name.

It was a lucky move. For only a few hours later the Patent Office received another claim to the invention of the telephone. This application came from Elisha Gray, an inventor who, independently of Bell, had been experimenting along the same lines.

VII

BELL RECEIVED HIS PATENT on his twenty-ninth birthday (March 3, 1876). It was a day of mental rejoicing, but not as yet of material success. For the telephone at this time was merely a toy. Nobody dreamed that it would ever become an instrument of practical use.

And thus the beginning of a new experiment for Bell. A heartbreaking struggle to compel a deaf world to hear. For the world still laughed at "Crazy Bell." Of what concern was this "silly little contraption" of his in the excitement of the Centennial Exhibition that was about to be opened at Philadelphia? Here was something real! Fireworks, brass bands, parades, games, merry-go-rounds, furs, jewels, shows, dances, songs—

everything to tickle the eye and the ear. And, to cap it all, the visit of a *real king*. Dom Pedro, the Emperor of Brazil!

Graham Bell had met Dom Pedro at the Boston School for the Deaf, where he had temporarily resumed his teaching to meet his expenses for food and rent. The Emperor was interested in education, and the two had enjoyed a long chat on the subject of visible speech.

And now Dom Pedro was the guest of honor at the Centennial; and Graham Bell, one of the obscurest of the exhibitors. His telephone had been relegated to an out-of-the-way corner in the educational exhibit from Massachusetts.

Sunday, June 25, 1876. Bell had received word that on this day the judges would reach the section containing his exhibit. He had come to Philadelphia for this one day—he could spare no further time because it was the examination period at the school.

A day of terrific heat. Bell was soaked in perspiration as he adjusted and readjusted the wires of his instrument. "What if something goes wrong!" But there's not time to think now. The judges are approaching the booth. They, too, are tired and disgruntled and hot. Accompanied by a handful of unofficial observers—among them the Emperor of Brazil —they have now reached the exhibit before his own. His heart sinks when he hears the announcement of their chairman: "This will be our last exhibit for today."

And so his telephone will not be examined today. Or *any* day. For tomorrow he must be back to his examinations in Boston.

The judges are now turning to leave. And for a moment they pause in deference for Dom Pedro to precede them. At this psychological moment Dom Pedro catches sight of the young inventor. "How do you do, Mr. Bell?"

While the judges are waiting fretfully for their imperial guest, Dom Pedro inquires about Bell's exhibit. He expresses a mild interest in the "speaking wires." He asks the judges to look at "this one more exhibit" before they go.

Reluctantly they consent. And then, the sensation of the Centennial. At one end of the exhibition hall Bell speaks into the transmitter. At the other end, five hundred feet away, the astonished judges pass the receiver from ear to ear. "The thing speaks!" Hamlet's Soliloquy—"'To be, or not to be: that is the question . . .'"

The chairman of the committee—the famous scientist Sir William Thomson (afterward Lord Kelvin)—announces that he will speak into the transmitter himself. A dash across the hall, and then, "'. . . ay, there's the rub . . .'" At the other end another member of the committee, Professor George F. Barker: "I can hear it plainly—Sir William's voice."

At the conclusion of the test the judges were no less excited than Graham Bell. "Young man," exclaimed Sir William, "you have achieved one of the marvels of the ages. I predict that this invention of yours definitely is *to be!*"

Yet even this tribute passed over the heads of most of the people— including the greater part of the press. The learned editors of the *Boston*

Transcript, for example, dismissed the event in a supercilious note: "The experiments of Professor Bell, made in the presence of the Emperor of Brazil, Sir William Thomson, and others interested in the subject, have been highly interesting . . ."

In other words—"Those who care for such things care for such things. As for the rest of us, *we* are concerned with the *important* things.

VIII

BELL WENT AHEAD with his almost impossible task to find recognition and capital for his new invention, while society shook its collective head and lamented—"there are no men of genius in the world today." Bell offered his patents to the Western Union Telegraph Company for one hundred thousand dollars. He knew it was a great sacrifice on his part, but he was anxious to get married.

The offer was flatly refused. "Preposterous!"

Bell tried to point out that with a little improvement—which of course, required capital—the telephone could be made to transmit speech over hundreds of miles, perhaps across the entire country.

The only reply was, "Nonsense!"

And so Bell was obliged to continue his experiments with his own slender means. And with the occasional "handouts" from his backers—Thomas Sanders and Gardiner Hubbard. But the public was still apathetic. "A pretty toy, to be sure, but it has no commercial possibilities."

Yet the toy, under the skillful fingers of Watson guided by the patient genius of Graham Bell, kept growing in precision and power. Now they could talk between Boston and Cambridge—an interval of two miles; now, between Boston and Salem—a stretch of sixteen miles; and finally, between Boston and New York—a distance of over two hundred miles.

The public at last began to wake up to a new thing under the sun. "Perhaps the thing *has* possibilities." The *Boston Post* devoted a substantial article to "Electric Telephony": "The application of this discovery promises to completely revolutionize the business of transmitting messages by electricity between distant points . . . Professor Bell is continually improving his invention, and he doubts not that he will ultimately be able to chat pleasantly with friends in Europe while sitting comfortably in his Boston home."

And now his patrons became a little more generous with their approval and their purse. Hubbard finally consented to Bell's petition for his daughter's hand. They were married (July 11, 1877), and they spent a year and a half abroad with every expectation that fame and fortune would await them on their return.

What they actually found on their return was a lawsuit that threatened to deprive Bell of all the fruits of his labors. The Western Union had purchased Elisha Gray's patents and was now trying to monopolize the entire field.

Bell was thoroughly disheartened at this new turn of affairs. He was an inventor, not a brawler. "I've had enough of the telephone. I'm through with the damn thing. I'm going back to teaching as soon as I get a job."

But for the present he was unable even to teach. The continuous repetition of his disappointments resulted in another physical breakdown. He was ordered to the Massachusetts General Hospital for a complete rest. To add to his misfortunes, he was now "hopelessly" in debt.

And then—a ray of light. The Western Union, convinced at last of Bell's prior claim to the telephone, settled the litigation out of court. The terms of the settlement—one fifth interest to the Western Union, four fifths to the Bell Company.

A ray of light between two thunderstorms—the second more threatening than the first.

This second lawsuit—or series of lawsuits—developed into the longest patent litigation in history. The longest, and the most bitterly contested. Bell was now faced not only with financial ruin but with personal disgrace. The petty chorus of his rivals had incited a universal and unreasonable hatred against Bell. "This man is a perjurer, a fraud, and a thief!" No less than six hundred claims were entered against Bell's "infringement of other people's rights." It was an amazing example of the parasitic human desire to eat at another man's table—and to poison their host.

The altercations dragged on for years; thousands upon thousands of pages of testimony were taken; several of the lawsuits were carried to the Supreme Court. But in every case the decision was in favor of Alexander Bell.

IX

AN INTERVAL OF TRANQUILLITY—the patience of an understanding wife— the adoration of two impulsive daughters—and then the greatest blow of them all. This time it was a charge of "collusion and bribery" entered against him by the Attorney General of the United States. This charge, instigated by the Pan-Electric Company, represented Bell as having connived with the Patent Office personnel to give him a claim to patents which he had stolen from other inventors. And thus the Government of the United States, as plaintiff, was indicting Bell for "having perpetrated the most gigantic fraud of the century."

A most gigantic fraud it was; but Bell was not the perpetrator. In the congressional investigation that followed—amid a deluge of journalistic garbage heaped upon Bell without the slightest shred of evidence—it was established that not only was Bell innocent of the charge but that the Attorney General was personally interested in the Pan-Electric Company to the extent of a million-dollar investment in that concern.

The case was becoming too "hot" for the Attorney General and the Pan-Electric Company—especially since the backers of this company were already under injunction for infringement of the Bell patents. The case against Bell was dropped—and from then on he was allowed to live in peace.

X

THE RICHES AND THE HONORS—and the disillusions—of old age. The Volta prize for scientific discovery; academic degrees; medals, statues, eulogies for his "unbounded services" to mankind. "Why do they offer all this to me now—what good is it to me now? It would have meant everything to me when I was a young man."

Yet Bell's was far from a bitter old age. He had built himself an estate—Beinn Bhreagh (Beautiful Mountain)—at Cape Breton. Here he "tinkered around" with gigantic box kites, investigated the currents of the air, and shared the results of his investigations with Professor Langley, the Wright brothers, Glenn Curtiss, and others who were trying to conquer the air. Indefatigable as ever, he devoted many hours a day to his flying tests. He generally worked till three in the morning and then took a walk to the hilltop under the stars before going to bed.

Once, when invited to attend President Taft's dinner for The League to Enforce Peace, he didn't go to bed at all. For he was to be one of the speakers at the dinner, and he was afraid that he might oversleep and miss his train.

On his arrival at the hotel, shortly before six, he was so tired from the trip that he lay down for a nap. The dinner was at eight. He awoke at ten-fifteen. "I was so ashamed of myself," he explained afterward, "that I didn't even show up." Instead he went to a movie and then took the train home.

He was extremely fond of "play-acting"—a relic of his early passion for Shakespeare. One of his favorite amusements was to arrange charades for the guests at Beinn Bhreagh. And he always insisted upon taking the leading part—an ancient Jehovah with long white hair and a glittering white beard, a black tam-o'-shanter perched obliquely on his head, and his long and still-animated figure dressed in a "working" blouse and homespun knickerbockers.

A child of elocution teachers and dramatic readers, he always dramatized himself—whether he undertook a lecture tour around the world or insisted on flying a kite in the midst of a hurricane. But always he acted his part with an eye to the future. When asked to write his reminiscences, he refused. "I am not interested in yesterday. I am interested only in tomorrow."

Always dictating scientific notes for tomorrow. When he lay on his deathbed, from pernicious anemia, he insisted upon his regular dictation. "Please don't hurry," implored his wife.

"But I have to," he murmured. "So little done. So much to do."

IMPORTANT DATES IN THE LIFE OF
ALEXANDER GRAHAM BELL

1847—Born, Edinburgh, Scotland.

1868—Entered London University.

1870—Moved to Canada.

1871—Became instructor to teachers of the deaf.

1873—Appointed professor of vocal physiology at Boston University.

1874—Invented harmonic multiple telegraph.

1875—Invented magneto-electric telephone.

1876—Exhibited telephone at Philadelphia Centennial Exposition.

1880—Awarded Volta prize of fifty thousand francs for electrical inventions.

1886—Received honorary degree of Doctor of Medicine from Heidelberg University.

1896—Received honorary degree of Doctor of Laws from Harvard.

1906—Received honorary degree of Doctor of Science from Oxford.

1906–12—Experimented with heavier-than-air flying machines.

1922—Died, Nova Scotia.

Thomas Alva Edison

[1847-1931]

GENIUS is the ability to do the hardest things the easiest way. One day, when Edison was working on a practical lamp for his newly discovered electric light, he found it necessary to get the cubical content of an irregular glass bulb. Too busy himself to attend to the job, he called in his most brilliant mathematician to help him. Arming himself with many sheets of foolscap, the great savant sat down to work. A week later Edison asked him how he was getting along.

"Very nicely, Mr. Edison, but I am not finished yet."

Edison looked at the formidable array of charts and figures submitted by the mathematician. "How much longer will it take you to solve the problem?"

"Oh, another week, I expect."

"Let me show you how to do it in a minute," said Edison.

He filled the bulb with water.

"Now measure the water, and you've got the answer."

II

EDISON POSSESSED not only a knack for hitting upon the obvious, but an infinite capacity for taking pains. In his effort to perfect the storage battery, he had made ten thousand unsuccessful tests on various chemical combinations. "Isn't it a shame," said a friend, "that with all this tremendous labor you haven't been able to get any results?"

"Why, man," said Edison, "I've got lots of results. I've discovered several thousand things that won't work."

Edison came by his energy from a stock of sturdy pioneers who were forever seeking for the things that worked through the discarding of things that wouldn't work. His great-grandfather, John Edison, fled from Staten Island to Nova Scotia in order to escape hanging as a Tory in the Revolutionary War. His grandfather, Samuel Edison, migrated from Nova Scotia in search of a better home and found it on the banks of the Otter River, in Upper Canada. His father, Samuel Edison—"a giant of a man" —became involved in a plot to overthrow the Tory regime in Canada and to replace it with a representative government like that of the United States. The plot was discovered, and "Sammy" Edison made his escape across trackless forests and icebound rivers—"it was my long legs that saved me"—until he found safety in the village of Milan, Ohio. Here he set up a mill and sent for his family through the kindly offices of a barge captain by the name of Alva Bradley. And here, in the midst of a blizzard on the morning of February 11, 1847, he greeted the arrival of his seventh child, a son. They christened the baby Thomas Alva—the second name in honor of Mr. Bradley.

From his very infancy Alva was preoccupied, ingenious, and ready to "learn something about everything." At six he set his father's barn on fire "just to see what it would do." It burned down to the ground, and almost burned Alva along with it. For this, the first of his experiments, his father punished him with a public spanking in the village square.

On another occasion he tried sitting on a nest of goose eggs to see if he could hatch them. All that he hatched was an omelet on the seat of his pants. Another spanking, another discovery of the things that wouldn't work.

His entire childhood was a succession of experiments. When he was seven years old his parents moved to Port Huron, Michigan. The new Edison home had a lofty tower overlooking Lake Huron and the St. Clair River. Young Alva—Al for short—spent a great part of his time scanning the horizon through an old telescope perched on top of the tower.

Watching the heavens above, and studying the elements below. In the cellar of his house he had set up a chemical laboratory with "Poison Don't Touch" labels on all the bottles, in order to keep them away from inquisitive fingers.

"An addled youngster," said the neighbors. One day he fed an enormous quantity of seidlitz powders to his little Dutch playmate, Michael Oates. "Why did you do it, son?" asked his father. "Well, Pop," said Alva, "I wanted to see if the seidlitz powders would form enough gas in his stomach to make him fly."

The children left him alone to his "crazy" games. The elders shook their heads. Even his father thought there was something queer about him. The only one who believed in him was his mother. She encouraged him in his experiments, and on his ninth birthday she bought him a copy of Parker's *School of Natural Philosophy*. "The greatest present I ever received," said Edison of this book many years later.

He used this book not only as a basis for his experiments but as a stimulant to his imagination. And he fed his healthy imagination on many another volume. By his tenth birthday he had familiarized himself with such works as Hume's *History of England,* Sears' *History of the World,* Burton's *Anatomy of Melancholy,* Gibbon's *Decline and Fall of the Roman Empire,* and the *Dictionary of Sciences.*

Yet Al Edison was no bookworm. On the contrary, he was a very practical youngster. When the railroad was built between Port Huron and Detroit, he applied for a job as "news-butcher" on the train. A "merchant on his own" at twelve, he wasn't content with only one occupation. In his spare moments, when he had finished peddling his newspapers, he busied himself in the baggage car, writing and printing a newspaper of his own, or in a chemical laboratory which he had set up in another car. This laboratory, incidentally, cost him his job on the train and thus indirectly led to his study of telegraphy and to his first invention. One day, as the train was bumping over a rough road, a stick of phosphorus from Edison's pile of chemicals fell to the floor and set fire to the baggage car. The conductor extinguished the flames and kicked Edison out of his railroad laboratory into the bigger laboratory of the world.

Al Edison—at that time he pronounced his name *Eadison*—was not sorry to lose his job as a news peddler. In his daily trips from city to city he had become acquainted with the telegraph operators at the railroad stations. Their work fascinated him. He decided to become one of them. Devoting as many as eighteen hours a day to practice, he soon mastered the job, stretched a wire between the drugstore and the depot at Port Huron, and set himself up as a "private merchant of local messages." But the businessmen of the town preferred to receive and to deliver their local messages in person. His earnings averaged less than fifty cents a month.

Yet his knowledge of telegraphy, combined with his mental resourcefulness, enabled him to come to the rescue of his townsmen on one occasion when an ice jam had severed the wires between Port Huron and Canada. Due to the floating ice, it was impossible to make the repairs. But this did not phase Tom—he had now changed from his second to his first name. He promised to deliver the messages across the lake to Canada if they would supply him with a locomotive and an engineer. Smiling skeptically, the railroad authorities granted his request. But their skepticism changed to admiration when they saw the simplicity of his plan. All he did was to toot out a telegraph message on the engine in whistles of dots and dashes. At first there was no answer; but when Edison had repeated the message several times, a Canadian operator caught on and tooted back a message in reply. It was perhaps the first instance of "wireless telegraphy" on record.

A remarkably clever young fellow. And remarkably untidy. He spent his money on books and left practically nothing for his clothes. One winter he went without an overcoat and nearly froze to death. An experimenting vagabond. From city to city he drifted, and from job to job. Easily hired, easily fired. His ideas were too "crazy" for his superiors. Talked about sending two messages over a wire. "Why, any damn fool knows that a wire can't be worked both ways at the same time." This "lunatic" was a bad influence upon the other fellows in the office. "Out you go!"

And out he kept going, until finally he found his way to Boston. It was on a midwinter day in 1868 when he walked into the Boston office of the Western Union and asked for a job as a telegraph operator. The superintendent, George F. Milliken, looked up from his desk. What a disreputable-looking hobo! Pants too short and too tight and all but waterproof with smudge. Shoes torn and twisted out of shape. Hat so ragged that one of his ears protruded through a hole. Shirt a patchwork of tatters that hadn't been washed for weeks. And hair a matted jumble that seemingly had never known the touch of a comb.

Tom Edison had written from Canada to a Boston friend about this job, and the friend had shown the letter to Milliken. "If he can take it off the wire in such a script," said Milliken as he looked at the printlike handwriting of the letter, "tell him he can have the job."

But when Milliken looked at Edison, with his unkempt hair and his unwashed shirt and his rickety shoes, he was not quite so sure of the young fellow's ability. "Come back at five-thirty," he said reluctantly, "and perhaps I'll give you a trial."

Edison came back at the appointed hour and found the clerks grinning at their desks. They had prepared a practical joke against their country bumpkin who dared to ask for a job as a city telegrapher. They had wired to one of the fastest New York operators to send a special news report of eight hundred words, and now they sat back to see the fun.

Picking up a bundle of blanks, Edison placed himself at the table assigned to him. "Ready!" he signaled, and the message began to pour in. Faster and faster came the words, but Edison was equal to the job. As his fingers flew over the sheets, he glanced up; and then for the first time he understood the grin on the other fellows' faces. So they wanted to show him up, did they? Very well, he would teach them a lesson! Opening the key of his instrument, he tapped to the galloping operator at the other end: "Come on, boy, don't go to sleep. Shake yourself and get busy with the other foot."

The New York operator surrendered, and the clerks in the Boston office rushed up to Edison and showered him with their congratulations. Right then and there they acknowledged him as the fastest telegraph operator in the Western Union.

III

"ANY DAMN FOOL knows that a wire can't be worked both ways." Again and again the skeptics kept reminding Edison of this natural "fact." But Edison persisted in his experiments and proved the "fact" to be a fiction. In the May issue of 1868 the *Journal of the Telegraph* made the announcement that Edison had "achieved the impossible." A few months later the following note appeared in the same journal:

"T. A. Edison has resigned his situation in the Western Union office, Boston, and will devote his time to bringing out his inventions."

A daring step for a penniless young man. It meant foodless days and sleepless nights. Offers to sell his inventions, delays, refusals, disappointments, but never despair. "You wait, they will come to me yet."

And they came to him sooner even than he had dreamed. A shrewd businessman for whom Edison had once worked, General Marshal Lefferts, was watching his inventions. He saw their financial possibilities. One day he summoned the hungry young wizard to his office. "How much will you take for all your contraptions?"

Edison thought quickly. Should he ask for three thousand? He could manage with that sum for the present. Five thousand? Oh no, that was preposterous! Lefferts would most likely kick him out of the office if he dared to mention that sum.

"Make me an offer, General."

"Very well, would you accept forty thousand?"

Until he received his check, Edison wasn't sure whether Lefferts had said *four* thousand or *forty* thousand. When he looked at the check he almost fainted. What would he do with all this fabulous amount of money?

Yet the fabulous amount melted away in a fabulously short time. His experiments always ran ahead of his cash. Opening a workshop in Newark, he paid the highest possible wages for the best possible workmen. "I have one shop which employs eighteen men," he wrote to his parents, "and I am fitting up another shop which will employ one hundred and fifty men." He had no accountant and kept no books. On one hook he hung all the bills he owed; on another, all the bills owed him. "This is the simplest sort of bookkeeping. Why ball myself up with all kinds of complicated figures?"

And thus, pouring his money and his mind into the secret crucibles of nature, he went on with his experiments. Multiple telegraphy—two, four, eight messages over a single wire at the same time. An electric stock-ticker instrument. An instrument that reproduced the human voice—"I'll bet you a barrel of apples against three dollars," he challenged the skeptics, "that this instrument will talk." An Aladdin's lamp that would light up the world with a new electric force. Crude discoveries thus far, mere foreshadowings of the miracles that he was to perform in these fields later on.

All work and work, save for a brief vacation to the "Wild West"—and time off to get married. Hardly a prepossessing bridegroom. Refused to wear white gloves at his wedding. "I've married a bear of a man," said his wife—the former Mary Stillwell—"but what an adorable bear!" Though gruff and absent-minded toward the rest of the world, he was all tenderness toward Mary.

And, later on, toward the children—Marion and Tommy. He nicknamed them *Dot* and *Dash*. It was his greatest pleasure to play the clown for them in his spare moments. "He would don Mary's dresses"—we are quoting his sister-in-law Alice, who lived with the Edisons—"and romp and play around the house with the youngsters. They had a stereopticon and he would sometimes go behind the screen and stand on his head, and go through various antics to amuse them."

And there were times when to amuse his children meant the greatest physical torture. "He was a great sufferer from earache"—again we are quoting Alice—"and I have seen him sit on the edge of a bed and fairly grind holes in the carpet with the heels of his shoes, he would be suffering such pain."

A little play, much work, incessant pain, and an infinite patience—these were the ingredients which, combined with a flaming imagination, enabled Edison to transmute matter into motion and light. But most important of all, perhaps, was his extraordinary memory for details—his ability to co-ordinate apparently isolated facts into a coherent unit. Edison's memory was the amazement of psychologists. It was almost photographic in its scope. One day, as he was working over the plans for a new mechanical device in a cement plant, he examined the old machine, went home without having jotted down a single note, and compiled a list of six hundred items in the old machine that required modification or improvement. Hardly a bolt or a screw had failed to impress itself upon the retina of his mental eye.

His retentive memory was like a well-stocked and well-organized mechanic's toolbox. Everything was in its logical place; and whenever he wanted to put several facts together, he could get at them without any waste of time or unnecessary fumbling. As a result of this faculty of orderly analysis, he was able to do more constructive thinking in a day than the average man is able to do in a lifetime.

But his inclusive memory and his ability to mold individual facts into related units would never have got him very far were it not for his endurance. As a general rule, he slept only four hours a day. "Life," he said, "is too important to waste in excessive snoring. There are too many things to be done. There are so many experiments waiting, and it takes so long to bring even a single experiment to a definite conclusion." It took him many years to perfect some of his inventions—years of incessant toil, fifteen hours, sixteen hours, seventeen hours, sometimes even eighteen hours a day. "I have no time for loafing as yet," he said on his sixty-seventh birthday. "I shall begin to loaf when I am eighty."

A sublime endurance, an equally sublime courage. In 1915 his laboratory at West Orange, consisting of six buildings, burned down to the ground. The buildings were not insured, and the loss amounted to five million dollars. "That's all right," he said, "I'll make a fresh start tomorrow morning. No one's ever too old to make a fresh start."

IV

WHILE he was in the midst of his experiments with the electric bulb there was a sudden blackout in his own household. His wife Mary died of a heart attack. Eighteen months of mourning, and then he married again. In his personal habits he was still very much of a baby and needed someone to mother him. And fortunately his second wife, Mina Miller, proved like his first wife to be a good mother and congenial companion. It takes great patience to live with a genius. But it gives great satisfaction. Mina was able not only to appreciate his inventions but to share his thoughts. He often discussed his philosophy with her at the dinner table. He was profoundly interested in the mystery of life. He believed that every atom within the body, like the entire body itself, possesses an individual intelligence. "Look at the thousand ways in which atoms of hydrogen combine with other atoms to form the most diverse substances. Do you mean to tell me that they do this without intelligence?"

And then he went on to clarify his thought. "Atoms in harmonious and useful combinations assume beautiful shapes and colors, or give forth a pleasant perfume. In sickness, death, decomposition, or filth, the disagreement of the component atoms immediately makes itself felt by bad odors."

And the upshot of it all? The final union of the most intelligent atoms into the most intelligent substance. "Gathered together in certain forms, the atoms constitute animals of the lower orders. At last they combine in man, who represents the total intelligence of all the atoms."

"But where," asked Mina, "does all this gradual combination come from?"

"From some power greater than ourselves."

"Then you believe in an intelligent Creator?"

"I certainly do. The existence of a personal God can to my mind almost be demonstrated by chemistry."

Edison was not only a great inventor but a constructive idealist. He was interested primarily in the things that further the plans of God. In his own experiments he aimed at the inventions that serve life, and not at those that produce death. "Making things which kill men," he once said, "is against my fiber. I would rather make people laugh."

This was the principal objective of his life—to bring laughter into the hearts of the people. More laughter and greater light. "The world has been steeped in darkness long enough."

V

THE INVENTION of the electric light was the direct outgrowth of Edison's philosophy. And it was as simple in its conception as it was eventful in its result. It was one of those surprising discoveries of the obvious. If electricity can produce power and heat, argued Edison, there is no reason why it shouldn't produce light—provided we can find something that will burn properly under the stimulus of heat and power. And so he began to seek a substance, which, like the bush of Moses, would burn without being consumed. In this quest Edison was not alone. Many others, on both sides of the Atlantic, had thought of electric lighting. An American inventor, J. W. Starr, had worked on incandescent lamps even before Edison was born. Another American, Moses G. Farmer, had provided his sitting room with a number of crude electric lamps twenty years before Edison's invention of incandescent light. In England, in France, and in Russia a number of scientists were producing equally crude lamps that would flare up for a short time and then flicker out. But Edison's chief rival in the search for the secret of practical and permanent electrical illumination was W. E. Sawyer. This American inventor had much of the brilliance but little of the patience of Edison. It was Edison who sat tirelessly in his laboratory, trying out one filament after another in his vacuum bulbs, ransacking every nook and cranny of the earth for the fiber that would give a brilliant and steady and, so far as possible, indestructible glow. And it was Edison who, refusing to admit defeat in the face of financial failure and the jeers of the scientific and journalistic world, finally discovered the magic fiber. On New Year's Eve, 1879, a throng of people from the surrounding cities had come to Edison's laboratory at Menlo Park, New Jersey. The ground of the little village was covered with snow. Suddenly, the switch of a button, and the darkness bloomed into a silver radiance under the flood of a dozen street lamps. On that New Year's Eve the genius of Edison had for the first time in history transformed night into day.

Just before the miracle had happened, a leading New York editor had exclaimed: "It has been absolutely proved that this sort of light is impossible—it is against the laws of Nature!"

VI

EDISON HAS BEEN ACCUSED of being a second-rate inventor and a first-rate businessman. He capitalized, it has been said, on the inventions of others. This accusation is, we believe, unfounded. It is true that others worked simultaneously with Edison on many of the inventions for which he is credited. But Edison worked harder and faster than the rest of them. And he worked under the handicap of his chronic earaches and his deafness. Indeed, he turned his handicap into an advantage. "It takes a deaf man to hear music," he remarked when he was experimenting on the phonograph. And when he was asked to explain this paradox, he said: "Most people hear only through their ears. I hear through my teeth and through my skull. Ordinarily I place my head against the phonograph. If there is some faint sound that I don't quite catch this way, I bite into the wood and I get it good and strong."

It was this faculty of hearing through his teeth and skull that enabled him to improve upon Alexander Graham Bell's invention of the telephone. Bell's instrument had been "hardly more than a mechanical curiosity," owing to the fact that it had been designed to serve both as a transmitter and a receiver. But Edison transformed it into an object of practical utility by giving it a separate mouthpiece and earpiece, instead of allowing the same tube to be used clumsily for both purposes. It sounds simple today. But it took Edison to think of it.

And many of the "simple" things that today make life worth living have had their origin in the magical laboratory of Edison's thought. Almost to the last day of his eighty-four years he worked on his experiments—an inspired, whimsical, untidy, modest, gentle, shrewd, and indefatigable Merlin. Out of his sorcerer's brain came an endless stream of electrical and mechanical servants to bring new amusements and new comforts to the human race. His inventions of the phonograph, the electric light, the motion picture, and the first crude "talkie" are merely the most popular of his hundreds of vital contributions to the applied science of the present day. His was perhaps the most universal mind in America during the nineteenth century. Once, when he visited Luther Burbank in his garden at Santa Rosa, the "plant wizard" asked him to register in his guest book. The pages of the guest book were divided into four columns, as follows:

Name   *Address*   *Occupation*   *Interested In*

Under the caption *Interested In,* Edison wrote: "Everything." He was satisfied with nothing short of the sum of practical human knowledge.

In his endless quest for the practical, he was never satisfied with his past achievement. Always he looked toward the future. His prophetic vision saw many years ahead of the contemporary needs of his country. It is interesting to note that one of his very last experiments when death overtook him (1931) was concerned with the production of synthetic rubber.

And death itself, he was convinced, is but the transition into a new laboratory for greater experiments. "I've lived my life. I've done my work. Now I am ready for the next job."

IMPORTANT DATES IN THE LIFE OF
THOMAS ALVA EDISON

1847—Born, Milan, Ohio.

1854—Family moved to Port Huron, Michigan.

1859—Became trainboy.

1862—Began to publish, for trainmen, the *Grand Trunk Herald.*

1863—Became telegraph operator.

1864—Invented automatic telegraph repeater.

1869—Came to New York. Invented improvements for stock tickers.

1872—Invented the kinetoscope (moving-picture machine).

1876—Moved to Menlo Park, New Jersey.

1877—Invented phonograph.

1878—Made chevalier of the French Legion of Honor.

1879—Demonstrated invention of electric light at Menlo Park.

1879-1931—Engaged in numerous inventions. Took out more than one thousand patents.

1931—Died, West Orange, New Jersey.

Eugene Victor Debs

[1855-1926]

EUGENE DEBS was a poet. But he didn't *write* his poetry; he *lived* it. With his life's work he created one of the epics of human progress. Instead of combining the letters of the alphabet into living words, he combined the longings of the workers into living hopes.

He was only twenty when he—and others too—became aware of this remarkable talent of his. Employed as a locomotive fireman at his native city of Terre Haute, he was invited to join the workers' Brotherhood and to help organize—if possible—its "aimless struggle for better things."

The workers needed an organizer of his type. Young as he was, many a poor devil had already turned to him for inspiration and advice. A tall and slender sapling of sturdy resolution—with a face full of pity and a heart full of love. When he spoke to you he bent over you as if in benediction. And when he clasped your hand he poured into your blood stream an electric current of strength.

When he first entered the hall in which the Brotherhood met, the oldest member came forward to greet the youngest. "How do you do, Gene? My name is Joshua Leach, and I bid you welcome here."

Debs looked into the eyes of the old man, and they both smiled. "I'm glad to be one of you, and I hope to do my share of the work if you'll only let me."

Mr. Leach placed his big, hairy hand on Gene's shoulder. "My boy, you're a bit young. But I *know* you'll make good."

Debs looked around at the men. Uncouth bodies, heavy boots, frayed collars, broken fingernails smudgy with coal dust. But frank and friendly faces. Something of the trustfulness of children in those homely features. Walt Whitman was right. "Here, too, the reflection of the divine." An exciting prospect, this—to work *with* them and *for* them.

And there was so much work to be done. The laboring masses were unorganized and inarticulate and poor. Like so many lumps of clay lying scattered over the ground. You could take each separate lump and torture it into whatever shape you liked. And then, if you got tired of it, you could just kick it out of your way. Too old and brittle for any further use.

And the workers, like the helpless lumps of clay that they were, had accepted their blows in silence and suffered on.

But Eugene Debs took hold of these pitiable clods of earth, and put the breath of life into them, and fused them into a single body. So that now, when one of them was hurt, the entire Brotherhood cried out in protest. To a world that had subscribed to the maxim "Everyone for himself and the Devil take the hindmost," the young crusader came with a new and more Christian motto—"All for one, and one for all."

Such was the poem that Debs had begun to compose when he joined the railroad Brotherhood in 1875. But at the time he had no inkling of the difficult road he was to travel and the heavy cross he was to bear.

II

BORN OF FRENCH PARENTS in Terre Haute, Indiana, Eugene Debs was brought up in a family of six children. There had been ten in all, but four of them had died. He was seven years old when he saw the soldiers marching to the Civil War. Hysterical rejoicing. And he was eleven when he saw them marching back. Again, hysterical joy. "Too bad," remarked his father, "that the young fellows killed in the war are not here to enjoy the speeches made in their honor."

Young Gene acquired an early hatred against war.

And against the callousness of a postwar world. At home, and in the homes of his friends, he heard many discussions about the high prices of food, the difficulty of finding houses and jobs for the returned soldiers, and the indifference of the rich toward the sufferings of the poor.

As he grew older he read in the papers about the corruption of business, the connivance of politics, and the numerous concrete examples of man's inhumanity to man. The Mobilier Scandal, the maneuvers of the Tweed Ring, the watered stocks of the railroads, the manipulations of Jim Fisk, Jay Gould, and Daniel Drew, the accumulation of intrigue, dishonesty, and greed that resulted in the stock-market crash of "Black Friday." And the cynicism of the times toward all this moral laxity. *Gold is God, and the public be damned.*

And the rich kept growing richer; and the poor, poorer. "Something will have to be done about this. But where is the man courageous enough to do it?"

As for Gene Debs, he was but a boy at the time—a mere cipher in many millions of the "damned public." At fourteen he was obliged to leave school and go to work. A job in the paint shops of the railroad at Terre Haute. A year of this apprenticeship, and at fifteen young Debs was big enough for a man's work. A full-sized job feeding coal into the furnace of the locomotive. A sweaty, grimy, muscle-straining, and heart-straining job. "Someday you may get out of this, and become one of the *brains* instead of a mere *hand* in the railroad business."

For Gene Debs was a bright youngster. After a full night's work in the locomotive he spent a good part of the day studying. His superiors saw possibilities in him. Good material to train for the executive office.

But Gene Debs was interested in other ideas. And in other people—his *own* sort of people. "I prefer to stay with the hunted rather than the hunters. I feel more at home there."

His father had a talk with him about this. "You have the guts, Gene, to rise to the top," said the elder Debs.

"Maybe I have," replied Gene. "But I prefer to fight in the ranks."

"The odds, you know, will be against you."

"It's fun to fight against odds."

What could you do with a youngster like that? Born for self-sacrifice. Maybe, though, it was lack of ambition. Had he no desire, like other normal boys, to become a rich man, to live in a spacious house? They glittered like jewels among the hills, those houses of the rich. The prizes held out to ability, determination, and push.

"I don't care for any of those things."

"Poor lad," thought his father. "No spirit of adventure in him."

But his father was unaware that the boy possessed a greater gift. The adventure of the spirit.

III

FROM A LOCOMOTIVE FIREMAN to a grocery clerk. No desire for ownership. But a flair for making friends. Among the workers. A Christlike sort of character. "Blessed are the poor." But it is up to you to show them the way to their heritage of bliss. A fairer distribution of the good things of the earth.

More comfort for your fellows, even though it may mean more suffering for yourself. Debs had given up his job in the grocery store to become a traveling organizer for the Brotherhood. But traveling was an expensive luxury—more than the union could afford. And so he generally tried to get free rides from friendly conductors. Now and then, however, he would run across a trainman who was not so good-natured as the rest. And then it meant an empty freight car until he was discovered and thrown out.

One night, in midwinter, he boarded a freight train that was passing through the state of New York. He was scheduled to give a lecture in Elmira. There was a blizzard blowing at the time. He shivered as he huddled into a corner of the freight car. Yet he was thankful even for this inadequate shelter. "What if I were out in that storm now?"

The next minute he *was* out in the storm. A none-too-sympathetic brakeman had found him and ejected him into the open fields.

A trek of several miles through the blizzard, and the lecture was delivered on schedule.

Debs had now developed into a dynamic speaker. A man who could stir an audience into any mood he desired. "Why don't you go into poli-

tics?" suggested his friends. A successful career, they insisted, lay ahead
of him. Member of the state legislature, mayor of Terre Haute, governor
of Indiana—and after that, who knows?

For a time he listened to the advice of his friends and tried to be a
politician. He joined the Democratic party and was elected to the Indiana
legislature. But at the end of a year he gave it up as a nasty job. "Politics
and ethics are incompatible bedfellows."

Eugene Debs was a strange fellow. Many people called him a *fool*. "Has
it within his grasp to become a power, a leader, a great success—and look
at him drift along with the mob."

But Eugene Debs didn't care for the power to lead; he merely wanted
the opportunity to help. He refused to ride to the top upon the backs of
other people. Instead of being a success, he preferred to be a man.

A fighter for human rights. A *peaceful* fighter. For Debs was not the
militant type of man. He went into the battle armed only with a caustic
tongue and a gentle heart. Caustic against the injustices of the strong,
gentle toward the supplications of the weak.

Debs had now fully decided upon his career. He would devote his life
to the righting of human wrongs.

A thankless life. "All you will gain for your trouble is derision and
poverty and hate." He was married now—another reason for "laying aside
your dreams and waking up to the realities of life." But Debs kept dreaming on, and fighting on.

IV

AND NOW he had a *real* fight on his hands. Eighteen hundred and ninety-
four. The workers of the American Railway Union were out on strike.
"They struck because their children were hungry; because they saw, in
their ill-ventilated shacks, too many pallid faces; because the eyes of their
little ones were full of a strange wonder that the world into which they
had been invited should promise so much to everybody and give so little
to the poor; they struck because death was too frequent a visitor to their
homes . . ."

Debs, who directed the strike, regarded it as "a holy crusade for justice." Stripped of Debs's somewhat overcharged language—he always
spoke out of a full heart—the facts were somewhat as follows: George M.
Pullman, the inventor of the "palace cars," had built a so-called "model
village" which he rented to his workmen. And then he had raised their
rents so high and cut their wages so low that they had practically nothing
left after they had paid for their housing. The workers complained that
they were being "squeezed at both ends." They requested that the matter
be submitted to arbitration. "We have nothing to arbitrate," declared
Pullman. Whereupon Debs declared a general strike of the Railway
Union. The railroad workers throughout the country refused to drive the
trains which had a Pullman car attached to them.

At this point the federal government stepped into the picture. At the instance of President Cleveland, it issued—for the first time in American history—a blanket injunction against labor's interference with the business of capital.

It was a hasty and ill-advised decision on Cleveland's part. Instead of insisting upon arbitration between the *two* sides, he had played into the hands of the *stronger* side. But he didn't stop there. Under cover of "protecting the mails," he sent two thousand federal troops into Chicago—the headquarters of the strike. There was a clash between the soldiers and the strikers—although Debs had insisted upon a *peaceful* strike—several of the strikers were killed, the strike collapsed, and Debs was sentenced to six months in jail on the charge of "interference with interstate commerce."

He emerged from the prison "a consecrated martyr." President Cleveland, in a sober but belated afterthought, appointed a commission to investigate the strike. The commission reported that Debs and the strikers had been in the right. But nothing could be done now to reverse the decision of the strike—or the verdict of the court. "With the help of government injunction, right has been violated by might."

From now on Debs was embarked upon a new campaign. A battle not only against the injustice of wealth but against any form of government that *championed* such injustice. "Let us drive the money-changers and their supporters out of the political arena. Let us replace them with men who, instead of protecting the strong against the weak, will protect the weak against the strong."

V

DEBS HAD CONCLUDED to enter politics once more. To enter it, in order to clean it up. He had become inflamed with the teachings of Karl Marx. "The development of machinery and its concentration in a few hands," read Debs, "brings the workers to their great opportunity . . . Let the workers take over this machinery *and work for themselves* . . . In this way, the many will no longer suffer because of the greed of the few."

This idea became the dominating dream of his life. Take over the machinery of industry by taking over the machinery of government. Not by violent *revolution,* but by peaceful *evolution.* Educate the masses to *vote* themselves into power. The ballot to replace the bullet. *The final battle of peace.* The words of Abraham Lincoln translated into their literal sense. A government *of* the people, *by* the people, and especially *for* the people. Applied Democracy, *Social* Democracy, *Socialism.*

To Eugene Debs, Socialism was more than a political formula. It was a form of religion. Christianity interpreted in the light of the present day. The scientific foundations of Socialism were perhaps a little over his head. He was interested primarily in its ethical implications. For Debs was not a scholar—he was a poet, the St. Francis of the Socialist creed.

And the sum and substance of this creed—*workers of the world, unite!* One world of friendly, peaceful, unenslaved, and unexploited men and women working harmoniously together toward a single end—the more abundant life for all the children of the human race.

The abolition of private property. Debs forgot that the instinct for property—for personal ownership—is innate not only in all humans but in all animals. The dog will fight for his bone, the tiger for his lair, the bird for his nest, the shopkeeper for his shop. But Debs was not so naïve as to advocate "the dividing up of all property." His socialism was based upon a somewhat more rational idea. The common ownership of the instruments of production. The collective use of capital for the individual enjoyment of life. Not only a *political government,* but an *industrial co-operation,* of the people, by the people, and for the people. Private property for private use, public property for public use.

But even to Debs the idea was, from a scientific point of view, rather vague. His criticism of property was—to quote H. G. Wells—"a passionate ferment" rather than a summation of facts. He didn't know exactly where to draw the dividing line between private and public property. Nor did anybody else know. To the owners of big property, Socialism meant nothing less than an attempt to dispossess them of everything that made their life worth while. And Debs was "a fiend incarnate who was inciting a mob to universal violence and theft."

From then on Debs looked upon himself as an apostle dedicated to a holy cause. And it was in this spirit that he led the Socialist party in five presidential campaigns—1900, 1904, 1908, 1912, 1920. "You are the victims of a conspiracy of the rich. Open your eyes and learn your rights. *Take whatever you make.* Not by cheating, and not by force of arms, but by sending your own comrades, toilers from among your own ranks, into the City Halls and the State Houses and the White House of the Nation."

A *holy* cause, and for the present—he realized—a *hopeless* cause. For the workers were politically uninformed. They had never had the opportunity—or the inclination—to acquaint themselves with the mechanism of political democracy. The Socialist press, poorly endowed and teetering continually on the verge of failure, could raise but a feeble voice in the political education of the workers. The general press, aided by the pulpit to a great extent, was aligned—in a good many cases with honest intent—on the side of "sane and sound government." And thus the workers heeded the "strident voice of oppression" and paid but little attention to the "feeble voice of hope."

Moreover, a great proportion of the workers had but recently migrated to America and had not as yet become naturalized. Many of them were too apathetic to take out their papers even after they were *entitled* to citizenship.

And thus Debs went crusading among millions of people who declared that they were ready to *die* for him. But very few of them were ready to *vote* for him. Yet even so his presidential vote increased from less than one hundred thousand in 1900 to nearly a million in 1920.

And even more important, the ideas that he advocated to his own generation of old reactionaries took root in the next generation of young radicals. Some of his measures were regarded as impossible dreams in

1900. In 1948 they had become an integral part of the American scene. Woman suffrage, income taxes, pensions for old age, federal insurance for depositors in savings banks, the abolition of child labor, the interdependence of the various groups and sections of the United States—of the entire world—these are but a few of the realizations of the "impossible dreams" that had issued from the heart of Eugene Debs.

VI

AN "IMPRACTICAL VISIONARY"—whose visions had a way of coming true. Yet one of them turned into a nightmare for himself. Nineteen hundred and fourteen—a world insanely plunged into war when a little sanity might have meant the preservation of peace. Debs, with the simplicity of a child, was unable to subscribe to the chess game of imperial ambition in which the millions of pawns are sacrificed for the handful of kings. "Honest desires and open hearts—what else do we need for our happiness here below?" Are the resources of the world unevenly distributed? Why not redistribute them on a basis equitable to all, without the tragic and ridiculous ordeal of war? To Debs it was as simple as all that. Cut across the complications of diplomatic chicanery and tell the truth. If the *masters* of the world are gone astray, let the *workers* of the world point out the road. Workers of the world, unite! Refuse to kill your comrades in other lands!

Such was the voice of Debs in the wilderness of World War I. So long as the United States was not involved, he was dismissed as a *fool*. But when the United States had entered the war, he was treated as a *dangerous fool*. "No time *now* to talk about peace. We have too serious a job on our hands."

And so he was told to refrain from his pacifist talk. But he refused to obey the order. It interfered, he said, with the freedom of his soul. In a speech delivered at Canton, Ohio, he declared: "I would rather a thousand times be a free soul in jail than a hypocrite or a coward on the streets." And then, with utter disregard of himself—and, as many believed, of the practical world in which he lived—he went on to propound his ideal of peace in a world at war. "Wars throughout history have been waged for conquest and plunder . . . You, the people, have never had a voice in declaring war . . . The masters have always declared the war . . . They never did any of the fighting. They have always sent the workers to fight for them . . .

". . . And we object on the part of the awakening workers of the nation! We object to being murdered! We object to murdering the citizens of other countries! We have no quarrel against them. We do not hate them. They are our brothers . . . There is no room in our hearts for hate . . . We have nothing but love and pity even for those who would . . . imprison us or put us to death . . .

"I for one am not afraid to go to jail. To me it is a great honor to suffer for being in the right. I am willing, if need be, to stand alone . . ."

And he did stand alone. He was arrested and put on trial for this speech. He knew what the verdict would be, and he awaited it calmly. When the district attorney had concluded his opening remarks against him, Debs leaned across the table and complimented him on the excellence of his summation. And when the young man commissioned by the government to take down Debs's speech repeated it to the jury—in a voice almost choked with tears—Debs patted him on the head. "Don't worry about it, my boy—you've only done your duty."

Debs was allowed to address the jury before the passing of the sentence. "I am prepared for the sentence," he said. "I will accept your verdict. What you do to me does not matter much. Years ago I recognized my kinship with all living beings, and I made up my mind that I was not one bit better than the meanest of earth. I said then, and I say now, that while there is a lower class, I am in it; while there is a criminal element, I am of it; while there is a soul in prison, I am not free."

The verdict was as expected. Under the circumstances, there was no other verdict possible. The jury found him guilty of sedition, and the judge sentenced him to ten years in the penitentiary.

Yet even in the announcing of the sentence the judge had nothing but gentle words for the gentleness that was Eugene Debs.

VII

WHEN Debs was incarcerated among a thousand thieves, he brought them the vision of a possible heaven on earth. He worked as an attendant at the prison hospital, and many a stricken prisoner had occasion to thank heaven that the maladjustments of society had sent this holy man to the penitentiary.

A prisoner at Atlanta, a prisoner in the world. "It sometimes seems to me," remarked one of his friends, "that the whole world is a prison, and that men like Debs, who deserve a much better fate than to be born into our midst, are nevertheless sent here to soften the bitterness and to lighten the loads of the rest of us, his fellow convicts in the prison-house of life."

He was released from the prison at Atlanta after a term of three years— and from "the prison-house of life" only a few years later. Just before he died he motioned for a pencil and paper—for he was no longer able to speak. And with the last flicker of strength that remained in his fingers, he traced upon the paper the words of Henley that were his lifelong creed:

> *It matters not how strait the gate,*
>   *How charged with punishments the scroll,*
> *I am the master of my fate,*
>   *I am the captain of my soul.*

IMPORTANT DATES IN THE LIFE OF
EUGENE VICTOR DEBS

1855—Born, Terre Haute, Indiana.

1871—Became locomotive fireman on Indianapolis Railroad.

1875—Joined Brotherhood of Locomotive Firemen.

1880—Elected secretary and treasurer of Brotherhood.

1885—Served as member of Indiana legislature.

1893—Organized and became president of the American Railway Union.

1894—Led winning strike of union against Great Northern Railway.

Led losing strike of union against Pullman Company. Imprisoned for his part in strike.

1900, 1904, 1908, 1912, 1920—Socialist candidate for presidency of United States.

1917—Arrested for pacifist speech. Sentenced to prison term of ten years.

1920—Pardoned after three years.

1926—Died, Elmhurst, Illinois.

Woodrow Wilson

[1856-1924]

ELECTION night, November 7, 1916. The tide had turned against Wilson, who was running for the second term. The East and the Middle West were rapidly drifting toward Charles Evans Hughes, the presidential candidate on the Republican ticket. At nine-thirty the *New York World,* Wilson's strongest newspaper supporter, conceded the election of Hughes. Wilson was resting in his New Jersey retreat at Shadow Lawn. At midnight his secretary, Joseph P. Tumulty, called him on the phone. "I'm sorry, Mr. President. It seems we're licked."

"Thank God!" was Wilson's reply.

The next morning, as he was shaving himself, his daughter Margaret tapped on the door of the bathroom. "Father, there's an extra edition of the *New York Times.* The West has swung in your favor. You've won the election!"

"Go tell it to the marines," retorted Wilson as he went on with his shaving.

Wilson dreaded the prospect of a second term in the White House. For it meant that he must lead his country into war. And he hated war with a hatred as intense as ever burned in the hearts of the ancient prophets. Both by training and temperament he was attuned to a life of constructive peace. He was a Celt, a visionary, a poet, a weaver of words, a dreamer of dreams. And a lover of his kind. He believed tenaciously in the might of right as against the right of might. As a child he had seen the devastation of the Civil War, and as a young man he had witnessed the degradation of its aftermath. He knew that when a country plunges into war it endangers the life not only of its body but of its soul. "Once lead the American people into war," he had remarked to Frank I. Cobb, editorial writer of the *New York World,* "and they will forget there was ever such a thing as tolerance. To fight, you must be brutal and ruthless. The spirit of ruthless brutality will enter into the very fiber of our national life . . ."

And so it was with a heavy heart that he allowed himself to be drafted into the campaign for the second term. "He kept us out of war" was the motto of his campaign managers. And, God willing, he *would* keep his country out of war. But he knew that he hoped against hope. In the avalanche of destruction let loose by the German military machine it was beyond the power of any man to keep America out of the war.

II

THOMAS WOODROW WILSON—he called himself "Tommy" until his senior year at Princeton—was a quiet child who preferred fairy tales to fights. When the soldiers paraded through the streets, he sat alone and aloof. He had a frail body and a strong mind. And a temper. He bossed his parents, and they in turn babied him. "Poor little Tommy is so delicate, we mustn't hurt his feelings." Flaxen-haired, freckled, with a rebellious stomach and bespectacled eyes, he was "predestined"—as his father jestingly remarked—to mental rather than to physical gymnastics. In his barn loft he organized a juvenile baseball nine, "the Lightfoots." He was not, however, their captain or their manager, but their "parliamentary leader." He taught them how to conduct their meetings in accordance with Roberts's *Rules of Order.* "Every one of the little chaps," Wilson recalled many years later, "knew perfectly well just what the previous question was, and that only two amendments to a resolution could be offered, which should be voted upon in the reverse order."

From earliest childhood he was a parliamentarian—and a disciplinarian. He was descended on both sides from a Scotch-Irish ancestry of printers and preachers. The love of, and the respect for, the Word was in his blood. It was not until his ninth year that he learned to read and to write —his parents wanted to shield him as long as possible from the hardships of a routine education. But he learned rapidly and he read voraciously. Night after night the light in his bedroom was on until long after nine, the prescribed bedtime hour for Tommy. But his parents never punished him. "Reading is the only dissipation I'm willing to allow him," said his father, the Reverend Doctor Joseph Wilson.

His father encouraged him in his reading—and in his writing. Both of them had a passion for the precise word. They delighted in verbal fencing. "You must wield the English language," Dr. Wilson advised him again and again, "into a flaming sword." Once, writes Newton D. Baker, Wilson took into his father's study an essay upon which he had spent much time and labor. "Dr. Wilson read the essay very slowly and then turned to his son. 'Exactly what did you intend to say in this?' The boy explained. 'Then why not say it?' And without further words, Dr. Wilson tore up the manuscript and let it flutter into the wastebasket."

But if the father was critical of the son, the son was equally critical of the father. He listened to Dr. Wilson's sermons with a severe—though proud—attention. And often after the sermon was over he pointed out how his father might have improved a passage by the insertion of a different phrase, a more picturesque figure, a word with a more resonant sound.

Like his father, Tommy was eager to become an eloquent speaker. Often on weekdays he would go into the church and "deliver a sermon" to the empty walls. On a midsummer afternoon, as he walked home from one of these "sermons," he was surprised to see the Negroes on the streets bowing to him obsequiously as he passed by them. Finally, his curiosity getting the better of his shyness, he asked one of the Negroes to explain the reason for their sudden outburst of reverence toward him. "We bow to you, Marse Wilson," replied the awed Negro, " 'cause you'se a great sup'rnatural preacher. We peeked in t'rough de window an' we seen you admonishin' de sperrits!"

III

BORN (December 28, 1856) in Virginia, Wilson was brought up in Georgia, whither his father had moved when Wilson was a year old. His training, therefore, was Southern. He was able at first hand to witness the bitterness of a defeat in war. He saw the trail of ashes left by Sherman's march to the sea. He spoke to rebel veterans, sullen, defiant men who, to use their own expression, were "conquered but unrepentant." He grew up with an overwhelming ambition—to help create a world without conquest or mastery or slavery or hate. And he trained his tongue and his pen to that end. His one hero was Lincoln. "When I remembered Lincoln and thought of all my greater material advantages . . . I believed I would be a poor creature indeed if, even without genius, I was not able to do some constructive work for the land that bore me and that I so loved."

"Even without genius." These words bothered him. Would he have the intellect necessary for the constructive work his country so desperately needed? In school he was mediocre—"neither good enough for distinction nor bad enough for censure." In September 1873 he entered Davidson College, and the following spring he returned home—a victim of physical and mental indigestion.

He retired to his room—his father was now pastor of the Presbyterian Church in Wilmington, North Carolina—and buried himself in his books. Especially books on history, philosophy, religion, and the science of government. He was in search of the Golden Grail of intellectual conviction. And one morning he discovered it. He had been sitting up until the small hours, "his elbows on his knees and his nose in a book on Gladstone," when the certainty he had been seeking flashed suddenly upon him. "Father," he cried as he burst into Dr. Wilson's study, "I have found it!"

"Found what?"

"The fact that I have a mind. A mind that can think and create."

His father blew a cloud of smoke from his pipe. "In that case, son, you had better go to Princeton." His own alma mater, Princeton was to Dr.

Wilson the one institution that could transform his son's intellectual yearning into practical achievement. His boy, he felt even at that time, was destined for something great.

And Wilson, too, shared this feeling. "Tommy," recalls a classmate, "seemed to have an uncanny sense that he was a man of destiny . . . He was always preparing himself, always looking forward to the time when he might be called to high service. When he walked alone it was, as he explained, to have opportunity for calm reflection." In the words of another classmate, "Tommy Wilson in his undergraduate days displayed a passion for three things—Gladstone, Government, and God."

He loved society—especially the society of those who preferred mental to physical games. "The play of the mind was as exhilarating to him as the play of the body is to athletes." He joined the college debating club, where he amazed the other students with the facile dexterity of his phrases. "He tossed them about like colored balls—and he never missed the mark."

True to his Calvinistic training, however, Wilson debated not to dazzle but to convince. On one occasion he was selected by lot to speak in favor of the protective tariff. He flatly refused to do this. "It is my principle to uphold only that which I believe."

His classmates derided and at the same time admired his stubborn honesty. "Tommy is different, but he is a jolly good mixer for all that." He took part in many of the leading college activities. He sang in the Glee Club, he edited the *Princetonian,* he joined the Athletic Association (as an adviser, not as a competitor), and he managed the varsity baseball team. And above all he "practiced forever" at the most zestful game of them all—the exciting game of making friends. Princeton, as his father had anticipated, played no little part in completing Tommy Wilson's education.

IV

WOODROW WILSON—he had now dropped the "Tommy" from his name—was determined to be "someone" in the public life of the nation. At Princeton, whenever he met a tough opponent in an argument, he jestingly remarked: "I'll thresh it out with you when I meet you in the United States Senate." And now, as a preliminary step toward the Senate, he decided upon a legal career. A year's study at the University of Virginia Law School—and once more, as at Davidson College, he was obliged to leave his course uncompleted. An attack of the same old trouble, indigestion.

He returned home—and went on with his legal studies in private. Failure never bothered Wilson. He merely cast it off like an old garment. Within two years he passed the bar and opened a law office in Atlanta.

Business was slack, and one day Wilson went on a picnic. When the company arrived at the grounds, Wilson got lost—and with him, Ellie Lou, the pretty and piquant young daughter of the Reverend Samuel Edward Axson. Lunch time, and everybody "hungry as a bear." Where in the world is Woodrow?

"I know," piped one of the children. "He's over there cutting a heart on a beech tree."

Shortly after the picnic their engagement was announced. "Woodrow Wilson," confided Ellie Lou to her brother, "is the greatest man in the world—and the best."

But the "greatest man and the best" couldn't make a go of the law. He had a disconcerting way of preferring justice to legality—a fatal error for a lawyer whose business it was to win cases and not to reform the world. "Your talents," Ellie Lou advised him, "are meant for the classroom and not for the courts."

And so he decided to prepare himself for an academic life. "There are more roads than one to a career of public service." He entered the Graduate School at Johns Hopkins and won his doctorate with a thesis on Congressional Government.

He married Ellie Lou and accepted an offer to teach at Bryn Mawr—a newly opened college for "masculine women." Wilson was unhappy at Bryn Mawr. He preferred to associate with feminine women. And his students preferred to associate with masculine men. They showed little respect for their young professor who instead of an athletic body had developed an athletic mind. Wilson was glad to be relieved of his duties at Bryn Mawr when he received an offer to teach at Wesleyan University (in Middletown, Connecticut).

Wilson understood men, and men understood Wilson. They disregarded his awkwardness, his short body stilted upon his long legs, his big ears, his northern Irish "horse face," his jutting jaw, and his large and sensuous mouth. They were interested mainly in the golden nuggets of wisdom that came tumbling out of that brave and homely mouth. And they forgave him for his inability to play football. For he had such an uncanny ability to devise winning formations for the players. Though never a member of a varsity team, he was appointed assistant football coach—and directed the Wesleyan team to a championship.

He acquired a national reputation as a teacher. In the spring of 1890, Princeton invited him to return as professor of political science. Wilson was elated. "If I cannot *lead* men, I can at least *teach* them to lead."

V

HIS CAREER AT PRINCETON is the story of an initial success and of a subsequent failure—a failure, however, which led to a greater success. Such was the destiny of Wilson. He was a man who never submitted to defeat. Even at the end of his life, as we shall see, it was not Wilson that failed. It was the world that failed Wilson.

But to return to Princeton. When Professor Wilson arrived at this "delightfully aristocratic" institution he set out to transform it into a *devotedly democratic* institution. And the students, with the exception of a handful of silver-plated snobs, responded with the enthusiasm of youngsters invited to new intellectual adventures. For several years in succession the senior class voted him the most popular member of the faculty. They listened to him with something akin to adoration when, in October 1896, Princeton College was formally reborn into Princeton University and "Godfather Wilson" was called upon to deliver the christening address. "The business of the world," he declared on that occasion, "is not individual success, but its own betterment, strengthening, and growth in spiritual insight." A new note in American education. A saner and humaner interpretation of the American credo.

And this note he repeated six years later when he was elected president of Princeton. "We must deal with the spirits of men, not with their fortunes." No longer would Princeton be an adolescent "country club." From now on it would become an experimental laboratory in the fine art of democratic living. He raised and stiffened the academic requirements, with the result that over a hundred "gentlemen loafers" were expelled for failure in their studies.

And then, while the fathers of these discredited youngsters were sharpening their axes, Wilson threw another bombshell into the academic sluggishness of the college campus. He proposed to abolish the aristocratic collegiate societies, with their exclusive eating halls and their luxurious clubhouses. In their place he outlined a group of democratic living quarters within a Gothic quadrangle—to be known as the "quad" system— eating commons and sleeping commons in which all the students were to be leveled up from social distinctions to simple devotions.

Wilson's bombshell exploded. The college world was in an uproar. "What—must a gentleman eat with a mucker?"

Wilson took up the fight for the muckers—and lost. The faculty refused to adopt his plan for the democratization of Princeton. But the loss of this battle led him to the winning of a far greater battle—the democratization of America. A number of political idealists had been following his fight. And as they watched this Scotch-Irish professor with the fearless heart and the peerless tongue, they saw in him the makings of a superior statesman. They offered him the candidacy for the governorship of New Jersey. He accepted the offer (1910) and won the election.

VI

THE POLITICAL IDEALISTS of New Jersey had brought about his election. And now the political bosses of New Jersey hoped to bring about his submission. "Sure, he promised to fight political graft. But we know them teacher birds. Lots of gab and no go." What was their surprise to find that the academic Dr. Wilson possessed not only "go" but a vigorous boot! One of his first acts as governor-elect was to denounce Boss Jim Smith of New Jersey, who was running for the United States Senate. "You can't do this to *me,* Mr. Wilson!" But Mr. Wilson went right ahead and kicked Jim Smith out of his senatorial dreams. The professional ward heelers throughout the country rubbed their eyes in amazement. Here was a new phenomenon under the sun—a politician who kept his word! But the political idealists saw themselves a step nearer to the fulfillment of their vision. Here was a man to whom the word Democracy was not merely a campaign slogan but a religious creed. Presidential timber this— a leader who was upright, clean, and unafraid.

And ambitious. Fortunately for the progress of America, Woodrow Wilson was selfish enough to crave for the glory as well as for the responsibility of leadership. His was not the humility of the saints, but the pride of the prophets. In order to be a great statesman, he knew that he must be a clever politician.

It was this double quality of adroit politics and solid statesmanship that won him the election to the presidency in 1912. And it was this double quality that enabled him to sway the sentiment of the Congress into the enactment of several laws designed to help the weak against the strong. He carried on from where Jackson and Lincoln and Theodore Roosevelt had left off. He reduced the tariff, enacted a graduated income-tax law based upon the principle "from each according to his ability to pay," dispersed the concentrated power of the banking interests into twelve federal units, imposed a legal curb upon the expansion of selfish corporations and unlawful monopolies, and strengthened the position of labor by legalizing trade unions and boycotts and picketing and by declaring that injunctions could not be issued against strikers except to prevent deliberate injury to property. Wilson was not a radical but a liberal. "We shall restore, not destroy," he had proclaimed in his inaugural. He was willing to leave the upperdog with his reasonable hunk of meat provided the underdog got his juicy bone. But it *must* be juicy, he insisted, and nourishing enough to sustain life and hope and the energy to emerge from the bottom of the heap. "Such is our national way of life."

His international, like his national, policy was based upon the principle of competitive fair play. In this principle of fair play he saw merely the modern application of the Golden Rule. He looked with approval upon every honest government that respected the rights and the opinions of the governed. He recognized the republic of Sun Yat-sen in China and he refused to recognize the dictatorship of Huerta in Mexico. The happiness of the people, he maintained, is of greater importance than the avarice of its rulers. Or of its investors. He put a drastic check upon the tendency to protect the foreign investments of American capitalists with the lives of American soldiers. It was his desire to abolish two false doctrines that stood in the way of human progress—the divine right of capital to rule the land, and the divine right of gunpowder to rule the world.

He was the happy leader of a peaceful nation. And then, in 1914, there came a double blow to him. His wife died, and Europe exploded into war. From that time on there was no happiness or peace for Wilson.

From the firing of the first gun he knew that unless the war came to a speedy end America would be dragged into it. The earth had grown too small for isolationism. The needs of humanity had become too complex, the exchange of world commerce too interdependent, the activity of every individual too closely related to the activity of every other individual, for any one country to remain unscathed when the other countries had been caught in a conflagration. When he accepted the burden of a second term, he did it as an unwilling soldier drafted into a hateful war. But the job had to be done. Perhaps, if he remained at the helm, he might make this a war to end war. A holy cause to die in—a noble vision for a man of peace.

When, on April 2, 1917, Wilson asked Congress to declare war, it was not Wilson nor the American Government nor the American people that made the decision. It was the ruthlessness of the German military machine. Or, if you will, the inexorable course of human destiny.

Wilson was a tragic figure on that gray spring morning in Washington. A prophet turned warrior. Like the prophets of old, he had prayed to God that the burden of the fatal message might never be his to proclaim. For a time he thought of resigning from the presidency. But a soldier must never desert.

As he rode back to the White House on that tragic day, Pennsylvania Avenue was lined with cheering crowds. But there was no cheer in the President's heart. "How strange to applaud a message of war," he remarked. "A message of death for our young men."

VII

THE ALLIES WON THE WAR and Wilson launched his Fourteen Points—a brave argosy of peace in a tempest of vindictive and selfish hatreds. Open covenants openly arrived at . . . an end to secret diplomacy . . . absolute freedom of the seas . . . free trade among equal races . . . reduction of armaments . . . the right of all countries to govern themselves . . . a league of nations to make war forever a thing of the past. And the blind leaders of men, both here and abroad, took these Fourteen Points and tore them up and turned them into the confetti of a rancorous victory parade. They cheered Wilson to the echo and rejected his dream. They corrupted his peace without victory into victory without peace. The cynical politicians of the day made two fatal mistakes. They were too harsh and too lenient—too harsh to the German people, too lenient to their military machine. They shut Germany off from the means of making an honest living, and they allowed her to develop the means of subsisting through dishonest force. The Treaty of Versailles was one of the most tragic paradoxes in history. It left the enemy both with the food for its venom and with the instrument for its sting.

Wilson foresaw this, and he knew that the scrapping of the Fourteen Points was but the prelude to another war. The world had failed him. The masters of the nations had betrayed his hopes—the hopes of their own people. His New Testament of international good will was too splendid for the spiritual astigmatism of 1919. "We are ruled," gibed Clemenceau with cynical candor, "by our dead."

But Wilson knew that his great vision would be judged by the living. And Wilson was right. At the end of another devastating war, humanity had learned its lesson. The historic year 1945 saw the laying of the cornerstone for the building of his utopian dream—the United Nations of the World.

IMPORTANT DATES IN THE LIFE OF
WOODROW WILSON

1856—Born, Staunton, Virginia.

1879—Graduated from Princeton.

1886—Received degree of Doctor of Philosophy from Johns Hopkins University.

1888—Appointed professor of history and politics at Wesleyan University.

1890–1910—Served first as professor of political jurisprudence and then as president of Princeton University.

1910—Elected governor of New Jersey.

1912—Elected the twenty-eighth President of the United States.

1912–16—Engineered the Federal Reserve Act, the Federal Trade Commission, and the Clayton Act (against the abuses of large monopolies).

1916—Re-elected to the presidency.

1917—Delivered message to Congress for declaration of war against Germany.

1918—Drew up the Fourteen Points and went to the Paris Peace Conference.

1919—Returned and laid before Congress the Versailles Treaty. Toured the country in behalf of the "League of Nations Covenant." Brokenhearted at the failure of his country to accept this covenant.

1924—Died, Washington, D. C.

Theodore Roosevelt
[1858-1919]

THERE were rivulets of many diverse races that emptied into the blood stream of his nationality. Some of it flowed from the businesslike stubbornness of the Dutch mingled with the freedom-loving impetuosity of the French Huguenots and the fearless defiance of the Protestants in the Rhineland. And some of it was the blood of the fighting Scotch Highlanders and of the fierce Irishmen of Ulster who had resisted the British kings. Here, too, was the spirit of the Welsh Quakers who had died by the thousands for the cause of free worship, and of the Quakers of Pennsylvania who had given the American Indian a "square deal" among his fellow men. All of it was the blood of rebels, of the *protesters* of the human race.

In his immediate background there was a conflict in the fusion. His earliest years were passed in the turmoil of the Civil War. His father was a Northerner whose heart was in the Union; his mother came from a prominent social family in Georgia. And the child, who upon his father's lap had acquired an aversion against the South, received a scolding at his mother's knee when he asked in his prayers for a blessing upon the North.

His undersized body was in conflict with his rugged mind. His eyes were poor, his speech was defective, and his chest was racked with asthma. He was too sickly to go to school. And throughout his life, in memory of his own suffering and weakness, he sympathized with all human weakness and suffering.

But at the same time he had grown to possess an exaggerated and almost fanatical worship of physical strength. "Make your own body, Ted," his father had urged him. And from the first the child had determined to become a self-made man—a daring knight of the New World. He lifted weights, and boxed, and chinned the bar. He spent every clear day of his boyhood in the open air, toughening his muscles and strengthening his lungs and taking deep draughts of the energy of life. And as he grew older he traveled with his father over forest trails and mountain roads and sailed the oceans and fished and hunted and built up a powerful body to shelter a vigorous mind.

When he entered Harvard at eighteen he was physically well equipped for life. "He was a little fellow five foot and a half high." But his small stature fooled none of his friends. A package of dynamite is also small.

II

At HARVARD "Mr. Roosevelt of Oyster Bay" drove a team and dogcart—the only one of its kind in the college—spent his money freely, and belonged to the most exclusive of the clubs. He had entered upon his education with the knowledge that he would never be forced to earn his living. In the gentleman's fashion of the day, he could choose the career that most interested him, or—if he preferred—no career at all. Too dynamic for a life of idleness, he thought for a time of becoming a naturalist adventurer like Humboldt or Darwin. In his senior year at Harvard he courted a young lady with such exuberant accounts of his "snakes and reptiles," which he kept in his college rooms, that he "frightened her out of her wits."

But before long he turned his imagination from the jungles of the lions to the labyrinths of the law. Here, too, was ground for exciting adventure. Yet not exciting enough for his superabundant energy. What to do? For do something he *must*. This young man who had inherited a life of ease had developed a hunger for work—the hardest sort of work. The paradox could be resolved only through the choice of the right career.

He married his fiancée and traveled with her over the continent of Europe. And when he returned home a new horizon had opened up in his reflections. The old childhood dream of knighthood in shining armor had taken on a sublimated form. There were intellectual as well as physical crusades to fight. Economic wrongs to be righted. Social injustices to be assailed. In this industrial struggle between the rich and the poor, each of the two sides blinded by a passionate self-interest to survive, was there not a crying need for a vigorous and cultured and disinterested Sir Galahad to insist upon a spirit of fair play? He, Theodore Roosevelt, would try to be this modern Sir Galahad. In the chaotic wilderness of politics he would search for the Holy Grail.

When he told his friends what he had in mind they were aghast. "Politics is a dirty business for ward heelers and machine bosses. Gentlemen are not welcome." But Roosevelt persisted with a logical stubbornness. Why should a gentleman shrink from the responsibilities of government? "If we were at war with a foreign enemy, I wouldn't for a moment think of hiring somebody else to do the shooting for me. Well, I intend to do my own shooting in the dirty war of politics. In this way, perhaps, I may be able to clean up some of the dirt."

He decided to start the cleaning in the boss-ridden saloons of his own city. "I am going to try to help the cause of better government right here in New York."

III

THEODORE ROOSEVELT entered the twenty-first district Republican Club of New York. It was the New York of Tammany Hall and of the Tweed Ring. The party bosses took one look at the "rich young man with an eyeglass, an evening dress, and a Harvard accent" and were convulsed with laughter. "A dude, the way he combed his hair, the way he talked, the *whole thing!*"

But Roosevelt took his seat at their councils and immediately commanded their respect. He let it be known that he intended to judge them not as freaks but as human beings, and that he expected the same treatment from them.

Soon the party bosses were spellbound by his energy and his fight. They forgot his "r-a-w-t-h-e-r" and placed him in nomination for the New York Assembly. Canvassing for votes among the saloonkeepers, he met one burly fellow who complained of the liquor taxes. "I hope you will do something for us when you get up to Albany, Mr. Roosevelt."

"Why should I?" replied the young candidate. "Your taxes aren't high enough by a long shot."

He won the election. The newsmen and the public were amused at the new legislator. "The exquisite Mr. Roosevelt of New York, a blond young man with English side whiskers and a Dundreary drawl in his speech, made his maiden effort as an orator . . ."

Roosevelt was fast learning things. The world was his oyster. And when he opened it he found it rotten. The moral concepts on which he had been raised, he was now told, were unseasonable. The *seasoned* politicians advised him that "the whole duty of a man consists in making the best of himself . . . but it is not part of his business to join with others in trying to make things better for the many by curbing the abnormal and excessive development of the few."

And now the press and the public in Albany were little short of amazed to find that "the exquisite Mr. Roosevelt" had become a roaring lion. He inspected the slums and introduced a bill to improve the conditions of the sweatshop workers in the crowded tenement houses. He led an investigation into the corrupt activities of a high judiciary officer. He lunged out against the attempts of the New York Elevated Railway to bribe the legislature for a reduction of its taxes. He exposed the venality of the big business corporations in the state. He insisted upon carrying "private morality into public office"—a thing almost unheard of in the political circles of the day.

And then suddenly a twofold blow in his domestic life halted him in his fight for "better government." Within twenty-four hours he lost his wife and his mother. The fighter was laid low. He bought a cattle ranch in the Dakotas as far from civilization as possible and left the city of New York for the wild lands in silence. His friends of the twenty-first political district understood and let him go. "You couldn't talk to him about it. You could see at once that it was a grief too deep . . . There was a sadness about his face that he never had before . . . He didn't want anybody to sympathize with him."

Here in the "Bad Lands" of Dakota, a country of elemental passions and elemental men, he began his emotional reconstruction. He drove his cattle and foregathered with sheriffs and helped keep the peace with his guns. Two years of hard adventure, and the realization that justice was only as strong as the weapons employed to enforce it. And then he turned East with the supreme conviction that the "guts" of the individual determined the goal of society.

He came back to the metropolis to carry on his fight. From now on there was no stopping him. The people knew him for a man of destiny.

IV

HE HAD ENTERED upon the political scene like a Don Quixote tilting at windmills. And he had changed the course of the wind. But the wishful politicians still persisted in the illusion that he was a knight in cardboard. They recommended him for an appointment to the Civil Service Commission—and they were further relieved when the reform mayor of New York appointed him police commissioner of the city. Here, away from the turmoil of elective office—they believed—he would paddle in the duckpond of petty reform and sink finally into the obscurity of a contented life.

They didn't know their man. He plunged into his work with a crusading fervor. He revitalized the police force. He scraped it of corruption and scoured it as clean as the shiny brass buttons upon the policemen's uniforms. He walked along the streets with a broom to sweep the taverns of their gunmen. "Teddy the Scorcher" had become the hero of New York. Before his term was ended there was no crooked policeman in New York and no figure in America more colorful than Commissioner Roosevelt.

The Republicans applauded him for the prestige he gave them and fearfully watched for his next step.

This step was from the "duckpond" to the sea. President McKinley had appointed him Assistant Secretary of the Navy—and immediately his voice was heard above the broadside of the navy's guns. When asked what we should do if we were ever attacked, he shouted: "Build a battleship in every creek!" Now at last the young fighter had come into his own. His eye fairly glistened with the spray of the sea.

He asked Congress for an appropriation of five hundred thousand dollars for ammunition. And a few months later he asked for an additional eight hundred thousand dollars. Congress wanted to know what had happened to the first sum. "Spent it on target practice," he replied. He was asked what he would do with the second sum. "Spend it the same way." He got his money.

And then once more the pent-up current of his energy burst forth in all its momentum. He went out to challenge the fates. America had declared war on Spain. The place for a knight was on the battlefield, not in the armchair. Roosevelt tossed aside his maps and his conference notes, collected a volunteer company of "Rough Riders," and went on the hunt for Spaniards in the swamps and the hills of Cuba. Always he believed not only in *denouncing* evil but in personally *fighting* against it.

It was a regiment of tough soldiers that he collected for his fight. For he loved to tame the coarsest fiber with the steady hand of his discipline. Amid a hailstorm of bullets he swung into the saddle—and the impetus of the charge carried him forward through the fighting and the peace and straight into the governorship of New York. His military exploits had been worth a hundred campaign speeches. With some of his shrewd good shooting he had set on fire the imagination of America.

And the bitter feelings of the politicians. They just couldn't cope with the unorthodox erratic who quoted Browning and busted broncos. An Andrew Jackson who wrote libraries of learned books. No such savage genius had ever joined Boss Platt's Republican party in all the history of its stormy campaigns. They made one final effort to put this "strange animal with the mind of a scholar and the heart of a lion" back into his cage. When his term as governor had expired they solicitously prepared a burial for him in the graveyard of American politics. McKinley was up before the Republican Convention for renomination as the party standard-bearer for the new term. And the practical members of the party had hit upon the simple idea of nominating Theodore Roosevelt for the vice-presidency. "Four years of this honorable and dignified seclusion will deprive him of the public ear and enable us to shelve him forever."

Yet Mark Hanna, the manager of the Republican campaign, threw up his hands in a tremble when the big vote for Roosevelt was counted on the night of the election. "I wonder whether any of you realize that there's only one life between this madman and the White House?" And almost before he could bring his hands down again, the "one life" was removed by an anarchist's bullet, and the "madman" reigned.

V

THROUGH the labyrinthine course of illogic and a path bristling with excitement, Roosevelt had risen from a gentleman's sinecure at Harvard to the presidency of the United States. Lady Luck had dealt him the ace cards in the deck of destiny. And now he was the ruler of all the people—those who had been consistently handed the joker and the deuce, as well as those who had been dishonestly shuffling the cards with the aces up their sleeves. Out in the "Bad Lands" of Dakota, Roosevelt had kept a gun by him to see that everybody got a square deal. And here in the White House he would use all the available machinery of the government to the same end. In the game of national industry as played between the businessman and the worker, the public and the private interests, the farmer, the banker, and the middleman, and in the game of international trade as played between the various countries of the world, "there shall be no crookedness in the dealing."

That was his commandment. And he struck his vigorous hand upon his desk and the altar and the lectern in the classroom. And he showed his "toothful" smile of triumph wherever he went, to hearten and to convince the people that his commandment would be obeyed.

He had become the gallant crusader for the Square Deal. "There can be no genuine feeling of patriotism of the kind that makes all men willing and eager to die for the land, unless there has been some measure of success in making the land worth living in for all alike." And the soldier of the Spanish war who himself had been ready to die now turned his deadly fire upon all the combinations of the private monopolists who made it difficult for their fellow Americans to live. He was determined to "bust" the giant "business trusts" that were flourishing with fixed prices and fancy profits in the restraint of all competitive trade. He established an Interstate Commerce Commission which checked the "selfish concentration" of the great railroads. He broke strikes that threatened the health and the safety of the general public. He invited the leader of the Negro race to dine with him in the White House. He laid plans to conserve the natural resources of the country—not only against the ravages of the weather but also against the rapacity of the "despoilers of the earth for their private gain."

And he told his people that he was building a bigger and better and happier nation, to the end that it might lead the way in the building of a bigger and better and happier world. "For such is the destiny of every great nation." He denounced the isolationists who were urging their countrymen to remain "cooped up" within their own little corner of the stage and to shut their eyes to the other actors and actions of the world's universal, interdependent drama. "We are not, and cannot, and never will be one of those nations that can progress from century to century doing little and suffering little, standing aside from the great world currents."

We must follow—he insisted—a vigorous and fearless foreign policy. No desire for peace should lower our sword when the stakes are decency and justice. He squared his shoulders to meet the taunts that the pacifists were hurling against him—"jingo, blusterer, warmonger." Even the Knights of the Holy Grail could never have kept the vows of Christ, save only by a handiness with the spear and a willingness to use the sword. He frankly confessed his "love for the blue steel unsheathed in the righteous cause." In 1902 the Monroe Doctrine had been put to the test. Kaiser Wilhelm had entered a financial claim against the government of Venezuela. And a German squadron had actually set sail to blockade the Venezuelan coast. Roosevelt's eyes narrowed. He was convinced that the German squadron was in American seas not merely to collect money. He believed that the Kaiser intended to take permanent possession of the seacoast of Venezuela and to make it a fortified jumping-off place for future aggression. And so Roosevelt requested the Reich to submit her financial claims to arbitration and to withdraw her battle fleet. With typical Prussian arrogance, the Reich refused his request. Whereupon Roosevelt assembled the United States fleet under Admiral Dewey and gave him orders to be ready to shoot. Then he sent the Kaiser an ultimatum. "Either you withdraw from Venezuela, or we open fire." The Kaiser withdrew. But Roosevelt, with a rare intuition into the Prussian mind, had won the respect of Kaiser Wilhelm. The German aggressor had at last met a man who could outguess him and outforce him.

Roosevelt was unafraid. He collected his fleet and sent it on a tour of "friendship" around the world. And as the huge guns flashed at every port and the marines marched through the capitals of many nations, he grimly declared: "This, in my judgment, is the most important service that I have rendered to peace."

His was the "peace of action." The realization had come to him that a canal must be built across the narrow neck of land which joins the two Americas. For—he reasoned—if this country were to be faced with a two-ocean war, "Japan in the Pacific and Germany in the Atlantic, for example," our Pacific and Atlantic fleets would be separated by the entire stretch of the long voyage around South America. Roosevelt selected the Isthmus of Panama as the best site for the canal. When the government of Colombia refused to permit the building of this canal, he encouraged a revolution by the Department of Panama and sent warships to aid the revolutionists. The Republic of Panama was proclaimed, and Roosevelt promptly recognized it.

The country was shocked at the "lack of nicety" in his procedure. But Roosevelt defended his action with honest bluntness. "I had two courses open. I might have taken the matter under advisement and put it before the Senate, in which case we would have had a number of most able speeches on the subject, and they would have been going on now, and the Panama Canal would be in the dim future yet. We would have had a half century of discussion, and then perhaps the Panama Canal," and his eyes flashed. "I preferred that we should have the Panama Canal first and the half century of discussion afterward."

The canal was built. But America felt at peace with the world. She had been lulled by sweet prosperity into an impractical dream, unaware of the importance of her role in the realistic struggle of the nations for existence. Roosevelt's warning was as welcome as a siren that blows in the middle of the night. The people dreamed on.

And when the two terms of his office were finished and he went off hunting in the jungles of Africa, a good many of his fellow Americans sighed with relief and declared, "That's where he belongs."

VI

INTO THE JUNGLES. And out again. Roosevelt was seeking to capture the biggest game of them all—an understanding of himself. To lay low his restlessness and to pluck out of his heart the meaning of the driving energy that would not give him peace.

But this prize eluded him. As he hunted the wild beasts in the African jungle he knew that there were many wild dragons of political injustice still unslain at home. For him there was no peace. He must be President again. He returned home. The ghost of his ambition—ambition not so much for splendor as for service—refused to lie still. But the flesh and the blood of him had bequeathed this ambition to Taft four years ago. The Republican party no longer wanted Roosevelt. Didn't this restless and erratic spirit who dared to gain entrance from another world realize that Theodore Roosevelt had died in March 1909?

But Roosevelt would not stay politically dead. Repudiated by the Republican Convention, he formed his own party of "Progressives" and once more stalked the country, making speeches, hunting votes. In vain. The people brushed him aside. Woodrow Wilson, the Democrat, was chosen chief of the nation. And Theodore Roosevelt once more took up his books and his guns and left America for another journey of exploration. To Brazil. As he paddled up the tropical rivers to their sources—always he was anxious to get at the *source* of things—an attack of jungle fever laid him low. His life of danger was finally threatening to take its toll. For many days he lay under the scorching skies in delirium. Slowly he fought his way back to his feet. Another victory for the happy warrior who refused to go down.

He came home again, and his eyes flashed as of old when he smiled. But he had left his strength behind him.

The old Rough Rider was hard upon his final journey. Suddenly across the seas a million-headed, steel-helmeted German monster swooped down upon Belgium on the way to Paris. The World War had begun!

Roosevelt rose from his bed and looked around for his armor. But the American Government refused to accept his services. There were millions of younger and sturdier crusaders eager to take his place. Among them was Roosevelt's own youngest son, Quentin. A gallant Rough Rider of the air. And one day they brought to the father the brief announcement about his son—"Died in the line of duty."

Good Lord, but this was *life,* this death of millions of Quentins. The father sat quietly on the porch of his home at Oyster Bay. He, too, was ready to be their soul's companion in the Great Adventure. "Only those are fit to live who do not fear to die."

IMPORTANT DATES IN THE LIFE OF
THEODORE ROOSEVELT

1858—Born, New York City.

1880—Graduated from Harvard College.

1881—Elected to the New York State Legislature.

1889—Appointed by President Harrison to the United States Civil Service Commission.

1895—Appointed president of the New York City Board of Police Commissioners.

1897—Appointed by President McKinley as Assistant Secretary of the Navy.

1898—Led the Rough Riders in the Spanish-American War.

1899—Served as governor of New York.

1900—Elected Vice-President of the United States.

1901—Became (upon the assassination of McKinley) the twenty-sixth President of the United States.

1902—Started "crusade of the people against the trusts."
Instituted policy of the "Square Deal."

1903—Sent a cruiser to Panama and secured the land for the Panama Canal.

1904—Re-elected to the presidency.

1905—Negotiated the Peace of Portsmouth to end the Russo-Japanese War.

1907—Sent the United States battle fleet on a cruise around the world.

1908—Called a conference of state governors for the conservation of the national soil and resources.

1912—Ran for the presidency on the Progressive ticket. Defeated.

1919—Died, New York City.

Jane Addams

[1860-1935]

IN 1881, Jane Addams entered the Women's Medical College in Philadelphia. The following year, however, she was obliged to give up
her scientific course. A painful curvature of the spine had laid her
low. The doctor prescribed an extended trip to Europe as a necessary
relaxation after her rigorous work in the laboratory. This trip was
destined to transform a stillborn physician into a successful philosopher.

It was in the slum district of London that the urge first came to her to
devote her life to the practice of social philosophy. One midnight she
was sitting on the top of a sight-seeing omnibus that made its way slowly
through the putrid garbage and the human derelicts of the East End
"lower depths." A huckster's truck had stopped at the curbstone. A rabble
of men and women were crowding around it—tattered rags, haggard
faces, raucous cries—haggling for the handful of vegetables that the huckster was auctioning off. The decayed leftovers of his day's business to
the decayed leftovers of the human family. Lurid haze of the gas lamps,
nauseating odor of death. A cabbage unfit for human consumption was
tossed into the hands of a bidder who held up the "extravagant" sum of
tuppence. The "lucky possessor of the prize" took the cabbage to the
curbstone and began to devour it, filthy and worm-eaten and raw, while
his less fortunate companions held up their hands to bid for the less
expensive remnants. "The final impression," writes Miss Addams, "was
not of ragged, tawdry clothing nor of pinched and sallow faces, but of
myriads of hands, empty, pathetic, nerveless and work-worn, showing
white in the uncertain light of the street, and clutching forward for food
which was already unfit to eat."

Throughout her subsequent stay in London, Jane Addams "went about
the city almost furtively, afraid to look down narrow streets and alleys
lest they disclose again this hideous human need and misery." A new
course in her education had begun. A daughter of the rich, she had beheld

suffering from the top of an omnibus. A sister of the poor, she would climb down from her height in order that she might alleviate some of this suffering. On that midnight tour of London, Jane Addams had joined the "universal fellowship" of mankind.

II

WHEN JANE was four and a half years old she came home one afternoon from her play and found a dark flag hoisted above the gateposts of her front yard. "Why did you put that flag up there?" she asked.

"A great man has died, child. The greatest man in the world."

"What was his name?"

"Abraham Lincoln."

On another occasion, when her father was sad and she asked him the reason for it, he told her that Joseph Mazzini, an ardent lover of mankind, had just died. Years later, when she wrote of her childhood, Jane Addams observed: "I was filled with pride that I knew a man who held converse with great minds."

Her Quaker father was all in all to her—her mother had died when Jane was two years old. He was a remarkable man, this state senator and prosperous miller of Cedarville, Illinois. Scrupulously honest himself, he had the utmost faith in the honesty of his neighbors. He never locked the front door of his house. Jane was sorry she had been born a girl. She was so anxious to grow up to be a great man, just like her father. She tried in every way to imitate him—even to the extent of rubbing the crushed grain in the mill in order that she might acquire his flattened miller's thumb. If ever she told him a falsehood, she couldn't go to sleep at night until she slipped out of her room and went down the dark stairway "to confess at his bedside."

He was so good and big, and she was so naughty and small. "Dear God, why didn't you give him the kind of a child he really deserves?" When strangers came to the Sunday school, she prayed that they wouldn't associate "that handsome man with this homely kid." On the way to church she deliberately walked with her uncle, who looked less distinguished than her father and was therefore more suitable company for her own insignificant little self.

Yet one day her father dissipated this feeling of inferiority on her part. It was on the main street of a neighboring city. She had come there with her uncle to do some shopping—a crooked, homely, shy little thing. Suddenly a tall, distinguished gentleman in a high silk hat stepped out of a bank. "Good Lord," she thought, all a-tremble, "I hope he doesn't recognize me in front of all these swell people!"

But he did. Removing his silk hat and swinging it wide, he made a courtly bow to his daughter. "How do you do, my dear?"

Jane could hardly speak for embarrassment. "Aren't you ashamed of me, Father?" she managed to blurt out.

"Why, you foolish child, I'm proud of you!"

III

So HER FATHER was proud of her! Well, she would try—oh, so very hard!
—to make herself *worthy* of his pride. She read the *Lives of Plutarch*—for
every one of these lives that she could report on he gave her five cents;
and she studied the lives of the signers of the Declaration of Independence
—for every one of *these* lives that she could report on he gave her *ten*
cents. But of all the lives, she believed, her father's was the greatest.
Throughout his legislative career, she tells us, nobody ever offered him
a bribe, "because bad men were instinctively afraid of him."

At seventeen Jane Addams entered Rockford College. And here she
learned to worhip two other heroes besides her father—the Sage of
Concord and the Carpenter of Galilee. So strong was her adoration for
Emerson that "in a state of ecstatic energy" she polished the shoes of one
of his mere disciples who delivered a lecture at the college.

The essays of Emerson introduced her to the service of beauty. The
parables of Jesus converted her to the beauty of service. Every Sunday
morning she read a chapter of the New Testament in the original Greek.
Here was a life to emulate! She would dedicate herself, like her Master,
to "the soothing of the afflicted and the healing of the sick."

But her lesson was not yet fully learned. She wanted to take up a
"superior" profession, to become a doctor, to lend a helping hand from
above. It was not until her sight-seeing tour of the London slum that she
glimpsed the first true vision of her career. The golden words of Emerson,
the Golden Rule of Jesus, pointed to the equal dignity of all the children
of men. Descend from the heights of your vanity and take your place
among your fellows. Enlist as a soldier in the common ranks of sorrow.

Her vision took gradual shape until it became crystallized into a
definite resolve. This happened on a day when she was visiting a bull-
fight at Madrid. The sight of the slaughter and the brutal applause aroused
within her a wave of resentment. Altogether too much of suffering was
due to human cruelty. She must do something to put an end to this
cruelty. At last she had found a concrete job for herself—to build a
"cathedral of humanity," a practical school of moral readjustment.

She had set herself a difficult task—a *terrifying* task. But she went
bravely ahead. "Always do," she said, "what you are afraid to do." And
so, inspired by her vision, she returned to Chicago, eager to undertake
her new work in spite of her fear. The metropolis of the Midwest had
grown from eight thousand in 1844 to one million in 1889. And seven
hundred and fifty thousand of them were foreign-born. Chicago was a
world in miniature—Englishmen, Germans, Jews, Negroes, Russians, Poles,
Irishmen, Italians, Frenchmen, Scandinavians, Bohemians, Swiss—these
were only a few of the many nationalities that had been swept together
by the winds of chance into a single community. Here were the human
factors for the working out of the problem of Practical Democracy. These
immigrants had brought with them the misunderstandings and the prej-

udices of a hundred countries. But they had also brought the hopes and the dreams of those countries. If Jane Addams could teach them to discard their prejudices and to unite their dreams, a new day would dawn in America—a day of justice and beauty and vigor and joy such as the world had never seen.

This, in brief, was her vision. Her life's work was to humanize and harmonize American society, and by the American example to harmonize and humanize the society of the world.

IV

SHE CREATED a new philosophy—the philosophy of social service. What this world needs, she said, is not an "uplift" of the immigrants by the Americans, or of the lower classes by the higher classes, but a mutual interdependence between alien and native and between class and class. The rich and the poor alike, she felt, had much to gain from their contact with one another. The rich were in need of greater sympathies; the poor, of greater comforts.

In order to establish this abstract theory upon a foundation of concrete fact, she rented a small house on Halsted Street—the Chicago desert of industrial sandstorms and material want. She called this little oasis of hers the Hull House, after the name of its architect and former occupant. A pleasant, homelike place, with wide halls, open fireplaces, and a piazza on three sides. She furnished the rooms with "luxurious simplicity"— handsome tables, inviting couches, bookcases and pictures and bric-a-brac she had picked up in Europe—everything, in short, that a wealthy person would want for a private home, and then she threw open the doors and extended a gracious welcome to the public. "All ye that are hungry, come in and eat. All ye that are weary, come in and rest."

At first the foreign population in the surrounding district—"a whirlpool of filthy and rotten tenements, foul stables, dilapidated outhouses, dives, saloons, flies, vermin, and children"—looked with suspicion upon this "strange American woman" who had moved into this "strange swell house" in their midst. What did she want of them with her invitations? They weren't used to this sort of thing from the "better" classes. There must be some trick behind that smile of hers. Best to stay away from that house.

A few daring souls, however, ventured into the house and found, to their astonishment, a human being like themselves. This Lady of Halsted Street was no "slummer" but a friendly neighbor. They spread word about the miracle, and little by little the "visits" to the Hull House be- came more frequent. One day a Greek woman rushed in with a sick baby in her arms. Her husband was away at work. She had no money for medicine or for doctors. Miss Addams secured a doctor and bought the medicine—and the child was saved. On another occasion an Italian bride of fifteen ran away from her husband to the Hull House because he had abused her for having lost her wedding ring. Miss Addams summoned the husband, gave the couple a friendly talk and the price of a new wedding ring, and husband and wife went off happily hand in hand.

Before long the Lady of Halsted Street had become the unofficial counselor of the entire district. "This rich lady is almost as nice as a poor woman." No service in behalf of her neighbors was too humble for her to perform. She not only *superintended* the work in the house, but lent a ready hand—and, what was even more important, a willing heart—in the *doing* of the work. She opened a day nursery for the babies of mothers who worked in the factories. In this nursery she fed and amused and cared for the children at the daily rate of five cents per child. "This, you understand, is no charity. You are paying good money for the service." For the older children she started a kindergarten—also at five cents a day —where they were not only fed and amused, but educated as well.

As for the fathers and the mothers of these children, Miss Addams studied their needs and found that they suffered from a twofold hunger —they were starved materially and aesthetically. And so she provided Hull House with a soup kitchen and an art gallery. And—in spite of the sneers of her wealthy friends at her "Quixotic" ideas—she was not surprised to find that her art gallery was more popular than her soup kitchen. It was not for bread alone that the European refugees had come to America.

V

THE "SUBMERGED TENTH" of Chicago paid Jane Addams the highest honor. They accepted her into their "exclusive" proletarian society. She was one of them, the genuine article, a Good Neighbor.

Slowly the little homestead on Halsted Street grew into a big community center. The idea of the Good Neighbor policy spread to other cities. Similar settlements of International Americanism sprang up throughout the country. Houses of Friendship. Playrooms and workrooms and study rooms—crucibles for the softening of the human heart into a more sympathetic understanding. "If only the various races could understand each other, there would be no need for hatred or war." Jane Addams undertook the "daring" project of interpreting the races to one another. And this led to an amusing but highly satisfactory incident. One evening the Irish women invited the Italian women to a reception. "But the Italian women," writes Miss Addams, "were almost Oriental in their habits. They stayed at home and sent their husbands . . . The Social Extension Committee of the Irish women entered the drawing room to find it occupied by rows of Italian workingmen. They were quite ready to be 'socially extended,' but plainly puzzled as to what it was all about." Fortunately the Italian men had a lively sense of humor. They proceeded to take the place of their wives in the entertainment of their Irish hostesses. "Untiring pairs of them danced the tarantella, their fascinating national dance, they sang Neapolitan songs, one of them performed some of those wonderful sleight-of-hand tricks . . . and all of them politely ate the 'quaint' Irish refreshments." The entertainment was a huge success. The Irish and the Italians were mutually delighted to find that "these strangers are just like other people." They thanked Miss Addams for having "cured" them of their "sick prejudices" against one another.

Jane Addams was the American pioneer in melting the differences of a hundred nations into a single democratic ideal. And now that the foundations of her "dream-cathedral of interracial understanding" had been laid, she went on to the next stage of her building. She wanted to see a happier race of children and a more peaceful race of men. And so she began to work for the abolition of child labor and for the establishment of universal peace.

In the 1890s child labor was one of the blots upon our civilization. The imposing structure of American prosperity had been grounded partially upon the backs of little children. In the industrial centers the children were overworked and underpaid to an appalling degree. Seven-year-olds were in some instances driven fourteen hours a day at four cents an hour. In the needle trades the children were often set to work at the age of four or five, pulling out the basting threads from the garments which their parents were sewing. Many children were maimed and not a few killed by the machines at which they were compelled to work before they were old enough or strong enough to handle them.

Jane Addams had a motherly instinct for children. She made their cause her own cause. In spite of her numerous other duties, she undertook a searching investigation into the problems of child labor. Indeed, she became America's foremost authority on the subject. Calling to her standard the various women's and workers' organizations in Illinois, she engineered the enactment of a state law (1903) forbidding "the employment of children under sixteen years before seven in the morning or after seven at night, and the employment of children under fourteen after six at night." This "Jane Addams Measure" was a good beginning in the right direction. It became a model for similar measures in other states. "If you want to prevent the evils of child labor," wrote the Boston *Journal of Education*, "get a copy of the law in your state and send it to Jane Addams. She will tell you, better than anybody else in the country, if it is wise."

Jane Addams, in her wisdom, planned not only to take the children . out of the factories but to keep them out of the streets. "In one short block," a contemporary investigator had observed, "I found seventy-five children playing in the gutter." Miss Addams undertook to remove them out of the gutters and into the playgrounds. Thanks to the maternal pity of the childless "St. Jane," the children of Chicago to this day enjoy one of the most extensive and best-managed playground systems in the United States.

Her sympathies, "warm as the sunlight, wide as the world," were always on the side of "the eager and the thwarted"—the children whose opportunity for education and whose capacity for happiness had become prematurely stunted. In her profound and tender book, *The Spirit of Youth,* she calls attention to the divine fire that lies smoldering in the heart of every child. "We may either smother this divine fire, or we may feed it. We may either stand stupidly staring as it sinks into a murky fire of crime . . . or we may tend it into a lambent flame with power to make clean and bright our dingy streets." And in thousands of cases she personally tended the divine fire into a lambent flame. Children of many nationalities came into Hull House. Some of them passed under her guiding hand through the universities into the professions. A greater number of them went into the ranks of business or labor. But nearly all of them became transmuted through the magic of her personality into better and happier and more understanding Americans.

Understanding Americans—this was the ultimate object of her life. Peace through understanding. The natives of many countries were migrating to America to become mutually acquainted. And here they learned to know and to admire one another. *And to co-operate with one another.* Though they couldn't follow the language of one another's tongues, they could interpret the language of one another's hearts. They realized that their Old World intolerances and hatreds and misrepresentations and fears were nothing but the bugaboos of foolish children. Russians, Frenchmen, Italians, Jews, Britons, Poles, Norwegians, Lithuanians, Czechs—all of them had the selfsame desire, the selfsame common yearning to feel the warm clasp of brotherhood between man and man. Jane Addams demonstrated the fact that in America a hundred quarrelsome nations could be united into one friendly family. Why couldn't she teach this vital lesson to the nations of Europe, of the entire world? She proceeded to initiate this new teaching. She became one of America's most passionate advocates of international good will. It seemed at times a hopeless task, but she never lost heart. Not even in 1914, when she saw the world engulfed in hatred. Nor in the following years, when she saw the collapse of civilization and the resurgence of barbaric dictatorships and fascist threats. For she had the patience of the true philosopher. She knew that the way to human understanding is precipitous and painful and slow. But she also knew that under the proper guidance the world would learn the lesson in the end. For she was sustained by that undying faith in the "continuity and interdependence of mankind."

In order to share her undying faith with her countrymen, she delivered a series of lectures against the barbarity of the military aggressors and their financial retainers. One of her friends described her as she looked on the platform: "A smallish, dark-faced woman, gentle of manner and soft of voice . . . She is dressed in a tailor-made suit of grayish blue . . . She is slightly stooped as she stands with her hands clasped behind her in a way touchingly childish, looking out at her audience . . . Her face is sad, though the eyes are luminous, and the lips adapt themselves readily to smiles." A frail and pallid wisp of a woman, insignificant in size, tremendous in magnetic power. And still modest to a fault. At one of her lectures the chairman introduced her as "the first citizen of Chicago, the first citizen of America, the first citizen of the world!" When she stood up to speak she raised her hand to silence the applause. And then, with a bashful smile, "I'm sorry, but your chairman must have meant somebody else."

VI

FOR A TIME during the (first) World War she stood almost alone. For she had foreseen, and she dared to proclaim, that our entry into the war would lead to no permanent peace. They stigmatized her as being pro-German. She was, of course, nothing of the kind. She was merely pro-human. And so she was "spiritually exiled" from her fellows for the sin of loving them too well. This spiritual loneliness was to her like an imprisonment. For she was by nature a woman who could not exist in solitude. Her very life needed the sustenance of social contact. She felt like an alien in her own country. Her very friends began to spy upon her as if she were a criminal.

But she took her blows, and went on proclaiming the new international ethics. "New ethics," she said in one of her speeches during the war, "are unpopular ethics." And in courting this unpopularity, she felt herself enlisted in a crusade no less sacred than the crusade of the enlisted men. The brave soldiers in the trenches were ready to die for war. The frail soldier in the Hull House was ready to suffer for peace. Theirs was the courage of an ordeal shared in comradeship. Hers was the heroism of a martyrdom endured in loneliness. Of the two kinds of sacrifice, which was the hardest?

When the war was over she felt that her crusade was only begun. She had organized, before the war, an American Women's Peace party. In the whirlwind of the war this movement had been torn apart. But with the return of calm weather the threads had been gathered up again, and Jane Addams proceeded to weave them into a new and larger pattern. The American Women's Peace party joined the Women's International League for Peace and Freedom, and Jane Addams became the president and guiding spirit of this league. "The dictators of the world will make you fight," she said, "but the women of the world will make you free." Half of her prophecy has come tragically true. But the other half, she was convinced, would at a not-too-distant date come *gloriously* true. In 1931 she shared, with Nicholas Murray Butler, the Nobel prize for peace. She donated her entire share—about sixteen thousand dollars—to the Women's International League. "The real cause of war," she said in making the donation, "is misunderstanding. Let this money be spent in the cause of international understanding." The understanding that the nations can live at peace if only they will unite to get rid of their individual aggressors.

This thought was like a refrain that ran throughout the symphony of her life. The children of the human family have been kept too long apart. The selfishness of their leaders has too long imposed upon their ignorance. They must be brought together, they must be educated, they must learn to know one another. "It is time," she said, "that we got better acquainted."

VII

IN THE SPRING OF 1935 she felt a sudden pain in the side. The doctors, suspecting a serious infection, advised immediate surgery. When the ambulance arrived to take her to the hospital, she begged the doctors to wait a few minutes. "I'd like to finish the novel I'm reading before I go. There are only a few pages left." And then, smiling through her pain, she added, "I'd hate to die without knowing how the plot came out."

"Nonsense! You're going to live!"

But when they operated on her they found a malignant tumor. Four days later she died.

As she lay in state her "family"—fifty thousand native and immigrant Americans—came to bid her Godspeed. And many of them wept, and not a few prayed, as they passed her coffin. For they were about to put away from their presence the all-embracing Mother of Men. As one of her "boys," a Greek workingman, expressed it, "Her no just one people, her no just one religion. Her all peoples, all religions."

And some of them thought they saw the faint, shy flicker of a smile on her face. "I'm sorry, but this good man must have meant somebody else."

IMPORTANT DATES IN THE LIFE OF
JANE ADDAMS

1860—Born, Cedarville, Illinois.

1881—Graduated at Rockford Female Seminary.

1889—Established Hull House in Chicago.

1910—Wrote *Twenty Years at Hull House.*

1915—Presided at the International League of Women.

1930—Published *Second Twenty Years at Hull House.*

1931—Shared, with Nicholas Murray Butler, the Nobel peace prize.

1935—Died, Chicago.

Henry Ford

[1863-1947]

A NEW monster had appeared on Main Street. A horseless carriage. "It shoots as it travels!" exclaimed the people as they heard it backfire. In Galveston, Texas, a prominent citizen was so terrified by the backfire that he drew a gun. "If that happens again," he yelled to the driver, "I'll kill you!"
In another state the new monster passed by a farmer and his wife in a wagon. The horses reared in alarm, and the woman leaped from the wagon and took to the woods. The driver stopped the car, walked over to the farmer, and asked whether he could help him tame the horses. "Hell, no," said the farmer. "But you can help me tame my wife!"

II

THE CREATOR of one of the world's most amazing miracles began life simply enough. His father was a Michigan farmer of intermingled Scotch, English, and Irish blood. A good basis for sobriety, imagination, and grit. "The young fellow," said his neighbors of William Ford, "has a clever hand and a kind heart." Always ready to help a fellow with the repairing of his tools and the plowing of his fields. A year after his marriage to Mary Litogot, when the papers were filled with the news of the Battle of Gettysburg, his first child Henry was born. "I want to see my son dedicated to the work of peace."

It was a peaceful home in which Henry grew up. One of the earliest incidents he could remember was watching his father at work in the fields. Long, straight furrows, so pretty to the sight. But here was a furrow that was not so straight. The plow had been turned aside at one point. "Why did you do it, Dad?" For answer, his father took his hand

and led him to the spot. There, on the ground, was a song sparrow's nest. "I didn't want to disturb it, son."

A peaceful home, and a busy one. Plenty of chores to do in the fields, in the barn, in the house. And, for a family living so far away from the supply stores, all sorts of gadgets to invent. Screw drivers out of shingle nails. Gimlets out of knitting needles. Tweezers out of corset stays. And, always, their own and their neighbors' watches and clocks to repair. "Has your timepiece stopped going? Leave it to Henry. *He'll* fix it!"

As often as not Henry would take a clock apart even when it needed no fixing. He wanted to see how well he could put it together again. "Every clock in the Ford home," remarked a friend jokingly, "shudders when it sees Henry coming."

In school Henry paid more attention to his gadgets than to his books. Indeed, his books served merely as a screen behind which he kept tinkering with his watches. The bigger the book, the better the shield between Henry's fingers and the teacher's eye. "Henry," said the teacher one day, "you seem to be more interested in your geography than in any other book."

But sometimes his teacher caught him at his "idle play." And then Henry had to sit in the corner with a girl—the regular punishment for misbehavior in school.

He found the punishment almost as pleasant as the crime.

But the pleasures of his childhood were arrested by an abrupt shock. He was only twelve when his mother died. "From that day on the house was like a watch without a mainspring."

Four more years of schooling and tinkering around with all sorts of machinery, and then he left home for a job in Detroit. Or, rather, two jobs. In the daytime he was an apprenticed mechanic; at night, a cleaner of clocks. His total pay for the two jobs was three dollars a week.

But he was ambitious. He wanted to become a mass producer of watches. Two thousand a day at a manufacturing cost of thirty cents and at a selling price of one dollar. A great boon to humanity, and a tidy profit for himself.

He went ahead with the idea, designed the machinery, cut the dies, and secured a partner. And then he had to give up the idea. "I could easily make two thousand watches a day. But how in the world could I sell them?"

A disappointed dream. But disappointments are only the seeds of future dreams. The idea of mass production had taken root in his mind. "Patience. It will come to flower in due time."

For the present Henry Ford yielded to his father's call for help on the farm. Nineteen years old. The golden age of courtship. It was on New Year's Eve that he met Clara Bryant, a dark-haired girl with a sun-bright smile. "Such a lovely young lady." "Such a sensible young man."

Apprenticeship for marriage. Six years of working and saving and planning; and then, on Clara's birthday (April 11) in 1888, she became his bride.

A new home, a new piano, and the reawakening of an old dream.

Something to be produced on a large scale. An inexpensive, serviceable, pleasure-giving gadget for his fellow men.

But what? Ah, he had it! A new kind of carriage. A sort of privately owned railway coach. Self-propelled, like a steam engine. He began to tinker with the idea on his farm. He took the cast-iron wheels of an old mowing machine, attached them to a crude locomotive with homemade cylinders, built a fire in the boiler, and tried it out. A spasmodic start, a splutter of steam, and the carriage came to a stop.

Another attempt, another, and still another—water tubes, fire tubes, flash designs. Same results. The thing wouldn't go. "The steam engine will never do for a common-road passenger car."

And then, an inspiration. One day in Detroit he saw a new kind of engine. It was operated by gasoline. That evening he explained the idea to his wife. He had read about it in the *World of Science*. "I've been on the wrong track, Clara. What I'd like to do is make an engine that'd sort of pump pop into pop bottles. A gasoline engine that'd take the place of a horse."

He drew a diagram on the back of a music sheet. "You see, if I could harness such an engine to four wheels——"

"Yes, Henry."

"But to do that, we'd have to give up the farm and move to Detroit. I'd need tools, and money, and all that sort of thing."

"I understand, Henry. I'll be ready when you say the word."

And so, on a late September day in 1891, they spread out the racks of their hay wagon, heaped all their belongings upon it, and started off in the direction of their dream.

III

DATE, August 12, 1896. Scene, the banquet room of the Oriental Hotel, Manhattan Beach, Long Island. Occasion, the convention of the officers of the Edison Electric Company. At the head sat Thomas Alva Edison himself.

Conversation about the presidential race between Bryan and McKinley, the plight of Cuba under the oppression of Spain, the expansion of American industry both at home and abroad. And then the talk drifted on to some of the latest industrial developments in the United States. One of the dinner guests touched Edison on the arm. "Do you see that young fellow across the table?"

"Yes. What about him?"

"Well, he's invented a gasoline car."

"Really? Sounds very interesting." And turning to Henry Ford, he said, "Young man, do you mind telling me about that new car of yours?"

The man who sat next to Edison vacated his chair and invited Ford to take his place. The young inventor began to explain his idea to the old inventor. Edison nodded approval. "Looks as if you've really got something." And then, "Tell me how you explode the gasoline in the cylinder."

"By electricity, sir." And taking a menu card from the table, Ford roughly sketched the principle of his make-and-break mechanism.

Edison's fist came down upon the table with a bang. "That's the thing, young man! Your car carries its own power plant—it's self-contained—no fire, no boiler. You've got it. Keep it up!"

Henry Ford kept it up. He was now the chief engineer at the Edison plant in Michigan. A very efficient young fellow, said the neighbors, but a little queer in the head. Spent all his evenings in a little alley shop behind the house, hammering away at some crazy contraption while everybody else was having a good time.

Wasting his time, and wasting his money. Didn't save up for a rainy day. Spent it all on useless tools. "Wonder what his wife must think? Doesn't she want to buy a new dress once in a while?"

But Clara Ford had the utmost faith in her husband. "Don't worry about me, Henry. My new dress can wait. Go right ahead."

At last his car was ready. "Like a strange, living creature from another world. You get into the seat, move a handle, and off it goes!"

Yet people were skeptical. A pretty enough toy, to be sure, but it would never do for practical purposes. Henry Ford, they said, was on the wrong track. Nobody but a fool would piddle around with a gasoline engine when everybody knew that the coming motive power was electricity.

And nobody but a fool—or a genius—would give up the security of an engineer's job for the insecurity of an inventor's dream. A "crank" with no future, a wife and a child to support, and a sputtering motor as the only collateral against want. Yet he managed to get the co-operation of a few other "cranks" like himself. They formed a little company with a capital of ten thousand dollars. The formation of this company was announced (August 19, 1899) in the *Detroit Free Press*. The item was sandwiched in between two advertisements—cucumbers at four cents a dozen, and cabbages at two cents a head.

The life of the company was short. One by one, Ford's backers lost heart and backed out.

But not Henry Ford. Slowly, patiently, fanatically, he went on with his dream. Another group of backers, another company dissolved. Two failures within three years. "Why don't you give up this crazy idea and go back to your job?" But Henry Ford "dug in with his toenails" and hung on. He built a racing car to enter in a meet against five other cars. A bicycle rider by the name of Barney Oldfield became interested in the car. "How do you run it?"

"Step in and find out."

Barney Oldfield stepped in. It took him but a few minutes to get the hang of the thing. "Let me race this car for you, Mr. Ford."

Henry Ford shook his head. "You've never driven a car before. It would be risking your life, you know."

Barney Oldfield insisted. "I might as well be dead as dead broke," he laughed.

Reluctantly Ford consented. Barney Oldfield drove the car and won the race.

From that day on financial backing was no longer a problem to Henry Ford.

IV

A NEW FORD COMPANY was organized with a cash investment of twenty-eight thousand dollars. The investors hoped for some profit, but had no idea to what a fantastic degree their hopes would be realized. One of them, the sister of James C. Couzens, put one hundred dollars into the company. In due time her one-hundred-dollar investment was worth three hundred and fifty-five thousand dollars.

These fabulous profits were due not only to the inventive skill but to the business genius of Henry Ford. His aim was, mass production to reduce the cost of every car; his motto, a better product at a lower price. With this objective in mind, he kept on increasing his capacity and improving his cars—Model A, Model B, Model C, and so on until he got just what he and the public wanted—Model T. The famous "Tin Lizzie" —the toast and the jest of America. "No show," wrote Roger Burlingame in *Engines of Democracy*, "was a complete success without a Ford joke. For six years, this is said to have taken the place of all paid advertising." The publishers issued anthologies of "uncanny stories about a canny car." The Ford cars were said to have overrun not only the entire world but the underworld. A magazine writer quoted His Satanic Majesty as saying to a visiting motorist, "Help yourself to one of these cars and take a spin around Hades."

"But, Your Majesty," replied the motorist, "these are all Fords."

"Sure," said the Devil. "That's the Hell of it."

The more they joked about the Ford, the more popular it became. "Two flies," wrote Luke McLuke in his *Phord Philosophy*, "can manufacture 48,876,552,154 new flies in six months, but they haven't anything on two Ford factories." In this joke, with all its exaggeration, there was almost more truth than travesty. In the summer of 1927 the output of the Ford Model T had reached the almost astronomical figure of fifteen million cars.

V

HENRY FORD was now the butt of every humorist in the country. Every paper must have its quota of witticisms about the Ford "flivver." Some of these witticisms were rather derogatory in tone. They got on the nerves of Ford's associate, James C. Couzens. One day he sent the following letter to the editor of the *Detroit News:*

SIR—*I hereby forbid you ever again to mention the name of the Ford Motor Company in your publication.*

JAMES COUZENS, *General Manager*

At the same time he canceled all the Ford advertisements in that paper. The editor sent out a representative to see Ford. "Jim has no sense of humor," laughed Ford. "I'll cancel his cancellation, and you can go right ahead with your jokes. I think they're funny. All good publicity."

Henry Ford had a strong sense of humor, and a heart full of compassion. When the first World War broke out he was horrified at the spectacle of man's inhumanity to man. At the suggestion of a number of idealists, he fitted out a ship to carry to Europe a delegation that might arrange for an armistice between the belligerent countries. "If I can be of any service whatever in helping end this war, I shall do it if it costs me every dollar and every friend I have."

The idea of the Peace Ship became a standing joke among the newspapers. "This Vessel of Mercy," wrote Walter Millis, "was launched, to the undying shame of American journalism, upon one vast sea of ridicule."

The mission was from the first doomed to failure. But Ford gave to it all his strength and energy and faith—"one of the few really rational and generous impulses of those insane years"—until February 1917, when the aggressiveness of the Prussians compelled the United States to sever diplomatic relations with Germany.

And then Ford threw himself heart and soul into the task of helping America prepare for the war. He converted his automobile plants into factories for the building of sea, air, and land weapons—Liberty motors, anti-submarine Eagles, caissons, helmets, ambulances, gas masks, battle tanks, and trucks. "I am a pacifist," he declared. "But if we can't have peace without fighting for it, by all means let us fight . . . And let us fight . . . with all our hearts and souls, until the end."

VI

HENRY FORD was a man with his head in the clouds but with his feet planted firmly upon the ground. Little by little he bought out his associates, until finally he alone controlled the Ford Motor Company. His organization had become an empire within a republic. It was a benevolent empire, to be sure. Like the more charitable of the Russian czars, he regarded himself as the Little Father of the men and the women who worked under his protection. He gave them good wages—too good, in fact, complained some of the professional economists. "Henry Ford," declared the *Wall Street Journal,* "has [in the establishing of a minimum wage] committed economic blunders if not crimes." He opened commissary stores where his workmen got the necessities of life at prices substantially lower than those prevailing in the rest of the country. He kept his workers employed even during the depression, when such employment meant a considerable financial loss to himself. His friends predicted his early bankruptcy. But Ford only smiled.

For he was a perfect mechanic. He knew that a machine is at its best when it is well oiled. His workers were human machines. Keep them in trim, and the wheels will turn around without any friction or delay.

The workers, therefore, must accept Mr. Ford's kindness and Mr. Ford's commands. They must have no minds, no desires, no complaints.

It was for him, and not for them, to decide whether their work was too hard or too speedy or too long. When his workers tried to organize themselves into a union and to join the CIO, he dismissed the eight "ringleaders." And when the workers, in retaliation, went on strike, he did everything within his power to put down the strike. He resented the interference of the workers, of the courts, even of the government, with his own "benevolent" way of doing things. Yet when the CIO was granted the legal right to organize his men, Henry Ford was big enough, in spite of his resentment, to accept the inevitable. "It's the law, and we're living up to it. If it's wrong, we'll find out. If it's right, we haven't anything to lose."

Henry Ford had his errors of judgment. Some of these errors resulted in inconvenience, and at times even in injustice, to others. But in every case, when convinced of his error, he made the necessary amends. In 1927, for example, a paper which he had founded—the *Dearborn Independent*—published a series of articles prejudicial to the Jews. These articles resulted in a libel suit against him. Believing in the accuracy of the statements as published in the articles, he spent more than a million dollars in preparation for his defense. In the course of the trial, however, he became convinced that the articles in question were unfair. Whereupon he made a public apology for the malignment of the Jewish race. "It has since been found," wrote the editor of the *Independent,* "that inaccuracies were present in the articles . . . Such statements . . . are withdrawn." In addition to this general retraction, Henry Ford issued a personal apology. "I deem it to be my duty as an honorable man to make amends for the wrong done to the Jews as fellow men and brothers, by asking their forgiveness for the harm I have unintentionally committed, by retracting so far as lies within my power the offensive charges laid at their door, and by giving them the unqualified assurance that henceforth they may look to me for friendship and good will."

The pettiness of error, the bigness of retraction, and the leavening grace of good will—these were among the fundamentals in the character of Henry Ford. In spite of his faults, he was intrinsically just and gentle and good. His goodness extended not only to his workers—among them there are fifty deaf-mutes, two hundred with crippled arms, and twelve hundred with only one eye—but to all helpless living things. Once, while he was having a new house built, he moved with his family into an old cottage. The cottage had been vacant for some time, and a couple of birds had made their nests just above the front door. When Ford noticed this he put up the following sign on the front porch:

"Please use the back door. There is a nest of young phoebes in one corner of the porch, and a robin's nest in the other corner. Mr. Ford does not want anyone to use the front door until the little birds have left their nests."

He built hospitals, established schools, and rehabilitated worn-out acreage for farming. "It is my aim to develop young men and to restore old men." One day he visited the distinguished Negro scientist, Dr. George

Washington Carver. He found him in poor health. "Pretty hard job to climb the stairs to your bedroom, isn't it, Doctor?"

"Oh, I manage it somehow," replied the old man.

Henry Ford turned the conversation to other matters. The next day, however, a number of workmen arrived at the home of Dr. Carver.

"What's the meaning of this?"

"We're going to install an automatic elevator, sir. Mr. Ford ordered it for you."

VII

HENRY FORD wanted to see a country happy at work, happy at play. As for himself, he enjoyed his play as much as his work. He loved to go off "gypsying" into the forest with his three cronies—Harvey Firestone, John Burroughs, and Thomas Edison. One day the four "vagabonds" were riding through the countryside in a Model T. A mazda lamp had burned out, and Ford stopped at a gas station to buy a new bulb. "By the way," he said to the owner of the station, "the man who invented the bulb is sitting out there in the car."

"You don't mean Thomas Edison?"

"Yes, I do." Ford's eyes roved to the rack behind the counter where he noticed a number of Firestone tires. "And it might interest you to know that one of the other men in the car is Harvey Firestone."

"Do tell!"

"And *my* name," with a twinkle in the eye, "is Henry Ford."

"Glad to meet you, Mr. —— Hey, hold on a minute. If you tell me that guy with the whiskers out there is Santa Claus, I'll call the sheriff!"

VIII

HENRY FORD in his seventies. Thin white hair, high forehead, blue-gray eyes, thin face furrowed with thought, firm lips that readily relax into a smile, long sensitive fingers, plain inexpensive clothes, plain inexpensive tastes. His greatest pleasures were the pleasures of the home. The one red-letter day of his old age was his fiftieth wedding anniversary. Bridegroom of half a century of golden honeymoons. "It is probable," observed the *New York Herald Tribune* on this occasion, "that the Fords are the richest couple on earth. Whether that fact is more astonishing than their record of having remained married fifty years is a matter for debate. And they remain essentially simple people . . . they still dance with each other. It may be that, in more matters than one, they are the richest people in the world."

In the course of the celebration Henry Ford submitted to a newspaper interview. "What," asked one of the reporters, "is your formula for a successful marriage?"

"The same as for a successful car," replied Ford. "Stick to one model."

A successful marriage, a fabulous portion of riches, and the common human cup of sorrow. A few years after the red-letter day came the black-letter day of his life. His only son, Edsel Ford, died.

But Henry Ford carried on. As in the first World War, he now turned all his resources and all his energy to helping his country win the second World War. His hatred of war had now matured into a hatred of aggression. Henry Ford was still true to his lifelong dream of peace. "What," he was asked, "do you think will come out of this war?"

"Out of this war," he replied, "will come the Great Awakening—the establishment of the Brotherhood of Man and the Federation of the World."

It was with this dream in his heart that he died—peacefully and simply as he had lived—on April 7, 1947.

IMPORTANT DATES IN THE LIFE OF HENRY FORD

1863—Born, Wayne County, Michigan.

1876—Became interested in repairing watches.

Became mechanic in Detroit.

1888—Married Clara Bryant.

Employed by Detroit Edison Company.

1892—Completed his first gasoline motorcar.

1899—Organized Detroit Automobile Company.

1902—Went into business for himself.

1903—Formed the Ford Motor Company.

1909—Began to specialize in Model T car.

1915—Chartered Peace Ship in effort to end World War I.

1918—Ran unsuccessfully for United States Senate.

1927—Completed car number 15,000,000.

1939-45—Devoted self to government war work.

1947—Died, Dearborn, Michigan.

George Washington Carver

[1864-1943]

ONE of the foremost agricultural scientists of the century, George Washington Carver, was born into slavery on a plantation near Diamond Grove, Missouri, during the Civil War. No human being had a less auspicious beginning to a distinguished career. His birthday was no more recorded by his owner than that of a chipmunk.

The years of the War between the States were among the most hectic in American history. Thieves rode high and handsome, plundering plantations and carrying off all movable property. One turbulent night a band of these pirates on horseback swooped down upon the stock of Moses Carver, an industrious German farmer of Newton County, Missouri. They made off with a slave mother and her son. Moses Carver, understanding the tricks of the trade, dispatched a neighbor to follow the thieves and offer them other goods in exchange for his blacks. His emissary tracked down the robbers and discovered that the mother had already been sold. But he bartered Moses Carver's race horse, valued at three hundred dollars, for the baby.

Cynical friends were amazed that Carver should yield a fine-blooded horse for an undernourished black baby, racked by whooping cough through long exposure to the cold. This sickly infant would never grow into a man fit for heavy manual duty on the plantation. In the business of slavery the only heart most men knew was the suit of red in a poker hand. But a miracle had taken place in the House of Carver—the miracle of love. Carver's wife had grown exceedingly fond of the child of her Negro servant. She gathered him in her arms and nursed him back to health. When the war was over and slavery was put to rest in the graves of the blue and the gray, the little Negro was adopted by his former owners. He was given their family name and, in addition, the Christian surname George Washington "because of his truthfulness."

The whooping cough signaled a long siege of illness for the little lad.

He grew frail as a plant. Since he was unable to labor in the fields, Mrs. Carver kept him in the kitchen and taught him to prepare meals, to bake and brew and iron and sew. After the day's work, however, the lad roamed in the forest around the farm. He loved to whittle the wood of the trees. With one of Moses Carver's hunting knives he fashioned crutches for a crippled boy in order that he might play with the other children.

No human being was ever more sensitive to the growth of life. Born an outcast from the society of men, he sought the society of plants. He perceived that flowers received an equal blessing from the rain and sunshine whether they were white or black or yellow. And he knew instinctively, before he was old enough to formulate his knowledge, that it was from this variety that the community of nature drew her beauty and her strength. He brought armfuls of flowers and shrubs to play with in his room. He went to sleep gripping these playmates in his hands. And whenever his little friends were sick, he transplanted them and healed them with uncanny skill.

With the men and women around him he was incurably shy. As a result of frequent attacks of the croup, he had developed a stammer in his speech, and much of the time no one could understand what he said. But the plants knew. He spoke to them in the touch of his fingers. And seeking additional ways of speaking the joy within him, he painted and sketched them. With all his being he felt that he had been appointed to make things grow. But his brain was enchained. One day he chanced across a blue-backed Webster speller. It was a formidable tool for self-expression. He plunged into a welter of words, much like Abraham Lincoln years before him, mastering countless cryptic spellings whose meanings he hadn't the slightest notion of.

But homespun learning was not sufficient. A school had been established for colored children in Neosho, eight miles from the Carver farm. To Neosho the ten-year-old George now turned his steps, with the blessings of his foster parents who had been impressed with his talents. When he reached his destination he found a stable for his first night's lodging. He lay down exhausted in the company of the horses.

He took his place by the other children on the bench of learning. After school hours he trekked from family to family, seeking work. A Negro family provided him with food and a bed in return for his services in the kitchen. Within a year he had absorbed all that the honest but limited teacher could offer. Folk spoke highly of the schools in the state of Kansas that were open to Negro and white pupils alike. George took the road to Fort Scott, Kansas. He hopped into a mule wagon on the way and arrived in the new community faced, as usual, with the problem of food and lodging and without a cent in his pockets.

Then commenced the pathetic routine. He knocked on doors to barter his services. He washed clothes, scrubbed floors, milked cows, snatching hungrily at an education. For seven years he remained at Fort Scott, going to school at odd hours. And then one night he came face to face with the stark tragedy of man's inhumanity to man. While performing an errand, he came to the town jail. An insane mob dragged a Negro prisoner from his cell and vent its vengeance upon him in the streets. George ran shuddering to his lodgings. In the thick of the night he slipped out of the town and picked his way along the road, searching for the dawn.

II

HE CONTINUED HIS QUEST for schooling and for work to keep his bones together while he learned to converse with savants and saints. Most of his time was consumed in scheming for his next loaf of bread or for a lesson book he required. But while he struggled with his bleak surroundings, God's gifts were maturing within him. Hounded and neglected and famished, he was yet one of fortune's princelings to whom destiny had bequeathed a priceless inner life that someday all men would envy. With his hands he wove intricate and dazzling crochet patterns, earning a few cents and satisfying his compulsion to create. Who could have acknowledged the bright world that was locked within the unprepossessing body of this Negro lad? When he received his high-school diploma at seventeen and took a train to Missouri to visit the Carvers, whom he hadn't seen in eight years, the ticket agent sold him a ticket at half fare, judging by his height that he was under the full-fare age.

Casting about for money to enter college and crown his long struggle for an education, he secured a room in Minneapolis, Kansas, for five dollars a month and opened a laundry service. His industriousness made many friends for him. The business venture proved profitable. Better food stimulated his growth, and he shot up almost as quickly as the beanstalk in the fable, until by the time he was twenty-one he reached nearly six feet.

He applied to Highland College in Kansas and was accepted by mail. Overjoyed, he sold his laundry, severed all business and social ties with Minneapolis, and set out for the school. But when he presented himself in person, the president found that he had made a serious error. It had never occurred to him that the candidate was not a white student. "Sorry, but we don't take Negroes here," he announced. And he shut the door on George.

It was a rude jolt for the Negro lad who had already suffered so many jolts. But he refused to lie down and play dead. Self-pity was a term he had not learned to spell in his Webster. The United States Government had opened lands in western Kansas for settlers, and many pioneer folk had grasped eagerly at the opportunity. Realizing that college was out of the question for the present, George migrated westward. He filed a claim for one hundred and sixty acres, built a sod house, and planted his crops. For two years he tended his farm and thought things out in the wind and sun and blizzards. But even in the Kansas desert he refused to relinquish his dream. Eastward lay the fulfillment of his destiny, a life of culture and learning. He had not survived a kidnaping on a plantation and lived through twenty-one years of misery merely to build upon the sand. Two years after the filing he proved upon his claim. He was too restless to remain the required five years on the property and obtain it free. He took out a mortgage for three hundred dollars and turned his steps toward Iowa.

And now fortune presented him with her first genuine smile. She gave him the key with which to unlock the final recesses of his intellectual self. An acquaintance informed him of a college at Indianola, Iowa, which had been established in accordance with the wishes of Bishop Matthew Simpson, an abolitionist and a lifelong friend of Abraham Lincoln. It was inconceivable that a college with such an origin would discriminate against a Negro. George hiked the twenty-five miles to Indianola and applied for admittance to Simpson. And he was accepted. Years later, when he had joined the ranks of the most renowned scientists of the age, sought after by governments and academic institutions everywhere, he remarked in a voice charged with feeling, "It was at Simpson that I first realized I was a human being."

Upon paying his entrance fees on his first day at Simpson, he discovered that he had ten cents left in his pocket. A woman offered him her woodshed to live in. Once again he turned his skill at needling and ironing clothes to financial account. He bought a washtub and went into the laundry business, servicing the college students and successfully meeting his bills. But his battle to earn a living was of minor importance now. The long struggle with a hostile world had ended in a victory for him.

The years at Simpson were the first genuinely happy years of his life. He began a systematic study of botany and the allied sciences. His fellow students, admiring his mental abilities, had accepted him as a companion in full. He assumed a leading musical role in student concerts, participated in the literary societies, and took piano lessons and paid for them with his paintings. His love for art competed with his enthusiasm for botany. He rapidly rose to the top position in his art class, and he permitted himself to dream that perhaps he would make a profession of his painting. He talked it over with his teacher, who declared that a career in art was not practical for him. Painting pictures would bring him personal satisfaction. But a colored man of his talents had no right to think in terms of private achievement. And George agreed. To enlist in the service of his fellow Negro, he needed more than the skill to paint canvases. "I can be of more service to my race in agriculture." With this decision firmly taken, he rounded out two years at Simpson and matriculated at Iowa State College of Agriculture and Mechanic Arts to broaden his training as an agricultural chemist.

Upon receiving his bachelor's degree in science, he was offered a job by a florist. He refused. "I did not earn my education in order to arrange flowers for the dead." A much more vital position was tendered him. So impressed were his professors by his wizardry in botany that they selected their first Negro graduate for an appointment on the faculty! It was a fascinating assignment. He was appointed assistant botanist and placed in charge of the greenhouse. Here he experimented in bacterial research and painted his beloved plants to his heart's content. He was like a young colt let loose in a pasture. His knowledge of plants astounded both his students and the professors alike. Stories of his achievements spread beyond the campus, and he accepted invitations to speak before horticultural societies throughout the state. By the time he obtained his master's degree in 1896, and his formal training at Iowa was finished, talk about his brilliance had reached the official ears of numerous university circles. He was sought after by some of the most important faculties in the country. Characteristically enough, he chose the one position most suited to his temperament and to his ideals.

In 1881, Booker T. Washington, born like Carver into slavery, had assumed direction of an educational institution whose aims were far more shining than its material assets. Several million Negroes, suddenly freed from the shackles of physical slavery, had been plunged into economic serfdom, mired helplessly on mortgaged farms, ignorant of the first principles of feeding and supporting themselves. Tuskegee was established to train teachers to impart to their people the elements of an education. Reports reached Washington, as he was organizing his faculty, of the brilliant young Negro botanist in Iowa. He immediately wrote to Carver requesting his services to direct the Department of Agriculture at Tuskegee. "If you are willing to come here," he wrote, "we can pay you fifteen hundred dollars a year and board, board to include all expenses except traveling. This perhaps may not seem a large salary, but from the first we have made a policy of trying to get teachers who come not . . . for the money but . . . for their deep interest in the race." And Carver answered the summons. "I will go to my people."

III

WHEN HE ARRIVED at Booker T. Washington's educational center, Carver discovered that Tuskegee had none of the facilities of Iowa State College. He couldn't find enough space even for the valuable mycological specimens he had collected. "My room is full of mice and they are damaging my boxes," he complained to Washington. There was no sewerage system at the institute, let alone an adequate laboratory for him to work in. Washington calmly answered his complaints. "The equipment must be in the head of the man and not in the laboratory." The young professor was not slow to take the hint. He set to work fashioning his materials by hand. He turned an old bottle of ink into a bunsen burner, stored his chemicals in teacups, collected the discarded zinc tops of fruit jars, and used a horseshoe for a bell with which to summon his classes. One day Washington, indicating the barren ground around the buildings of the institute, declared to the young botanist: "Our people have always been challenged with signs telling them to 'Keep off the grass.' Do you think you can grow grass out there for them?" And Carver, with the skill that was in his fingers and the knowledge of soils in his mind, covered the grounds with a rug of grass.

Cotton, the cash crop of the South, had pretty well exhausted the farm land of its fertility for food crops. Carver made a thorough analysis of the Alabama soil and discovered just what elements had to be added to transform it into a productive land. And when he had devised methods for turning the desert into Canaan, he visited the farmer and brought him the results of his laboratory research. For Tuskegee was not only a university for students, it was an experimental center for the benefit of the whole community.

He originated an "experiment wagon," from which he gave portable demonstrations of the results of his research. He remained for several days at a farm settlement, frequently setting up headquarters in the county courthouse. A field was plowed for demonstrations in planting, a garden selected for vegetable displays; wives were instructed in model housekeeping. He examined blighted crops and, with the uncanny instinct of a doctor diagnosing ailments in human beings, he invariably tracked down the disease and saved them. His success at plant doctoring became legendary.

Devotedly he continued his dual role, teaching students and performing public service for the community. To free him from the minor jobs that plagued a teacher at Tuskegee, Washington created a Department of Agricultural Research. Now that Carver was at liberty to indulge in limitless research, he produced results that rivaled the fabled alchemists. He investigated the clays of the countryside and extracted from them tints and stains which the Negro farmers were able to employ with startling success on the walls of their houses. Shoveling up red clay and processing it through successive stages of oxidization, he rediscovered the royal blue with which the Egyptians had painted the tombs of their kings and which had been lost to man for centuries. He developed from the clay also a powder to scour silver and a dust to kill the Colorado beetle on white potatoes. In addition he devised fifty-three different products from the feathers of domestic fowls. "And I have only begun to show their wonderful possibilities."

He found new methods for curing and pickling meats, provided a hundred ways to serve the tomato, and discovered more than two hundred and fifty medicinal properties of plants. When war came to the United States in 1917, and American markets were cut off from the aniline dyes of Germany, he perfected an amazing series of vegetable dyes as a substitute, processing more than five hundred varieties from the roots and stems and fruits of twenty-eight plants. The country suffered from a wheat shortage. And this Negro Paracelsus demonstrated the possibilities of using the sweet potato as a bread maker. For years he had been making eggs from the Puerto Rican sweet potato.

But the results of one investigation in particular were so startlingly picturesque that they won for him instant recognition in the hearts of millions of his fellow men. Since 1912 the boll weevil had swept from Mexico into Dixie Land and had systematically destroyed the cotton. This struck a vital blow at Southern prosperity. And it became evident that salvation lay only in the discovery of another crop that could be used as a business substitute. Carver, convinced that the "Creator had deposited somewhere in the ground something that could take cotton's place," began a long, arduous research, hunting for a clue to the plant. He tore apart the sweet potato and put its chemical elements together into different syntheses. He extracted starch and sugar and more than one hundred other products before he was finished. But none of these were as marketable as cotton. Then he examined the pecan but decided it wouldn't do. Finally he turned to the peanut, whose properties had intrigued him for years. But was it worth while to try to break the peanut? It seemed a pretty worthless plant, used chiefly to feed hogs.

Years later he was fond of relating to his students how he began his successful experiments with the peanut. "I went into my laboratory and said, 'Dear Creator, please tell me what the universe was made for.' And the Creator declared, 'You want to know too much for such a little mind. Ask for something your size.' Then I asked, 'Dear Creator, tell me what man was made for.' Again the great Creator answered, 'Little one, you are still asking too much. Make your request a more proportionate one.' 'Tell me then, Creator, what the peanut was made for.' Then the great Creator taught me how to take the peanut apart and put it together again. And out of this came all these products which the Creator taught me to make."

In 1921 an association of peanut growers in the South, witnessing what the Tuskegee professor had done with the "lowly" peanut, requested that he appear on their behalf before a Senate committee for a tariff to protect their product. Carver arrived at the Capitol carrying a box crammed with the fantastic products he had extracted in his laboratory. He entered the committee room and sat down quietly in the rear while a score of speakers argued for and against the legislation. By the time his name was called, the senators were weary with statistics and anxious to go home. Some regarded the Negro listlessly, some with amused tolerance. What did this old fellow know about the tariff? they asked themselves.

The chairman of the committee warned Carver that he had only ten minutes of speaking time. The professor nodded and plunged into his story of the peanut. When his ten minutes were over, the senators shouted for him to continue. He did, for an hour and a half. Never before had they witnessed such a demonstration! He drew from his box milk, cereal, coffee, Worcestershire sauce, face cream, printer's ink, mock oysters, soaps, salads, vinegar, butter, oil dyes, wood stains, paints, flavors, axle grease, shampoos. And as he presented each item he told the politicos that he had extracted each one from the peanut!

At the conclusion of the amazing performance John Nance Garner rose and declared in behalf of his colleagues: "You have made the most wonderful exhibition ever presented to this committee." And all the senators rose to their feet and applauded. Although Carver declared that he had not appeared in behalf of the tariff but in the interests of science, the Senate wrote into the Smoot-Hawley Bill the steepest rate ever accorded the peanut growers, and a new high-powered Southern industry was born.

Indeed, "Mr. Creator" had played a smart trick on men. Through the genius of a scientist who had been born a slave, a quarter-of-a-billion-dollar industry sprang up in the South, bringing it great wealth. But

Carver refused to take a cent of the profits. "Mr. Creator did not charge anything to grow a peanut, and I cannot accept money for my work with it." Before he died Carver had wrested more than three hundred products from the peanut. He had shown mankind how it was possible to live almost entirely on it alone.

A certain Mr. Tom Huston, who had established a business on Dr. Carver's investigations, once asked the scientist what gift he would most like to receive. "A diamond," instantly replied Carver. Huston purchased a diamond set in a platinum ring. He sent it to Carver. Then he dispatched a friend to find out if the professor was pleased with the present. When the visitor asked Carver where his diamond was, the scientist opened a case of geological specimens—and there it lay among his minerals!

IV

AT THE TIME when George Washington Carver's demonstrations with the peanut first brought him to the attention of men everywhere, he was nearing sixty. His hair had silvered. He walked with a slight stoop. His sense of humor was as fertile as the soils he nourished. Once a reporter for a national magazine described him as being toothless. "Fiddlesticks!" exploded Carver. "What a pity he didn't ask! Then he would not have made such a shameful error. If he had taken the trouble to inquire, I could have proved I am not toothless. I had my teeth right in my pocket all the time."

His colleagues were often shocked at his "lack of dignity." He was incorrigible in his dress. He donned scarves and ties dyed in his own plant juices to determine their wearing characteristics. Daily he picked for his lapel a native flower, and it refused to wilt even in the hottest weather. In 1937, when he attended the unveiling of a bronze bust of himself, he wore the suit in which he had graduated from Iowa State College more than forty years before. At Tuskegee commencements he yielded to custom and appeared in an academic gown—with the tassel of his cap dangling on the wrong side.

He was not interested in making money. At the crest of his fame he continued to draw his fifteen hundred dollars a year from Tuskegee. The treasurer had to follow him and plead with him to cash his salary checks, some of which had gathered dust for months, so that the books could be cleared. Edison offered him one hundred and seventy-five thousand dollars a year if he would join his research staff. But he was unwilling to leave Tuskegee. Henry Ford, who became an intimate friend and enthusiastic admirer, tried time and again to wean him from the institute. But the Detroit industrialist failed to win his services. "Mr. Washington is not with us any more in person, and I wouldn't be true to this great cause if I should leave here."

Lavish honors were tendered him. He received a Doctor of Science degree from Simpson College, his alma mater. He was elected a fellow of the Royal Society of London, one of the most exalted of scientific bodies. Governments wooed him. Before the first World War, Germany requested his advice on the best means of growing cotton in her African colonies. In 1931 Joseph Stalin invited Carver to visit the Soviet Union and assist in the cotton industry. But Carver declined to go because of his age. In 1935 the United States Government appointed him consultant to the Division of Mycology and Disease Survey in the Department of Agriculture, but he was permitted to carry out his duties from Tuskegee Institute.

For the greater bulk of his life Carver had worked without any assistants, carrying on his tremendous researches down to the last detail with his own hands. But when he passed his seventieth year he at last became anxious to train someone in his philosophy and methods so that his work would not die with him. And he selected as the inheritor of his professional knowledge Austin W. Curtis, Jr., a Negro graduate of Cornell University. The indoctrination of Curtis was a leading incentive that kept Carver alive during the remaining seven and a half years of his life. The professor and assistant worked side by side in the laboratory, traveled together, and gave lectures on the same platform. Inevitably the scientific mind of Curtis was fashioned in the image of his teacher.

As a further preparation to extend the life of his labors, the professor contributed his savings, over thirty thousand dollars, to the endowment of the George Washington Carver Foundation, a research center for promising Negro scientists. Meanwhile he continued his own experiments to make happier the fortune of man.

His lean body was bent and his steps dragged. But he entered his laboratory daily, as long as he was able, and watered his flowers. When an attack of pernicious anemia laid him low, his greatest sorrow was his inability to inspect the new greenhouse which the institute had recently built. When he gained sufficient strength to leave the hospital, he resumed his walks in the woods at dawn and he painted with his fingers in the pigments of the Alabama clay.

Finally Tuskegee, to whom he had remained loyal, was ready to receive him in her warm friendly earth. Booker T. Washington had already been put to rest, and there was a bed beside him waiting. In January 1943 the aged scientist took leave of the plants in this life.

IMPORTANT DATES IN THE LIFE OF
GEORGE WASHINGTON CARVER

1864—Born near Diamond Grove, Missouri.

1890—Entered Simpson College, Iowa.

1896—Received master's degree in science from Iowa State College of Agriculture and Mechanic Arts.

Appointed to faculty at Tuskegee Institute in Alabama.

1916—Named a fellow in the Royal Society of Arts, London.

1921—Displayed more than one hundred extracts from the peanut before United States Senate committee.

1923—Awarded the Spingarn Medal for most distinguished contribution by a Negro to science.

1935—Appointed to United States Department of Agriculture.

1940—Established the George Washington Carver Foundation.

1943—Died, Tuskegee, Alabama.

Charles Proteus Steinmetz

[1865-1923]

HE WAS born deformed. The left leg wasn't "just straight" and there was a hump on his back. "But he'll get along all right," the doctor assured his father.

Karl Heinrich stiffened. "Oh yes, he'll get along all right." All the Steinmetzes did. In spite of their handicaps. For generations they had toiled and suffered on the constantly shifting frontiers of Germany and Poland. They had lived by their shrewdness. They had been innkeepers and shopmen, small-town bourgeoisie who knew how to bargain and how to eke a narrow margin of profit out of life. Never had they asked for quarter. Never fear for the newcomer. "He'll manage somehow."

And within a year little Karl had to manage without his mother. His father, a lithographer for a German railroad, placed him under the care of his grandmother.

In the large room of the house on Tauenzienstrasse in Breslau the frolicsome child played with his *Grossmutter* and learned how far he could exploit her love. She entertained him with folk tales of her native Poland and with biblical stories about the ancient Hebrew cities of splendor and gold.

"We too have miracle cities, have we not, Grossmutter?" asked the child. "Perhaps when I grow up I can help to build one of them."

With his wooden blocks he constructed the Temple of Solomon, and when Grandmother wasn't looking he set a candle inside "to light it up." But the flame fed on the blocks and threatened to grow into a conflagration until his grandmother rushed over and deluged the building in water.

Karl was hurt and mystified. So *this* is what happens when you try to give too much light. As he grew older his mind laid plans to seek for a light that would shine in the temple without reducing it to ashes.

He entered the gymnasium at an age when he was "scarcely beyond his infancy." At five he conjugated Latin verbs. At seven he learned Greek and a smattering of Hebrew. At eight he possessed a "respectable knowl-edge" of algebra and geometry. Upon his completion of ten years of study he was ready to graduate with the highest honors. Nervously he awaited the event.

It was the custom for the graduating class to appear on the platform in full dress and to participate in an oral examination. Karl could not afford to own a formal suit. But he rented one. And then, on the morning before the great occasion, there appeared on the bulletin board of the school the following notice:

"Karl August Rudolph Steinmetz, by reason of his exceptional scholar-ship, is not required to submit to the oral examination."

Slowly he folded his formal suit and put it away. The tears on his cheeks were hot. He understood the reason for his exemption. The crip-pled body of the student. The crippled minds of the teachers. They were ashamed to show him before the public. They had singled him out, alone among the students, only to make him the more painfully aware of his loneliness. Karl Steinmetz never wore a full-dress suit again.

II

SHORTLY AFTER he entered the University of Breslau he gave evidence of a prodigious intellect. His professors were amazed at his "magical juggling" of figures. They nicknamed him "Proteus."

The ancient little hunchback of the sea. According to the Greek legend, Proteus was no bigger than the human hand. When trapped, he could change himself into a thousand different shapes. But if the captor held firm, he would gradually resume his real shape and whisper into the ear the secrets of the world. For the wrinkled little god possessed all the knowledge that men were searching for. . . . So, too, did this little Proteus of a Steinmetz, said the students with an uneasy smile. They were somewhat afraid of his "uncanny mind."

But Steinmetz craved companionship, and he sought for the society of his more serious fellow students. One day a classmate invited him to tea and told him about the plans of the German workers for a new social order—a world free from want, a co-operative commonwealth whose motto, based upon the Golden Rule, would be, *One for all and all for one.* "Will you join us socialists?" asked his classmate.

Karl's heart leaped with excitement. Here was a young man interested in matters beyond the usual frolics and duels of the average student. Of course he would join him and his socialists!

At first his new "crusade" was a pleasant diversion from his studies. For the early socialism of Germany was a peaceful movement to secure, by political means, many of the reforms that we in America have gained within the past ten years. But due to the arrogant stupidity of Bismarck the movement was driven underground. As a result of this suppression the "cause" of socialism gained momentum. But the members of the so-cialist party had won the badge of martyrdom.

The "movement" had now become an exciting adventure for Steinmetz. He wrote letters in invisible ink to fellow agitators who were detained by the authorities. He undertook to edit the socialist weekly—*The People's Voice*—with its challenging and somewhat absurd motto: "We don't know what the government wants, but we are against it."

Karl Steinmetz had found congenial company at last. He was a full-fledged member of the "Noble Order of the Dispossessed." Gradually his mathematical problems took up less and less of his time as the "larger social problem" began to occupy the foremost place in his mind.

And just now this problem called for an immediate and personal solution. *The People's Voice* was in financial straits. One day the printer and the paper merchant appeared together, demanding the immediate payment of a bill that had been overdue for several months. But Karl's sense of humor didn't desert him. He led his two creditors into the rear office of *The People's Voice* and offered to give them in payment a complete file of the weekly's back numbers. "Very interesting historical matter," he explained, "quite unobtainable elsewhere."

Finally a bailiff appeared to attach the furniture. "May I offer you a complete file of our back numbers?" inquired the intrepid editor. "Quite unobtainable elsewhere."

It was a gay life. And it was coming to an end. For he was about to graduate from college—with the highest honors in mathematics, to the great joy of his father. It was rumored that the authorities were planning to publish his senior thesis in the official scientific journal. A brilliant career was ahead.

One evening Steinmetz rounded up his socialist friends and announced that he wanted to give a beer party in celebration of his success. It was a merry company that swarmed into the restaurant. Each man called for a stein of beer. Each man proposed a toast, to which the entire company responded in chorus. As the evening wore on, the voices grew louder and the humor broader. They sang in complete disorder.

And then Steinmetz proposed a final toast. "To my father, whose greatest desire it has been to see me graduate with honors. To my escape over the Swiss border from the police who, as I have been tipped off, are planning to arrest me as a socialist. To my senior thesis that might have come to a glorious end in publication rather than in a hideaway suitcase. To the world and its irony, let's drink!"

In the dawn he tiptoed into his father's room. The older man stirred in his sleep. "I have had such a pleasant dream, Karl—your future——"

"Yes, Father," he murmured. "My future . . . It *was* a pleasant dream, was it not?"

A few hours later he left Germany and his father forever.

III

AT ZURICH he earned a scant income writing articles on astronomy. He attended courses at the Polytechnic Institute, rooming with a fellow student

"on the top floor of the last house at the end of the final street at the edge
of the town." And here came an important turn in his life. His fellow
lodger, Asmussen, told him of a country which he had visited—"a land of
magic" where the "social question" did not exist. "If you came to America
you could discard your preoccupation with politics and devote yourself
exclusively to mathematics. There is a crying need for engineers in
America."

A land of opportunity where everyone was given a second chance—even
a cripple who was hounded by the German police. Perhaps in the West he
might find the light that glowed but didn't scorch. His roommate had
spoken of the Goddess of Liberty who held in her uplifted hand the torch
that lighted the gateway of the New World.

It mightn't be a bad idea to sail for America. But how was he to raise
the money for the passage?

It was his fellow lodger who—involuntarily—found an answer to the
question. He had fallen in love with a Swiss girl and he had written about
his "blessed romance" to an uncle who lived in San Francisco and who
supplied him with his monthly allowance. The answer was a stern command that Asmussen come to America at once. Furthermore, he gave
notice to his nephew that he was cutting off his allowance.

The saddened lover fingered his bank roll reflectively. "I'll pay your
expenses to New York, Karl, if you come along with me."

Steinmetz hesitated for an instant. "What can you do here, Karl? You
can't return to Germany. The only good business in Switzerland is that of
a hotelkeeper. Have you got a hotel?"

And so it was decided. They came by steerage. The steamship, *Le
Champagne,* docked in the New York harbor on a warm June day. The
officials looked over the shipload of prospective Americans. They were not
at all impressed by the little dwarf of a man who limped up to them.
Could he speak English? He didn't understand, didn't answer. Asmussen,
who spoke English fluently, interpreted the question. "A few——" mumbled Steinmetz sheepishly.

Had he any money? *"Nein."* Had he any job? *"Nein."* Undesirable
alien! They would ship him home. No one asked to see the treatise on
higher mathematics that he had along with him—a work that singled him
out as one of the few geniuses of his generation. To the detention room
with him!

But Asmussen stepped in. He showed the officials a bank roll. He asserted that these funds were at the disposal of Steinmetz. "I will personally see to it that my friend does not become a public charge."

The authorities yielded. The unprepossessing young cripple limped up
the busy streets of New York, with only a few letters of recommendation
to electrical firms, a capital of mathematical symbols, and a slender lug-
gage of hope. He moved with Asmussen into a tenement in Brooklyn and
started immediately to look for a job. He applied to the chief engineer of
the Edison Electric Company and received a curt rebuff. "There are too
many engineers coming to America these days."

He visited the manufacturing establishment of Rudolph Eickemeyer.

The secretary, taking him for a tramp, was preparing to shoo him away when Mr. Eickemeyer himself strode into the office. The young foreigner made a stumbling attempt to introduce himself. Rudolph Eickemeyer looked at him kindly. Here was a fellow German. *"Sprechen Sie Deutsch?"* Within an hour's conversation he had learned all about Steinmetz. "I too am a political refugee," he remarked. "I fled from Germany in 1848. Come around in a week. There may be a job waiting."

There *was* a job waiting—the position of draughtsman at twelve dollars a week. Eickemeyer was a manufacturer of hats. But in his spare moments he experimented with electrical gadgets of his own devising. "Are you interested in electricity?" he asked Steinmetz. "If so, you may study some of the generators I've been tinkering with. Clumsy contraptions, I admit—elementary attempts to supply the world with power and light. Most of us are still groping blindly in this field. We blunder and stumble and snatch here and there at a little electricity, an incandescent lamp, a wire, but mostly we know nothing about the general laws. We do not as yet understand how to control electricity."

And then he took Steinmetz to a window overlooking the busy street. "There is a throne awaiting some man—a seat of untold power over vast cities and industries and millions of men and women—such is the kingdom of light lying in wait for its lawgiver . . ."

Even for a friendless immigrant who had eluded the police in his native land? That night, when work was over, there was a flush on the face of a little hunchback as he hitched his way home.

IV

WITHIN THREE YEARS Karl Steinmetz had assumed the throne in the kingdom of light. He had joined the American Institute of Electrical Engineers. He had reviewed the notes he had taken on electrical transformers at the Polytechnic in Switzerland. And he had made a thorough study of Eickemeyer's generators. Did the industry need an expert mathematician? The entire realm of mathematics had limped its way to America in that summer month of 1889. The electrical engineers were complaining that they were unable to estimate beforehand the efficiency of any generators which they were planning to build. And this inability to foretell the power capacity of an engine under construction was due to *hysteresis*—an (unpredictable) loss of energy. The engineers had noticed that a current passing through a core of iron sets up a magnetic north pole and a magnetic south pole, and that when the current reverses its direction, so also are the poles reversed. This alternating magnetism, the engineers had further noticed, meant a loss of power and efficiency. But nobody knew how to estimate the amount of this loss in advance, and therefore nobody knew how to build a machine that would reduce the hysteresis to a minimum. It was a hit-or-miss method, and the misses were far more frequent than the hits.

Such was the electrical state of affairs in the 1880s. A race of engineers in the wilderness of experimental electricity was looking for a Moses to lead them to the promised land of mathematical certainty. But for a long stretch of time no voice spoke to them.

And then at a meeting of the American Institute of Electrical Engineers in January 1892, one of its most obscure members walked to the platform and in halting, broken English read to the assemblage a mathematical paper. In this paper he formulated, definitely and for all time, the exact law of hysteresis. No need any longer to build a generator blindly. Karl Steinmetz had tamed electricity to the service of man.

Now he was no longer a German "alien" but an American pioneer. Accordingly he must adopt an American name. Charles August Rudolph Steinmetz? Charles Rudolph Steinmetz? Charles August Steinmetz? No —none of these would do—they were too hyphenated. Charles Steinmetz? That was better. But still something was wrong. Most Americans, he had noticed, had middle names. And then a puckish laugh shook his little frame of five foot three. Why not Proteus for a middle name? The old nickname of his student days. Proteus, the god of a thousand shapes, the guardian of a thousand secrets, the interpreter of the mystery of the tempest and the fire and the sea . . . From that day on he signed his name Charles Proteus Steinmetz.

V

IN THIS SAME YEAR which marked the discovery of the law of hysteresis (1892) the Edison General Electric Company of New York merged with a rival company and formed the gigantic trust of the General Electric Works. This new organization bought out the firm of Rudolph Eickemeyer and received, along with its other assets, the services of young Steinmetz. The company moved its general offices to Lynn, Massachusetts, and Steinmetz went to that city together with the rest of the office personnel.

A friend who had known him in New York paid him a visit a month after his removal to Lynn and was amazed to find him in sad straits. His clothes were ragged. He looked pale and thin. He had not paid the rent for his room. Through a clerical oversight his name had been omitted from the pay roll. For four weeks he had received no salary and he was too shy to make inquiries. "Perhaps," he told his friend, "they don't think I'm worth a salary as yet. Perhaps they feel that I ought to be grateful for the experience I'm getting with the firm."

It was soon made clear to him, however, that he was not expected to work for nothing. Indeed, he learned that his financial worries were over for the rest of his life. For the executives of the company realized that they had captured a Merlin of the modern age and they would never let him go. They sealed him in comfort and turned the key. The little man blinked in bewilderment as he looked at his new shoes and his new clothes and the platters of tasty meats that were set up before him. He pinched himself to see if he were really awake.

And then, satisfied that this was no dream, he took out his wand and worked another miracle. He had observed that alternating current had gradually begun to replace direct current as the best means of transmitting electricity over great distances. But as a result of this replacement a new difficulty had arisen. It was easy enough to calculate the regular flow of direct current according to Ohm's law. But no mathematical law had as yet been discovered to measure the irregular flow of alternating current. Steinmetz now discovered this law. It was a mathematical formula that required three volumes of complicated equations.

"This man," declared the chairman of the board of directors, "isn't cut out to be an engineer. He isn't a toolmaker but a lawgiver—a thinker in a class with Newton." From that day on they gave him no orders, made for him no regulations, and classified him for no particular job. "Here is our entire plant. Do anything you want with it. Dream all day, if you wish. We'll pay you for dreaming."

The company moved from Lynn to Schenectady and dressed the city out in a constellation of light. And into this Bagdad on the Mohawk rode the pygmy king in triumph. As the lights streamed from the humming dynamos and a thousand suns danced in the midnight air, Steinmetz knew at last that he had come home. This was the miracle shrine that had been awaiting him from his childhood days. Here in the electric city alive with batteries and wires of power devised largely out of his abstract mathematical formulas he sat hunched at the switch—a modern Jehovah ready to wield his thunderbolts over the cities of men. A Jehovah with a little red beard and a stogie in his mouth. A flibbertigibbet of a celebrity. Newsmen cornered him and photographed him and made much ado about "selling" him to the public. But still he was timid. He fancied that people were fascinated by his picturesque personality rather than by any appreciation of his thoughts or his feelings.

Did they know, for example, why he had moved into a big house on Wendell Avenue? And did they realize how lonely he was in the midst of these luxurious surroundings? At first he had taken lodgings with a landlady. But he was ill at ease. He burned her carpets with his acids, damaged her walls with his gadgets, ruined her disposition with his noises in his homemade laboratory at all hours of the day and the night. And that was why he had built himself a mansion—a hermitage for the housing of all his laboratory needs, a spacious temple of light. But he trembled at the thought of moving into the vast palace—a king without a family, without a friend. The reporters waxed enthusiastic about the splendor of the house and never bothered themselves about the loneliness of the owner.

But he tried to conquer his loneliness. One evening he paid a visit to his laboratory assistant—a young man who had just taken a wife. Timidly he invited the young couple to come and live with him. "In this way, you see, my house can become a home." Soon there might be a family in this house—children of sounder flesh than his own. Someday, perhaps, they would call him godfather. . . .

The young couple accepted his invitation and moved into the house on Wendell Avenue. But Steinmetz still remained alone—shrinking from the company of his fellows who were fashioned so differently from himself. Out of his suffering for his own ugliness he had developed a tenderness toward all ugly things. In the conservatory adjoining his house he cultivated a "distorted paradise"—of cacti plants. No delicate flowers for him. No foliage of beauty. But ugly misshapen cacti.

"If you want to make me really happy," he told his acquaintances, "send me alligators." He built a pool for five of them and decorated it with lilies. Accompanying him as he limped through the grounds of his estate was a homely mongrel who would never have gained his master's affection had he been slick and pedigreed. "Send me sick fowl and anemic kittens. I will fatten them." The outcast animals reached him in swarms.

And then came the climax to his collection in the "garden of the horrible and the misfit"—a Gila monster. The more curious among the people of Schenectady went to their encyclopedias for an account of this monster. "A huge, sluggish lizard . . . Its head equals the size of its body, and its tail equals the size of its head . . . With its two spearlike teeth it holds on to its victim while the saliva oozes from its venomous mouth . . ."

Such was the gentle pet. Steinmetz kept him in a cage and every year placed a dozen eggs by his side. Once a month the creature roused himself from his slumbers in the sun and ate an egg. And then he shut his scaly eyelids.

Ugly creatures, these. Nobody cared for them, yet somehow they made their way in life. Steinmetz closed his eyes whimsically over his cigar.

VI

HE WAS RAISED (in 1901) to the presidency of the American Institute of Electrical Engineers. The following year he was given an honorary degree at Harvard University. "I confer this degree upon you," said President Eliot, "as the foremost electrical engineer in the United States and therefore in the world."

When George R. Lunn entered upon his term as the socialist mayor of Schenectady, he appointed his fellow socialist of Breslau president of the Board of Education. Steinmetz was happy at the opportunity to put some of his social theories into practice. He increased the number of city playgrounds, he instituted special classes for the mentally slow and for the immigrants unfamiliar with the English language, and he introduced glass-enclosed classrooms on the roofs of the schoolhouses for the tubercular children. "Bring light into the lives of people—a light that does not destroy but only heals."

The skeptics wagged their heads over his social activities. How could this engineer of a great monopoly reconcile his capitalistic profession with his socialistic idealism? In answer to this question Steinmetz wrote a book—*America and the New Epoch*. It is precisely through the expansion of capitalism that we shall bring about state socialism, he declared. From the large-scale corporation to the corporate state. "Eventually private ownership will give way to government ownership under private management." And all this through the peaceful use of the ballot.

He was a great believer in economic reform through political means. In 1922 he ran on the socialist ticket for the office of state engineer. His specific platform was the harnessing of water power. "For this in a large measure means the liberation of man." Puffing vigorously at his cigar, he terrified all the lovers of beauty with his proposal that the water of the Niagara Falls be channeled into a huge plant for hydroelectrical purposes. What was the esthetic pleasure of a honeymooning couple as compared to the physical welfare of the human race? He estimated that the potential energy of Niagara Falls was six million horsepower. "This would bring to the state about two billions of dollars annually—to be spent on housing, playgrounds, and schools." And then, as he enumerated these advantages, his face softened into a puckish smile. For a compromise suggestion had occurred to him. On the six working days of the week the water could be diverted to supply the power for the hydroelectric machinery. But on Sundays the power could be closed down and the water could then be allowed to tumble over the precipice "in all its holiday beauty." His eyes beamed with excitement as the full glory—and the full humor—of the vision dawned upon him. "What a spectacle it would make, with the water beginning to trickle, slowly at first, then tumbling more and more impetuously until it became the thundering Niagara that we know! Wouldn't that be a display infinitely more impressive than what we have now?" He was defeated at the polls.

But he went on with his utopian dreams. "The progress of the human race," he once remarked, "is merely a matter of intelligent engineering." And then he went on to cite an example in order to clarify his idea. "If the Bering Strait were blown up and widened and deepened, we would be able to divert the whole course of that current to the north of North America. If that current ran above our continent, it would melt all the ice and snow of Canada and Alaska, and there would be no more glaciers in Greenland or icebergs in the Atlantic. . . . It would make all of North America warmer in the winter and milder in the summer. It would double the habitable area of the globe. It would remake the world."

And on another occasion: "I believe that the engineers of the future will bring about a four-hour working day. Work is a curse. The chief aim of society should be the abolition of it."

As for himself, however, he sought no cessation from his work. His beard was graying even as he grew young with his thoughts of the future. The total of cigar stubs that he had thrown away mounted appallingly. And still Steinmetz continued with his experiments.

Now he was studying lightning arresters—devices to protect electrical machinery from the bolts of an angry sky. Now he was building electric condensers that succeeded in capturing some of the characteristics of these celestial bolts. All around him his associates were clamoring for more power, more light—higher currents to press through the wires— higher voltage!

And now at last Charles Proteus Steinmetz was ready for his final experiment. "Come in, gentlemen," he told the group of reporters and distinguished scientists who had gathered at the door of his laboratory. "I have manufactured lightning!"

Quietly they entered. In the corner of the room they saw a monster generator. Spread out before them was a miniature village with houses and trees and a white-steepled church. "If you please, gentlemen, I will show you the devastating power of electricity."

There was a subdued hum and a glow in the vacuum tubes as they warmed up to discharge their power. And then—a terrific crash. A zigzag flame broke over the village. The trees and the houses and the steeple were enveloped in a whirlpool of smoke.

As the smoke cleared, the trees were dust, the houses were a heap of ruins, and the white steeple of the church had entirely disappeared.

Steinmetz looked at his astonished audience with a whimsical smile. "Incalculable is the power of electricity to destroy," he said, "when wielded by a foolish hand. . . . But equally incalculable, when wielded by a *wise* hand, is the power of electricity to *build*."

VII

SIDE BY SIDE with the cacti the owner of the Wendell House had planted the grounds with orchards lovely and fragrant. But the shadows threatened all the beauty, all the ugliness. Steinmetz was getting old and wayworn. One autumn morning (October 26, 1923) his adopted son, Joseph Hayden, entered the bedroom of the engineer. He had sensed that Dr. Steinmetz had passed a restless night. "I'll bring up the breakfast tray," he suggested. "Better to eat a snack before you try to get up."

"All right. I will lie down again."

A few minutes later Hayden's son came into the room with the breakfast. He drew close to the bed. The little man was sound asleep.

Somewhere in the silent air lurked a voice speaking words that only a little child in Breslau and a kindly old grandmother would understand. "I am tired building with my blocks, Grossmutter. I will lie down again. And when the morning comes, I will make another temple so much better than the one I built today."

IMPORTANT DATES IN THE LIFE OF
CHARLES PROTEUS STEINMETZ

1865—Born, Breslau, Germany.

1889—Came to America.
Secured work at Osterheid and Eickemeyer factory at Yonkers.

1893—Made consulting engineer at General Electric Company, Schenectady, New York.

1902—Appointed (in addition to his regular job) professor of electrical engineering at Union College, Schenectady.

1923—Died, Schenectady, New York.

The Wright Brothers
[Wilbur Wright, 1867-1912
Orville Wright, 1871-1948]

ON DECEMBER 17, 1903, Orville Wright made the first historic flight in a heavier-than-air machine. Five years later, after many successful flights witnessed by hundreds of spectators, there were a number of scientists and editors who were still unconvinced. "Human flight," wrote Professor Simon Newcomb, "is not only impossible, it is illogical." And the editor of one of America's leading magazines returned a report on an authentic flight with the following comment:

"While your manuscript has been read with much interest, it does not seem to qualify either as fact or fiction."

II

IN SPITE of its terrible destructiveness in war, the airplane, we believe, will prove to be the instrument that marks the shortest distance between human hearts. For this instrument will have succeeded more than any other in drawing the earth into a unit, in combining widely separated communities into a friendly next-door neighborliness. The airplane is the final conqueror of time and space and isolation. In 1852 it took Ezra Meeker six months to travel by ox team over the Oregon Trail to Washington. In 1924 this ninety-three-year-old pioneer sped over the same distance, by airplane, in one day.

III

FOR THOUSANDS OF YEARS the secret of air travel had eluded the ingenuity of the world's greatest scholars. Yet the magicians who finally discovered it were two uneducated bicycle mechanics. Wilbur and Orville Wright were the sons of a clergyman. Their two older brothers and their sister were college graduates. But they themselves had only a few years of schooling. Like Benjamin Franklin, Walt Whitman, Mark Twain, Thomas Edison, and Henry Ford, the Wright brothers proved that a college degree is no passport to immortal achievement.

But if Wilbur and Orville Wright were no scholars, they were, in the true sense of the word, poets. A *poet*, by its Greek definition, is a *maker*, a *creator*, a man who transforms dreams into actualities—in short, an *inventor*. There is very little difference between the creative genius of a Shakespeare and inventive faculty of an Edison. The one forges dead syllables into a living poem, and the other combines lifeless materials into a throbbing machine. The process is the same—the fusing of odd old bits of memory into some hitherto-undiscovered aspect of the sublime.

The Wright brothers shared in this faculty of fusing old memories into new discoveries. Like Edison, they developed at an early age an almost uncanny ability for remembering details. Added to this, they both displayed a passion for mental and physical gymnastics. It was his excessive fondness for "idle" reading and for athletics that prevented Wilbur's graduation from high school. But their reading helped them to spread the wings of their imagination. And their athletic training enabled them to come safely down to earth when they took their first ride on the bucking bronco of the air.

The two boys became interested in flight when their father one day brought them a mechanical toy called a *helicopter*. This "flying top" had two propellers that caused it to whizz into the air when it was wound up. The two boys took the helicopter apart, put it together, and then took it apart again, in order to discover the secret of its flight. They noticed that the propellers of this toy pushed against the air just as the paddles of a boat push against the water. Throwing the dismantled toy into a rubbish heap, they stored up in their memory the lesson that they had learned from it.

Later they watched the flight of a box kite, and then they turned to the birds. For hours they would lie on their backs, their eyes intent upon the lifting and the drifting of the wings against the sky. They noticed that some of the birds, especially the sea gulls, had a slight warp, or dip, to their wings. It was this warp, they observed, that enabled the birds to maintain their balance and to make their turns in the air. This fact, too, the boys carefully stored away in their memory for future use.

A couple of restless youngsters, with observant eyes and active minds. And fingers always on the itch to be puttering with tools. They built and sold kites for pocket money, constructed a wooden lathe with a foot treadle and with marbles for ball bearings, invented an improvement on a hay-baling machine, and designed an original device for folding newspapers. All this before they were out of their teens. "The boys," said their teachers, "are bright, but they are unable to concentrate on their school textbooks." True enough. Their minds were centered upon the far more important mechanical textbook of the universe.

Their thinking was almost entirely extracurricular. They delved into the mysteries of nature. They pondered upon one of the most baffling of these mysteries—the sustaining power of the air. They began to read up on the history of man's attempts at flight. They learned about the mythical wings of Icarus, the crude experiments of Leonardo da Vinci, the enthusiastic but fruitless efforts of Chanute, Mouillard, Ader, and Lilienthal, and the scientific researches of Maxim and Langley. They noted that there were two schools of thought with regard to the possible conquest of the air—those who believed in the kitelike gliders, and those who experimented with the birdlike motor machines. They decided to begin their own experiments with the motorless gliders.

From the very start they found themselves handicapped. Men like Ader and Maxim and Langley had the advantage of a large working capital for their experiments. But the only capital in the possession of these two young mechanics—they had opened a bicycle shop at Dayton, Ohio—was an inexhaustible supply of enthusiasm and a daredevil willingness to take risks.

With these two assets, Orville and Wilbur set to work in the back yard of their bicycle shop, laying their "crazy" plans and collecting homespun and rubbish for the building of their first glider. "And with this contraption," laughed their father, "you expect to conquer the kingdom of the birds!"

The neighbors shared the good-natured ridicule of the father. So the Wright boys were planning to fly, were they? Well, it couldn't be done! Men were meant to stay down on the earth. Otherwise they'd have been given wings. And that was that!

But the Wright boys believed they could do it. They had made an intensive study of Lilienthal's papers on *The Problem of Flying and Practical Experiments in Soaring*. True enough, Lilienthal had been killed in a crash of his gliding machine. But before his fatal accident he had made several successful hops through the air in his glider. "What Lilienthal has done with a glider, we can do with a motor machine."

First, however, they would begin where Lilienthal had left off—with a gliding machine. They had studied the causes of Lilienthal's failures— and these failures had been far more numerous than his successes; they had calculated the lifting and the balancing power of flat and of curved wings; they had measured, by means of a funnel which they had invented for the purpose, the pressure of the air on moving bodies; and they had reached the conclusion that the secret of aerial navigation lay in the proper equilibrium between the airship and the air. And thus they completed their first scientific glider—at a cost of fifteen dollars. It was a peculiar-looking object—a box kite of cloth and wooden ribs that resembled an enormous chicken coop.

In order to try out this glider, they asked the Weather Bureau at Washington to recommend a spot where they could find steady winds, low hills for take-off, and soft sand dunes for landing. Willis L. Moore, chief of the bureau, informed them that Kitty Hawk, North Carolina, was such a spot.

Here the two brothers took their aircraft on September 25, 1900. And here, without any fuss or witness, they began their practical experiments. At first they tried to send their glider up like a kite. It took to the air without any trouble. Their calculations had been correct. There was plenty of *lift* to the creature. Then they proceeded to the next step. Pulling their wood-and-canvas Pegasus down to earth, they prepared it for its first aerial ride with a human being upon its back. Wilbur stretched himself out on the lower wing, face down, took the controlling reins in his hands, and the next minute found himself flying through the air.

It was one of the strangest experiences within the memory of man. Wilbur Wright had set himself adrift in the Nowhere, without any roads to guide him and without any anchor under his feet. It was a terrifying moment. He grew panicky. "Let me down," he cried, *"let me down!"*

In later years, when Wilbur had become an expert pilot, he recalled this episode with a smile. The "appalling" altitude to which he had been lifted from the ground in his first flight was eight feet.

IV

THE WRIGHT BROTHERS had now proved that man could *glide* through the air. But the more important question still remained unanswered. Could man *fly* through the air? For three years they experimented with motors and propellers in an effort to supply the answer. Years of hard work and continual disappointment. At one time Wilbur was so discouraged that he was ready to give up. "Not in a thousand years will man ever learn to fly."

But Orville, the younger and the more daring of the two, kept urging his brother to go on. New wind tunnels, new airplane models with wings of various edges and curvatures, and tables upon tables of calculations and resultant figures for their subsequent tests. "Will you boys ever stop working?" asked their father, with a skeptical smile.

"Not until we have built a machine that can fly," replied Wilbur.

"And *that*," rejoined Orville, "will be only the *beginning* of our work."

See them now at their work in the back yard of their bicycle shop. Wilbur, thirty-six years old, tall and rangy, face closely shaved, firm thin lips, muscles of steel, and a steel-like glint of determination in his gray-blue eyes. Orville, thirty-two, shorter and more compact, with a heavy dark mustache that conceals the firmness of the upper lip, but with the same determined gray-blue glint in his eyes. Two dynamic machine men, their feet planted upon the ground, their hearts uplifted toward the skies.

And at last their heart's desire seemed about to be fulfilled. Toward the end of 1903 they had finished their first motorplane—the result of several years of theoretical calculation. They took it to Kitty Hawk for its practical test in the air.

But just then they received bad news. The scientific world had come to the "final conclusion" that flight in heavier-than-air machines was impossible. Professor Langley of the Smithsonian Institution had built, with the aid of government funds, an intricate and costly airplane. An imposing group of scientists had gathered on the banks of the Potomac to watch its initial flight. But it refused to fly. The dream of the ages, agreed the scientists, must remain an unattainable dream.

It was under these discouraging conditions that Wilbur and Orville prepared to make their first attempt with their modest little "air toy." Like the Langley machine, it was equipped with propellers and a motor. But unlike the Langley machine—and this was a secret which the Wright brothers were keeping to themselves—it was built upon an entirely new principle. As a result of their persistent experimentation, the two unschooled but observant young mechanics had at last discovered the true principles of air pressure—a discovery which had eluded the mathematical calculations of all the trained scientists. Their airplane, crude and inexpensive as it was, had been designed in accordance with these newly discovered principles. Theoretically, it ought to work. But *would* it? What business had they, a couple of bungling tinkers who hadn't even had a college education, to set themselves up against the scientific verdict of the greatest contemporary scholars? And so it was with a mingled feeling of hope and misgiving that they got ready for their take-off.

Monday, December 14, 1903. The two brothers toss a coin for the opportunity to make the first test. Wilbur wins the toss.

The test results in complete failure. The plane, after staying in the air for three and a half seconds, topples sideways to the ground.

Two days of repairing the broken parts, and the Wrights are ready for the next attempt. It is now Orville's turn.

December 17. The day is overcast. A raw northeaster blows in from the Atlantic half a mile away. The two pioneer airmen, their blood thinned from too much confinement in the bicycle shop, are stamping their feet and flapping their arms to keep themselves warm. They wear no overcoats, for an overcoat would hamper their movements in this dangerous experiment. As they prepare their clumsy mechanical bird for its tentative flight, they observe a flock of sea gulls soaring gracefully overhead. A raucous shriek from the gulls, as if in mocking challenge to the men below. The brothers are practically alone on the dunes. Only five spectators have taken the trouble to come from the near-by village. One of them looks from the birds to the plane and remarks with a sneer. "So *that* rigamajig is a-goin' to fly?" "Sure it is," rejoins another of the spectators, "in a hundred-mile tornado!"

The brothers, paying no attention to the jeering remarks, tune up the motor. With a roar that drowns out the beating of the surf, the engine begins to spit fire and smoke from the open exhaust. Orville climbs into the wings. "Let her go!"

A moment of breathless expectation—the moment for which a hundred million years had been waiting. Orville grasped the controls—and then the miracle happened. The first mechanical airship began its historic flight.

V

A YOUNG REPORTER, H. P. Moore of the Norfolk *Virginian-Pilot*, heard about the flight and set his imagination to work. He prepared a wholly fictitious story about a "long journey" through the air, at the end of which the operator of the machine ran over the ground yelling "Eureka." He sent the story to twenty-one newspapers, only three of which took the trouble to print it. When Orville learned of this incredulity on the part of the editors, he merely shrugged his shoulders and laughed. "No wonder they disbelieved the story. It was an amazing piece of work. And yet, though 99 per cent wrong, it did contain one correct fact. There *had* been a flight."

But neither the editors nor the public would recognize this fact. "A couple of silly boys bucking against the eternal laws of nature." Some of their Dayton acquaintances were even sarcastic about it. "Flying and perpetual motion will come at the same time," sneered one of them. And another, "There is only one thing that could lift a machine off the ground—spirit power. And the Wright boys are not even spiritualists."

No, the Wright boys were just a couple of mischievous youngsters. Especially Orville. He had a habit of storming up the steps to his bedroom on all fours, like a child. It didn't bother him or Wilbur that the world looked skeptically upon their work. Their invention was a fascinating game, nothing more. Even in after years, when the world had come to recognize their work, they refused to be puffed up. They had merely "pulled off" a good play in their game. They retained their good-natured modesty when colleges showered them with honorary degrees and kings favored them with their smiles. They came both to the college presidents and to the kings dressed in their ordinary street clothes and their caps.

They felt no pompous awe in the presence of royalty and they expected the public to feel no pompous adulation in their own presence. Again and again they refused to make public speeches. "I know of only one bird, the parrot, that talks," said Wilbur, "and the parrot can't fly very high." They were careless about the medals and the ribbons which they received from scientific societies. They carried them around, together with other commonplace doodads like screws and bolts and scraps of paper, in their pockets. And they felt more chagrined when they mislaid a bolt than when they lost a medal. They possessed, in other words, the simplicity of greatness.

They never married. Their sister Katharine, who taught at the local high school, provided them with all the feminine companionship that they needed. Together with their old clergyman-father, they enjoyed that most perfect of human relationships—a harmonious family.

But suddenly the harmony was shattered. On May 30, 1912, Wilbur died of typhoid fever. He was only forty-five at the time, and his death meant the ending of one of the greatest inventive partnerships in history.

Throughout their work the two Wright brothers supplemented each other. Together, they formed one supreme intellect. But apart, neither of them could accomplish much. In spite of his genius, Orville felt physically and mentally lost without his brother. And he never found himself. The invention of the airplane had come out of the interplay of their ideas. It was like a spark generated by the clashing of two swords. And when one of the two swords lay broken, the other remained inactive in its sheath. For a little while after his brother's death Orville tried to go on. He experimented and made improvements on the stability of the airplane. But his heart was no longer in the work. With the passing of Wilbur, Orville had grown from a boy into a man. Aviation had ceased to be a game for him. It was now a business. And Orville hated business. After three years as president of the Wright Company, he resigned.

VI

On DECEMBER 17, 1928, the United States celebrated the twenty-fifth anniversary of human flight. A monument had been erected at Kitty Hawk in honor of the Wright brothers. Orville had been invited as the principal guest. He stood beside the monument and smiled sadly at the cheering crowd. "Mighty eagle of the air!" they called him. But it was a broken eagle that stood there, with his frail gray head uncovered to the sky. His eyes roamed over the sand dunes. Drifting sands—drifting years. Past landmarks obliterated—past friendships buried. He felt suddenly cold and alone in the great crowd. His mind went back to the Ohio graveyard, where his brother lay cold and alone. Two brave eagles, equally indifferent to the jeers and the cheers of the world.

IMPORTANT DATES IN THE LIVES OF
THE WRIGHT BROTHERS

WILBUR WRIGHT

1867—Born, Millville, Indiana.

1903—Constructed first successful airplane.

1904-08—Continued successful airplane experiments.

1908—Won Michelin Prize in France.

1909—Flew from Governors Island to Grant's Tomb and back. Received gold medal from French Academy of Sciences.

1912—Died, Dayton, Ohio.

ORVILLE WRIGHT

1871—Born, Dayton, Ohio.

1888—Finished high-school education.

1903—Finished, with Wilbur, first successful airplane.

1905—Made first long-distance flight near Dayton, Ohio.

1909—Received gold medal from French Academy.

1915—Sold his interest in Wright Aeroplane Company.

1917—Awarded Albert Medal from Royal Society.

1920—Won John Fritz Medal.

1925—Received John Scott Medal.

1948—Died, Dayton, Ohio.

Bernard Mannes Baruch

[1870-   ]

THE story of Bernard Baruch is an American legend. A Greek scholar and a Wall Street financier, an adviser to five Presidents, and the recipient of not a single political office, a speculator, idealist, elder statesman, and country squire, Baruch is the unique product of a unique society.

He was the son of a physician, an emigrant from East Prussia, who married a daughter of impoverished Southern planters. Portuguese Jews, they had settled in America seven generations before. As a lad of fifteen, Dr. Simon Baruch, despising German militarism, migrated to the United States to commence life anew. He learned English by reading an American history with the help of a dictionary, and eventually he received a degree in medicine. During the Civil War he joined the Confederate Army as a surgeon. Several times he was captured by Federal troops. In the course of a confinement in Fort McHenry he wrote a book on bayonet wounds of the chest which became a classic in medicine. He settled in Camden, South Carolina, and here, in 1870, his son Bernard was born. Baruch in Hebrew means "blessed." Bernard's birth was indeed a "blessed" event.

He was a fat, dumpy little boy who hunted with an old breech-loading rifle and labored on the farm which his father maintained for agricultural research. He fought in the neighborhood street gangs and employed barrel staves as a weapon with which to defend himself against the stronger "toughs." On one occasion he filched candy from the desk of a schoolmate. He was filled with such remorse that he never stole again. Gradually he evolved an inflexible code of ethics: honesty, good fellowship, and skill in the science of self-defense.

His father, who experimented in methods of hydropathy—water for medical treatment—decided to further his research in the East. And the family moved to New York. Dr. Baruch was appointed professor at the College of Physicians and Surgeons of Columbia University, and he earned a splendid name for his achievements. Among other things, he pioneered in the treatment of appendicitis.

Barney was eleven when he arrived in New York. He grew up with a skill for classical languages and an educated fist. He boxed for hours in a gymnasium on Twenty-eighth Street. One of those who witnessed his punching was the former heavyweight champion, Bob Fitzsimmons, who declared in after years: "The ring lost a good man when Barney Baruch decided to take up another profession."

At fourteen Baruch entered the College of the City of New York. He practiced the strictest economy. Until his final year he was given an allowance of twenty-five cents a week. In bad weather he received ten cents extra for carfare, but he walked to school to save the dime for himself. He was fascinated by his classes in political economy. And he participated in the political life of the campus. In his senior year he was selected chairman of the class-day exercises. He refused, however, to compete for the office of class orator, for he shied away from speaking in public. In later life he frequently referred to this quality of bashfulness. "I have never been able to speak well before people."

On one occasion he planned to resign from college. He was offered an appointment at West Point. But upon examination it developed that this young athletic man of six feet three, who, at first glance, seemed a sturdy enough physical specimen, was almost totally deaf in one ear through an injury he had received while playing baseball. Hitting a tremendous wallop, he had slid home on a close decision. During the riot that ensued between the members of the teams, he had been struck on the ear with a bat. This tragedy has not dampened Baruch's love for the game. But years after the event, when he served as industrial mobilizer of the nation's resources during the first World War, he frequently mused how he might have been a major general offering service on the field of combat if only he had been accepted at West Point.

His mother was greatly concerned over his future. She took him to a phrenologist. He ran his fingers over young Barney's skull and inquired, "What are you planning to do with this boy?" "We would like to have him study medicine," she replied. "A doctor? No! Put this lad into business or finance. He will do big things."

The fate of Bernard Baruch rested on the bumps of his head. He became a businessman.

II

AT FIRST he did not take the citadel of finance by storm. No merchant was ready to invest heavily on a phrenologist's diagnosis. Baruch received a modest position with wholesale dealers in glassware. He ran errands, dispatched invoices, and copied letters for three dollars a week. His pay was meager, but his schemes were luxurious. A gambler by nature, doting on the excitement of stakes, he played cards with a zest and attended the race tracks with a professional zeal. The essential proc-

ess of his life was the wager. One evening his father, surprising him
in a gambling den, took him home and measured him with stern words
—in vain. His gambling, vulgar as it seemed to his parents, was a release
for a deeply felt need of self-expression. In after years he would play with
the same sure instinct for the raw materials of the world. And his winnings would be the victory of the American war machine over Germany.

He discovered his proper milieu when he entered Wall Street to work
for a retired clothing merchant, Julius A. Kohn. The firm was chiefly
concerned with trading in securities between nations. Baruch throve on
this atmosphere. It was as if he had been handed a key to the cabala
wherein lay the exact meaning of his life. He familiarized himself with
stock quotations in the international marts of exchanges, learned the
mechanics of transferring sums into various currencies, and served faithfully at the observation post of global speculation. Gradually his eyes
opened wide at the possibilities and power of the speculator. And he
learned how a mortal could build and rule over a kingdom of gold.

But in the midst of this secret initiation the ever-surging restlessness
in Baruch reasserted itself. He left the little cockpit of Wall Street for
the vast spaces beyond the Mississippi. He took a job as mucker in a
San Francisco mine shaft; toiled with the pick and bucket; joined a
crew to blast the bowels of the earth. And he played his cards in the
gambling "dives," dreaming of systems to "break" the banker. Finally
he invested his winnings from the table in a mining proposition, and lost
every cent.

This terminated his adventure in the West. He returned to Wall Street
determined to speculate hereafter in commodities rather than to gamble
on the turn of a wheel. He took a job with the firm of A. A. Houseman
and Company, Wall Street brokers, at a salary of five dollars a week, and
he devoted a mind that had mastered Latin and philosophy to the business
of correlating the facts of finance into a system of knowledge. He became a student of corporations, their organization, personnel, history. He
saturated himself in the industrial geography of the United States until
he could draw from memory the location of the leading industries and
railroads. He deduced the effect of weather fluctuations on commodities,
crops, and freight movements. Brokers grew to know him for his vast
immediate knowledge of their business. Instead of looking up data on a
stock for its dividends, earnings, and book value, they came to him for
the facts. Gradually "Ask Barney, he knows," became a matter of casual
statement.

Senior clerks quipped humorously at the lanky youth who bustled in
and out of offices, always in a hurry. "Young fellow, get down off that
stool!" His firm, recognizing his unusual ability, took him into partnership, according him an eighth of the profits. His share for the first year
was six thousand dollars.

Quietly, professionally, in the meantime, he had begun to speculate
in the market. "Speculation" is hardly the word. No man brought greater
knowledge or competency to a task. He felt his way cautiously, like a
prize fighter, sparring for an opening. He scored his first major coup in

sugar, buying on margin at a time when the sugar interests were anxiously awaiting the decision of Congress on the tariff. Calculating that Congress would not reduce the tariff, he continued to invest heavily. His judgment was confirmed; he closed the deal with a profit of sixty thousand dollars.

Then came a series of dazzling coups. On the night of July 3, 1898, during the war with Spain, while Baruch was vacationing on the Jersey coast with the senior partner of his firm, a friendly reporter brought news to them which had not yet reached the headlines. It was a portentous item. The United States Navy had sunk substantially the entire Spanish fleet in Santiago harbor. The Spanish war was to all intents finished. Baruch and his partner, realizing that they alone among financiers were in the possession of a "tip" that could send the stock market booming, decided to act upon it at once. The following day was Monday, July 4. All business would be suspended. This gave them an immense advantage. It was imperative that they cable London and make purchases that would take advantage of the expected rise of prices on the New York Stock Exchange when it opened on Tuesday. But it was already late in the evening. There were no trains running from Long Branch to New York. They hired a locomotive and tender and rode up to the city in a manner worthy of a melodrama. From their office they wired London, buying stocks right and left. And when the New York Exchange opened with a rise they made a handsome "killing."

Baruch now investigated dealings in the tobacco industry. He got in touch with Thomas Fortune Ryan, the wizard financier, and represented him in negotiations to purchase the Liggett and Myers Tobacco Company. He received fifty thousand dollars as a commission, and bought himself a seat on the Exchange.

Now he met with a really incredible stroke of good fortune. He had invested heavily in Amalgamated Copper. With his usual thoroughness, he had studied the stock carefully and had come to the conclusion that its price was too high. He commenced to sell. The stock, true to his predictions, began slumping. At the most critical phase, as Baruch watched with eagle eye to see whether the stock would continue to decline, his mother telephoned him. "Son, do you know that Monday is Yom Kippur? I expect you home." Without a word he left his post and spent the Jewish holiday with his family, shutting himself off from all communication with his business associates. When the Exchange opened, the stock continued to fall. Several times his assistants tried to reach him by phone and urge him to sell. In vain. They were unable to reach him. By midday, however, the fortunes of Amalgamated Copper turned. The company had declared a dividend. The stock shot upward. When Baruch returned to his office he discovered that he was richer by almost a million dollars.

In the course of accumulating his wealth, Baruch resigned from his partnership with Houseman and entered business for himself. He refused to associate with any group of investors. "Men called him the lone eagle," wrote a correspondent. "They turned to whisper as he passed, tall, aquiline, smiling but uncommunicative, among the excited stock traders."

Time and again he staked his judgment against the leading financiers of the Street, and won. "I piled up one million and another. . . . And then I really began to make money," he confessed.

He speculated in pioneering industries. He subsidized Texas Gulf Sulphur, which enabled the United States to retain control over the world's market in sulphur. He financed a process for mining porphyry low-grade rock, a technique that doubled the world's output of copper. Convinced that Far Eastern rubber producers were exacting excessive profits, he developed plantations in Mexico to manufacture rubber from the guayule plant at a low price for American consumers.

At thirty-two he held a substantial interest in the vital commodities of the world's economy. The wheel of fortune had indicated his number with monotonous regularity. But he was dissatisfied. He was unhappy with the mere game of making money. He felt that he was destined to do something more important than just accumulate wealth. He was sensitive of the term "gambler" which folk applied to him. In the hard bed of his business shrewdness there had always existed a vein of idealism at times extravagant in its quality. Friends, realizing this, had often told him, "You know, Barney, you are not a Wall Street man at heart. You should go into public life, and someday you will."

Surely enough, an opportunity to work for his fellow countrymen presented itself to this young man replete with the material goods of the world. A Southerner whose father once wore the Confederate gray, Baruch for years had given generously to the campaign funds of the Democrats. Since most of the men of wealth in the country were normally Republicans, Baruch loomed in the financial schemes of the party. In 1912 a group of liberal Democrats determined to support Woodrow Wilson, the governor of New Jersey, for the presidency. Seeking the monetary backing of Baruch for their candidate, they introduced him to Wilson. This meeting changed the entire course of Baruch's life. The presidential candidate and the financier took a strong liking to each other. The one was no more a mere politician than the other was a mere businessman. In culture and in idealism these two Americans met on common ground.

Baruch supported the nominee generously. But when Wilson, upon being elected President, desired to name him Secretary of the Treasury, he declined the offer. He wanted no reward for his loyalty. The tide of international affairs, however, drew Baruch to Washington. There was one summons he could not fail to answer. The call to arms.

III

Up to the eve of the European conflict in 1914, few Americans had any idea that warfare required anything more than a military mobilization of the people. But with the advent of the World War, civilians behind the trenches discovered that modern combat was not a responsibility of the soldier alone. Wars were won by the massed power of a nation's industry. An embattled people required not only a commander in chief of armed men, but a commander in chief of armed industry. And America discovered this new type of general in Bernard Baruch. It was a new kind of challenge for a man whose entire life had been a series of challenges. It was a gamble for a gambler.

Baruch's first assignment was a preliminary to an even greater one. Early in 1917, Wilson appointed him a member of the Council of National Defense, chief of the Division of Raw Materials. Tongues wagged. It was rumored that Wilson, through this uncrowned monarch of the Stock Exchange, was "selling out" to the nation's "vested interests." But Wilson knew his man. Before accepting his post with the government, Baruch sold his seat on the Exchange and disposed of all the securities he held in businesses that might be affected by the war effort. A master bargainer who knew the "ins" and "outs" of the battle, he entered upon his role as negotiator for the people with typical zest. The price for copper, boomed by the war abroad, was thirty cents a pound. He persuaded the copper barons to sell to the government for a little more than sixteen cents a pound. And he obtained steel for half the market price.

But there were greater tasks ahead. For the first time in history the government found it necessary to harness American industry to meet the unprecedented demands of war. The job of pooling industries, arranging prices, controlling the allocation of raw materials, restraining the desires of individual businessmen for unlimited profits and unlimited competition was one that literally staggered the imagination. Various methods had been tested by the Administration to harness American business, but indecision and lack of imagination had greatly frustrated its efforts.

Finally, on March 5, 1918, Wilson appointed Baruch chairman of a War Industries Board to cope with the problem. In selecting Baruch, the President referred to him as the "general eye" of the mobilization. He gave him life-and-death powers over American business. Baruch's task was nothing less than to organize the largest industrial combination the world had ever seen. And this son of an immigrant who had fled from Prussian militarism, this American who had grown up as a boy amid the devastation induced by a Civil War, now spoke earnestly of the task forced upon a people to complete a war against aggression. "There is only one business for America and Americans—war. . . . War is the business of America."

He slashed the red tape which had bridled his predecessors. He did not call a dozen board meetings to arrange details. He acted. Although he possessed the power to commandeer plants, if necessary, and to throttle the activities of recalcitrant producers, he wielded his authority with such tact and restraint that not a single businessman made a genuinely hostile declaration against him. In a single year, 1917, he purchased more than ten billion dollars' worth of food and material.

To France alone he sent enough steel to manufacture one hundred and sixty million 75-millimeter shells and enough food to feed twelve million Frenchmen for a year and a half. That was the magnitude of his assignment. He managed matters with lightning speed. Within forty-eight hours after the French ambassador requested gasoline, two tank steamers were on their way to a French port. When Wilson one afternoon directed him to acquire all Austrian shipping in American harbors, he phoned back the next morning: "The Austrian shipping has been purchased, Mr. President."

He employed a masterly psychology in his dealings. The United States, on one occasion, found itself desperately short of Chilean nitrate for munitions. Chile, exploiting the shortage, had boosted the price of nitrates to an exorbitant level. Baruch caused word to be spread that the United States had developed new plants for extracting nitrogen from the air. This report reached business interests in Chile who immediately offered to ship an enormous supply of nitrates to the United States at a reasonable price. The chairman of the War Industries Board had succeeded on a bluff.

Baruch was the despair of all his colleagues in Washington. He carried the data of his business so easily in his mind that he became neglectful of records. His lack of an orthodox sense of organization bewildered his associates no less than his amazing insight. Although he exercised more power than any other American, he appeared outwardly the least disturbed individual in the capital. He always seemed to have considerable time to relax, to talk with people, to make friends. Wilson dubbed him "Dr. Facts." His mental processes were a miracle to himself as well as to everybody else. His mind exercised itself in flashes of brilliant hunches. He seemed to possess the secret of a sixth sense, the quality of which he was unable to explain in words. "His ability," wrote Mark Sullivan, "is something of the nature of artistic genius. Many a man has made money who doesn't conform to the characteristics of the businessman. They make money as other men paint . . . pictures or compose music."

Baruch indeed was not a typical businessman. Upon completing his stupendous assignment, he told his friends that he would not return to Wall Street. He had acquired so much "inside information" as chairman of the War Industries Board, he declared, that it would be improper for him ever to go into the market again. He shrugged aside all praise for his public service. "When God and the community have been good to a man, isn't it natural that he should try to make some payment?"

IV

Bernard baruch remained a public counselor to the world. He traveled to Paris as Wilson's adviser and helped to frame the economic terms of the peace treaty. He welcomed the League of Nations. However, he was convinced that the issue of America's entrance into the League was a national and not a party question. And he urged the Democrats to conciliate the Republicans who expressed fears at certain extreme articles of the Covenant. He believed that the President should accept the treaty with reservations, for he knew that the great decisions of the country must be taken in a spirit of compromise, especially when the future of the world is at stake. But Wilson hewed to an inflexible course of principle. Americans refused to ratify the Covenant, and the United States declined to enter the League.

Baruch held his ear close to the squabble of the Allies over the war reparations. He witnessed the insistency of the nations on their sovereign privileges. He talked frequently with Winston Churchill, then British War Minister of Munitions, and with Clemenceau, who in his trenchant admiration had dubbed the American financier "Prince d'Israel." All activity and discussions at Paris pointed to one thing—humanity was by no means guaranteed a lasting peace.

Baruch returned to the United States and warned his countrymen of this. He established himself as a "committee of preparedness," a watchman on the alert through the night. Counseling his fellow citizens not to permit the machinery which had so effectively mobilized the resources of the nation in one war to disintegrate in an era of counterfeit peace, he advised them to maintain a skeleton organization which should be constantly at work on industrial preparedness. And he hammered away at a principle: "Take the profits out of war." He gave lectures at the Army Industrial College, and he financed a school of international relations at Williamstown, Massachusetts, at which leading statesmen and economists gathered to diagnose the social and political ills of the nations.

In addition to his activity on an international level, he was concerned with domestic problems. As an adult he retained his childhood memories of the poverty-stricken sharecropper in the South. And American farmers, overwhelmed by the recession following the war boom, turned to the former chairman of the War Industries Board to succor them in their hour of trouble. In so doing, they paid a rare tribute to a rare individual.

In 1921, at the request of the Kansas State Board of Agriculture, Baruch devised a program which has been called a "Magna Charta" for the farmer. Realizing that agriculture lagged a half century behind the development of industrial civilization, he urged the farmer to adapt salient practices of industry to agriculture. He freed the cultivators of the soil of their prejudices, convincing them, for instance, that it was no disgrace to sit at an office desk and "boss" a job. He worked out a method of co-operative marketing, prescribed specific means for reducing a surplus of the tobacco crop, and solved problems peculiar to the grain growers. In demonstrating to farmers the means for transforming their production and marketing into big business, he revolutionized the economy of the soil.

The role Baruch assumed of a Wall Street speculator transformed into the farmer's Messiah was no more extraordinary than the part he played during this period in national politics. A Democrat, for twelve years following the war he served as an influential adviser to three Republican Presidents. He accepted no public office. He followed the tradition of Socrates, the Gadfly. He pricked and he prodded, a persuasive, relentless, ubiquitous, insistent public conscience. Since he had established himself as a counselor for the world, what better place was there for him to carry on his business than from a park bench!

This tall, lean, aging Socrates of modern America selected a bench in

Lafayette Park, where he stretched his legs mornings in fair weather and foul. He sat under a chestnut to the rear of an equestrian statue of Andrew Jackson, alert for any summons to the White House, which stood diagonally across from him. He continued to serve, whether the sun shone or the sky thundered, in a job from which there was no retirement. And the people continued to respond to his philosophy of common sense. "He was the greatest living exponent of two times two makes four."

Finally, as Baruch had foreseen, America went to war again. For the second time in a generation she joined forces against aggression. A chastened nation called upon its elder statesman for assistance. He was assigned to unravel a succession of critical problems. With the co-operation of two scientists, Dr. Conant and Dr. Compton, he devised means for the country to cope with a deficient supply of rubber. He dealt with the war man-power problem successfully, applying a budget system to the allocation of labor in industry. Finally, when the conflict reached a climax, he was appointed by James F. Byrnes, director of the Office of War Mobilization, to explore thoroughly the task of readjusting the nation's postwar economy.

He delivered a comprehensive report by way of answer to the prophets of despair who bowed their heads before the inevitability of a cycle of depressions in a society of free enterprise. He answered with a declaration of faith in the productivity of the American people. To the Communists he retorted: "You don't distribute wealth; you distribute poverty." And he added, for the followers of all the "isms" but Americanism to hear, "The fiscal strength of a nation lies not in what the government owns but in what its people own. The sinews of production are not dollars—they are efforts."

Production for construction, not destruction. He eagerly accepted an invitation by President Truman to serve as American delegate on the Atomic Energy Commission, and he comprehensively studied the means whereby the world might eliminate the weapons of mass destruction and use the atom creatively in a warless age. The Baruch Report on Atomic Energy has become the foundation on which the international edifice for the control of this stupendous power is being built.

Close to eighty, straight as a ramrod, with clear blue eyes, Baruch remains today an active warrior for peace.

IMPORTANT DATES IN THE LIFE OF
BERNARD MANNES BARUCH

1870—Born, Camden, South Carolina.

1889—Graduated from the College of the City of New York.

1897—Accorded partnership in brokerage firm of Houseman and Company.

1912—Met Woodrow Wilson; supported him financially for President.

1916—Named a member of the Advisory Committee of the Council of National Defense.

1918—Appointed chairman of the War Industries Board.

1919—Served on the Supreme Economic Council of the Peace Conference in Paris.

1921—Advised Kansas State Board of Agriculture on ways to industrialize farming.

1942—Developed rubber program for war industry.

1943—Developed man-power program.
Worked out a program of postwar economic adjustment.

1946—Appointed American delegate to the Atomic Energy Commission.

Alfred Emanuel Smith

[1873-1944]

ONE afternoon the members of the New York State Assembly were engaged in a lively debate over a controversial bill. As a young Democrat reached the most impressive portion of his rebuttal, and the Chamber had grown quiet enough for the dropping of a penny to be heard, a messenger entered and whispered something to the speaker. He paused for breath and then declared, "Pardon me for interrupting my political discussion, but I have received news I know the Assembly desires to hear. Cornell has just won the boat race."

Applause swept the Chamber.

Then a loud piping voice exclaimed, "I really don't give a hoot. I'm a Princeton man." A lanky Republican rose to his feet and seconded this sentiment. "I'm not very much impressed myself. Harvard was my university."

The speaker on the floor grinned. His blue eyes telegraphed an imminent burst of humor. "I sympathize with you gentlemen who have never attended Cornell. There's no reason, for instance, for a Dartmouth or a Stanford alumnus to shout himself hoarse over a Cornell victory on the river. As a matter of fact, I have nothing to applaud about either. I'm an F.F.M. man."

"What's that?" asked several voices.

"Fulton Fish Market," replied Al Smith.

II

SOME AMERICANS learn the science of government in school. Al Smith's classroom was the East Side of New York. Son of an Irish truck driver who loved to swap lusty stories in the barrooms, Al mingled on the water front with the longshoremen who unloaded fabulous cargoes from every country of the globe. His neighborhood contained the greatest number of immigrant nationalities in the city. The East Side, with its smells and filth and hash of languages and customs, was the testing ground of democracy.

Above the swarming nationalities loomed the newly completed Brooklyn Bridge, a network of steel across the sky. The bridge was the setting for Al Smith's first experience in human tragedy. On Decoration Day, 1883, as people promenaded over the great span, voices shouted that the bridge was on the point of collapsing. Instantly the panic-stricken multitude rushed for the banks. About twenty persons were trampled to death. Al pressed as closely to the disaster as the police would allow. "That was my first view of a great calamity. I did not sleep for nights."

When the lad reached fourteen his father, whose health had broken down, was compelled to leave his trucking business for the only job available to an unskilled semi-invalid—the post of a night watchman. Within a short time he passed on. Al was grief-stricken. He had been his father's frequent companion on excursions to Coney Island, and to the Bowery music halls where he had been permitted a sip of beer while the band played sprightly melodies.

And now life for the Smiths changed drastically. The death of the head of the house had left the family penniless. Neighbors scraped together money for the funeral expenses. Al's mother went into business for herself. She moved into a basement and opened a little candy store with the money she borrowed from her landlady. Al took over a newspaper route and relieved his mother in the evening behind the counter.

And then, in pursuit of higher wages, he left the St. James Parochial School which he had entered as a boy of seven. Thus he terminated his eight years of formal education. He never entered a classroom again. He received a job as "truck chaser" along the water front, hailing drivers and transmitting to them orders from the front office. Frequently he made a detour to visit the firehouses, where he lent a hand in polishing the engines. Ever since childhood he had frequently brought sandwiches to the firemen, whom he regarded as his older brothers.

For two years he retained his job as chaser. And then he went to work as assistant to the shipping clerk in the oil firm of Clarkson and Ford—at the unprecedented salary of five dollars a week. This increase in wages enabled him to experiment in larger cigars and better beer. He wore his narrow brown derby as rakishly as any young "Bowery buck" in his middle teens. He was definitely "getting ahead."

His neighbors, meanwhile, discovered him to be a lad of talents. In school he had won several medals in debates. He became actively interested in the dramatic society of St. James, which presented performances in the basement of the church for the parish. And he rapidly developed into the star of the company, playing villains with particular gusto. After witnessing the performances of famous actors from the gallery of the Broadway Theater, he returned to the St. James's basement and applied the lessons he had learned. His impersonations received praiseworthy notices in the local press.

And all this time he worked industriously to earn a living. He resigned his position at Clarkson and Ford for a job at the Fulton Fish Market, which paid him twelve dollars a week. Not only was the income attractive, but he was permitted to take home as much fish as his family could eat. For the next few years he shuffled aimlessly from one employment to another, attracted simply by the size of the pay check. He seemed destined to share the permanent obscurity of thousands of uneducated poor boys. But suddenly an opportunity arose which changed the course of his life.

Upon the recommendation of a friend, he was assigned to the law office of ex-Judge Allison to serve summonses for jury duty. Al loved the job. The relatively disagreeable role of a summons server was no handicap to him. He had been born with a genius for mingling with people. Soon he was promoted to the position of investigator, to hunt down individuals whom the regular process servers were unable to find.

Meantime he had joined the downtown Tammany Club, which was the nerve center of all the social life in the community. The local politicians —acute observers of political talent—had been keeping their eye on Al since his childhood. They were convinced that he was excellent timber. At last they gave him his chance. Nineteen hundred and three was an election year for state assemblymen. The candidate whom Tom Foley, the district boss, had previously sent to Albany had proved disloyal to the party. Foley decided to abandon him. But he was uncertain as to whom to select in his place. An associate declared, "Have you considered Al Smith, Tom? I don't know of a finer bet among the young men in the club."

Once Al had received the nomination, his election was assured. Everybody in the neighborhood knew him and liked him. He campaigned vigorously from the back of a truck. His rough-and-tumble voice could be heard over the rattle of horsecars and all the other noises of the street. His opponents—a Republican, a Socialist, and a Prohibitionist—waged a futile struggle. Al received almost five thousand votes. The Republican ran second, with approximately fifteen hundred votes. The Socialist received one hundred and six, and the Prohibitionist five.

And now, to bestow on him the outward appearance of his newly acquired dignity, Al's friends bought him a full-dress suit with a cutaway coat. They were determined that their representative in the legislature should be dressed as prosperously as the upstate "swells."

III

WHEN AL SET OUT for Albany as freshman assemblyman at a salary of fifteen hundred dollars a year, he hadn't the slightest awareness of the difficulties that awaited him. He entered the legislature "well grounded in the Ten Commandments and in nothing else." The constitutional procedure of the Assembly, the language of the bills, and the speeches delivered were an unfathomable puzzle to him. He couldn't make head or tail out of such matters. Valiantly he took the bills home and forced an undeveloped mind to study them. He sat in the last row of the Chamber. Frequently he couldn't see or hear what was taking place. It was not until three days before the adjournment of the first session that the speaker of the Assembly became acquainted with him. No one lent a helping hand to sharpen his untrained mind into a useful tool. When the first term came to a close, there was no evidence to show that he had sat in the Assembly.

But he had voted with the party on every measure. He had attended sessions faithfully. Foley was satisfied. And Smith was elected to a second term. During this session he was selected to serve on two committees— Banking and Public Lands. "I had never been in a bank except to serve a jury notice, and I had never seen a forest."

The young assemblyman was deeply discouraged, and several times he announced his intention of retiring to a simpler kind of existence. But Tom Foley would hear none of this. He was grooming his protégé for a bigger role. And he handled Smith with the utmost shrewdness, returning him to Albany term after term.

Foley's judgment was gradually becoming vindicated. During Al's third term James W. Wadsworth, the Republican speaker of the Assembly, became interested in him and assigned to him a fair amount of committee work. In 1907, Al spoke from the floor for the first time—and his speech impressed the members of both parties with its clarity and common sense.

The long years of rigorous self-discipline were bearing fruit at last. Imperceptibly he was gaining mastery over the business into which Foley had guided him. And his abilities propelled him to the forefront of his party in the Assembly. By 1911, when the Democrats gained control of both chambers of the legislature, Smith was the acknowledged leader of his party in the Assembly. He was appointed chairman of the influential Committee on Ways and Means.

But it was a public catastrophe that first brought him to the recognition of the people beyond the confines of Albany. On March 26, 1911, six hundred employees of the Triangle Shirtwaist Company in New York City were trapped by a fire which had broken out suddenly in the factory building. Almost one hundred and fifty of the workers—mostly women and young girls—perished in the flames. Indignation swept the city. Demands were made for an investigation to fix the responsibility. Robert F. Wagner and Al Smith, Democratic leaders of the Senate and Assembly, appointed a commission to investigate. As vice-chairman of this commission, Smith traveled from one end of the state to the other, acquiring a liberal education in the grim conditions prevailing in factories. As an East Sider, he had personally shared the load of the underprivileged. Now he gained an insight into the practical steps that could be taken to lighten this load.

Armed with his facts, Smith returned to the floor of the Assembly and battled to correct the abuses he had witnessed. He fought for accident-prevention measures, for legislation to prohibit night labor by women. During his investigations he had seen whole families—fathers, mothers, and children—toiling seven days a week. He demanded that workers be entitled by law to one day's rest. When the cannery interests requested exemption from this legislation, Smith stood up and made the briefest speech in the history of the Assembly. "I have read carefully the commandment, 'Remember the Sabbath Day, to keep it holy,' but I am unable to find any language in it that says 'except in the canneries.' " The opposition was annihilated.

In 1913, when Smith was elected speaker of the Assembly, he broadened his fight for social welfare. With a witty, lashing tongue and blue eyes that flashed steel, he battled against the private interests who sought to impede public control of water power and electricity. He championed financial compensation for workingmen who sustained injuries at their jobs. He continued his struggle for the reform of the factory code.

The press spoke with humor of this Irish crusader. "Speaker Smith is running the Assembly and nobody else. . . . Nobody has to cup his ear in his hands to catch what he is saying." His voice was harsh and his manner impetuous; but his heart was eloquent. "Smith . . . pounds his gavel," remarked one witness of his earnestness, "as if he were challenging one of those sledge-hammer affairs at Coney Island which are supposed to show you how strong you are."

Smith's popularity was tremendous. Friends and foes were fascinated by him. They roared at his stories, applauded his genius for dialect, his ability to act. And whether he sat in the speaker's chair or—humbled by the perverse wind of political fortune—rejoined the ranks of the minority, he delivered speeches which for their simple effectiveness had never been heard before. On one occasion, in support of a child-welfare measure, he stood up and declared: "We have been in a great hurry to legislate for the interests. We have been in a great hurry to conserve that which means to the state dollars and cents. We have been slow to legislate along the direction that means thanksgiving to the poorest man recorded in history —to Him who was born in the stable at Bethlehem. . . ." The child-welfare measure became law.

For more than a decade Smith matched his wits successfully with his colleagues in the Assembly. And he was subsequently accorded the opportunity of matching them with the greatest legal minds in the state. It was the practice for New Yorkers to summon a convention every twenty years to consider a revision of the constitution. And in 1915 such an assembly convened at Albany. At the convention Smith impressed his fellow delegates with his intellectual acumen and his Hibernian charm.

He walked out of the convention the most admired young political figure in the state. His fellow Democrats were determined to reward him. He had served for twelve years in the Assembly at a nominal salary. The leaders of the party now offered him a more lucrative assignment. They nominated him to run for sheriff of New York County. The job paid twelve thousand dollars a year, but the fees accruing to the office were four times the salary. Even the leading Republican papers deplored his retirement from the Assembly. The *Tribune* declared, "The City of New York could well afford to pay Alfred E. Smith all the prospective emoluments of the sheriff's office as a consideration for his continuing to represent a local assembly district at Albany."

He was elected sheriff without difficulty. During his two years in this office he became a wealthy man. But he was not happy at his job. He was anxious to continue his fight for social welfare. Within a short time he was destined to re-enter the lists. But when he returned to Albany, it was as governor of New York.

IV

In 1918 the state chiefs of the Democratic party selected Al Smith to lead their ticket. In accepting the nomination, Smith resigned from the presidency of the Board of Aldermen, to which he had been elected in 1917. He entered the campaign with vigor. A number of Republicans and independent progressive voters rallied to his support. Women prepared to cast their vote for the first time, and a substantial number in New York were attracted by Smith's concern for the "human side of government." Prominent among them was a capable social worker, Belle Moskowitz, who joined ranks with Smith at this time and for the remainder of his political life rendered him the services of a highly trained social scientist.

This was a curious state of affairs: Progressives supporting a Tammany-sponsored candidate! But this nominee, molded in machine politics, had risen by some gift of genius above his environment and had spoken to the human heart. In the first address a Democratic candidate ever delivered to a female electorate, at the Women's University Club, Smith declared: "I know what is right. If I ever do anything that is wrong, it will not be because I don't know it to be so, and you can mark it down as being willful and deliberate and hold me to account for it."

It was unconventional talk for a politician. The voters were impressed. Smith was elected governor by a margin of fifteen thousand votes, half of which came from the soldiers in camps. His mother was the first woman in the state to cast a vote for her son.

At the age of forty-five Smith had reached the Executive Mansion. Educated liberals had discovered a successful spokesman at last. These intellectual liberals lacked the practical touch. But Al Smith, untrammeled by the textbook theories of political science, turned complex facts into pictures of human life. He made government live. He demonstrated to intelligent businessmen that the social welfare of the worker was financially as well as morally desirable. He was unsurpassed in the art of getting opponents to discuss their differences. "I am one of the easiest men to sit down with," he declared. "I was brought up in such a way that I cannot lean way back in my chair. I always bend over when I am talking to anybody." Frequently, when a newspaper printed an editorial that he deemed an unfair presentation of his policy, he paid a visit to the writer with facts he considered vital for a just appraisal. His most implacable opponents in the legislature were his dinner companions. One Republican politico thus grudgingly summed up the magnetism of his personality: "If everybody in New York State had a personal acquaintance with Al Smith, there would be no votes on the other side."

Through a miracle of mind and character, he fashioned the state into a more effective instrument for social justice. Instead of adhering to the time-honored custom of selecting Tammany politicians for posts, he found it desirable to surround himself with a kitchen cabinet of specialists and educational experts in progressive government. When he selected a prominent engineer for the job of superintendent of the highways, and the appointee confessed that he knew nothing about politics, Smith retorted: "We have had a good many political superintendents of highways. Now we want one who knows how to build roads." He assigned Miss Frances Perkins, who afterward became Secretary of Labor in the Franklin Roosevelt administration, a seat on the State Industrial Commission. Leaders of industry were shocked that the governor should appoint a woman. When, however, Miss Perkins successfully negotiated several labor settlements, they realized the shrewdness of his choice.

Impressed with the efficiency of industrial corporations, the governor applied the methods of business to government. "We are all stockholders in the great corporation of the United States. We own it. It belongs to us." He sharpened the physical tools of state, consolidating one hundred and sixty-five departments into eighteen. Since this meant a drastic elimination of political patronage, he encountered a stubborn opposition from all "interested" parties. But he took his program to the people and won the fight. To his opponents who charged him with the desire "to make himself a king," he smiled and replied ironically, "Yes, meet the King, the King of the East Side."

Under his direction, Robert Moses, a graduate of Yale and a student of jurisprudence at Columbia and Oxford, devised plans for transforming poorly graded roads into broad highways and forests into parks. People of wealth were infuriated that the state planned to buy woodland which they desired for their own private uses and to build highways which would render these preserves accessible to workingmen on Sundays. They battled vigorously against what they termed was legislation for the rabble. "The rabble!" Smith bellowed. "*I* am the rabble." He fought for a bill to replace slum tenements by modern low-priced dwellings. He liberalized the salaries of teachers and raised the standards of schooling in rural districts, maintaining a competent body of educators throughout the state.

No one so completely reveled in a battle as he. No one so thoroughly enjoyed the struggle to put his measures into law. He was, as Franklin Roosevelt declared in a speech sponsoring him for President, the "Happy Warrior."

He made regular public accountings of the state's financial budget, unraveling the whole "Chinese" puzzle of appropriations and taxes in such a vivid and exciting manner as to make it an adventure in learning for the "man in the street." In his campaign to render government truly popular, he gave a remarkable demonstration of political tolerance. In 1919, when the Assembly refused to seat five members of the Socialist party who had been elected in the recent campaign, the governor issued a statement excoriating the legislators. "Although I am unalterably opposed to the fundamental principles of the Socialist party, it is inconceivable that a minority . . . should be deprived of its right of expression."

And all the while he battled under a standard with the flaming device: "The cure for the evils of democracy is more democracy."

V

FOUR TIMES he was elected governor by the people of New York. One other man alone had received this honor, George Clinton more than a century before.

Only once was Smith repudiated by the people. In 1920, while running for a second term, he became a victim, along with other Democrats, of the Republican landslide that swept the country. He declared that he would never run for office again. And he entered business as the president of the United Trucking Company. However, on the eve of a new election in 1922, Democrats, liberal Republicans, and non-partisan progressives from all over the state pleaded with him to offer himself as candidate once more. Franklin Roosevelt wrote from Hyde Park: "You represent the hope of . . . the average citizen."

Smith re-entered politics, relinquishing a handsome business salary. He was elected governor by a plurality of almost four hundred thousand votes. At the end of his second term he enjoyed a greater popularity than any other political leader in the history of the state. When John W. Davis was chosen presidential candidate at the 1924 Democratic convention, he beseeched the governor to campaign for a third term to strengthen the party's national chances. And Smith was re-elected, although Davis met with overwhelming defeat. In 1926 his admirers demanded that he accept the nomination for a fourth term. And once more he was elected, this time by a plurality of a quarter of a million votes.

A leading national figure whose legislative program had stirred the imagination of Americans in all forty-eight states, Smith entered the Democratic National Convention at Houston, Texas, in 1928, the outstanding candidate for the presidential nomination. He was named on the first ballot. But the people who loved him feared for his political life. Advisers urged the governor, whose idiosyncrasies had been accepted by the people of New York, to groom himself for the wider electorate beyond the Hudson. They counseled him to polish his East Side accent, to suppress his "ain'ts," his double negatives, his penchant for speaking of the "raddio." To his board of strategy Smith replied, "I won't change now, even to get into the White House. I'm going to run just as God made me."

Answering an attack by an influential American in a national magazine that a President of the Catholic faith would be compelled to place his allegiance to the Papacy above his loyalty to his country, Smith vigorously denied that there was any incompatability between his religion and his Americanism. He concluded with an appeal. " . . . I join with fellow Americans of all creeds in a fervent prayer that never again in this land will any public servant be challenged because of the faith in which he has tried to walk humbly with God."

But it was an impossible task Al Smith had set for himself. Powerful forces were aligned against him. He was a Catholic, he was against Prohibition, he was a Democrat in a political era dominated on the national level by Republicans. Herbert Hoover, the Republican candidate, won the election by some six million votes.

Al Smith lost the campaign, but he won a far more substantial victory. He had selected, as his party nominee to the governorship of New York, Franklin Delano Roosevelt. By designating Roosevelt as his successor, he had unwittingly placed a Democrat of his political faith of embattled liberalism in a position of influence from whence he would ride into the White House four years later. But his own journey into politics was over now, at fifty-eight. "Your husband is among the unemployed," he told his wife. He wrote his autobiography, dictated political articles, and for a time served as an editor of the *New Outlook*. Appointed president of the Empire State, Inc., he moved, upon completion of the building, into an office on the thirty-second floor of the tallest skyscraper on earth.

The years passed. Although newspapers no longer carried headlines about him, and election celebrations were tendered others, people everywhere warmed to memories of the Bowery prince who had glimpsed a better world beyond the water front. Al Smith did not reach the White House, but his principles have. The basic features of his experiments in human justice have been assimilated into the policy of both major parties. No political candidate today would dare to return the American people to the social jungle that existed forty years ago when Smith first sat in the Albany Assembly.

In October 1944, at the age of seventy, the "Happy Warrior" passed away. More than one hundred and sixty thousand of his fellow citizens filed past his bier in St. Patrick's Cathedral. And many of them recalled the words he had spoken: "The cure for the evils of democracy is more democracy."

IMPORTANT DATES IN THE LIFE OF
ALFRED EMANUEL SMITH

1873—Born, New York City.

1895—Appointed a clerk in the office of Commissioner of Jurors.

1903—Elected to the New York State Assembly.

1911—Served as vice-chairman of factory commission investigating labor conditions.

1913—Chosen speaker of the Assembly.

1915—Named delegate to the state constitutional convention.

1915–17—Served as sheriff of New York County.

1917—Elected president of the Board of Aldermen of New York City.

1919–20—Served first term as governor of New York State.

1923–28—Served three additional terms as governor.

1928—Nominated by Democrats for President.

1932—Became head of the Empire State Building.

1944—Died, New York City.

George Michael Cohan

[1878-1942]

ONE night George M. Cohan was sitting at a table at Jim Churchill's, the rendezvous for theatrical celebrities. A down-and-out and consumptive ex-trouper, George Fuller Golden, walked over to the table.

"Anything I can do for you, George?"

"Yes, Mr. Cohan. I'm writing a book on vaudeville, and I'm selling advertising space in it."

"What's the cost?"

"Not much, Mr. Cohan. Twenty-five dollars a quarter page, fifty dollars a half page, a hundred dollars a full page."

"All right, George, put me down for half a page."

"Thanks, Mr. Cohan." Golden looked on, a trifle disappointed, as the Song and Dance Man took out his checkbook. He had expected a full-page ad from George M. Cohan.

"Here you are, kid, take care of yourself," said Cohan as he handed the check to Golden.

Golden looked at the check and fainted. It was made out for ten thousand dollars.

George M. Cohan was so skillful in portraying other people's lives because he was so gentle in getting under other people's skins and into their hearts.

II

AT THE HEIGHT of their successful partnership, Cohan and Harris were looked upon as "just a couple of lucky Jews." Cohan was often taken for a Jew because of his Semitic-seeming name. As a matter of fact, however, he was a full-blooded Irishman whose original family name was Keohane —pronounced Ca-han or Co-han.

His father, Jeremiah John Cohan, and his mother, Nellie Costigan Cohan, were among the "aristocrats" of the nineteenth-century troupers. Fiddler and mimic and dancer and singer, Jerry Cohan organized his own troupes, wrote his own sketches, invented his own dances, and was generally regarded in the profession as a man with too big a heart and too empty a purse. In the spring of 1874, having no money and no plans, he decided to marry. "It's more fun to starve in company"—especially in the company of a young and pretty and vivacious Irish colleen. From now on it was the team of "Mr. and Mrs. Jerry Cohan" in their favorite melodrama, *The Owls of New York*.

A merry, tumultuous, knockabout life between the footlights and the boardinghouses. No time for rest—not even when their three children, Maude, Josephine, and George Michael, were born. Maude died at nine months, and Josephine was two years old when George Michael uttered his first little song-cry to an unheeding world.

Scene, the home of a cousin of the Cohans in Providence, Rhode Island. Time, July 3, 1878—a date which the dramatic-minded Jerry changed, for the official record, to July 4. "The birthday of American independence, the birthday of a great American actor."

But to the people of Providence the date or even the event of George's birth made little difference. "A good but shiftless family. Can't afford too many children. Got to be on the go all the time."

And on the go they were, only a few weeks after George's arrival. The Four Cohans—father and mother dancing on the stage, the babies sleeping in a hotel. One evening, in Albany, the hotel room in which the two babies were asleep—one in a crib and the other on a trunk—caught fire. Fortunately the fire was put out and Josie and Georgie were carried to safety. When the parents returned from their performance they found the babies still asleep.

As Georgie grew older his parents tried to introduce him to a little "schooling and fiddling." Georgie developed an equal aversion both to his music and to his books. Many years later, when George and Jerry were dining at an expensive hotel in Cincinnati, they listened entranced to an expertly rendered violin solo. "Say, Dad," exclaimed George when the solo was over, "if I had paid more attention to my violin lessons, I might now be playing here."

"Yes, son," replied Jerry, "but you wouldn't be eating here."

It was in his eighth year that Georgie gave up his schoolbooks and his violin to take his place as a professional actor upon the stage. The part in which he made his first hit was that of Henry Peck in *Peck's Bad Boy*. He played this character—"the incorrigible lad with a heart of gold"—to the hilt because it was himself that he portrayed. "Never was so mischievous a leprechaun let loose upon an unsuspecting world." Always playing pranks upon prompters, managers, musicians, actors, property men, mechanics—every molested member of the cast and the backstage crew. And always warding off a blow with his warm and disarming smile. A laughter-loving and popular gang, the Four Cohans—Josie, too, "America's Youngest and Most Graceful Skirt Dancer," had joined them on the stage.

Talented parents, precocious kids. At eleven Georgie was already writing his own sketches and songs. He knew very little about grammar and even less about music, but he had an inborn genius for the universal language that reaches from heart to heart. "I never had time to learn how to write, I was always so busy writing."

Writing, and living, and restlessly roaming from town to town. The tide of adventure was in his blood. At fifteen he tried to elope with a female baritone. A detective hired by his father brought him home—the family was staying at a Rhode Island summer resort at the time. As Georgie and his would-be bride got off the train they were greeted by the local band. The bandmaster, a friend of the Cohans, winked at the musicians. "Go to it, boys!" And the disappointed lover was compelled, to his chagrin, to walk past the bandstand to the tune of "The Cat Came Back." "It's all right, boys," he waved sheepishly to the players. "When I run away with my next girl, you'll have to play 'The Cat Got Lost.'"

Always getting into scrapes, he yet managed to guide the Four Cohans into bigger and bigger time until finally they reached New York. George was now the acknowledged business manager of the team.

And at twenty-one he brought a new member to the team. It was in the summer of 1899 that he married Ethel Levey, an Irish actress who had assumed the name of her Jewish stepfather for her stage career. George wrote her a song—"I Guess I'll Have to Telegraph My Baby"—which became one of the high spots of the show. The Cohans had reached top billing and top money. Their act was now good for one thousand dollars a week.

And so they sang and danced their way into the twentieth century—the staid Jerry, the gentle Nellie, Josie of the "light fantastic toe," Ethel of the hearty, husky voice, and George, with straw hat and bamboo cane, jerky gait and bobbing head and corner of the mouth uplifted in a perpetual grin, a Pied Piper leading his audiences of grown-up children out of the workaday world into the fairyland of whimsy and wisecracks and dreams. "The squarest little shooter and the smartest little guy of them all."

III

THE MARRIED LIFE of George and Ethel staggered along the rocky road to the divorce courts. Two fiery temperaments, they generated between them the sparks of many a flare-up and misunderstanding. On one of the train jumps during their vaudeville circuit there was an unusually heated discussion in which the entire family took sides. Unable to stifle his mounting anger, George finally stormed out of the car and went off to sulk in the smoker.

A few minutes later the conductor came along. "Ticket, please."

"Out there with the company," barked George.

"What company?"

"The damnedest company you ever saw!"

But for the present he stuck to the company, and to Ethel Levey. The birth of a girl—they named her Georgette—and for a while there was peace in the family. But then the fire of their conflicting temperaments flared up anew. The end of their marriage, if not yet in sight, was nevertheless a foregone conclusion. "They'll never stick it out. Oil and fire burn fine, but they burn down too soon."

For the present, however, his domestic excitement spurred him along to artistic success. Songs, vaudeville sketches, full-length plays—*I Love Everyone in the Wide Wide World, The Story of the Wedding March, The Governor's Son, Running for Office, Shades of Night, I Long to See the Sunrise in the East*—came tumbling like a cataract from the magic of his pen. Again and again he would sell a play before he had written a line, before even he had definitely worked out the plot. But once the sale was made, he would sit at his desk twelve, sixteen, twenty hours a day, spinning out the story with indefatigable invention and incredible speed. "There are half a dozen geniuses in that compact little body of his." He wrote his plays, he produced them, he staged them, and he played the leading part in them. In one of his plays he brought the house down singing "If I Were Only Mr. Morgan." Referring to this occasion, the *New York World* wrote: "Master Cohan is a fair-sized trust in himself. Why he should wish he were Mr. Morgan is . . . difficult to understand."

Twenty-five now, and already one of the most familiar figures in New York, gaining friends wherever he went—and enemies, sometimes through other people's envy, sometimes through his own generosity. "I once made Filson a present of a sketch of mine—and now he is one of the stanchest enemies I have." If you want people to avoid you, said an Eastern sage, put them in debt to your kindness. What people hate most is to pay a debt.

A cynical and a sensible little guy, this kid who had danced his way into the affections of New York. A fellow who loved to put his foot on the brass rail and to buy drinks for everybody in the house—actors, writers, singers, agents, publishers, prize fighters, baseball players, anybody who happened to be in the mood for a spicy snip or a cheering word.

And yet he was not satisfied. "I've been in this stage business since I was a kid. I've written all sorts of trash—but nothing ever that was good, real!" And now he had something good in his mind—at least, the title for it. *Little Johnny Jones.* He spoke about it to Abe Erlanger, the "Czar" of the show business. "Kid, I've got a play for you that'll bowl 'em over."

"Fine!" said Erlanger. "Tell me the story."

"It's about a jockey, little Johnny Jones. You'll like it, kid!"

"But what's the story?"

"It gives me a real part. Scenery, songs, dances, dialogue—best thing I've ever done, no fooling."

"But the story?"

"It's a knockout, kid! Come on, let's start rehearsals."

Erlanger, however, was in no mood to start rehearsals on a story he knew nothing about. Later that day, conversing with a number of his pals at the Metropole, Cohan chuckled: "How the hell was I going to tell the story to Erlanger when I didn't know it myself?"

Shortly after his interview with Erlanger, Cohan formed a much more important partnership for the production of his play—and of many other plays. He was sitting at his desk in the offices of the Miner Lithograph Company, a general meeting place for theatrical folk. Walter J. Moore, the New York manager of the company, walked over and sat down beside him. "How's that new play of yours coming along, Georgie?"

"Just fine, kid."

"Got Abe Erlanger interested?"

"I guess so," was the noncommittal answer.

Moore pulled his chair up closer. "Listen, Georgie. You've got a full-sized job on your hands. Too big for any one man. Even for the great little Cohan."

"Then what do you expect me to do?"

"Get yourself a partner, Georgie. Somebody to take the business worries off your hands."

"Have anybody in mind?"

"Yes, Georgie. That fellow over there talking to Al Woods. His name's Harris, Sam Harris. A guy with imagination, a good business head, and a square shooter."

"Sounds all right. Bring him over."

Moore raised his voice. "Hey, Sam! Come here and meet a friend of mine . . . Sam, this is Georgie Cohan . . . George, meet Sam Harris."

"Glad to meet you, Mr. Cohan."

"How're you, kid."

And thus began one of the most famous partnerships in the American theater.

IV

SAM HARRIS, a product of New York's East Side, was small, wiry, astute, honest to a fault, and a wizard in diagnosing and correcting the weak parts in a play. He had something of the Midas touch in his managerial make-up. Whatever play he touched was likely to turn into gold.

His first venture under the partnership of Cohan and Harris—no contracts were ever signed between them—was *Little Johnny Jones*. The play opened at Hartford on October 8, 1904. On the opening night Cohan and Harris counted their available funds. They had less than fifty dollars between them. And their pockets were full of unpaid bills—for costumes, properties, scenery, salaries, and what not. They entered the theater with a sinking heart. Three hours later they emerged triumphant. They had an unmistakable hit on their hands—a play with a lively plot, sparkling dialogue, three superb songs ("Yankee Doodle Boy," "Give My Regards to Broadway," and "Good-bye, Flo"), and an inimitable monologue (*Life's a Funny Proposition After All*) recited by George M. Cohan himself.

The success of this play convinced Erlanger that George M. Cohan was a good man to have around. He sent for him and asked him to write a musical play for Fay Templeton—a small-town girl who had made good on Broadway. "Have you any idea on the subject?"

"Sure," said Cohan, whose "idea on the subject" had popped into his head the moment he heard the name of Fay Templeton. "It's to be a small-town play—a 'rube' show somewhere around New York." His brain and his tongue worked simultaneously. "How about a place like New Rochelle? . . . Great idea, don't you think? I'll get to work right away. Tomorrow you'll have the plot and the song titles and the whole outline ready. And we'll have Victor Moore for the male part. And what do you say to Cleveland or Cincinnati or Columbus for the opening?"

In reply to the tornado, Abe Erlanger could only gasp. "Yes," he managed to blurt out, "Columbus *might* be a good place for the opening. . . ."

A whirlwind period of production, a whirlwind success, and a sad aftermath. George M. Cohan and Ethel Levey had decided to go their separate ways. They were divorced in the winter of 1907.

V

AND NOW came one of the most tumultuous years of his life. Divorce, courtship, marriage—to Agnes Nolan of Boston, whose fireman father didn't consider an actor good enough for his daughter—a quarrel with his parents, a reconciliation, with George crying like a child in his mother's lap, three successful plays on Broadway, a bon-voyage party in the grand ballroom of the Hotel Knickerbocker, and a trip to Europe with his winsome young bride, whose father had at last been convinced that even a New York actorman can make a desirable son-in-law for a Boston fireman.

Return from Europe, reunion with his family, new successes for the Four Cohans—"My mother thanks you, my father thanks you, my sister thanks you, and I thank you"—a new relationship established through the marriage of Sam Harris to Agnes Nolan's sister, Alice, and five productions within a single year under the management of Cohan and Harris. Yet George was still unhappy. Though popular with the "gallery," he had failed to win the approval of the critics. "A smart little guy, but no real substance to him—too versatile to be deep." So that's what they thought of him! Well, he would show them they were wrong. Someday he would retire from his acting and devote himself entirely to his writing. And then he would give the world something *real*—"a regular play, a sane play, about things I know and people I know."

In 1909 he actually tried "retiring" for several months. He sat at his desk and wrote and wrote and wrote—and produced nothing. That is, nothing complete. But the time was not wasted. For in that period he laid the groundwork for some of his later works—*Get-Rich-Quick Wallingford, Seven Keys to Baldpate, Broadway Jones*—plays that were to come pretty close to being real.

The actual writing of these plays, however, was but an item in a crowded routine. George M. Cohan worked best under pressure. By training and by instinct he was a "variety" man. He found his ideal workshop in a hotel room, and his favorite retreat for meditation in the hubbub of a rehearsal. It was under such conditions that he dramatized George Randolph Chester's short stories about J. Rufus Wallingford—a "straight" comedy without songs or dances.

It was his first artistic success. "I take my hat off to George M. Cohan," wrote Channing Pollock in the *Green Book*. Here, agreed the critics with hardly a dissenting voice, was a "new Cohan"—a man who surpassed all the contemporary American playwrights in the hilarity of his satire and the brilliance of his lines.

Get-Rich-Quick Wallingford was not only his first *artistic* success, but one of his greatest *financial* triumphs. After the play had run 424 times in New York, Cohan one evening walked into the Metropole and spoke to one of his cronies, Edmund Plohn: "Kid, take a good look at me. You're looking at a millionaire."

At this stage George M. Cohan owned not only a million, but "all Broadway." A new theater bearing his name had been opened in Times Square; the Friars Club and the Society of American Dramatists and Composers gave dinners in his honor; the leading American newspapers, including even the sedate *Boston Transcript,* regarded him as little less than a god. The key to the city, to every footlight-loving city in the country, was his for the asking.

A man with a ready plot, a ready purse, and a ready wit. One evening he attended the première of Paul Armstrong's fascinating melodrama, *The Deep Purple.* After the first act he sought out the author. "Great stuff, kid. You ought to thank George Tyler for the cast."

"I'm not speaking to Tyler," said Armstrong.

After the second act Cohan said to Armstrong, "It's a sure hit, Paul. You ought to thank Hugh Ford for the direction."

"I'm not speaking to Ford," said Armstrong.

After the play Cohan met his press agent, Edwin Dunn, in the lobby of the theater. "I wonder," said Dunn, "why Paul Armstrong didn't make a curtain speech."

"I know why," flashed Cohan with a grin. "He's not speaking to the audience."

VI

SUNLIGHT, and storm cloud, and sunlight again. George M. Cohan had reached the meridian of his career. Wealth, popularity, genius, friendship, love—all these he had in overflowing measure. He was head now of one of the great families of America—they still lived and traveled and, whenever possible, played together. "There's a great and tender understanding in that Cohan family." Once when they were on tour with a company of sixty, George and his father occupied different sleepers. Every morning George made his way through the train until he came to his father's berth and greeted him with a "Hello, Dad" and a kiss. "Never in the annals of mankind," observes Cohan's biographer, Ward Morehouse, "has there been a son more devoted to his parents." And, he might have added, a brother more devoted to his sister. When his sister and his father died, within a few months of each other, Cohan felt for a time completely lost. "It was then," he confided later to a friend, "that I went on the only period of hard and sustained drinking in all my life."

Death, desolation, war. April 6, 1917. The Germans had torpedoed an American ship. Congress had declared that a state of hostility existed between the United States and Germany. Life, Cohan realized, had its brutal as well as its tender face. He was sitting at his desk trying to work at one of his plays. But the characters refused to come to life. No time now for comedy. The world was attuned to a more serious note. He took up a piece of paper and began to scribble aimlessly. Soon the thoughts and the words and the music began to take shape, and within a few minutes they came to life in a marching song for ten million men:

> Over there, over there,
> Send the word, send the word over there,
> That the Yanks are coming, the Yanks are coming,
> The drums rum-tumming everywhere.
> So prepare, say a prayer,
> Send the word, send the word to beware,
> We'll be over, we're coming over,
> And we won't come back till
> It's over over there.

A sadder and wiser Cohan now. A man not only of impetuous activity, but of serious thought. Yet masterful and independent as ever. Having quarreled with Sam Harris, he dissolved the partnership and went on producing alone. And having been defied by the officers of the Actors' Equity Association, he fought them throughout the actors' strike of 1919 and refused to make peace with the Equity even after he had lost the fight. A strange role for a man who had always been on the side of the underdog. But Cohan was a strange man—a sort of benevolent despot, a man with a great heart but with an equally great pride. When the strike was over he declared, "I don't think I'll produce any more; I don't think I'll act any more; I'll go to Great Neck and hide . . . And that's the kind of a little guy I am."

But that was not "the kind of a little guy" he was. He could no more separate himself from the theater than he could separate himself from the breath of his life. Before long he was at work on another play, *The Tavern* —a script which was submitted to him as a melodrama and which he rewrote into a farce. As usual, he engaged the actors and went into rehearsal before the play was finished. "The last act," relates the co-producer of the play, Brock Pemberton, "was fed to the director and cast in short takes and the suspense was terrific." The leading character in the play, a vagabond, appeared to the very last scene as a romantic hero. The man who played this part was Arnold Daly. On the day before the opening, when the final scene came galloping in fresh from Cohan's desk, Arnold Daly almost had a fit. His romantic hero turned out to be an escaped lunatic.

The surprise was as great to the public as it was to Arnold Daly. *The Tavern* was a huge success.

VII

SUNSET, and evening star, and after that the dark. Cohan was now regarded not only as an outstanding playwright, but as a first-rate actor. "It is an annual surprise," wrote Alexander Woollcott, "to find how deft, how artful, how quiet, how winning, and how gently pathetic a comedian is George M. Cohan." An older generation of critics had condemned him as "a symbol of brash violence—a disciple of perpetual motion." The newer generation had seen him grow into "the softest-spoken and the most subtle of our male comedians." Somebody, observed Heywood Broun, should create a foundation which would endow all stage aspirants with tickets to see Cohan act. With a single low inflection of the voice, he could transform a lifeless sequence into a living scene. When he appeared in *Ah, Wilderness!*, one of Eugene O'Neill's lesser plays, his acting hypnotized the audience into hailing it as a masterpiece. But the mastery, as Gilbert Gabriel observed in the *New York American*, "remains that of Mr. Cohan."

And it was the mastery of Mr. Cohan's acting—he played the part of President Franklin D. Roosevelt—that turned *I'd Rather Be Right,* a musical comedy by George S. Kaufman and Moss Hart, into "the most important and talked-about enterprise in the theater of its time."

This play, too, was a landmark in another respect. It marked the resumption of the partnership of Cohan and Harris. The reconciliation of the two "friendly enemies" had come about in a simple manner. One evening they met at the Plaza. "George," said Harris, "why did we ever split?"

"Dunno, kid," replied Cohan. "Couple of damn fools, I guess."

It was Tennyson, we believe, who wrote, "Blessings on the falling out that all the more endears." Cohan and Harris had now become greater friends than ever. Each tried to outdo the other in generosity. One day they sat at Dinty Moore's, buying drinks for all their cronies who happened to drop in. Finally the waiter was ready with their check. It was for about seventy dollars. Both of them made a grab for it. Cohan got it.

"If you let Mr. Cohan pay the check," cried Harris, "you'll never see me here again!"

"If you take the money from Mr. Harris," growled Cohan, "I'll never again step into this place, so help me!"

They continued this altercation, to the embarrassment of the waiter, until Billy Moore, son of the proprietor, came along. The waiter explained the trouble.

"I'll tell you what we'll do," said Moore, who reached for the check and tore it into bits.

Whereupon Cohan leaped forward, held out his hand to Harris, and grinned: "Shake, kid. The old gag works every time."

Cohan was sixty now. Threescore years, threescore plays, and hundreds of songs. Yet he was still dissatisfied. "I should have done more, much more." He felt ill at ease among the so-called highbrows. "I'm nothing but an ignorant little guy." Once, when Irving Berlin proclaimed him as "the greatest natural song writer America has ever produced," he grinned sheepishly at Berlin and said, *"There,* kid, is a guy who can *really* write a song."

A gray-headed, sulky, quarrelsome, blustering, temperamental, big-hearted little trouper—an Irishman of many moods and infinite charm. Always he had a circle of friends around him, and always he paid their bills. And the tips he gave to waiters and to other servants were, as a friend expressed it, "out of this world."

Still exuberant as ever; but his exuberance was now of the spirit rather than of the flesh. The flame of his life was flickering low. Too uninterruptedly energetic, too early exhausted. He smiled sadly when on his final tour he heard a Pittsburgh girl remark: "So this is the great Cohan who wrote all those corny old tunes. Looks on his last legs, poor guy!"

His last legs—too tired for dancing now, but still sturdy enough to take him occasionally around the reservoir in Central Park. "Look at that Fifth Avenue skyline. When I first started going around this lake—it was twenty-five years ago—those high buildings weren't there . . . Funny thing, life—buildings go up, men go down."

Men were going down too rapidly around him—relatives, acquaintances, friends. Most of all he missed his "more than partner, my very brother," Sam Harris. His footsteps dragged as he followed Harris to his last resting place in the midsummer of 1941.

And now, no more walks around the lake. A bedridden invalid, who saw in a projection room an advance showing of a picture based on his life. "Great stuff," he said. "That's the kind of a little guy I would have liked to have been."

When he died (November 4, 1942), a whole nation mourned. That's the kind of a little guy he was.

IMPORTANT DATES IN THE LIFE OF
GEORGE MICHAEL COHAN

1878—Born, Providence, Rhode Island.

1891—Sold his first song.

1899—Married Ethel Levey.

1901—Produced his first full-length play, *The Governor's Son.*

1904—Formed partnership with Sam H. Harris.

1905—Scored success in *Forty-five Minutes from Broadway.*

1910—Produced *Get-Rich-Quick Wallingford.*

1913—Produced *Seven Keys to Baldpate.*

1917—Wrote war song, "Over There."

1920—Dissolved partnership with Sam Harris.

1924—Wrote autobiography, *Twenty Years on Broadway.*

1928—Produced *Elmer the Great.*

1934—Played in Eugene O'Neill's *Ah, Wilderness!*

1937—Resumed partnership with Sam Harris.

1928—Played part of President F. D. Roosevelt in *I'd Rather Be Right.*

1942—Died, New York.

Will Rogers

[1879-1935]

WILL Rogers was one eighth Cherokee Indian—and proud of the fact. One day he was delivering a lecture at the citadel of blue-blooded Americanism, the Boston Symphony Hall. "I am honored," he began in his Western drawl, "by the presence of so many descendants of the pioneer Americans. My own forefathers, I gotta confess, didn't come over like yours on the *Mayflower*. But," he added with a chuckle, "they met the boat."

II

TWO PECULIAR LEGENDS have grown up around the name of Will Rogers: the first, that he was an illiterate cowpuncher who paraded as a philosopher; the second, that he was an Oxford graduate who masqueraded as a clown. Neither of these two legends is true. Will Rogers was the fairly well educated son of an Oklahoma ranchman and banker. He could have had a college education if he had wanted it. But he was too restless a spirit to sit in the stuffy classroom of the academy. He preferred to roam at large in the wider academy of the open road. In everything he thought and said, in his profound observations as well as in his careless speech, he was always frankly and absolutely himself. This was the keynote to his greatness. His words were the perfect mirror of his heart.

Yet it took the world, it took even his own family, a long time to recognize him for what he was. As a child, Will Rogers was a disappointment to his parents. "Doesn't like his school. Plays truant every other day. It must be the Indian in him." Like his father, he was a good horseman. But it was not as a horseman that his father wanted to bring him up. "I've done enough riding for the whole family. I want *you* to grow up into an educated man."

In his effort to educate his boy, Clem Rogers—affectionately known in the neighborhood as "Uncle Clem"—sent Willie (of all places!) to a girls' school. Here an effort was made to have Willie "genteeled" not only in the three Rs, but in painting and in music as well. "I was doing nicely at the piano," he wrote years later, "until an angry teacher slapped me off the stool."

And now there came a tragedy into his life, the death of his mother. And a change from a girls' into a boys' school. But there was no change in Will's distaste for academic learning. From one school to another he was hustled, in the hope that somewhere along the line he would "perk up" and begin to study. In vain. "The boy is untidy, impetuous, and a spoiled brat." From some of the schools he was taken away at his own request; from others, at the request of his teachers. "The trouble with Willie," said one of his teachers, "is that his mind is too idle while his hands are too busy." He was too fond of playing with the lariat. He roped everything in sight—desks, tables, chairs, cats, dogs, boys on the way to and from school. "How I wish I could rope the headmaster!" This he didn't quite dare, but one day he dared the next thing to it. He roped the headmaster's colt. Unfortunately, however, Willie let go of the lasso. The frightened colt, with the rope dangling from its neck, bolted across the campus and disappeared beyond the limits of the town. "The headmaster," writes Betty Rogers in the story of her husband's life, "decided then that maybe Willie couldn't do without his lariat, but that the school could do without Willie."

His father, in the hope that a stricter discipline would be good for Willie, sent him to the Kemper Military Academy (1897). Here the young "loafer" received the highest mark for elocution—"he's such a good mimic"—and a less than average grade for scholastic attainment. Not that his mind was slow—indeed, he could memorize his lessons faster than anybody else in the school. But he was such a clown when he stood up to recite. His slouchy manner, the lift of his eyebrow, the shrug of his shoulders, the grin upon his face—all these "antics" would disrupt the class before he opened his mouth. "Sit down!" the exasperated teacher would cry and give him a "failure" mark.

Two years at the academy was all he could stand. Summarizing his entire school career, Will Rogers wrote with comic exaggeration: "I spent ten years in the fourth grade and knew more about *McGuffey's Fourth Reader* than McGuffey did."

But he had developed into a fine athlete—he had played baseball and football at Kemper—he could now ride and rope almost as well as his father, and he felt an insatiable urge to shut his books and to open the world. And so, after two years at Kemper, he borrowed thirty dollars from his three sisters, bought himself a "spooky old" horse, and set off on a ghost ride to the cow country of Amarillo, Texas.

Here he got his first job as a cowboy. "We helped drive a herd to Western Kansas . . . No greater, no happier life in the world . . . That was the prettiest country I ever saw in my life, flat as a beauty contest winner's stomach, and prairie lakes scattered all over it. And mirages! You could see anything in the world—just ahead of you."

And this, from now on, was to be the restless adventure of his life—to be always on the trail, seeking out the mirages of the world, and interpreting their false but nonetheless fascinating allure to his fellow men. A strange phenomenon in history—a philosopher on horseback.

III

IN BETWEEN ADVENTURES Will Rogers met Betty Blake. Strangely enough, she lived in a town named Rogers (Arkansas). On a visit to her sister in Oologah, Oklahoma, she met this "lithe, shy little fellow" who looked so little like a cowpuncher. They were having supper at the house of a mutual friend. "Will was awkward and very still during supper, but later . . . he thawed out and began to sing . . . He had a high tenor voice . . . I remember my delight as he sang song after song . . ."

She returned to her home in Arkansas. A few weeks later she received a letter from Will. "No doubt you will be madly surprised on receipt of this epistle but never the less I could not resist the temptation . . . Hoping you will take pity on this poor heart broken Cow pealer and having him rejoicing over these bold prairies on receipt of a few words from you I remain your True Friend and Injun Cowboy."

An exchange of letters—the early sunrise flushes of a bashful love—and Will suddenly left on a pilgrimage that was to take him around the globe. His first objective was the Argentine, a place which he had heard was good "cow country." He got to that country in a blundering, roundabout way—from Oklahoma to New Orleans, from New Orleans to Galveston, from Galveston to New York, from New York to Liverpool, from Liverpool to Buenos Aires.

Arrived in the Argentine, he became intimate with two unwholesome companions—hunger and disillusion. "The workers here get about five dollars a month . . . and have to live like dogs." And even this dog-life was denied to him for a time. He was reduced to sleeping in the park and going without meals before he got a job on a South American ranch.

But he couldn't stay put. Too eager to go on with the business of learning through living. On to the next page in the open book of the world. He shipped as a cattle tender on a boat that sailed for South Africa with a cargo of livestock.

It was in South Africa that he caught up with his destiny for the first time. He got a job in the show business—the place where he naturally belonged. "I was hired to do roping in Texas Jack's Wild West Circus." This circus was touring the South African cities. "We generally stay in a town two or three days . . . I am called 'The Cherokee Kid' on the program."

A kid, the adoration of all the other kids. "The matinee is especially for children and is always crowded . . . I am their ideal."

And so he traveled over South Africa, delighting his audiences—"this fellow can lasso the tail off a blowfly"—depositing good will wherever he went, and waiting for the chance to return to America.

This chance came by way of Australia, where he joined the circus of the Wirth Brothers as "the champion trick rough rider and lasso thrower of the world." From Australia to New Zealand—"Don't get excited when you look on the map and see where I am now"—and then back to America. He had been gone for two years. "I started out first class. Then I traveled second class, then third class. And when I was companion to the she-cows, was what might be called no class at all." He came back empty-handed—he had lost all his savings to professional gamblers in a card game. But he was rich in experience. "I would not take a fortune for my trip."

His father now urged him to settle down to the "respectable" business of ranching. But Will refused. The show business had got into his blood. Uncle Clem gave him up in disgust. "No boy who wastes his time in the circus will ever amount to anything."

And thus, too, believed Betty Blake. "I had a wide streak of conventionality in me," she writes, "and I was not particularly thrilled about Will's profession."

But when he proposed to her, she accepted—on condition that he would give up the theater.

A brief honeymoon, plans to settle down in Oklahoma, the theft of their presents and their savings in Butte, Montana—and then there came an offer to play the Percy Williams vaudeville circuit at three hundred dollars a week. This time even Betty was willing to accept the offer. Will Rogers was wedded to the stage for life.

IV

THERE WAS A NEW FEATURE now in his act—a running patter of observations as he rode around the stage and roped his animals. It was by accident that he had hit upon his added feature. One day a friend suggested that it might be a good idea for him to announce the most difficult catch of his act. Will did so, and the audience laughed. He was furious. "So they made fun of me, did they?"

"Why, no," said the manager after the show. "They thought you were grand. A laugh is the best thing you can get out of an audience."

Will tried it again. It worked. Once he tried to jump with both feet inside a spinning rope. He missed. "Well," he drawled to the audience, "got all my feet through but one." It brought the house down. From that day on Will kept his tongue busy on the stage as well as his hands and his feet.

Gradually his monologue acquired a definite personality. It had developed from a scattering of wisecracks to a philosophical point of view. He dispensed pills of bitter truth in the sugar-coating of his impertinent jests. "I once explained to my audience why I was able to tell the truth. It is because I never mixed up in politics." The devious ways of politics had become the continual butt of his satire. "You know, the more you read about politics the more you have to admit that each party looks worse than the other." There wasn't an officeholder who was free from his lashing tongue. He played no favorites either in party or in personality. Democrat, Republican, Wilson, Harding, Hoover, Coolidge, Roosevelt—not one of them was free from his caustic observations. Yet not one of them harbored any grudge against him. He was so good-natured in his scorn. His criticism was not the deadly poison of a foe, but the healing medicine of a friend.

And there was much that in his opinion needed healing in the political and social sickness of his day. Oppressive labor conditions. "Judge Gary reported for *one hour* in favor of a *twelve-hour* day. Then he was so exhausted they had to carry him out." The diplomatic muddle with Mexico. "We chased Villa over the border for five miles, but run into a lot of government red tape and had to come back." Our too-easy attitude toward the panhandlers of Europe. "Our foreign dealings are an open book—generally a checkbook." Our amateurishness in our international relationships. "The United States never lost a war or won a conference." The Geneva Peace Convention. "The Convention is off to a flying start. There is nothing to prevent their succeeding but human nature." And our unpreparedness—this was in 1934—in the face of aggressive dictatorship. "Walked into a barbershop today . . . Heard the radio going and somebody raising Old Ned with somebody. I says, 'Who's that?' They says, 'Why, that's the President giving some folks fits for being against military preparedness.' I says, 'Amen.' Sic 'em, Franklin. Pour it on 'em. If they want to know what 'not having a gun will do for you,' they can point out China and India."

The saddest truths, observed G. K. Chesterton, are often spoken in jest.

V

WILL ROGERS was one prophet who was not without honor in his country. Generous praise and lavish offers were heaped upon him from every side. One or two colleges even tried to give him an honorary degree. But he had too fine a sense of humor to accept this distinction. "Degrees have lost prestige enough as it is without handing 'em around to comedians, and it's this handing 'em out promiscuously that has helped to cheapen 'em. Let a guy get in there and battle four years if he wants one."

This was the quality that people loved best about Will Rogers—his freedom from all affectation. Whether on or off the stage, he was always informal. He was equally opposed to full-dress clothes and full-dress speech. He talked to his audiences as a man talks to a visiting friend. Again and again, after his intimate chat on the stage, he would sit down on the edge with his feet dangling over the orchestra pit. "Now, folks, please go home. I'm tired of messing with you."

He regarded himself as an ordinary fellow talking with his ordinary neighbors. He felt embarrassed when critics referred to him as a public figure, a statesman, and a sage. "I am just an entertainer. All I do is to watch the Government and report the facts." He even refused to call himself a humorist. "The facts themselves are humorous enough."

He saw the ridiculous sadness of the human show. Yet he was modest enough to refrain from suggesting any improvements. Once, after a meeting with Bernard Shaw, he remarked, "We've got a great deal in common. Both of us know the world is wrong, but we don't know what's the matter with it."

His mind couldn't grasp the evils of the world, but his instincts rebelled against them. There was too much distrust between man and man. Too many contracts, too little faith. Will Rogers never signed a contract, and he never broke his word.

There was too much cruelty between man and man, and between man and beast. This instinct for cruelty was a trait that just never found its way into the character of Will Rogers. His sympathies always went out to his fellow men. During the entire World War I he contributed, out of a salary none too large, one hundred dollars a week to the Red Cross. After the Nicaragua earthquake of 1931 he contributed five thousand dollars for the relief of the victims. These were but drops in the bucket of his lifelong generosity. "I've been lucky more than I deserve. I'd better pay up the score."

He paid up the score not only to his fellow men, but to all living things. "You know, it's funny," he once said to Fred Stone, "but I guess I'm about the only cowboy who never owned a gun. When I was a kid I used to go jack-rabbit hunting with the boys, but they did all the shooting, I never killed anything in my life."

VI

In his person and in his talk Will Rogers remained casual, even careless, to the end. "Will had a rule," writes his wife. "He dressed only once a day." On one occasion he was invited to attend a dinner given in honor of the mayor of Los Angeles. His wife laid out a clean shirt and a freshly pressed suit on his bed.

"What's wrong with *this* suit?" he protested when he arrived from his work at the studio. "And with this shirt? They're clean enough. I just put them on this morning." And he left for the dinner dressed in his old and comfortable clothes.

And, too, he always went to his performances dressed in his old and comfortable words. "I got me a dictionary one time," he said, "but it didn't last long . . . Here's one good thing about language, there is always a short word for it. 'Course the Greeks have a word for it, the dictionary has a word for it. I love words but I don't like strange ones. You don't understand them, and they don't understand you. Old words is like old friends—you know 'em the minute you see 'em."

The slovenly twist to the old tie, the ungrammatical turn of the old phrase, but the familiar lovable warmth underneath—this was the careless unconventional charm of Will Rogers at his best.

VII

HE WAS RESTLESS AS EVER. Though he had built himself a substantial estate at Santa Monica, his spirit was always on the wing. "I like to go away just for the fun of coming back." Vaudeville and lecture tours, trips to collect funds for charity, and pleasure jaunts around the world. At times he was so far away from home that "it took me a month before I found out that Notre Dame had lost a game." But everywhere the same human folk with the same human needs and the same human tastes. "The countryside here," he wrote from Siberia, "resembles the countryside in Oklahoma. And the farmers," he added, "are just as bad off." From Harbin he wrote: "What do you think I found here? A war? A revolution? No! *Abie's Irish Rose!* Played by Russians and Chinese combined."

And always the blessedness of coming home—to his wife and four children, and the simple Western food. "About all I do when I come back is just shake hands and eat . . . Beans, and what beans—kinder soupy navy beans cooked with plenty of real fat meat. And then the ham . . . Then the cream gravy . . . Ham gravy is just about the last word in gravys . . . Now then comes the corn bread. Not the corn bread like you mean. I mean corn pone, made with nothing but meal, and hot water and salt . . . Beans, corn bread, country ham, and gravy! Then for dessert? Don't have room for any dessert. Had any more room, would eat some more beans."

A brief rest, a satisfying bellyful of the home food and the home affection, and then off again on the wing.

Nineteen hundred and thirty-five. Will Rogers had worked and traveled strenuously for several years. He was tired. "Time to take a rest, Will," said his wife. But no. His friend, Wiley Post, was about to start on an air trip across Siberia to Moscow. Will Rogers decided to go along.

"The California night was cool," writes his wife. "Will and I were sitting in the grandstand at Gilmore Stadium, watching a rodeo . . . I watched him grin and wave to the contestants as they rode by on the tanbark . . . Will knew most of the boys in the show; and one by one, as the evening wore on, the old-timers came over to shake hands with him . . .

"That night in Los Angeles we drove from Gilmore Stadium to the airport. The waiting room was crowded and we slipped outside to talk until the plane was ready to go. Then we said good-by, and with his overcoat over his shoulder and a roll of midnight editions under his arm, Will stepped aboard. The plane taxied down the field, turned around and came back for the take-off. As the ship nosed up I caught a fleeting glimpse through the window—he was smiling—and I stood looking up at the red and green lights of the plane until they disappeared in the darkness. . . ."

Ten days later the news flashed around the world—"Will Rogers dead in an airplane crash on the tundras of Alaska."

VIII

"SHE HAD LIVED SUCH A LIFE," wrote Will Rogers when one of his sisters had died, "that it was a privilege to pass away. Death didn't scare her. It was only an episode in her life. If you live right, death is a joke to you, so far as fear is concerned."

These words were prophetic of the manner in which he himself died. When they discovered his mangled body, there was a smile upon his lips.

IMPORTANT DATES IN THE LIFE OF WILL ROGERS

1879—Born, Oologah, Indian Territory (later Oklahoma).

1889—Lost mother.

1893—Recognized as top-notch cowhand and steer-roper.

1897—Entered Kemper Military Academy.

1898—Ran away from Kemper Academy.
Got job as cowhand at Ewing Ranch, Texas.

1899—Won steer-roping prize at Claremore.

1902—Went to South America, and from there to South Africa.

1903—Worked in a circus in Australia.

1904—Returned to America.
Became vaudeville "cowhand."

1906—Met Fred Stone.

1908—Married Betty Blake.

1911—Lost father.

1914—Joined Ziegfeld Follies.

1919-22—Acted in silent pictures.

1922—Began to write for McNaught Syndicate.
Started on lecture tour.

1934—Voted most popular screen actor.

1935—Killed in airplane accident, Alaska.

Helen Keller

[1880-   ]

PETER Finley Dunne and Mark Twain were discussing the blindness of Helen Keller. "God, how dull it must be for her," exclaimed the author of *Mr. Dooley*. "Every day the same, and every night the same as the day!"

"You're damned wrong there," retorted Mark Twain. "Blindness is an exciting business, I tell you. If you don't believe it, get up some dark night on the wrong side of your bed when the house is on fire and try to find the door."

Helen Keller, because of her handicap, has enjoyed the excitement of trying to find the door out of the darkness—not only for herself but for the rest of mankind. Hers is the cause of the blind leading the blind, and of the seeing as well, to a new vision of life.

II

AT HER BIRTH she was normal, like other children. When she was twenty months old, however, she was stricken with an illness—the doctors called it "an acute congestion of the brain"—which deprived her of her sight and her hearing and consequently of her speech. Her parents looked pityingly upon her. Another of those human creatures condemned to the existence of an animal. How could she ever be expected to have *sense* if she was deprived of two fifths of her *senses*? People who were merely blind, or merely deaf-mute, could be taught somehow to communicate with the rest of the world. But this child who was blind and deaf and mute—what hope was there ever for *her*?

A pathetic little animal who could neither understand nor make herself understood. Instinctively she felt that she was different from the rest of the world, and this feeling made her furious. She kicked and she screamed and she scratched at the people who tried to approach her. Unable to play like other children, she amused herself by tearing their clothes and snipping their hair with a scissors. A pitiable nuisance. There was no way of teaching her to behave. One day she locked her mother in the pantry, and she laughed as she felt the vibration of her mother's pounding against the door.

A nuisance and a danger. She had a baby doll and a baby sister. She loved her doll, because she was allowed to play with it. But she didn't love her baby sister, because she wasn't allowed to play with *it*. Once she found the baby sleeping in the cradle which belonged to the doll. In a fit of temper she overturned the cradle, but her mother fortunately caught the baby as it fell to the floor.

A danger not only to others but to herself. Accidentally spilling a glass of water on her apron, she spread it out to dry before the smoldering fireplace. When the apron failed to dry quickly enough, she drew nearer and threw it over the live coals. In an instant her clothes were ablaze. Her old nurse barely managed to save her life by throwing a blanket over her. "Poor thing," said her relatives, "it might have been more merciful if she had burned to death."

And then there dawned a miraculous day when a teacher came to her and made her a member of the living world.

III

IT WAS THANKS to Alexander Graham Bell, inventor of the telephone, that Helen's parents were able to get the "miracle teacher" for their child. Mr. Bell, who had a tender feeling for the "imperfect specimens of the potter's clay," had suggested that Mr. Keller write to the Perkins Institute for the Blind with reference to Helen's problem. As a result of Mr. Keller's letter, the director of the institute recommended Miss Anne Mansfield Sullivan as a suitable teacher for the six-year-old Helen.

Anne Sullivan, a graduate of the Perkins Institute, was one of those rare geniuses who flower out of the muck of poverty and disease. Her father was a ne'er-do-well drunkard, her brother had died of tuberculosis, and she herself had been threatened with total blindness up to the age of eighteen, when a successful operation had partially cured her. At twenty, when she became Helen's teacher, she had recovered enough of her vision to read for the child and to lead her into a new world.

But how to begin? How to transform thoughts into words when the child had no conception of human language? Anne Sullivan found a way. The morning after she arrived she gave Helen a doll—an object with which the stricken child was most familiar. And then, using the code for the blind, she slowly spelled out with her fingers into Helen's hand the word *d-o-l-l*. This finger play, to Helen, was a fascinating game. Flushed with excitement, she clumsily imitated the motions, *d-o-l-l*. Then she ran downstairs to her mother and traced those funny motions into *her* hand. "At that time," writes Miss Keller in *The Story of My Life*, "I did not know that I was spelling a word or even that words existed; I was simply making my fingers go in monkeylike imitation." Little by little, however, Miss Sullivan got her to realize that these motions had a meaning. *They pointed out a thing.* Something she played with. Something for which she had once thrown her baby sister out of of her cradle. And there were other motions that pointed out other things. *D-o-g* meant something with a fuzzy snout that romped around you. *C-u-p* meant something out of which you drank. *H-a-t* meant something you put on your head when your mother took you out visiting. What a wonderful game! What a wonderful world! It was so full of so many things. *And everything had a name!*

One day she learned a new set of words—*mother, father, sister.* So that's what they were called. She had known them all her life without knowing it. And *teacher.* The name of that lovely new playmate of hers. Come, let's keep on playing the game. It's such fun! Give me more names, more, more. The child's hunger for knowledge was insatiable, and Miss Sullivan fed it with a resourcefulness that was amazing. In the springtime, when the daisies and the buttercups arrived and the birds and the squirrels awoke to new life, her teacher gave her blind little scholar an "insight" into the secrets of nature. And, "as my knowledge of things grew, I felt more and more the delight of the world I was in."

And then Miss Sullivan opened up for her a new delightful world—the world of books. She taught the child to read by supplying her with slips of cardboard on which various words had been printed in raised letters. New things, new names, new ideas. Stories. Poems. Pretty thoughts, pretty rhymes. She couldn't hear those rhymes, but she could feel with her fingers the same sorts of letters at the ends of the lines. Like the pattern of pretty trimmings on her Sunday dress. After all, you don't have to hear and you don't have to see the beautiful things of the world. You get to know them anyhow. You sort of *feel* your way to them.

Why, even those who can see and hear—Anne Sullivan had told her—must *feel* their way toward lots of things. *Hope,* for instance, or *joy,* or *love.*

"Now take love, Helen. Nobody can see it or hear it or taste it or smell it or touch it. Yet it's there just the same, strong and beautiful and real. How do you know? You can just *feel* it, that's how you know."

"Yes, Anne, *I* can feel it. I love *you.*"

And thus the soul of Helen unfolded gradually, until one day—miracle of miracles!—she learned to speak. The process was long and laborious and at times seemingly hopeless. The method, briefly, was as follows: Her teacher pronounced certain sounds while Helen passed her fingers over her teacher's tongue and lips and throat as these sounds were being pronounced. Then, passing her fingers over her own organs of speech, Helen tried to imitate the sounds by imitating the positions of these organs. After a seemingly endless succession of failures, the child—she was ten years old at the time—finally succeeded in articulating the letters of the alphabet. And then came the great moment of her life when she stammered out her first connected sentence—"It is warm."

The barrier between herself and the rest of the world had at last broken down. She was—almost—like other people! Her preliminary training had rescued her from the prison of her isolated helplessness. And now she was ready to enter with her peers into the competitive race of higher education.

IV

IN 1896, accompanied by her teacher, she entered the Cambridge (Massachusetts) School for Young Ladies in preparation for Radcliffe College. Miss Sullivan attended the classes with her, took the necessary notes and then interpreted them to Helen in the code language for the blind. Her examinations Helen took at home under the supervision of the principal who had learned the "manual alphabet" and who spelled out the questions into her hand. She answered the questions on a typewriter by means of the touch system. "She'll never make it," said her teachers at the start. But she made it, and within a comparatively short time. Only a year after her admission to the Cambridge School she passed her preliminary examinations for Radcliffe—and received "honors" in English and in German. Two years later she passed the final examinations and entered Radcliffe College—still inseparable from her "beloved" Anne Sullivan.

And now she was no longer aware of her handicaps. Together with the rest of the students she was ready to plunge eagerly into the hidden world of knowledge. "In the wonderland of Mind I felt as free as the next." She studied Shakespeare under Professor Kittredge and English composition under Professor Copeland—"men who were able to give new sight to the blind." It was Charles Townsend Copeland—known affectionately to his students as "Copey"—who discovered her genius as a writer. "You have something of your own to say, Miss Keller, and you have a manner of your own in saying it." He suggested that she expand some of her classroom compositions into a story of her life. She followed the suggestion and gave to the world one of the rarest of human documents—the struggle of a soul, hedged in by excessive limitations, to penetrate an unlimited universe. And the universe, as she found it in her undergraduate days and throughout her later life, was a magical place of "large loves and heavenly charities." Blindness, she declares, is nothing; and deafness, nothing. We are all blind and deaf to the eternal things. But nature is kind to us all in her very unkindness. She has endowed all of us, possessors of five puny senses at most, with an infinite sixth sense—"a sense which sees, hears, feels, all in one."

The Story of My Life was published in the *Ladies' Home Journal,* and later in book form. In the meantime Helen Keller had been graduated from Radcliffe—*cum laude*. With the money she received from the sale of her manuscript she settled down with Anne Sullivan on a farm in Wrentham, Massachusetts, for a life of writing and contemplation. A silent, soothing, yet exciting world. Rambles into the woodland—Anne Sullivan had strung a wire from tree to tree, so that Helen could go walking all alone without being lost. Excursions with her friends in her rowboat on the lake—"It is fun to try to steer by the scent of water-grasses and lilies, and of bushes that grow on the shore." Canoeing in the moonlight—"I cannot, it is true, see the moon behind the pines, but I can fancy that I feel the shimmer of her garments as I trail my hand in the water." Imagining the world as it really is—"Has anyone ever known the *real* world?" Translating the sensations of sight into the sensations of touch—"Often I had felt petals showered upon me by a passing breeze, and so I could imagine the sunset as a vast rose garden from which the petals had been shaken and were drifting through the sky." And, most joyous experience of them all, reading books—"Literature is my Utopia." Anne supplied her with all the classics printed in Braille, and her sensitive fingers were kept constantly busy "looking" into the hearts of the masters. No need to pity Helen Keller on her Wrentham farm, with Anne Sullivan for her guardian and the entire world for her company.

And then a third person joined their rich and exciting world. John Macy, one of her English instructors at Radcliffe. He married Anne Sullivan and came to live with them at Wrentham. "I cannot enumerate the helpful kindnesses with which he smoothed my paths . . . Once, when I was tired with the manual labor of my copying, he sat up all night and typed forty pages of my manuscript, so that they might reach the press in time." A new variation in the old triangle of two women and a man. A triangle not of passion and jealousy and revenge, but of faith and charity and love.

V

FOR A BRIEF SPRINGTIME of ecstasy Helen Keller was herself to experience the love of a woman for a man. During a brief vacation of Anne Sullivan and John Macy a young man had come to her as her secretary. Love laughs at locksmiths—and at the makers of all other sorts of barriers. The young man proposed to Helen; and Helen, in a moment of yearning forgetfulness, accepted him. "For a brief space I danced in and out of the gates of Heaven, wrapped up in a web of bright imaginings." But she rapidly awoke to the reality. Physical love, marriage, the joys and the responsibilities of motherhood—these things were not for her. She must remain content in this world of her own, surrounded by her dreams and her books.

And her friends. It has been granted to few to enjoy so many and such abiding friendships as were Helen Keller's. Among those who gave her of their very hearts—to mention only a handful—were the philanthropists H. H. Rogers and Andrew Carnegie and Otto Kahn, who tided her over many a dismal bog when her finances were low; Mark Twain, that sad man of laughter who always used to tell her that she saw better than most people—"The world, Helen, is full of unseeing eyes, vacant, staring, soulless eyes"; Frank Doubleday, her publisher, "whose kindness to me has been the kindness not only of a friend but of a father"; Eugene Debs, "that neglected St. Francis of the twentieth century"; and Alexander Graham Bell, of whom she wrote at the time of his death—"Although life has never seemed the same since we learned . . . that Dr. Bell was dead, yet the mist of tears is resplendent with the part of himself that lives on in me."

Her life was saddened by the departure of her friends. But she went on with her work of teaching both the seeing and the blind. She traveled across the country on a lecture tour—she had learned to speak with sufficient clearness to make herself understood on the platform—and she was hailed everywhere as a "miraculous freak of nature." She was amused at the picture that she got of herself through the newspapers. "I learned for the first time that I was *born* blind, deaf, and dumb, that I educated myself, that I could distinguish colors, hear telephone messages . . . that I was never sad, never discouraged, never pessimistic, that I applied myself with celestial energy to being happy . . . We supplied [the newspapers] with the facts when we were asked for them; but we never knew what became of these facts." What the stunt-seeking public failed to recognize about Helen Keller was merely this—that she was a human being with somewhat more than her share of mortal affliction and decidedly more than her share of immortal genius. The gods had given her less sight but more vision than the ordinary.

Her vision enabled her to see into the future of mankind. She believed that the salvation of humanity would come through an intelligent application of Socialism—food for the hungry, shelter for the homeless, education for the ignorant, peace among the nations, and justice for all. "There is in the world today too much thoughtlessness and too little joy." If the greedy were able to *think* better, the needy would be able to *live* better. In her contemplation of human progress, she said, she was neither too sanguine nor too despondent. "Like the poet Henry van Dyke"—she wrote—"I am not an optimist; there's too much evil in the world and in me. Nor am I a pessimist; there is too much good in the world and in God. So I am just a meliorist, believing that He wills to make the world better, and trying to do my bit to help and wishing that it were more."

And so, like a sundial—"I record only the serene hours of life"—she lived in her beautiful world and tried to do her bit to help make it more beautiful. And when the shadows fell across her path she brushed away her tears and waited patiently for the next bright day. One of the darkest shadows of her life fell when Anne Sullivan died (1936). It was as if a part of her own soul had died. "I suppose," observes Dr. Richard C. Cabot, "that such an extraordinary partnership of two human souls has never existed before upon this earth." For a time Helen Keller was like a lost creature. But finally she shook off her despondency, and with the help of her new secretary, Miss Polly Thompson, she went on with her work. Went on interpreting through her sensitive mind the world which she "saw" through her sensitive fingers. And how vividly she could see with those fingers of hers! One day she visited the studio of the sculptress, Malvina Hoffman. Among the statuary that she studied, she came upon the figure of a man. She felt the folds of the cloak, the rope girdle, the sandals on the feet. "A monk," she said. Then she went on and felt a wolf pressing its head to the man's side, a rabbit resting in his arms, a bird nestled in the fold of his cowl. She traced her fingers back to the man's face. It was raised toward the sky. "A lover of God and a friend of the animals . . ." And then, "I see! It is St. Francis!"

Like St. Francis of Assisi, Helen Keller is convinced that the end of the road toward which she is so patiently groping is but the beginning of a more beautiful road. "I cannot understand the poor faith that fears to look into the eyes of death." For beyond lies the city of the sun, where she knows that she will meet again her departed friends. A confirmed Swedenborgian, she declares that after her death she will for the first time be *truly* able to see. And so, "with steadfast thought I follow sight beyond all seeing, until my soul stands up in spiritual light and cries, 'Life and death are one!' "

IMPORTANT DATES IN THE LIFE OF HELEN KELLER

1880—Born, Tuscumbia, Alabama.

1882—Deprived of sight and hearing and speech through severe illness.

1887—Got Anne Mansfield Sullivan as her teacher.

1890—First learned to speak.

1896—Entered Cambridge School for Young Ladies.

1900—Entered Radcliffe College.

1902—Wrote *The Story of My Life*.

1904—Graduated with honors. Entered upon a lifelong career of writing and lecturing.

1936—Lost, through death, her "dearest friend and teacher," Anne Sullivan.

1938—Published *Helen Keller's Journal*.

1940—Published *Let Us Have Faith*.

George Catlett Marshall

[1880-   ]

THE man who organized and led to victory the army of the United States during the most critical war in history, George Catlett Marshall, descended from the breed of statesmen, soldiers, and judges, one of whom was the celebrated John Marshall, first Chief Justice of the Supreme Court. Members of the family fought in the wars of Charles I on the royal fields of France, at Brandywine, and at Valley Forge. Marshalls served with the Union and Confederate armies.

The father of the future Chief of Staff, however, was neither a soldier nor a statesman nor a judge. He was a prosaic businessman who, along with scores of other Americans, tied his fortunes to the kite of industrial expansion. A Kentuckian, he bought coal properties in Pennsylvania and rapidly rose to local prominence in Uniontown, his adopted home.

George, born on December 31, 1880, became one of the most popular boys in Uniontown. He was sandy-haired and freckled, and he had a pug nose that gave him a saucy piquancy. His companions dubbed him "Flicker." Like Huck Finn, Mark Twain's eternal boy, "Flicker" adored pets. He had a company of dogs. His friends whispered that he even kept a caged wildcat somewhere concealed. He owned a share in a favorite stock of the juvenile community, gamecocks. And he would spring these "Fightin' Chickens" from their secret lodgings in the woods to battle all newcomers in matches that excited the sporting bloods of the neighborhood. George was a practical lad. He wanted to learn the "know-how" of things. One morning on his way to school he ducked into an alley and spent the day in a blacksmith's shop learning the tricks of the trade.

When he reached sixteen his father, anxious to send his son to a distinguished military academy, tried to obtain an appointment for him at West Point, but he had as much chance to hike to the moon. He was a Democrat from Kentucky in a Republican district of Pennsylvania. His efforts to open the doors of the Point were fruitless. Somewhat chastened, he compromised by sending George instead to Virginia Military Institute. Thanks to the political eccentricities of our democracy, V.M.I. gained a magnificent general of the future.

The glory, however, was strictly of the future. The lean, clumsy recruit who entered V.M.I. in 1897 seemed hardly a candidate to add to the reputation of any institution. A colleague, General Johnson Hagood, later wrote of Marshall's inauspicious commencement to a military career: "He landed in the awkward squad, and he stayed there on and on. He could not march. All that he could do was sweat, look uncomfortable, and be embarrassed whenever he was spoken to." But his "brother rats" soon discovered that George, for all his initial maladjustment to the mechanics of soldiering, possessed the genuine military heart. Stonewall Jackson had been a teacher at V.M.I. "Flicker" Marshall studied every scrap of information he could find on the doughty general. And when the band played "Dixie," he responded with a feeling that lifted him clear out of the mundane world of dress-parade shoes and close-order drill.

He was powerfully moved by the ceremonies commemorating the Battle of New Market, which took place during Grant's Wilderness Campaign. The cadet corps of V.M.I., deploying from the center of the rebel line, had succeeded in hurling back the Union forces across the Shenandoah River at a serious cost in lives. George thoroughly investigated the battle. He diagramed the positions of the engaging forces for his fellow cadets and spent long hours night after night explaining in detail the intricacies of each maneuver. In vain his roommates tried to escape the wearing intensity of this enthusiasm. He would corner them, lecture to them, plague them assiduously with his knowledge of history and tactics to such an extent that for years afterward, whenever Marshall's name was mentioned to any one of them, he would involuntarily look for a means of escape.

During his senior year Marshall made a reputation playing football on the academy team. His skill at tackle won eulogies from the press. And he was named on the All-Southern Eleven. He weighed a mere one hundred and seventy pounds at the position, but he ran rings around much heavier opponents by outthinking them, developing a strategy which invariably knocked them out of the play.

His classroom marks were not distinguished. He graduated fifteenth in a class of twenty-five. But he received the highest honor the cadets could pay one of their number. He was voted First Captain of Corps. It was a significant augury of things to come.

He had wooed and won, in the meantime, Elizabeth Carter Coles, a much-sought-after belle of Lexington, Virginia, and one of the most beautiful women in the South. She was an invalid. A thyroid condition had affected her heart. And Marshall entered into the marriage realizing the omnipresent possibility of sudden tragedy. Nevertheless he faced the future unafraid. The marriage took place in February 1902, shortly after the groom received his commission as second lieutenant in the infantry. Immediately the young honeymooners became acquainted with the sacrifices called for by a military career. Marshall received orders to join the 30th Infantry in the Philippines. The islands were still smoldering with the recent insurrection against the United States. Army wives were not permitted to accompany their husbands. Marshall spent two months with his bride—months that passed all too briefly. Then he embarked on his first mission.

II

HE REPORTED to Company G of the 30th Infantry on the island of Mindoro. Within short order he assumed command of the company with headquarters at Mangarin. This outpost was situated in one of the most unhealthy areas on the islands. It was cut off from all civilization for weeks at a time. There were no roads and no wireless. During Marshall's assignment the troops on one occasion went without pay for four months. The paymaster from Manila had failed to put in an appearance for this length of time.

It was not an easy task for a young lieutenant to deal with soldiers whose tempers were on edge. But the veteran troops of Company G, inured though they were to warfare with the islanders, sized up this tenderfoot officer with clear blue eyes and sandy hair, fresh from classes at V.M.I., and they recognized instantly the authority and wealth of power inherent in him. They respected him.

Marshall returned from the Philippines in November 1903, having successfully mastered his first lesson in the art of dealing with men. But he was not destined to practice his skill at leadership to the full. After he had experienced a little more than two years of garrison duty, his superiors dispatched him to the School of the Line at Leavenworth, Kansas, for staff training.

Since the war with Spain, in which the army barely survived the mismanagement of officials concerned with transportation and supply, voices had spoken out for the formation of a staff which would supervise and co-ordinate troop maneuvers before the tactical commanders took the field. Secretary of War Elihu Root proposed the appointment of an army chief who would be responsible to the war secretary, and a staff consisting of personnel, intelligence, operations and supply officers, to assist him in his over-all planning. The bill was signed by President Theodore Roosevelt in 1903. And the foundation of the modern American Army was laid.

Young promising officers were assigned to a school at Fort Leavenworth to be trained in staff duties. At Fort Leavenworth the spirit of the new army was born. It was hard, factual, mechanistic, as businesslike as an industry. The emphasis was no longer upon spit and polish and dress parade. The days of the drum-and-bugle technique of winning wars were over. The cheerleaders were replaced by scientists.

Marshall became imbued with the psychology of the new professionalism at the School of the Line. He graduated at the head of a class which contained some of the most brilliant students in uniform. He was immediately assigned to the higher grade of the Staff College. And here too he finished at the top of his class. Detailed as an instructor in the Engineering Department of the Service Schools, he spent the following three years teaching at Leavenworth. But the lure of field service proved strong. In the summer of 1910, disturbed at his prolonged absence from the infantry, he departed the cloister at Leavenworth, attended the rifle matches at Camp Perry, Ohio, and settled down for a year as instructor with the Massachusetts National Guard.

And then in 1913, having served at home for almost ten years, the thirty-three-year-old officer sailed for another tour of duty in the Philippines. In the midst of his final year of service in the islands, a Marshall legend was born.

During maneuvers in which close to fifteen thousand troops were engaged on Luzon, the chief of staff of the force committed to the defense of Corregidor and Bataan fell suddenly ill with malaria, and his command was thrown into consternation. The ranking officer sent for Marshall, who, as adjutant at headquarters, had not been in touch with the detailed operational phase of the maneuvers.

"Lieutenant," asked the commander, "do you know how to draw up a field order?"

The tall, thin adjutant, who had been summoned in haste and who stood bareheaded, in his shirt sleeves, nodded. "I think I do."

"Very well, go ahead and draw one up."

In a twinkle of an eye Marshall had become chief of staff in charge of operations. The staff attached to headquarters was apprehensive. Marshall had been given no clue to the latest battle situation. But he was not one to waste time. He instantly sent for the regimental commanders and placed them under a running barrage of questions. He had them indicate the positions of the infantry, the cavalry, the medical troops, the supply trains, and the remaining components. Then he ordered an immediate attack. While the umpires and the officers at headquarters looked on in amazement, he dictated for several minutes a field order, calmly and slowly without reference to any notes. When he finished he had provided detailed and complex instructions for every element taking part in the engagement. Not a single factor had been overlooked, not a word was revised or a comma corrected. Marshall did not even reread his command.

The troops carried out his orders and brought the maneuver to a decisive victory. The top leaders of the army took due notice of Marshall's achievement. A few days after the maneuver General Franklin Bell, the departmental commander, assembled his entire staff and made a remarkable statement: "Gentlemen . . . as you know, I fought all over these islands in the early days, and I know them from end to end. . . . I have seen a great many plans for the protection of Manila . . . but the best plan that I have ever laid eyes upon, the most complete, the most concise, and the most effective, I hold in my hand. It is written in pencil and was dictated in the field by a lieutenant of infantry unexpectedly called from other duty. This lieutenant is one of those rare men who live and dream in their profession. . . . Keep your eyes on George Marshall. He is the greatest military genius of America since Stonewall Jackson."

III

WHEN America entered the war in 1917, Marshall, along with every other officer in the army, was eager for an assignment to France. "I'd do anything to get there," he told his friends. "I'd be an orderly." His wish to join the American Expeditionary Forces was realized. Late in June he received orders detailing him to the General Staff Corps. He reported to the Quartermaster Depot in New York City and sailed for Europe as operations officer of the First Division.

Several times the young lieutenant colonel requested to be relieved from staff duties for service with troops in the field. But his superiors turned down his request. Major General Bullard, commanding the First Division, reported on one occasion: "I cannot approve because I know that Lieutenant Colonel Marshall's special fitness is for staff work and because I doubt that in this, whether it be teaching or practice, he has an equal in the Army today." On another occasion, when an officer attempted to transfer Marshall from the First Division for duty with a higher command, he was told that reassignment was impossible. "Marshall *is* the First Division."

However, in July 1918, Headquarters at Chaumont provided Marshall with the chance to exercise his talents on a larger scale than a division. He was detailed under Colonel Fox Canner (G-3) to plan operations for all American troops in France. Here he put his vast abilities to work. He prepared plans for the reduction of the St. Mihiel salient in Lorraine, but before the actual offensive (which succeeded beyond all expectations) got under way he was assigned an even more ambitious task. By the summer of 1918 the German armies were retreating all along the western front. The Allies had decided to launch a broad offensive in the Meuse-Argonne sector designed to break the supply lines of the Wehrmacht and to end the war. In preparation for the greatest single offensive ever undertaken by American troops, Marshall familiarized himself with all aspects of the situation. The size and complexity of the maneuver was unparalleled for those times. Almost a million men had to be moved into position over six meager supply routes. Almost four thousand artillery pieces and forty thousand tons of ammunition had been earmarked for concentration. Thirty-five hundred trucks, ninety thousand horses and mules were destined for transportation. In addition it was necessary to establish chemical warfare, medical, signal, tank, motor, ordnance, and quartermaster supply depots to insure the success of the offensive. Marshall had handled the problems with audacity and skill. Within two weeks this tremendous force of men and supplies was moved into line with such secrecy that the enemy received notice of the attack only after it had begun.

The soldiers of the First Army battled through German entrenchments in an advance that was terminated by the armistice. Marshall had launched the most magnificent staff operation of the war. But to his fellow officers, who warmly congratulated him, he confided, "I would rather have commanded a regiment than anything they could have given me."

IV

MARSHALL RETURNED to America in September 1919 as an aide-de-camp to General Pershing, the hero of the A.E.F. He accompanied the general on his triumphant appearances before crowds who thronged the streets to see him in the South, the Middle and the Far West. And when the last speech was made and the final banquet tendered, he joined Pershing on a tour to inspect the Panama Canal.

In 1923 he was promoted to the permanent rank of lieutenant colonel. And the following year he was detailed for duty with the 15th Infantry at Tientsin, China. Then a tragedy which had been stalking him for twenty-five years overtook him. Upon the couple's return from China, Mrs. Marshall's heart trouble became critical. On September 15, 1927, she died in the Walter Reed Hospital in Washington.

Army officials, realizing that Marshall would welcome an assignment away from Washington, dispatched him to the Infantry School at Fort Benning, Georgia. Here he displayed his genius in the role of a builder. He found the Infantry School in a rut. The instructors, basing their teachings on their own experience in the World War, espoused a defensive strategy of tactics much as their French colleagues advocated in the shadow of the Maginot Line. When an instructor declared to Marshall upon his arrival, "The whole faculty is indoctrinated with formalized defense," he answered sharply, "Well, we'll just un-doctrinate them."

In the fall of 1930, Marshall took as his second mate Mrs. Katherine Tupper Brown, the widow of a Baltimore lawyer and a former Shakespearean actress. Husband and wife emerged from personal tragedies to give each other the benefit of a mellow companionship and mature love.

Marshall, in the meantime, had been plodding along in the traces of army red tape, bridled by the misfortune of painfully slow promotions. Although he had been glowingly commended by his superiors and recommended for the rank of general during the first World War, fifteen years after the conflict he possessed only the rank of a colonel assigned to a series of relatively minor jobs. He had served in the armed forces for more than thirty years. He was approaching sixty, and it seemed to him that before long he would be retired from the army as a colonel. The fact that he had graduated from V.M.I. militated against him. The top jobs in the service went to West Pointers.

However, the hour was at hand when his loyalty would be fully repaid. Powerful friends, cognizant of his ability, had for years been waging a vigorous campaign for him. In 1936 he received the star of a brigadier general. At the very moment he attained the rank of general, Hitler was arming his Wehrmacht for an assault on humanity. Significantly enough, Marshall's fortunes now rose suddenly in tempo to the increasing threat of Nazism.

In the summer of 1938 he was summoned from Vancouver Barracks, where he commanded the 5th Infantry Brigade, to enter the War Plans

Division of the General Staff in Washington. It was an assignment indicating that he was a man marked for distinction. Events in Europe had stirred the army and American students of foreign affairs into extreme uneasiness. With the uncanny instinct that impels Americans frequently to choose for their leaders in a crisis men they have neglected in times of normality, important people in Washington suddenly became alive to the indispensable qualities of the new brigadier who twenty-five years before had been called the greatest military genius since Stonewall Jackson.

Marshall remained three months with W.P.D. as assistant chief of staff. Then affairs moved quickly. The four-year term of the Chief of Staff of the Army, General Malin Craig, was almost over. Someone had to be selected in his place. Pershing contacted President Roosevelt and suggested that Marshall was the man for the job. The assistant secretary of war, Louis Johnson, also urged the President to make the appointment. Finally, in August 1939, Roosevelt, passing over twenty major generals and fourteen brigadiers who were Marshall's seniors, several of whom loomed as illustrious personalities in the public eye, named the junior brigadier to succeed General Craig as Chief of Staff. As far as the American people were concerned, the President had plucked an unknown officer out of obscurity. They were unaware of the long years of brilliant service and patient waiting.

V

MARSHALL became Chief of Staff on the very day that Hitler ordered his panzers into Poland and set the fuse for war. Within an hour he had been summoned from an assignment in which he had concerned himself merely with local problems to a post that required experienced judgment in affairs of international scope. On incredibly short order he matured from an obscure army officer into an acknowledged military statesman.

Unlike the German military leaders, who were free to plan a war without public interference, Marshall not only was called upon to organize the greatest army in American history, but to win over public opinion at every critical step of the way. He needed the qualities of a Job as well as those of a general. One military man alone before him had faced a problem of comparable magnitude—George Washington. And before Marshall had resigned his post he was the only citizen among his contemporaries, like Washington, who could have won a unanimous vote of confidence from Congress.

He had not the slightest military arrogance. In dealing with Congress, he refused to employ technical lingo. Requesting money for maneuvers before America entered the war, he declared to the legislators: "You wouldn't send a team against Notre Dame before it had scrimmaged, would you?" He received the appropriation.

He had no use for the army's reliance on wasteful paper work. He amazed the Senate Military Affairs Committee by testifying without reference to notes. He demanded that his assistants reduce their problems to their salient features and bring them to him orally. The speed of his thinking processes awed those associated with him, also his propensity for concentrated work. Secretary of War Stimson had to order him to take time off and relax at a football game. Even the chestnut Marshall rode for exercise at Fort Meyer he named "Prepare."

He brought his talent for trimming down office work to the organization of the army. He was dissatisfied with the unwieldy staff and command organization he had inherited, and he made a decision that required courage. Few other generals would have dared tamper with the organization of troops while they were in the process of being trained and deployed in a world war. But early in 1942, Marshall, acting on the results of a study by the assistant chief of staff, General McNarney, ordered the military grouped into three major commands, the Army Ground Forces, the Army Air Forces, and the Army Service Forces. He selected for commanding generals men he had observed carefully through the years: General Lesley McNair for the AGF, and General Henry Arnold and General Brehon Somervell for the Air and Service forces respectively. Around this greatly simplified structure the army grew to more than eight million troops. Marshall was able to deal efficiently with nine theaters of operations joined by fifty thousand miles of communication lines.

In addition to achieving unity within the American Army, Marshall hammered away at the broader issue of achieving unity among the Allies. He insisted that all land, sea, and air forces be welded into a team; and he won a reluctant concession from Churchill that even His Majesty's Navy would, under certain circumstances, serve under American direction.

As early as June 1941 he prepared for the ultimate invasion of Normandy, and he refused to be budged from the plan. He battled against the insistence of the British that the main thrust be directed against the Balkans, the so-called "underbelly" of Europe. And although he permitted an American assault upon North Africa, he stubbornly adhered to his basic strategy, convinced that a landing in France would be the quickest way to end the war.

From the first he had hoped privately that he would be permitted to lead the invasion of Europe himself. His desire throughout his army life to command combat troops on the field burned more strongly than ever now. For forty-one years he had been denied the opportunity. And the Allied commanders, convinced that Marshall had earned the right, decided in the summer of 1943 to name him to the greatest field command in history. However, immediately after the secret decision was taken, Admiral Leahy, Admiral King, and General Arnold, each torn by misgivings, went to President Roosevelt and pleaded with him to keep Marshall in Washington. Pershing himself wrote to the President, stating that to deprive the Allies of Marshall's brilliant service as Chief of Staff would be a grave error in policy. Leaders of the American public, deeply disturbed by the rumors of Marshall's appointment, launched a campaign to retain him in his job. In the midst of the hubbub the President invited the Chief of Staff to make his own decision. Marshall refused to reveal his personal wishes to Roosevelt. He told him preferences were of no account, that it was up to the President to say the final word. Then Roosevelt confessed, "I feel . . . that I will not be able to sleep at night with you out of the country." And he selected General Dwight Eisenhower for the European command.

Stubbornly refusing the limelight under any circumstances, General Marshall became wrathful when a group of Democrats, preparing for the 1944 election, declared that they would sponsor him for the presidency of the United States. When these Democrats put out feelers to Marshall's close associates, they were told abruptly, "The General would no more think of lending himself to such a proposal than he would resign his post in the midst of a battle."

Consistently Marshall rejected all honors. When Congress introduced a bill to create a new rank for him, that of five-star General of the Army, he told the solons that he regarded a bill that would give him a higher rank than George Washington an absurdity. "I'm against the whole thing. If I am called to testify on the bill, I shall refuse to go." "Besides," he later remarked to his wife, dryly, "Marshal Marshall sounds very silly to me." Nevertheless the rank was conferred on him. General Marshall's fellow citizens insisted on recording their tremendous gratitude.

Secretary Stimson expressed this gratitude of a nation in a splendid manner. On noon of the day on which the German Army surrendered he summoned Marshall to his office, and before an assembly of high-ranking officers of the War Department he spoke words that brought a tear to many a rough-and-tumble general present. "I have seen a great many soldiers in my lifetime, and you, sir, are the finest soldier I have known." And the citation for an oak-leaf cluster to his Distinguished Service Medal summed up for Marshall in the best possible fashion the feelings of the people who had borne with him daily the struggle of seeing the conflict through. "Millions of Americans gave their country outstanding service. General of the Army George C. Marshall gave it victory."

VI

During the midnight of the war the Chief of Staff envisaged the day when he would return to his country home as a private citizen. "Soon you and I," he repeatedly told his wife, "shall retire and garden together." He was a very tired man. In addition to the heartache of public service, he had suffered in common with thousands of citizens a great personal loss. Lieutenant Allen Tupper Brown, Mrs. Marshall's second son, had been killed in action on the Anzio beachhead. "War is the most terrible tragedy of the human race," remarked the bereaved foster father who had dedicated almost a half century of his life to the armed service of his country.

In August 1945, after the defeat of Japan, Marshall sought from President Truman permission to retire from his job. And on November first, the time for his release, he cleared the desk that had once belonged to

General Phil Sheridan of his final papers, took down his oil painting of Pershing, and departed from the Pentagon for his home at Leesburg, Virginia.

But there was no rest ahead for him. As soon as he reached Leesburg he received an urgent phone call from President Truman. China was on the verge of bloody civil war. An American with tremendous prestige must instantly be sent to attempt to bring the dissident factions together and avert a threat to world peace. This American Cincinnatus dropped his plow and journeyed to China as the Special Representative of the President with personal rank of Ambassador. For more than a year Marshall tried to reason with the Kuomintang and the Communists; he urged them to drop their differences and unite to build a peaceful China. Valiantly he labored to rally the half-awakened forces of liberalism.

But in the midst of his efforts he was recalled to Washington. The United States Government had decided that a man of Marshall's talent was needed to play an even greater role as pacifier on a global scale. And in January 1947 the President appointed him Secretary of State. Marshall thus became the first professional soldier in the history of his country to enter the Cabinet and assume leadership of American foreign policy.

The citizen who led an embattled army to victory has been given the opportunity to keep that victory secure. It is an impressive commentary on the quality of her soldiers that America can voluntarily call upon a sixty-seven-year-old general to lead her out of the wilderness of political and economic contention. And this general who hates war, who remained Chief of Staff when he could have become one of the greatest field commanders in history, who nursed an invalid wife for a generation and stood over the grave of a foster son, is amply qualified to help the world survive its tragedies.

IMPORTANT DATES IN THE LIFE OF
GEORGE CATLETT MARSHALL

1880—Born, Uniontown, Pennsylvania.

1901—Graduated from Virginia Military Institute.

1908—Graduated from Army Staff College.

1913–16—Served in the Philippine Islands.

1918—Drafted plans for the Meuse-Argonne offensive.

1919–24—Served as aide-de-camp to General Pershing.

1927–32—Named assistant commandant of the Infantry School, Fort Benning, Georgia.

1936—Promoted to the rank of brigadier general.

1939—Appointed Chief of Staff.

1945—Named Special Representative of the President in China.

1947—Appointed Secretary of State.

Franklin Delano Roosevelt
[1882-1945]

FROM too close a view it is difficult to see a forest because of the trees. Similarly, from too close a view it is difficult to see a man's character because of his characteristics. The perspective of time and space will be necessary for a final evaluation of Roosevelt's personality. Those of us among his contemporaries who try to appraise him are likely to slip into the dangerous pitfall of his too-ardent admirers, who call him a St. Francis in politics, or into the equally dangerous pitfall of his too-bitter opponents, who look upon him as a ravenous wolf in sheep's clothing. To an impartial observer—and at such a stormy period no observer can be altogether impartial—Roosevelt seems to have been a dynamo of energy dominated by an instinct for justice. His energy often drove him into error, but his justice generally brought him back to the right course. "Roosevelt is a man who loves to fight—and who fights to love."

II

HE CAME by his love for fighting and his instinct for affection through the Roosevelt ancestral strain. The Roosevelts are a peculiar tribe—a family of strong, rich adventurers who possess a friendly sympathy for those that are not strong enough to adventure for riches. Born on the banks of the Hudson, he grew up to look upon humanity as a stream of travelers going up and down the river—an endless and living unit of interdependent motion. His father, like many of the other Roosevelts a combination of the successful businessman and the practical philosopher, explained and strengthened in his growing boy this American sense of active interdependence. Not only this, but the constitutional and the ethical right of every human creature to his life, his liberty, and his pursuit of happiness. On Sundays he pointed out the pleasure yachts that took the wealthy upon their cruises and the passenger boats that carried the workers upon their excursions. "God has made the same river and the same sky for us all. And he wants all of us alike to share in their bounty."

The only child of his father's second marriage—he had a grown-up half brother by his father's first marriage—young Franklin developed a great hunger for companionship. And his father encouraged, rather than hindered, this wholesome hunger. Although he educated him at home, he allowed him to make the acquaintance of the village youngsters—the children of the farmers and the butchers and the coachmen and the grocers and the gardeners of Hyde Park. These children, Franklin was surprised to learn, were—save for their clothes and other such unimportant externals—just as human and just as likeable as the wealthier children who came to visit them at their Hyde Park estate. This so-called *estate,* his father maintained, was in reality just a mere *farm*. There was nothing pretentious about James Roosevelt. A simple, companionable, democratic, human father who possessed a rare gift—he knew how to train a sensitive child into a sensible man.

From his father and from his companions young Roosevelt got his love for human beings. And from his mother he derived his love for the sea. She told him how her father had captained his own sailing ship and had brought his cargoes of tea from China. As a child she had sailed on her father's ship, and once in a storm she had come dangerously close to losing her life. But, added his mother, she was never afraid.

Excellent environment for the unfolding of an impressionable character. In his father he found a superior teacher, in his mother a superb playmate. She was so very much nearer to Franklin's own age—there was a difference of thirty years between his father and his mother. The Roosevelt family represented *three* rather than *two* generations—a long stretch of years and experiences for young Franklin to absorb.

Such was the heritage of Franklin Roosevelt: an eagerness to see humanity on the go, a passion for universal companionship, a longing for adventure, and a laughing fearlessness in the face of danger. He was growing up into fit timber either for the captain of a ship or the leader of a state. Whatever might be his future career, he was pretty certain to show the necessary spunk.

And the proper kind of education. His father saw to that. As a supplement to his book study, James Roosevelt enabled him to travel and to study places and men. For eight successive years, between the ages of seven and fourteen, young Roosevelt spent his vacations abroad in the company of his parents. And thus he learned to know the peoples of Europe and their languages and their ways. And, too, he got to know the difference between free nations and those that were led by the leash. In London he and his tutor were once stopped at the door of the Kensington Museum. "Sorry," said the attendant, "but you can't go in. The Prince of Wales is inside." Whereupon Roosevelt showed his membership card in a nature club to which his father had once in a playful moment elected him. "Oh well," remarked the attendant, "in that case you can go right in." And within a few moments Roosevelt found himself face to face with the future king of England.

Quite different, however, was his experience in Germany, where he once spent a cycling holiday with his tutor. As they were passing through the countryside near Strasbourg they were arrested four times within a single day—once for picking cherries, once for taking their bicycles into a railroad station, and twice for other inadvertent infringements of the universal German *Verboten*. "The German credo," laughed Roosevelt, "is—*Forbidden to live!*"

III

HIS FREQUENT VACATIONS on shipboard had aroused in him a desire to go to sea like his grandfather. But his parents advised him that he must first round out his education. They must send him to a good preparatory school and to a good college. Groton and Harvard.

He entered Groton, where his hearty voice and his handsome features stamped him at once as a "regular guy." He displayed not the slightest arrogance toward anybody—except the arrogant. For these "blustering cymbals of gilded brass" he had little sympathy. He criticized them for their boastfulness about their fathers' income. "How much does that income add to the value of your character?"

Yet Roosevelt was no prig. Even when he criticized he did so with a good-natured smile. If some of his classmates acted foolishly at times— "Well, we are all of us fools, most of the time." He held out the hand of unaffected friendship to all those who were unaffectedly willing to meet him halfway. "There goes a real thoroughbred!" said the boys at Groton.

And at Harvard. They elected him to their clubs, they took him into their confidence, and they appointed him to the editorial board of the *Crimson*. Here, too, as at Groton, he insisted upon taking a fellow for what he *was* rather than for what he *had*. In an editorial which he wrote just prior to the election of the class-day officers, he insisted that these officers be elected on the basis of fitness rather than on the basis of friendship. "There is a higher duty than to vote for one's personal friend, and that is to secure for the whole class leaders who really deserve the position." Let the class poet and the class orator, for example, be selected from among those who were most highly gifted rather than from among those who were most highly pedigreed.

Already he was feeling his way toward a new kind of politics—democracy based upon honest common sense.

And it was about this time that he became definitely interested in a political rather than in a naval career. His fifth cousin, Theodore Roosevelt, had just been elevated to the presidency of the United States. It was like a bugle call to Franklin. Cousin Theodore was a fighter for justice. Had been so all his life. A fine man to emulate. A fine career to follow—this setting to right the wrongs of his fellow men.

Yet the call at the start was none too insistent. He was a young man just out of college, with a personal income of five thousand dollars a year—his father had recently died and left him a substantial fortune—with a healthy appetite for living and a resplendent and congenial world in which to live. A carefree and pursefree Prince Charming, adored by the ladies, admired by the men. A favorite of fortune, destined for an early marriage and a life of contented ease.

He married. But he did not settle down to an easy life. For his young wife was, like himself, a Roosevelt. A fighter of the good fight and a righter of wrong. Eleanor Roosevelt, a niece of Theodore Roosevelt, was as sensitive as Franklin. But her sensitiveness was translated into thought rather than into action. She represented the poetry, as he represented the prose, of the human quest for justice. Like Franklin, she was an ardent observer of life; but, unlike him, she was an equally ardent reader of books. Franklin had noticed some of the ills of society. Eleanor had studied to discover their remedies. While a student at a fashionable school in London, she had taken excursions into the slums to see how the poor lived. She had noted their hardships and she had listened to their grievances. And she had studied the literature of labor, of Henry George, of Karl Marx. Once she had marched in a workers' parade. Her sense of obligation had been aroused. Something *must* be done to make the hard lot of the poor easier. "And you, Franklin, are the man to do it."

And thus it was through the road of social service that Roosevelt started upon his stony climb to political fame.

IV

In 1910 he entered upon his first political campaign—a Democrat running for the state senate in a Republican district. And he won. "The Roosevelt smile," said the voters, "is irresistible."

But, his colleagues in the senate soon discovered to their surprise, his independence was also irresistible. "That young Roosevelt has a mind of his own." "Yes, and a *dangerous* mind, too." He had set himself against the boss politicians of his own party—a bad precedent, they insisted, for a young upstart in public office. And the worst of it was that he couldn't be bribed. He was too well off. And he couldn't be ousted. He was too well liked. The bosses tried to fight him—in secret, in the open. But he couldn't be budged. "There is nothing," he laughed, "that I love as much as a good fight." What in the world were they going to do with this "fresh college kid"?

And the "fresh college kid" threw himself into another fight—for a reduction of the working week in New York State to fifty-four hours. And won.

It was in the same spirit of fighting independence that he went as an anti-Tammany Wilson delegate to the Democratic National Convention in 1912. At this convention, as one of the Tammany bosses put it, "the two educated guys"—Wilson and Roosevelt—"stole the show." Franklin

Roosevelt played no unimportant part in bringing about the nomination and the election of Woodrow Wilson.

When Wilson was elected he offered Roosevelt his choice of three posts. He could become either Collector of the Port of New York, Assistant Secretary of the Treasury, or Assistant Secretary of the Navy. Without a moment's hesitation, Roosevelt decided to throw in his lot with the navy. For that was where his heart lay.

He immediately set to work advocating a larger and more effective American "patrol of the seas." For the world, as he had realized in his travels, is but a little cluster of trading posts, not *separated* but *connected* by the universal highway of the ocean. An easy road for the merchant, an equally easy road for the aggressor. A war in one continent, therefore, is a direct threat to the peace of the other continents. This elementary fact of modern geography Roosevelt recognized even before the first World War. America, he insisted, must have a navy big enough and strong enough to guard against any aggression from whatsoever source it might suddenly arise.

And he succeeded in strengthening the navy despite the opposition of those who couldn't see beyond the horizon. When America entered the war (in 1917), the young Assistant Secretary of the Navy had become, next to the President, perhaps the hardest-working man in the government. "At times," Mrs. Roosevelt tells us, "sleep was practically eliminated for days." He personally scrutinized the repairing, the fueling, and the arming of the ships, the building and the fortifying of adequate supply bases and arsenals and training stations, and the allocation of the necessary funds for the designated needs without any wasting of red tape or time. In his effort to generate action, and still more action, he broke enough laws, as he himself laughingly remarked, to send him to jail for nine hundred and ninety-nine years. Here, for example, is just one of his admirable though "illegal" transactions as related by the New York contractor, Elliot C. Brown, to Roosevelt's biographer, Ernest K. Lindley: On June 27, 1917, Roosevelt examined a site for a receiving-ship cantonment in New York City. On June 28 he gave the contractor an order to go ahead with the work. On June 29 the plans were on the way; on July 5 the ground was broken; on August 4 the work was completed; on August 11 breakfast was served at the new cantonment to sixty-eight hundred men. And then, two months later, Roosevelt received from the government an official authorization to build that cantonment!

But Roosevelt was not content with his activities as a government official. He wanted to see action on the battlefield. He was young and healthy and eager to risk his life when so many other young Americans were risking theirs. He pleaded with the President to release him from his post. Wilson refused his plea—Roosevelt was too valuable a man where he was. The President did, however, allow his young subordinate to sail on an inspection tour of the fifty-odd American naval stations in the war zone. A dangerous job, but Roosevelt loved danger. He traveled over the submarine-infested Atlantic, visited the Azores, Corfu, and the Orkney Islands, called on King George in London and on Clemenceau in

Paris. On his return trip he contracted the flu and came home a very sick man.

But soon he recovered sufficiently to take another journey to France—this time in connection with the Peace Conference. Not as a member of the conference, but as a supervisor for the demobilizing of the naval stations abroad. Again he had an opportunity to meet Clemenceau. And a remark that Clemenceau made to him on this occasion must have given Roosevelt much deep thought. "You wonder why we want to end this war with such a hard peace? Don't forget this tragic fact—that for the last century and a half every Frenchman who ever reached the age of seventy has been compelled to take part in a struggle against an aggressive Germany."

Roosevelt's return from this second trip was on the *George Washington,* the same ship that was bringing Wilson back a victor in the war and a victim of the peace. Roosevelt saw a great deal of his sad but still hopeful old prophet-chieftain on this trip. Someone pointed out to him the chair and the table on which Wilson had written the first draft of the League of Nations Covenant. Roosevelt asked his President for this "memento of a great historic occasion," and the President graciously presented it to him.

And thus Franklin Roosevelt inherited the desk and the dream of Woodrow Wilson.

V

In 1920 Roosevelt resigned from his post in the navy to run for the vice-presidency on the Democratic ticket. He conducted the campaign with his usual strength and sincerity and fire. He went on a speaking tour that took him into every state in the Union and kept him busy with an average of eleven speeches a day. The theme of his campaign was the perpetuation of Wilson's League of Justice. It proved too noble a message for too selfish an age. Roosevelt was defeated.

And then suddenly there came another and greater defeat. It was in the summer of 1921. A plunge into the ice-cold water of his summer home at Campobello, an hour of careless lolling in a wet bathing suit, a slight chill —and then years of silent suffering in the grip of a paralysis that seemed determined to kill. But Roosevelt was even more determined to live. He came out of this tragedy with weakened limbs and a strengthened soul. Illness is the best teacher of philosophy. The world offers many a curious angle to a man who is compelled to study it from an invalid's pillow. The ancient Greek philosophers had an apt saying—"Wisdom comes through suffering." Before his illness, Roosevelt had been an honest politician. After it, he became a devoted statesman.

While Roosevelt was making his fight for life, Alfred E. Smith had risen to the top of the Democratic party. And now that Roosevelt had won his fight, he joined forces with Al Smith for the regeneration of the political life of America. It was a union between the poor little rich boy and the rich little poor boy—a combination of the Harvard and the Bowery accents into a new American dialect. A new though unnamed party arose as a result. This new party, which may be termed as the Aristodemocracy of 1928, cut deeply into both of the old parties. It united the progressive elements both in the Democratic and in the Republican camps. It fell short of electing Al Smith to the presidency, but it succeeded in sweeping Franklin Delano Roosevelt into the New York State House and, four years later, into the White House.

VI

ROOSEVELT came into the White House with a vision, and he summarized this vision in four words—*the more abundant life*. As a convalescent at Warm Springs, in Georgia, he had witnessed physical suffering; and on his recovery he had devoted more than half of his fortune to the relief of such suffering. And now, in the midst of the depression, he witnessed economic suffering throughout the country and decided to devote all of his strength to the relief of *this* suffering.

When he took over the reins of the government he found himself at the head of a hopeless, spiritless, and strengthless nation. He revived its hope and its spirit and he began slowly to restore its strength.

His program at the outset was chaotic. But, in a crisis, deliberate planning is impractical. While the rescuer is trying to make up his mind as to whether to take a boat or to swim out to a drowning person, the poor victim is likely to die. What is needed in such an emergency is—first, quick action for survival; and only then, leisurely planning for recovery.

This is what President Roosevelt tried to do. The entire banking system, the heart that was pumping the economic lifeblood into the nation, was on the verge of collapse. He promptly performed an emergency operation. Declaring a bank holiday, he closed all the banks in the country, subjected them to a thorough examination, and then removed the unsound institutions and reopened those that satisfied the Treasury Department as to their soundness.

His next step was to try to provide food for the hungry. There were fifteen millions of them when he stepped into his executive office on March 4, 1933. The next morning, at breakfast, a friend asked him about his immediate plans. "I have seen," said Roosevelt, "the aged and the infirm, the poor and the helpless, standing for hours in breadlines waiting for their crust of bread and bowl of thin soup. The first thing I want to do is to take them out of those lines, rehabilitate them, feed them, make them happy once more. No nation can ever amount to anything while its people are in want."

This, throughout his first two terms in the White House, was his primary objective. To get the American people out of want. In order to accomplish this objective, he initiated his New Deal. This New Deal, to our contemporary and therefore limited point of view, resembles a labyrinth of wisdom and foolishness and compassion and justice and jumbles and contradictions and mistakes. Its general direction, however, appears to have been rightward and lightward—the conservation of the national resources for the common good; the harmonious balance of the various group interests in the United States; the reorganization of the spirit of the Supreme Court; the utilization of the federal subsidies for local needs; and the development of a policy of good neighborliness throughout the Western Hemisphere with a view to its ultimate fruition into a Pan-American League of Nations. Above all, the right of every American to enjoy the "four freedoms"—freedom of speech, freedom of worship, freedom from want, and freedom from fear.

But a brief summary—indeed, *any* summary—is altogether inadequate to encompass the rapid kaleidoscope of intermingled permanent laws and emergency measures known as the New Deal. In an effort to answer the question, "What is the New Deal?" the editors of the London *Economist* wrote a thoughtful and factful book of one hundred and fifty pages—and confessed at the end that "the answer is still incomplete." For the blueprint of the New Deal was no less than an attempt to break the ground for a new road to ethical, social, and economic fair play.

But hardly had the work begun when a horde of international brigands blocked the way. Roosevelt had to turn his attention from the establishment of national justice to the building of a national defense. Aware of his fitness as a pilot through dangerous waters, the country drafted him for a third term. And elected him, in spite of the unquestioned ability of his Republican opponent, Wendell Willkie.

And then, a year after his election, the storm broke. The treacherous attack on Pearl Harbor. Before the attack our country had been divided —our enemy thought, *irreconcilably* divided—both on the domestic and on the foreign policy of President Roosevelt. The radicals complained that he was creeping too slowly on the road to salvation; the conservatives, that he was rushing too rapidly on the way to perdition. The employers insisted that he had allied himself with the labor agitators against honest enterprise; the workers, that he had united himself with the greedy exploiters against honest labor. The interventionists contended that he was giving aid and comfort to the aggressors with his policy of appeasement; the isolationists, that he was giving unnecessary provocation to one of the belligerents in a war that was none of our business.

But the attack on Pearl Harbor (December 7, 1941) produced a miracle. It united the country into a single passionate resolve for victory against the forces of evil. No more radicals or conservatives, employers or workers, interventionists or isolationists, Democrats or Republicans—but Americans all, eager and determined to follow the leadership of the Commander in Chief.

And from the beginning of the war to his untimely death (April 1945), Roosevelt stood forth as a commander whom his countrymen followed with the utmost faith. For he was a master of world politics and a fighter of unconquerable grit. For him the word *defeat* simply did not exist. He had already fought a war, more terrible than Hitler's, and he had come off victorious. His attack of infantile paralysis, his doctors had declared, would either kill him or leave him helpless for the rest of his days. But he had stubbornly refused to die or to submit to a life of invalid despair. For many years he had fought against destiny—and had come out smiling at the end. In the darkest days of his illness he had kept on encouraging his doctors, who held out not a single word of encouragement for him. Again and again he had told them: "Never fear, I'll beat this thing yet!"

This was the man, and this the motto, around whom America rallied to win the war. And is still rallying, some years after the war, to win the peace.

IMPORTANT DATES IN THE LIFE OF
FRANKLIN DELANO ROOSEVELT

1882—Born, Hyde Park, New York.

1904—Graduated from Harvard University.

1907—Admitted to the bar.

1911–12—Served in the New York state legislature.

1912—Appointed Assistant Secretary of the Navy under President Wilson.

1920—Defeated as the Democratic candidate for the vice-presidency.

1921—Stricken with infantile paralysis.

1924—Conquered the disease.

1928—Elected governor of New York.

1930—Re-elected to the governorship of New York.

1932—Elected the thirty-second President of the United States.

1933—Unsuccessful attempt to assassinate him at Miami, Florida.

1933–36—Inaugurated the "New Deal" in the economic and social life of America.

1936—Elected to a second term in the White House.

1940—Elected to a third term in the White House—an act without precedent in American history.

1941—Drew up, with Winston Churchill, the "Atlantic Charter."
Assumed duties as Commander in Chief of a united nation in the war against Germany, Italy, and Japan.

1944—Elected to a fourth term in the White House.

1945—Died, Warm Springs, Georgia.

Knute Rockne

[1888-1931]

KNUTE Rockne came from the Land of the Midnight Sun, the cold, hard country where the mountains glower in challenge to the fainthearted. He sprang from a simple people who lived in the village of Voss on the road from Oslo to Bergen. The males of the Rockne family had clever fingers. They pounded sparks from the horse's hoof and chanted lustily in the heat of hard workmanship. They fashioned wagons and buggies with springs of steel. It was no small matter to forge a wheel that rolled over the crusted slopes of the mountain against the weather, carrying people and supplies.

Knute learned as a yougster to live by his muscles. He swam and fished in the chilled, lucid mountain lakes. He explored the resourcefulness of his body, feeling the marrowness of himself. He was a rough, tough child who clung to a dare like a leech. When a stableman offered him a horse—Satan, whose wildness fitted his name—if he could keep to the saddle, the five-year-old boy accepted the challenge and hung gamely to the mane of the devil.

Knute's father came to America in 1891 to display his carriages at the World's Fair at Chicago. He made a sufficient impression to obtain a job as machinist, and he sent for his family. Miraculously, a lad was whisked from the Voss Mountains. Knute emerged from childhood in Norway to find himself on Logan Square in Chicago. This square was the workground and playground of immigrants. Two nationalities predominated, the Scandinavians and the Irish. The grownups went to night school to learn Americanism. The youngsters went out into the corner lots, kicked around a football, punched each other in the eye—and *were* Americans.

There was a fierce competitive spirit in the games of the immigrant nationalities in Logan Square. On Wednesdays and Fridays the Irish met the "Swedes"—all Scandinavians were referred to by Hibernians as Swedes—to practice the refined art of crashing through the line for a touchdown. These contests were held under the critical eye of a corner policeman, O'Goole. During the first few contests, as the Irish devoted themselves systematically to annihilating their opponents, O'Goole rubbed his hands. "A fine game for youngsters, this football," he beamed. But the Scandinavians drew a trick out of their badly cocked hats. They sent for reinforcements, in the shape of two bulky Italian lads who proceeded to introduce the Irish players to mouthfuls of mud. O'Goole strode quickly into the pitched battle and parted the pigskin gladiators. "The game is unfit for young lads," he declared in consternation.

Knute took to sports like a whippet released from the barrier. He was clumsy when he attempted to do chores at home, and his father called him "all thumbs." But out on the playground his awkwardness suddenly became grace. This slight chap with the blue eyes and flaxen hair of a Viking could run and jump and hurdle like an American Indian.

He felt no more at home in the classroom than an Iroquois brave. He was unable to concentrate on a lesson book when the winds were calling him to race them. One cannot interest an antelope in mathematics. He was expelled from high school one afternoon when the principal caught him playing hooky to practice the hundred-yard dash. He entered another school, but his mind would simply not be bothered with square roots and Shakespeare. In a burst of restlessness, he quit classes altogether.

This overspecialization in the education of the muscles deeply disturbed his parents. They had come to America to give their children the finest education possible. And how did Knute manage his golden opportunity? He became a pole vaulter! But there was little they could do. They permitted him to take a job, and they awaited developments.

Knute found employment in the Chicago post office. Declining a desk assignment, he went to work as a mail dispatcher. And he lugged bags, weighing fifty pounds on the average, to the trains. In his free hours he participated in track events with various athletic clubs in the city. No ancient Greek athlete ever devoted more serious effort to a hobby than did this Norwegian bantam who strove for the laurel wreath.

For four years he lugged the mail and saved his earnings so that one day he would be able to take an entrance examination for the University of Illinois. He had matured greatly during these years of working, and he desired at last to acquire an education. In 1910, at the opening of the fall college term, two of Knute's comrades who had competed with him in numerous track events announced that they were going to enter Notre Dame. They invited him to join them. This little Catholic university at South Bend, Indiana, was only a name to Knute. It couldn't possibly compare with the University of Illinois! "Why, how many people have ever heard of Notre Dame?" he retorted. "They've never won a football game in their lives!" His companions pointed out that it would be an easy matter for him to find employment on the college campus. And a job would ease the burden of tuition fees.

Knute found the idea reasonable. He put aside his dispatch bags and prepared for the entrance examination. Hereafter he would "carry the mail" for Notre Dame.

II

ROCKNE'S STUDENT YEARS were colorful ones. A Norwegian Protestant studying under priests in a Catholic institution (in after years he became a Catholic himself), he made numerous friends of the fathers and students alike, thrilling the track coach with his speed on the cinder tracks and "raising the roof" of the playhouse with his portrayal of flaxen-haired ladies in the college dramatics.

He received honors in chemistry. In addition he performed the duties of a laboratory janitor to earn money. In the midst of his studies his father died, and he decided to leave school so that he could support the family. But his sister interceded. "If you quit now, you will make a living but it will be as a mail dispatcher," she declared. And he remained at college.

Naturally Rockne's chief interest at Notre Dame was athletics. In the fall of his freshman year, when the pigskins soared over the end zone, he presented himself as a candidate for the football team. The coach, on the lookout for two-hundred-and-twenty-pound behemoths who could strike their opponents with the impact of a battering-ram, took one glance at the little one-hundred-and-forty-five-pound Norwegian and shook his head dubiously. Watching Rockne perform in a practice session did not reassure him. He sent him to one of the dormitory teams. He wanted bulls, not calves, for the varsity.

The coach, however, had not reckoned with this freshman's shrewdness. Rockne realized that he had one asset—speed afoot. He decided to try for the track team, convinced that he would be able to compete successfully for football only after he had established a reputation as a sprinter. He estimated his chance correctly. His ability to run won him ultimately an assignment with the varsity. But he absorbed a merciless physical pounding, finding himself more often on his seat than on his feet.

The game, as played in the early 1900s, was a grinding contest in which eleven men on the offense bulled and bucked and gouged eleven men on the defense, advancing the ball to the goal line at the pace of a snail. Speed and deception were as welcome as untouchables in a Brahmin temple. There was definitely no opportunity for fast, clever little men. But as Rockne underwent the ritual of bodily punishment his brain teemed with heresies. Why shouldn't clever little men be given a greater chance in football?

A few teams had recently experimented with a new weapon of attack —the forward pass. But they hurled the ball through the air only on rare occasions, employing it as a novelty to give the spectators a thrill. According to the football cognoscenti, the forward pass had no serious function. The sharp-witted little speedster at Notre Dame thought differently, however. Self-preservation is the surest incentive to invention. Rockne resolved to develop this "toy" weapon into an integrated and deadly instrument of offense, and by means of it to transform the character of the game from ancient siege warfare into a modern blitzkrieg. And he communicated his enthusiasm to Gus Dorais, the Notre Dame quarterback.

In the summer months of 1913, before the fall season during which Notre Dame was scheduled to play Army, the supreme ruler of the football realm, the quarterback and the end explored the potentialities of the forward pass. They discarded the clumsy method of hurling the pass like a steam shovel and receiving it against the chest. Instead they tossed and caught the pigskin in the manner of a baseball. On the beach along Lake Erie, Dorais threw the ball to Rockne from all conceivable angles and at various speeds until they had perfected the maneuver to the last detail.

On November 1, 1913, the Notre Dame team arrived at West Point for the game. It was the first time Notre Dame had been invited to play in the East. The team was known to only a handful of sport followers. The contest, as a matter of fact, had been scheduled by Army to provide a "warm-up" exercise for its difficult games ahead. The stands were sparsely filled when the teams trotted out for the game. The New York sports editors had sent their second-string reporters to cover the event. None of the football wise had any suspicion that the football would suddenly take a sustained flight through the air! The Army was no more prepared for Notre Dame's passes than an ancient foot soldier for a four-engine bomber.

The game began in an orthodox enough manner. Army, outweighing Notre Dame by fifteen pounds to the man, pressed forward with the massed strength of a Roman legion. But the legionnaires who overpowered the armies of the world never had to face a hand grenade. As the Army eleven charged, Dorais stepped back and flipped the pigskin over its heads. When the flabbergasted cadets drew back to defend themselves against the constant barrage of passes, Dorais sent Notre Dame halfbacks through the line or around the ends. The climax was reached when Rockne, limping sufficiently to hoodwink the opposing halfback, suddenly caught a pass from Dorais and raced forty yards for a touchdown on as sound a pair of legs as an outwitted pass defender ever had the misfortune to witness.

Before the debacle had run its course, the South Benders had amassed a total of thirty-five points to Army's thirteen, completing fourteen passes out of seventeen. And the following morning sports readers scanned the papers to learn that a new game of football had been born.

III

ROCKNE'S DESTINY, thereafter, was football. Upon graduating with honors, he became an assistant football coach at Notre Dame. In 1918 he succeeded the head coach, Jess Harper, and he commenced to train his teams for victories on his own.

Americans demonstrate an enthusiasm for their athletes that is rivaled only by the ardor with which the ancient Greeks welcomed the skilled young participants of their Olympic contests. And Rockne, above all others, raised the performance of American athletics to the level of an art. He transformed a contest which had hitherto been an ungainly scramble of young men into a spectacle beautiful to the eye. A skilled performer on the flute and a connoisseur of the theater, he injected music and drama into the sport he loved.

Emphasizing brains, fancy footwork, and deception, he drilled his teams in rhythm and synchronization. He developed a "shift" through which his team suddenly concentrated its attack upon any weak spot of the defense. And a welterweight was thus able to envelop a giant. This "shift" in the backfield contained all the harmony and precision of a dance in moleskins. Each man swung his arms, nodded his head, stepped in unison. Each play depended upon an exquisite sense of timing. Every movement counted for something. There was not a single wasted motion.

He had an uncanny realization that the game was fundamentally a drama and that it should be staged as one. But the contest had this advantage over the play: it was not confined to repetitions of the same script. Into the game was introduced the immeasurable element of surprise. It was a conflict, a comedy, a tragedy, whose ending was foreseen by none. And the typical Rockne-fashioned protagonist of this drama was the small, slight youth who snaked his way through his large-sized opponents for touchdown after touchdown.

Rockne's philosophy of football was his philosophy of life. Bald, stumpy, with a nose whose bridge had been broken in his youth by a baseball bat, he nevertheless evoked the virility of a nation to respond to him from its depths. "Demosthenes wasn't exactly an Adonis either," he would reply to those who kidded him about his appearance. Like Demosthenes, this homely little Norwegian-American had a persuasive tongue. He inspired young men not only to play winningly but to live winningly for him.

He taught chemistry, as well as football, at Notre Dame. He was an instructor who galvanized his pupils into dynamic self-expression. Students who had no special knowledge of either subject flocked into the laboratory and swarmed to the practice field to witness his skill and exuberance. When he discussed football plays on the blackboard for his squad, lads who had never held a pigskin in their hands attended the session merely to sit at his feet.

He understood his young men, sensed the unreleased springs of activity in them. He was able to pat a boy on the head without inducing in him an overweening sense of pride; he could ignore a lad without having him feel overlooked, and scold him without causing the slightest degree of anger. He took lads who appeared outwardly ordinary and transformed them into All-Americans in character as well as football skill.

In Rockne's thirteen years as coach at Notre Dame his teams won one hundred and five games, tied five, and lost twelve. They enjoyed three undefeated seasons, scoring three national championships as a result. Sporting folk marveled at Rockne's football wizardry. Coaches generally have limited control over the performance of their athletes. "A good football coach knows what physical condition his boys are in. He knows just about how much football they understand. But there is one thing he cannot tell: he cannot fathom what's in their hearts."

Rockne, however, was one coach who knew intuitively what was in the human heart. And this was a fundamental reason for his success.

Although he encouraged a style of football that stressed the team rather than individual stars, he coached a number of athletes who achieved national renown. The greatest of these was George Gipp. One afternoon in 1916, Rockne discovered a tall, lithe young man punting a football for recreation. The grace and power of the young fellow in street clothes intrigued Rockne. He invited the youth to report for the team. The young prospect—Gipp—replied that he had never played a game of football. He agreed, however, to attend the next practice.

During that session Gipp astounded Rockne and the varsity with his ball-carrying. Rockne realized that here was one of nature's perfect children of the flesh—the kind of athlete who comes along once in a generation. He possessed the physique of the ancient Greek discus throwers, and he ran like a nervous deer.

In his first game as a freshman he displayed a single-mindedness which in someone inferior would have led to catastrophe. The score was tied. There were three minutes left to play. Notre Dame had the ball in her own territory. The quarterback called for a long punt to move the team out of danger. Gipp received the ball. Instead of punting, he coolly drop-kicked the pigskin from his own thirty-eight-yard line over the opponent's goal post. This sixty-two-yard field goal won the game.

Gipp was audaciously defiant. During one game he announced loudly enough for the opposing eleven to hear that he was going to throw a series of forward passes. After brazenly handing them a blueprint of his plans, he proceeded to carry them out to the smallest item. The defenders were unable to smother the pass attack, even though they were alerted for it. And so Gipp spun and swivel-hipped his way through maneuver after maneuver of pigskin legerdemain.

It required a rare teacher to handle this rare boy. And Rockne cultivated his virtuosity into its finer expression. But nature, which had so generously bequeathed Gipp her abundance, suddenly presented him with a devastating bill of account. In 1920, just after he was selected All-American back of the year, Gipp contracted a fatal case of pneumonia. To Rockne, who kept a vigil at his bedside day and night, he whispered as he lay dying: "I've got to go, Rock. . . . I'm not afraid. . . . Sometime when the team is up against it, when things go wrong and the breaks are beating the boys—tell them—to win one for the Gipper."

No human life is ever really finished so long as there is someone to remember it. Eight years after Gipp's death in 1928, when Notre Dame athletes limped into the clubhouse between halves after having thus far absorbed a sound drubbing at the hands of a superior Army eleven, Rockne for the first time broke his silence and revealed to the players the final words of a dying man. When the Notre Dame team returned to the field to resume the game, George Gipp came alive again. He passed and punted and blocked and tackled and galloped berserk as of old. Time had not broken his stride.

As Chevigny, the Notre Dame quarterback, carried the ball over for the

crucial touchdown, he called, "Here's one for the Gipper." Notre Dame
had turned defeat into victory for its invisible captain.

Rockne never ceased to marvel at the miracle of the process whereby
nature harmonized human athletes to perform to perfection with one
another. And he was grateful that he had a hand in helping the process.
One season four awkward freshmen reported to the team. One of them,
a halfback, looked sleepy enough to be dreaming football rather than
playing it. The quarterback made as many errors as the number of plays
he called. Their backfield companions appeared as alien to their element
as a pair of roosters in the clouds. Yet within a couple of seasons these
four young welterweights, Harry Stuhldreher, Jim Crowley, Elmer Layden,
and Don Miller, were synchronized into the most famous backfield quar-
tet in modern football annals. Riding roughshod over all other American
youths who took the field against them, these masters of gridiron presti-
digitation became known as the galloping "Four Horsemen" of Notre
Dame.

Truly the surprises of the game delighted Rockne, the creator. "How it
came to pass that four young men so eminently qualified by temperament,
physique, and instinctive pacing to complement one another so perfectly
and thus produce the best-co-ordinated and most picturesque backfield in
the recent history of football—how that came about is one of the inscrutable achievements. . . ."

Inscrutable achievements continued to baffle Rockne's colleagues as
team after team of his victory-bewitched young men swept the football
stakes of the nation. Boys of every faith were enrolled in Rockne's winning combinations. Eager youth from the villages and lake fronts and the
Logan Squares of America. They broke their legs and broke their hearts
together, the stars who dominated the game and the scrubs who elbowed
glory for a single play: "Art," the left-handed French passer, and "Jumping Joe," the hard-running Italian; the Protestant who pounded through
the line with a dislocated shoulder and the Catholic who performed sixty
minutes of a game without his helmet; the poor boy who booted the ball
for the "coffin corners"; and the well-to-do lad who defended with his
body the poor boy's freedom to kick.

The "Fighting Irish" of Notre Dame. "With your Carideos . . . and
Kizer . . . and Parisian and Salvoldi and Bach and Larson . . . where in
the world are your Irish?" newsmen inquired of Rockne.

And his eye lit up with a twinkle. "They're all fighting Irish to me!"

IV

During the spring of 1929, Knute Rockne was tackled and laid low by
disease. As the result of four ailing teeth, he suffered an infection in the
leg. Physicians diagnosed his condition as a thrombo-phlebitis, a partial
closing of the veins. Whenever he attempted to use his feet the pressure
on his weakened veins caused him agony.

The life of an invalid was intolerable to a man as restless as Rockne.

Despite his doctor's advice, he left his bed and drove out to the practice field, instructing his athletes over a loud-speaker from the seat of his auto. When the fall season arrived and the team traveled out of town for their games, Rockne listened at first to a broadcast of the contest. But the excitement proved too much for him, and the radio was removed from his room.

He insisted upon accompanying his boys to Pittsburgh for a climactic struggle. The vibrations of the train aggravated his condition, and he watched the game from the side lines in a wheel chair, experiencing immeasurable pain. When his associates, however, warned him against leaving his bed in the future, arguing that a football game wasn't worth the risk, he retorted crisply: "Don't forget these are my boys. I'm willing to do anything to help them out. I'm the one who is suffering this, not you."

And the little Vossing, who so frequently in his life had turned defeat into a triumph, now proceeded to astound the doctors with his recuperative powers. During the fall of the new 1930 football season his condition had improved to such a degree that he was able to conduct practice sessions from a chair, careful not to become excessively tense. His team responded to his recovery by presenting him with an undefeated season, winning nine successive contests and receiving the national football championship for the third time.

At the close of the season the mayor of New York planned a charity contest to aid the city's thousands of unemployed. He suggested that Rockne select an eleven of the greatest athletes who had played under him and lead them into a game with the New York Giants at the Polo Grounds. And although Rockne's physicians had ordered him to take a complete vacation after the regular season, he agreed to the mayor's request.

He sent telegrams to his old pupils who were scattered over the country, and every one of them left their jobs and flocked to South Bend for a few days' practice before the game. These football demigods of yesterday no longer had the stamina and the youth to sparkle the gridirons of today. The game they played before a crowd of fifty thousand spectators was hardly a football triumph. They were decisively beaten. But Rockne never enjoyed the zest of victory as much as this defeat of the "old" men who had risked their bodies to re-enact the saga of the past.

The audience applauded the spectacle and wished Knute Rockne fortune in his fast-returning health. Only the Umpire above realized that this was to be his final football contest on earth.

In March 1931, Knute Rockne boarded an airplane for California. He had joined the sales division of the Studebaker Corporation, bringing his vigorous talents to business in his hours away from the gridiron. Now he was flying to Los Angeles to address a sales meeting. In addition he planned to visit Hollywood and arrange for the production of football films.

But the wing of the plane broke over Kansas, and the ship plummeted to earth like a huge, helpless prairie bird riddled by a broadside of shot. At forty-three Rockne had survived disease only to enter a plane that failed to reach its destination. He was humbled by an uncompleted forward pass.

IMPORTANT DATES IN THE LIFE OF
KNUTE ROCKNE

1888—Born, Voss, Norway.

1893—Came to America.

1906-10—Worked in Chicago post office.

1910—Entered the University of Notre Dame.

1913—Became captain of grid team which defeated Army and revolutionized football.

1914—Named assistant coach of football at Notre Dame.

1918-31—Served as head football coach at Notre Dame.

1919—Led team in his first undefeated season.

1920—Scored second undefeated season.

1924—Coached third undefeated team; final season of the "Four Horsemen."

1929—Stricken with thrombo-phlebitis.

Led team in his fourth unbeaten season.

1930—Scored his fifth undefeated season.

1931—Died in an airplane crash over Kansas.

Dwight David Eisenhower

[1890-   ]

IN 1942, when the Allied invasion of Europe was being planned, a number of generals were prominently discussed in the press as the possible leaders of that invasion. One man was completely overlooked —Eisenhower. "Just another cipher" among the twenty million unknown soldiers who were fighting in the war.

And when Eisenhower was selected as the commander in chief of the invading forces, the news came crashing like a bombshell into an astonished world. "Never heard of the man. . . . Who is he? . . . How did they know about him? . . . What has he done to be singled out above all the rest?"

The answer to these questions constitutes the substance of our story. The invisible development of a seed until it suddenly springs into flower. The latent evolution of a genius until it suddenly flames into achievement. Success is frequently a combination of little incidents and a great soul. The incidents come from without; their transformation into an essence of greatness comes from within.

Such, in brief, is the structure of Eisenhower's life.

II

BORN in Denison, Texas, he was christened David Dwight Eisenhower. Later he transposed the first two names. Still later he accepted the nickname "Ike" as the most suitable to his character. Homespun and friendly and unassuming and frank. Familiar as a blade of grass, congenial as the light of the sun.

His German ancestors, like the Puritans of England, had come to America in quest of religious freedom. They belonged to a group called Brethren in Christ—a Quakerlike sect of lovers of justice and haters of war. His grandfather was a lay preacher among the Brethren. His father, an engineer by profession, was a religious teacher by conviction. With the help of his wife, whose parents were also members of the Brethren in Christ, he tried to inspire his children with a hateless and spiteless courtesy toward the world. "For all of us belong to a single family—and the love of our Father extends to us all."

The selfsame spirit of tolerance toward the people of Europe, where Ike's ancestors had lived; of Texas, where he first saw the light of day; and of Kansas, where he grew to be a man. He was only two years old when his parents moved to the Kansas city of Abilene. Here his father got a job as engineer at the Belle Springs Creamery, and Ike—"barefoot boy with cheek of tan"—grew up in the give-and-take spirit of American democracy. Learn to get along with your brothers, to respect your parents, to demand justice for yourself, and to dispense justice to all. The American creed of mutual helpfulness. The Eisenhower boys took their turn building the kitchen fire at four-thirty in the morning. "A disagreeable job, but it has to be done." More pleasant, however, was the cooking of the family dinner on Sunday. In this job all the boys participated—to give their parents a rest. Great fun preparing the mush and puddin', and especially making the piecrust. For the dough could be rolled into a ball for a game of catch. And, also, you could play catch with the dishes. Big Ike —Edgar—would wash them and toss them to little Ike, who would dry them and then in turn toss them to Arthur, who would stack them on the shelves. "Work isn't half bad if only you can turn it into play."

And schooling, too, if you can season it with athletic games. Ike had developed into a good football player. Practice on the gridiron, home lessons, and firing the boiler at the creamery—his father had secured him this job. A good life, this—full of mental and physical excitement, interesting companions, and devoted friends. Friends with whom you could discuss things, play ball, and—in your rare spare moments—play poker. Ike Eisenhower had become the best poker player in town. For he had an amazing memory and an uncanny skill in outguessing his opponents. "The entire trick in poker," one of his older friends—"Joner" Callahan— had pointed out, "is to know the percentages, to calculate the chances, and to figure out what the other fellow has in mind."

The entire trick in poker and—as Eisenhower was to prove many years later—in war. For the present, however, his thoughts were far from the idea of war. This idea was not within the precinct of the Eisenhower way of life. At the time of the Spanish-American War the Eisenhower boys had tried to play "soldiers"—to their mother's displeasure and their own smarting backsides. After the thrashing she had explained her ideas on the subject. As a child in Virginia, she had seen her home ransacked first by the Confederate soldiers and then by the Yankee troops. "That's what the war did to them, turned them into savage animals . . . God forbid that you boys should ever go to war."

Yet the game of war had a fascination for Ike. Not as a struggle of beasts in the jungle, but as a conflict of human wits. He was fond of reading Clausewitz. "Of all the branches of human activity," this military expert had declared, "war is most like a game of cards."

A sporting fondness for the intricacies of poker, a scientific interest in the complexities of war. But, above all, a sincere effort to finish the day's work before he entered upon the evening's play.

III

AT HIS GRADUATION from the Abilene High School, the "class prophet" expressed the opinion that "Ike will wind up as a professor of history at Yale." Not so wild a prediction for a youngster who was to be appointed president of Columbia. But none of his classmates suspected the road over which he was to travel to that post.

It was a year after his graduation that he entered upon the first milestone of that road. At the suggestion of his classmate, Everett Hazlett, he took the examinations both for Annapolis and for West Point. And to his surprise—"I never was much of a student"—he was top man in the navy test and runner-up in the army test. The power of concentration, and the determination to win.

He was appointed to Annapolis, but the appointment could not be confirmed. The maximum age limit for entrance to the naval academy was twenty; and Eisenhower, who had gone to work when he was through with his high-school course, was now twenty-one. The age limit for the military academy, however, was twenty-two. Eisenhower requested his senator, Joseph L. Bristow, to change his appointment to West Point; and when the ranking candidate failed in his physical test, Ike was chosen in his place.

At West Point he starred in football and was a little better than average in his studies. Owing to an injured knee, he failed to develop into an all-American athlete. But he succeeded in developing into an all-American character. Everybody loved his friendliness, his optimism, his ability to take orders with a smile, his fondness for practical jokes—even though the laughs were at his own expense—his enthusiasm for work, and especially his courage in the face of danger and his courtesy toward all men of whatever religion or race.

It was during one of his vacations from West Point that his townsmen were able to see something of this manhood and magnanimity that had become so integral a part of his character. Envious of his reputation as a West Pointer, some of the old "gang" inveigled him into challenging Dirk Tyler, a professional Negro prize fighter, to a boxing match. When Ike saw the gigantic Negro, his bulging muscles and impassive face, he felt literally sick. But he put on a bold face and threw down the challenge.

"When do you wanna fight?" asked Dirk.

"Right now."

They repaired to a public "gym," where they stripped for the fight. A large crowd had collected. They were anxious to see the "kill."

And they saw it. Not, however, as they had expected. It was Ike who knocked out the Negro. And in the very first round.

For a time after the fight it was a dismal world for Dirk Tyler. They taunted him as a "no-account bastard and a yellow-livered coon." The little boys took to throwing stones at him, and the older fellows "ganged up" on him in a sadistic reaction to their former fear.

But Ike didn't like this. "Come on, fellows, lay off. He did the best he could. It's no fault of his that he lost. Or that his skin is black."

And when some of the fellows still persisted in their abuse, Ike took matters into his own hands. "Brave guys, hey? Well, if you're so brave, stop picking on Dirk and start picking on me!"

IV

WHEN he was graduated from West Point (June 12, 1915) he ranked 61 in a class of 168. He stood high, however, in engineering, military science, and drill.

Commissioned as a second lieutenant in the 19th Infantry, he looked upon the opening battles of the first World War with a professional but somewhat detached interest. A chess game played by foreign experts. Intriguing enough, but no American championship at stake. He studied the campaigns, applauded the good plays, criticized the bad ones—and executed one outstanding play for himself. He got married. To Mamie Geneva Doud, the daughter of a successful meat packer.

There was a great difference in their social rank, for the Douds were very wealthy. But there was no difference in their love. And so they took their unequal union in stride and soon learned to march in mutual adoration and harmonious step. Mamie's father offered no financial assistance— "Let the youngsters stand on their own pins." And Ike was quite willing and able to stand on his own feet.

But it meant a long and patient and at times disheartening stand before anything worth while turned up. Football coach at the Peacock Military Academy; instructor of the National Guard at Camp Travis; teacher in the Officers' Training Camp at Fort Oglethorpe, and afterward at Fort Leavenworth; commander of the Tank Training Center at Camp Colt. From second to first lieutenant, to captain, to major, to lieutenant colonel. But no orders for active duty. America had now entered the war. But no opportunity for Eisenhower to get into the line-up. He was too valuable as a teacher, a side-line director, a coach. The youngster had too rare a talent to be wasted in field duty. He knew how to turn civilians into soldiers. For he understood people, and could get them to understand him.

To trust him, to obey him, and, if necessary, to contradict him. He knew how to *give* and *take*. Above all, he disliked the rubber-stamp type of man, the "yes-man." If a subordinate disapproved of his ideas, and had a good reason for his disapproval, let him come out with it! One of his lieutenants at Camp Colt kept applauding him for his ability as a commander. "Nobody else could have done such a perfect job, sir."

"Do you really think so?"

"Yes, sir!"

"Find everything here just right?"

"Yes, *sir!*"

"Well," snapped Eisenhower, "get out and find something wrong with the place. No camp can be *that* good. Either you're a flatterer or you're as big a fool as you think *I* am."

Yet Eisenhower's work at Camp Colt, while not *that* good, was good enough to receive the Distinguished Service Medal. For his "unusual zeal, foresight, and marked administrative ability in the organization and preparation for overseas service of technical troops of the Tank Corps."

Superior ability in preparing other men for overseas service. But no luck in getting an overseas assignment for himself.

At last, however, the long-deferred hope was about to be realized. Early in November 1918 he rushed into his house waving a piece of paper and shouting triumphantly to his wife. "I've made it, darling! My orders for sailing to France!"

His wife, with a smiling face and a sinking heart, held out her hand for the paper. "It's wonderful, Ike. When do you go?"

"Here, read it."

She took the paper. "You will proceed to Camp Dix for embarkation on November 18."

But on November 11 the war was at an end. Ike Eisenhower seemed destined for a job behind the scenes.

V

NINETEEN TWENTY-ONE—a year that brought to Eisenhower a great tragedy and, though he was unaware of it at the time, the opportunity that was to culminate in his final success.

Three years earlier he had been blessed with a son—little Icky. A bright and playful and lovable little "rascal" of a child. Never after his most difficult days at the army post was Eisenhower too tired for a game of tag with Icky. The child played so eagerly, and so hard. Too hard, perhaps. One day in December 1920 he caught cold. It developed into scarlet fever. On January 2, 1921, he died in his father's arms.

Every year thereafter, wherever he happened to be stationed, Eisenhower sent flowers to his wife on Icky's birthday.

His immediate grief at Icky's death, however, was somewhat assuaged by a new set of duties under a new command. Chief of staff to General Fox Connor, commander of the 20th Infantry in the Canal Zone. General Connor had met the young officer through George Patton. He had admired his enthusiasm, his geniality, his ability to get along with people, his quickness in sizing up a situation, and his thorough understanding of military technique. A good man to pacify the natives and to organize the defenses of the Panama Canal.

Eisenhower accepted the job with alacrity. Just what he needed to make him forget. The 20th consisted largely of Puerto Ricans—men of boiling tempers and sluggish limbs. Eisenhower didn't blame them for either of these faults. They were merely the product of their tropical environment.

And so, instead of bullying them into a discipline to which they had not been accustomed, he set them an example of efficiency and cheerfulness and self-restraint which many of them were only too anxious to emulate. "Look at the Headquarters—white-painted fences, pretty flower beds, spotless furniture, dusted floors. Better keep our own quarters like that." A spick-and-span commander, a spick-and-span outfit. No slovenliness in any camp with a man like *that* at the head.

And no fooling around, either. Ike Eisenhower was a combination of tactfulness and tenacity—when a friendly reminder failed, it was followed by a strict command. His soldiers loved his smile, but shriveled up before his frown. "The young man," observed General Connor, "is definitely headed for higher things."

But, for the present, his fortunes were definitely on the downgrade. In the peacetime contraction of the army, his rank had been reduced consecutively from lieutenant colonel to major and from major to captain. "No prospect of another war, and no chance for advancement in times of peace." General Connor tried repeatedly to get him into the School for the General Staff, at Leavenworth. But in vain. Instead he was appointed —once again—as a football coach. The Third Area Eleven at Camp Meade.

General Connor tried to console him. "Cheer up, son. This job, too, may have its use. Study your tactics on the football field. Try to outguess the other coach. All this knowledge will come in handy someday."

For Connor was certain that another war was coming. "And sooner than anyone thinks. Everything in Europe points to it—and in the Pacific, too." And the general was equally certain that Eisenhower possessed the necessary qualities for leadership in that war. He had observed him at his command, and he had talked to him again and again. A superb capacity for absorbing and remembering facts, for sizing up a situation and making a quick and logical decision, and for *getting things done*. "Men will follow you because they like you . . . When the time comes, I and my generation will be too old . . . It will be up to you youngsters . . . I mean you in particular . . . I want you to be ready to answer the call."

But the next call was for another "useless" job. Recruiting officer at Fort Logan. Again it was General Connor who kept up his spirits. "A good place to mark time . . . and to keep up with your studies . . . I still have faith in your star."

Perhaps, thought Ike with a grim smile. For the present his star was but an invisible flicker among the hundred million others in the American sky.

Yet life had its compensations. His presence at the recruiting office in Colorado brought his wife more closely to her parents. His wife, and their new son. All their affection was now centered in this child. It softened their pain at the loss of their other child and their disappointment at the comparative obscurity of Eisenhower's career. Happiness is not only in the glare of the sun. "Even the shadow can outline the image of God."

And thus Eisenhower, like a good soldier, was faithful to his little jobs and—at the same time—on the alert for something big. And the big opening came in the form of a telegram from General Connor. "Be ready—make no move—don't even breathe—Fox Connor."

Appointment to the General Staff School at Leavenworth.

VI

EISENHOWER had traveled a long way from West Point. Against the keenest competition of some of the army's "smartest" brains, he came out first in his class. "You are now [June 1926] marked for advancement on the Eligible List of the General Staff."

An overseas order, to prepare *A Guide to American Battlefields in Europe*. A golden opportunity to study at first hand the terrain and the tactics of World War I. When he returned from Europe he was an encyclopedia of information about the gigantic chessboard upon which any future war game might be played.

And then some further intensive training in the art of war. A student-officer at the War College in Washington. Major Eisenhower—he had been promoted now—had at last attracted the attention of the military leaders in the United States. An officer with a superior mind.

Nineteen hundred and thirty to 1938. The years of *depression* and *oppression*. Business failures, idle workers, closed banks. And the inevitable result of economic anarchy—political dictatorship. Madness in the saddle, savagery on the gallop without bridle or rein. Yet even now the world was asleep. Very few saw the approaching danger. Especially in the United States. "We are so far away . . . protected by two oceans . . . safe and snug in our isolated home."

But a few men with a keener vision could sense the coming storm. And one of these farsighted men was Major Eisenhower. Assigned to several important tasks—in the office of the Assistant Secretary of War, on a second mission to the battlefields of France, on the staff of General Mac-Arthur during a military inspection tour of the Philippines—he became more and more insistently aware of the military unpreparedness at home and the threatening catastrophe from abroad. Both in the East and in the West.

And yet he was descended from a long line of pacifist men. He had an intense hatred against war. When Chamberlain came back from Hitler with a promise of "peace in our time," Eisenhower defended the English statesman. "Next to the loss of freedom," he explained to his son, who was now studying at a private school in the Philippines, "war is the ultimate calamity which can befall a nation . . . It is so horrible that imagination cannot grasp it in all its hideous aspects."

"But what are the chances against war," asked his son, "so long as Hitler is in power?"

"Well," smiled Ike, "there's always a chance that somebody might shoot the s.o.b."

Nineteen hundred and thirty-nine—and Eisenhower still hoped for peace. And prepared strenuously for war. He helped organize the defenses of the Philippines. The Filipinos adored him—his infectious good nature, his democratic camaraderie, his simple code of honor, his amazing capacity for work, and his utter relaxation in play.

He left the Philippines on December 13, 1939—and sailed immediately into troubled seas.

VII

WHEN HE RETURNED TO AMERICA he was amazed at its complacency. Everybody ridiculed the "phony" war in Europe and the "silly" fracas in China. "Don't you understand what the hell's going on?" he insisted. "The Germans and the Japs are aiming at the conquest of the world. *They're aiming at us!* They've been preparing for this for the past twenty years. And what have we done about it? What are we going to do when they strike?"

Nothing but jeers and boos for an answer. "Alarmist Ike!"

But Ike wasn't content with being an alarmist. He turned his sense of alarm into creative action. Defense against imminent attack. He was ordered to Fort Lewis as executive officer of the 15th Infantry. A wide-awake regiment which had just returned from China. The men had seen the Japanese invasion and they knew what it meant.

Knew, but remained unafraid. Their regimental crest bore the inscription, *Can Do.* "Fellows after my own heart!" said Ike.

A reciprocal feeling. The boys took their "Exec" immediately to *their* hearts. One day, as he inspected the kitchen, he saw a pile of raw meat freshly ground for hamburgers. With one hand he grabbed an onion and with the other a fistful of meat, and continued his inspection as he munched his spicy tidbit. "My God," muttered the cook, "raw meat! Tough guy!"

Tough guy, and *good* guy. Knew how to settle a soldier's quarrels without a fight. There had been a long-standing feud between two privates. There was bad blood between them, and they were always "itching for a scrap." Ike sent for them and ordered them to wash a window—one on the outside and one on the inside. For a time he watched them scowling at each other across the pane, and then he burst into laughter. The two men forgot their scowls and joined in the laugh. It was the end of their feud.

Always good-natured when his men behaved. But a whiplash of fury when they disobeyed. There was never any "monkey business" under Eisenhower's command.

And yet, fifty years old now, and only lieutenant colonel at a regimental post. But from now on the action grows faster, and more dramatic. The actors are attuned to a more accelerated peace, and those who are the most efficiently trained are hurried to the fore. Colonel Eisenhower, and then chief of staff of the Third Army, and now Brigadier General Ike. He has won his first star as official recognition for his defensive tactics in the

maneuvers between the "Red" Army and the "Blue." As a result of these
tactics, the battle has ended in the total "annihilation" of the "enemy's"
tanks.

But it has meant terrific work. Relax for a while now and catch your
breath. A December Sunday at Fort Houston. "I'm dead tired, boys. Guess
I'll treat myself to a nap. Call me if anything happens."

A few minutes later it happened. The attack on Pearl Harbor.

VIII

THEY CALLED HIM TO WASHINGTON. Assistant to General Gerow, Chief of
War Plans. A period of darkness and defeat. Yet here is a man who is
preparing the strategy for an attack. A job for a football coach. The best
defense is a good *offense*.

A most *efficient* coach. In March 1942 promoted to major general. Next
month appointed head of operations for the United States Army. A
month later ordered by General Marshall to England. On an inspection
tour. To inspect and—though Eisenhower was unaware of it—to be inspected. "Let's see if he's the man."

On his return from England, General Marshall asked his British colleagues whether they would approve the assignment of Eisenhower to the
chief command of the American forces in the European theater. The answer was a unanimous and enthusiastic *yes*.

General Marshall summoned Eisenhower to his office. They discussed
the plans for the invasion of Africa. "In your opinion," asked the Chief of
Staff, "are the plans as nearly complete as is humanly possible?"

"Yes, sir," replied Ike, "I think they are."

"And you are ready to O.K. them?"

"Most heartily, sir."

"I'm glad to hear this," said Marshall, "because you're the man to carry
them out."

As he walked down the steps in the Munitions Building he met an old
friend of his—General Francis B. Wilby. "What's the matter, Ike?" asked
Wilby. "You look as if you had just swallowed a camel."

"Brother, I have!" And then, with a catch in his throat, "They're sending me over in charge of the whole shebang."

IX

GENERAL EISENHOWER'S ACHIEVEMENTS in the European theater are familiar
history. Asked to deliver a message to America on the Fourth of July, he
replied: "There is no time for messages until we can say them with bombs
and shells."

And this is precisely how he spoke to the world until the job was completed. Dynamite for the enemy, dynamic inspiration for the allies. Here
was a general who knew his *job*—a lifelong application to military science

had prepared him for it—and who knew his *men*. An expert in the geography of the battlefield and in the terrain of the human soul. Cheerful—at least on the surface—when others were despondent, friendly when others were captious, daring when others were hesitant, and sincerely democratic at all times and to all men. His character was an amalgamation that cemented the soldiers of many countries into a single army. No separate Americans, or British, or Russians, or French, or Negroes, or Jews—just an undivided unit of co-operating "buddies" inspired with a single aim— Victory. Once he had occasion to praise an officer to General Hastings Ismay. "Was he British or American?" asked the general. "I honestly don't remember," grinned Eisenhower. On another occasion he dismissed an officer for calling a fellow officer a "British bastard." "I don't mind your calling him a bastard if he is one," said Ike, "but I'm damned if I'll let you call him a *British* bastard."

The selfsame unruffled courtesy in victory and defeat. Jealousy against him within the army, criticism at home—"Why did he do this, and why didn't he do that?"—accusations that he was playing politics—"What business had he to negotiate with Darlan?"—clamors for his removal during the Battle of the Bulge—"Why didn't he anticipate von Rundstedt's attack?"—and through it all he acknowledged his mistakes, accepted his defeats, and worked indefatigably toward the final day. "I *know* we shall win!"

And every last soldier in the ranks had caught fire from this dynamic leadership; and they, too, knew that they would win. When he visited a contingent in the field, they shouted themselves hoarse in their adoration for "Ike, Ike, Ike!"

And then, as the invasion was nearing the end, even his critics were convinced. His mistakes had meant but the human groping of genius instinctively bent upon the one right course. In the international rivalry of human affairs there can be no greater tribute to a man than the homage of a foreign press. "The charge entrusted to Supreme Commander Eisenhower," wrote the *London Times*, "meant nothing less than the liberation of the continent . . . No choice could have been more acceptable to all the Allied Services."

X

HE CAME BACK FROM THE WAR with the "same size hat." Throughout the ovations that greeted him across the land, he remained the selfsame man that he had always been. An American with a democratic vision, a brilliant mind, and a modest soul. More than ever now he hated war and longed for a world-wide co-operation in which the common man would be able to "preserve his freedom of worship, his equality before the law, his liberty to speak and act as he sees fit, subject only to provisions that he trespass not upon the similar rights of others."

Appointed to the presidency of Columbia University (1947), he accepted this latest honor—like all the others—with humility and a smile.

Asked, in a press interview, whether he preferred to be called General Eisenhower or President Eisenhower, he replied: "Please call me by the name I like best of all. Just plain Ike."

And this was the name the people liked best of all when they elected him, in 1952, to the Presidency of the United States. "I like Ike" was the slogan that helped to sweep him into the White House by the biggest popular vote in American History.

IMPORTANT DATES IN THE LIFE OF
DWIGHT DAVID EISENHOWER

1890—Born, Denison, Texas.

1892—Parents moved to Abilene, Kansas.

1915—Graduated from West Point.

1918-19—Served as instructor at tank-training centers in United States.

1921—Appointed to staff of General Connor in Canal Zone.

1930-38—Instructor at various camps, two inspection trips to France, and preparation of manual on *American Battlefields in Europe*.

1939—Served on staff of General MacArthur in the Philippines.

1942—Appointed commander of allied forces in invasion of Africa.

1944—Appointed commander in chief of allied forces in invasion of Europe.

1945—Represented United States in Allied Military Government of Germany.
Appointed Chief of Staff of United States Army.

1947—Chosen president of Columbia University.

1952—Elected President of the United States.

George Gershwin

[1898-1937]

GEORGE Gershwin was born in Brooklyn, New York, two years before the turn of the century. He came from Jewish business people. One ancestor had been a successful furrier in Russia, another had sold a model gun to the Czar. There was not a drop of music in his lineage.

George's father was a nomad. Hardly was he settled in a job than, like the Arabs, he folded his tent and slipped away. He was, by turn, a designer for women's footwear, proprietor of a cigar store and a billiard parlor, part owner of a Turkish bath, and a restaurateur. Like Micawber, he was convinced that something would turn up to make him wealthy.

Since Papa Gershwin insisted upon living within walking distance of his business, the family was constantly "on the go." When George was still an infant the Gershwins moved from Brooklyn to the lower East Side. George was a Dead End kid. He used his fists and asserted his leadership over boys who were potential candidates for reform schools. He played baseball, hockey—and hooky. He had all the prejudices of the street arab. He wouldn't stay quiet long enough even to read the dime thrillers that his brother Ira and the rest of the gamin-reading population were devouring by the carload. When anybody talked of playing a musical instrument, he hissed "Maggie," which was the pavement jargon for "Sissie." He wouldn't be caught dead with a violin!

But the popular songs of the day sang themselves into the heart of this East Sider as into the fancy of all the other arabs in town. When he was only six he stood outside a penny arcade listening to Rubinstein's "Melody in F." "The peculiar jumps in the music held me rooted." Then, when he grew a little older, the strange charm of music again took hold of him. One of the students at his school, Maxie Rosenzweig, a violin prodigy who became a celebrated virtuoso, gave a recital in the auditorium after classes. George, with his usual scorn for such business, did not bother to attend. Instead he went outside to play ball. While he was batting the horsehide, the strains of Maxie's violin came to him from an open window of the auditorium. It was the tender melodious music of Dvořák's "Humoresque." He lost heart for his game. He dropped his bat and stood enthralled.

He determined to make the acquaintance of this fellow Maxie Rosenzweig, to whom he had never bothered to nod. He must be friends with a kid who played music like that! He remained outside the door of the school, waiting for the violinist to appear once the concert was over. He waited an hour and a half. It began to rain, and he got soaked to the skin. Finally, calculating that Maxie must have made his exit through another door, he inquired where the violinist lived, and he ran, as if in a dream, to his home, only to find that Maxie had left for an evening engagement.

George persisted until he was introduced to Maxie. The two boys took to one another. Maxie was altogether different from the other boys George knew. He was small, sensitive, with alert, eloquent eyes. He never talked of prize fights and hockey and gangsters. He spoke of Mozart and Schubert and of other composers who starved for the stars. And George, listening to the stories of these music makers, secretly felt an urge to play the piano in the house of one of his friends. Somewhat ashamed to declare this "vice" before the gang, he stole unobtrusively up to the piano and picked out melodies with his fingers. Every spare moment he retreated to his instrument and sought new tricks from it.

And then a momentous thing happened at home. It was decided that Ira, the older and more studious boy, should take music lessons. The Gershwins bought a piano, and one incredible day it was hoisted through the window into the parlor. But to his parents' astonishment, it was George who welcomed the instrument and tackled it as though he belonged to it. Mama Gershwin arranged for him to receive instruction.

His first teacher was a woman in the neighborhood who charged fifty cents an hour. George learned elementary technique. He kept to the scales without a murmur. But the moment his teacher's back was turned he launched out in improvisations. The sunless yearning of the gutter children broke forth into a rhapsody. The newsies and the bootblacks and the banana pilferers and the scumbums of all colors and all languages found their way into his tentative tunes.

George progressed from lady teachers to the ex-conductor of a Hungarian band, and finally he came under the tutorship of Charles Hambitzer, a concert pianist. Within a short while Hambitzer wrote to his sister: "I have a new pupil who will make his mark in music if anybody will. The boy is a genius, without a doubt. He wants to go in for this modern stuff, jazz and what not. But I'm not going to let him for a while. I'll see that he gets a firm foundation in the standard music first." Hambitzer, in this letter, touched upon a quality in George that irked and puzzled him—George's passion for jazz music. This brilliant young student expressed his appreciation for the classical composers, listened to all they had to offer—and insisted upon playing American dance melodies at every opportunity.

Hambitzer, like most serious musicians, turned up his nose at American popular music. Hour after hour he argued with his promising pupil on the matter of aesthetics. "These jazz men are brassy and shallow, George. Many of them pick out their tunes with one finger. Here I am trying to prepare you for Carnegie Hall and you flirt with Tin Pan Alley." And George would reply: "This music of the common people is *my* music. It expresses *me*. Besides, didn't Verdi write tunes that are played by every organ-grinder? I'll stick to my rhythms of the street."

At fifteen George had learned all he could from conservatory teachers. There was no seat in the classroom for the new campus beauty, Jazz. There was only one conservatory where he could continue his education in the strange rhythms of the slums, and that was Tin Pan Alley, then a stretch of Twenty-sixth Street in New York, where the nation's top publishers rolled out music hits that were sung from coast to coast.

George put a startling proposal before his parents. He wanted to leave the High School of Commerce he was attending and take a job as pianist with a music publisher. Papa Gershwin, who had nursed hopes that his son would become a respectable bookkeeper, shrugged his shoulders with an air of fatalism. As far as he was concerned, Tin Pan Alley was the direct route to a hobo jungle, if not to a prison yard. Mama Gershwin remonstrated with George that if he wished to devote his life to music let him at least become a serious pianist, not a musical gangster. But George had his way. He was interviewed by the head of Remick's Publishing House, and he received a job as staff pianist for fifteen dollars a week. The die was cast. And it rolled through the years right into the crap game that Porgy shot in Catfish Row.

II

GERSHWIN "CLERKED AT THE PIANO" along with a battery of other music makers from morning till night in a "veritable madhouse" of sound. He played banal ditties to client singers who couldn't read a note, plugging a tune for each customer's fancy. Two years of bartering the penny songs of uninspired songsmiths filled him "up to the ears." Yet these two years afforded him valuable clinical experience. He became an expert in the anatomy of the jazz tune. He studied the typical defects of the Tin Pan Alley music, its bathos and insistence on clichés, its adherence to an unimaginative formula. One song was like every other. No wonder the popular song was in low repute with all "high-brow" musicians.

He refused, however, to lose faith in the essential vitality of the Alley. There was nothing aesthetically wrong with popular folk music. "I regard jazz as an American folk music. Jazz *is* music; it uses the same notes that Bach used." There was need for an American composer who would take the American dance tune and lift it into the concert hall.

Strange new rhythms and daring musical nuances bubbled from his pen. Frequently, while playing a Remick tune to a client, he would interpolate one of his own melodies, in the vain hope that the customer would listen with amazement, cast aside all the old folderol, and say, "By God, I want this tune of Gershwin's!" Finally, however, the ice was broken. He sent a song to Harry Von Tilzer and actually made a sale for five dollars. He followed his sale to Von Tilzer with a melody for a show at the Winter Garden, and he took a part-time assignment as rehearsal pianist for a musical comedy written by Victor Herbert and Jerome Kern. The theater gripped him as the sea grips the sailor. When rehearsals were over he sat for hours in the darkened auditorium envisioning the day when the girls and comedians would "hoof" across the stage in a show by George Gershwin.

Suddenly the job at Remick's became a solitary confinement. He kicked the traces and went hunting for new employment. He stuck to nothing long, passing from one job to another with a restlessness that was symptomatic of great things stirring within him. Then a storybook opportunity presented itself. George was introduced to Max Dreyfus, head of Harms' Musical House. Dreyfus had a genius for picking out talent and exploiting it. He had discovered Kern and Vincent Youmans. He would in the future discover Richard Rodgers. Gershwin had published only two songs, but Dreyfus was, on the basis of these, willing to make him an incredible offer. "I feel that you have the stuff in you, George," Dreyfus told him. "It will come out. It may take months, it may take years, but it will come out. I tell you what I'll do. I'll give you thirty-five dollars a week without any set duties. Just write music and step in every morning to say 'hello.'"

It was a bonanza, this leisure with pay. And it was a blue-ribbon investment for Dreyfus. He garnered a fortune on Gershwin. George took full advantage of his opportunity. Under Dreyfus's protection, he hammered out melodies of a novelty that stamped them far above the contemporary output. His reputation was solid but hardly sensational. In 1919, however, he wrote a song, "Swanee," which impressed Al Jolson so deeply that he purchased it for his musical show *Sinbad*. And Gershwin skyrocketed to fame. For Jolson, with his magic mammying, sang "Swanee" into a sale of two and a half million phonograph records and millions of sheet music to the four corners of the earth. At this time Gershwin was just past his twenty-first birthday.

III

AFTER "SWANEE," Gershwin made "music talk." His piquant blues were news. His spiced harmonies and startling rhythms cured the jaded Broadwayites of jazz claustrophobia with a release of fresh new air. He burst wide open the patterns of the popular song, split the atoms of the waltz and foxtrot, and liberated a universe of music energy for the millions.

Here the story of George Gershwin might have ended—if he were not George Gershwin. Had his life followed the routine of many American success stories, Gershwin could have died right then and there artistically. He would have lived out merely the ghost of his creative life, turning out the same songs year after year, dead from the mind down. But Gershwin was curious enough to explore and develop his own potentialities into something more than "Swanee." He had too much intellectual inquisitiveness to doze under the sun of the American dollar. He realized that to continue to produce Broadway hits for people who were already sworn friends of jazz was like carrying coals to Newcastle. As a composer who believed passionately in the right of popular music to take its place in the concert hall, he knew he must reach the "high-brows" with his talents.

On November 1, 1923, at Aeolian Hall in New York City, a concert singer, Eva Gauthier, introduced into a program of classical music, which featured Hindemith and Purcell, a jazz medley of tunes by Berlin, Kern, and Gershwin. It was the first time in the history of American music that jazz had been invited, even tentatively, to take a place by the side of the classics. The concert was a distinct success. Among those at the concert who were deeply impressed was Paul Whiteman. An émigré from symphony orchestras, Whiteman had assembled a dance band with a definite goal in mind. He believed that popular musicians performed in too cheap and haphazard a fashion; that only if dance ensembles developed the technical efficiency and serious purpose of concert orchestras would the jazz-girl reveal her own true aristocracy.

Whiteman had made an initial bow with his band in Los Angeles, and his style of "symphonic jazz" attracted the attention of the entire West Coast. Then he had toured America and finally Europe in triumph. Now he approached George Gershwin with a challenge. "Write me a large work for my orchestra, and I'll hire Aeolian Hall to play it in!" George dismissed Whiteman's suggestion lightly. He was psychologically and technically unprepared to do the kind of large work Whiteman desired. But once Whiteman got his teeth into an idea he hung on like a cub. He had selected his man, and now he went about calmly making arrangements. One morning George picked up the *New York Herald Tribune* and was astonished to read an announcement by Whiteman of a jazz concert to be held within a few weeks at Aeolian Hall. The major work on the program was to be a large symphonic composition written in the jazz medium by George Gershwin!

George got Whiteman on the telephone. "How in the devil can I write a piece on such short notice, three weeks?" he demanded. "Do you think it's like dashing off a song for a musical? Besides, Paul, I've never written a symphonic work. I don't know how." Gershwin was won over by the insistency of the band leader. But he hadn't the slightest idea around which to build such a piece. His knowledge of harmony and counterpoint and all that went into the texture of a sustained musical composition was slight and never before tested. How would he begin?

"Suddenly an idea occurred to me. There had been so much talk about the limitations of jazz, not to speak of the manifest misunderstanding of its function . . . I resolved, if possible, to kill that misconception with one sturdy blow. Inspired by this aim, I set to work composing. . . . I had no set plan, no structure to which my music could conform. I had worked out a few themes, but just at this time I had to appear in Boston for the première of *Sweet Little Devil*. It was on the train with its steely rhythms, its rattly-bang that is so often stimulating to a composer . . .

that I suddenly heard—even saw on paper—the complete construction of the 'Rhapsody' from beginning to end. . . . I heard it as a sort of musical kaleidoscope of America—of our vast melting pot, of our incomparable national pep, our blues, our metropolitan madness. By the time I reached Boston, I had the definite plot of the piece."

The concert was held on Lincoln's birthday, 1924. Seats had been reserved for the aristocracy of the musical world, Rachmaninoff, Stravinsky, Stokowski, Victor Herbert, Damrosch, Heifetz, Kreisler, Elman. Whiteman conducted preliminary groups of jazz songs, contrasting old popular music with the new, and then, as a wave of restlessness passed through the hall, Gershwin made his appearance to play his "Rhapsody in Blue." The first "rooster-whoop" of the clarinet lifted the audience to its toes. "Somewhere in the middle of the score," admitted Whiteman, "I began crying. When I came to myself I was eleven pages along, and to this day I cannot tell you how I conducted that far."

People were electrified. They have been ever since. The jazz-volley of the "Rhapsody in Blue" was a Declaration of American Musical Independence, heard round the globe. Distinguished serious composers, startled into the realization that Tin Pan Alley was an important highway in the world of music after all, poured forth a torrent of jazz in the medium of operas and concert suites. But none of them infused into their music the vitality of a Gershwin. The "Rhapsody" survives today as the most popular music in American symphonic literature. "It has become," in the words of a leading music scholar, "one of the theme songs of our nation . . . a great national quotation in tone."

IV

No sooner had Gershwin made a reputation as a serious composer than people began to nibble away at it. Certain critics, eager to witness a funeral of talent, declared that the "Rhapsody" was a lucky inspiration by a young musical illiterate who had exhausted his creative powers in one outpouring and would never be heard from again. To call the bluff of his detractors, Gershwin decided that he would compose an even more ambitious piece than the "Rhapsody." He signed a contract with Walter Damrosch of the New York Symphony Society to write a jazz concerto for piano and orchestra within a year.

The "Concerto in F"—the first jazz concerto for the piano in history— was duly delivered to Damrosch. Gershwin himself appeared as the soloist at a concert in Carnegie Hall, December 3, 1925. And the audience was carried away by his performance. Once again, as in the case of the "Rhapsody," serious musicians took the jazz baby to their hearts.

In the spring of 1928, Gershwin, not quite thirty, decided to leave New York, where his constant commissions for shows kept him in a whirl. He planned to go abroad for musical study. But he was mistaken if he thought he would find peace in Europe. The moment he landed, people from all walks of life, who had been singing his songs for a decade, mobbed him. Everywhere he went orchestras struck up the "Rhapsody in Blue," as if it were the national anthem. However, despite the social merry-go-round, Gershwin returned from Europe with a tone poem, "An American in Paris"—"a frank humoresque indulging freely in unbuttoned humor." Then on a trip through the Caribbean, he investigated the infectious dances of Havana and expressed them in a "Cuban Overture." Rhythm was second nature with him.

For his next major work he wrote the score for a musical comedy in which he departed radically from the usual mood of his Broadway offerings. In *Of Thee I Sing,* Kaufman and Ryskind fashioned a satirical book on American politics. Gershwin contributed music of a pungent humor that place him on a level with Sullivan.

In his middle thirties, at the height of his prestige, wealthy, charming, a brilliant performer of his own works on the piano at parties, Gershwin had become the lion of New York society. He was taut as the strings of a violin keyed to concert performance. His smile was tinged with cynicism, as though he were forever asking a question. He had a habit of jerking his neck, as if trying to straighten out a kink. Next to his music he was passionately fond of tennis and ping-pong. He boxed in a small-sized gymnasium specially built in his apartment. The rhythm for many a song was suggested to him as he punched the bag. His music is the music of an athlete. "I feel that I was meant for hard physical work, to chop down trees, to use my muscles," he frequently declared. "When I'm in my normal mood my tunes come dripping off my fingers. And they're lively tunes, full of outdoor pep."

He composed, frequently to the lyrics of his brother Ira, in the still hours of the morning, playing dreamily at the piano, half dressed, with a cigar in his mouth. His melodies came easily and unprovoked, but he sweated over them painstakingly as he worked them into finished form. He called himself a "modern romantic." There is, however, nothing slushy in Gershwin's tunes. On the contrary, they are crisp, sharp, scintillating with a kind of Gallic wit, malicious, and full of surprise. He was amazingly objective about his work. He told his friends that he would gladly exchange his prestige for the genius to write Schubert's "Ave Maria."

At the height of his fame something occurred at a party in Gershwin's honor that set him thinking. Otto Kahn, patron of the arts, in a speech on his music, turned to the composer and told him that for all its wit and melody there was one essential element lacking: "The legacy of sorrow, the note that springs from the deepest stirrings of the race." He hinted that Gershwin had been hog-tied by his own success, by the circumstance that he had never experienced the suffering in which the music of the really great composers was seeded. "The long drip of human tears, my dear George. . . . They fertilize the deepest roots of art."

As a matter of fact, Gershwin had planned for several years to write an opera which would sound the sorrow as well as the gaiety of the American personality. He had searched unceasingly for a proper libretto. It would be an American opera, patterned not after European traditions, but an

opera in which Gershwin would have the opportunity to express his un-orthodox talents. At first he considered the idea of using as a theme the melting pot of races in New York City. "I should like to catch the rhythms of these interfusing peoples." And then he recalled a Theater Guild production of the play *Porgy* by DuBose Heyward which had fasci-nated New York audiences. In the love of a crippled Negro beggar for a girl named Bess, he sensed the perfect story. The idea continued to haunt him until he finally decided to drop everything else that he was doing and write the music for *Porgy*.

He ceased work on more than two hundred thousand dollars' worth of contracts and, together with DuBose Heyward, rented a shack at the water front in Charleston in the midst of the Negroes he wished to study for his music. "Under the baking suns of July and August," writes Hey-ward of these days, "we established ourselves on Folly Island. . . James Island, with its large population of primitive Gullah Negroes, lay adja-cent and furnished us with . . . an inexhaustible source of folk material. The most interesting discovery to me . . . was that to George it was more like a homecoming than an exploration. The quality in him which had produced the 'Rhapsody in Blue' in the most sophisticated city in America found its counterpoint in . . . the music and bodily rhythms of the simple Negro peasant of the South."

Gershwin worked eleven months on his score, traveling up and down the coast. And he spent another nine months orchestrating it. When he was finished he presented the Theater Guild with several hundred closely written pages of music. The Guild put into rehearsal an all-Negro cast headed by Todd Duncan and Anne Brown, and on October 10, 1935, it offered the first performance of *Porgy and Bess* to a New York audience. An America that had been eagerly awaiting the Gershwin opera was not disappointed. The cries of the street vendors selling their fish cakes in Catfish Row, the praying of the mourners who wailed a terrifying invo-cation in a hurricane, the savage rhythms of the Negro dances, and, above all, the haunting melodies of "Summertime" and "I've Got Plenty of Nothin'," written to the lyrics of his brother Ira, intrigued the nation. Into this music had truly seeped the suffering of the Negro race.

V

Gershwin, in writing *Porgy and Bess*, had passed a milestone in the prog-ress of his art. He was brimming with optimism about the future. He was convinced that all the music he had hitherto written was a warm-up exer-cise for the music he was about to write. Among other things he planned a chorale setting to Lincoln's *Gettysburg Address*—an inspiring libretto by the great social Emancipator to serve a great musical emancipator! "I'm intensely interested in the project. . . . While I'm working on it I might learn something about harmony!"

To equip himself, he had been taking lessons in musical theory with Joseph Schillinger. It was the most thoroughgoing technical preparation he had ever undergone. His notebooks were filled with ingenuities in harmonies and rhythms for the future.

Welcoming a "breather," as he phrased it, before he engaged in serious composition, he settled in Hollywood to write the music for the *Goldwyn Follies*. During the summer of 1937 he complained of headaches and dizzy spells, but he shrugged them off as symptoms of nervousness. Yet disturbing things continued to occur. One evening, while performing his "Concerto in F" for a concert audience, his fingers stumbled on passages he had played fluently dozens of times before. He had a curious odor in his mouth, a burning smell in his nostrils. And then suddenly, at work on the *Goldwyn* score, he collapsed. The doctors who examined him found nothing alarming about his condition. They permitted him to return to his composition. But he suffered a relapse. And the worst fears of the physicians were realized. It was a tumor of the brain. Gershwin was instantly rushed to the hospital for an emergency operation—too late. He passed away on Sunday, July 10, 1937, at the age of thirty-eight, without learning that he had just received Italy's highest award to a foreign composer—an honorary membership in the St. Cecilia Academy of Music in Rome.

But, in a real sense, the story of George Gershwin only began on the day he died. For, from that day until the present, the music, disassociated from the personality of the living man, has sung its way on its own absolute merit into a greater popularity than Gershwin had achieved even during his lifetime. He is still the prince of fortune. For he has the luck that no other composer from Tin Pan Alley ever possessed, the luck of life everlasting.

IMPORTANT DATES IN THE LIFE OF GEORGE GERSHWIN

1898—Born, Brooklyn, New York.

1914—Obtained job as a staff pianist with Remick's Publishing Company.

1919—Composed his first complete score for a Broadway musical show, *La, La, Lucille*. Wrote first national song hit, "Swanee."

1924—Performed on piano at première of the "Rhapsody in Blue" at Aeolian Hall.

1925—Participated as soloist in first performance of the "Concerto in F."

1928—Wrote "An American in Paris."

1931—Composed score for Pulitzer-prize musical comedy, *Of Thee I Sing*.

1935—Completed score for *Porgy and Bess*.

1937—Died of brain tumor, Hollywood, California.